ARK OF THE COVENANT

According to the Bible, the Ark was a gold-covered wooden chest containing the Tablets of the Covenant, the stones engraved with the ten commandments which were dictated to Moses by God at Mount Sinai.

The Ark was used as a mobile temple while the Jewish people were wandering in the desert after their Exodus from Egypt. A sacred artifact representing God's presence on earth, it was believed to have mystical powers. The early Hebrews carried the Ark as a talisman in front of their army when going into battle. Later, the Ark was placed in the Temple in Jerusalem and religious ceremonies were performed around it.

Nobody knows what happened to the Ark of the Covenant. It is mentioned in biblical text for the last time around 600 BC, in connection with the renovations of the Temple. In the year 568 BC, the Babylonians conquered Jerusalem and exiled its inhabitants. There is no mention of the Ark on the Babylonians' list of looted treasures or the Bible's account of this list.

Many legends have evolved about the Ark and its whereabouts. Archaeologists, mystics, and adventurers still seek for it in vain.

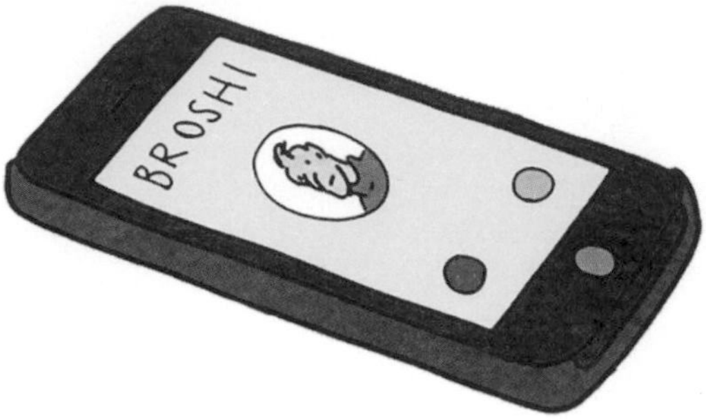
BROSHI

OTHER WORKS BY RUTU MODAN
The Property
Exit Wounds
Jamilti and Other Stories

drawnandquarterly.com

ISBN 978-1-77046-466-7
First edition: October 2021
Printed in China
10 9 8 7 6 5 4 3 2 1

Cataloguing data available from Library and Archives Canada.

Published in the USA by Drawn & Quarterly, a client publisher of Farrar, Straus and Giroux.
Published in Canada by Drawn & Quarterly, a client publisher of Raincoast Books.
Published in the United Kingdom by Drawn & Quarterly, a client publisher of Publishers Group UK.

Mifal Hapais

The book was produced with the support of
the Israel Lottery Council For Culture & Arts

TUNNELS

RUTU MODAN

Translation by **ISHAI MISHORY**
Story edits by **NOAH STOLLMAN**

drawn & quarterly

Part 1: The Inscription

5700
THE GATEKEEPER
6200
THE GATEKEEPER
80%
22:07
Broshi
mobile
Ring-ring
Message
Accept
Remind Me
Decline
80%
22:07
Broshi
mobile
Ring-ring
Message
Accept
Click
Remind Me
6400
HAUNTED STAIRS
6400
DARK WELL
80%
Broshi
mobile
Ring-ring
Message
Accept
Remind Me
Decline
80%
22:07
Ring-ring
Message
Accept
Click
Remind Me

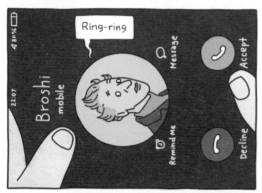

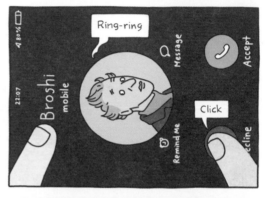

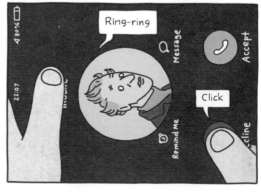

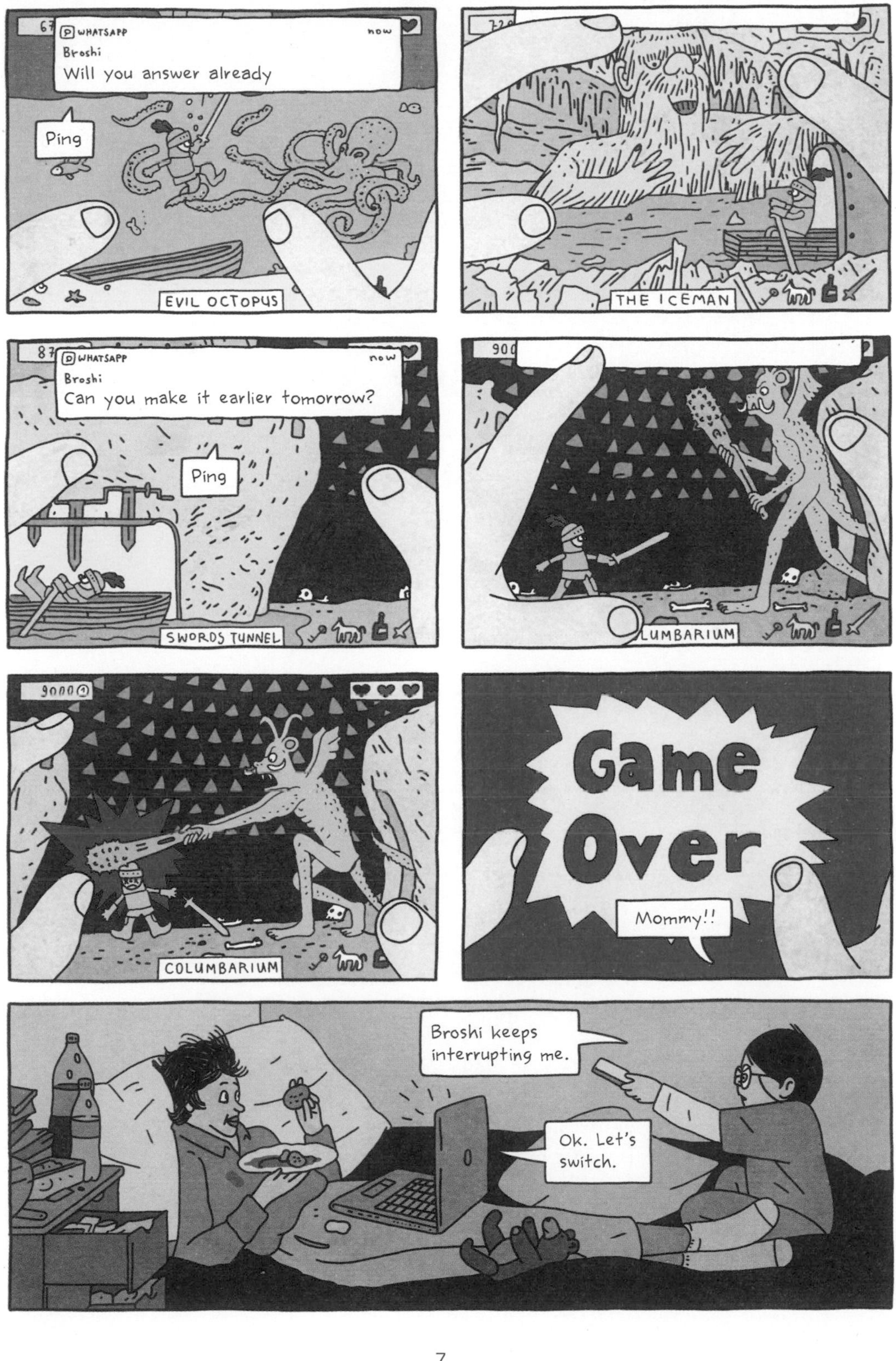
WHATSAPP
now
Broshi
Will you answer already
Ping
EVIL OCTOPUS
THE ICEMAN
WHATSAPP
now
Broshi
Can you make it earlier tomorrow?
Ping
SWORDS TUNNEL
9000
COLUMBARIUM
Game Over
Mommy!!
Broshi keeps interrupting me.
Ok. Let's switch.

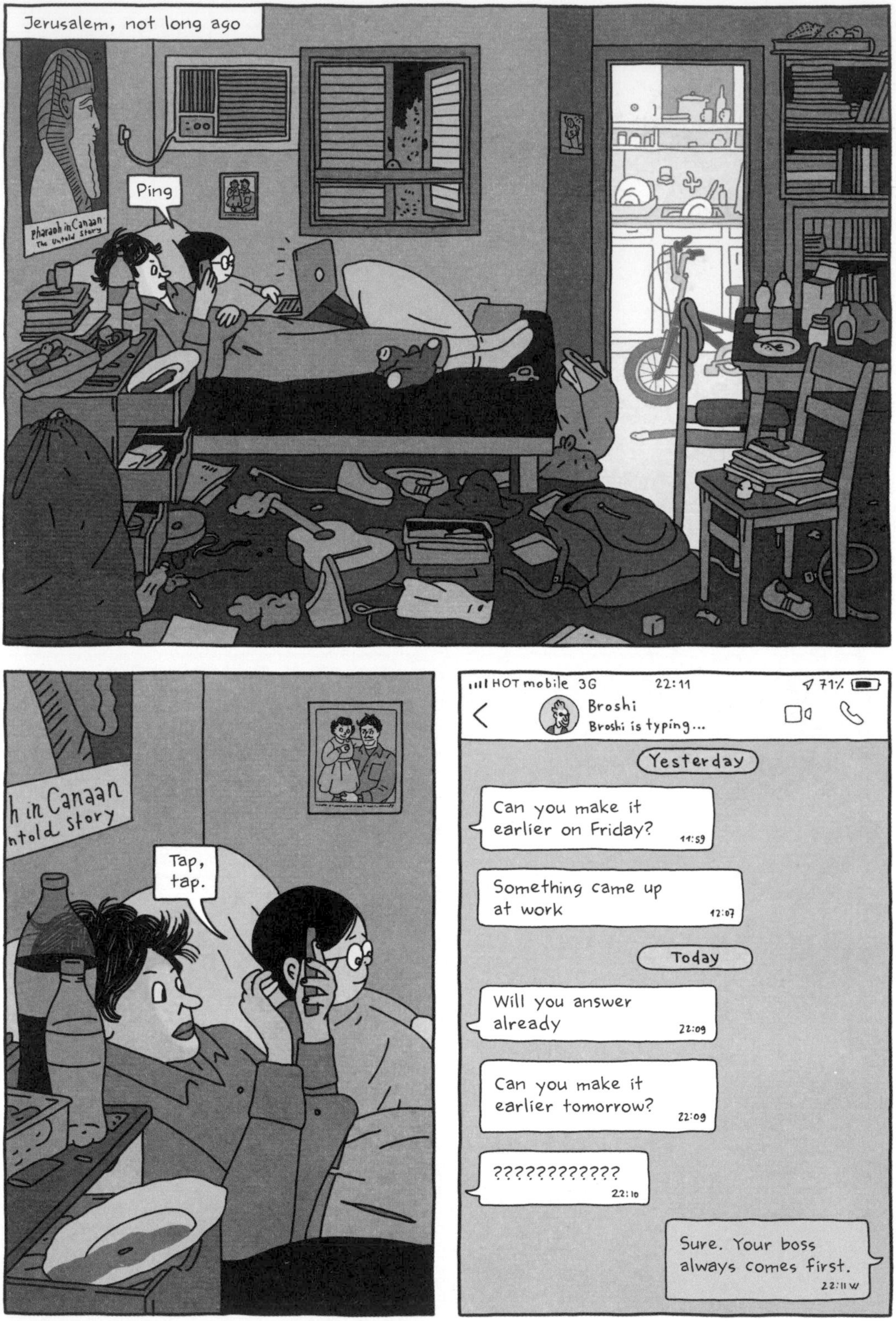

Jerusalem, not long ago
Pharaoh in Canaan
The Untold Story
Ping
h in Canaan
ntold story
Tap, tap.
HOT mobile 3G
22:11
71%
Broshi
Broshi is typing...
Yesterday
Can you make it earlier on Friday?
11:59
Something came up at work
12:07
Today
Will you answer already
22:09
Can you make it earlier tomorrow?
22:09
????????????
22:10
Sure. Your boss always comes first.
22:11

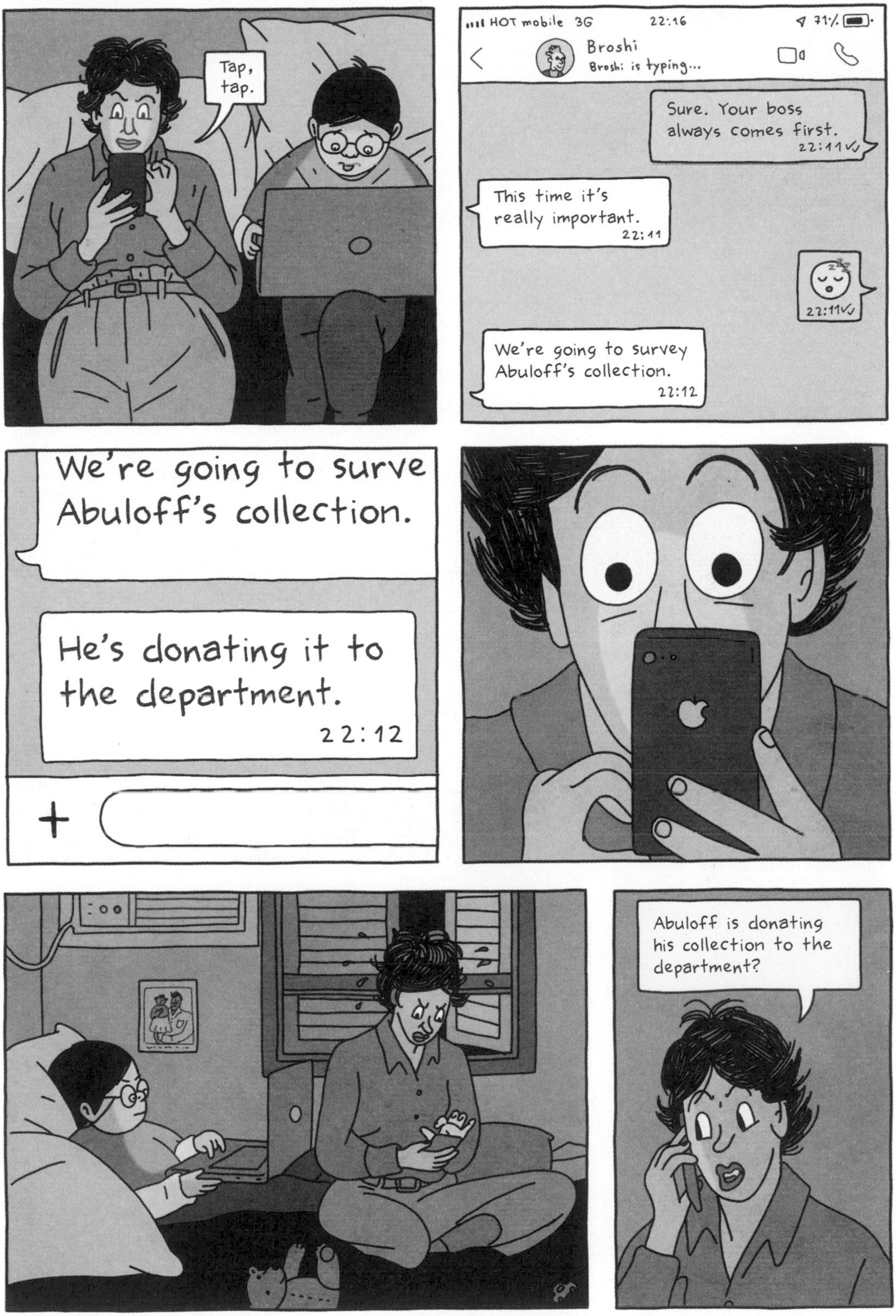
Tap, tap.
HOT mobile 3G 22:16 71%
Broshi
Broshi is typing...
Sure. Your boss always comes first. 22:11
This time it's really important. 22:11
22:11
We're going to survey Abuloff's collection. 22:12
We're going to surve Abuloff's collection.
He's donating it to the department. 22:12
Abuloff is donating his collection to the department?

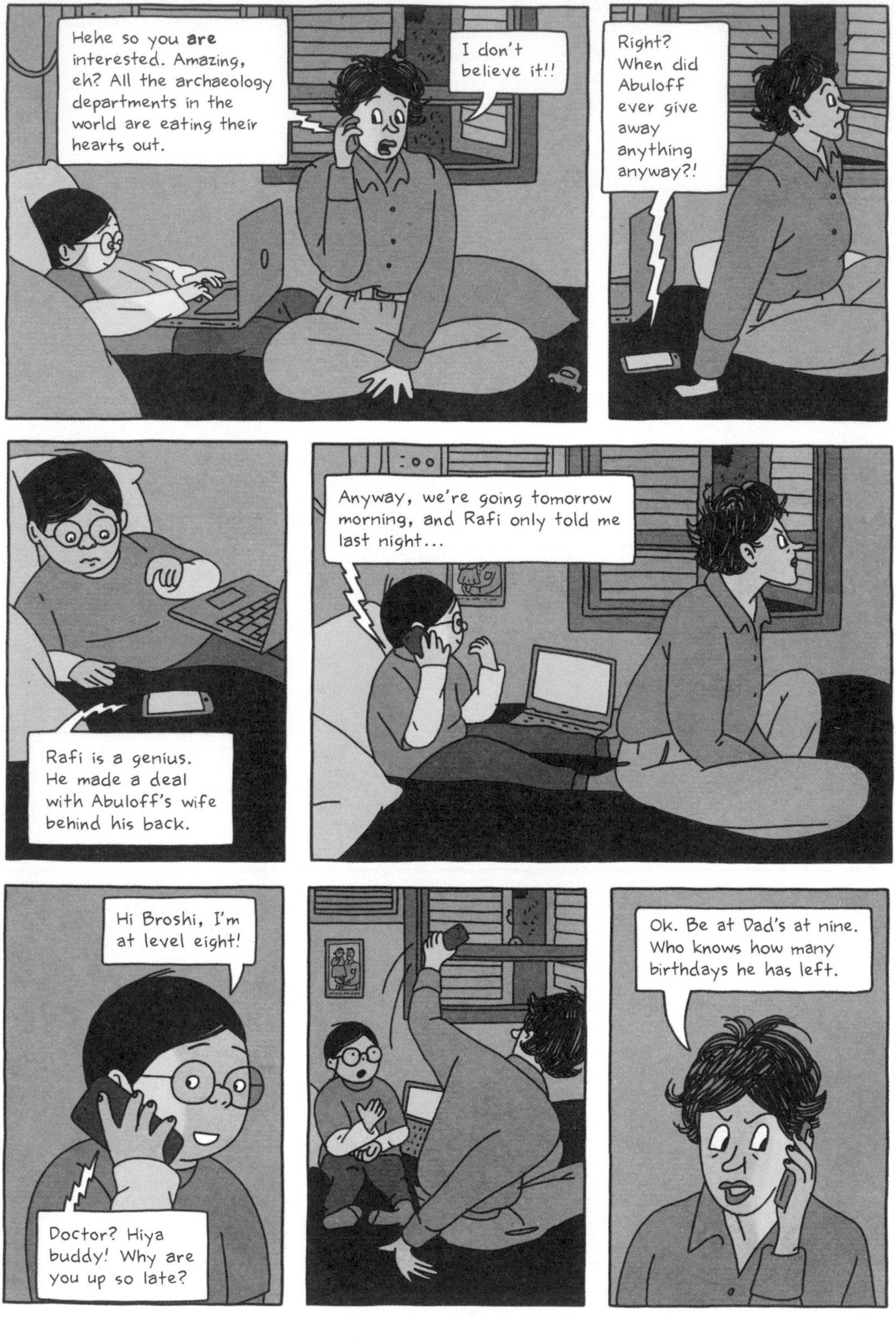
Hehe so you **are** interested. Amazing, eh? All the archaeology departments in the world are eating their hearts out.
I don't believe it!!
Right? When did Abuloff ever give away anything anyway?!
Rafi is a genius. He made a deal with Abuloff's wife behind his back.
Anyway, we're going tomorrow morning, and Rafi only told me last night...
Hi Broshi, I'm at level eight!
Doctor? Hiya buddy! Why are you up so late?
Ok. Be at Dad's at nine. Who knows how many birthdays he has left.

Next morning, 7am.

Gling-glong

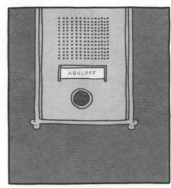

Gling-glong

Gling-glong

Emil, open the door! I'm on the phone!

I'm not opening for those vultures!

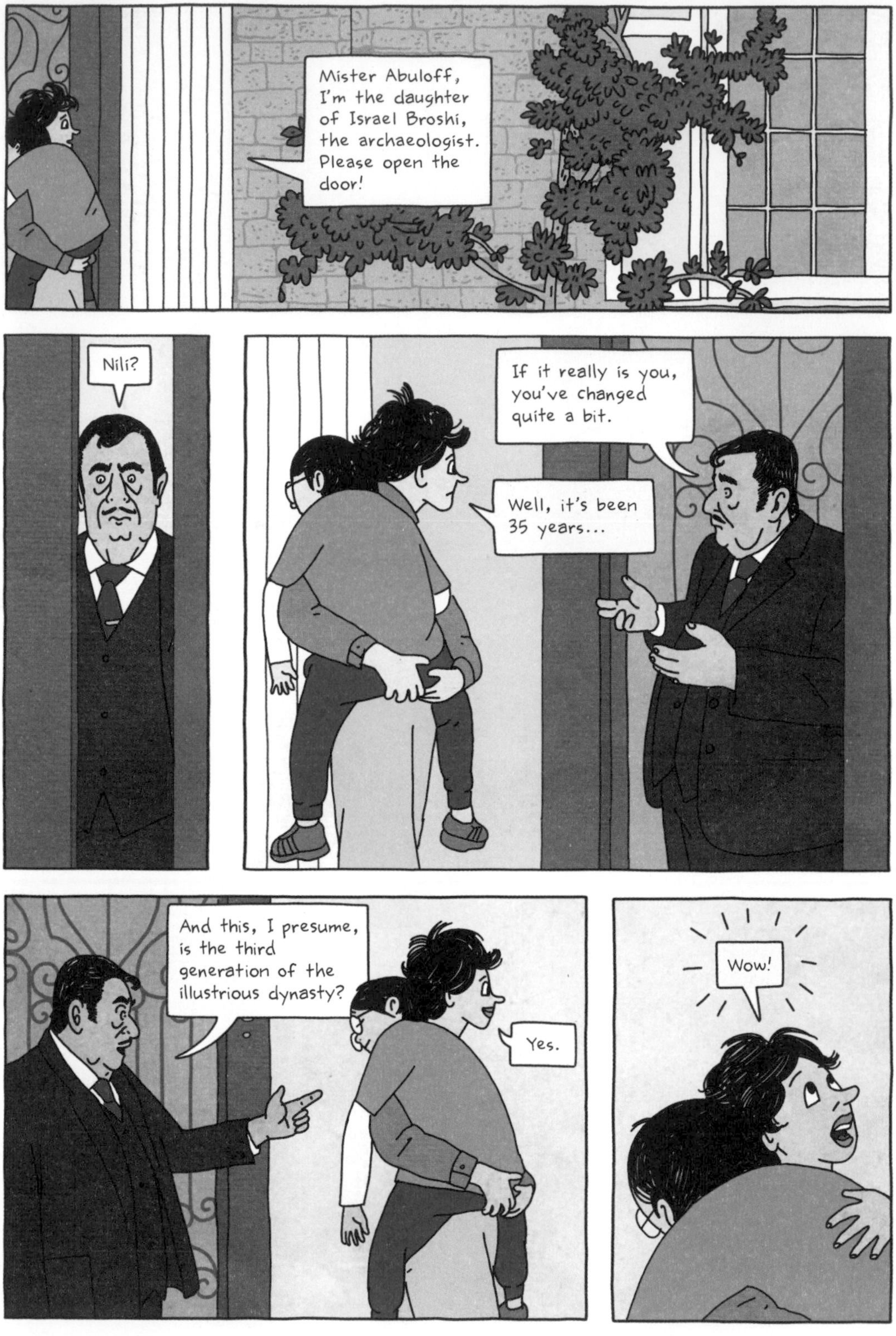
Mister Abuloff, I'm the daughter of Israel Broshi, the archaeologist. Please open the door!
Nili?
If it really is you, you've changed quite a bit.
Well, it's been 35 years...
And this, I presume, is the third generation of the illustrious dynasty?
Yes.
Wow!

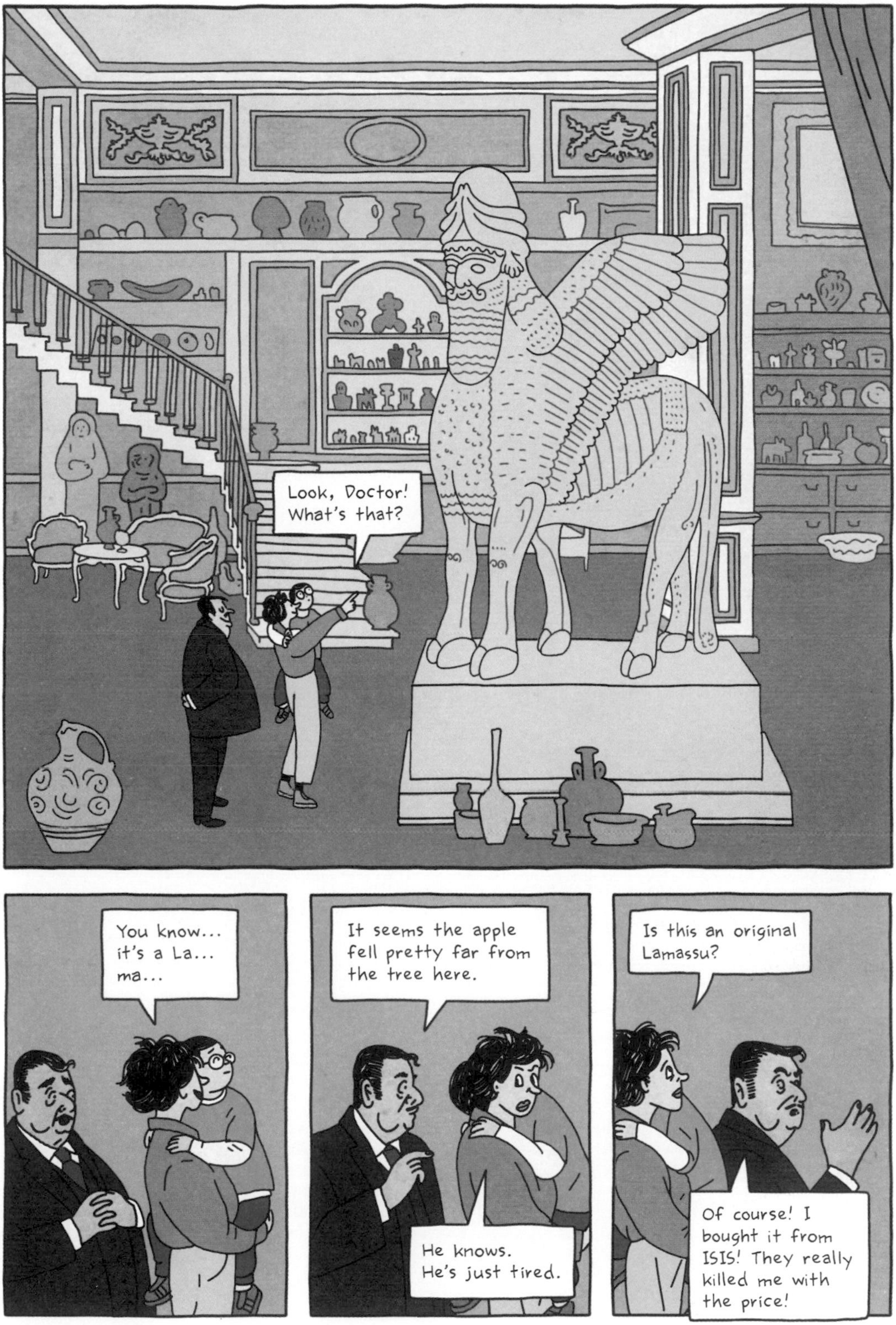
Look, Doctor! What's that?
You know... it's a La... ma...
It seems the apple fell pretty far from the tree here.
He knows. He's just tired.
Is this an original Lamassu?
Of course! I bought it from ISIS! They really killed me with the price!

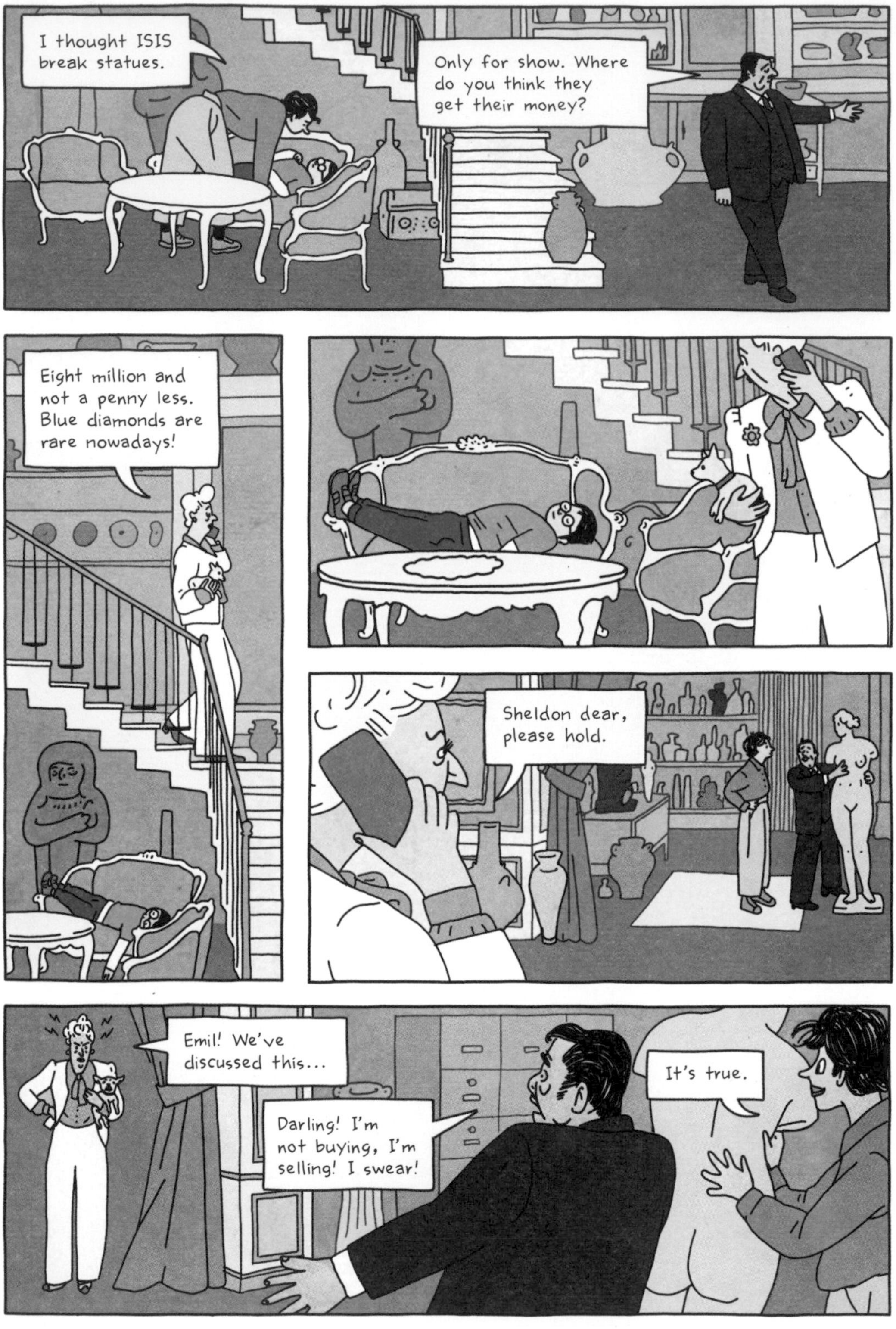
I thought ISIS break statues.
Only for show. Where do you think they get their money?
Eight million and not a penny less. Blue diamonds are rare nowadays!
Sheldon dear, please hold.
Emil! We've discussed this...
Darling! I'm not buying, I'm selling! I swear!
It's true.

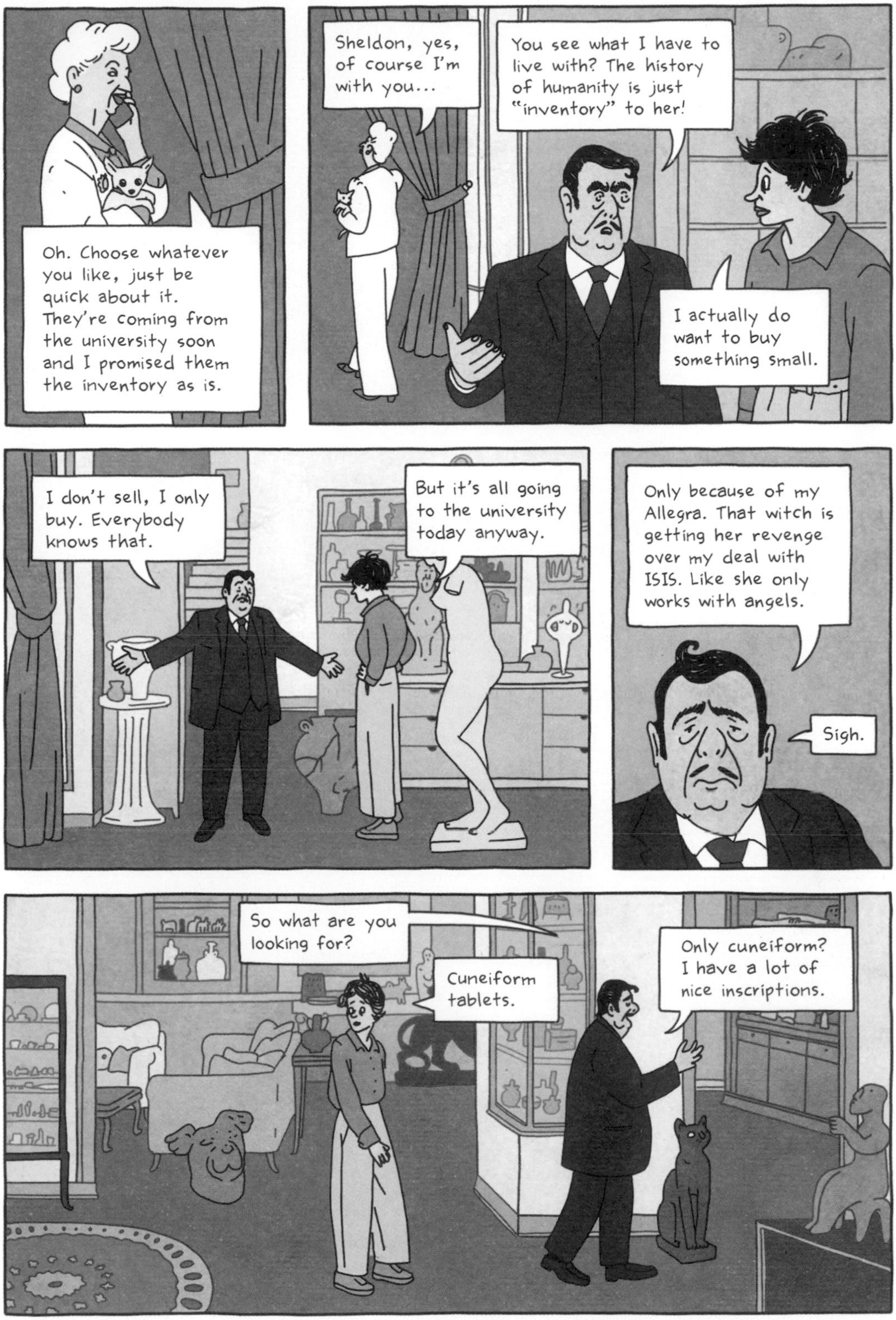
Oh. Choose whatever you like, just be quick about it. They're coming from the university soon and I promised them the inventory as is.
Sheldon, yes, of course I'm with you...
You see what I have to live with? The history of humanity is just "inventory" to her!
I actually do want to buy something small.
I don't sell, I only buy. Everybody knows that.
But it's all going to the university today anyway.
Only because of my Allegra. That witch is getting her revenge over my deal with ISIS. Like she only works with angels.
Sigh.
So what are you looking for?
Cuneiform tablets.
Only cuneiform? I have a lot of nice inscriptions.

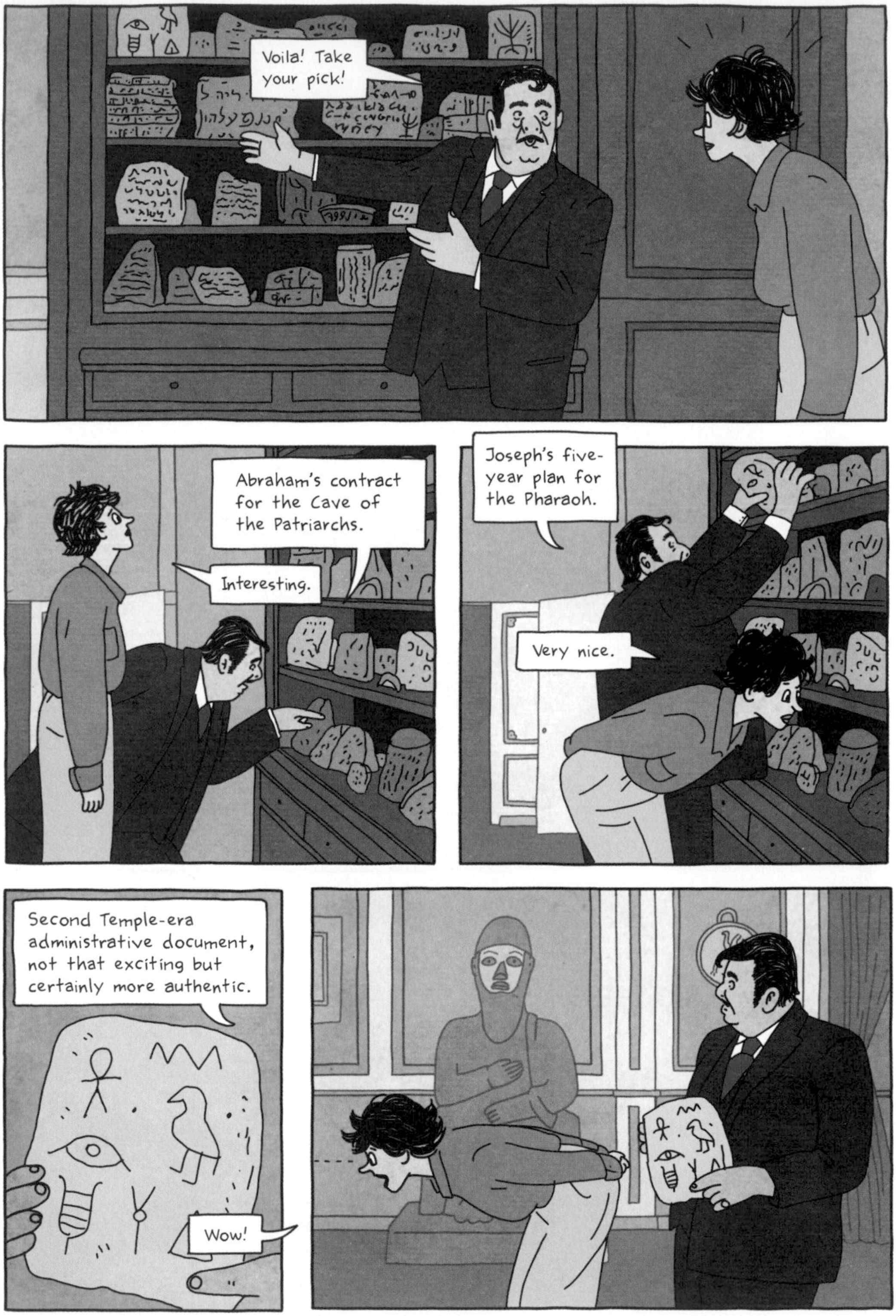
Voila! Take your pick!
Abraham's contract for the Cave of the Patriarchs.
Interesting.
Joseph's five-year plan for the Pharaoh.
Very nice.
Second Temple-era administrative document, not that exciting but certainly more authentic.
Wow!

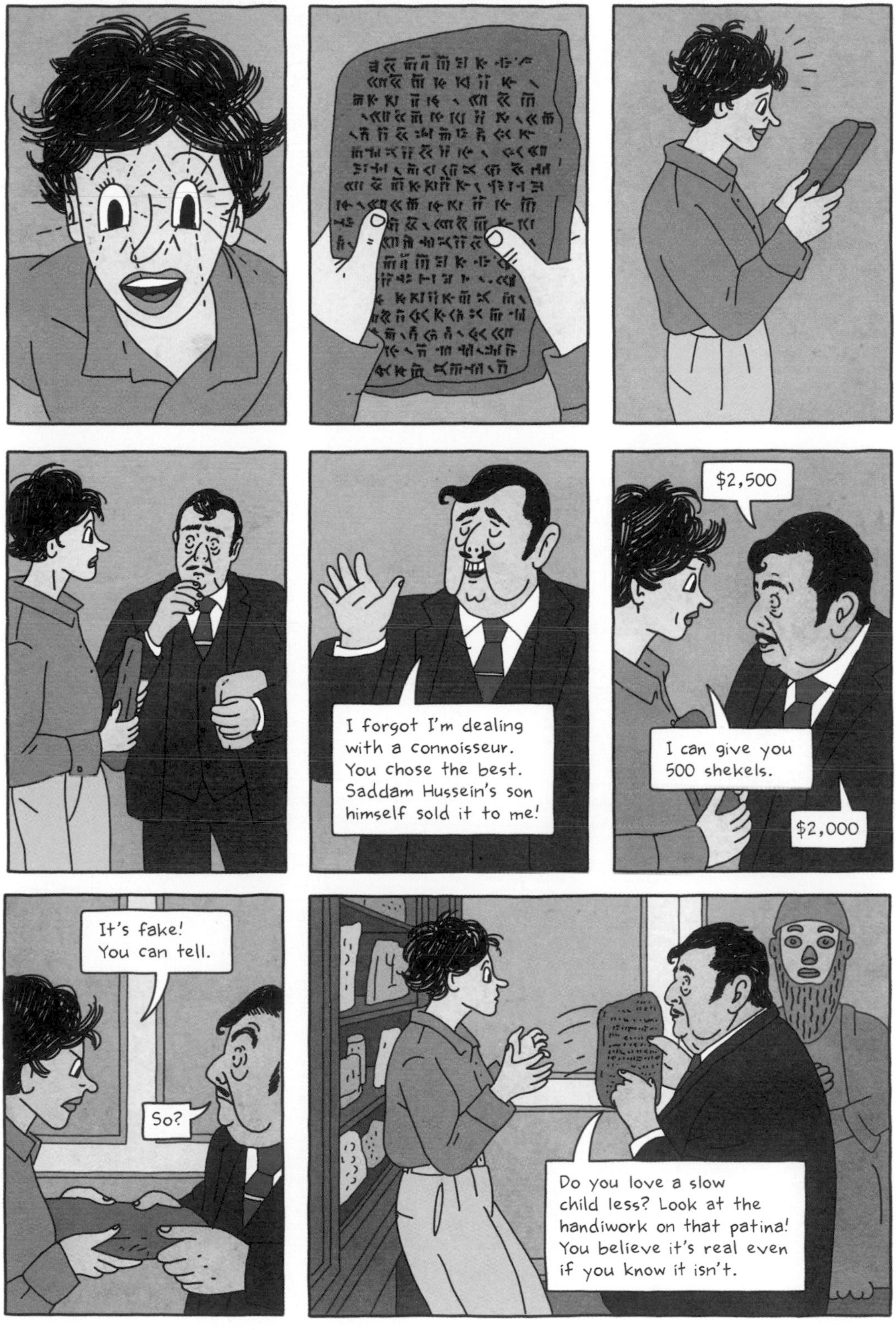
I forgot I'm dealing with a connoisseur. You chose the best. Saddam Hussein's son himself sold it to me!
$2,500
I can give you 500 shekels.
$2,000
It's fake! You can tell.
So?
Do you love a slow child less? Look at the handiwork on that patina! You believe it's real even if you know it isn't.

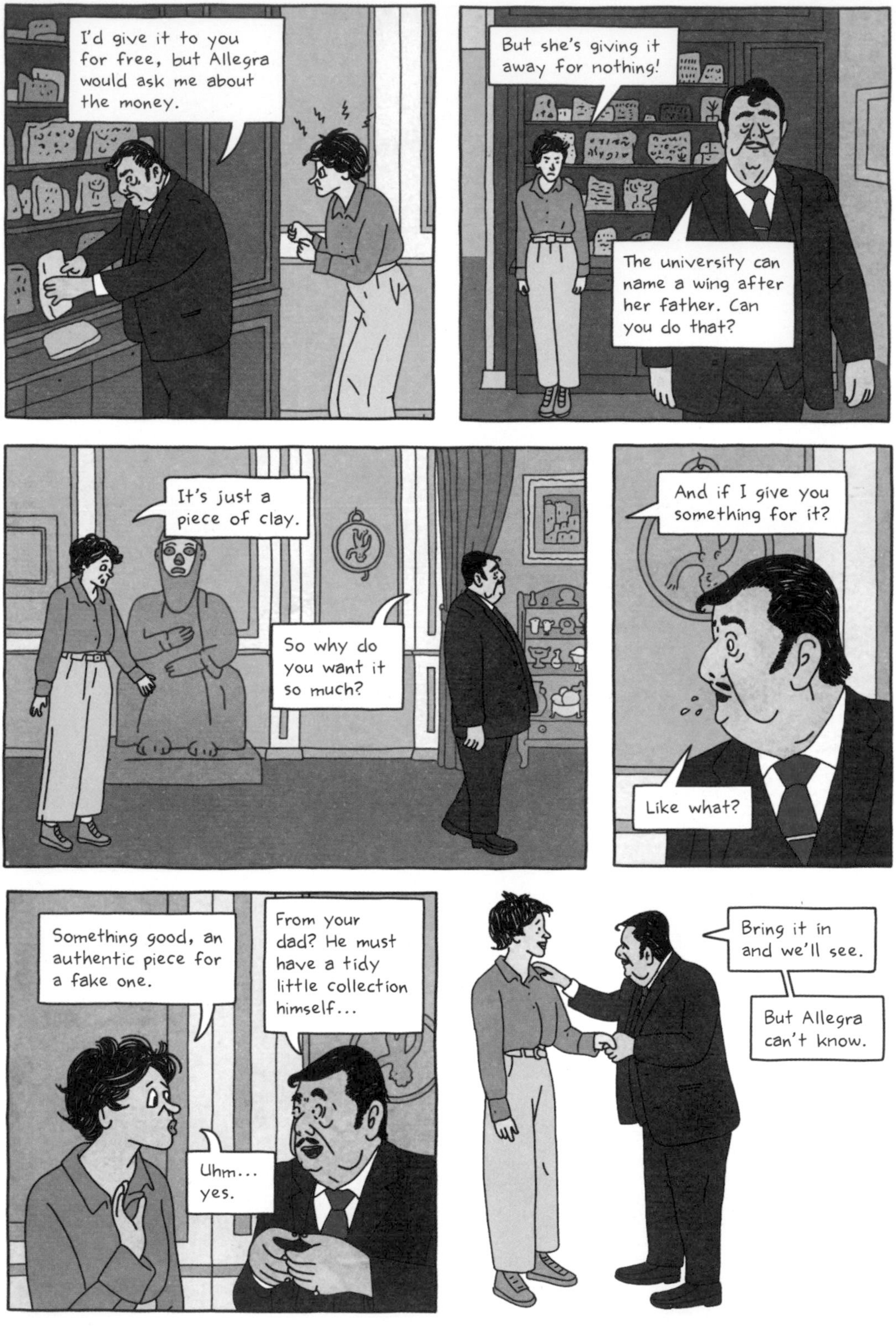

I'd give it to you for free, but Allegra would ask me about the money.
But she's giving it away for nothing!
The university can name a wing after her father. Can you do that?
It's just a piece of clay.
So why do you want it so much?
And if I give you something for it?
Like what?
Something good, an authentic piece for a fake one.
From your dad? He must have a tidy little collection himself...
Uhm... yes.
Bring it in and we'll see.
But Allegra can't know.

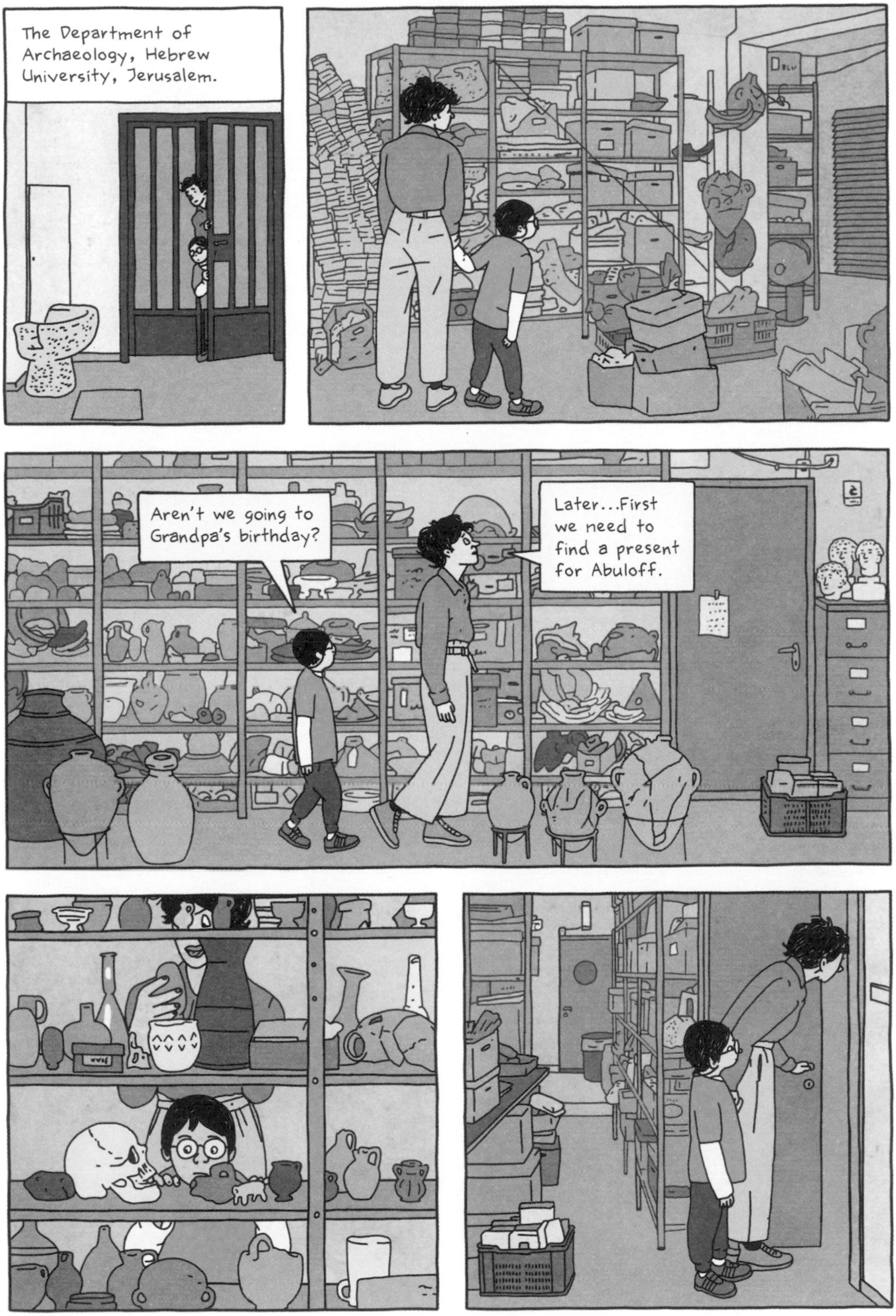
The Department of Archaeology, Hebrew University, Jerusalem.
Aren't we going to Grandpa's birthday?
Later...First we need to find a present for Abuloff.

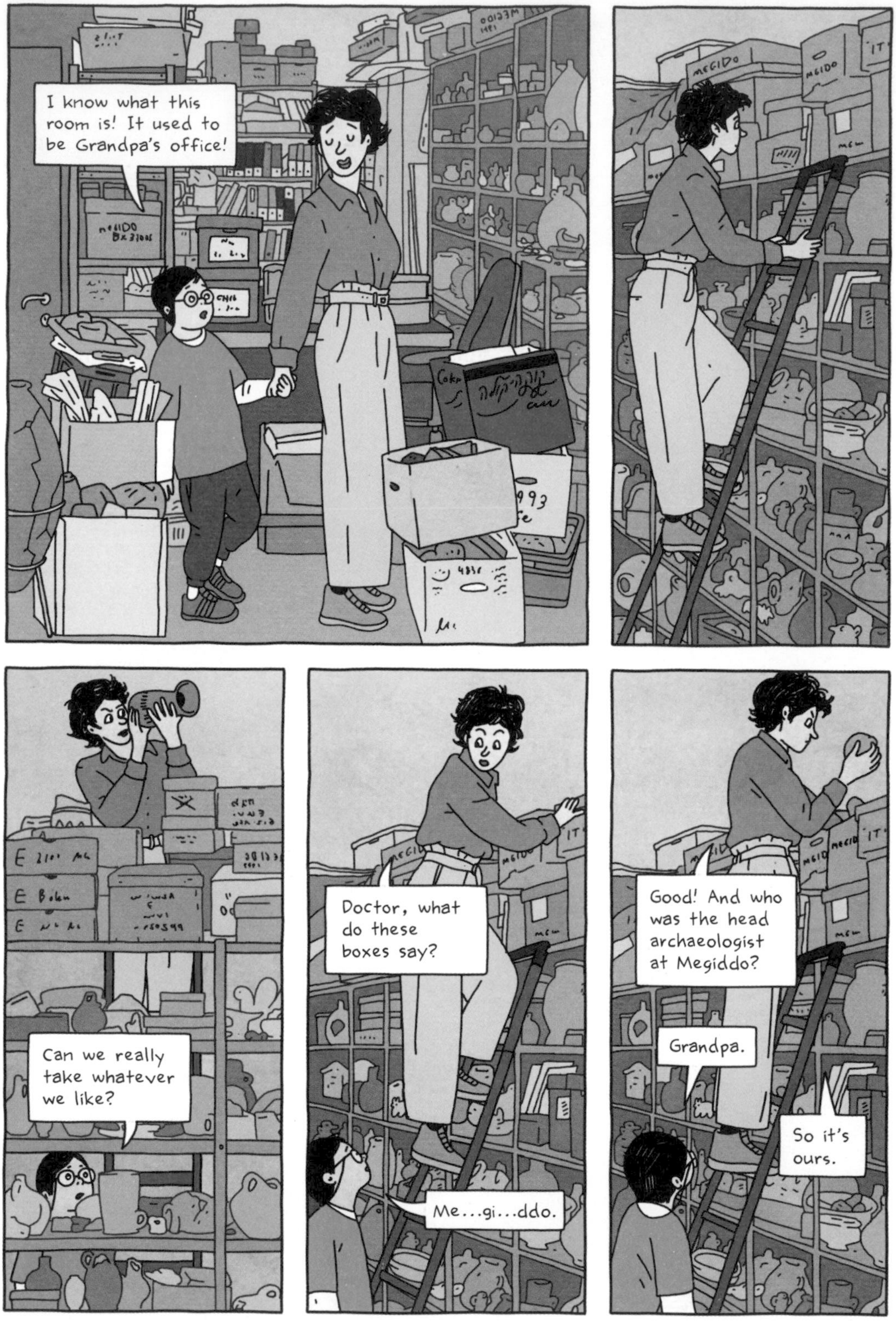
I know what this room is! It used to be Grandpa's office!
MEGIDO
MEGIDO
Can we really take whatever we like?
Doctor, what do these boxes say?
Me...gi...ddo.
Good! And who was the head archaeologist at Megiddo?
Grandpa.
So it's ours.

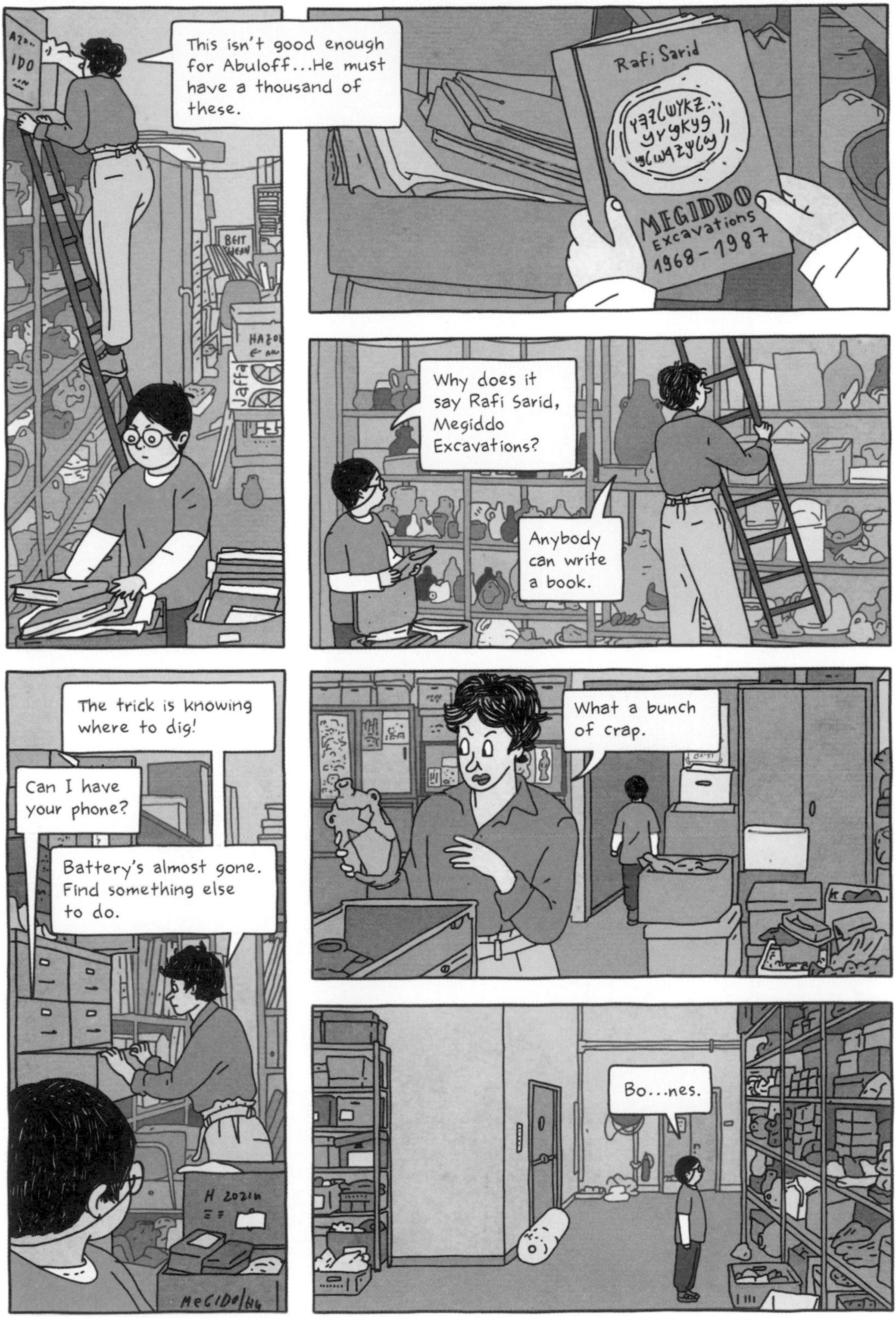

This isn't good enough for Abuloff...He must have a thousand of these.
Rafi Sarid
MEGIDDO
Excavations
1968-1987
Why does it say Rafi Sarid, Megiddo Excavations?
Anybody can write a book.
The trick is knowing where to dig!
Can I have your phone?
Battery's almost gone. Find something else to do.
What a bunch of crap.
Bo...nes.

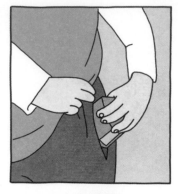

Prof. Rafi Sarid
Department Chair

Prof...Ra... fi...Sarid.

Esteemed President of the State of Israel, ladies and gentlemen...

It is with pride, humility, and some degree of sincere astonishment that I find myself on this platform today...

Accepting the Future of the Past Award.

22

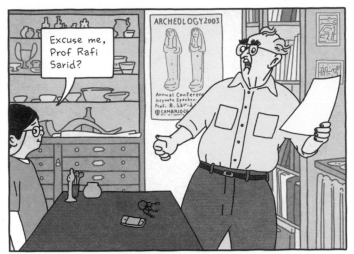

Excuse me, Prof Rafi Sarid?

ARCHEOLOGY 2003

Annual Conference
Keynote Speaker
Prof. R. Sarid
CAMBRIDGE

What percentage do you have?

You're Broshi's nephew, no? Is he here?

No, I came with Mommy.

What on earth is she after?

Grandpa's findings.

What?! How dare she!

BEIT SHEAN

The nerve!

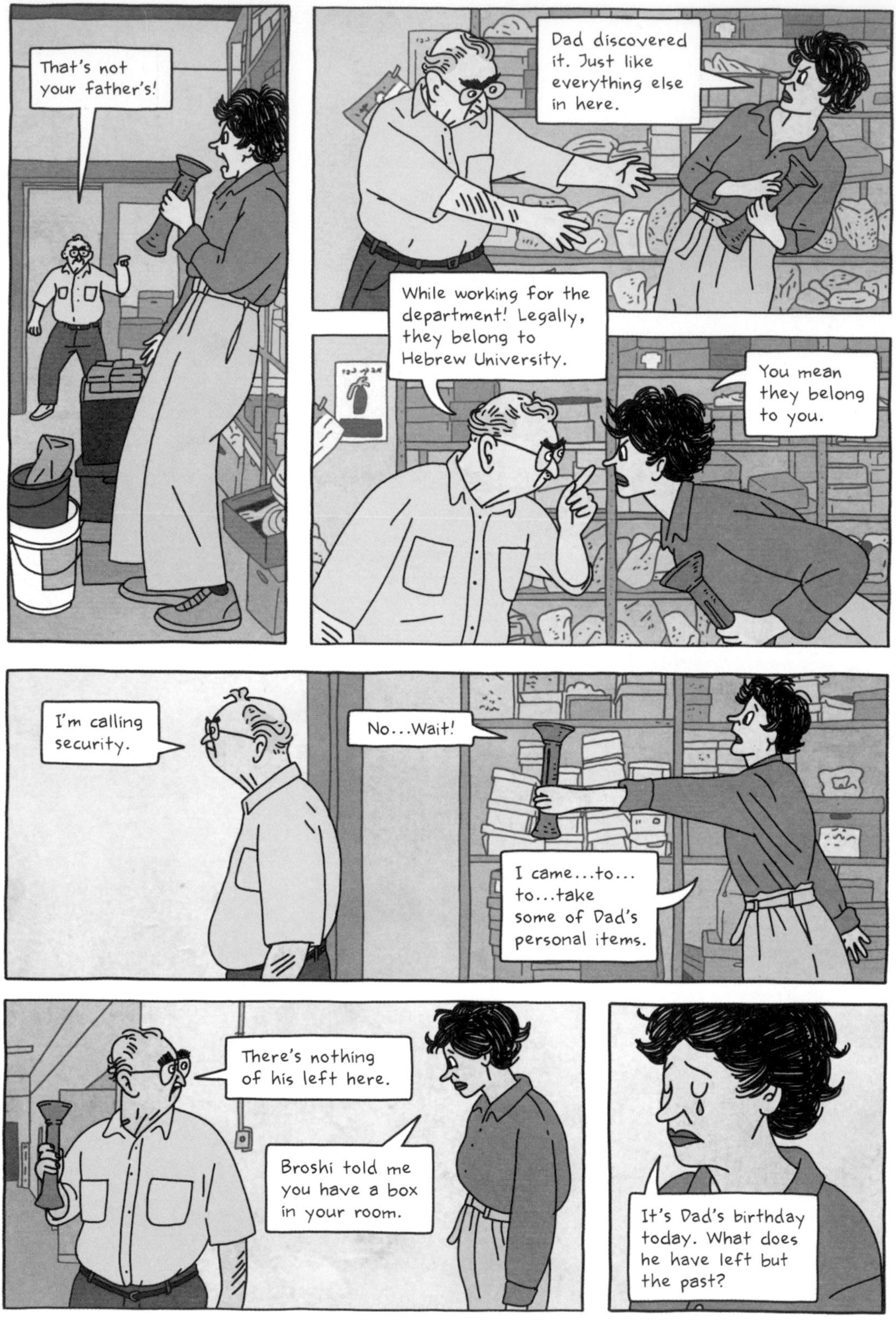
That's not your father's!
Dad discovered it. Just like everything else in here.
While working for the department! Legally, they belong to Hebrew University.
You mean they belong to you.
I'm calling security.
No...Wait!
I came...to... to...take some of Dad's personal items.
There's nothing of his left here.
Broshi told me you have a box in your room.
It's Dad's birthday today. What does he have left but the past?

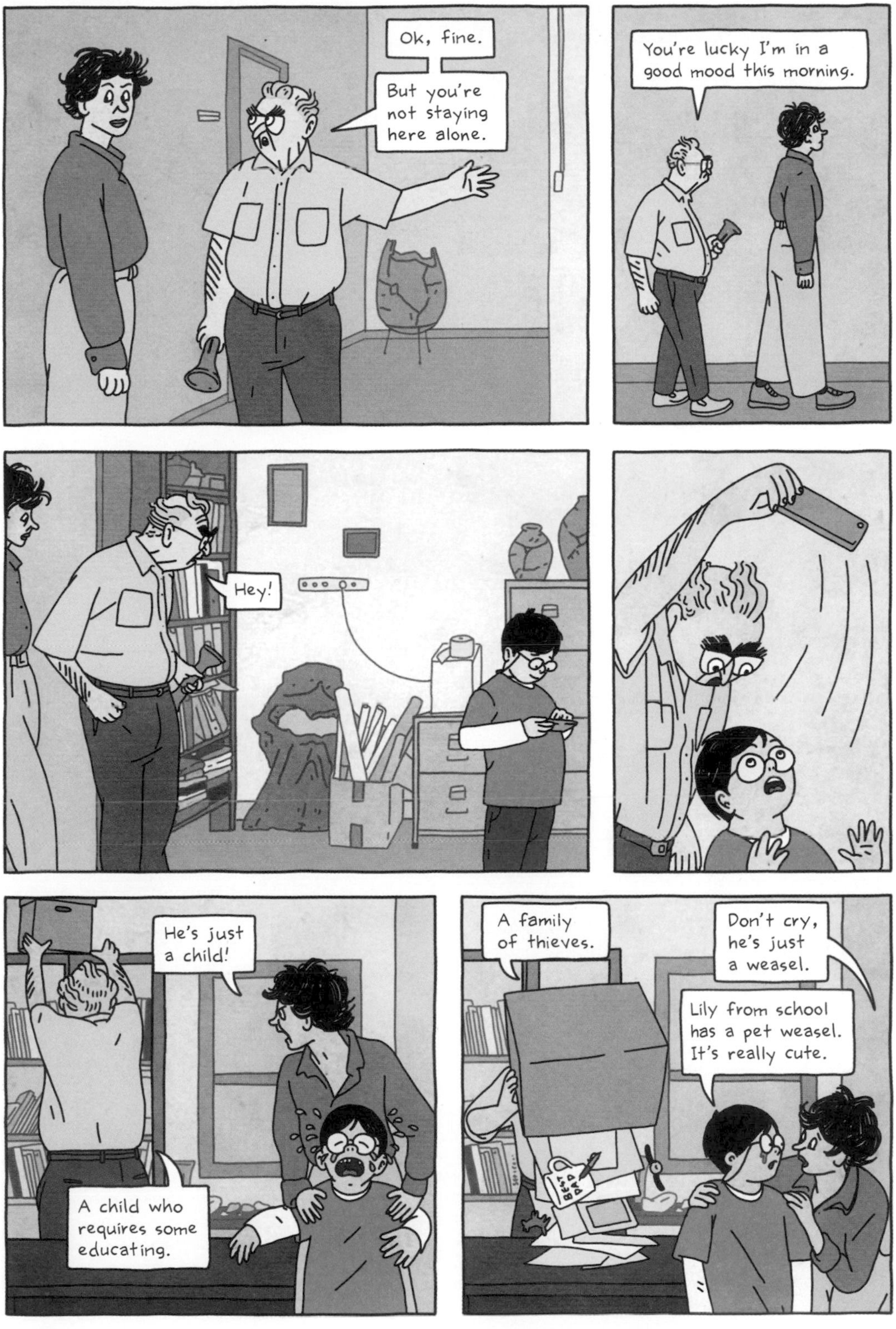
Ok, fine.
But you're not staying here alone.
You're lucky I'm in a good mood this morning.
Hey!
He's just a child!
A child who requires some educating.
A family of thieves.
Don't cry, he's just a weasel.
Lily from school has a pet weasel. It's really cute.
BEST DAD

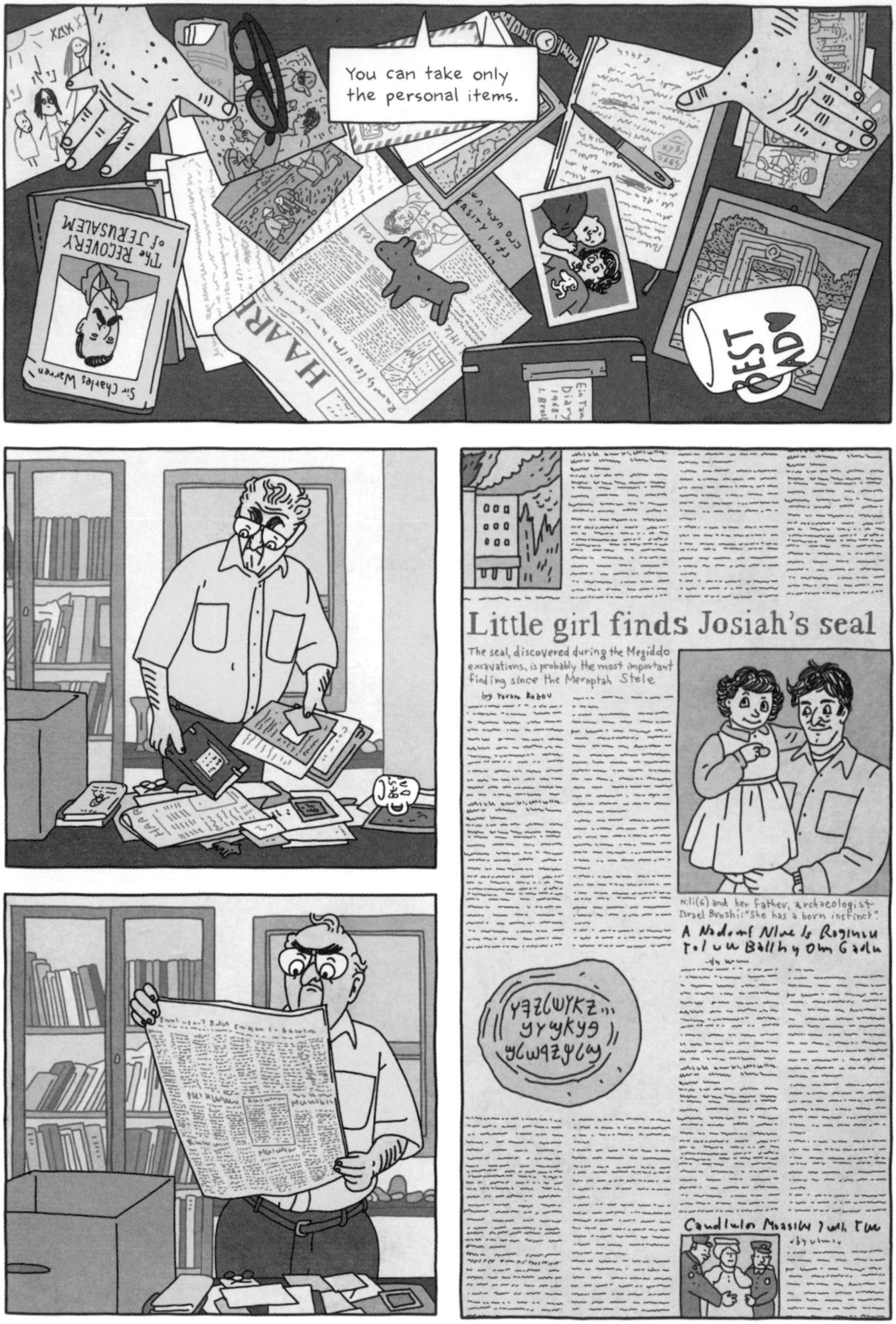
You can take only the personal items.
The RECOVERY of JERUSALEM
Sir Charles Warren
Little girl finds Josiah's seal
The seal, discovered during the Megiddo excavations, is probably the most important finding since the Merneptah Stele
by Yoram Rabov
Nili(6) and her father, archaeologist Israel Broshi: "She has a born instinct".

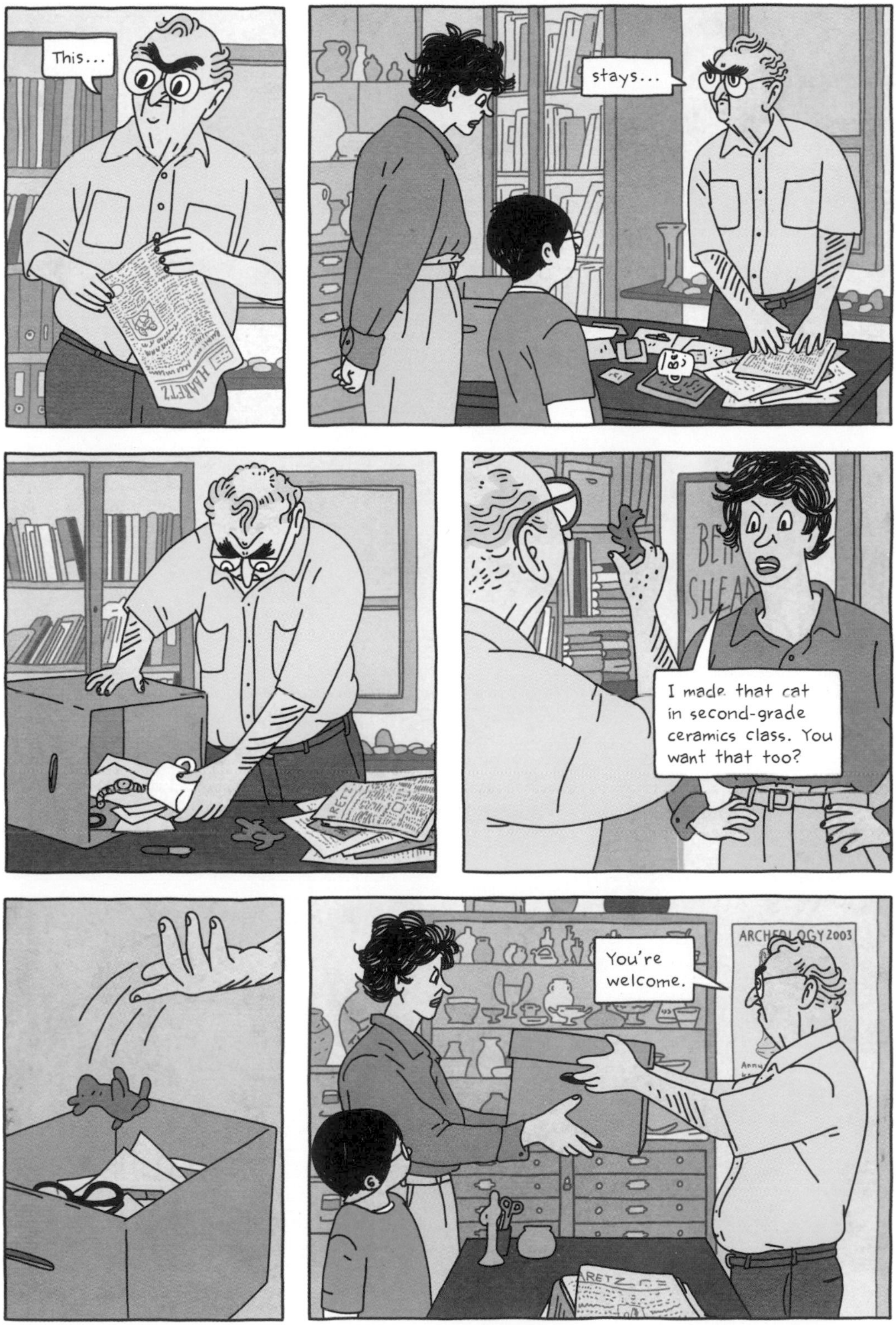
This...
stays...
I made that cat in second-grade ceramics class. You want that too?
You're welcome.

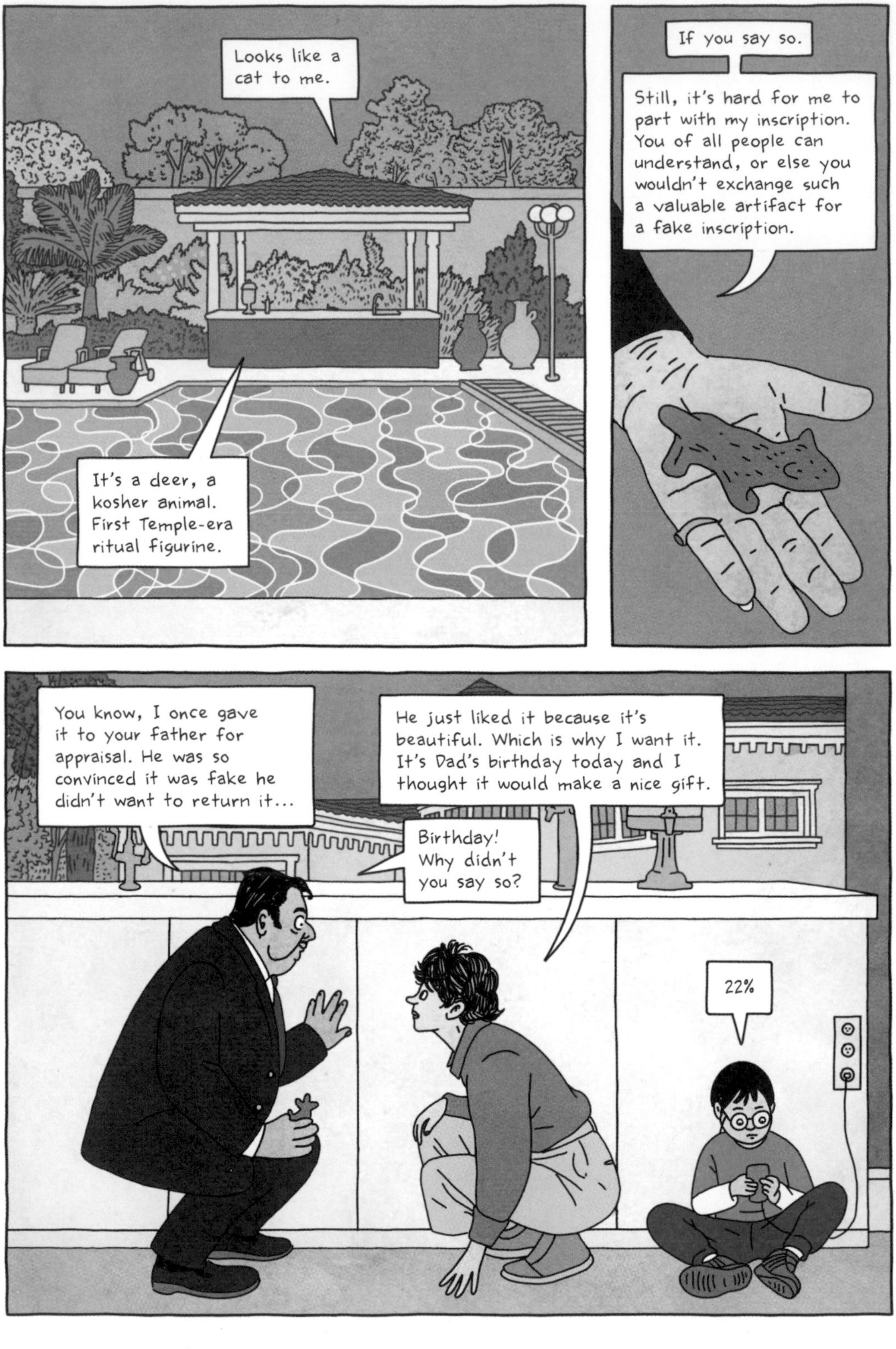
Looks like a cat to me.
It's a deer, a kosher animal. First Temple-era ritual figurine.
If you say so.
Still, it's hard for me to part with my inscription. You of all people can understand, or else you wouldn't exchange such a valuable artifact for a fake inscription.
You know, I once gave it to your father for appraisal. He was so convinced it was fake he didn't want to return it...
He just liked it because it's beautiful. Which is why I want it. It's Dad's birthday today and I thought it would make a nice gift.
Birthday! Why didn't you say so?
22%

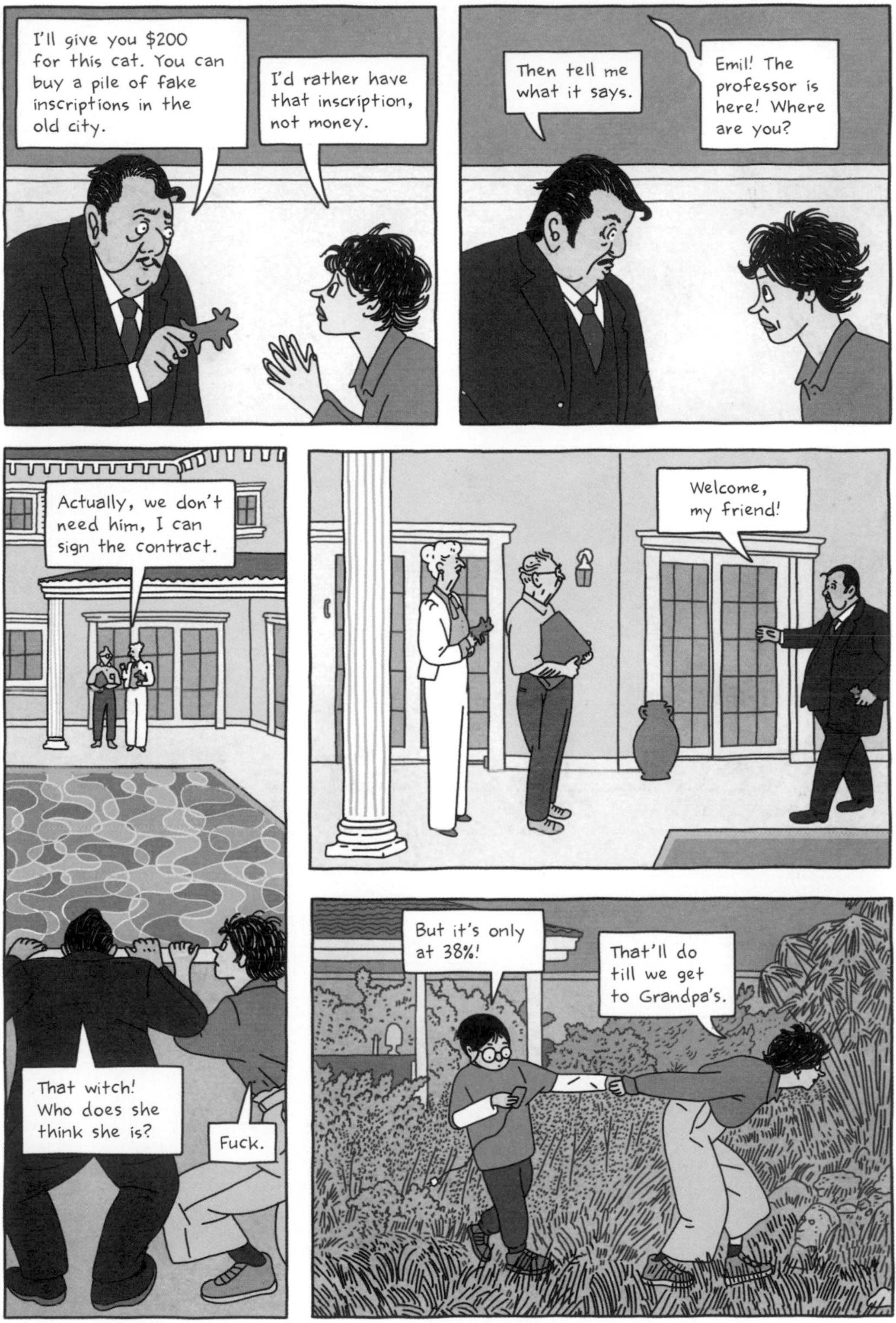
I'll give you $200 for this cat. You can buy a pile of fake inscriptions in the old city.
I'd rather have that inscription, not money.
Then tell me what it says.
Emil! The professor is here! Where are you?
Actually, we don't need him, I can sign the contract.
Welcome, my friend!
That witch! Who does she think she is?
Fuck.
But it's only at 38%!
That'll do till we get to Grandpa's.

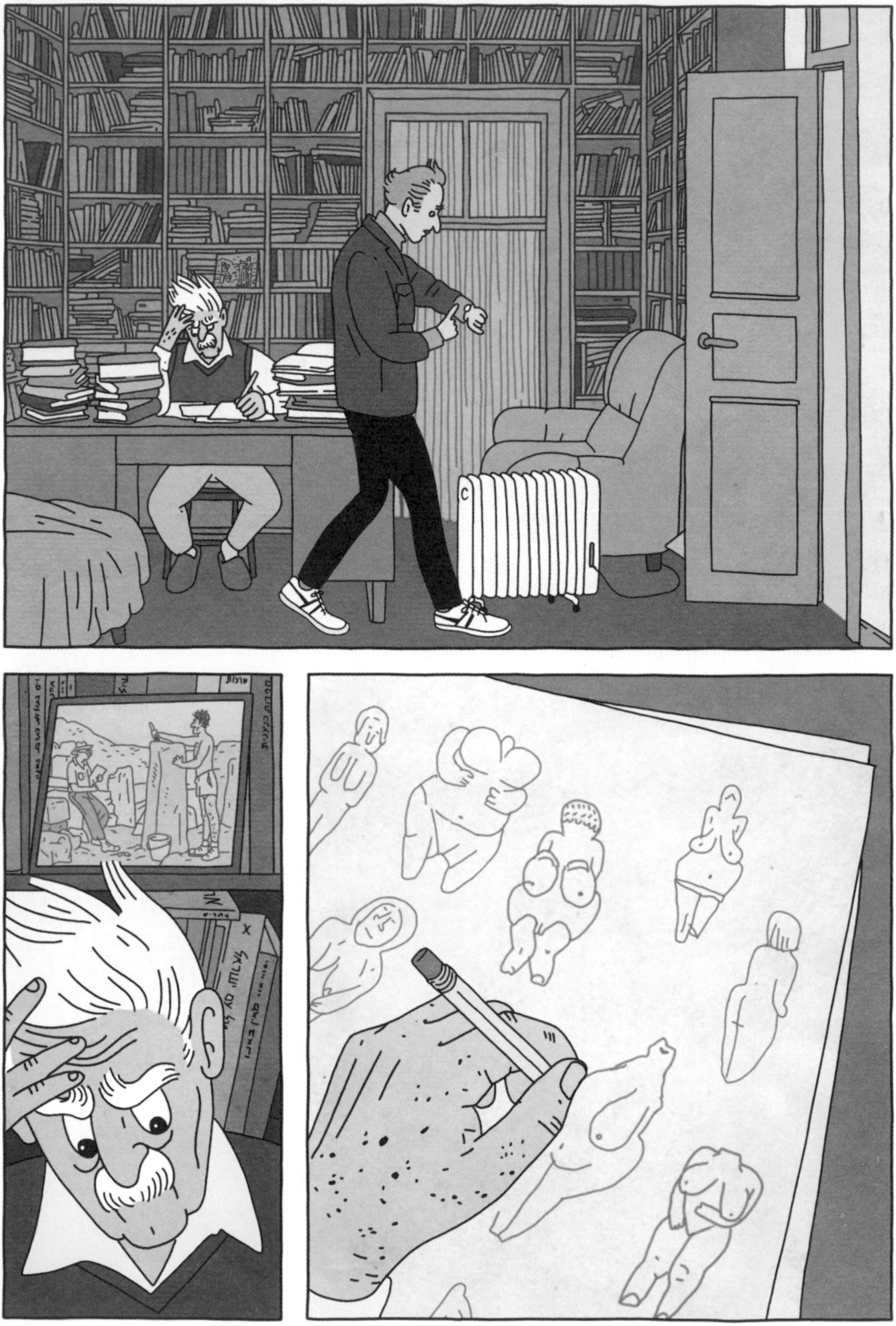

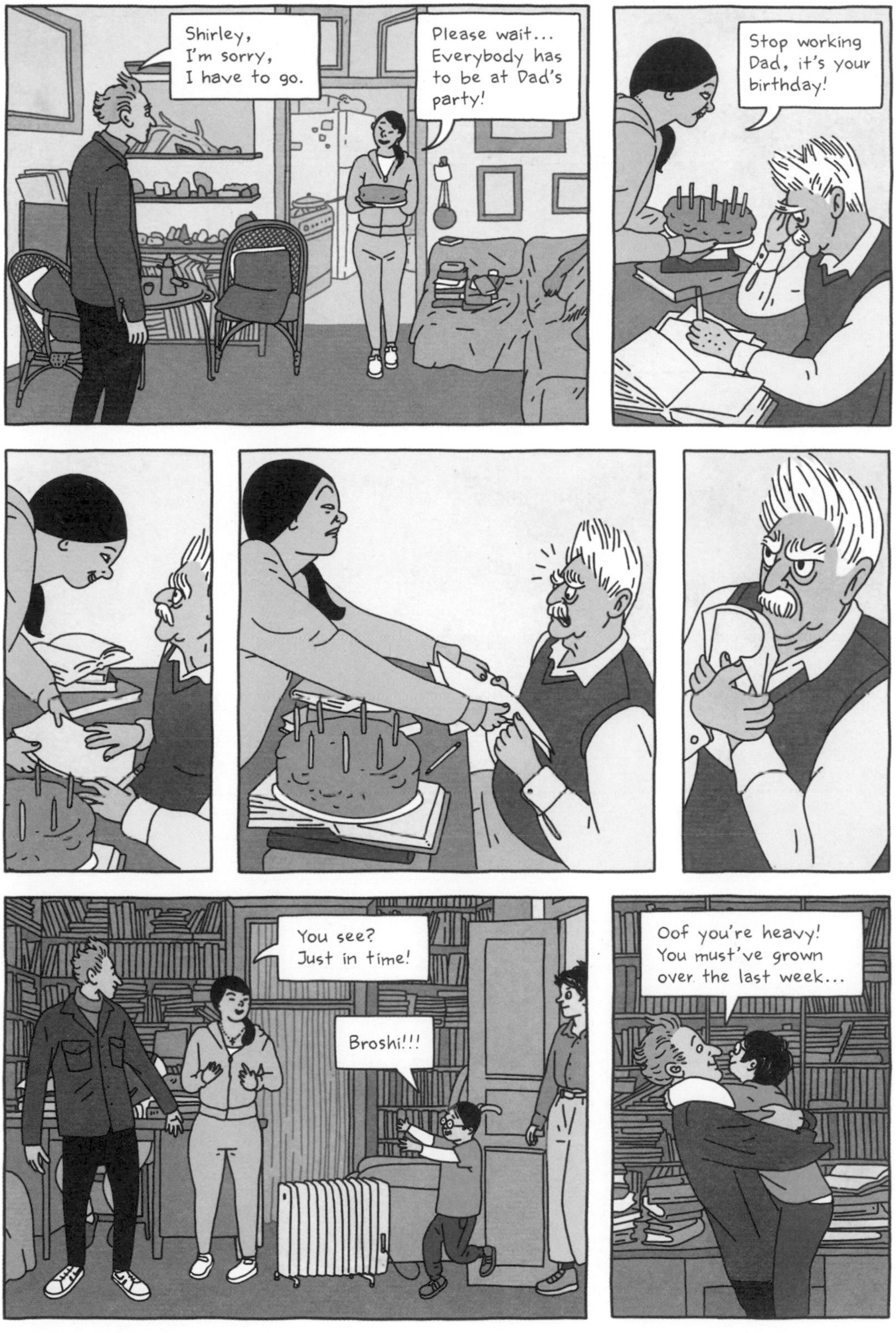
Shirley, I'm sorry, I have to go.
Please wait... Everybody has to be at Dad's party!
Stop working Dad, it's your birthday!
You see? Just in time!
Broshi!!!
Oof you're heavy! You must've grown over the last week...

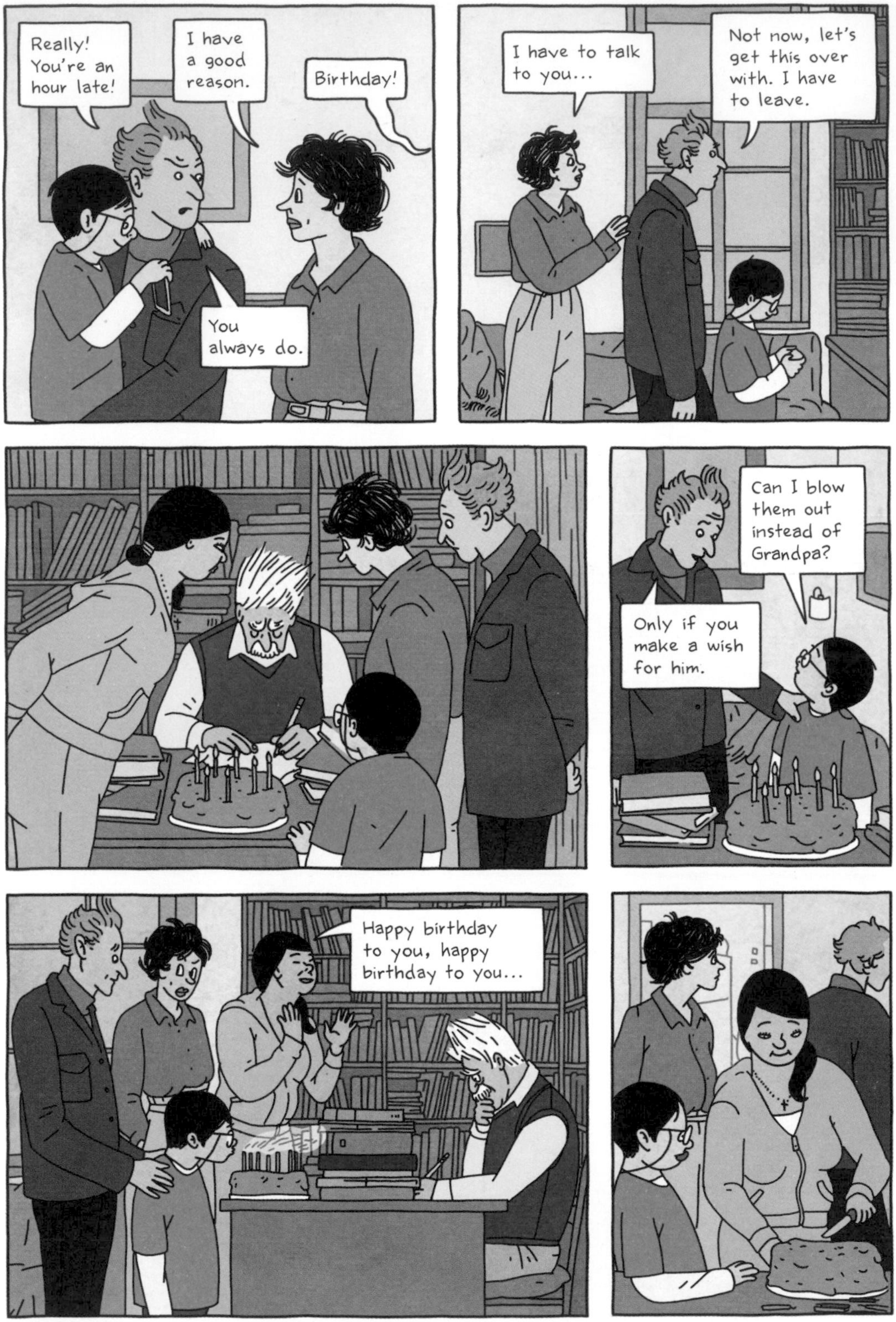
Really! You're an hour late!
I have a good reason.
Birthday!
You always do.
I have to talk to you...
Not now, let's get this over with. I have to leave.
Can I blow them out instead of Grandpa?
Only if you make a wish for him.
Happy birthday to you, happy birthday to you...

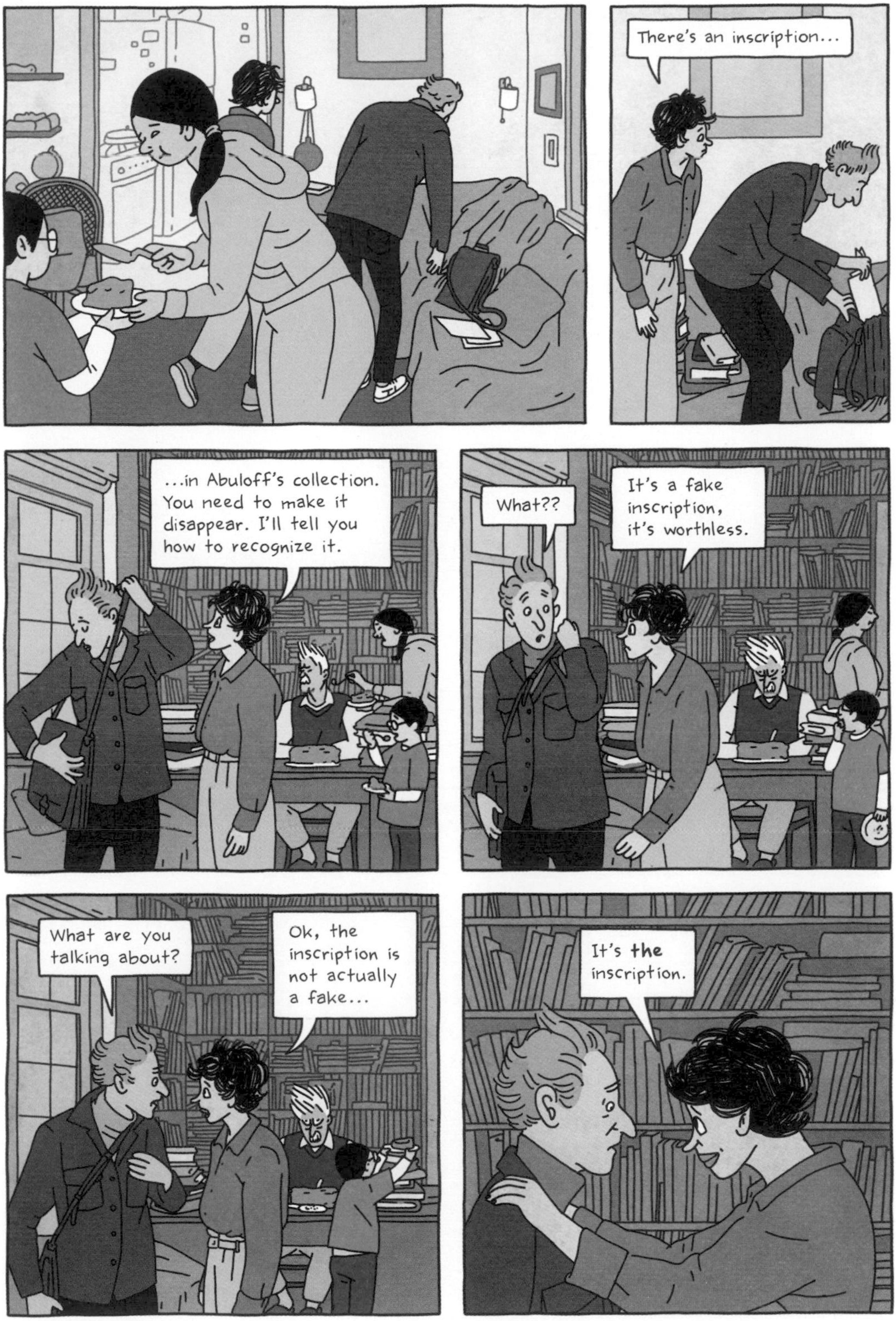
There's an inscription...
...in Abuloff's collection. You need to make it disappear. I'll tell you how to recognize it.
What??
It's a fake inscription, it's worthless.
What are you talking about?
Ok, the inscription is not actually a fake...
It's **the** inscription.

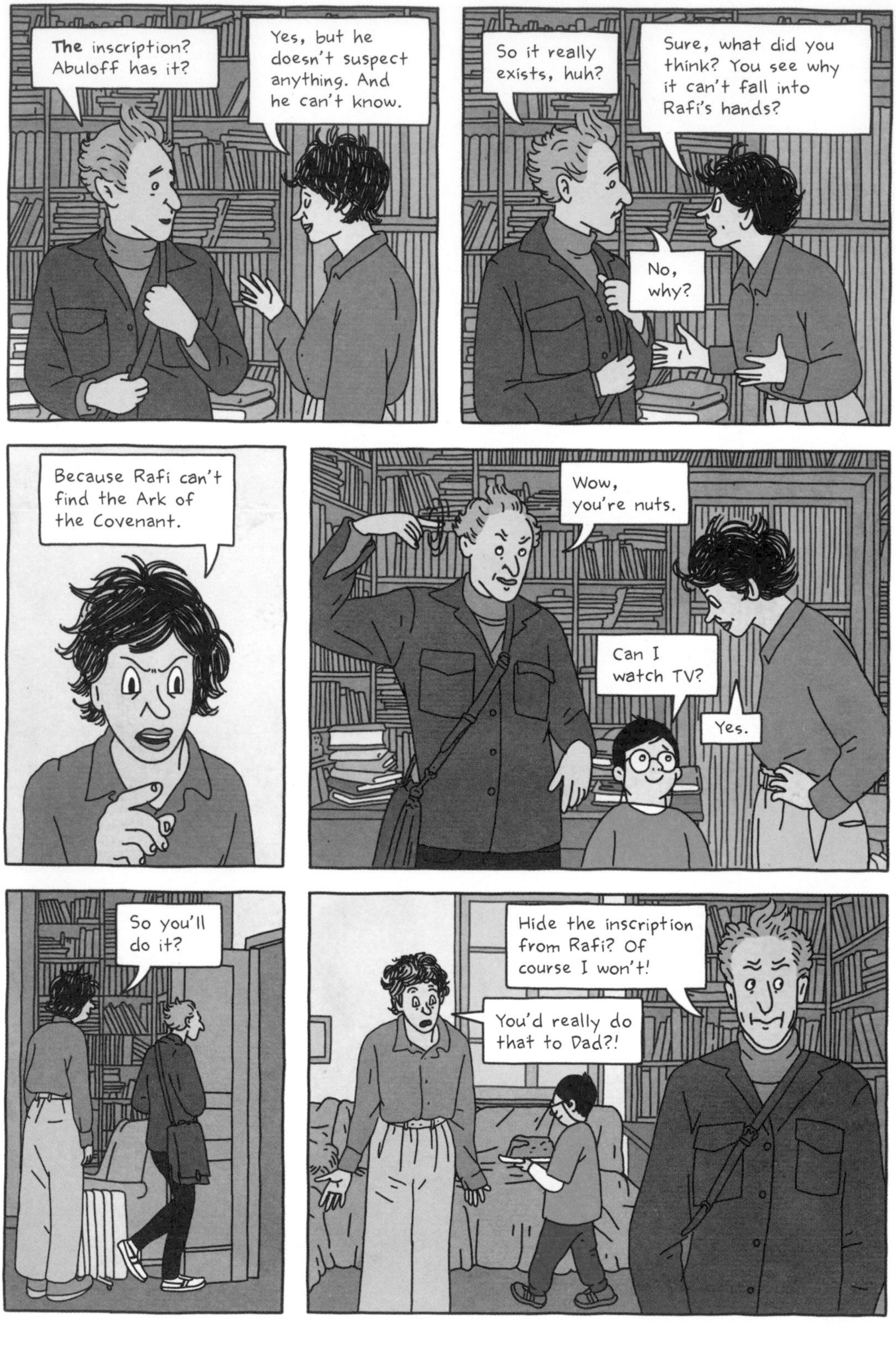

The inscription? Abuloff has it?
Yes, but he doesn't suspect anything. And he can't know.
So it really exists, huh?
Sure, what did you think? You see why it can't fall into Rafi's hands?
No, why?
Because Rafi can't find the Ark of the Covenant.
Wow, you're nuts.
Can I watch TV?
Yes.
So you'll do it?
Hide the inscription from Rafi? Of course I won't!
You'd really do that to Dad?!

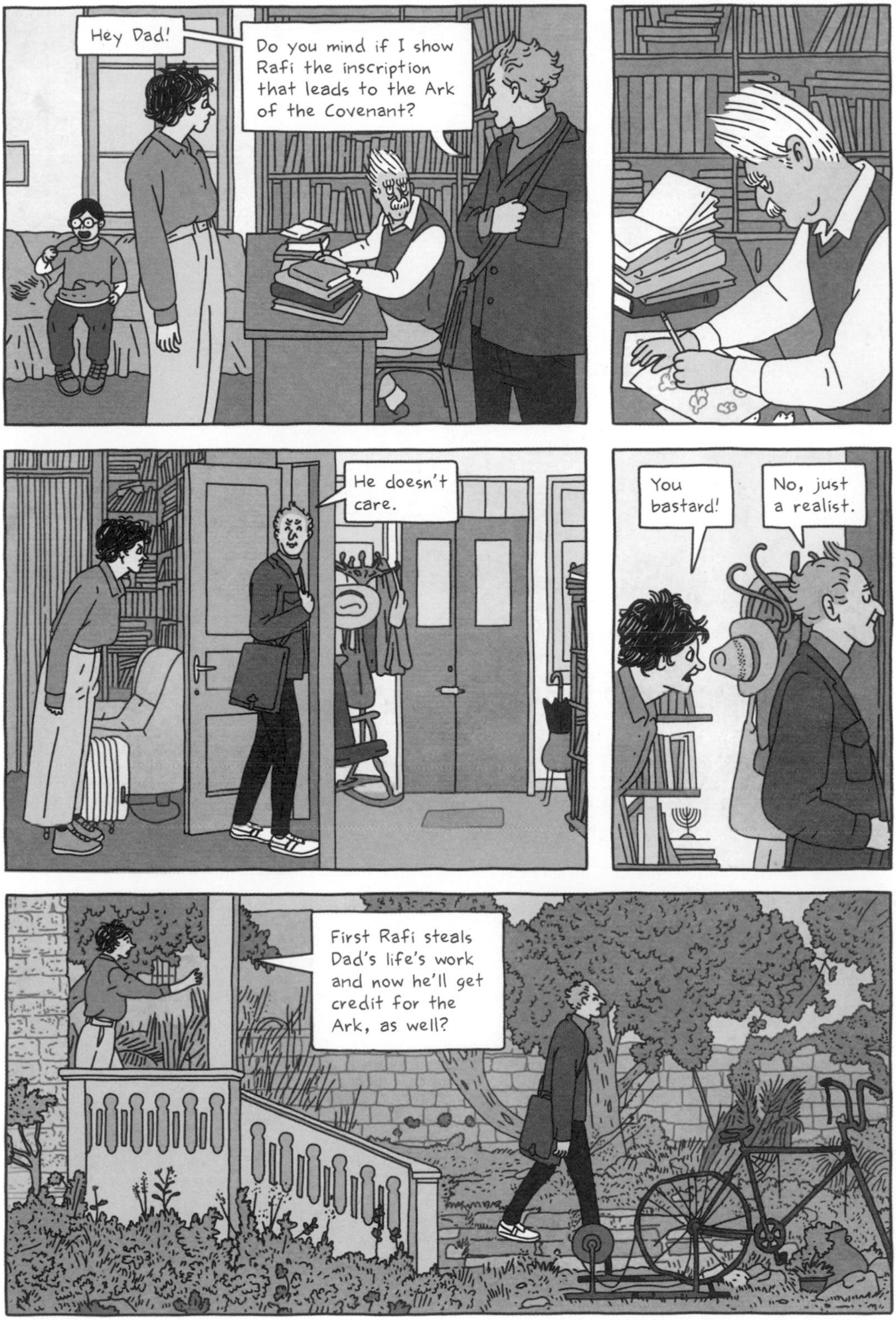
Hey Dad!
Do you mind if I show Rafi the inscription that leads to the Ark of the Covenant?
He doesn't care.
You bastard!
No, just a realist.
First Rafi steals Dad's life's work and now he'll get credit for the Ark, as well?

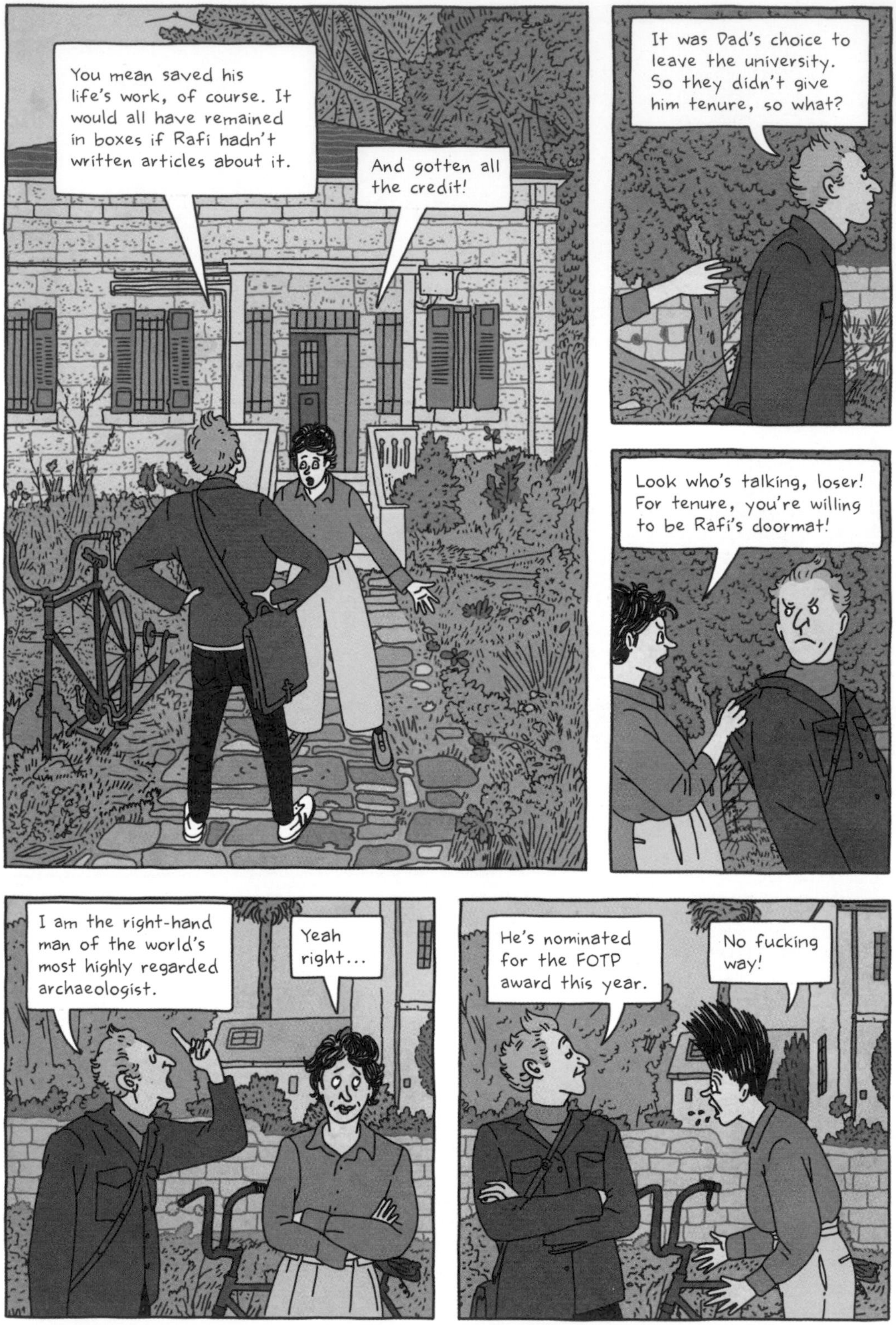
You mean saved his life's work, of course. It would all have remained in boxes if Rafi hadn't written articles about it.
And gotten all the credit!
It was Dad's choice to leave the university. So they didn't give him tenure, so what?
Look who's talking, loser! For tenure, you're willing to be Rafi's doormat!
I am the right-hand man of the world's most highly regarded archaeologist.
Yeah right...
He's nominated for the FOTP award this year.
No fucking way!

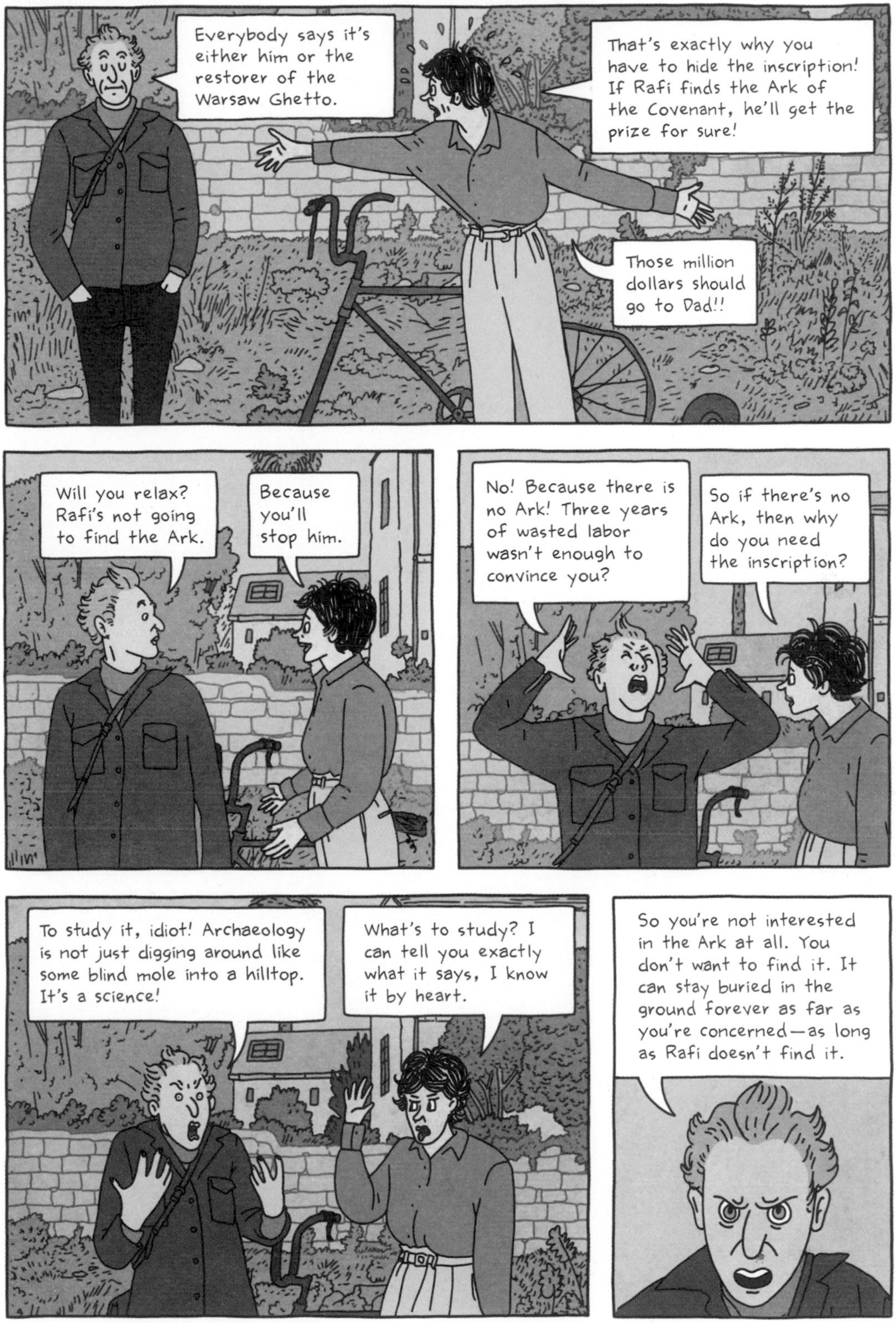

Everybody says it's either him or the restorer of the Warsaw Ghetto.
That's exactly why you have to hide the inscription! If Rafi finds the Ark of the Covenant, he'll get the prize for sure!
Those million dollars should go to Dad!!
Will you relax? Rafi's not going to find the Ark.
Because you'll stop him.
No! Because there is no Ark! Three years of wasted labor wasn't enough to convince you?
So if there's no Ark, then why do you need the inscription?
To study it, idiot! Archaeology is not just digging around like some blind mole into a hilltop. It's a science!
What's to study? I can tell you exactly what it says, I know it by heart.
So you're not interested in the Ark at all. You don't want to find it. It can stay buried in the ground forever as far as you're concerned—as long as Rafi doesn't find it.

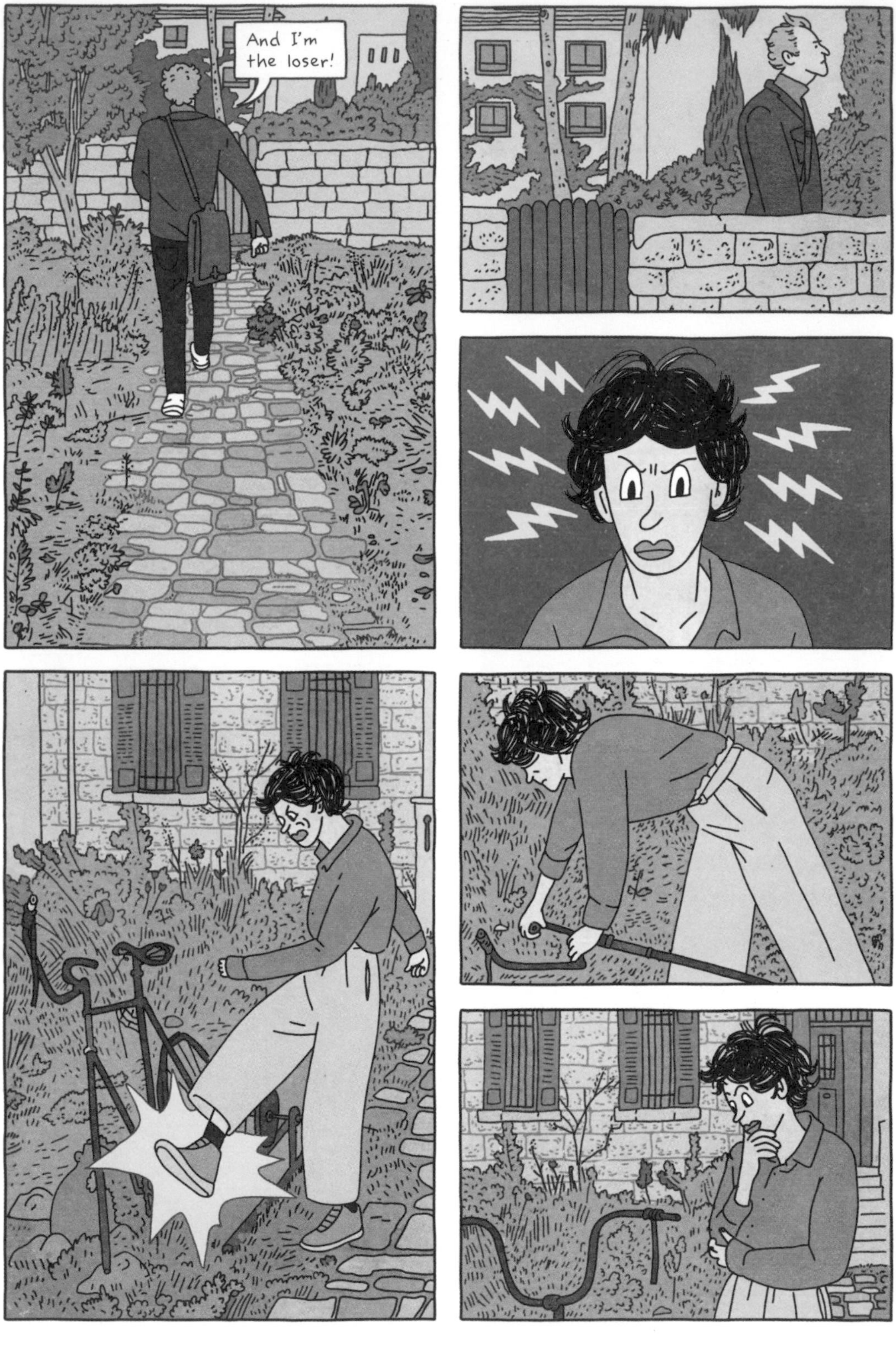
And I'm the loser!

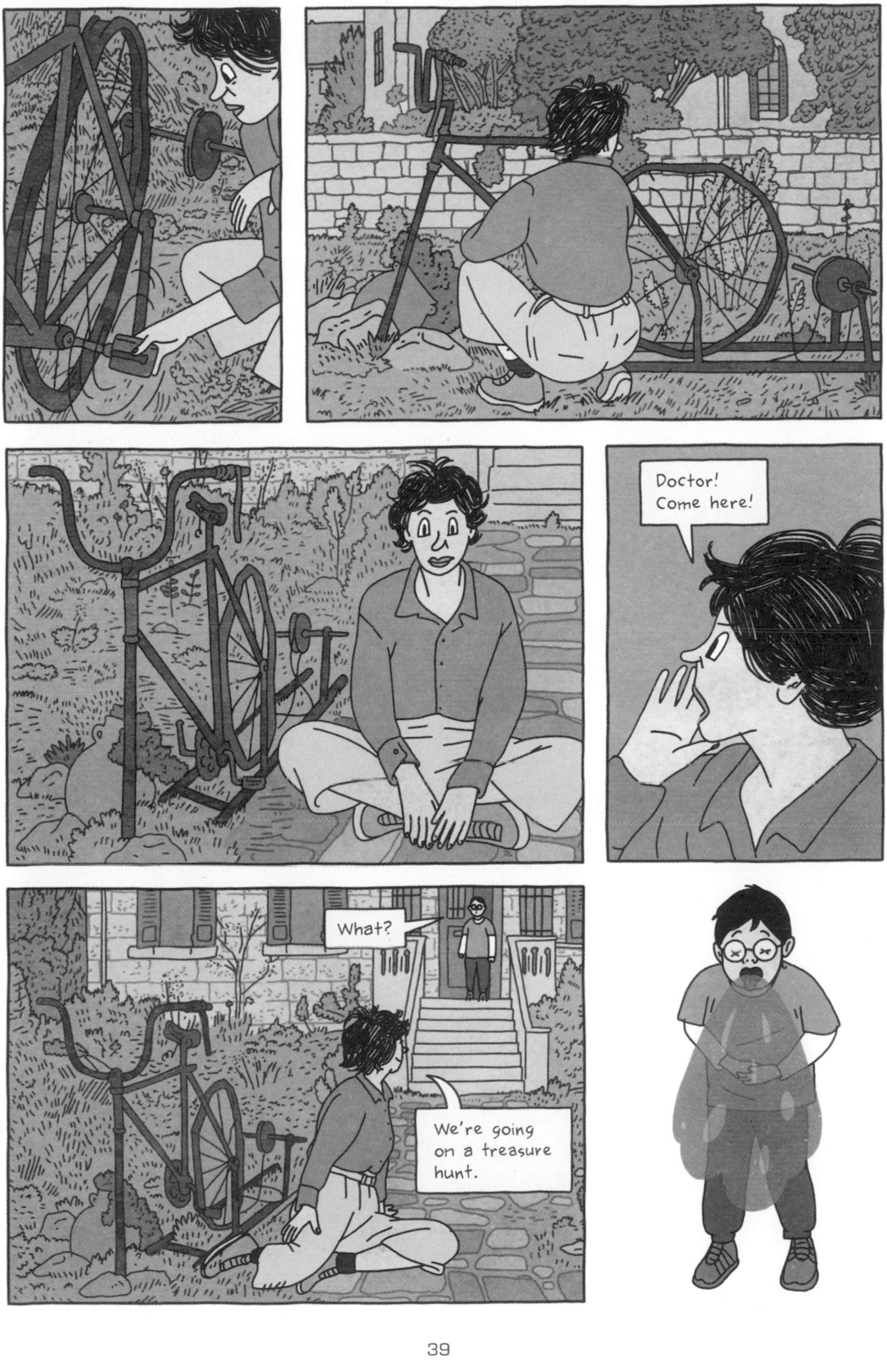
Doctor! Come here!
What?
We're going on a treasure hunt.

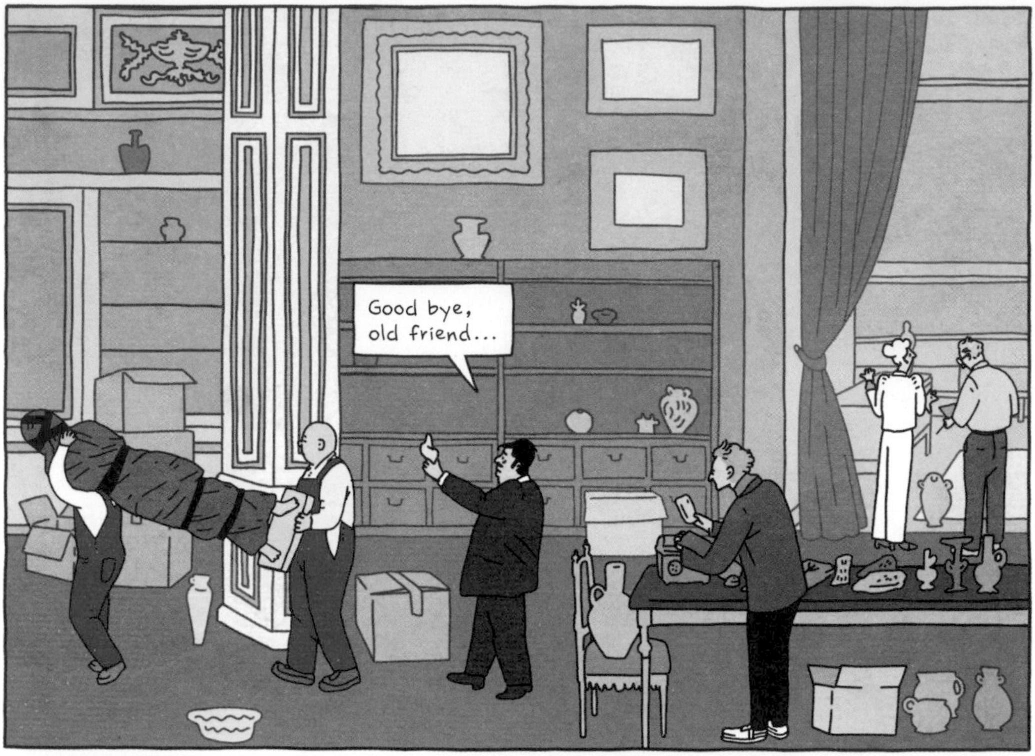
Good bye, old friend...

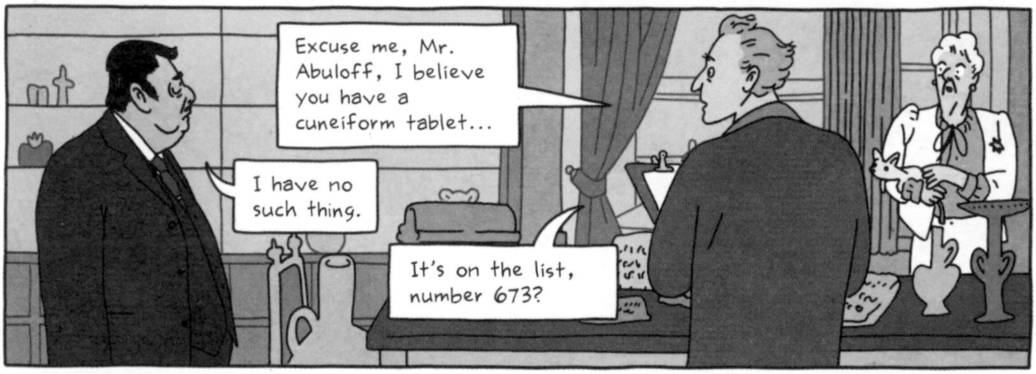
Excuse me, Mr. Abuloff, I believe you have a cuneiform tablet...
I have no such thing.
It's on the list, number 673?

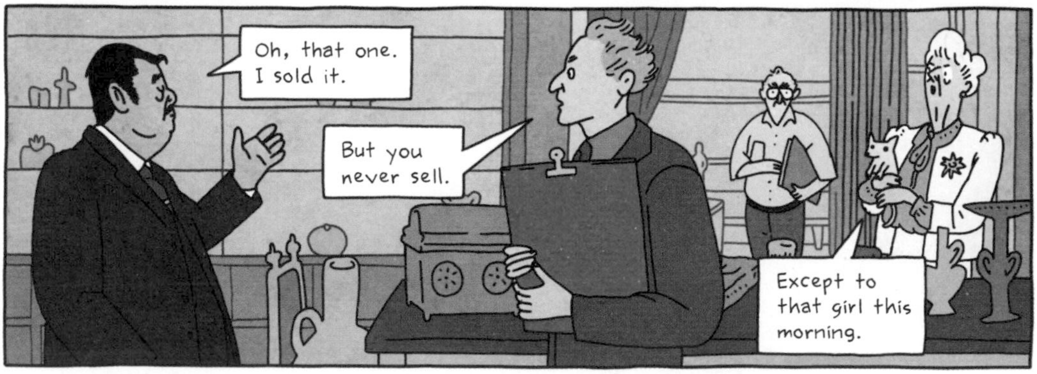
Oh, that one. I sold it.
But you never sell.
Except to that girl this morning.

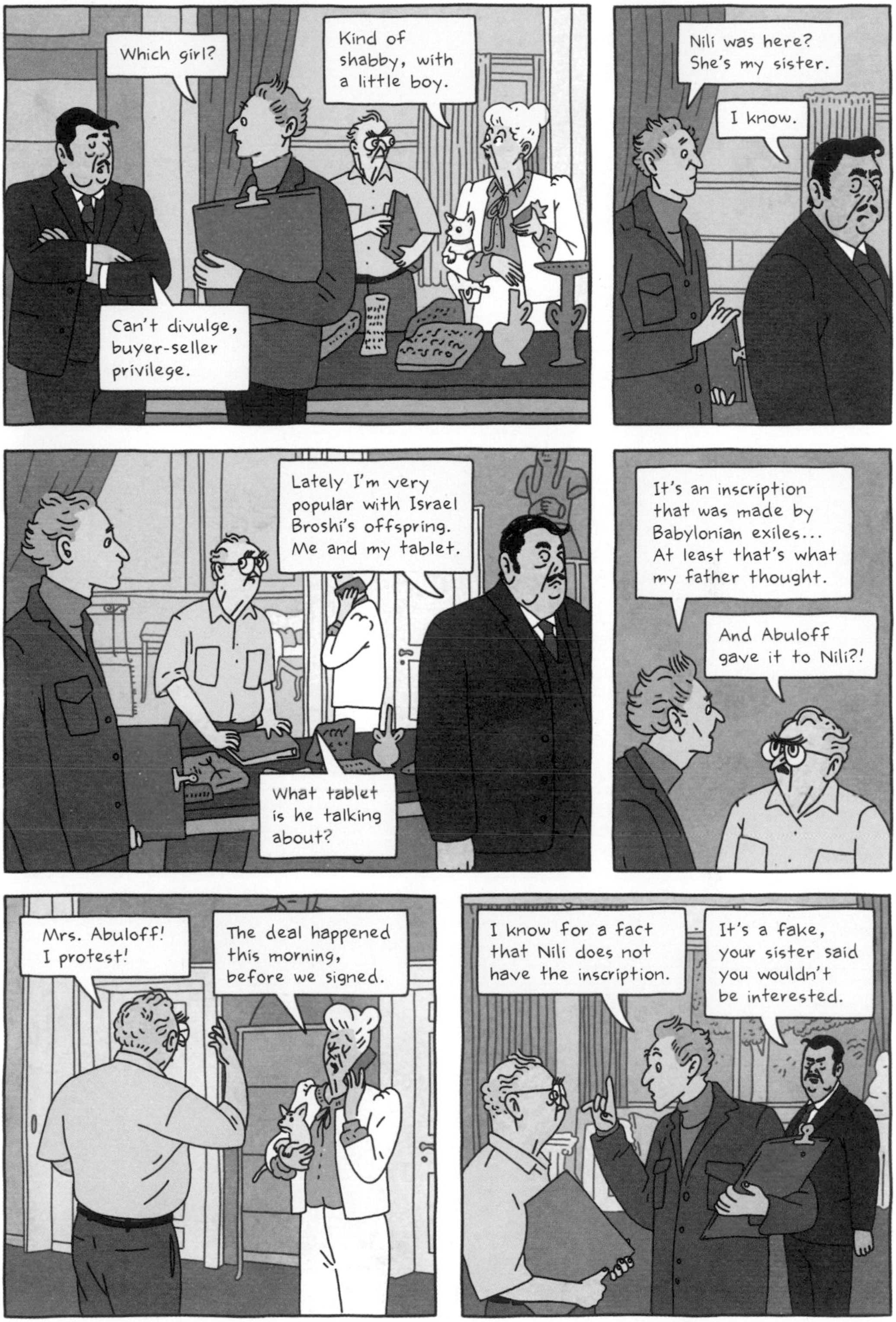

Which girl?
Kind of shabby, with a little boy.
Can't divulge, buyer-seller privilege.
Nili was here? She's my sister.
I know.
Lately I'm very popular with Israel Broshi's offspring. Me and my tablet.
What tablet is he talking about?
It's an inscription that was made by Babylonian exiles... At least that's what my father thought.
And Abuloff gave it to Nili?!
Mrs. Abuloff! I protest!
The deal happened this morning, before we signed.
I know for a fact that Nili does not have the inscription.
It's a fake, your sister said you wouldn't be interested.

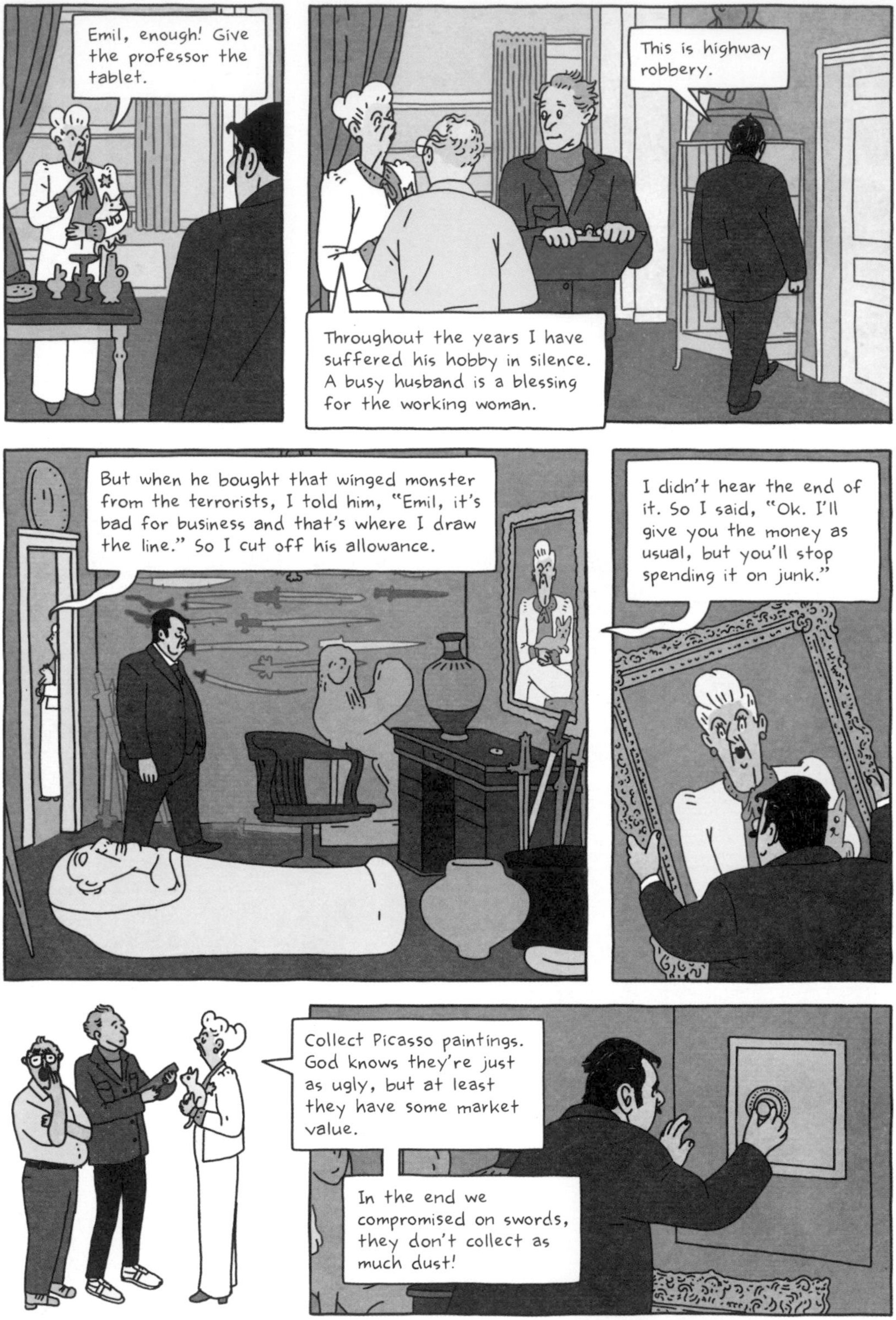
Emil, enough! Give the professor the tablet.
This is highway robbery.
Throughout the years I have suffered his hobby in silence. A busy husband is a blessing for the working woman.
But when he bought that winged monster from the terrorists, I told him, "Emil, it's bad for business and that's where I draw the line." So I cut off his allowance.
I didn't hear the end of it. So I said, "Ok. I'll give you the money as usual, but you'll stop spending it on junk."
Collect Picasso paintings. God knows they're just as ugly, but at least they have some market value.
In the end we compromised on swords, they don't collect as much dust!

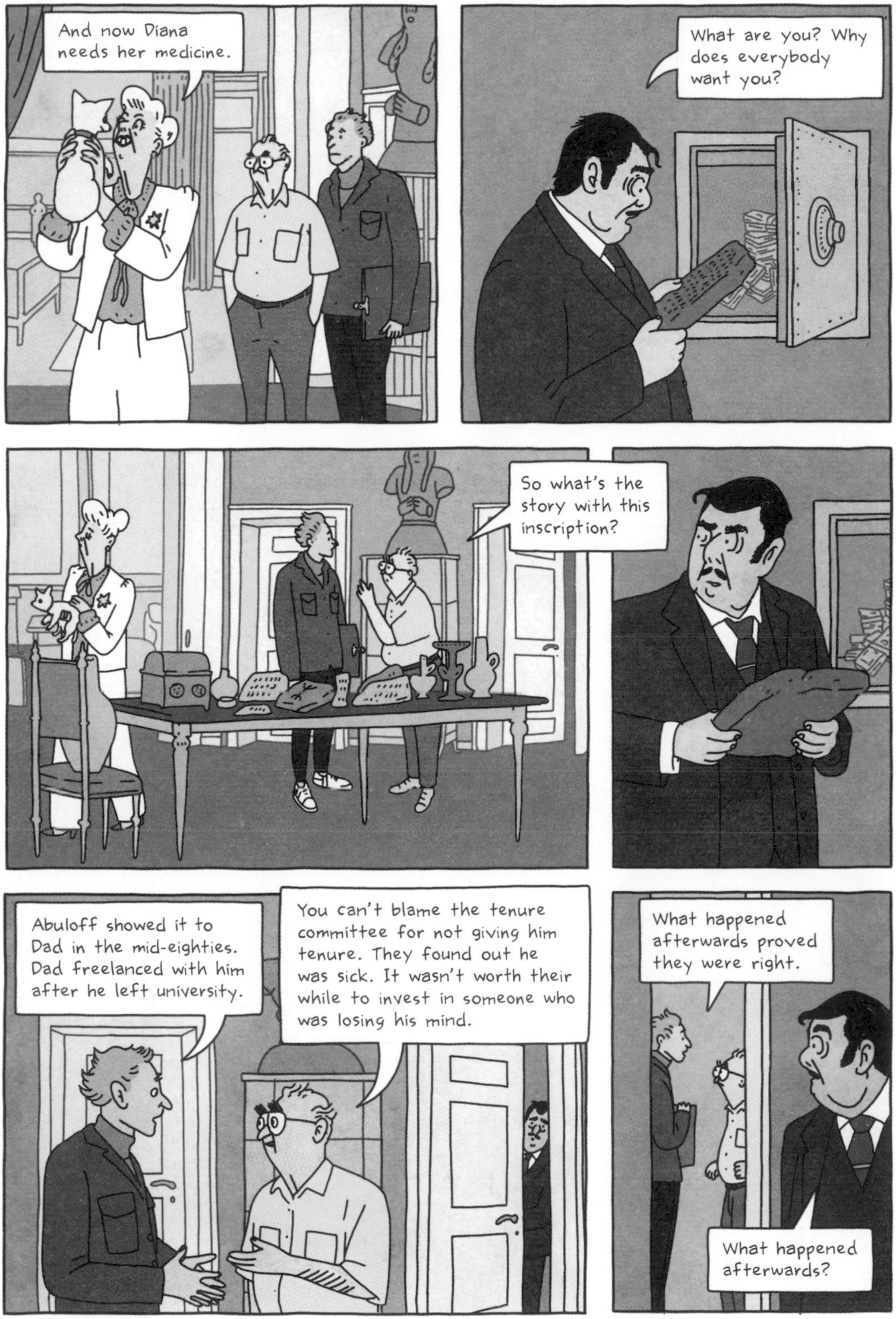
And now Diana needs her medicine.
What are you? Why does everybody want you?
So what's the story with this inscription?
Abuloff showed it to Dad in the mid-eighties. Dad freelanced with him after he left university.
You can't blame the tenure committee for not giving him tenure. They found out he was sick. It wasn't worth their while to invest in someone who was losing his mind.
What happened afterwards proved they were right.
What happened afterwards?

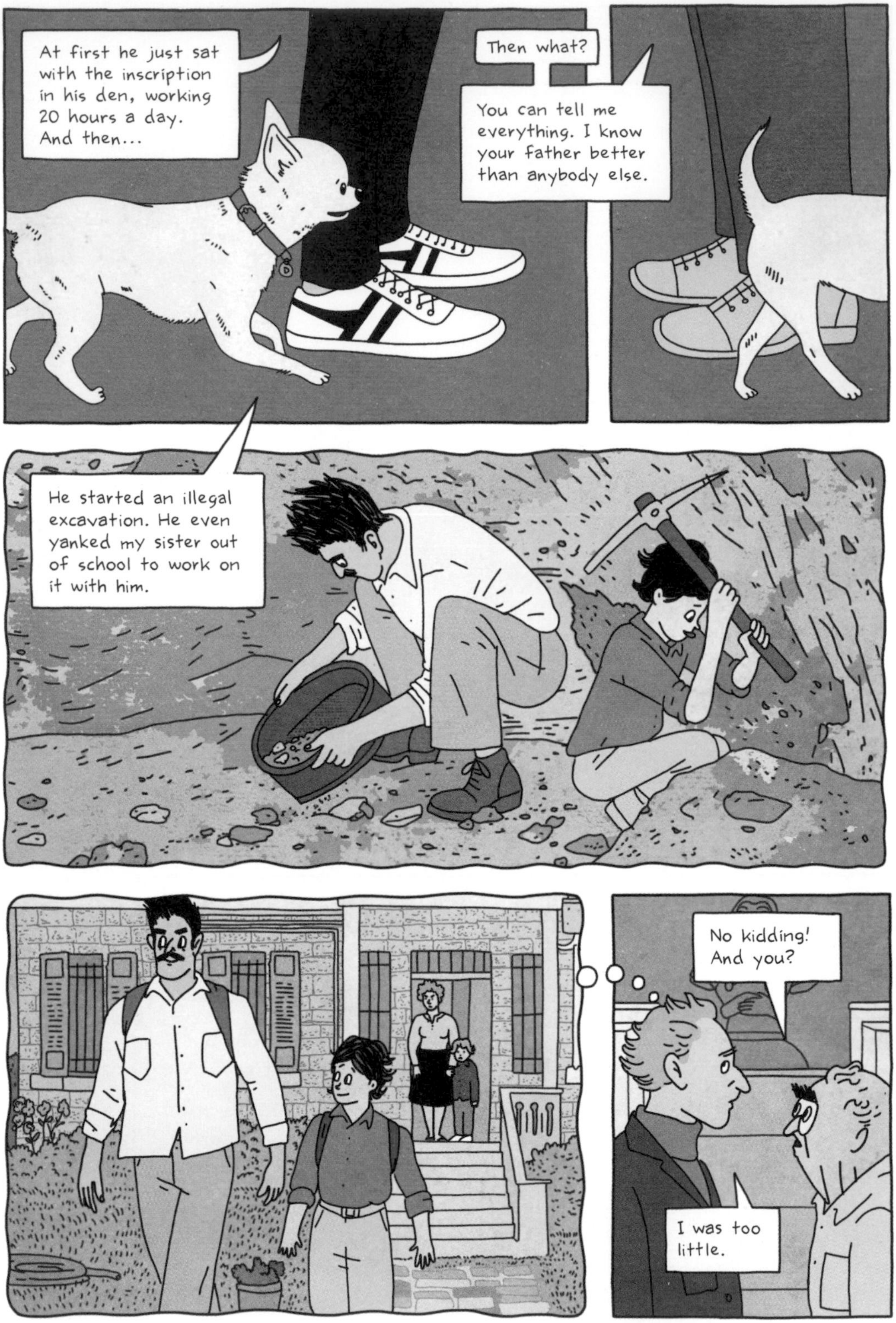
At first he just sat with the inscription in his den, working 20 hours a day. And then...
Then what?
You can tell me everything. I know your father better than anybody else.
He started an illegal excavation. He even yanked my sister out of school to work on it with him.
No kidding! And you?
I was too little.

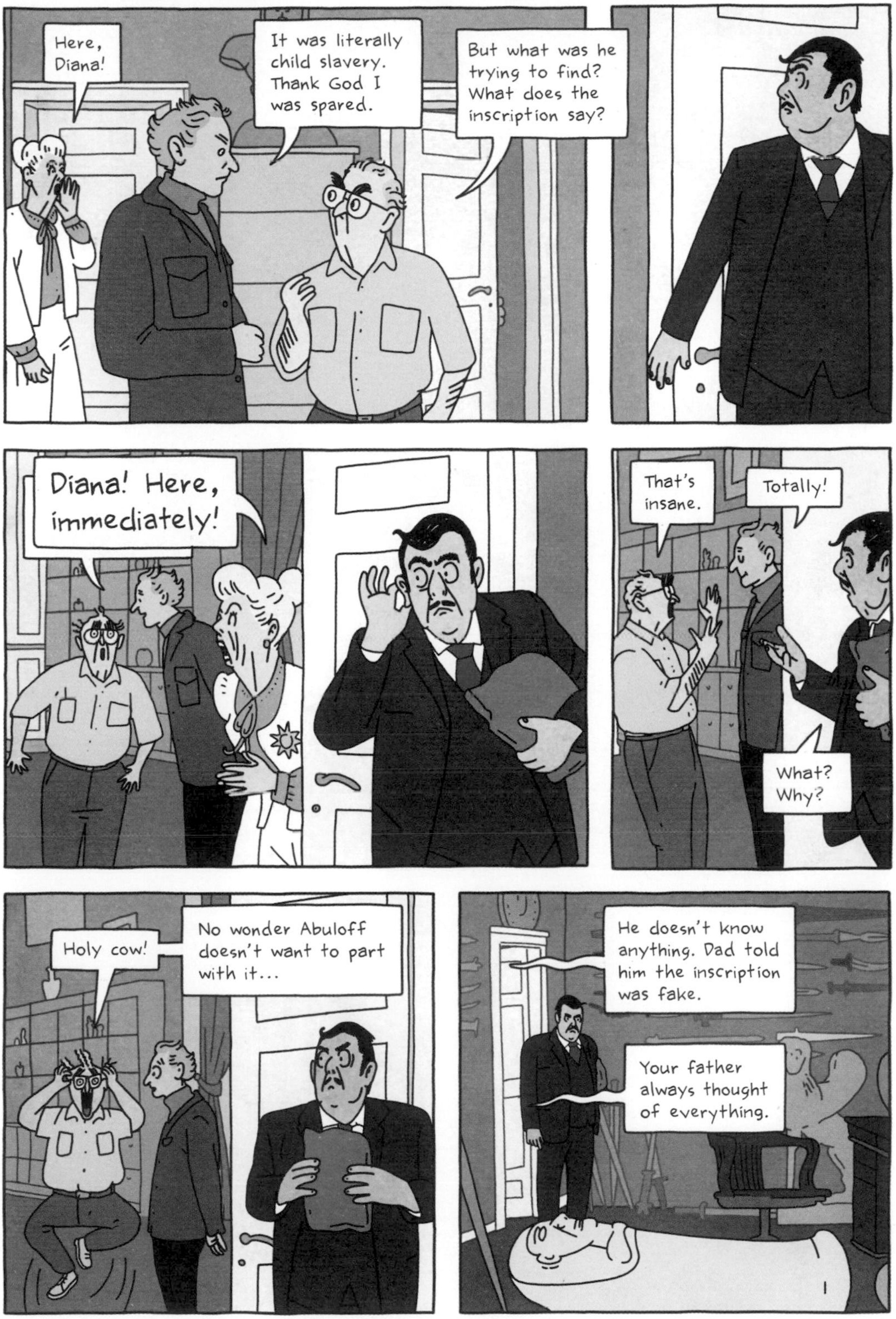
Here, Diana!
It was literally child slavery. Thank God I was spared.
But what was he trying to find? What does the inscription say?
Diana! Here, immediately!
That's insane.
Totally!
What? Why?
Holy cow!
No wonder Abuloff doesn't want to part with it...
He doesn't know anything. Dad told him the inscription was fake.
Your father always thought of everything.

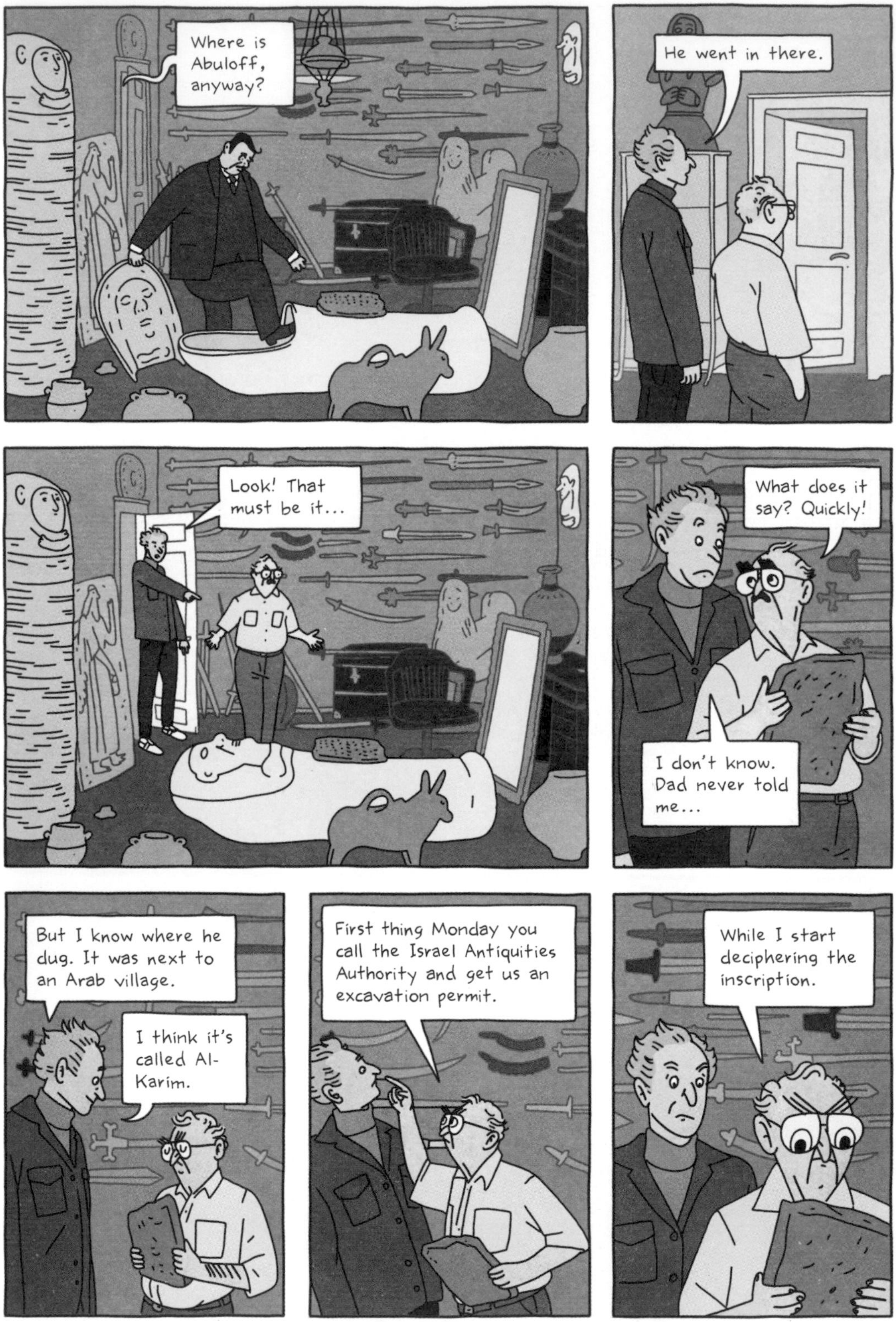
Where is Abuloff, anyway?
He went in there.
Look! That must be it...
What does it say? Quickly!
I don't know. Dad never told me...
But I know where he dug. It was next to an Arab village.
I think it's called Al-Karim.
First thing Monday you call the Israel Antiquities Authority and get us an excavation permit.
While I start deciphering the inscription.

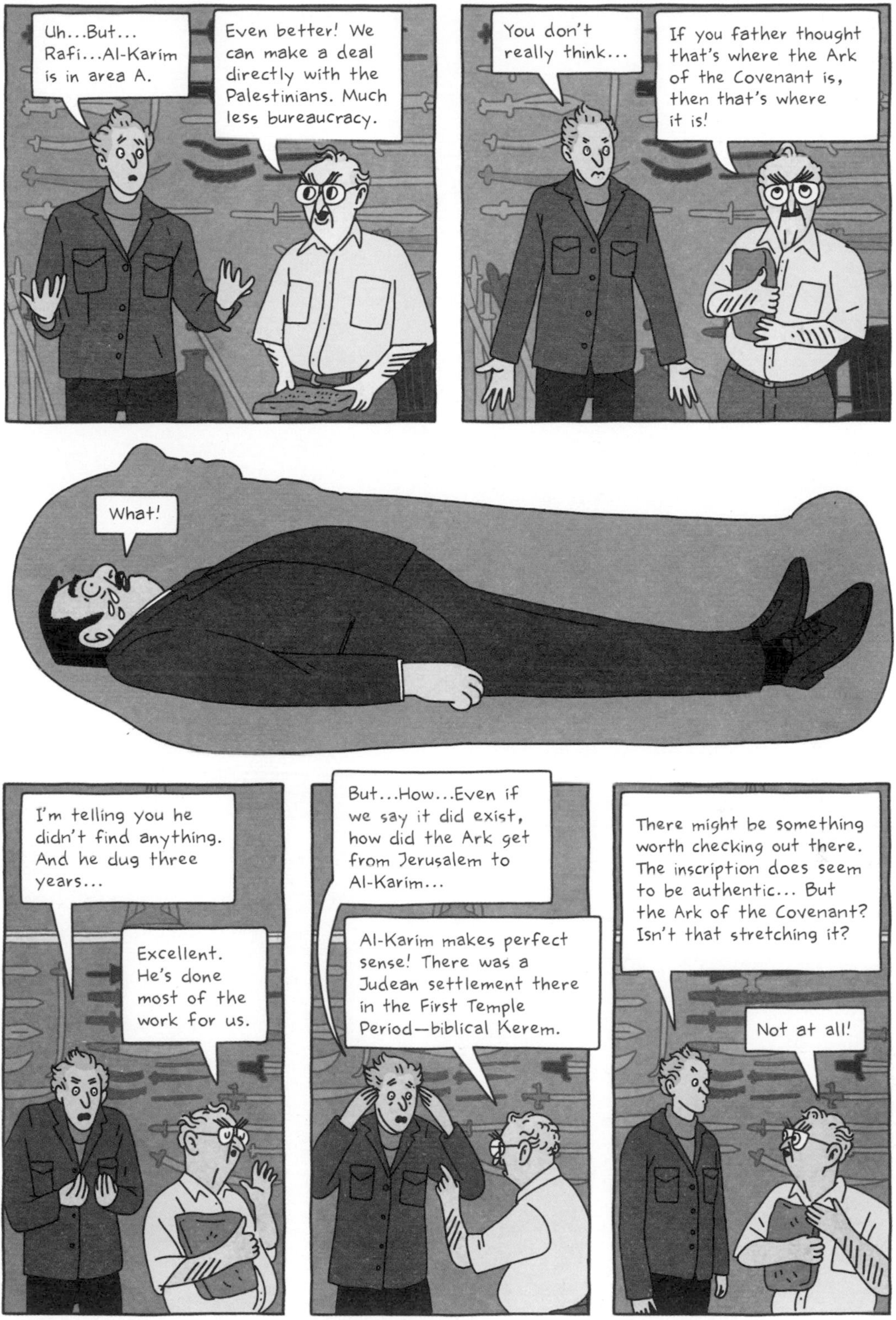
Uh...But... Rafi...Al-Karim is in area A.
Even better! We can make a deal directly with the Palestinians. Much less bureaucracy.
You don't really think...
If you father thought that's where the Ark of the Covenant is, then that's where it is!
What!
I'm telling you he didn't find anything. And he dug three years...
Excellent. He's done most of the work for us.
But...How...Even if we say it did exist, how did the Ark get from Jerusalem to Al-Karim...
Al-Karim makes perfect sense! There was a Judean settlement there in the First Temple Period—biblical Kerem.
There might be something worth checking out there. The inscription does seem to be authentic... But the Ark of the Covenant? Isn't that stretching it?
Not at all!

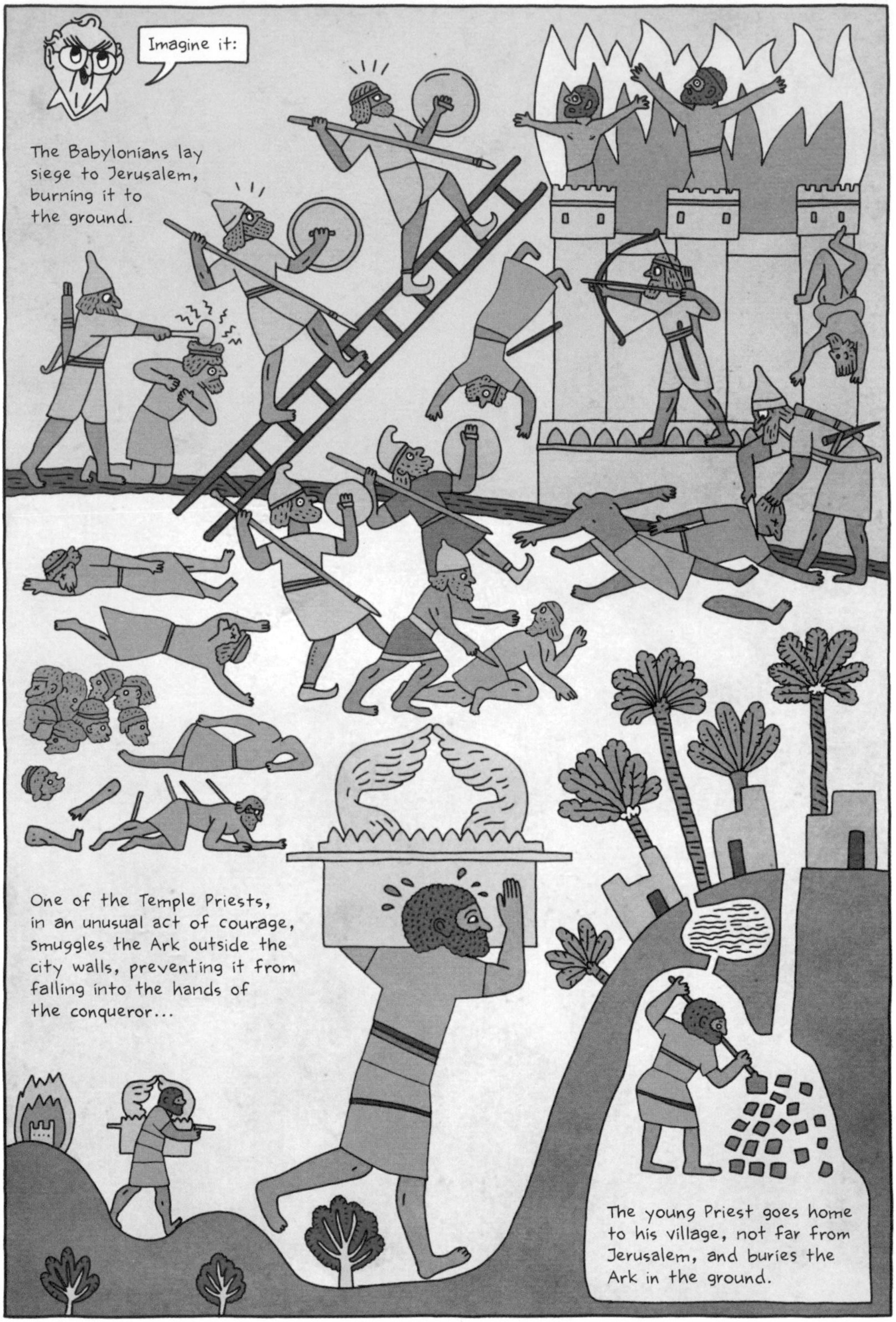
Imagine it:
The Babylonians lay siege to Jerusalem, burning it to the ground.
One of the Temple Priests, in an unusual act of courage, smuggles the Ark outside the city walls, preventing it from falling into the hands of the conqueror...
The young Priest goes home to his village, not far from Jerusalem, and buries the Ark in the ground.

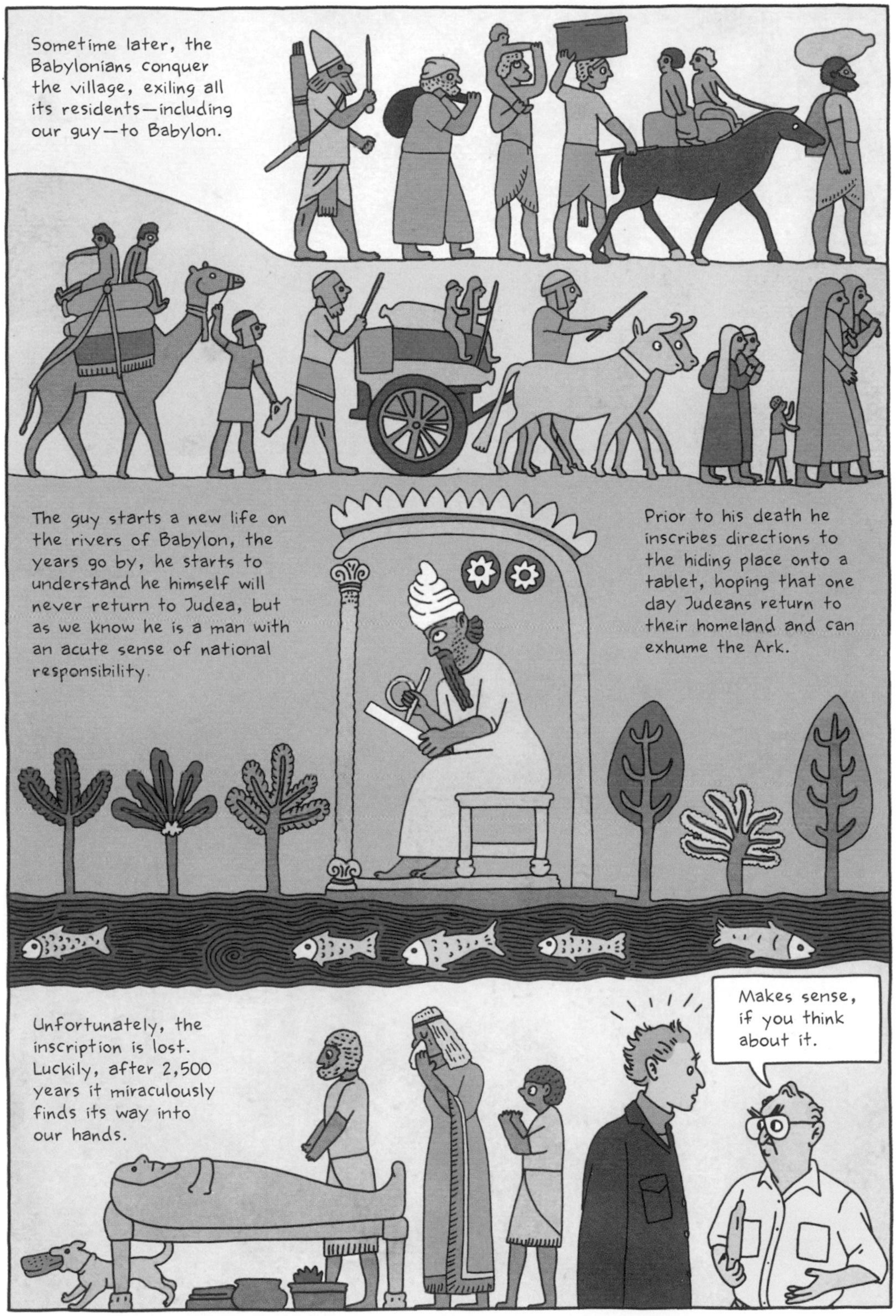
Sometime later, the Babylonians conquer the village, exiling all its residents—including our guy—to Babylon.
The guy starts a new life on the rivers of Babylon, the years go by, he starts to understand he himself will never return to Judea, but as we know he is a man with an acute sense of national responsibility.
Prior to his death he inscribes directions to the hiding place onto a tablet, hoping that one day Judeans return to their homeland and can exhume the Ark.
Unfortunately, the inscription is lost. Luckily, after 2,500 years it miraculously finds its way into our hands.
Makes sense, if you think about it.

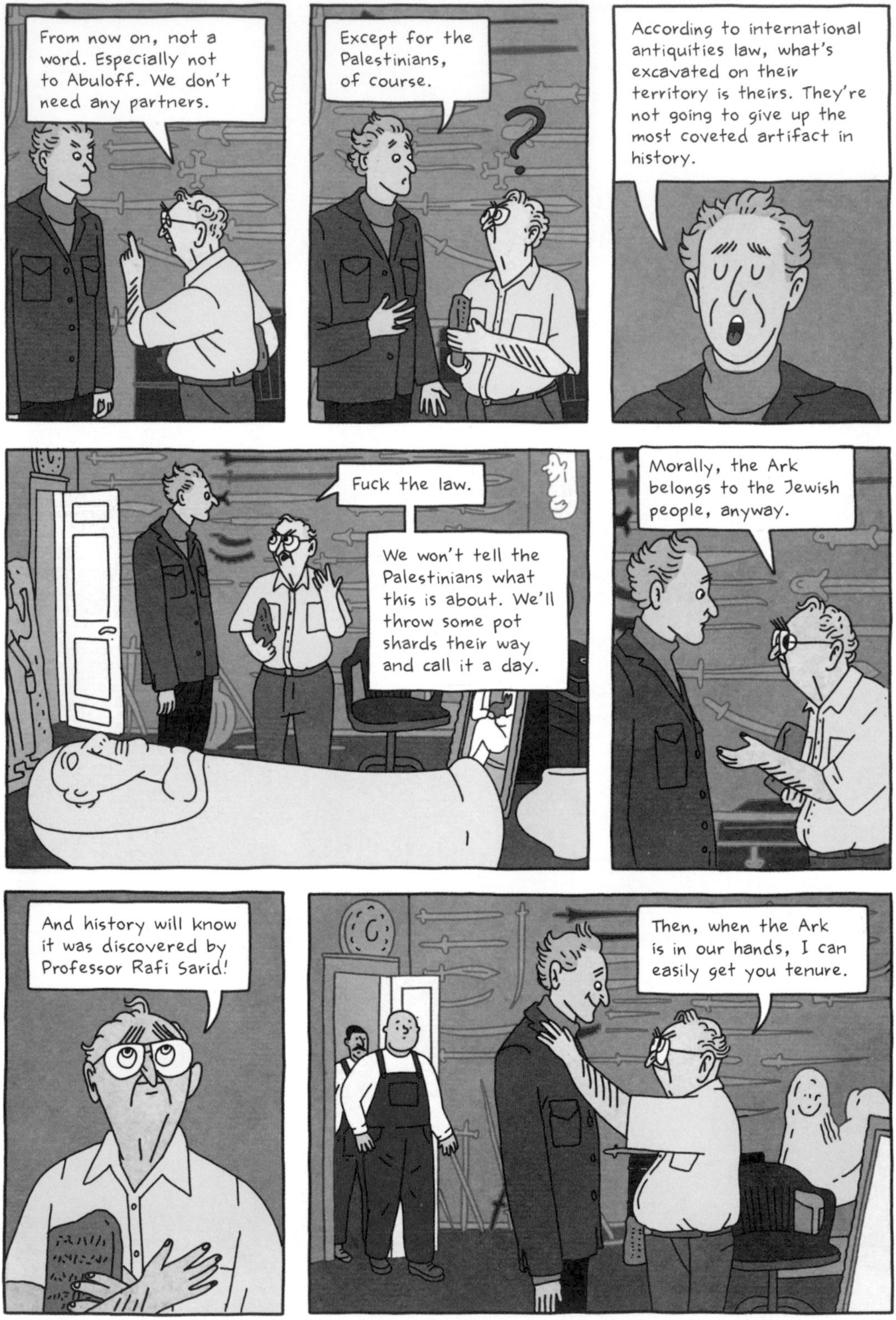
From now on, not a word. Especially not to Abuloff. We don't need any partners.
Except for the Palestinians, of course.
?
According to international antiquities law, what's excavated on their territory is theirs. They're not going to give up the most coveted artifact in history.
Fuck the law.
We won't tell the Palestinians what this is about. We'll throw some pot shards their way and call it a day.
Morally, the Ark belongs to the Jewish people, anyway.
And history will know it was discovered by Professor Rafi Sarid!
Then, when the Ark is in our hands, I can easily get you tenure.

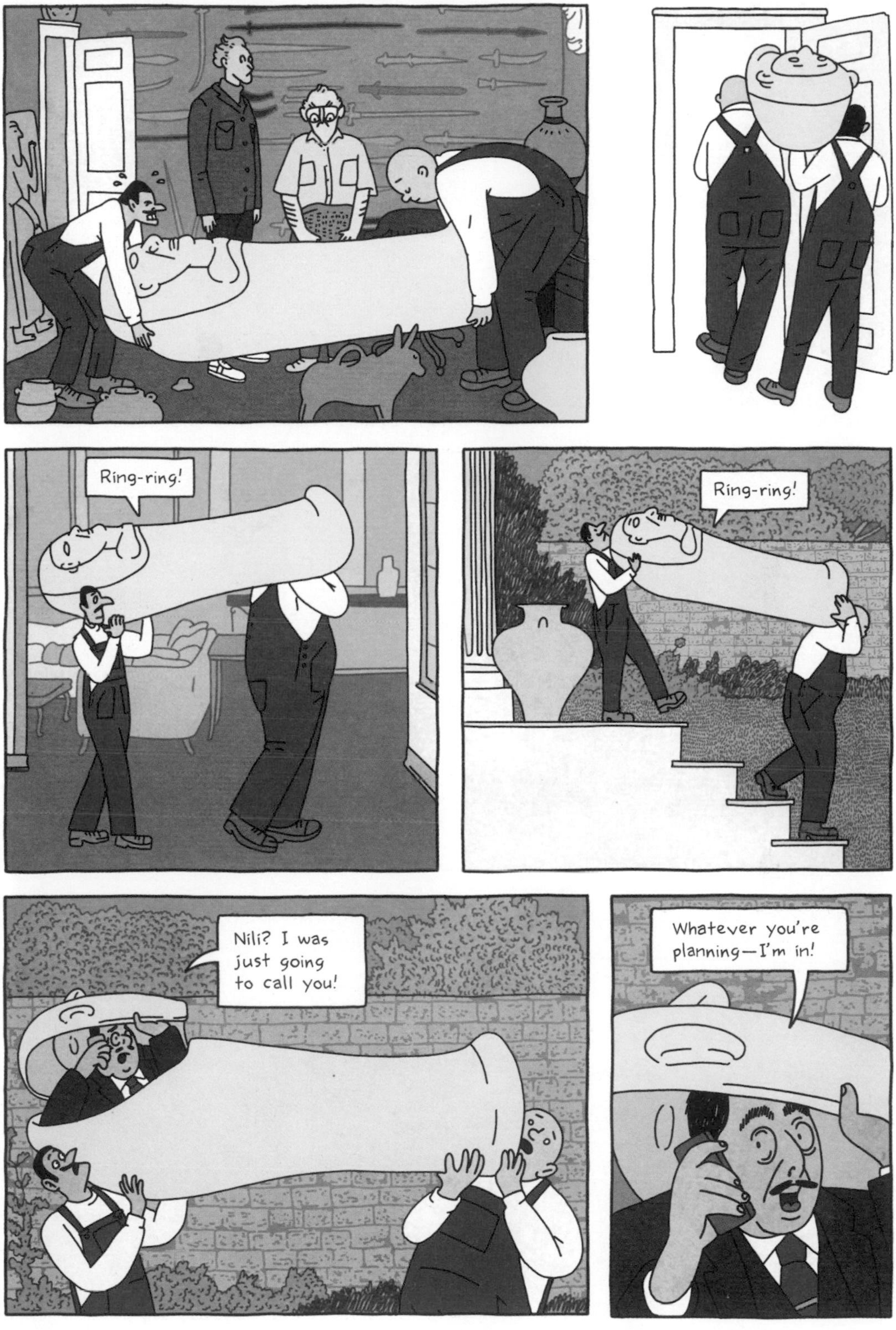

Ring-ring!
Ring-ring!
Nili? I was just going to call you!
Whatever you're planning—I'm in!

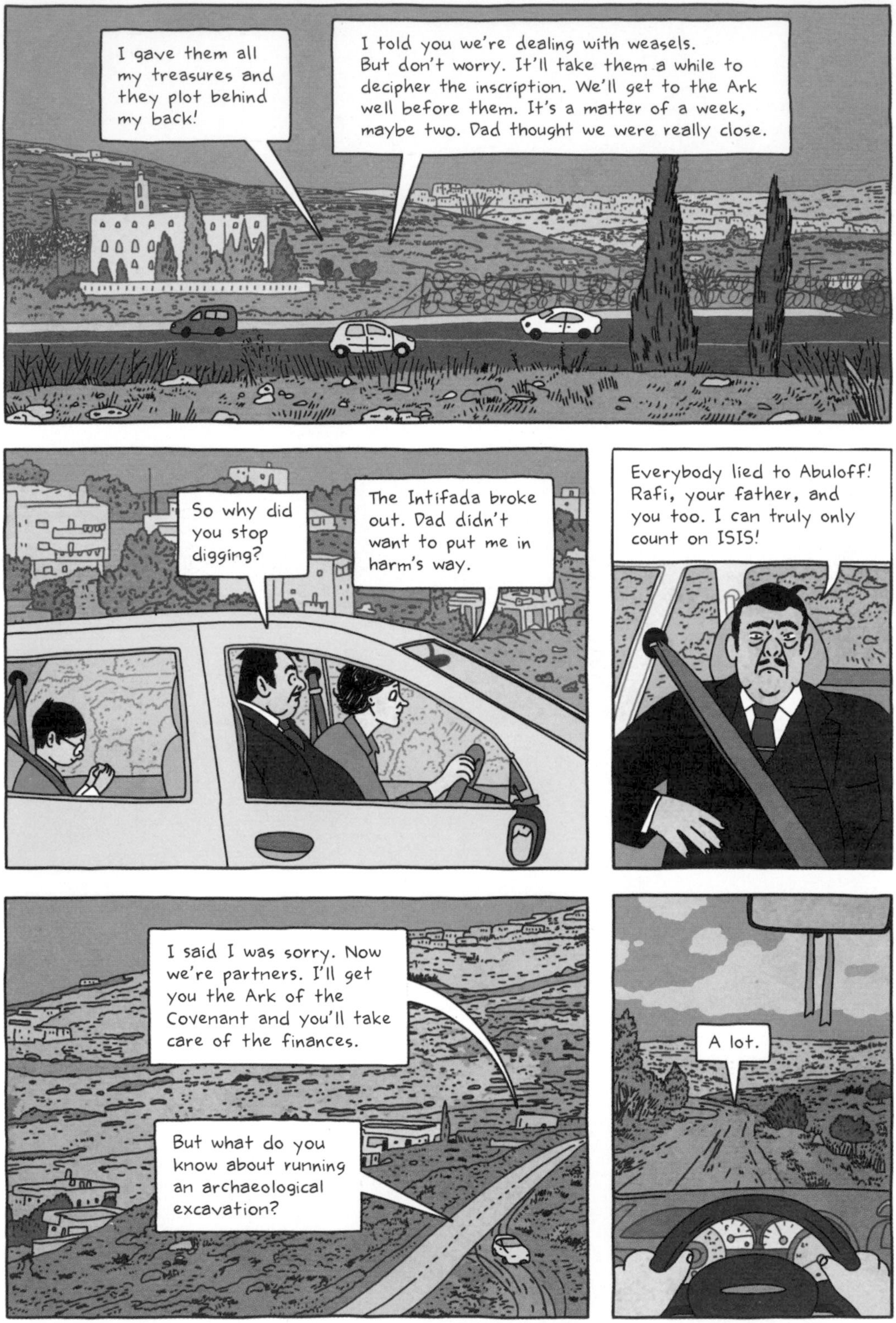
I gave them all my treasures and they plot behind my back!
I told you we're dealing with weasels. But don't worry. It'll take them a while to decipher the inscription. We'll get to the Ark well before them. It's a matter of a week, maybe two. Dad thought we were really close.
So why did you stop digging?
The Intifada broke out. Dad didn't want to put me in harm's way.
Everybody lied to Abuloff! Rafi, your father, and you too. I can truly only count on ISIS!
I said I was sorry. Now we're partners. I'll get you the Ark of the Covenant and you'll take care of the finances.
But what do you know about running an archaeological excavation?
A lot.

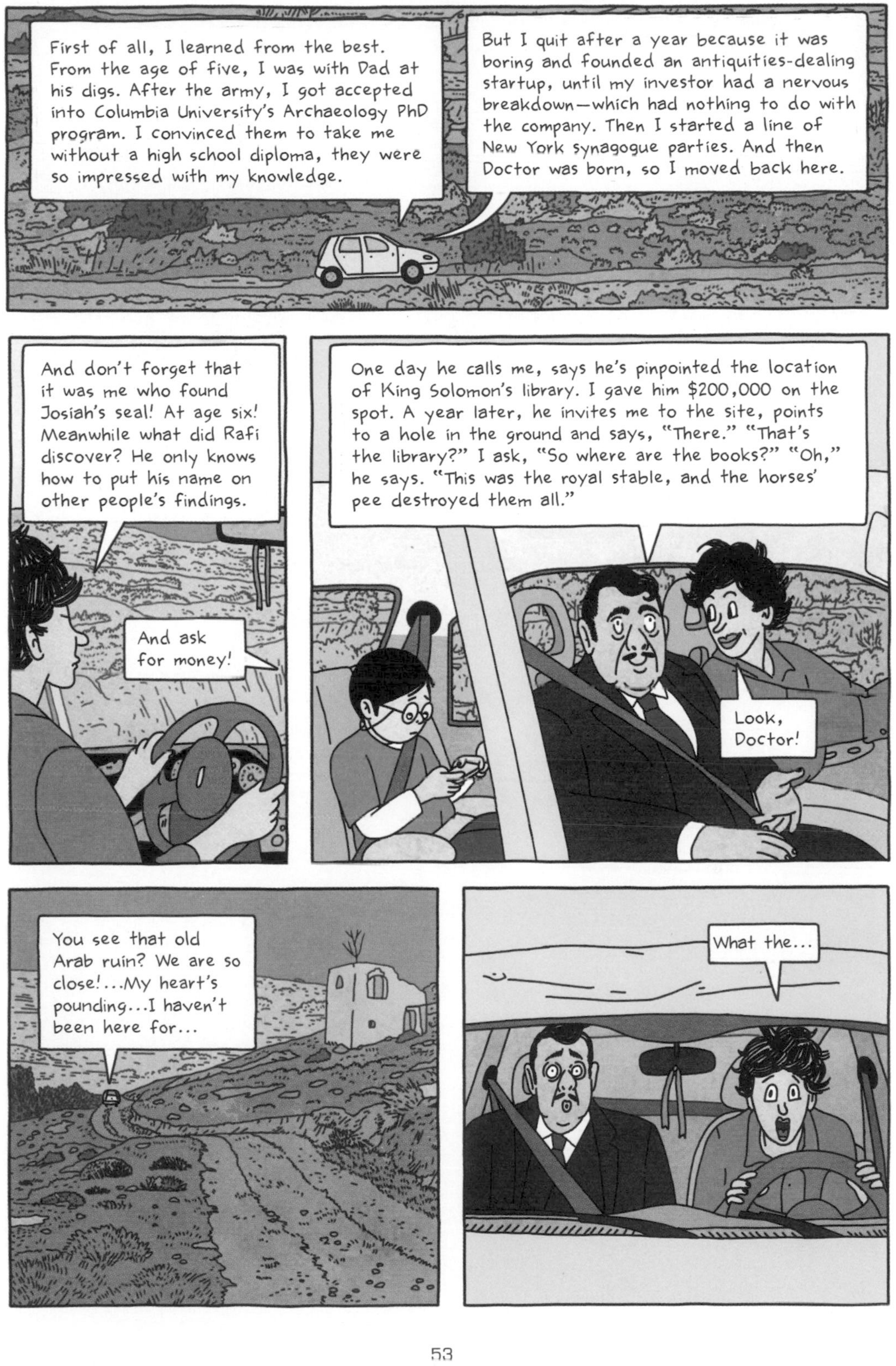
First of all, I learned from the best. From the age of five, I was with Dad at his digs. After the army, I got accepted into Columbia University's Archaeology PhD program. I convinced them to take me without a high school diploma, they were so impressed with my knowledge.
But I quit after a year because it was boring and founded an antiquities-dealing startup, until my investor had a nervous breakdown—which had nothing to do with the company. Then I started a line of New York synagogue parties. And then Doctor was born, so I moved back here.
And don't forget that it was me who found Josiah's seal! At age six! Meanwhile what did Rafi discover? He only knows how to put his name on other people's findings.
And ask for money!
One day he calls me, says he's pinpointed the location of King Solomon's library. I gave him $200,000 on the spot. A year later, he invites me to the site, points to a hole in the ground and says, "There." "That's the library?" I ask, "So where are the books?" "Oh," he says. "This was the royal stable, and the horses' pee destroyed them all."
Look, Doctor!
You see that old Arab ruin? We are so close!...My heart's pounding...I haven't been here for...
What the...

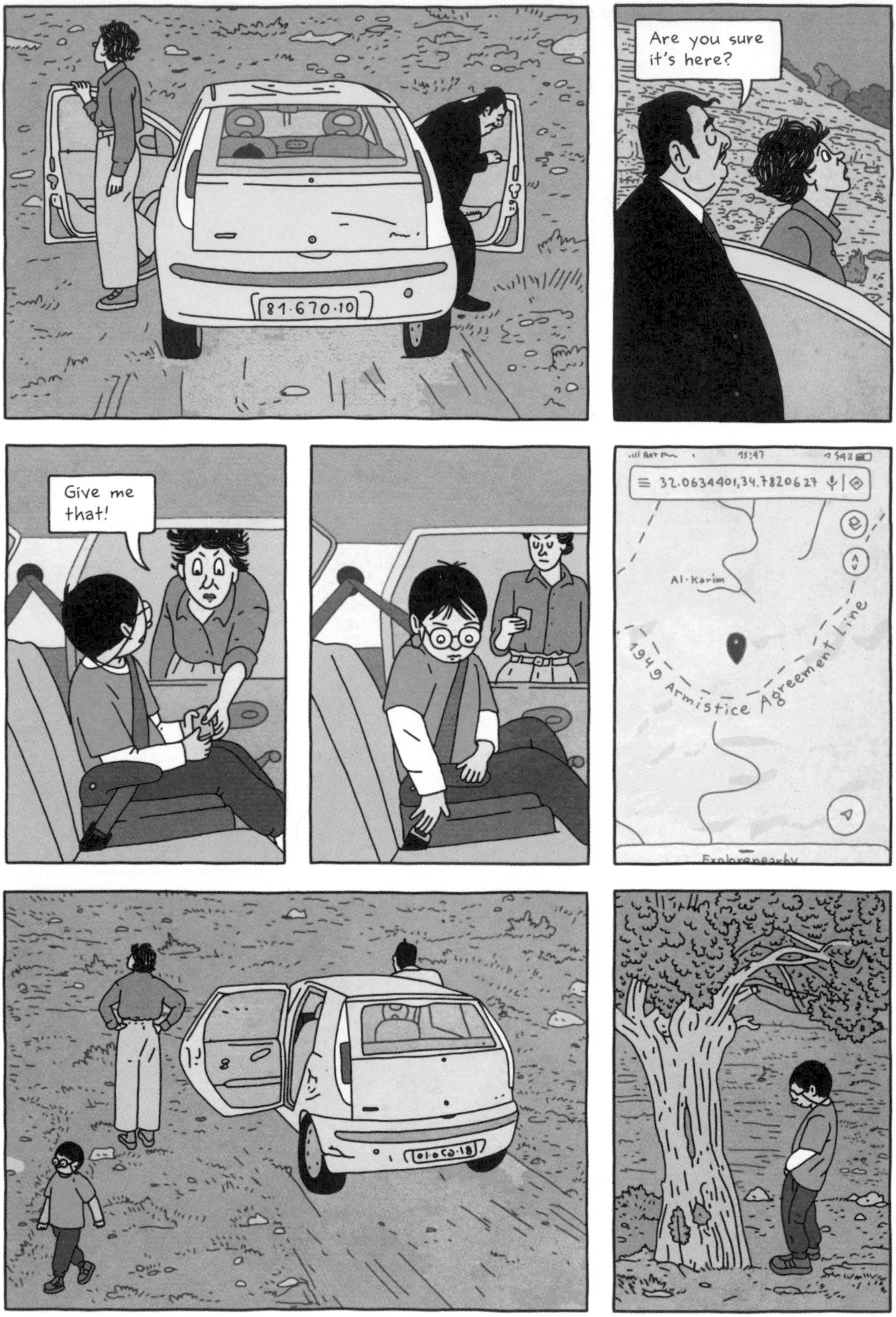
81·670·10
Are you sure it's here?
Give me that!
15:47
32.0634401,34.7820627
Al-Karim
1949 Armistice Agreement Line

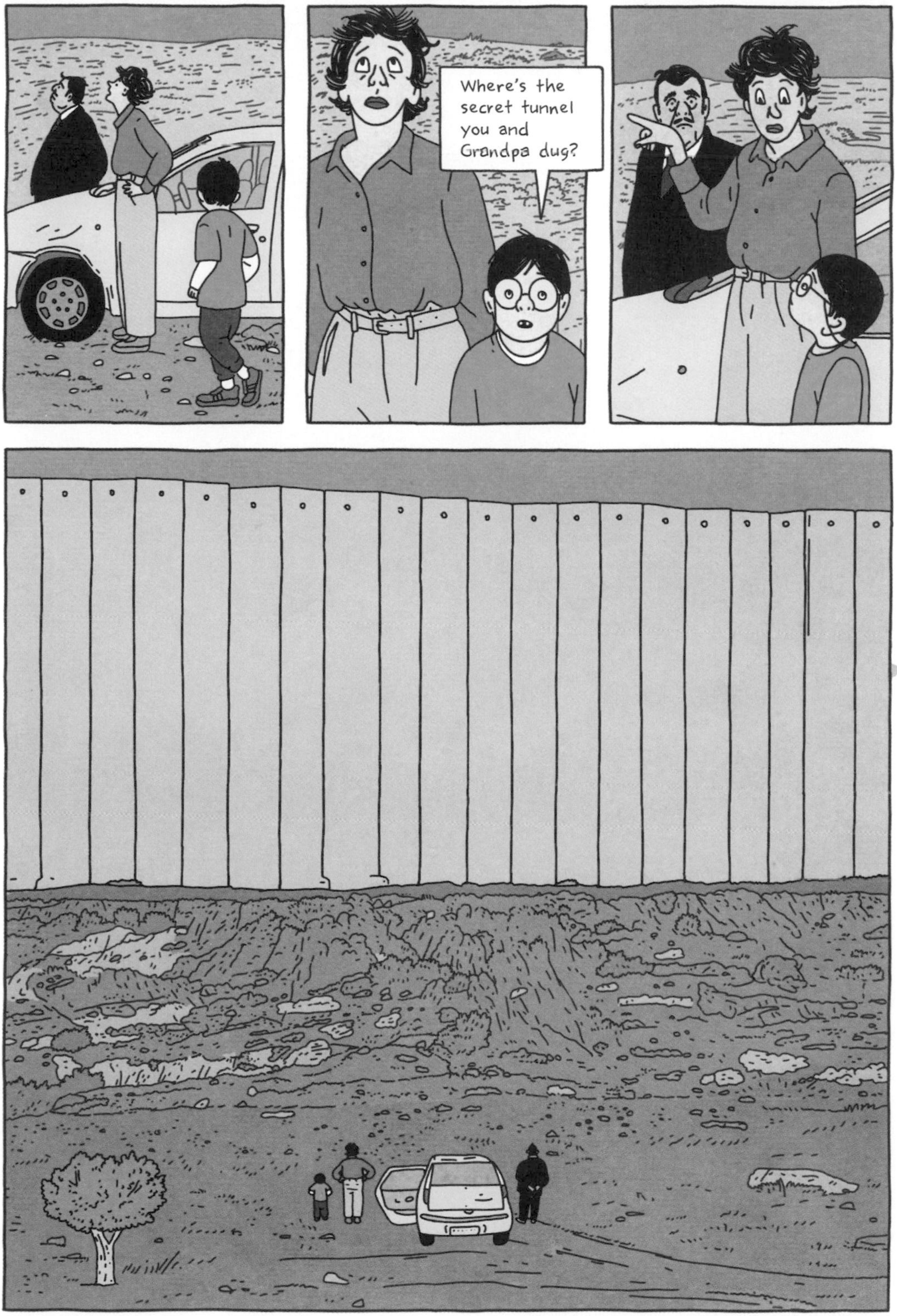
Where's the secret tunnel you and Grandpa dug?

Part 2: The New Tunnel

City of David excavation, Silwan village, East Jerusalem.
DON'T WORRY BE HAPPY
MINI MARKET & BAKERY
TICKETS

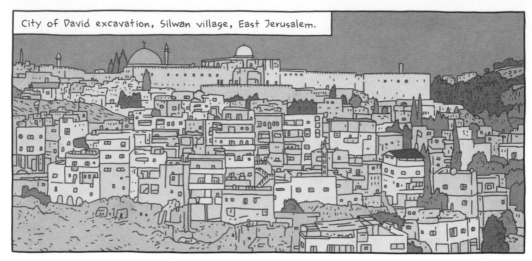

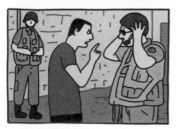

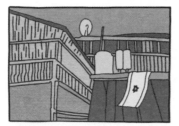

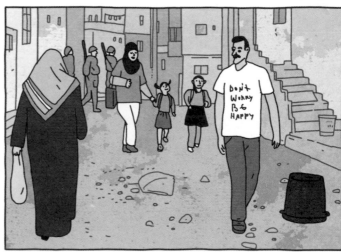

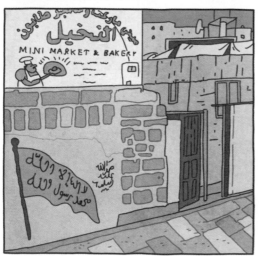

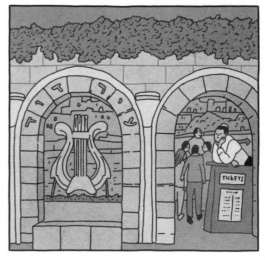

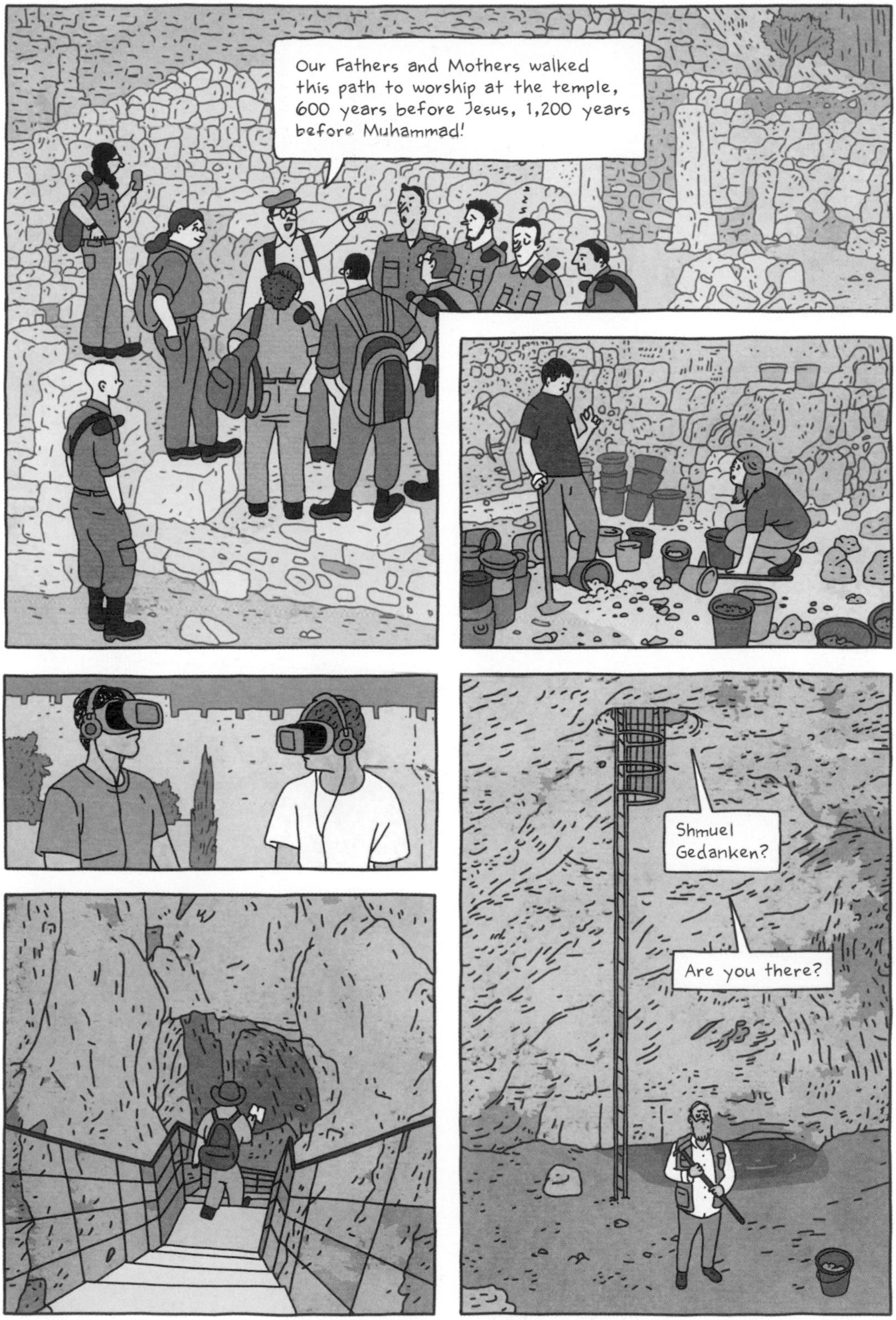
Our Fathers and Mothers walked this path to worship at the temple, 600 years before Jesus, 1,200 years before Muhammad!
Shmuel Gedanken?
Are you there?

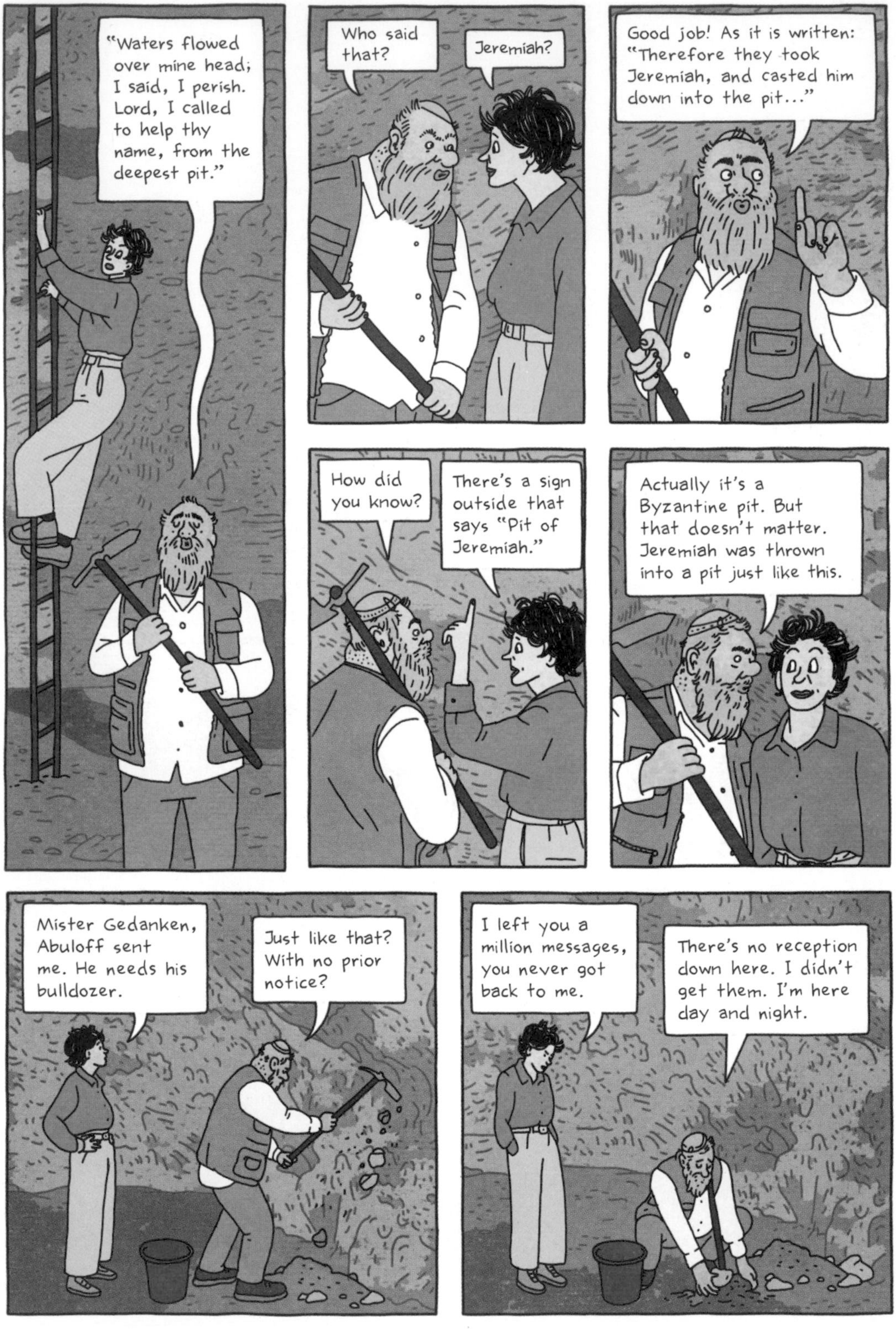
"Waters flowed over mine head; I said, I perish. Lord, I called to help thy name, from the deepest pit."
Who said that?
Jeremiah?
Good job! As it is written: "Therefore they took Jeremiah, and casted him down into the pit..."
How did you know?
There's a sign outside that says "Pit of Jeremiah."
Actually it's a Byzantine pit. But that doesn't matter. Jeremiah was thrown into a pit just like this.
Mister Gedanken, Abuloff sent me. He needs his bulldozer.
Just like that? With no prior notice?
I left you a million messages, you never got back to me.
There's no reception down here. I didn't get them. I'm here day and night.

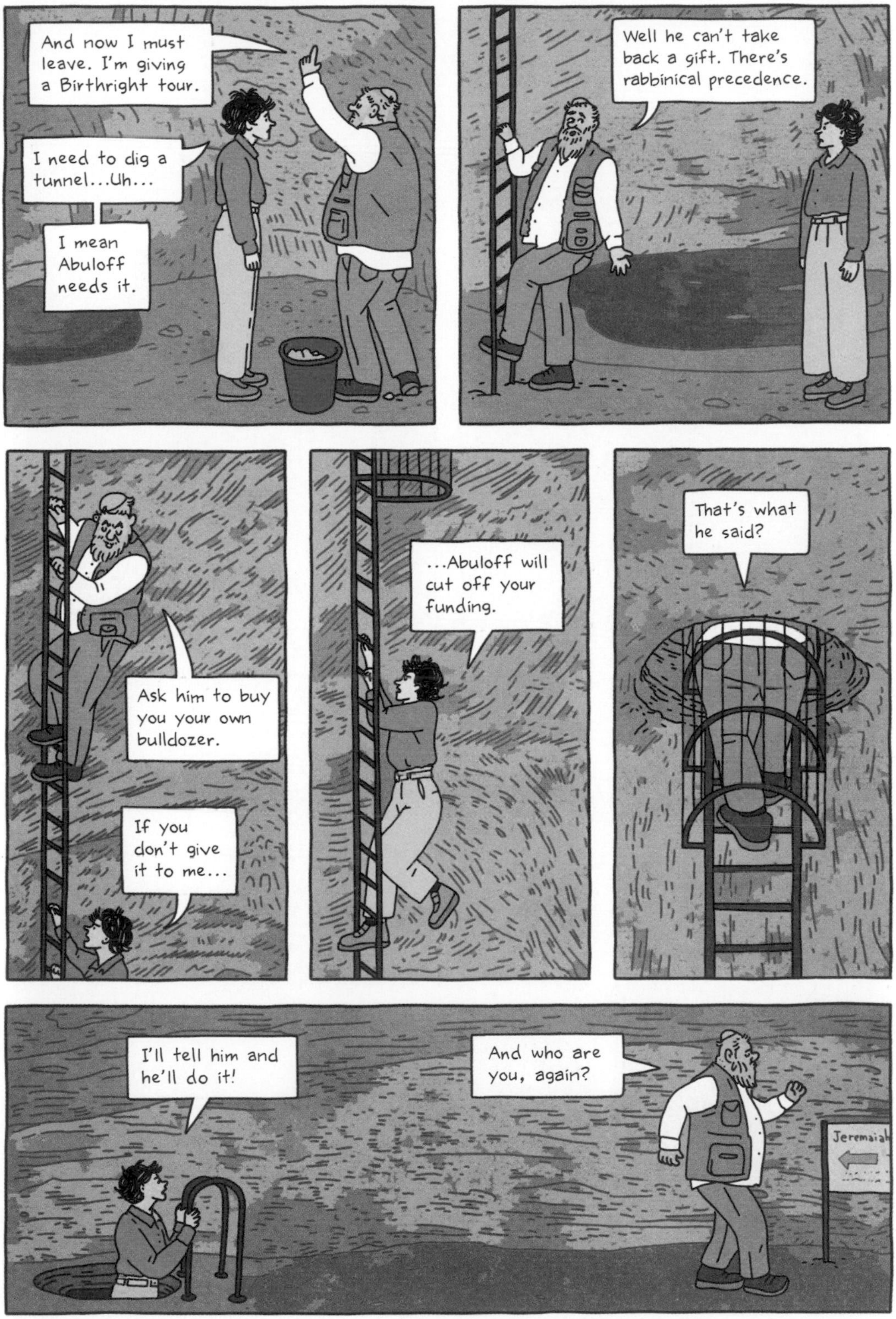
And now I must leave. I'm giving a Birthright tour.
I need to dig a tunnel...Uh...
I mean Abuloff needs it.
Well he can't take back a gift. There's rabbinical precedence.
Ask him to buy you your own bulldozer.
If you don't give it to me...
...Abuloff will cut off your funding.
That's what he said?
I'll tell him and he'll do it!
And who are you, again?
Jeremaiah

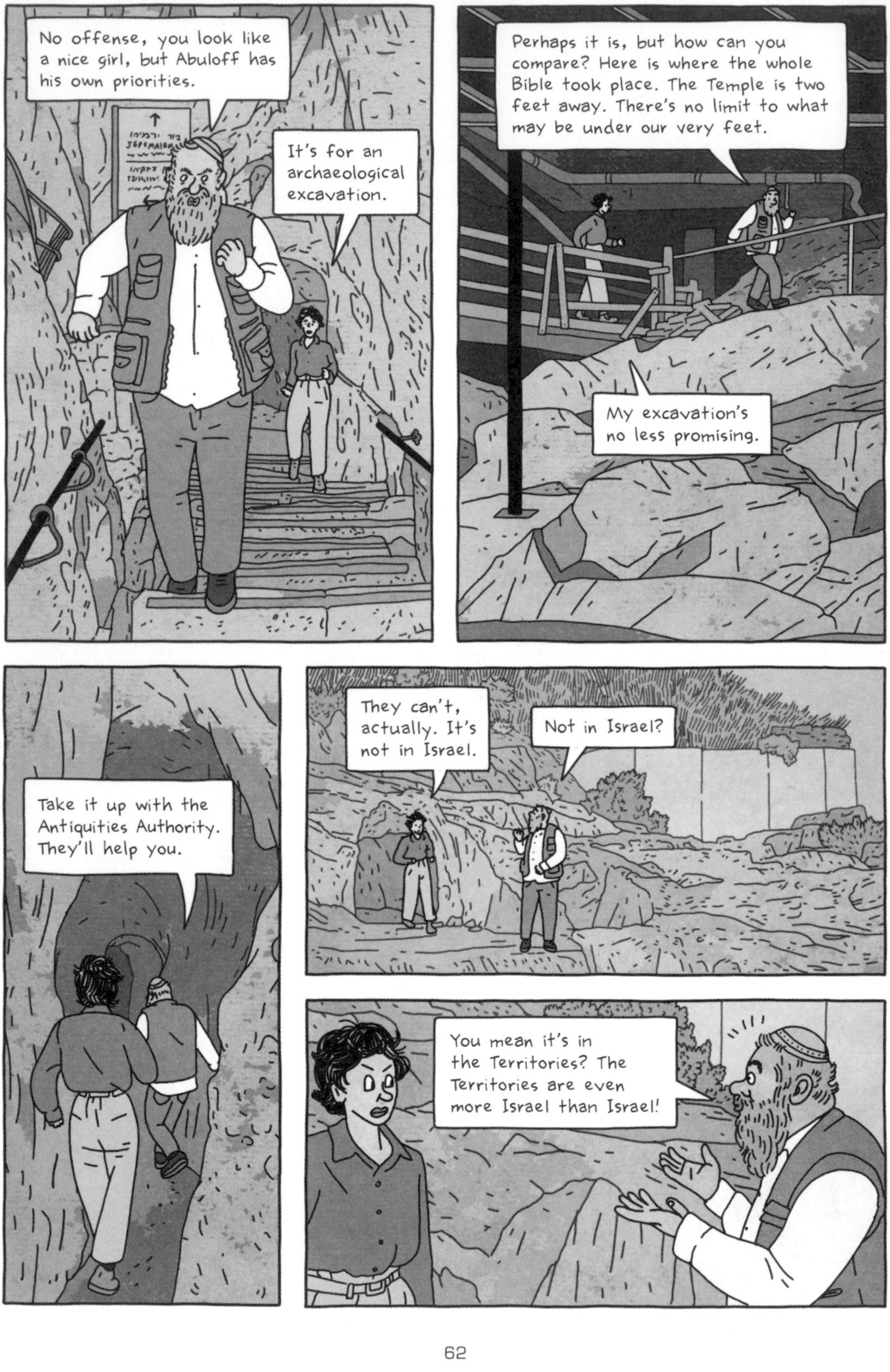
No offense, you look like a nice girl, but Abuloff has his own priorities.
It's for an archaeological excavation.
Perhaps it is, but how can you compare? Here is where the whole Bible took place. The Temple is two feet away. There's no limit to what may be under our very feet.
My excavation's no less promising.
Take it up with the Antiquities Authority. They'll help you.
They can't, actually. It's not in Israel.
Not in Israel?
You mean it's in the Territories? The Territories are even more Israel than Israel!

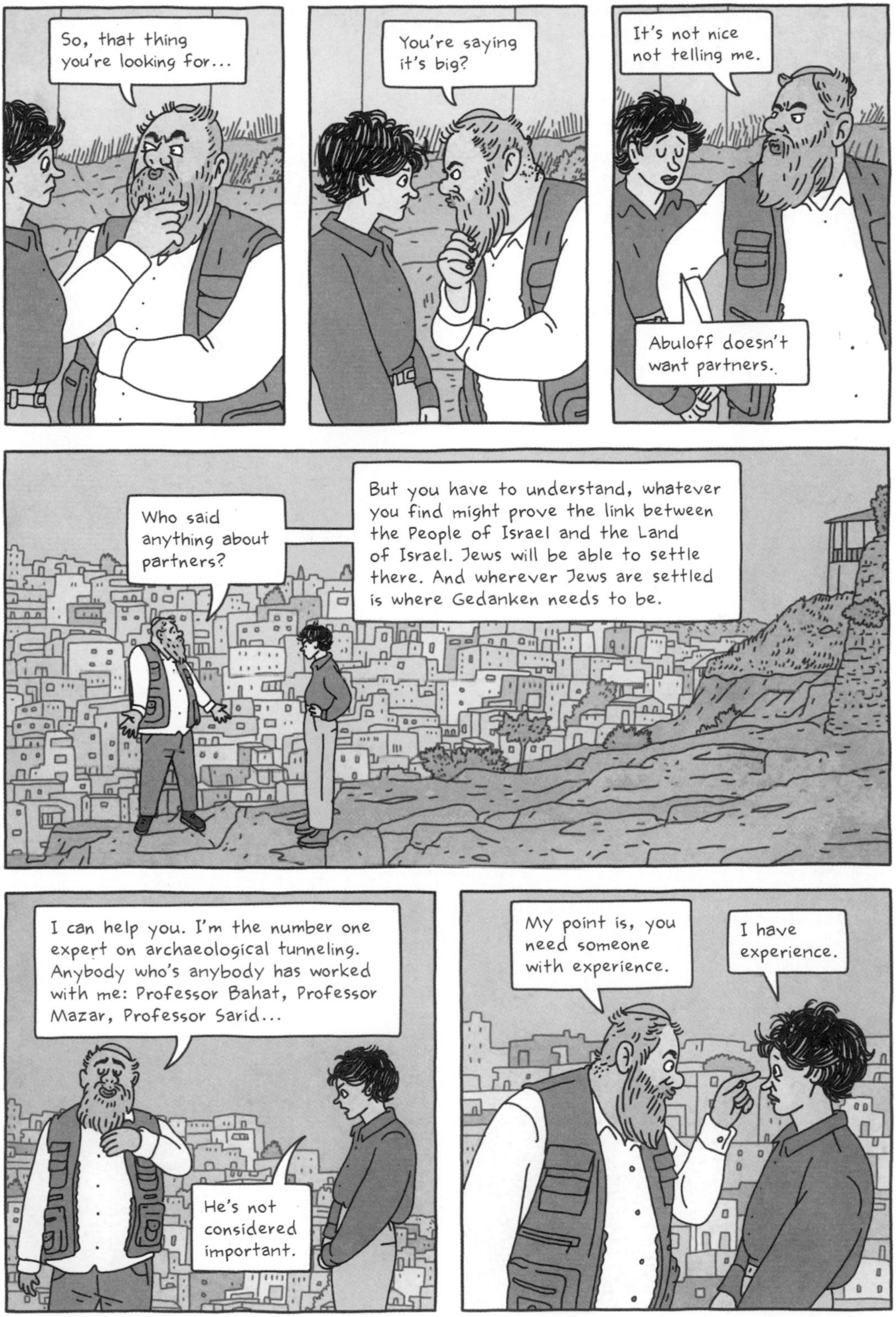
So, that thing you're looking for...
You're saying it's big?
It's not nice not telling me.
Abuloff doesn't want partners.
Who said anything about partners?
But you have to understand, whatever you find might prove the link between the People of Israel and the Land of Israel. Jews will be able to settle there. And wherever Jews are settled is where Gedanken needs to be.
I can help you. I'm the number one expert on archaeological tunneling. Anybody who's anybody has worked with me: Professor Bahat, Professor Mazar, Professor Sarid...
He's not considered important.
My point is, you need someone with experience.
I have experience.

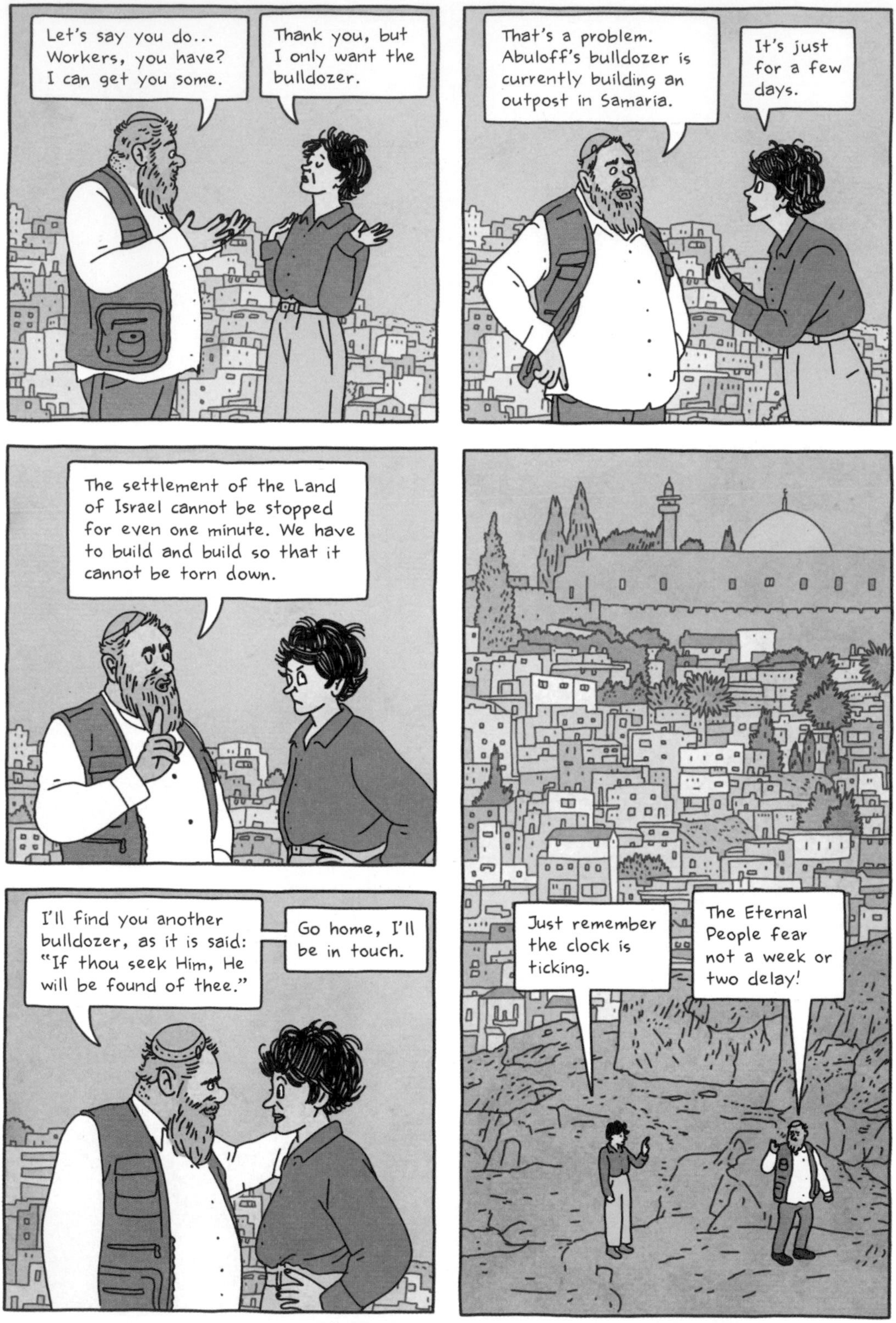

Let's say you do... Workers, you have? I can get you some.
Thank you, but I only want the bulldozer.
That's a problem. Abuloff's bulldozer is currently building an outpost in Samaria.
It's just for a few days.
The settlement of the Land of Israel cannot be stopped for even one minute. We have to build and build so that it cannot be torn down.
I'll find you another bulldozer, as it is said: "If thou seek Him, He will be found of thee."
Go home, I'll be in touch.
Just remember the clock is ticking.
The Eternal People fear not a week or two delay!

Weeks pass...

Careful, the doorframe!

Hold the pick at a 45-degree angle...

Gedanken

Tap, tap.

Any news?

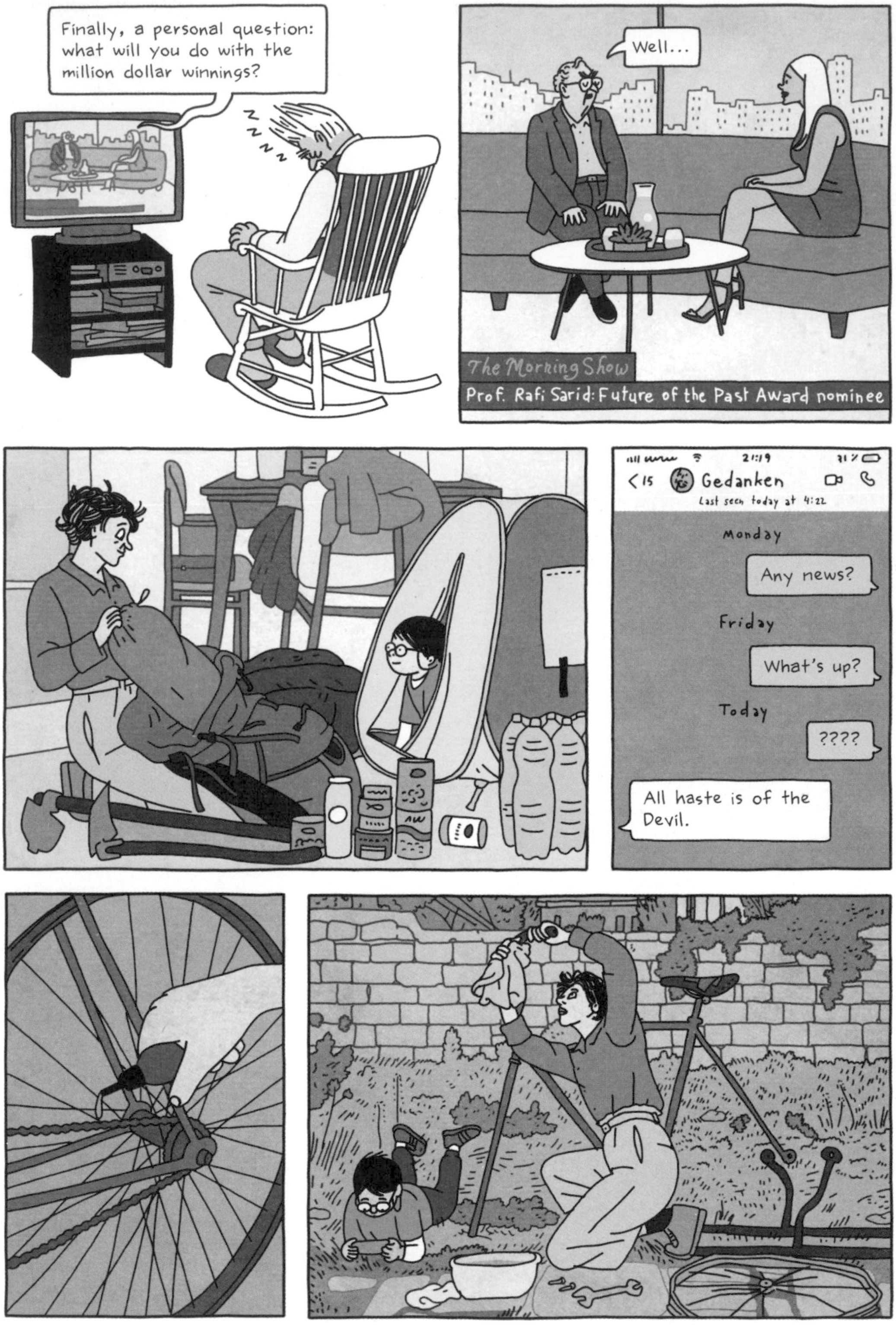

Finally, a personal question: what will you do with the million dollar winnings?
Z Z Z Z Z
Well...
The Morning Show
Prof. Rafi Sarid: Future of the Past Award nominee
21:19
<15 Gedanken
Last seen today at 4:22
Monday
Any news?
Friday
What's up?
Today
????
All haste is of the Devil.

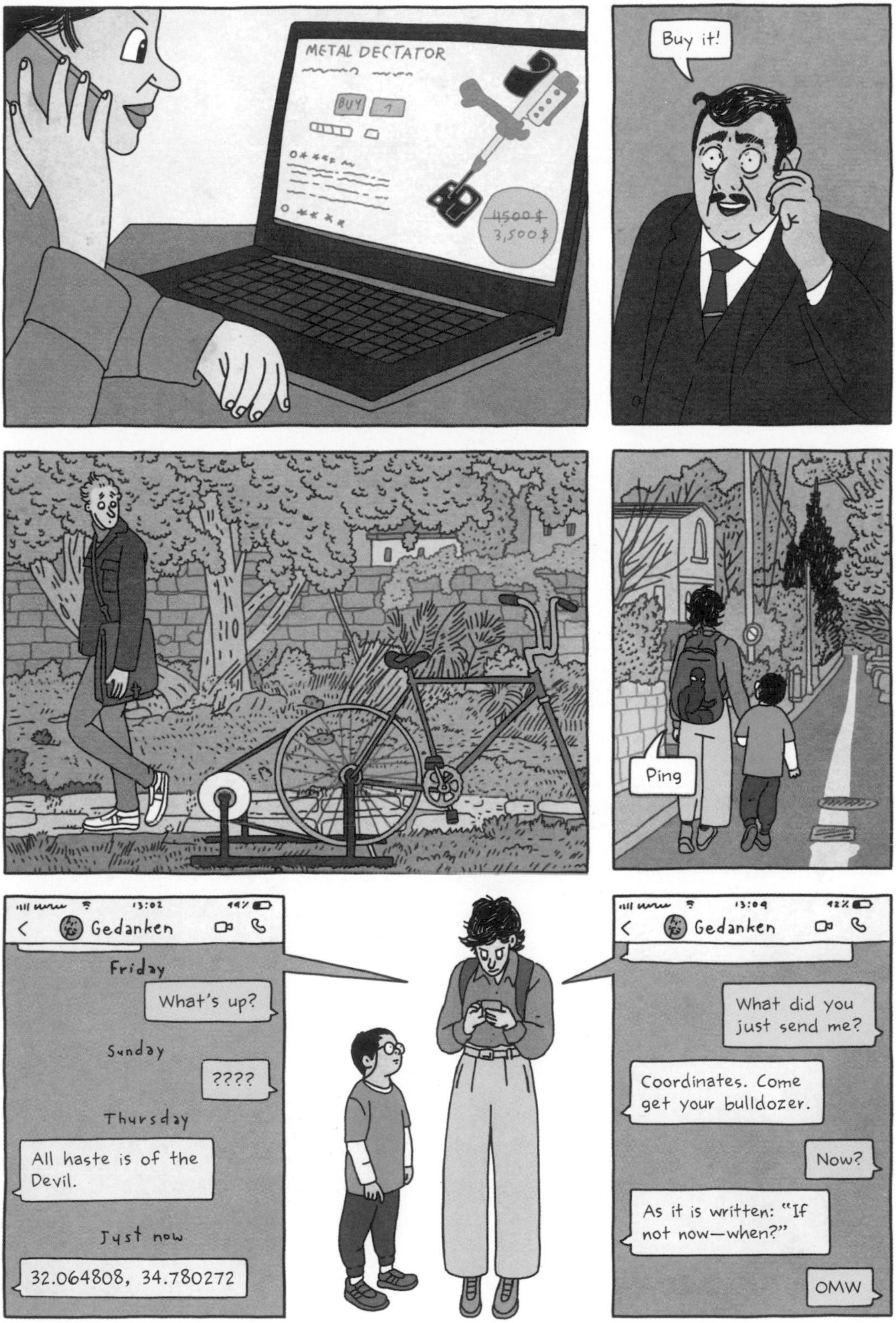
METAL DECTATOR
BUY
4500 $
3,500 $
Buy it!
Ping
Gedanken
Friday
What's up?
Sunday
????
Thursday
All haste is of the Devil.
Just now
32.064808, 34.780272
Gedanken
What did you just send me?
Coordinates. Come get your bulldozer.
Now?
As it is written: "If not now—when?"
OMW

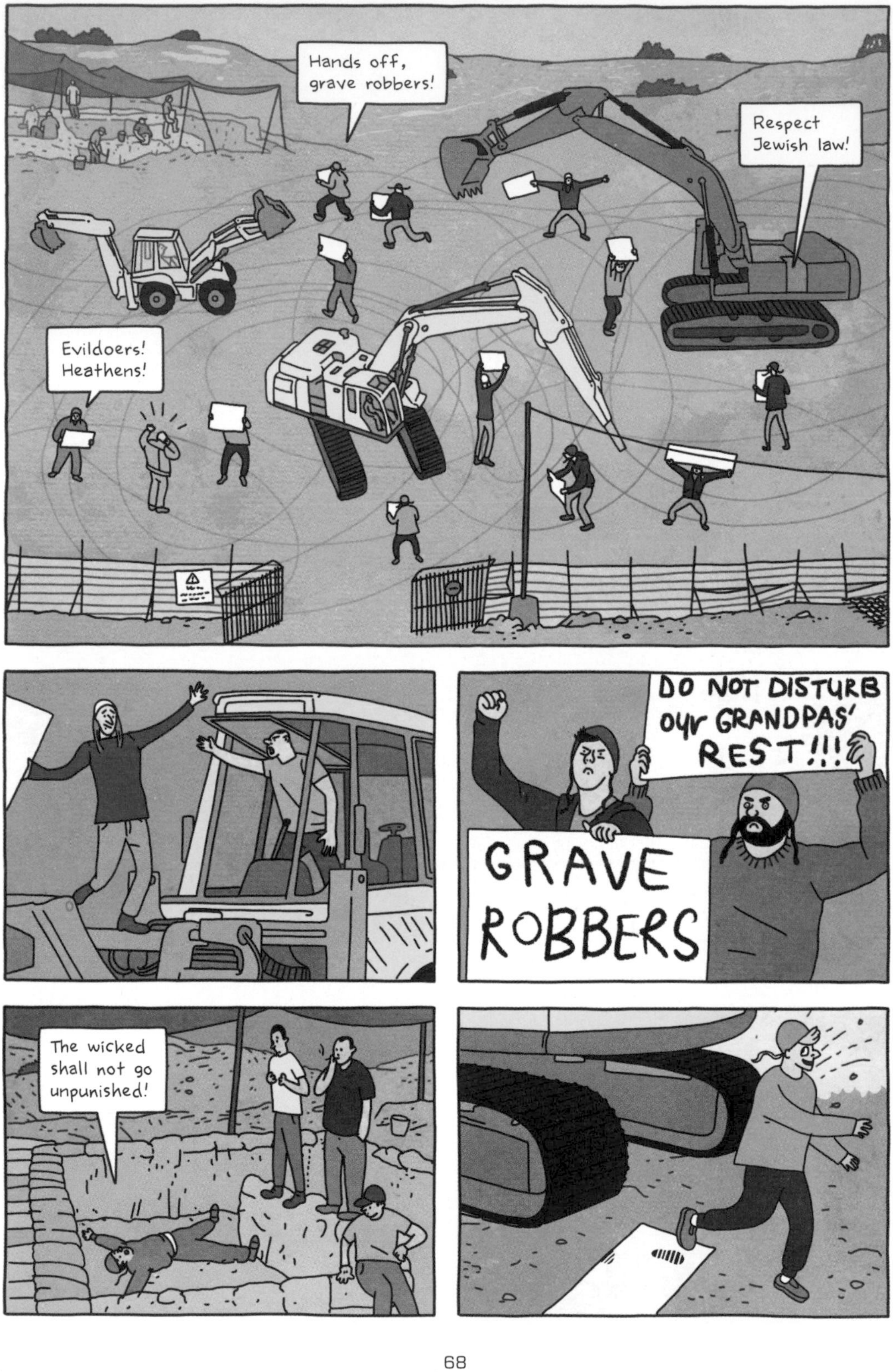
Hands off, grave robbers!
Respect Jewish law!
Evildoers! Heathens!
DO NOT DISTURB OUR GRANDPAS' REST!!!
GRAVE ROBBERS
The wicked shall not go unpunished!

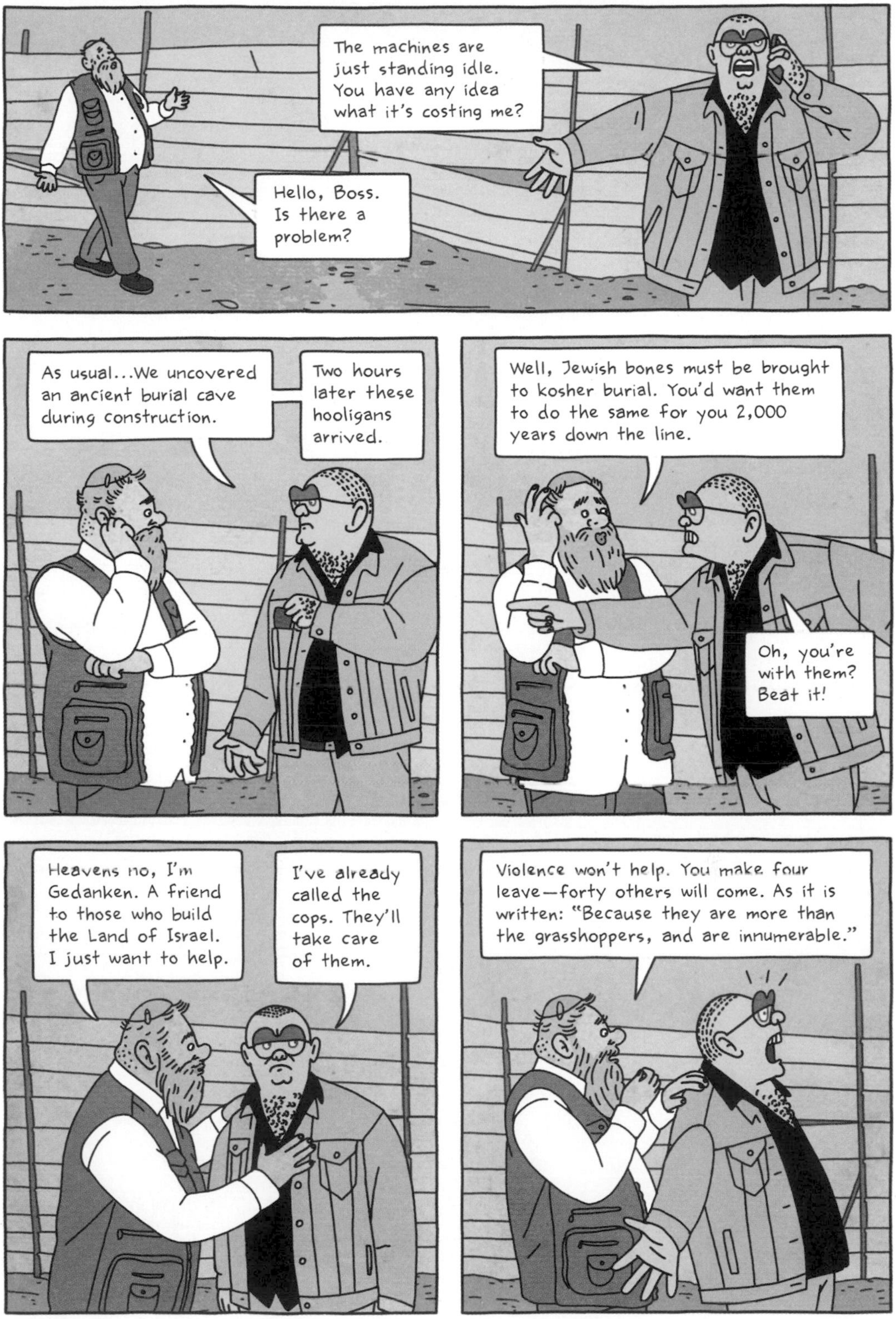

The machines are just standing idle. You have any idea what it's costing me?
Hello, Boss. Is there a problem?
As usual...We uncovered an ancient burial cave during construction.
Two hours later these hooligans arrived.
Well, Jewish bones must be brought to kosher burial. You'd want them to do the same for you 2,000 years down the line.
Oh, you're with them? Beat it!
Heavens no, I'm Gedanken. A friend to those who build the Land of Israel. I just want to help.
I've already called the cops. They'll take care of them.
Violence won't help. You make four leave—forty others will come. As it is written: "Because they are more than the grasshoppers, and are innumerable."

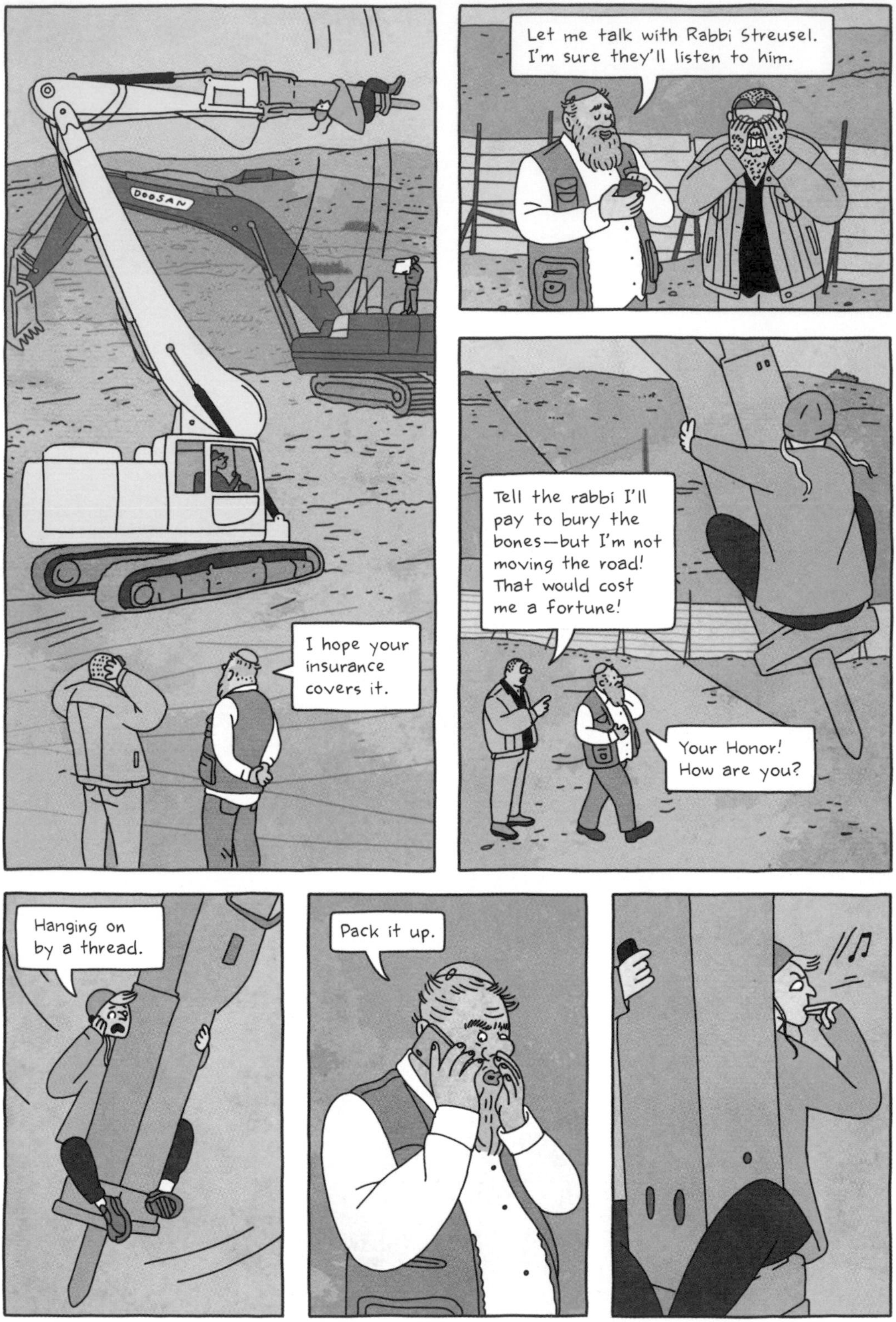
Let me talk with Rabbi Streusel. I'm sure they'll listen to him.
I hope your insurance covers it.
Tell the rabbi I'll pay to bury the bones—but I'm not moving the road! That would cost me a fortune!
Your Honor! How are you?
Hanging on by a thread.
Pack it up.

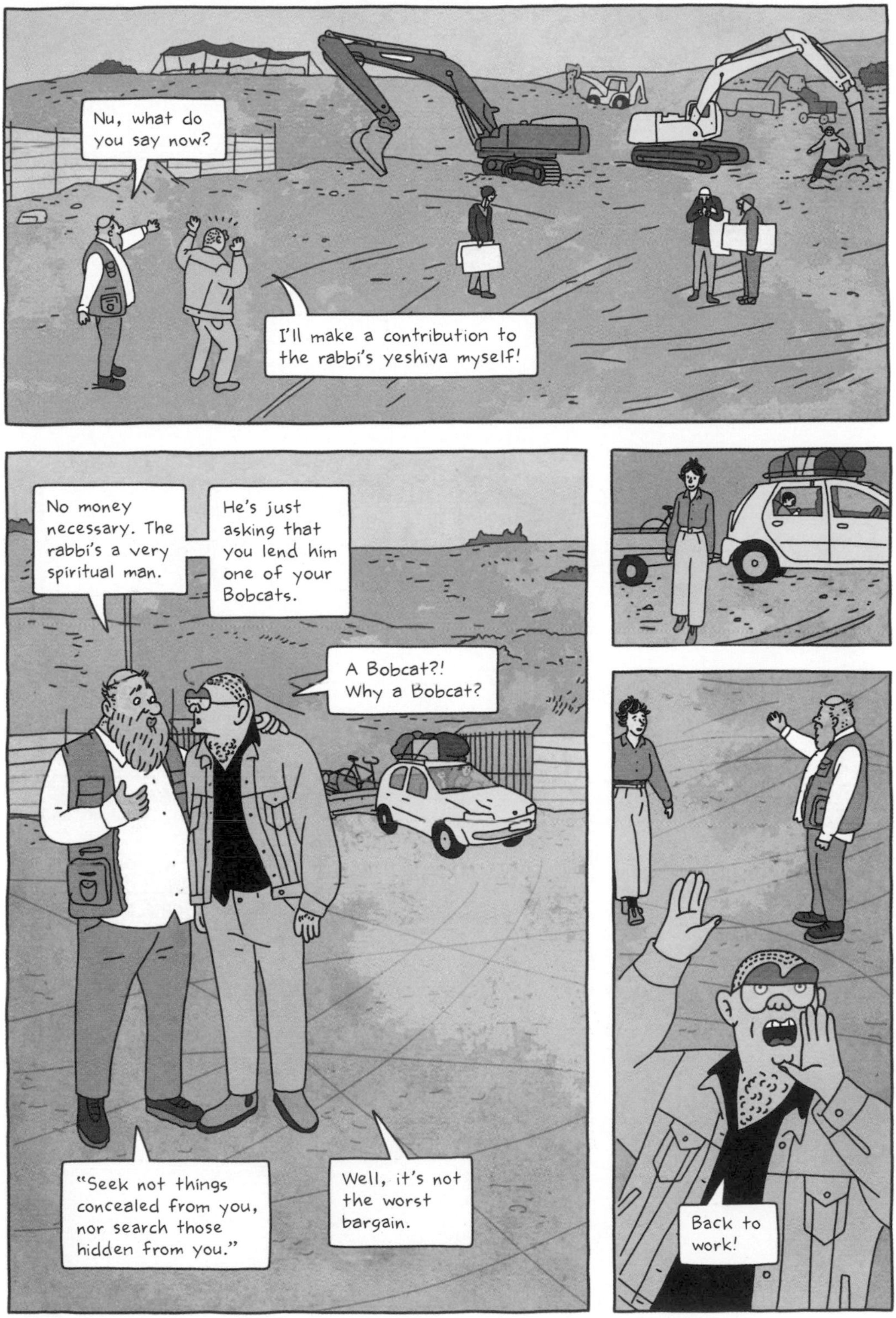
Nu, what do you say now?
I'll make a contribution to the rabbi's yeshiva myself!
No money necessary. The rabbi's a very spiritual man.
He's just asking that you lend him one of your Bobcats.
A Bobcat?! Why a Bobcat?
"Seek not things concealed from you, nor search those hidden from you."
Well, it's not the worst bargain.
Back to work!

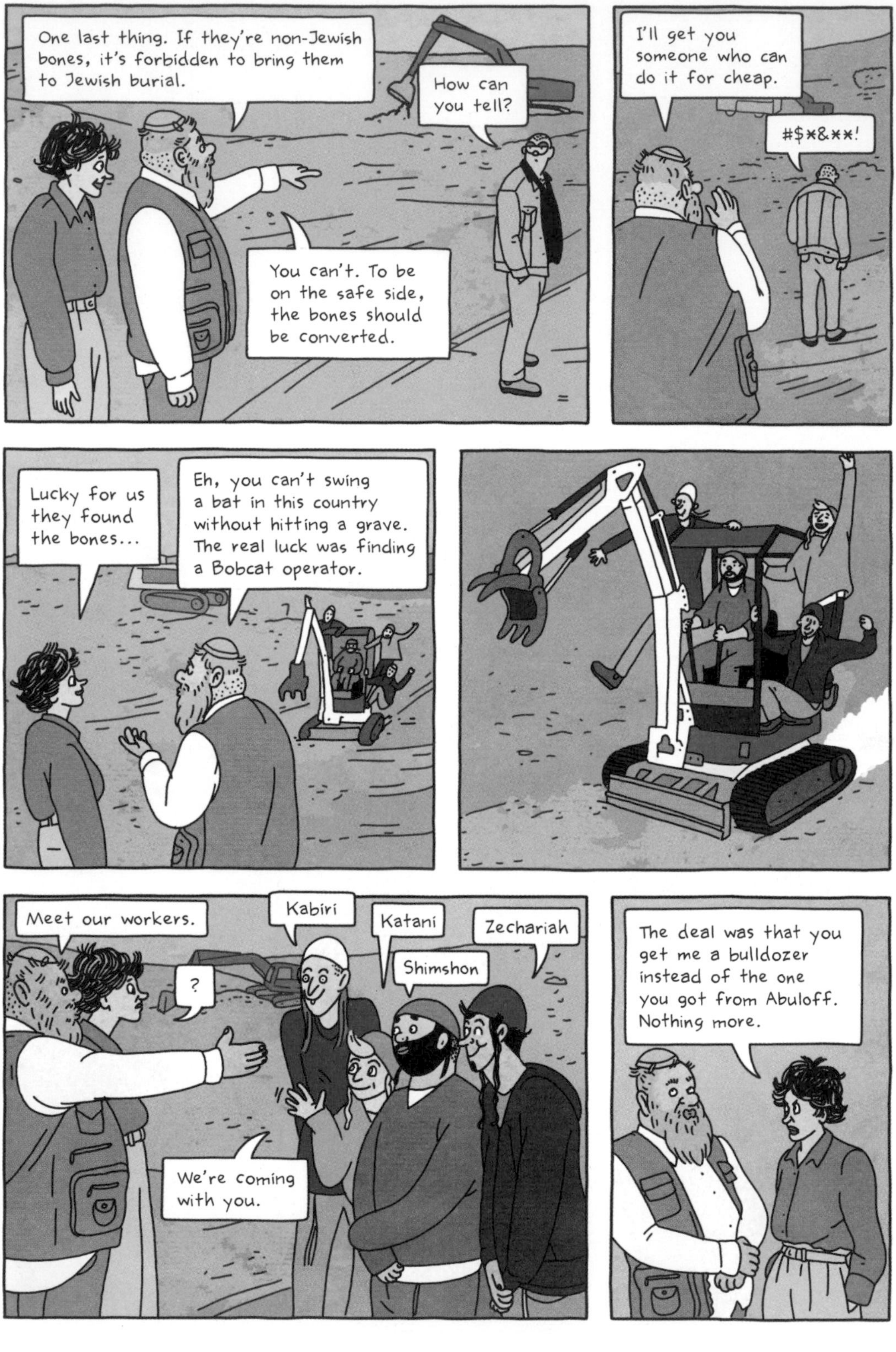

One last thing. If they're non-Jewish bones, it's forbidden to bring them to Jewish burial.
How can you tell?
You can't. To be on the safe side, the bones should be converted.
I'll get you someone who can do it for cheap.
#$*&**!
Lucky for us they found the bones...
Eh, you can't swing a bat in this country without hitting a grave. The real luck was finding a Bobcat operator.
Meet our workers.
?
Kabiri
Katani
Shimshon
Zechariah
We're coming with you.
The deal was that you get me a bulldozer instead of the one you got from Abuloff. Nothing more.

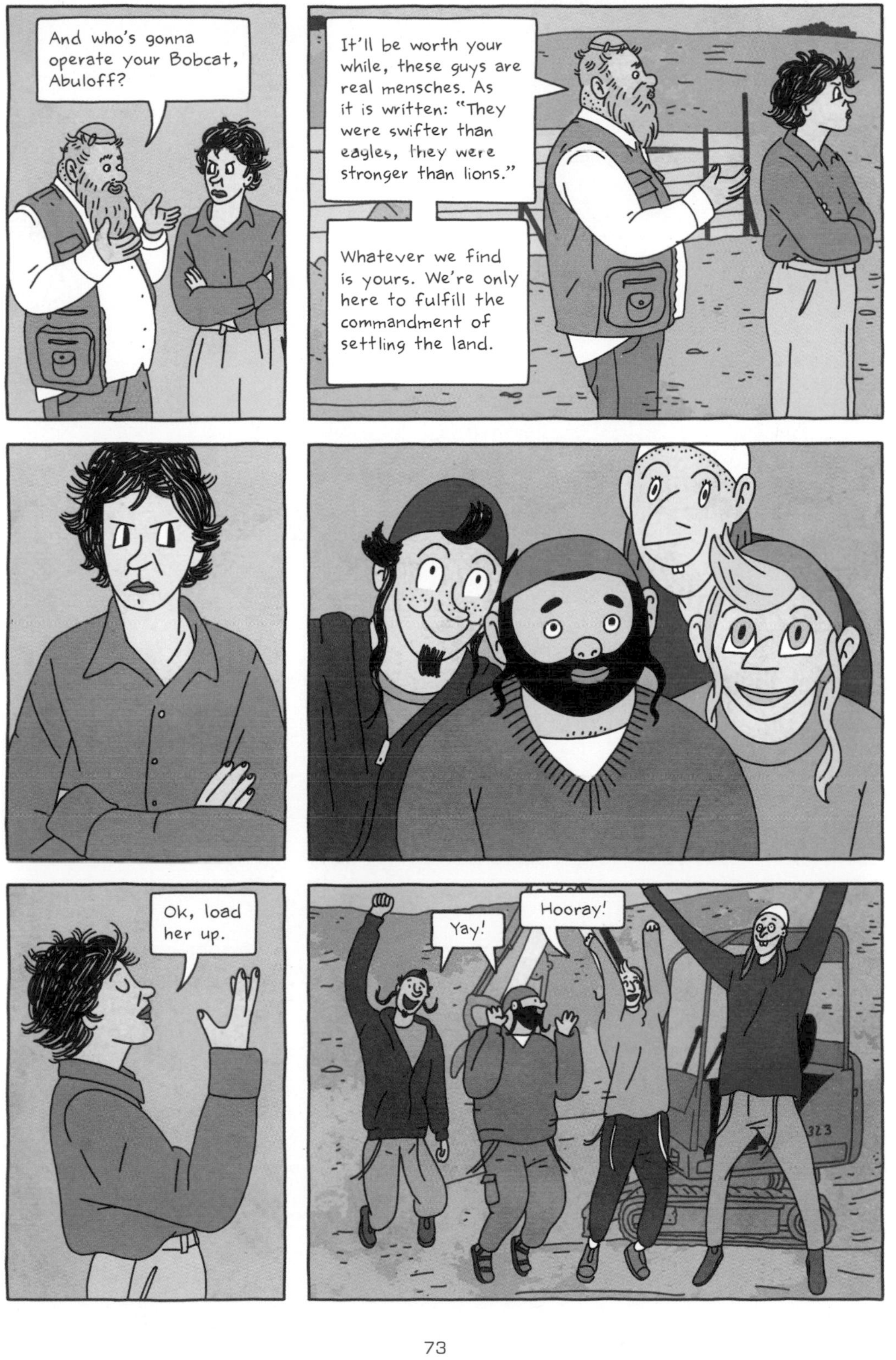

And who's gonna operate your Bobcat, Abuloff?
It'll be worth your while, these guys are real mensches. As it is written: "They were swifter than eagles, they were stronger than lions."
Whatever we find is yours. We're only here to fulfill the commandment of settling the land.
Ok, load her up.
Yay!
Hooray!
323

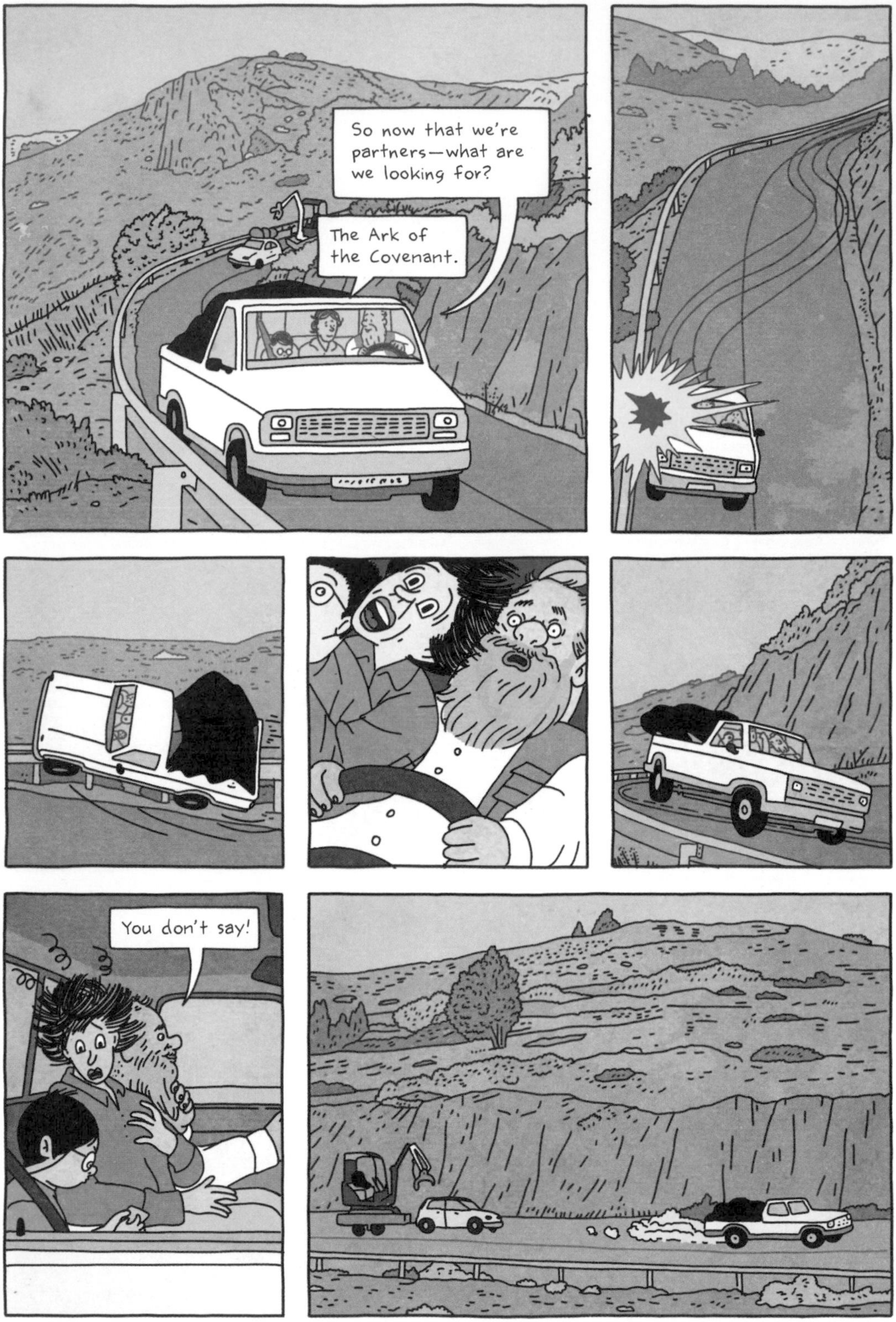
So now that we're partners—what are we looking for?
The Ark of the Covenant.
You don't say!

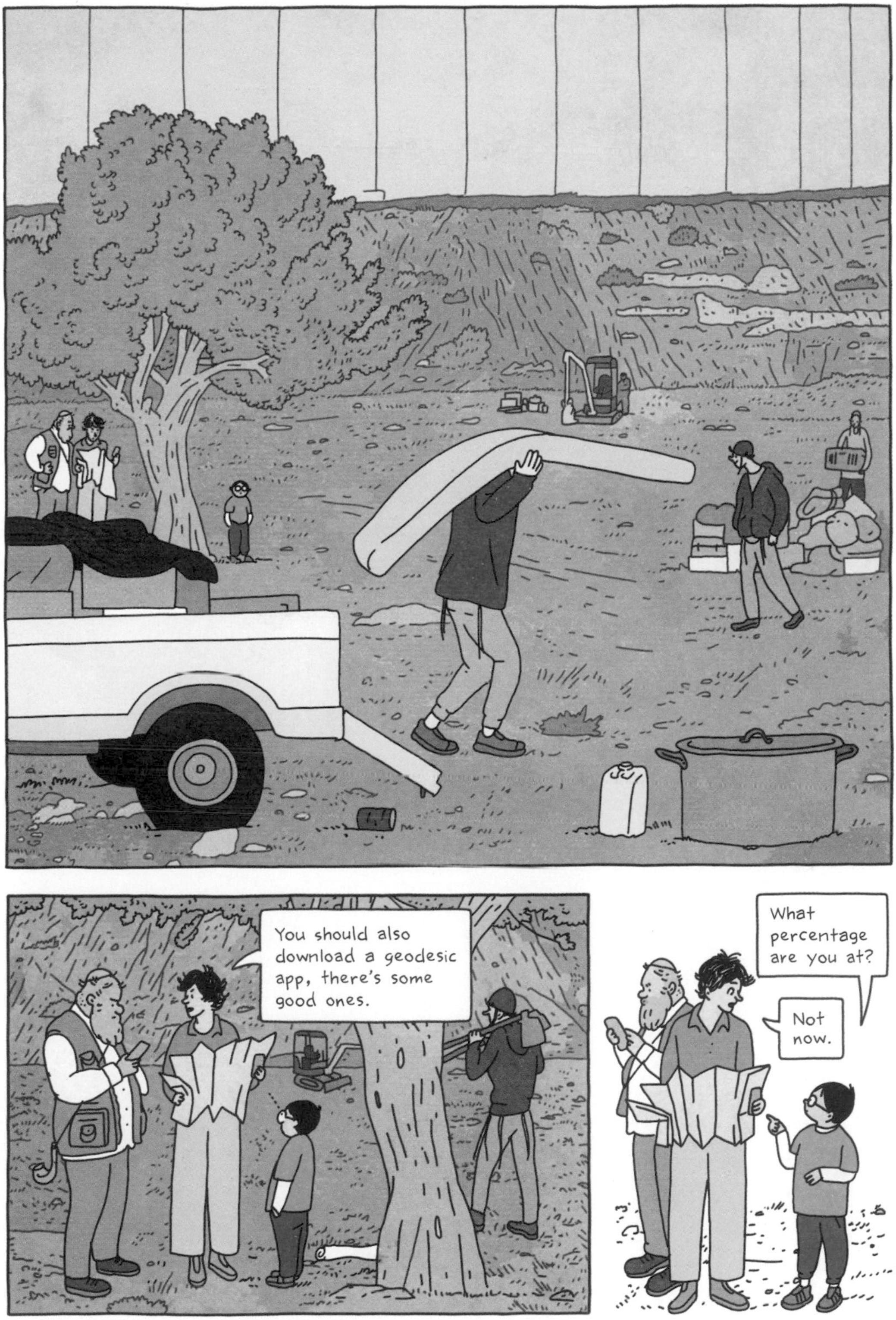
You should also download a geodesic app, there's some good ones.
What percentage are you at?
Not now.

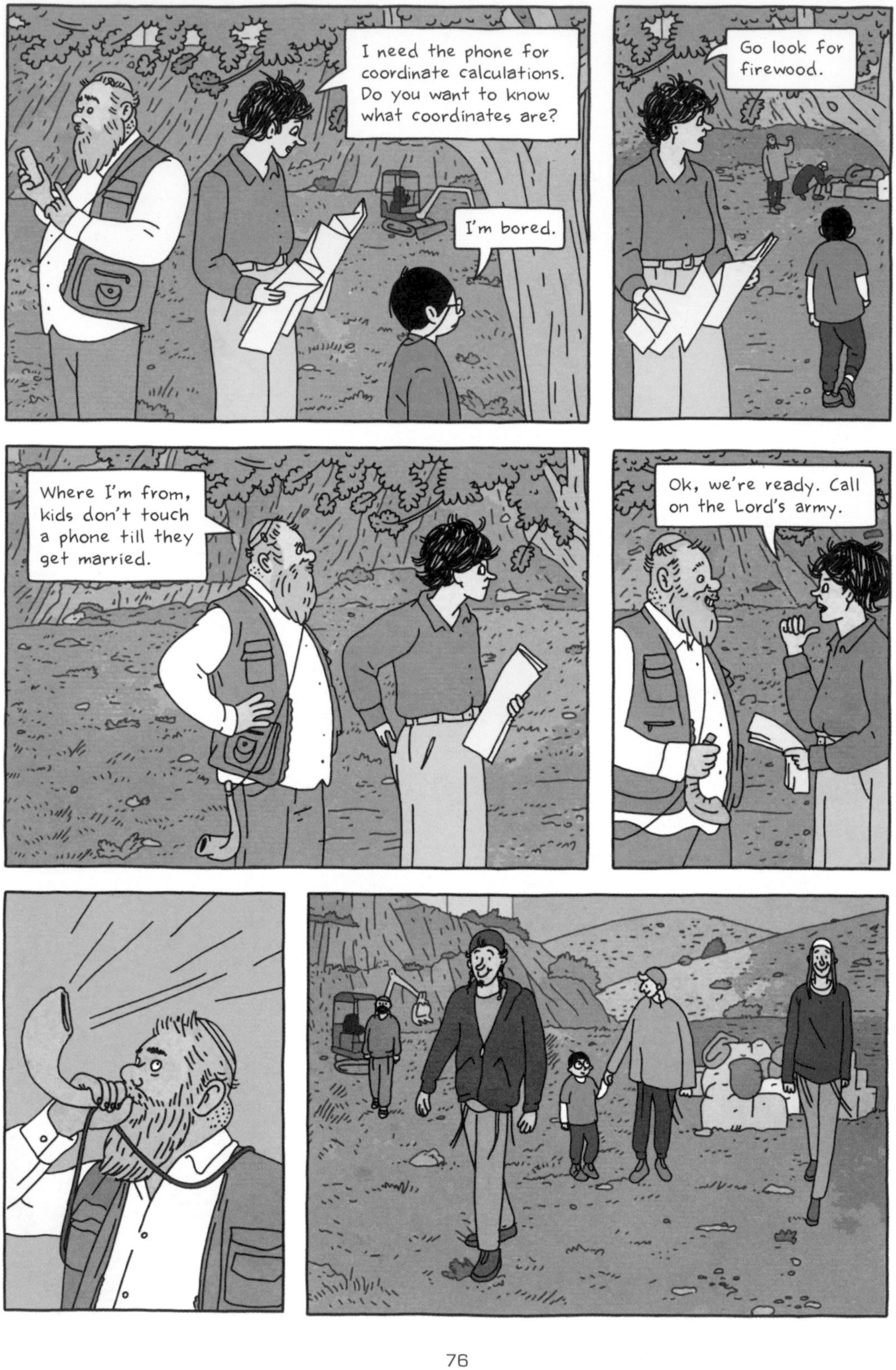
I need the phone for coordinate calculations. Do you want to know what coordinates are?
I'm bored.
Go look for firewood.
Where I'm from, kids don't touch a phone till they get married.
Ok, we're ready. Call on the Lord's army.

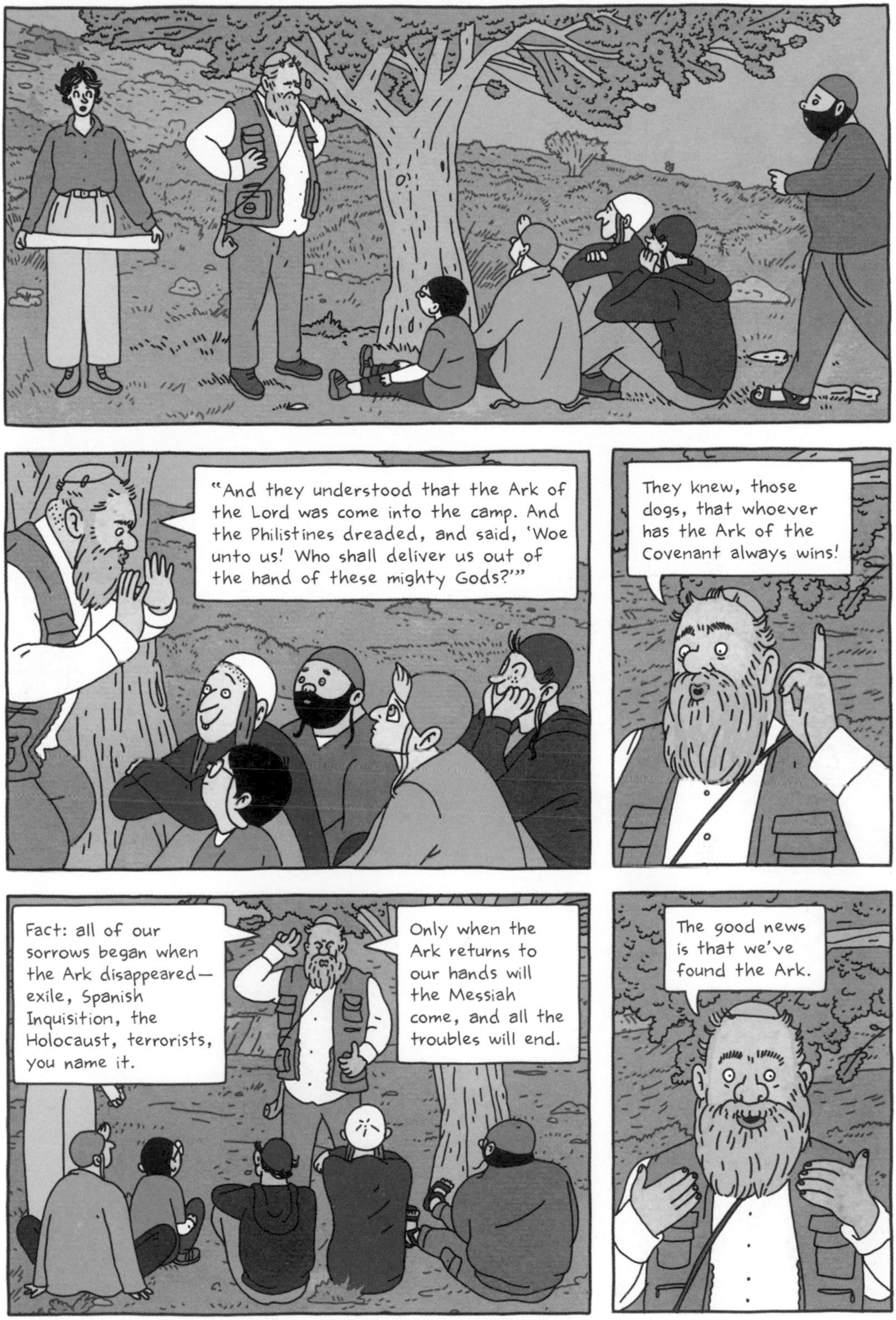
"And they understood that the Ark of the Lord was come into the camp. And the Philistines dreaded, and said, 'Woe unto us! Who shall deliver us out of the hand of these mighty Gods?'"
They knew, those dogs, that whoever has the Ark of the Covenant always wins!
Fact: all of our sorrows began when the Ark disappeared—exile, Spanish Inquisition, the Holocaust, terrorists, you name it.
Only when the Ark returns to our hands will the Messiah come, and all the troubles will end.
The good news is that we've found the Ark.

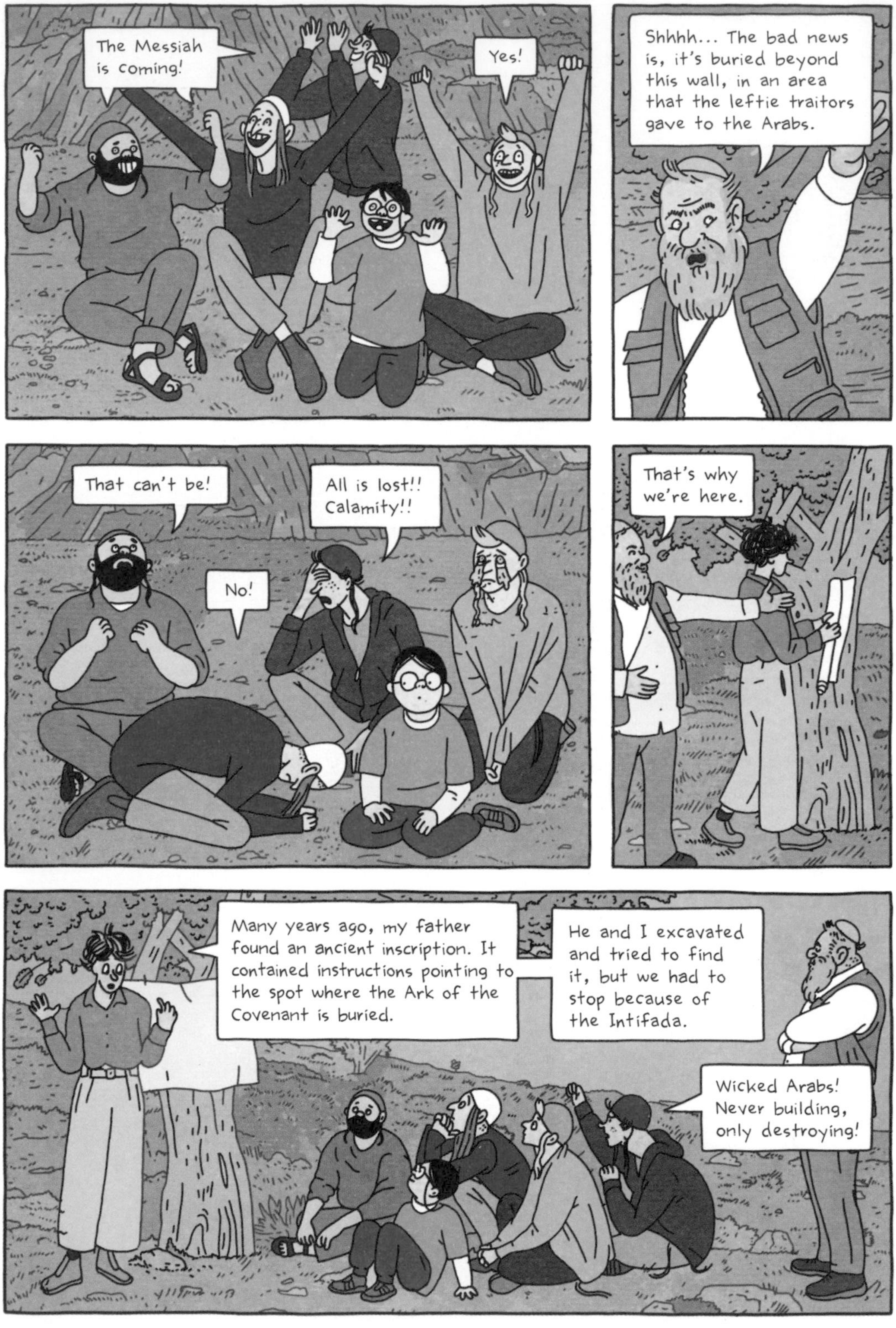
The Messiah is coming!
Yes!
Shhhh... The bad news is, it's buried beyond this wall, in an area that the leftie traitors gave to the Arabs.
That can't be!
No!
All is lost!! Calamity!!
That's why we're here.
Many years ago, my father found an ancient inscription. It contained instructions pointing to the spot where the Ark of the Covenant is buried.
He and I excavated and tried to find it, but we had to stop because of the Intifada.
Wicked Arabs! Never building, only destroying!

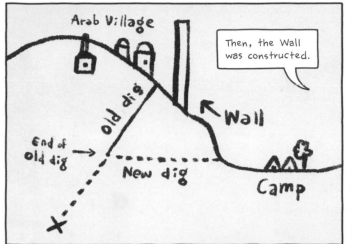

Arab Village

Wall

End of old dig →

Old dig

New dig

Camp

X

Then, the Wall was constructed.

So, what we're going to do is to tunnel under the Wall with the bulldozer, until we connect to Dad's tunnel. From there...

...We keep tunneling until we get to...

...The Ark of the Covenant!

Yes. Well, sort of.

With God's help. Questions?

Are we getting paid?

How long are we going to be here?

Payment—in the world to come. Timeline—the coming of the Messiah. Next question?

Isn't it dangerous? I've heard the Ark is radioactive.

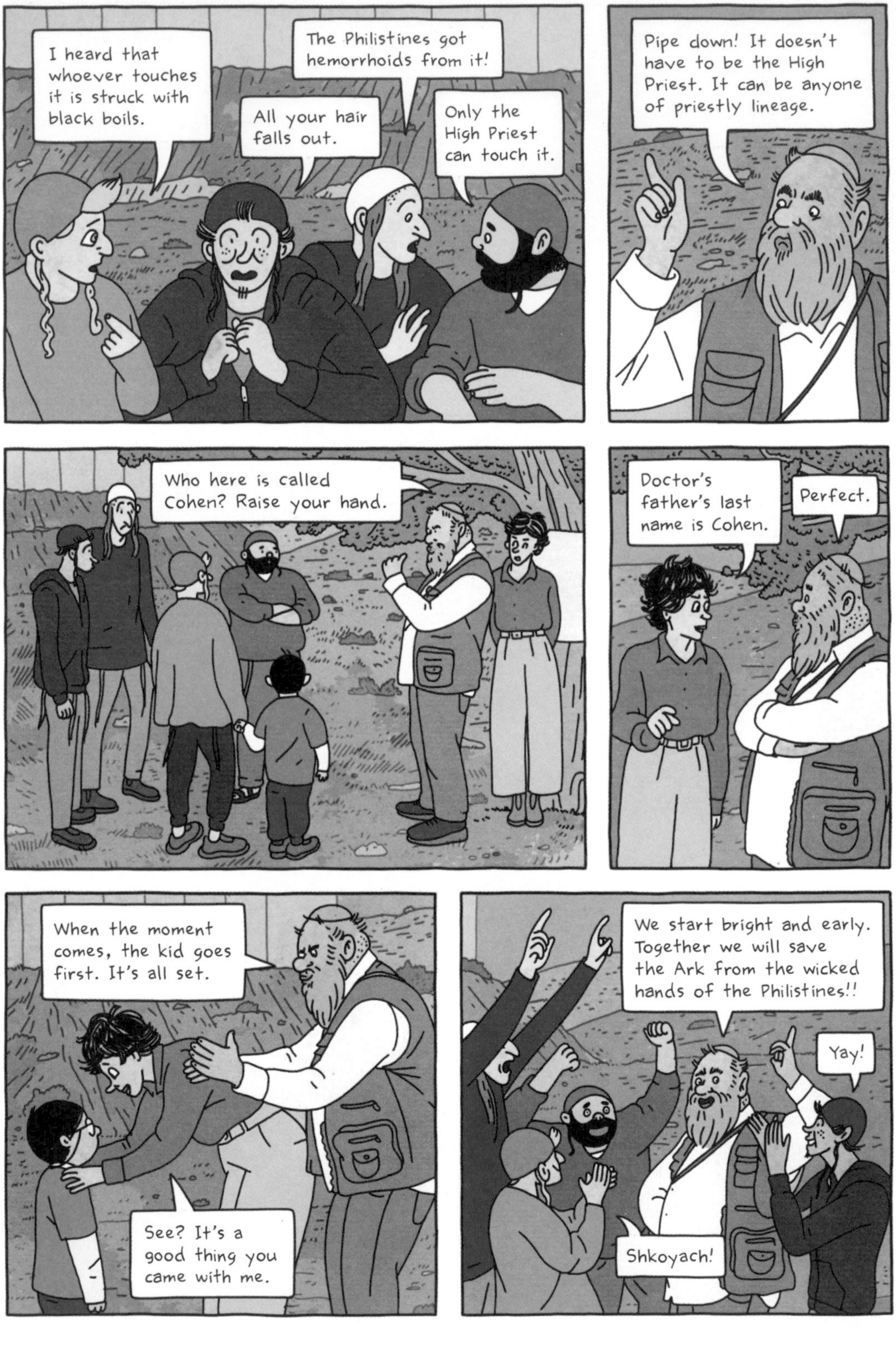
I heard that whoever touches it is struck with black boils.
The Philistines got hemorrhoids from it!
All your hair falls out.
Only the High Priest can touch it.
Pipe down! It doesn't have to be the High Priest. It can be anyone of priestly lineage.
Who here is called Cohen? Raise your hand.
Doctor's father's last name is Cohen.
Perfect.
When the moment comes, the kid goes first. It's all set.
See? It's a good thing you came with me.
We start bright and early. Together we will save the Ark from the wicked hands of the Philistines!!
Yay!
Shkoyach!

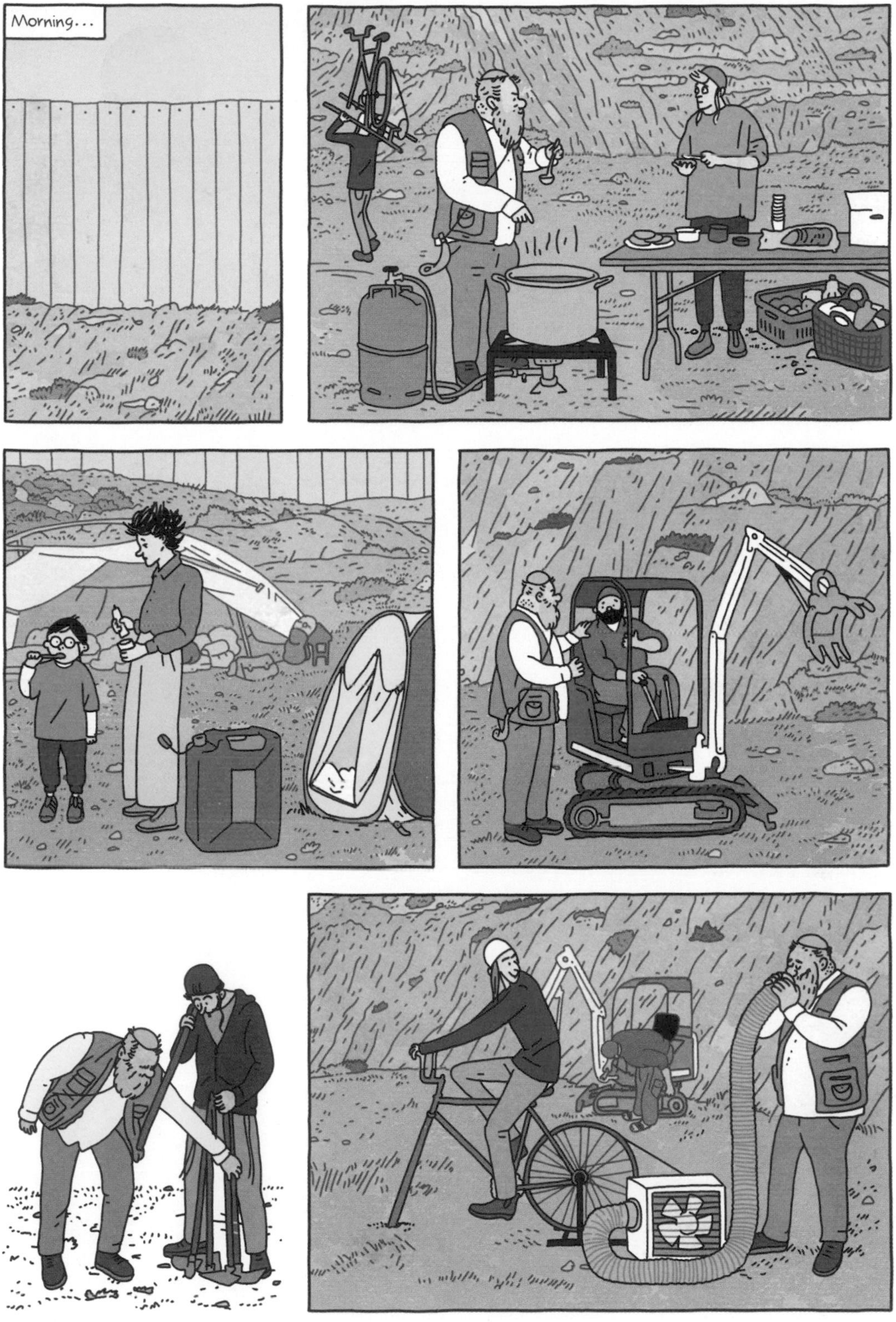
Morning...

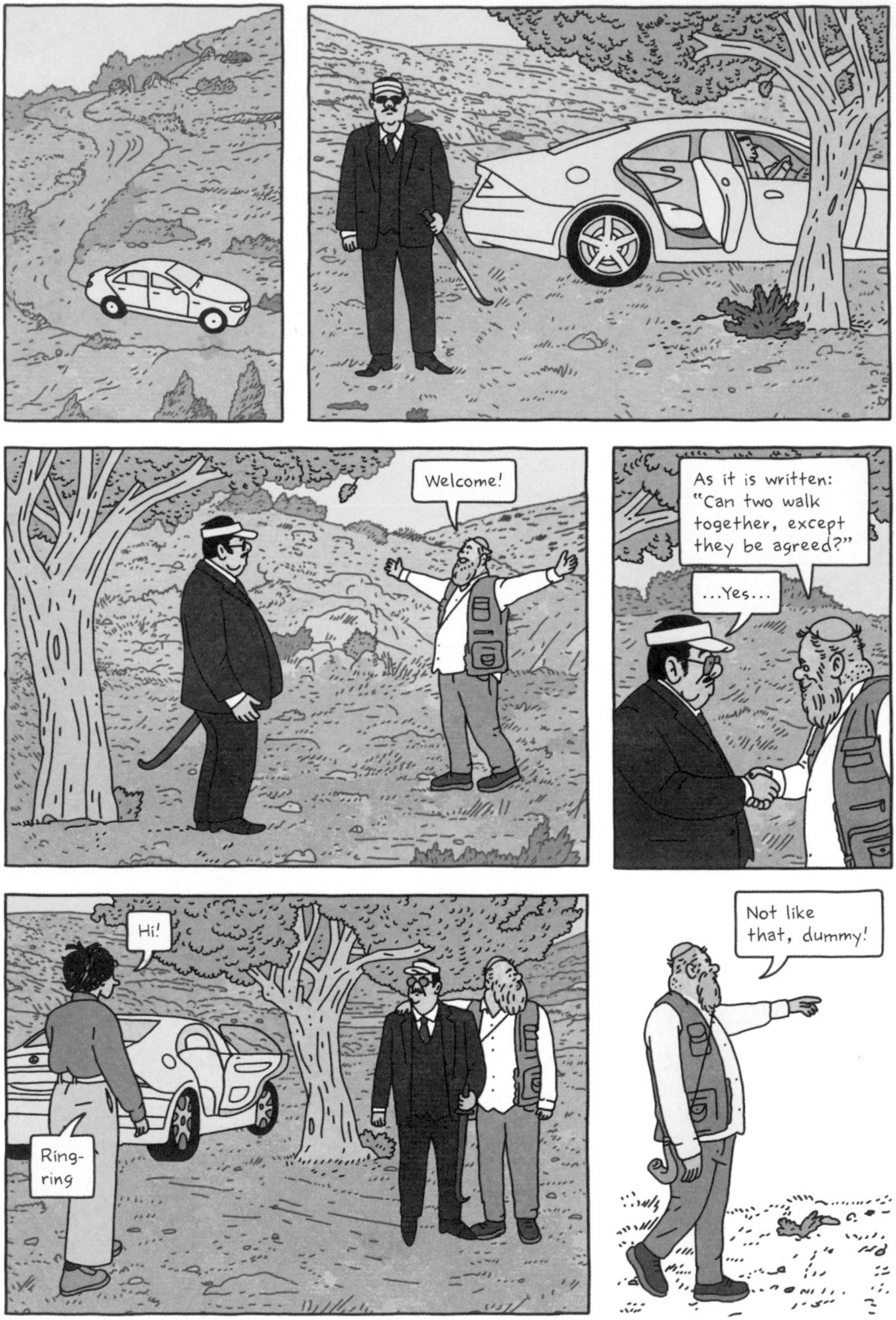
Welcome!
As it is written: "Can two walk together, except they be agreed?"
...Yes...
Hi!
Ring-ring
Not like that, dummy!

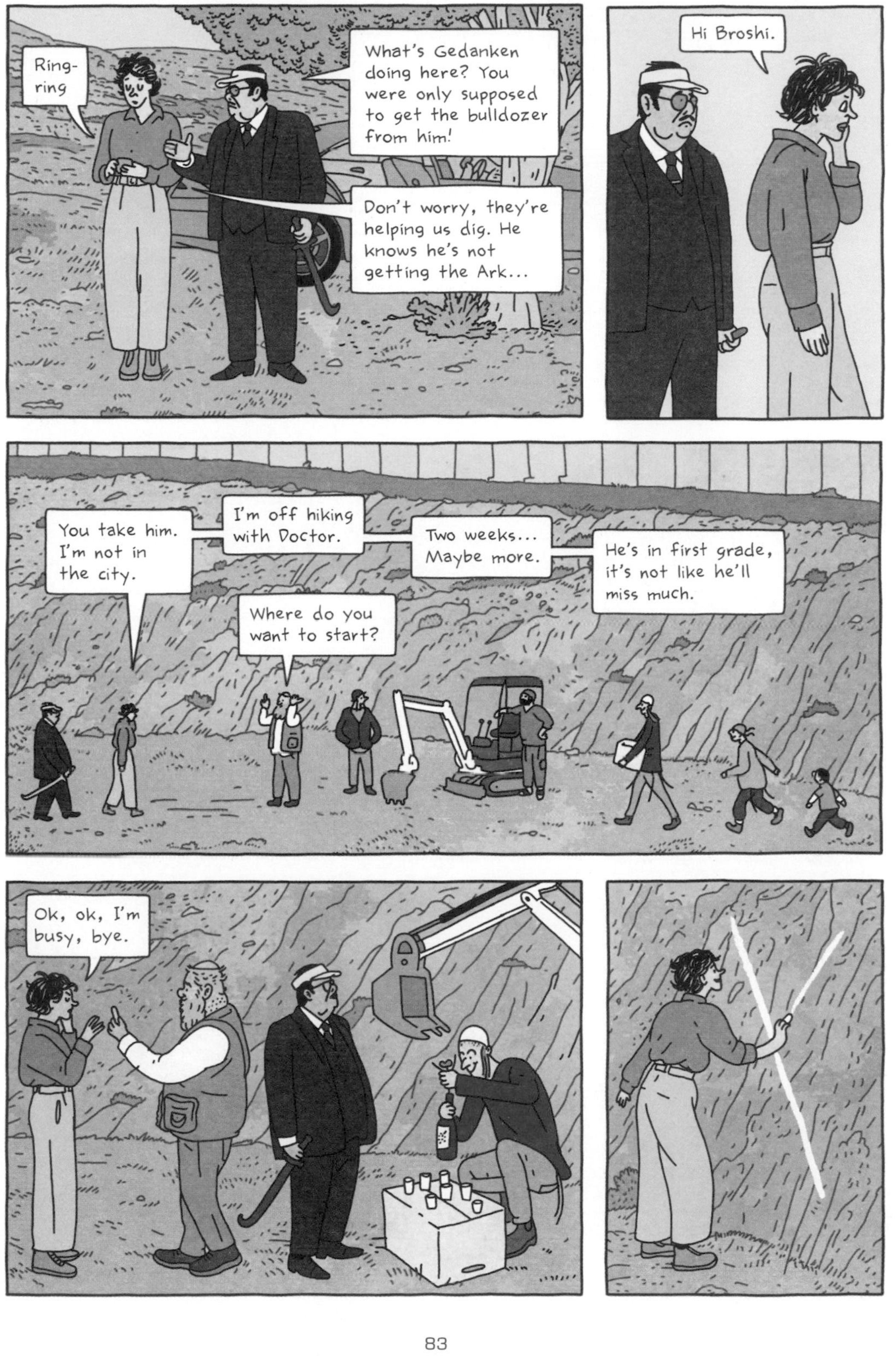
Ring-ring
What's Gedanken doing here? You were only supposed to get the bulldozer from him!
Don't worry, they're helping us dig. He knows he's not getting the Ark...
Hi Broshi.
You take him. I'm not in the city.
I'm off hiking with Doctor.
Two weeks... Maybe more.
He's in first grade, it's not like he'll miss much.
Where do you want to start?
Ok, ok, I'm busy, bye.

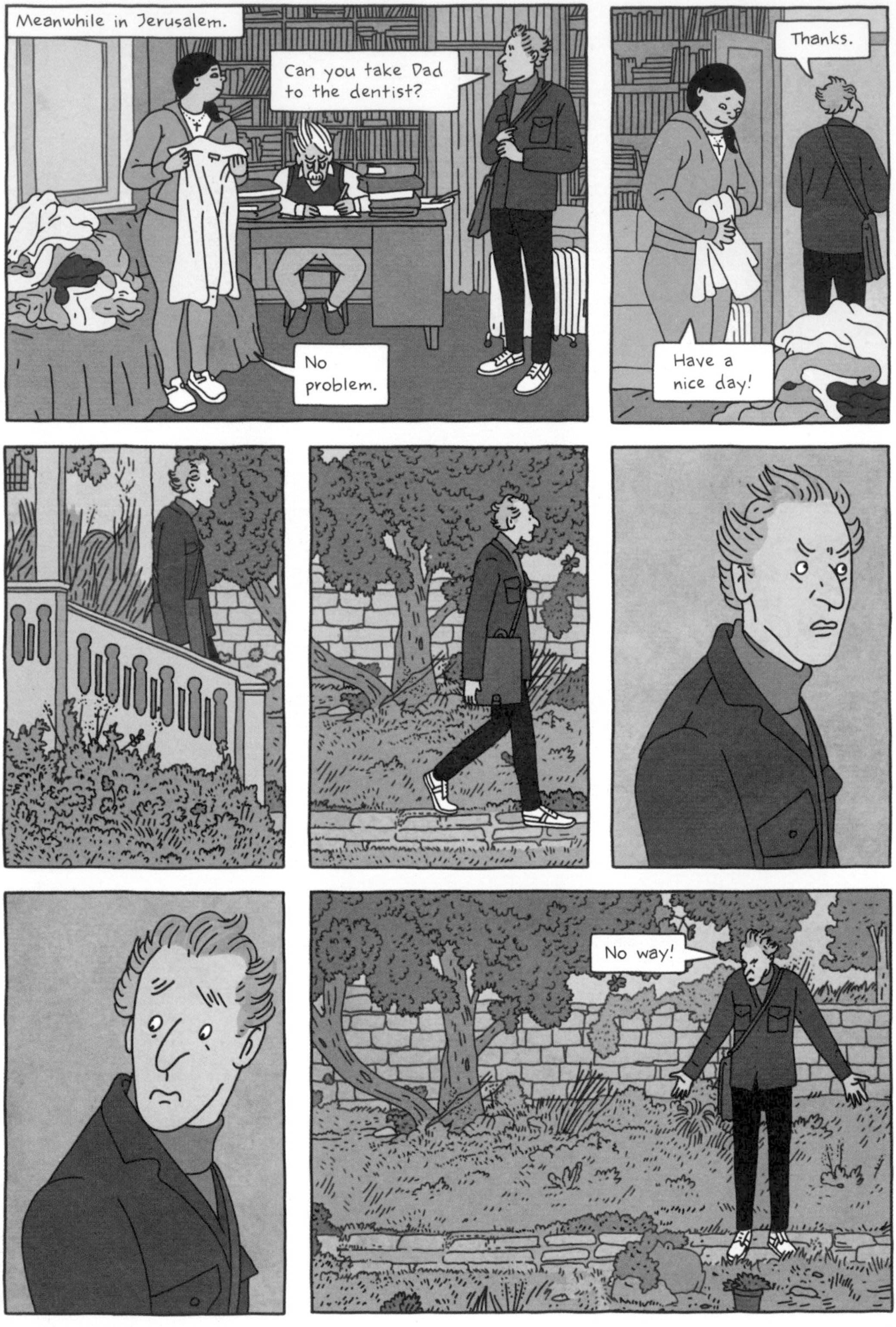
Meanwhile in Jerusalem.
Can you take Dad to the dentist?
No problem.
Thanks.
Have a nice day!
No way!

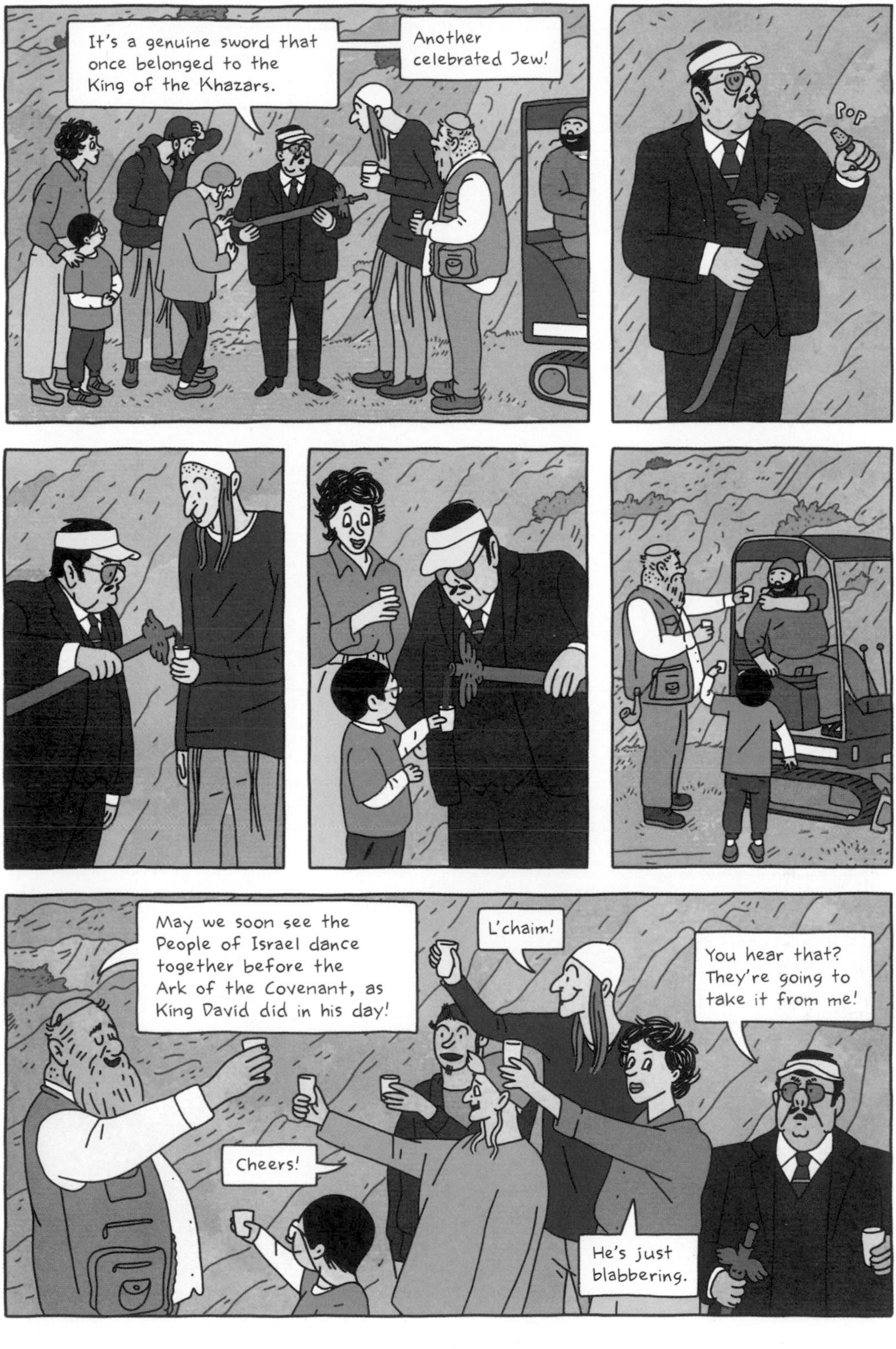
It's a genuine sword that once belonged to the King of the Khazars.
Another celebrated Jew!
POP
May we soon see the People of Israel dance together before the Ark of the Covenant, as King David did in his day!
L'chaim!
You hear that? They're going to take it from me!
Cheers!
He's just blabbering.

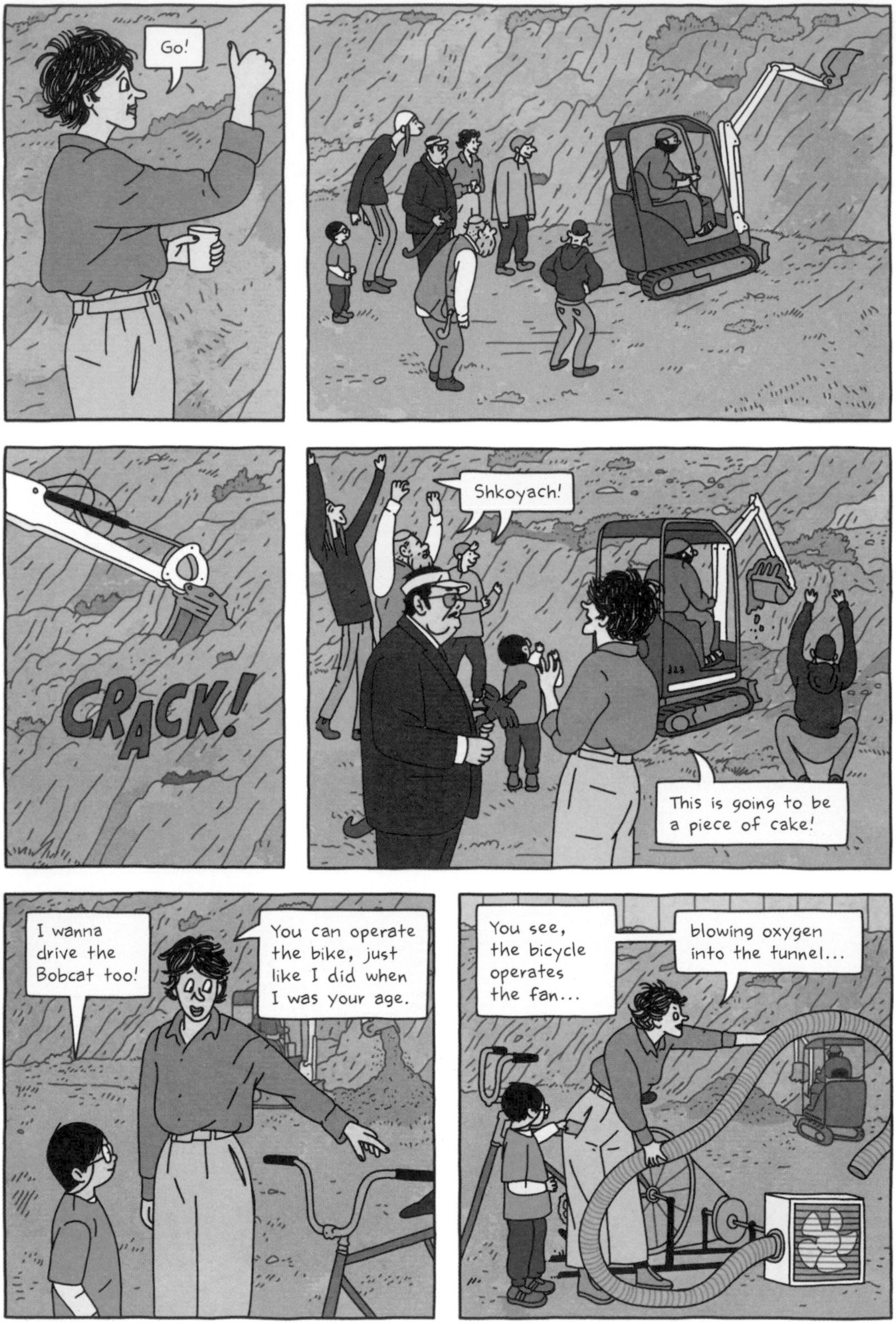
Go!
CRACK!
Shkoyach!
This is going to be a piece of cake!
I wanna drive the Bobcat too!
You can operate the bike, just like I did when I was your age.
You see, the bicycle operates the fan...
blowing oxygen into the tunnel...

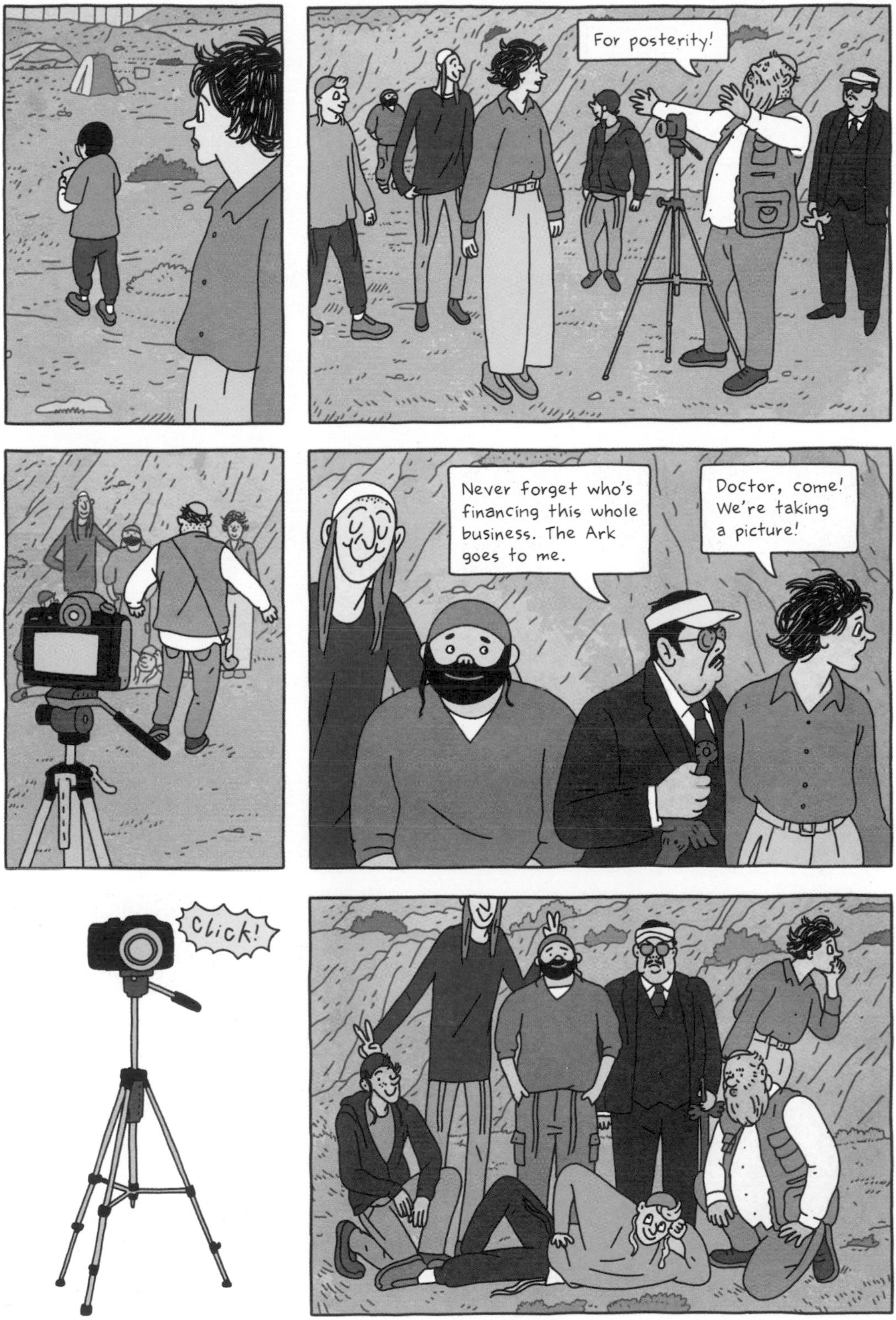
For posterity!
Never forget who's financing this whole business. The Ark goes to me.
Doctor, come! We're taking a picture!
Click!

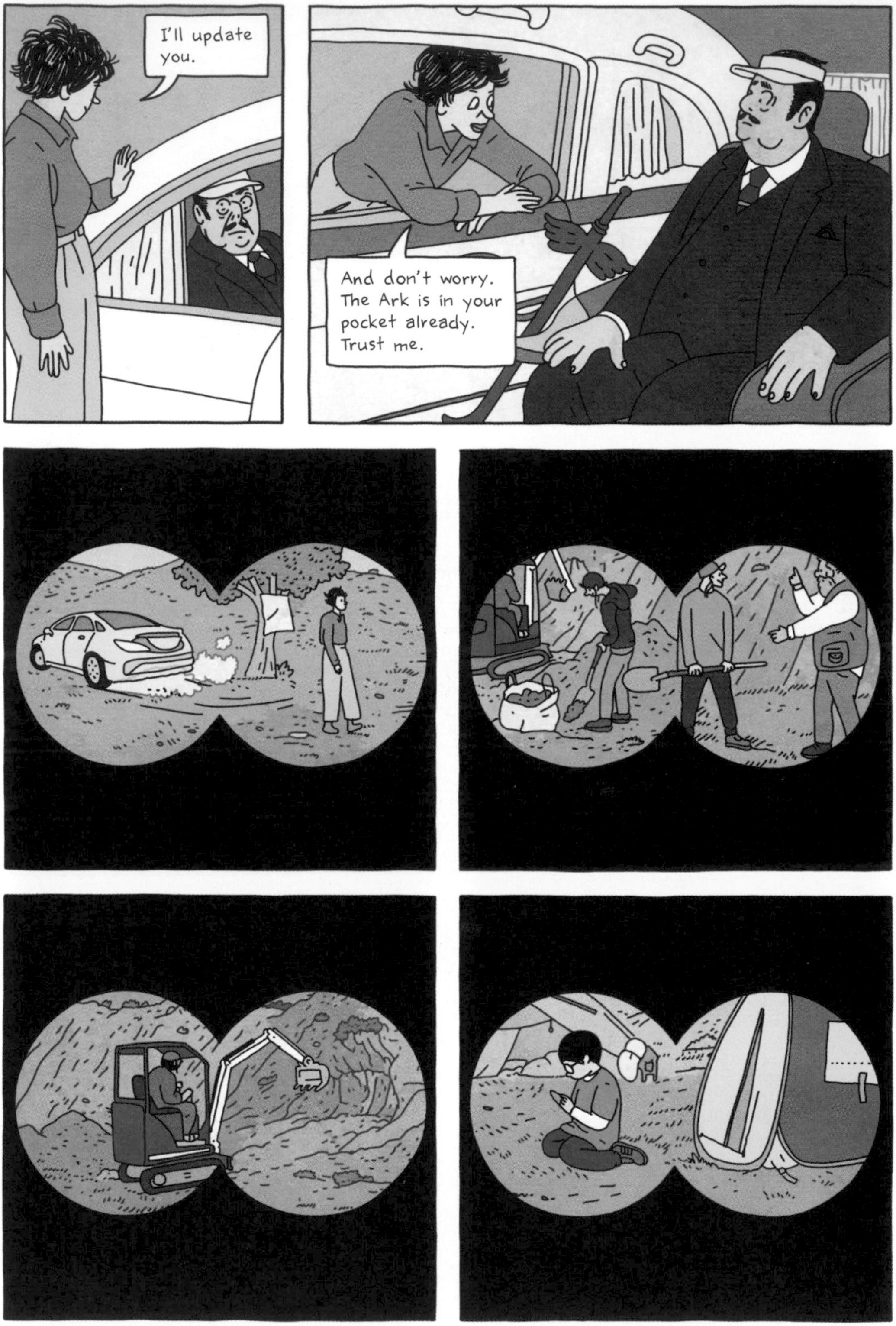

I'll update you.
And don't worry. The Ark is in your pocket already. Trust me.

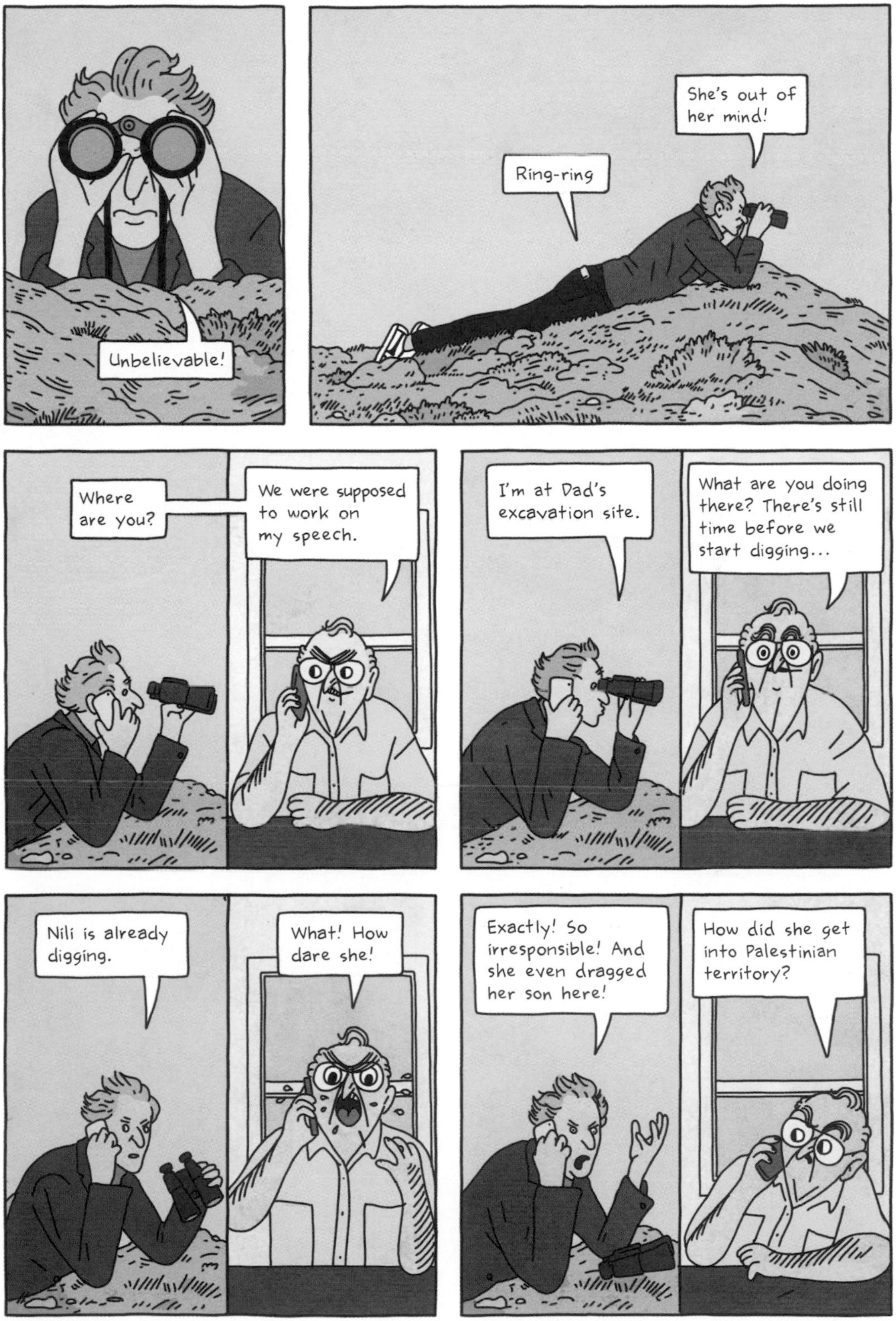
Unbelievable!
Ring-ring
She's out of her mind!
Where are you?
We were supposed to work on my speech.
I'm at Dad's excavation site.
What are you doing there? There's still time before we start digging...
Nili is already digging.
What! How dare she!
Exactly! So irresponsible! And she even dragged her son here!
How did she get into Palestinian territory?

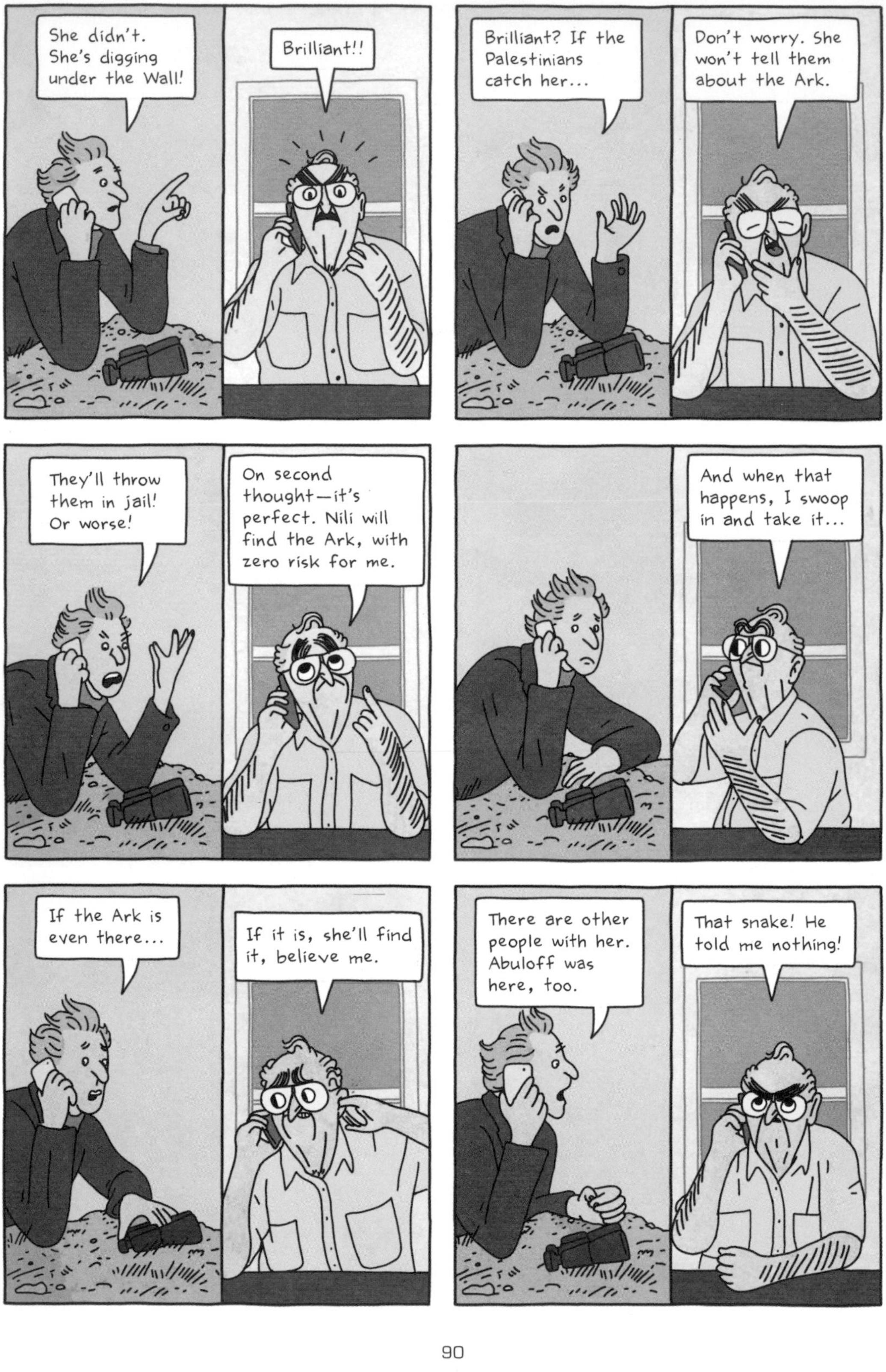
She didn't. She's digging under the Wall!
Brilliant!!
Brilliant? If the Palestinians catch her...
Don't worry. She won't tell them about the Ark.
They'll throw them in jail! Or worse!
On second thought—it's perfect. Nili will find the Ark, with zero risk for me.
And when that happens, I swoop in and take it...
If the Ark is even there...
If it is, she'll find it, believe me.
There are other people with her. Abuloff was here, too.
That snake! He told me nothing!

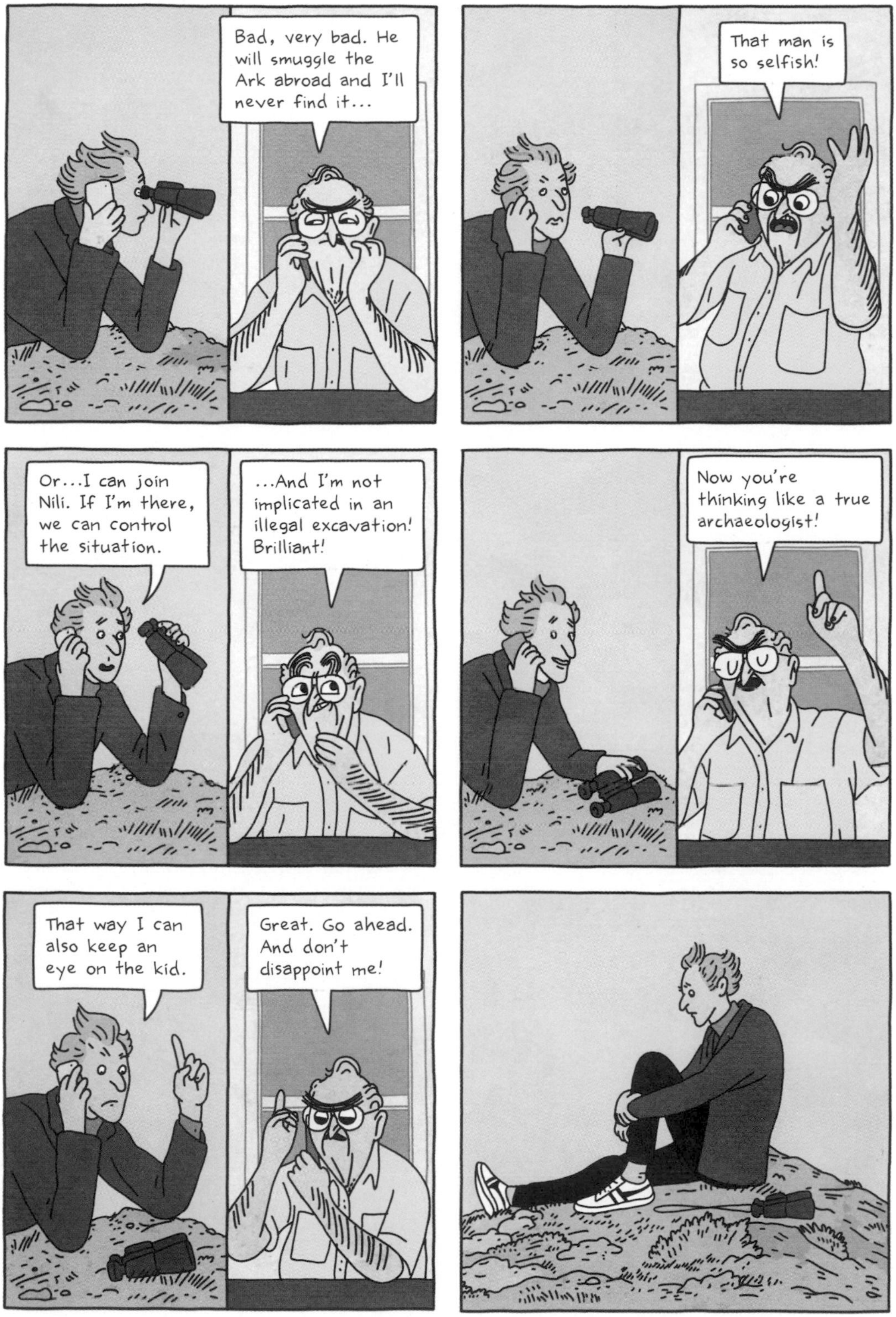
Bad, very bad. He will smuggle the Ark abroad and I'll never find it...
That man is so selfish!
Or...I can join Nili. If I'm there, we can control the situation.
...And I'm not implicated in an illegal excavation! Brilliant!
Now you're thinking like a true archaeologist!
That way I can also keep an eye on the kid.
Great. Go ahead. And don't disappoint me!

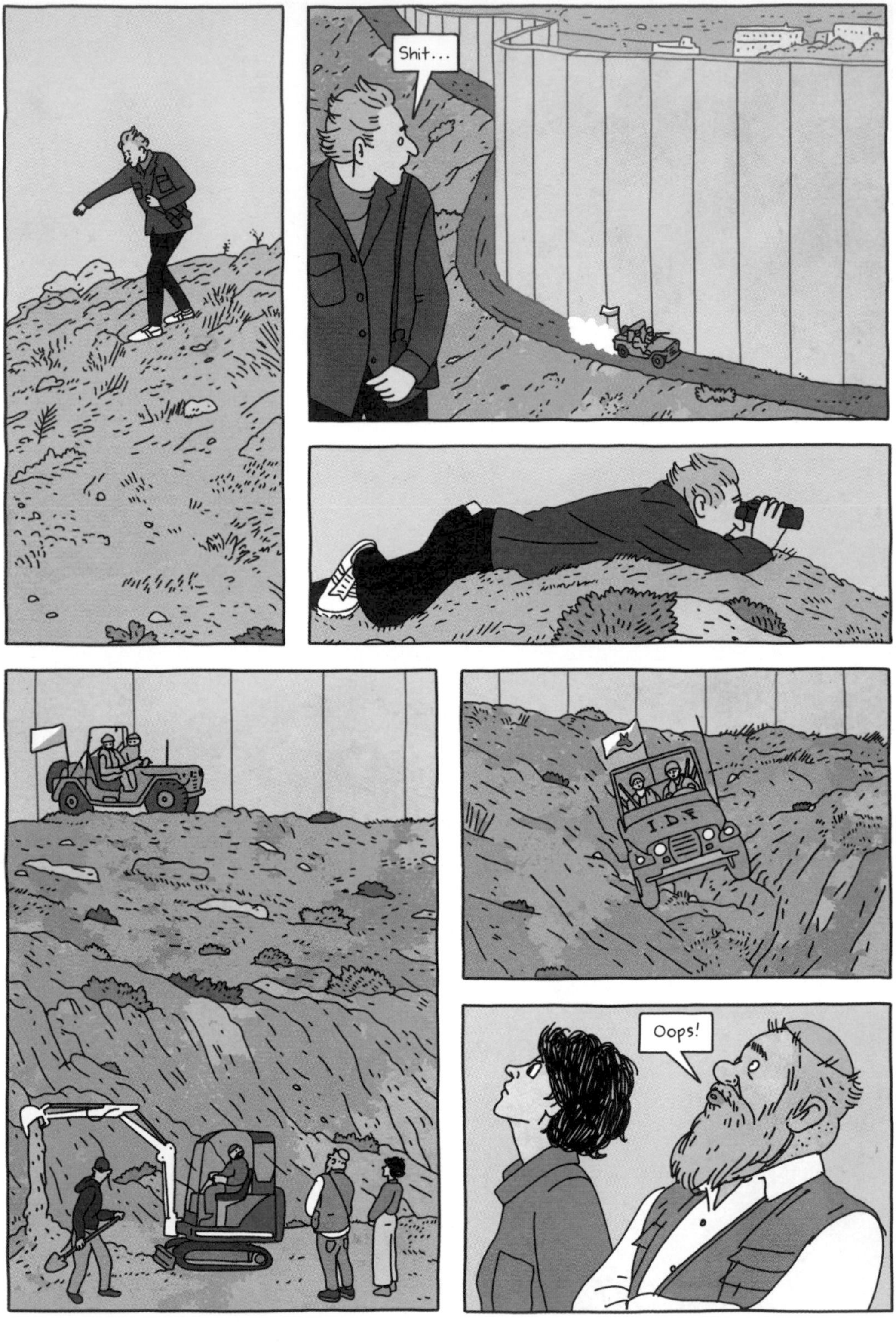
Shit...
I.D.F
Oops!

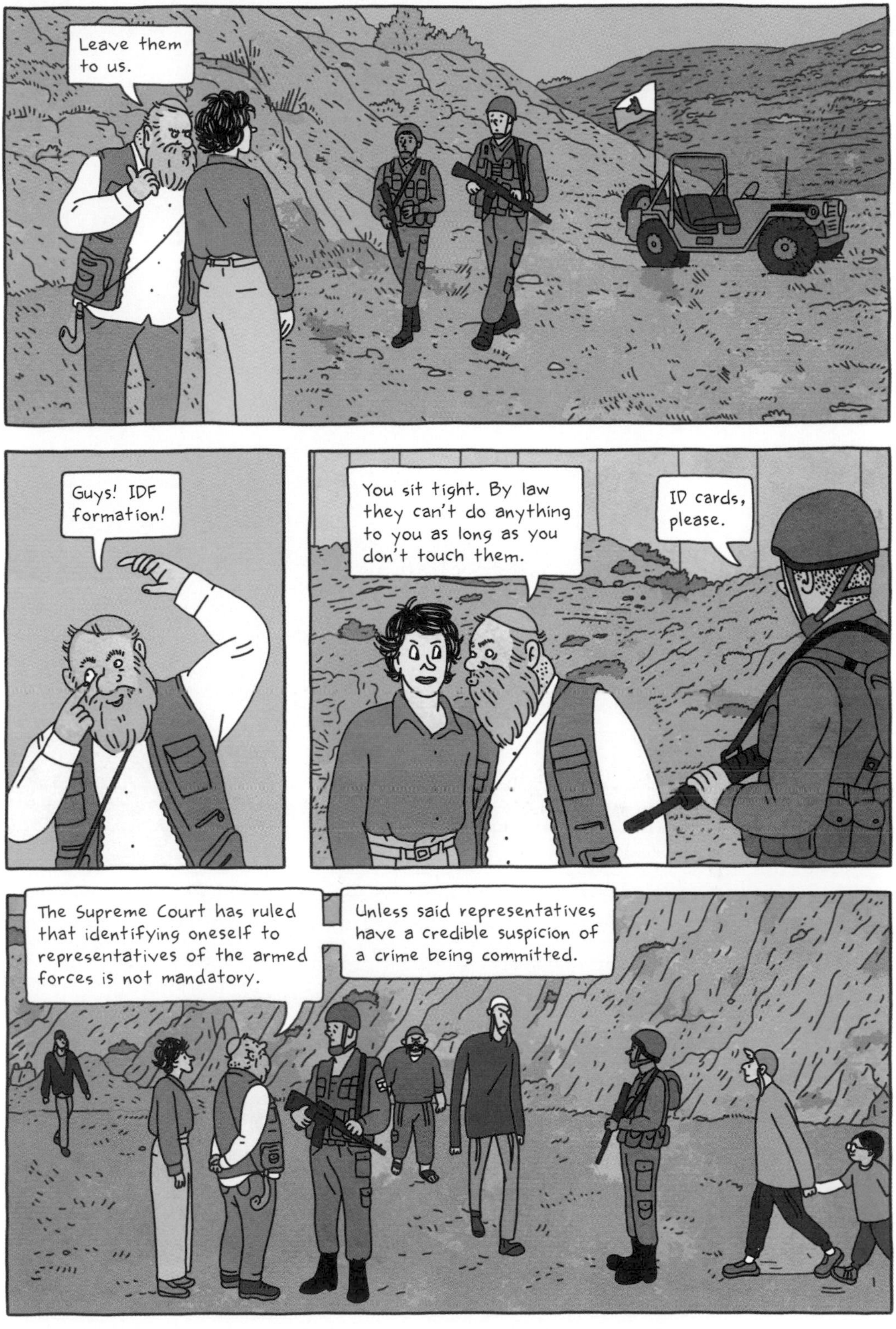

Leave them to us.
Guys! IDF formation!
You sit tight. By law they can't do anything to you as long as you don't touch them.
ID cards, please.
The Supreme Court has ruled that identifying oneself to representatives of the armed forces is not mandatory.
Unless said representatives have a credible suspicion of a crime being committed.

Are you calling us criminals?
Dunno, who are you?
Dance with us!
Who do you think we are?
Settlers?
Deeedel deidl deedel dum
Deeedel deidl deedel dum
She looks like a settler to you?
"Anarchists Against the Wall"?
You have your Anarchist card?
La la la la
La la la la
La la la la

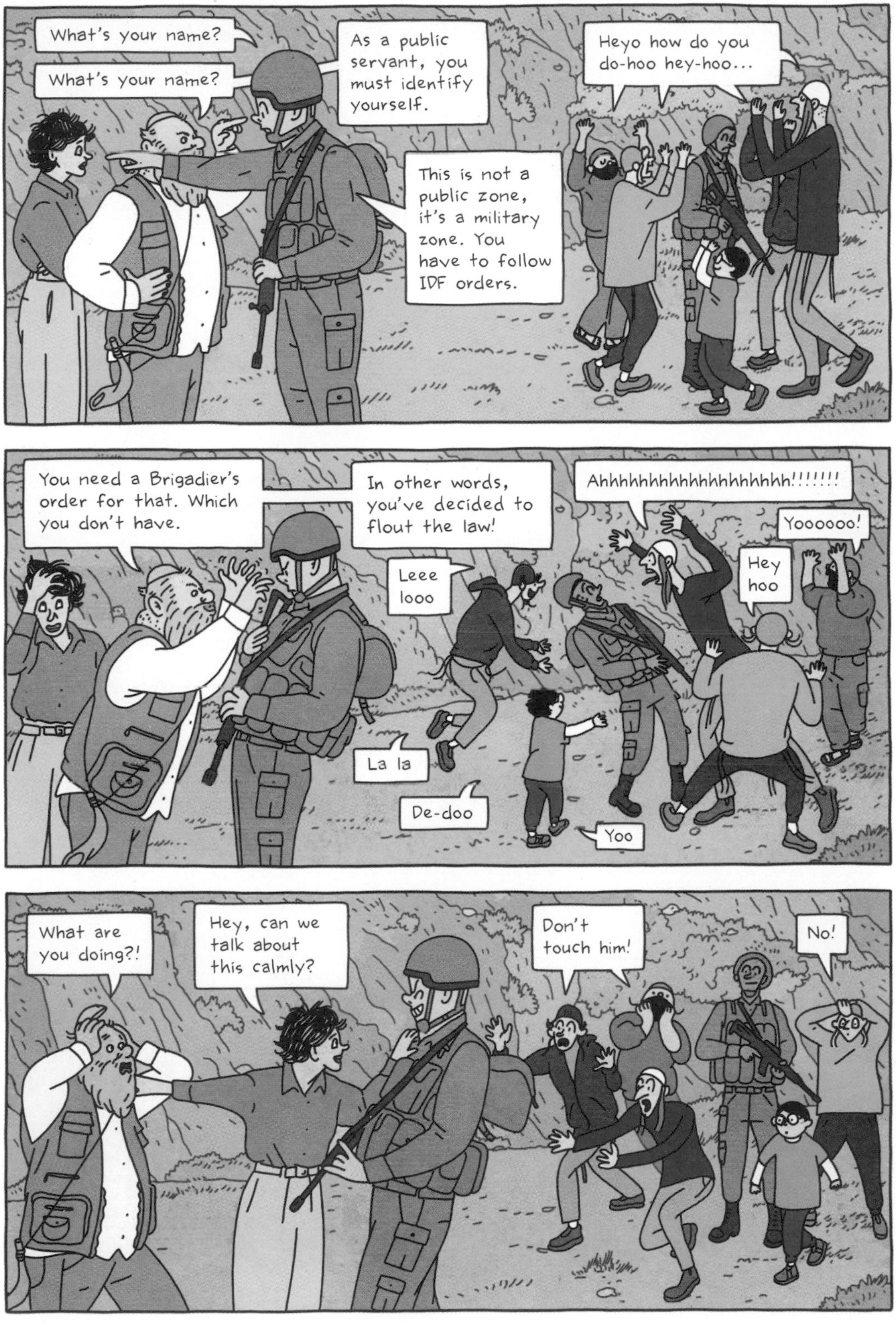
What's your name?
What's your name?
As a public servant, you must identify yourself.
This is not a public zone, it's a military zone. You have to follow IDF orders.
Heyo how do you do-hoo hey-hoo...
You need a Brigadier's order for that. Which you don't have.
In other words, you've decided to flout the law!
Leee looo
La la
De-doo
Ahhhhhhhhhhhhhhhhhh!!!!!!!
Yoo
Hey hoo
Yoooooo!
What are you doing?!
Hey, can we talk about this calmly?
Don't touch him!
No!

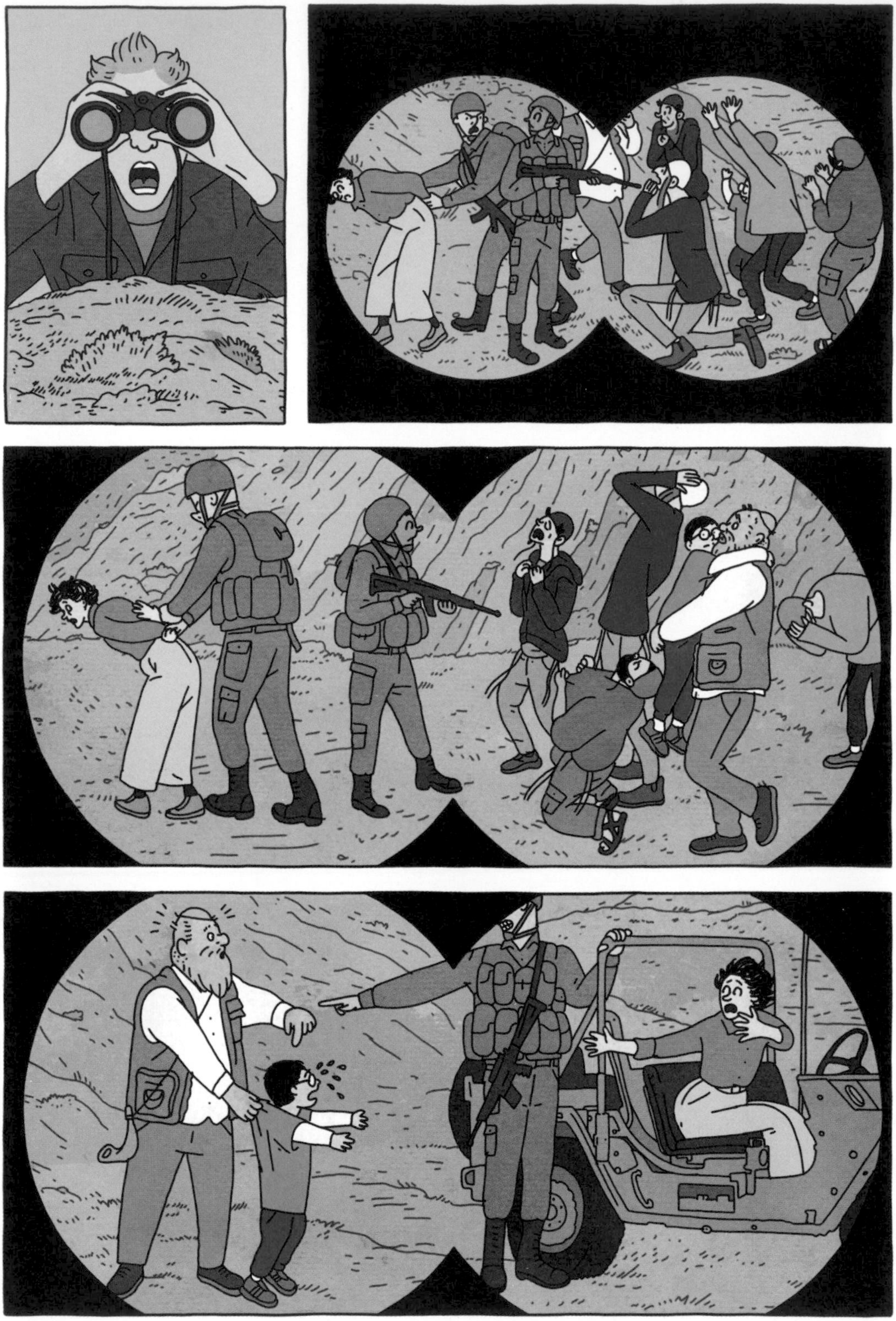

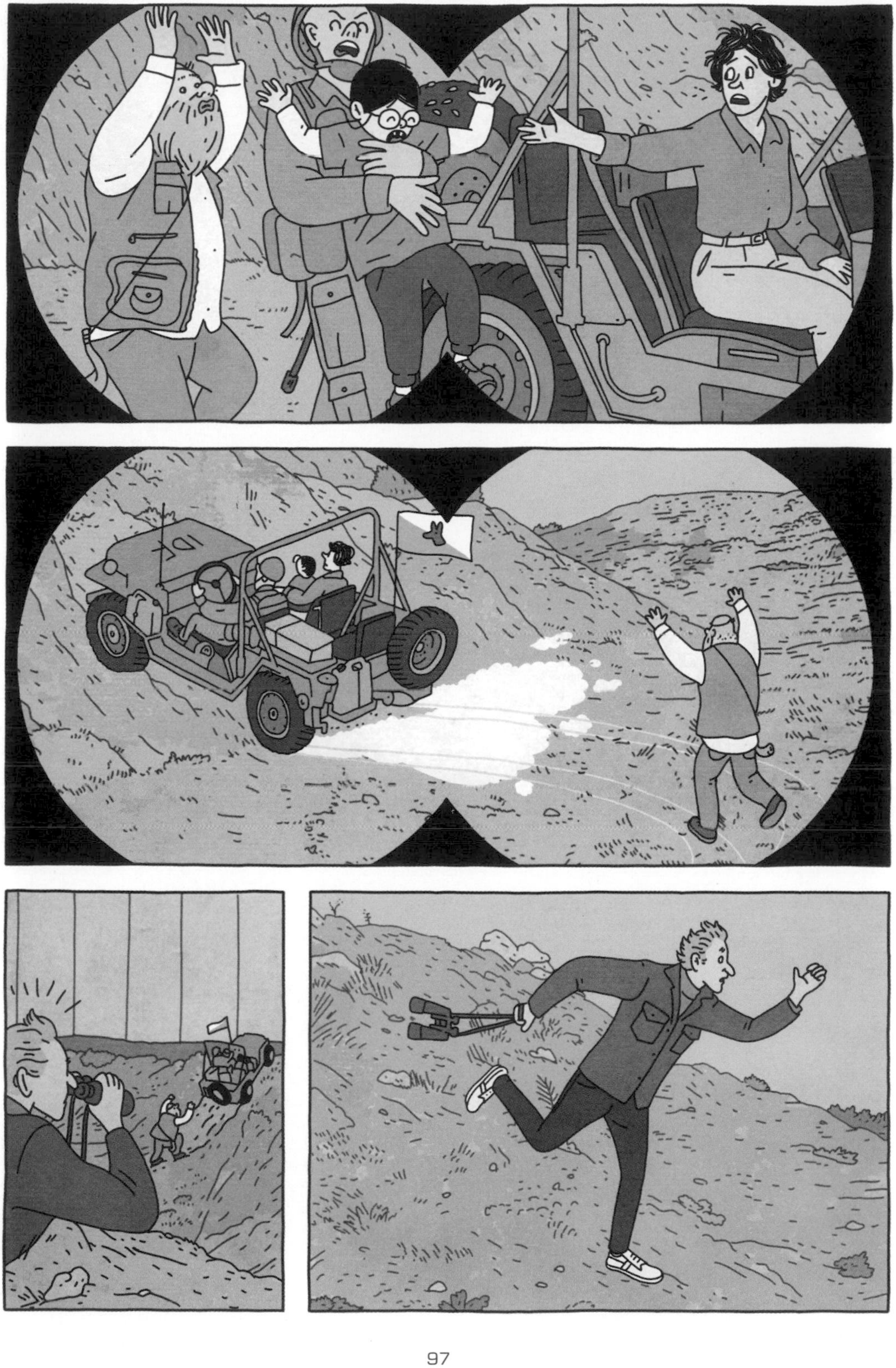

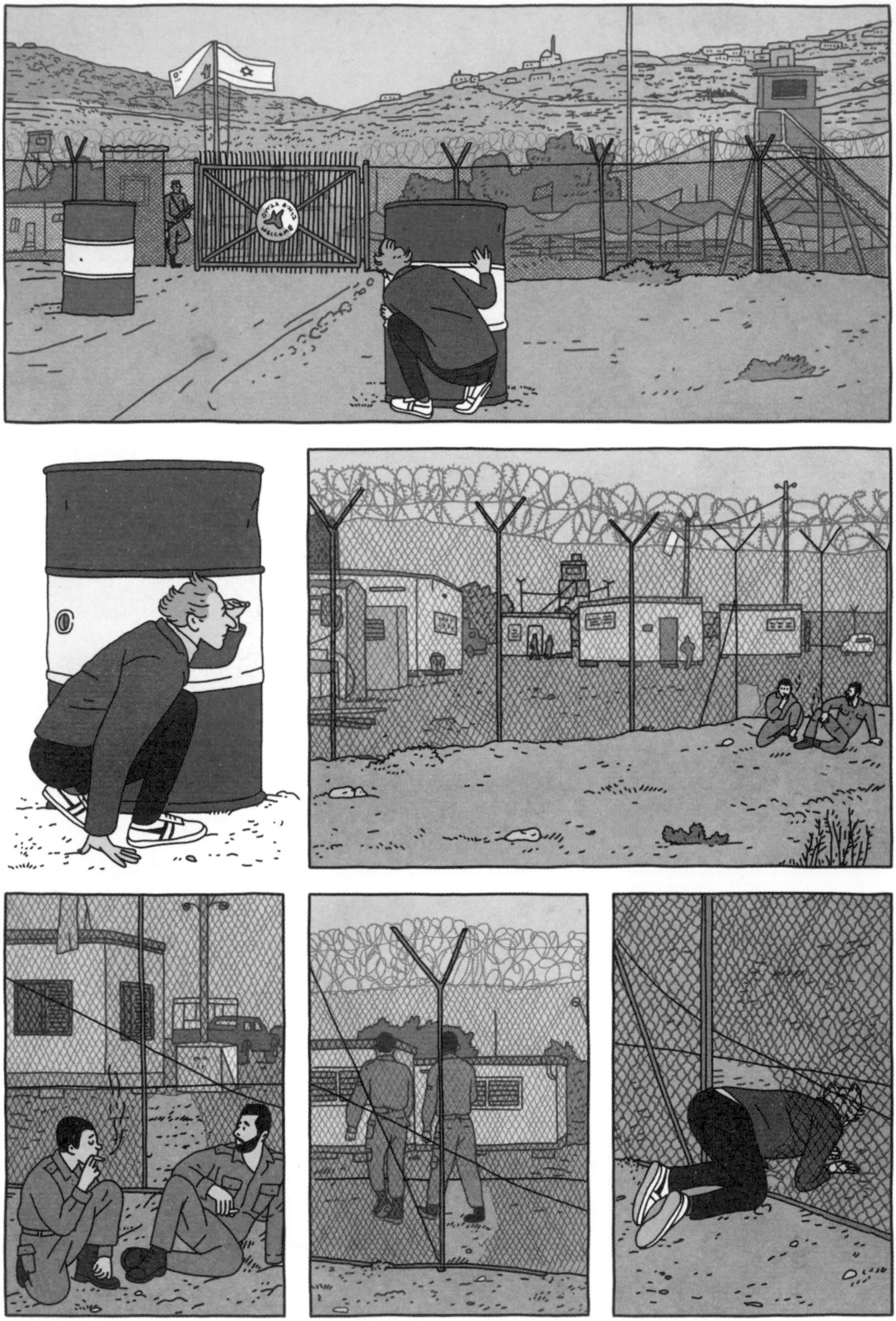
WELCOME

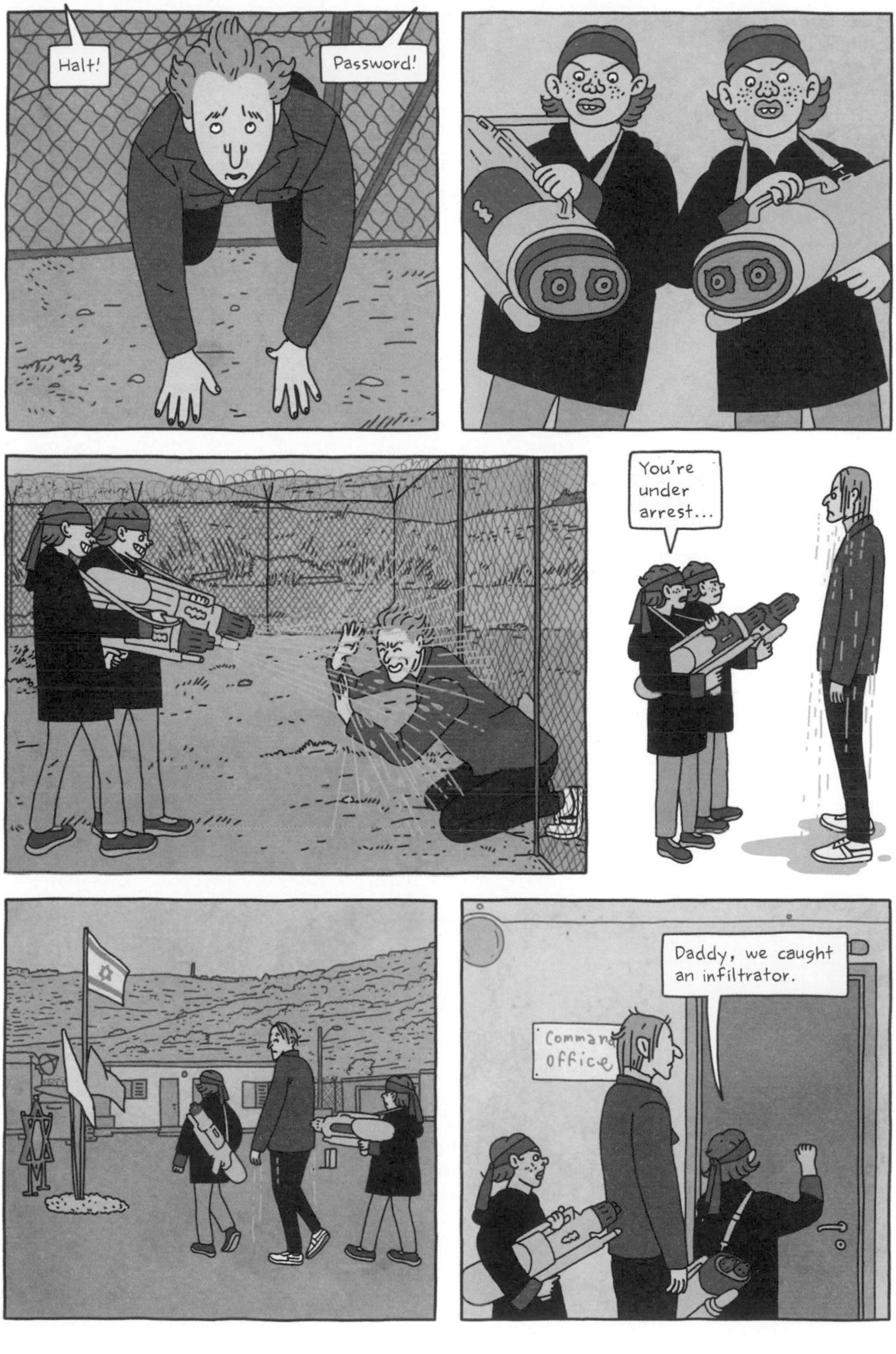
Halt!
Password!
You're under arrest...
Command office
Daddy, we caught an infiltrator.

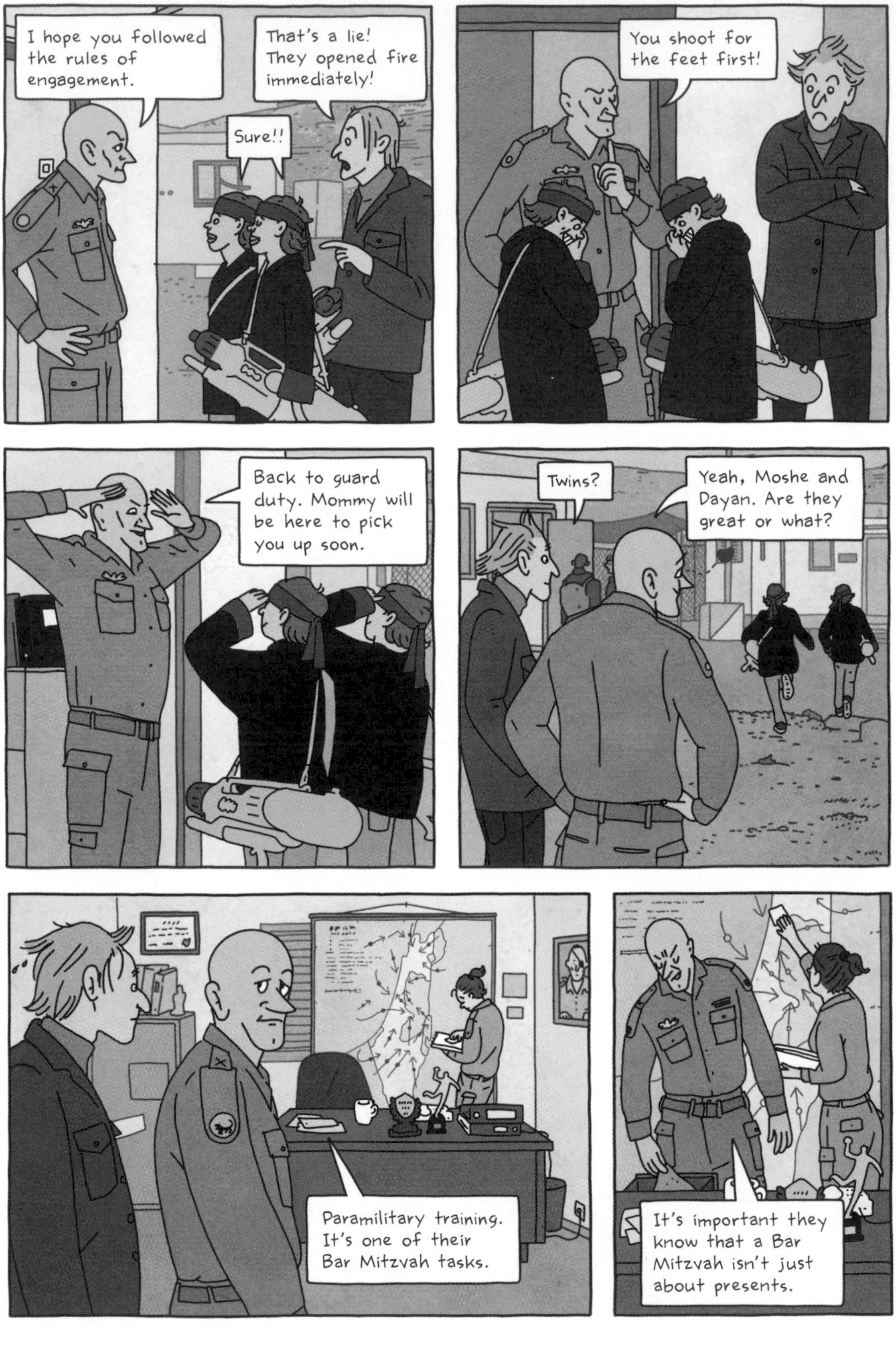
I hope you followed the rules of engagement.
Sure!!
That's a lie! They opened fire immediately!
You shoot for the feet first!
Back to guard duty. Mommy will be here to pick you up soon.
Twins?
Yeah, Moshe and Dayan. Are they great or what?
Paramilitary training. It's one of their Bar Mitzvah tasks.
It's important they know that a Bar Mitzvah isn't just about presents.

OPERATION
BAR-MITZVA

Which task goes here?

Break-in to Atlit naval base. Don't forget to liaise with Sharvit.

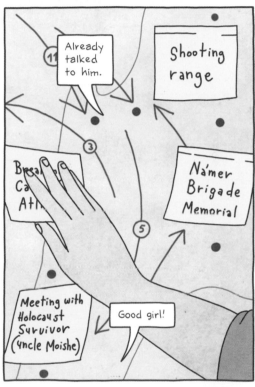

Already talked to him.

Shooting range

11

3

Brea... Ca... Atl...

5

Na'mer Brigade Memorial

Meeting with Holocaust Survivor (uncle Moishe)

Good girl!

Your suicide case is waiting for you at the infirmary, Doc.

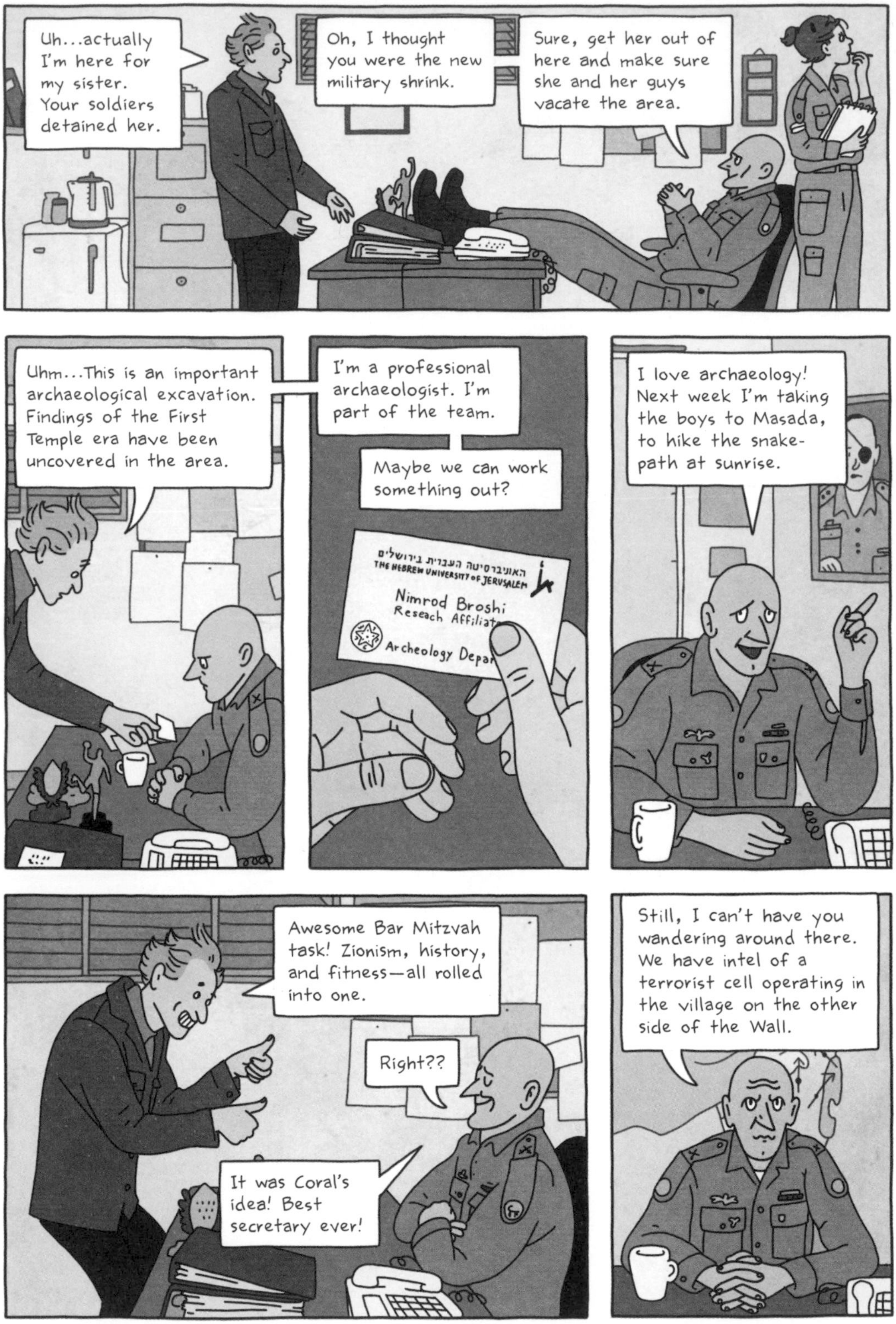
Uh...actually I'm here for my sister. Your soldiers detained her.
Oh, I thought you were the new military shrink.
Sure, get her out of here and make sure she and her guys vacate the area.
Uhm...This is an important archaeological excavation. Findings of the First Temple era have been uncovered in the area.
I'm a professional archaeologist. I'm part of the team.
Maybe we can work something out?
האוניברסיטה העברית בירושלים
THE HEBREW UNIVERSITY OF JERUSALEM
Nimrod Broshi
Reseach Affiliat
Archeology Depar
I love archaeology! Next week I'm taking the boys to Masada, to hike the snake-path at sunrise.
Awesome Bar Mitzvah task! Zionism, history, and fitness—all rolled into one.
Right??
It was Coral's idea! Best secretary ever!
Still, I can't have you wandering around there. We have intel of a terrorist cell operating in the village on the other side of the Wall.

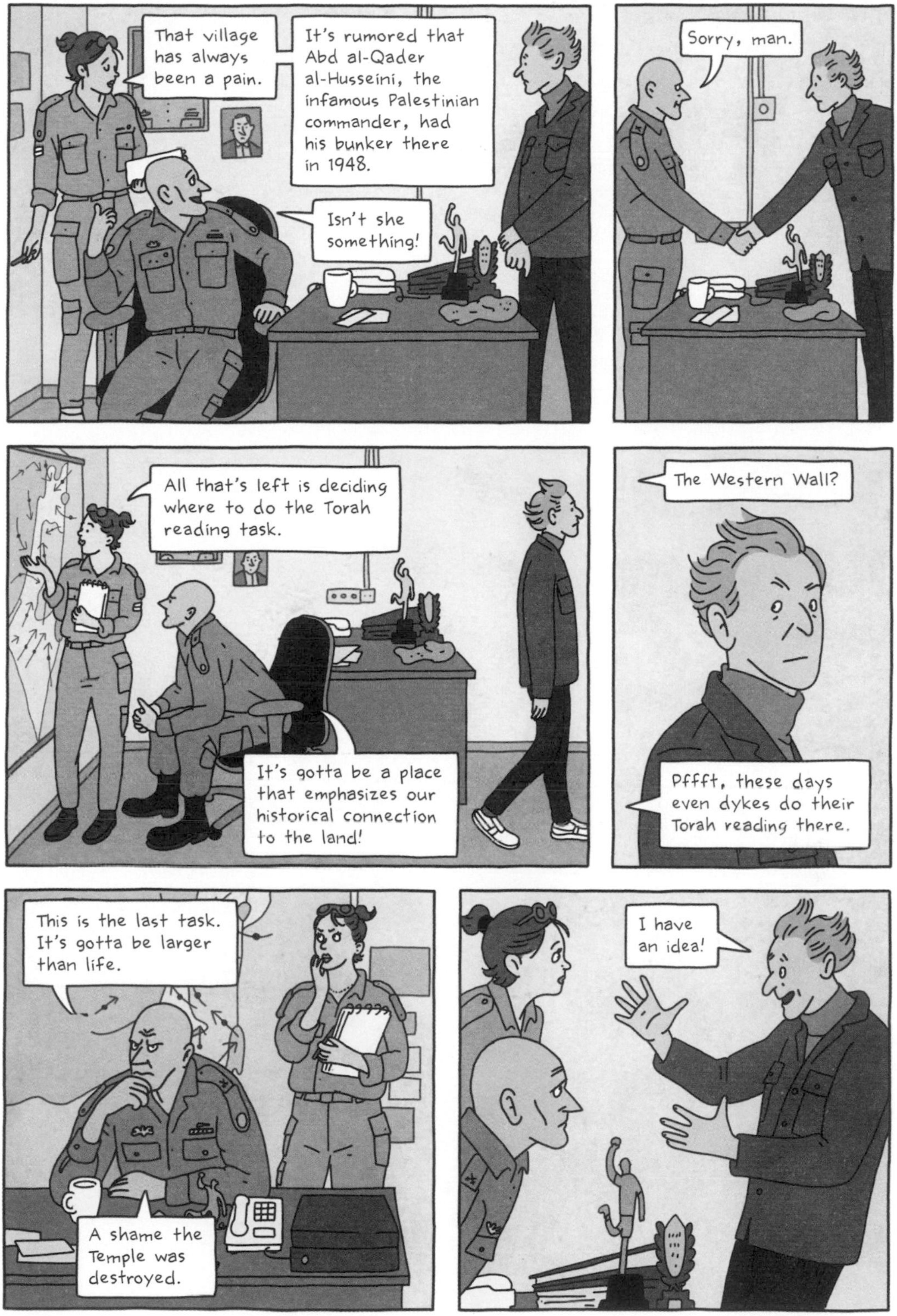
That village has always been a pain.
It's rumored that Abd al-Qader al-Husseini, the infamous Palestinian commander, had his bunker there in 1948.
Isn't she something!
Sorry, man.
All that's left is deciding where to do the Torah reading task.
It's gotta be a place that emphasizes our historical connection to the land!
The Western Wall?
Pffft, these days even dykes do their Torah reading there.
This is the last task. It's gotta be larger than life.
A shame the Temple was destroyed.
I have an idea!

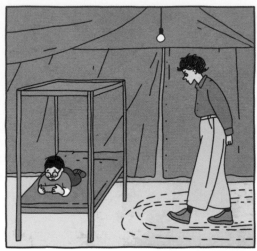

Broshi! What are you doing here?!

Saving your ass.

Really, what were you thinking?

So I blew it. Don't be smug.

Take a look.

The Commander is going to support your dig.

He'll provide you with water, food, an electric generator...

What...How...

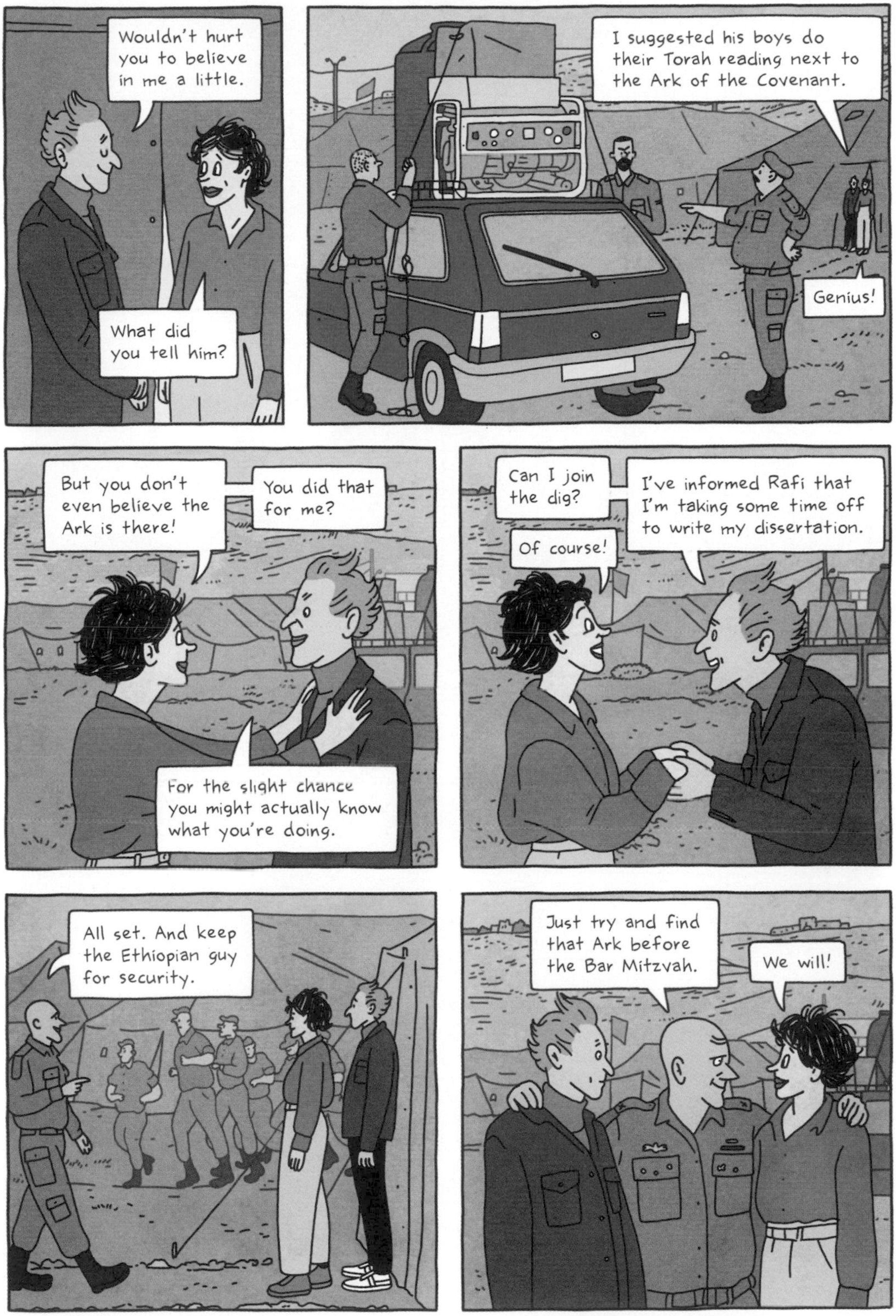
Wouldn't hurt you to believe in me a little.
What did you tell him?
I suggested his boys do their Torah reading next to the Ark of the Covenant.
Genius!
But you don't even believe the Ark is there!
You did that for me?
For the slight chance you might actually know what you're doing.
Can I join the dig?
Of course!
I've informed Rafi that I'm taking some time off to write my dissertation.
All set. And keep the Ethiopian guy for security.
Just try and find that Ark before the Bar Mitzvah.
We will!

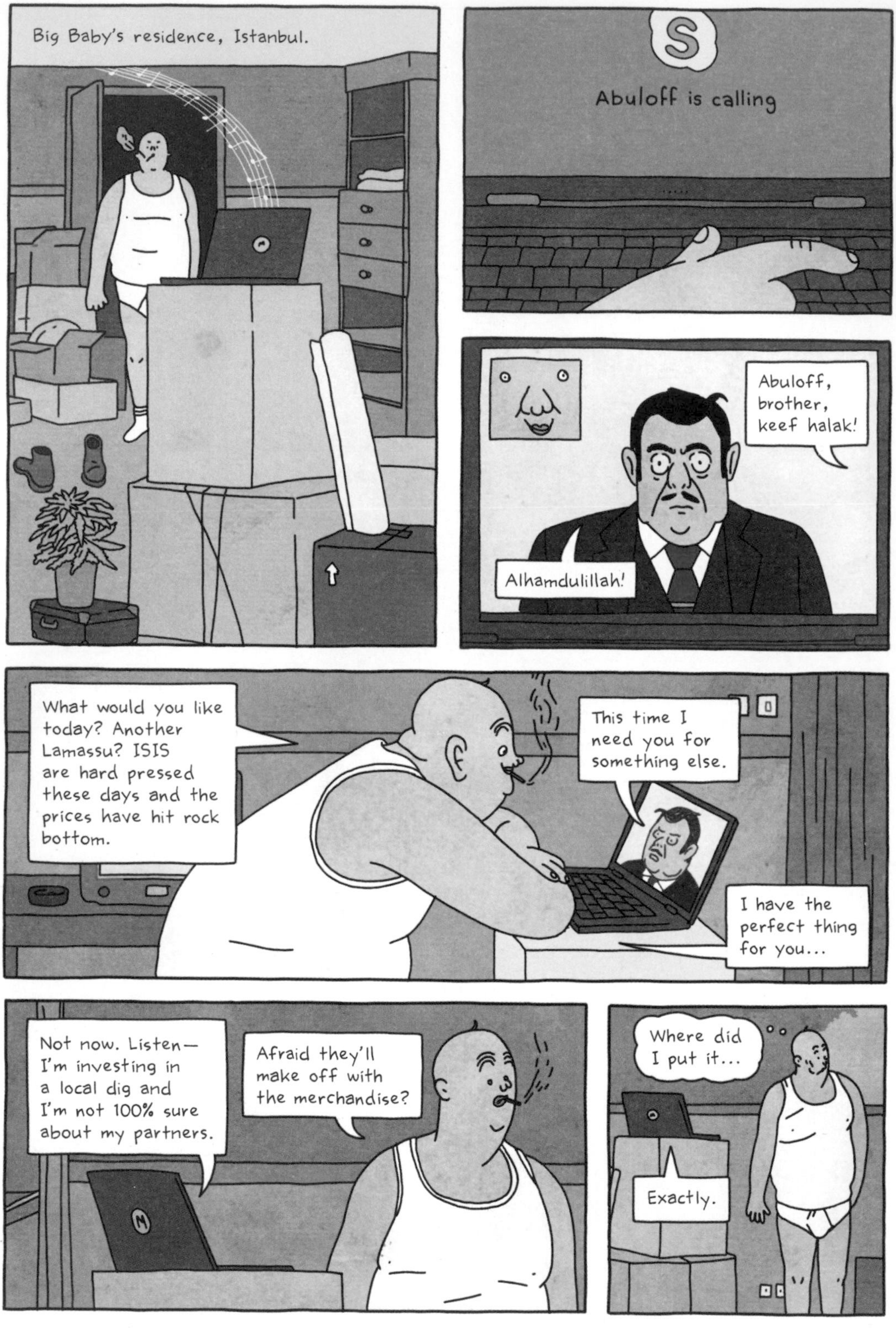
Big Baby's residence, Istanbul.
Abuloff is calling
Abuloff, brother, keef halak!
Alhamdulillah!
What would you like today? Another Lamassu? ISIS are hard pressed these days and the prices have hit rock bottom.
This time I need you for something else.
I have the perfect thing for you...
Not now. Listen— I'm investing in a local dig and I'm not 100% sure about my partners.
Afraid they'll make off with the merchandise?
Where did I put it...
Exactly.

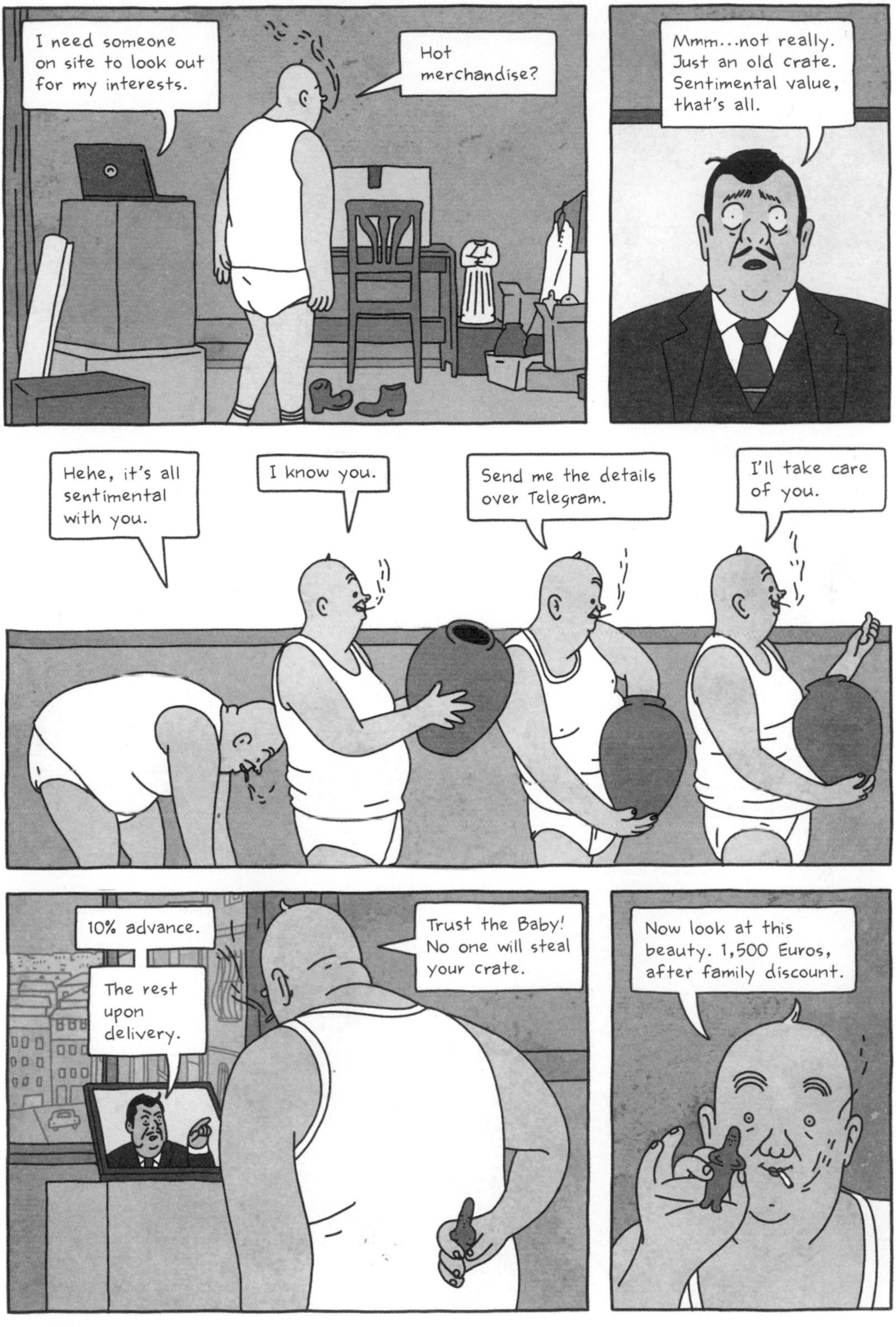
I need someone on site to look out for my interests.
Hot merchandise?
Mmm...not really. Just an old crate. Sentimental value, that's all.
Hehe, it's all sentimental with you.
I know you.
Send me the details over Telegram.
I'll take care of you.
10% advance.
The rest upon delivery.
Trust the Baby! No one will steal your crate.
Now look at this beauty. 1,500 Euros, after family discount.

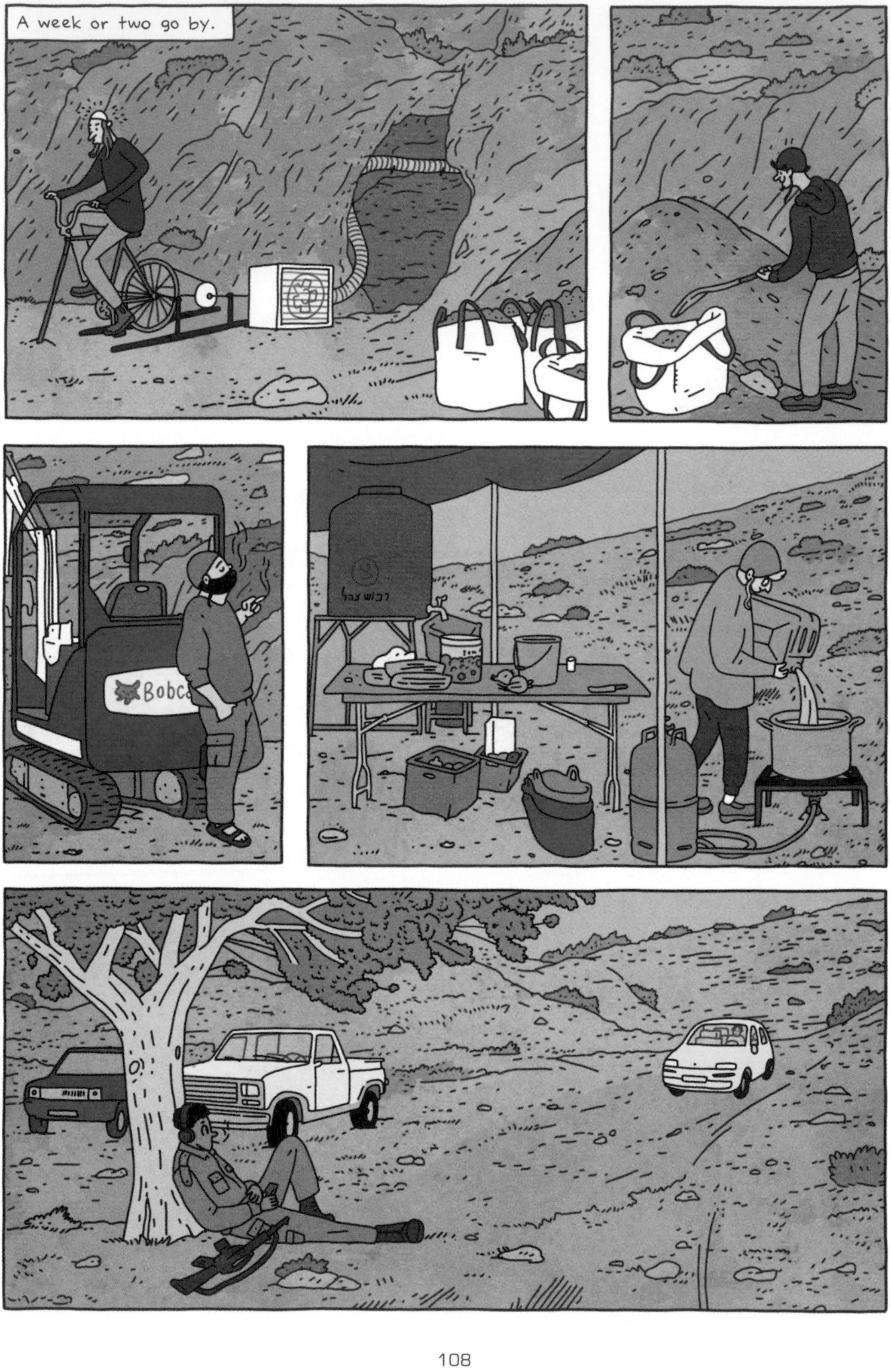
A week or two go by.
Bobca

Katani!
Scoot!

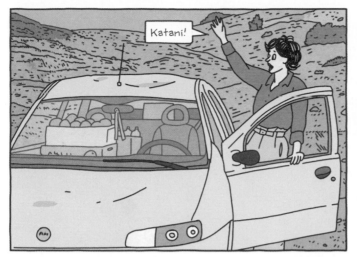

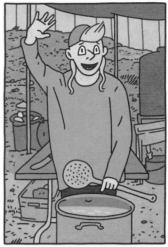

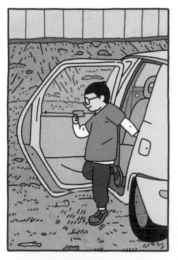

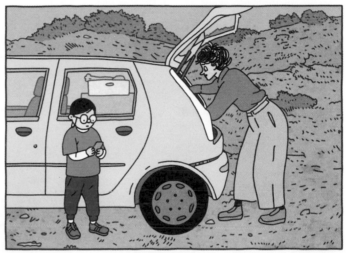

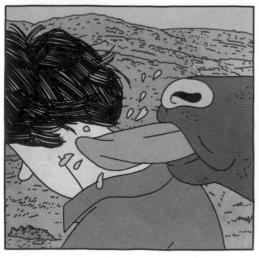

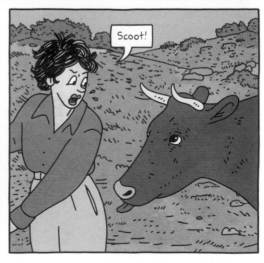

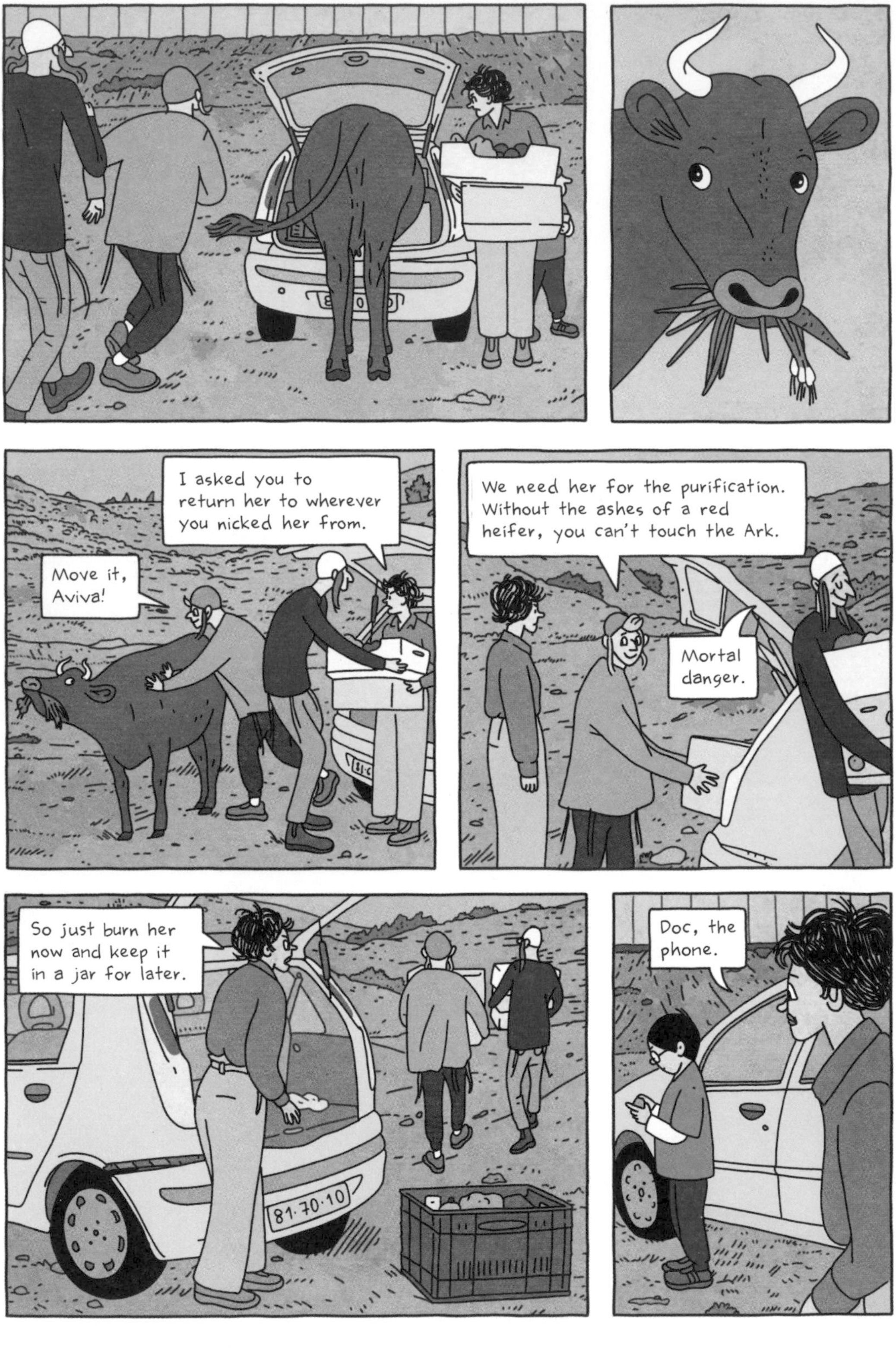
I asked you to return her to wherever you nicked her from.
Move it, Aviva!
We need her for the purification. Without the ashes of a red heifer, you can't touch the Ark.
Mortal danger.
So just burn her now and keep it in a jar for later.
Doc, the phone.

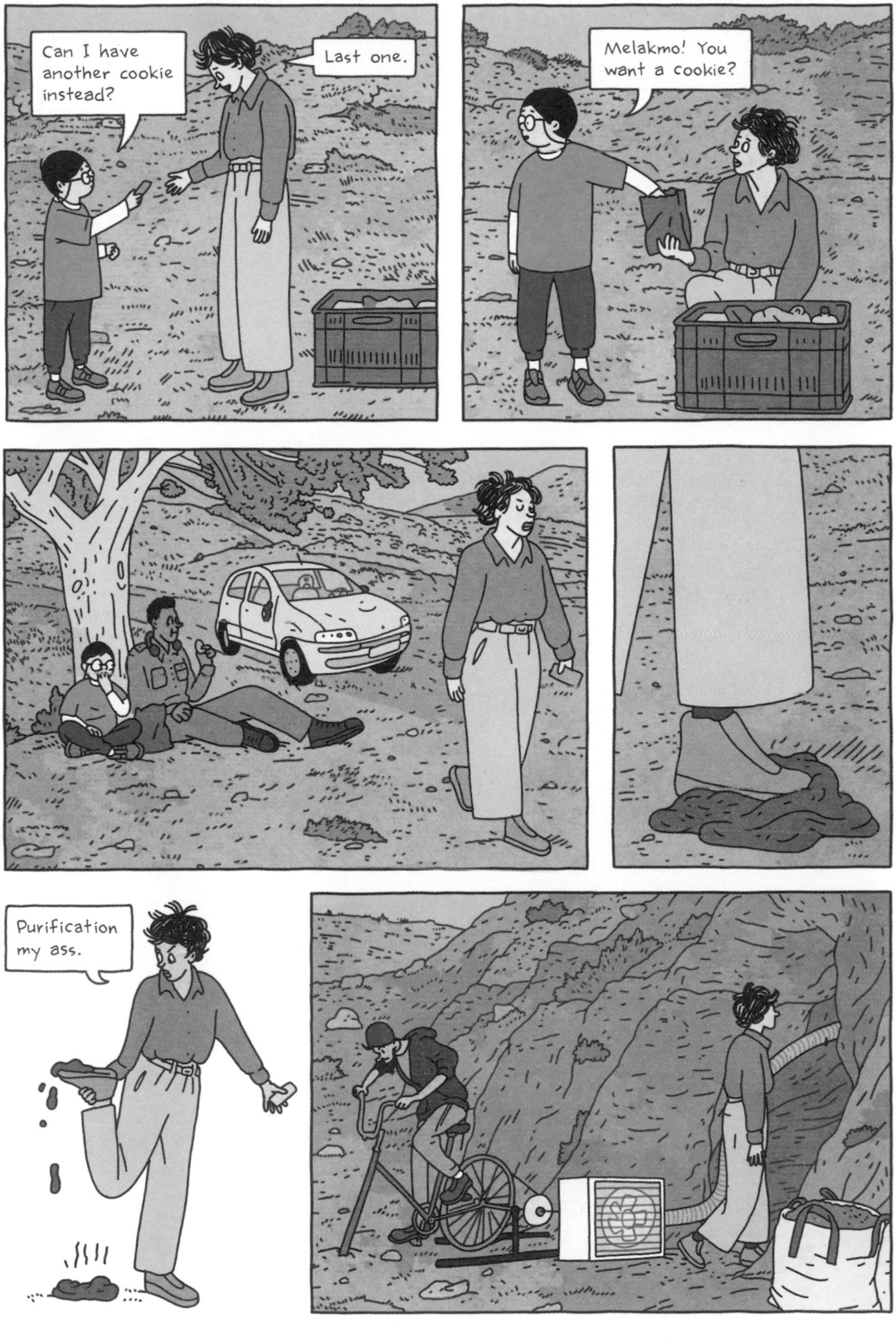
Can I have another cookie instead?
Last one.
Melakmo! You want a cookie?
Purification my ass.

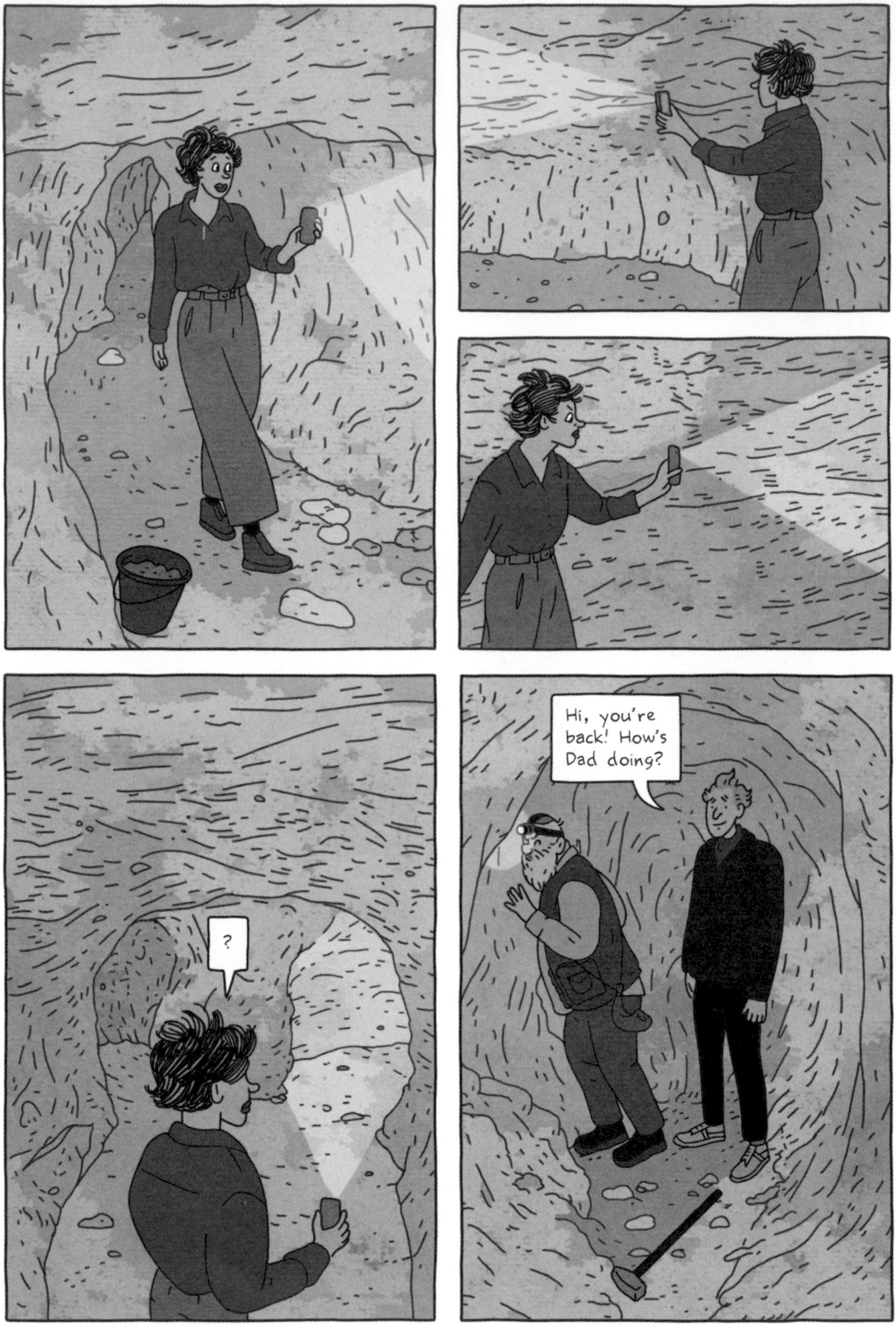
?
Hi, you're back! How's Dad doing?

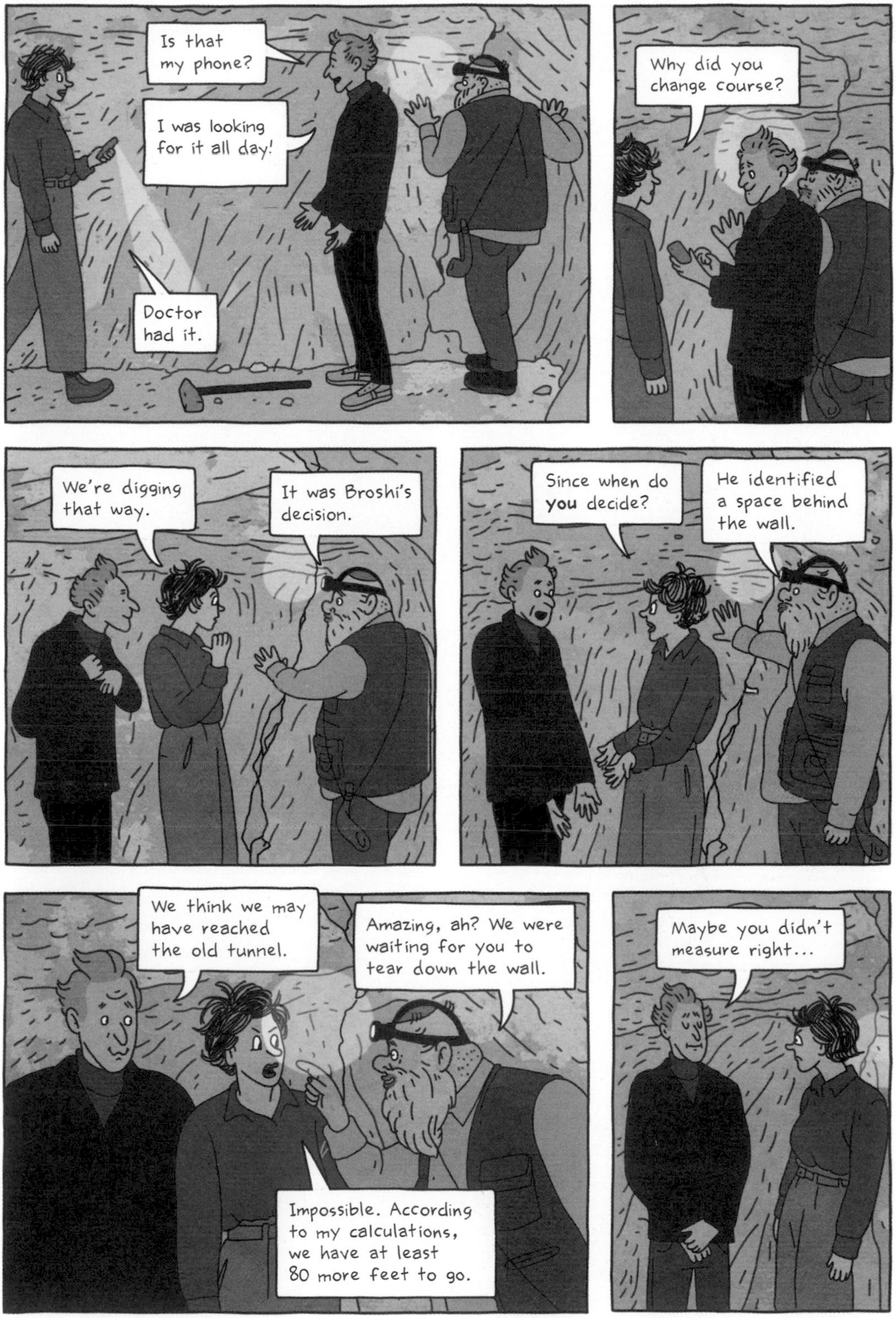

Is that my phone?
I was looking for it all day!
Doctor had it.
Why did you change course?
We're digging that way.
It was Broshi's decision.
Since when do **you** decide?
He identified a space behind the wall.
We think we may have reached the old tunnel.
Amazing, ah? We were waiting for you to tear down the wall.
Impossible. According to my calculations, we have at least 80 more feet to go.
Maybe you didn't measure right...

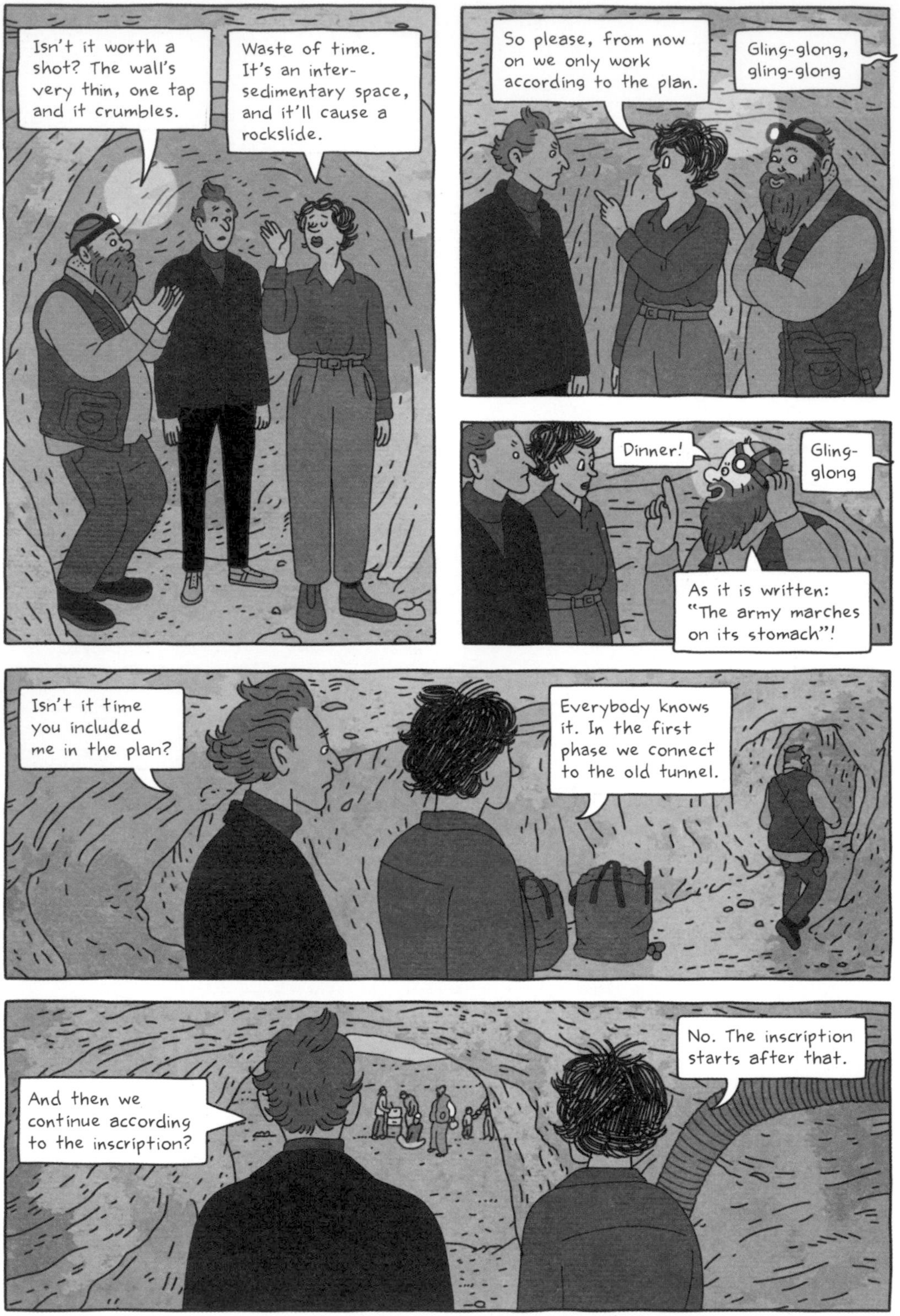
Isn't it worth a shot? The wall's very thin, one tap and it crumbles.
Waste of time. It's an inter-sedimentary space, and it'll cause a rockslide.
So please, from now on we only work according to the plan.
Gling-glong, gling-glong
Dinner!
Gling-glong
As it is written: "The army marches on its stomach"!
Isn't it time you included me in the plan?
Everybody knows it. In the first phase we connect to the old tunnel.
And then we continue according to the inscription?
No. The inscription starts after that.

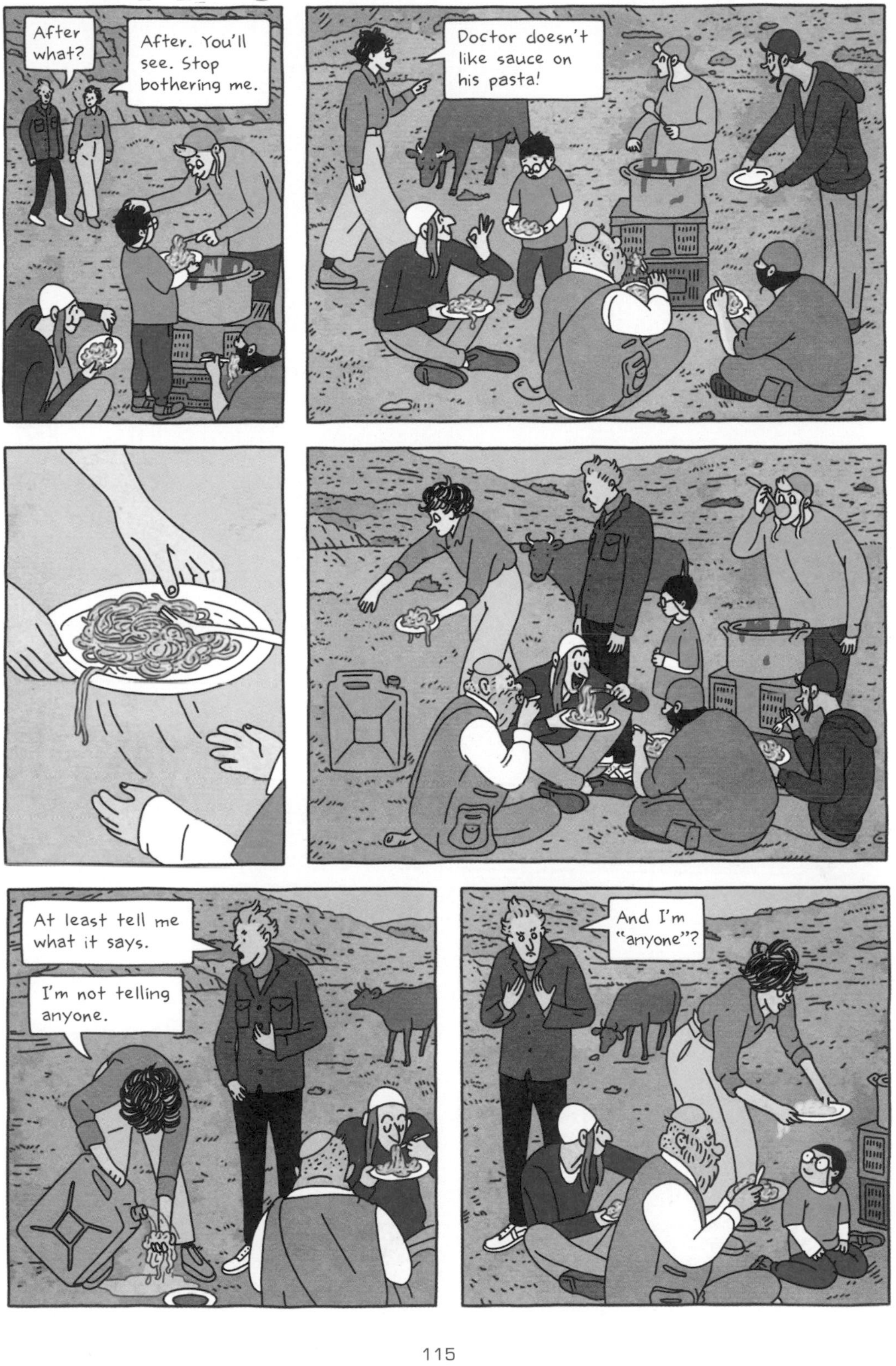
After what?
After. You'll see. Stop bothering me.
Doctor doesn't like sauce on his pasta!
At least tell me what it says.
I'm not telling anyone.
And I'm "anyone"?

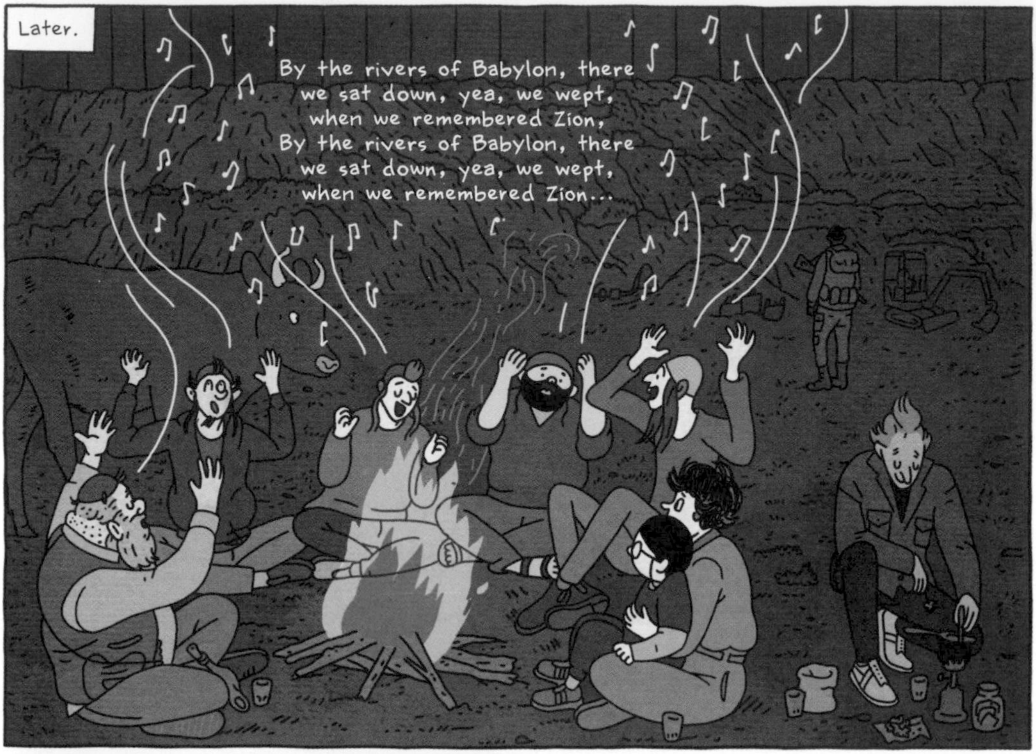
Later.
By the rivers of Babylon, there we sat down, yea, we wept, when we remembered Zion, By the rivers of Babylon, there we sat down, yea, we wept, when we remembered Zion...

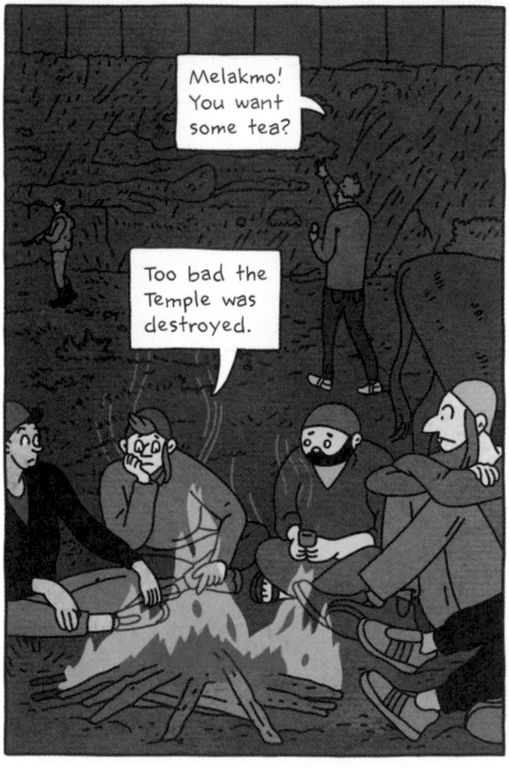
Melakmo! You want some tea?
Too bad the Temple was destroyed.

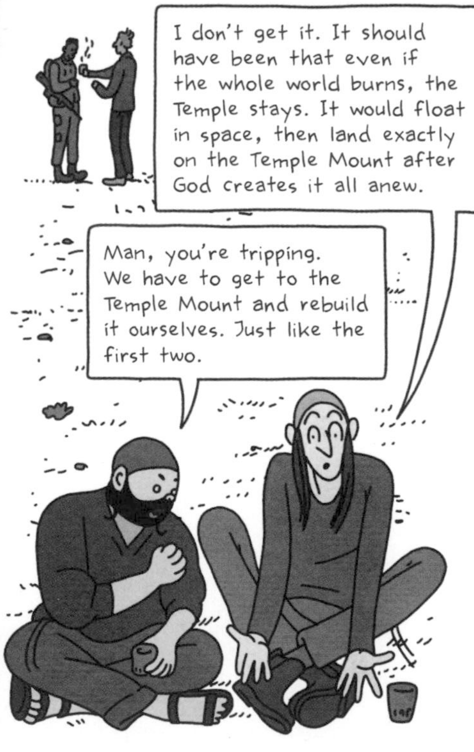
I don't get it. It should have been that even if the whole world burns, the Temple stays. It would float in space, then land exactly on the Temple Mount after God creates it all anew.
Man, you're tripping. We have to get to the Temple Mount and rebuild it ourselves. Just like the first two.

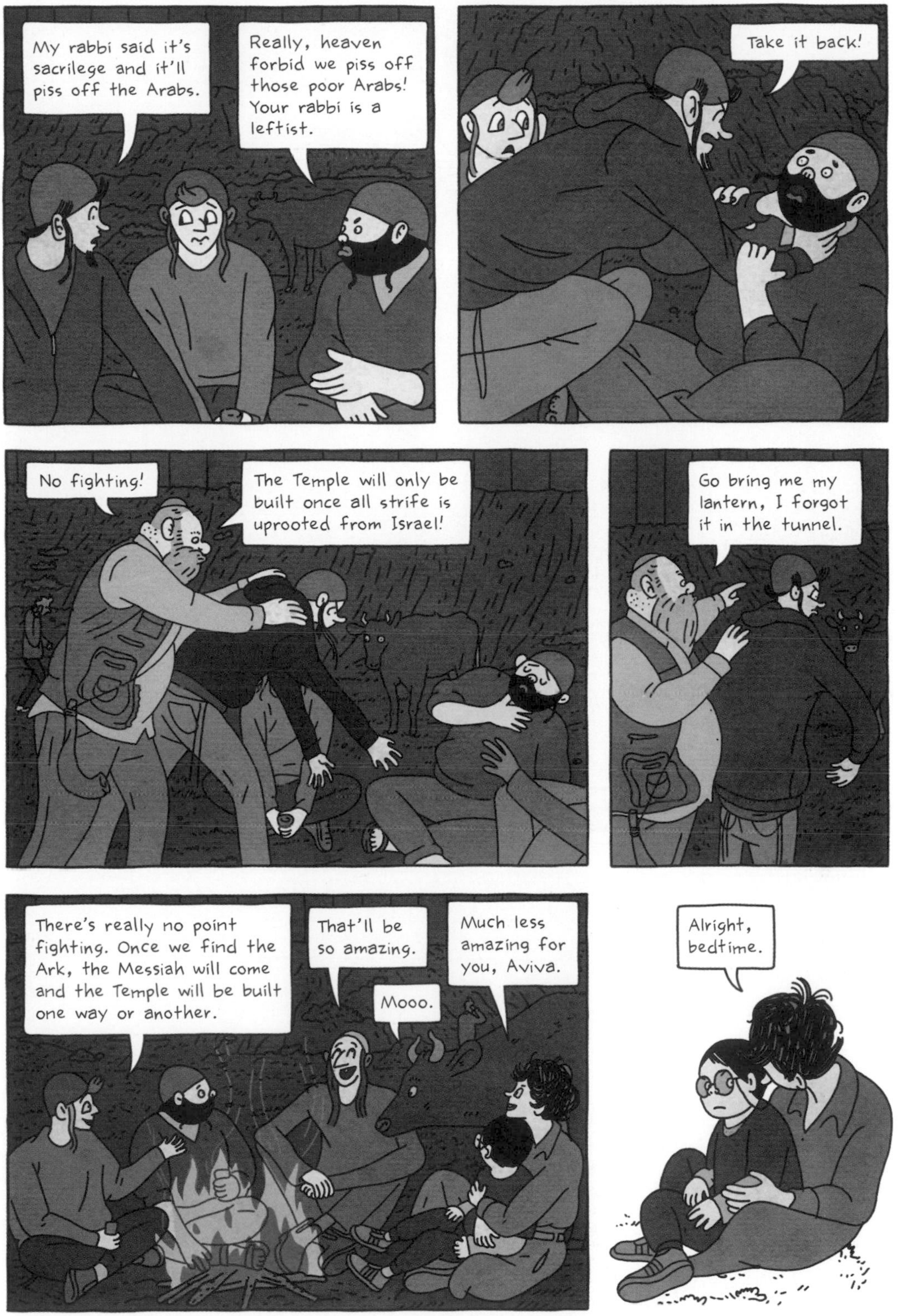

My rabbi said it's sacrilege and it'll piss off the Arabs.
Really, heaven forbid we piss off those poor Arabs! Your rabbi is a leftist.
Take it back!
No fighting!
The Temple will only be built once all strife is uprooted from Israel!
Go bring me my lantern, I forgot it in the tunnel.
There's really no point fighting. Once we find the Ark, the Messiah will come and the Temple will be built one way or another.
That'll be so amazing.
Mooo.
Much less amazing for you, Aviva.
Alright, bedtime.

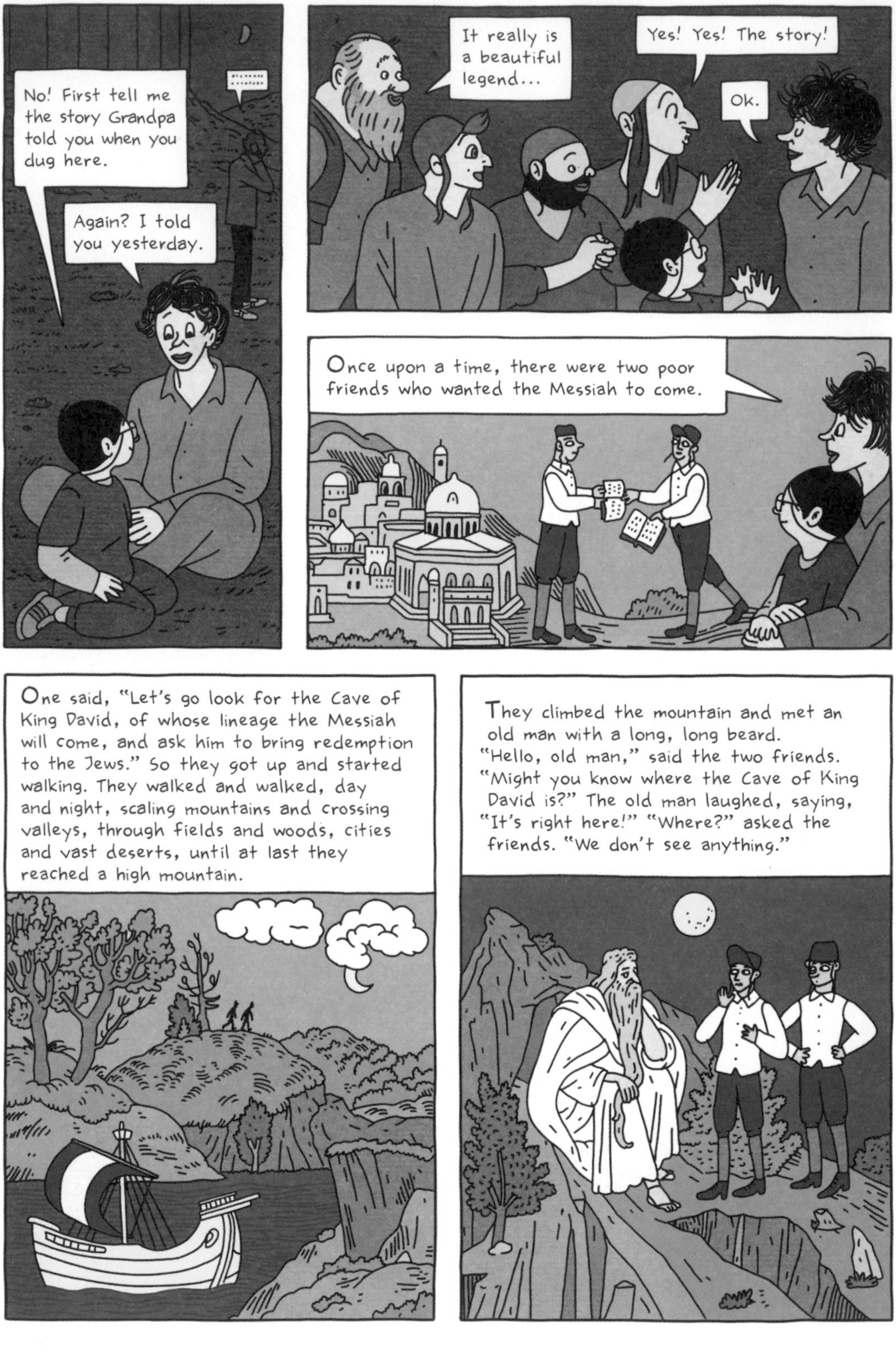
No! First tell me the story Grandpa told you when you dug here.
Again? I told you yesterday.
It really is a beautiful legend...
Yes! Yes! The story!
Ok.
Once upon a time, there were two poor friends who wanted the Messiah to come.
One said, "Let's go look for the Cave of King David, of whose lineage the Messiah will come, and ask him to bring redemption to the Jews." So they got up and started walking. They walked and walked, day and night, scaling mountains and crossing valleys, through fields and woods, cities and vast deserts, until at last they reached a high mountain.
They climbed the mountain and met an old man with a long, long beard. "Hello, old man," said the two friends. "Might you know where the Cave of King David is?" The old man laughed, saying, "It's right here!" "Where?" asked the friends. "We don't see anything."

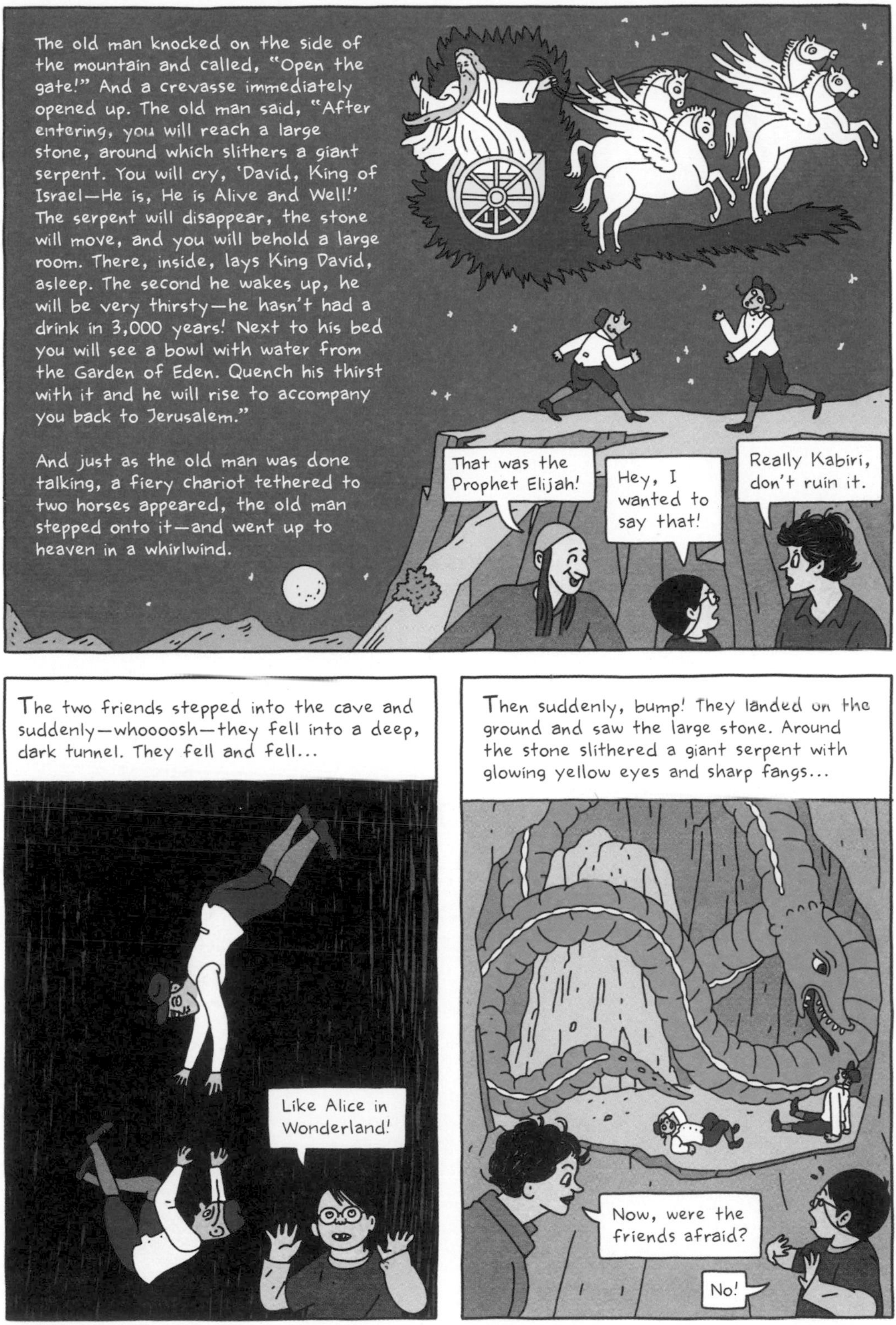
The old man knocked on the side of the mountain and called, "Open the gate!" And a crevasse immediately opened up. The old man said, "After entering, you will reach a large stone, around which slithers a giant serpent. You will cry, 'David, King of Israel—He is, He is Alive and Well!' The serpent will disappear, the stone will move, and you will behold a large room. There, inside, lays King David, asleep. The second he wakes up, he will be very thirsty—he hasn't had a drink in 3,000 years! Next to his bed you will see a bowl with water from the Garden of Eden. Quench his thirst with it and he will rise to accompany you back to Jerusalem."
And just as the old man was done talking, a fiery chariot tethered to two horses appeared, the old man stepped onto it—and went up to heaven in a whirlwind.
That was the Prophet Elijah!
Hey, I wanted to say that!
Really Kabiri, don't ruin it.
The two friends stepped into the cave and suddenly—whoooosh—they fell into a deep, dark tunnel. They fell and fell...
Like Alice in Wonderland!
Then suddenly, bump! They landed on the ground and saw the large stone. Around the stone slithered a giant serpent with glowing yellow eyes and sharp fangs...
Now, were the friends afraid?
No!

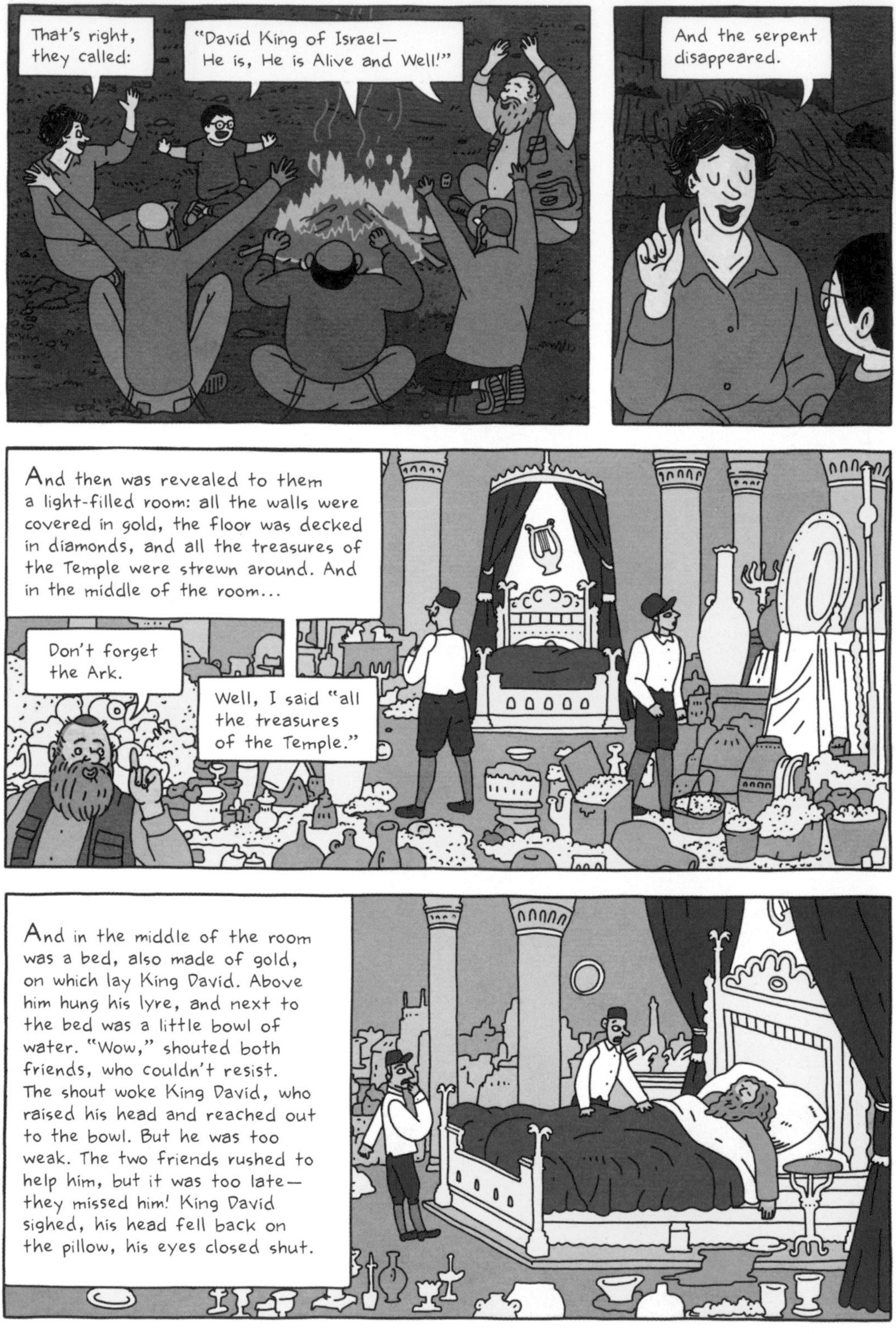
That's right, they called:
"David King of Israel— He is, He is Alive and Well!"
And the serpent disappeared.
And then was revealed to them a light-filled room: all the walls were covered in gold, the floor was decked in diamonds, and all the treasures of the Temple were strewn around. And in the middle of the room...
Don't forget the Ark.
Well, I said "all the treasures of the Temple."
And in the middle of the room was a bed, also made of gold, on which lay King David. Above him hung his lyre, and next to the bed was a little bowl of water. "Wow," shouted both friends, who couldn't resist. The shout woke King David, who raised his head and reached out to the bowl. But he was too weak. The two friends rushed to help him, but it was too late— they missed him! King David sighed, his head fell back on the pillow, his eyes closed shut.

At that moment, a terrible storm erupted, the light went out, loud thundering could be heard, and...Pooof! It was all gone.

And all the two friends could see now was only dark skies and desert.

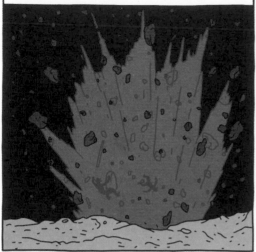

Is it a true story?

There's... There's...

There's someone inside the mountain!

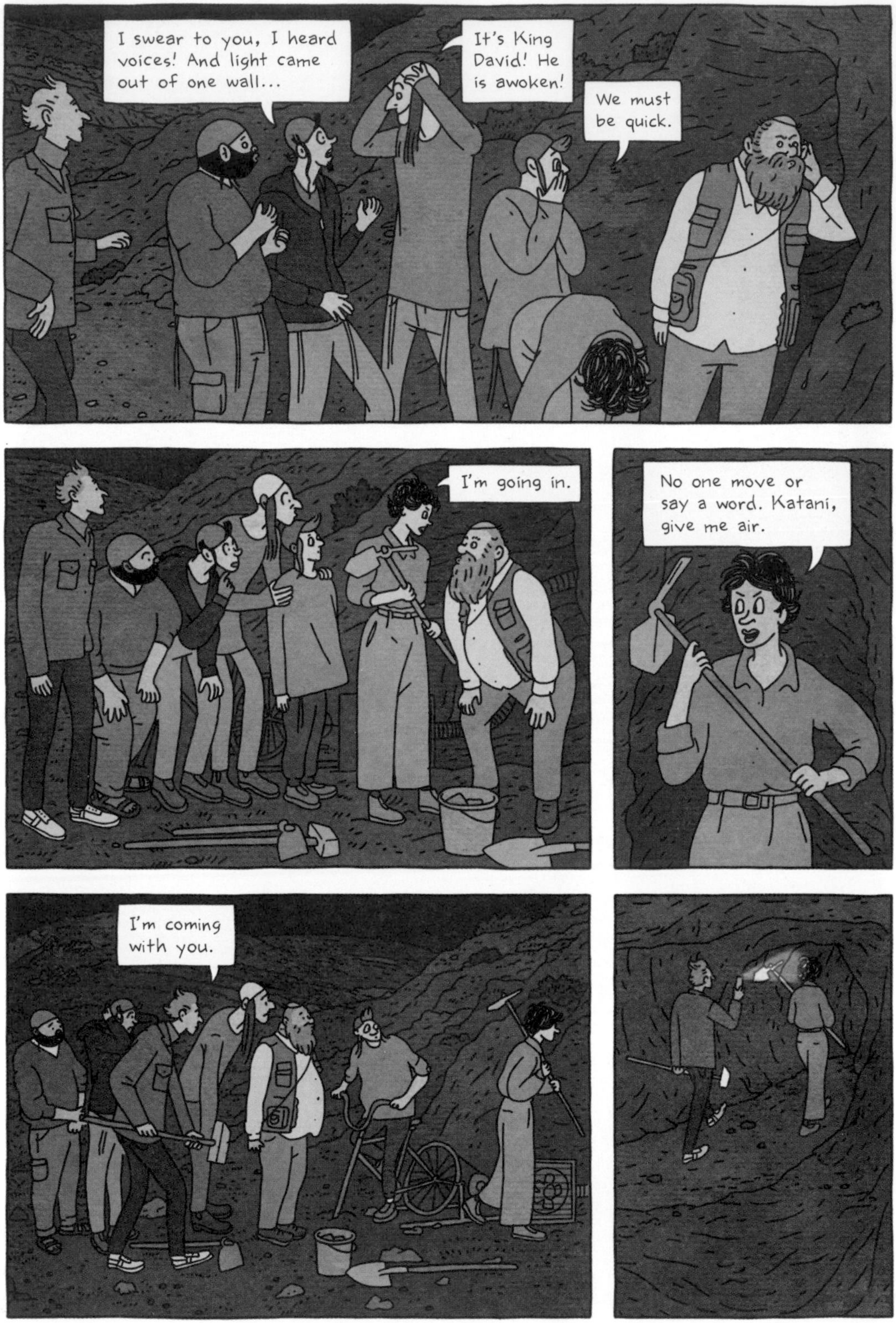
I swear to you, I heard voices! And light came out of one wall...
It's King David! He is awoken!
We must be quick.
I'm going in.
No one move or say a word. Katani, give me air.
I'm coming with you.

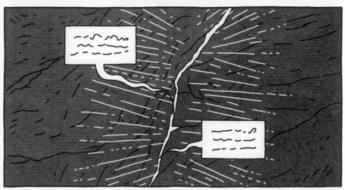

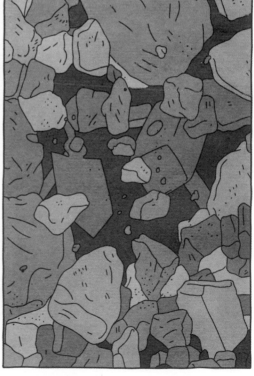

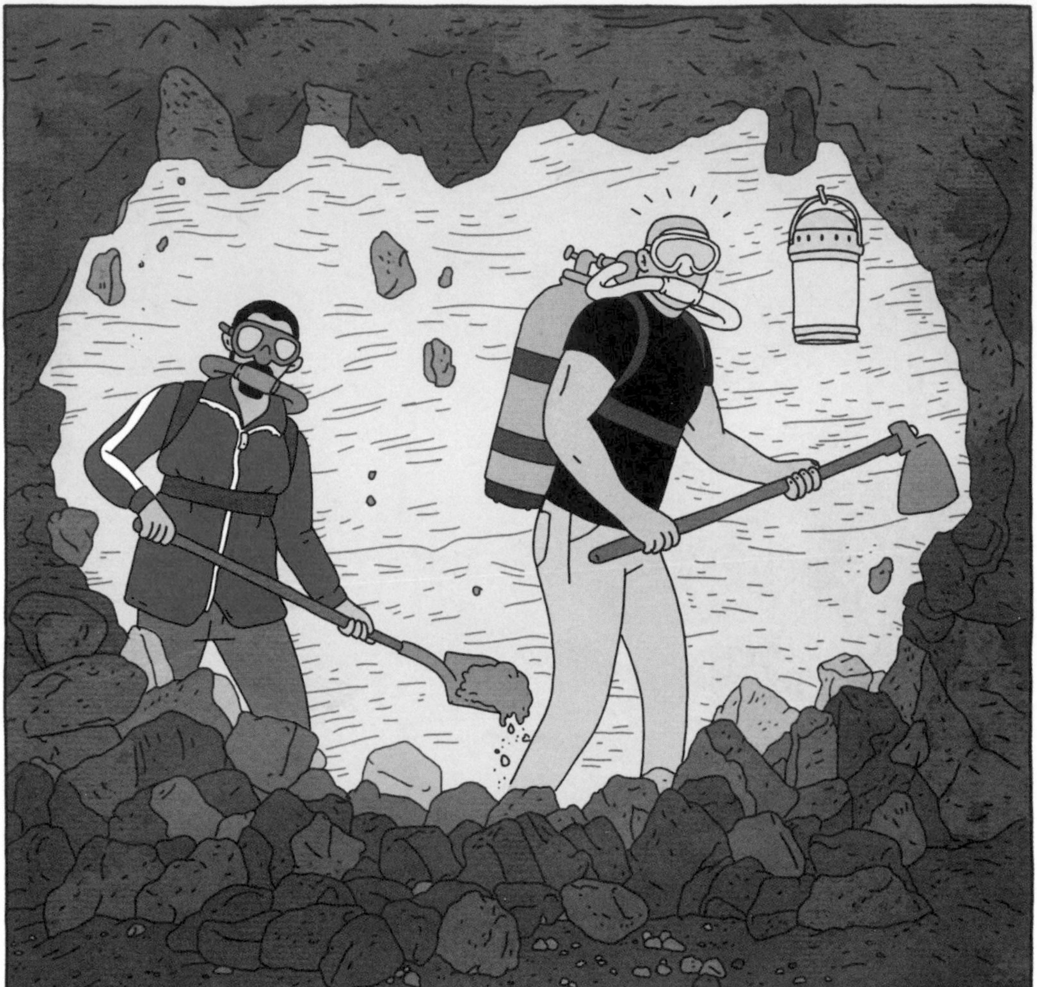

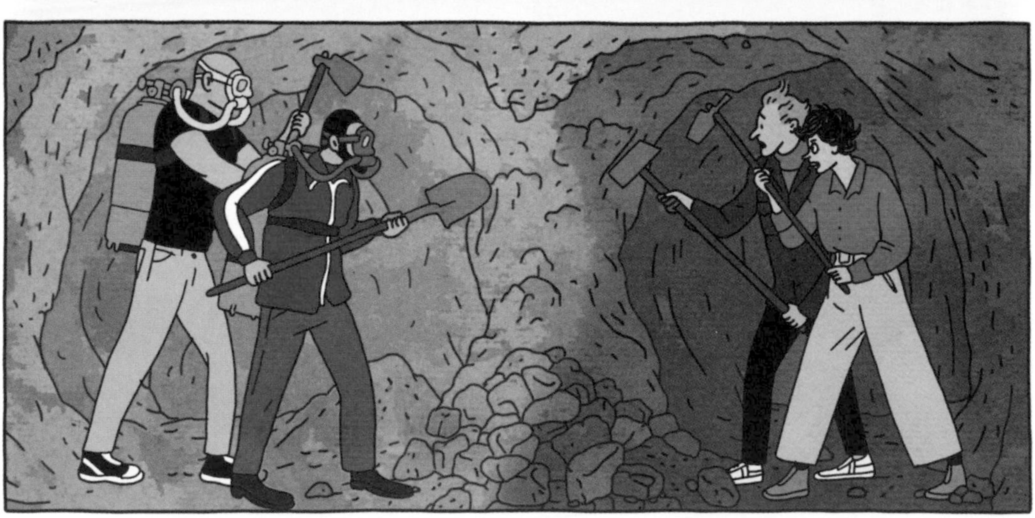

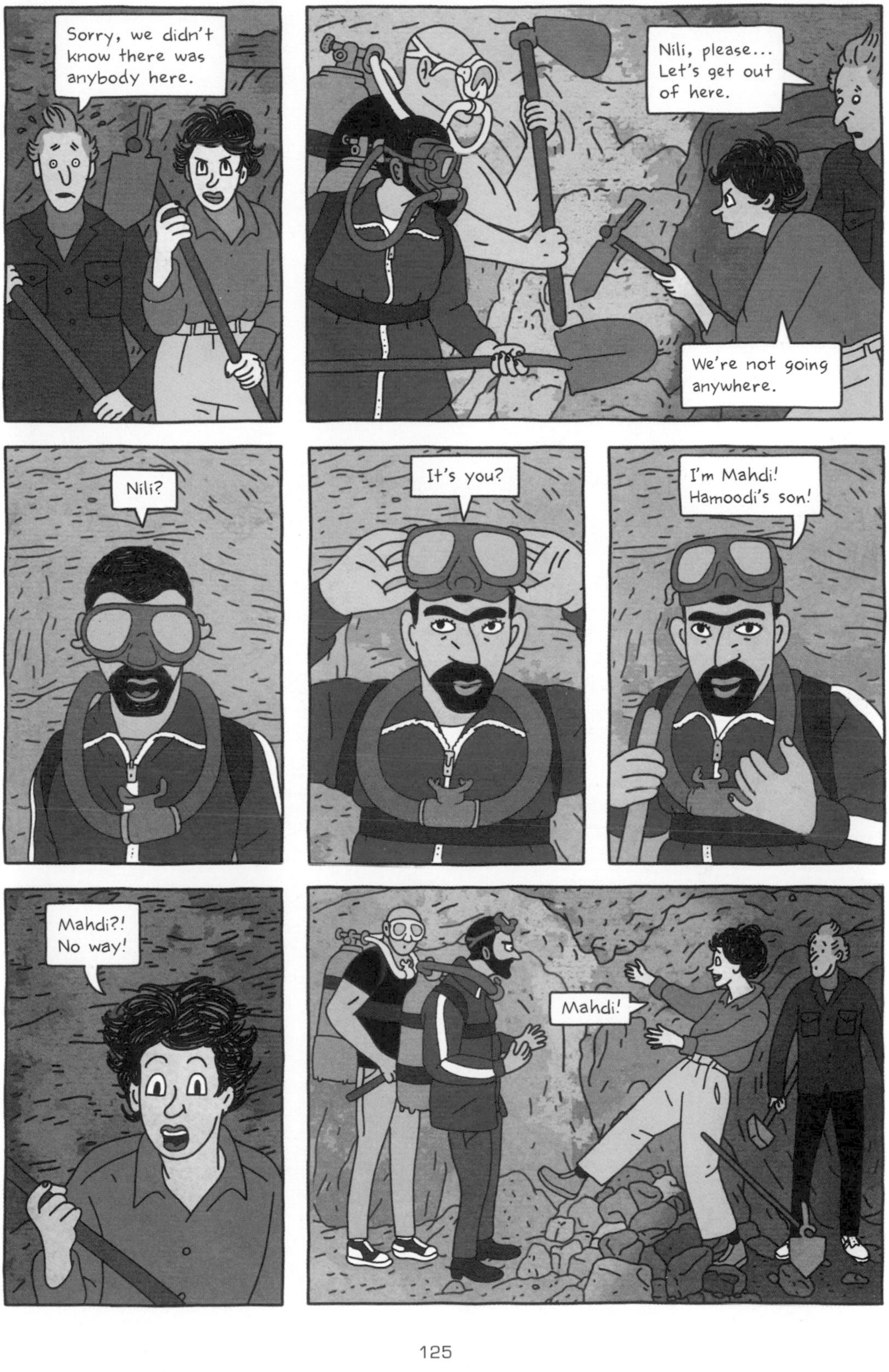

Sorry, we didn't know there was anybody here.
Nili, please... Let's get out of here.
We're not going anywhere.
Nili?
It's you?
I'm Mahdi! Hamoodi's son!
Mahdi?! No way!
Mahdi!

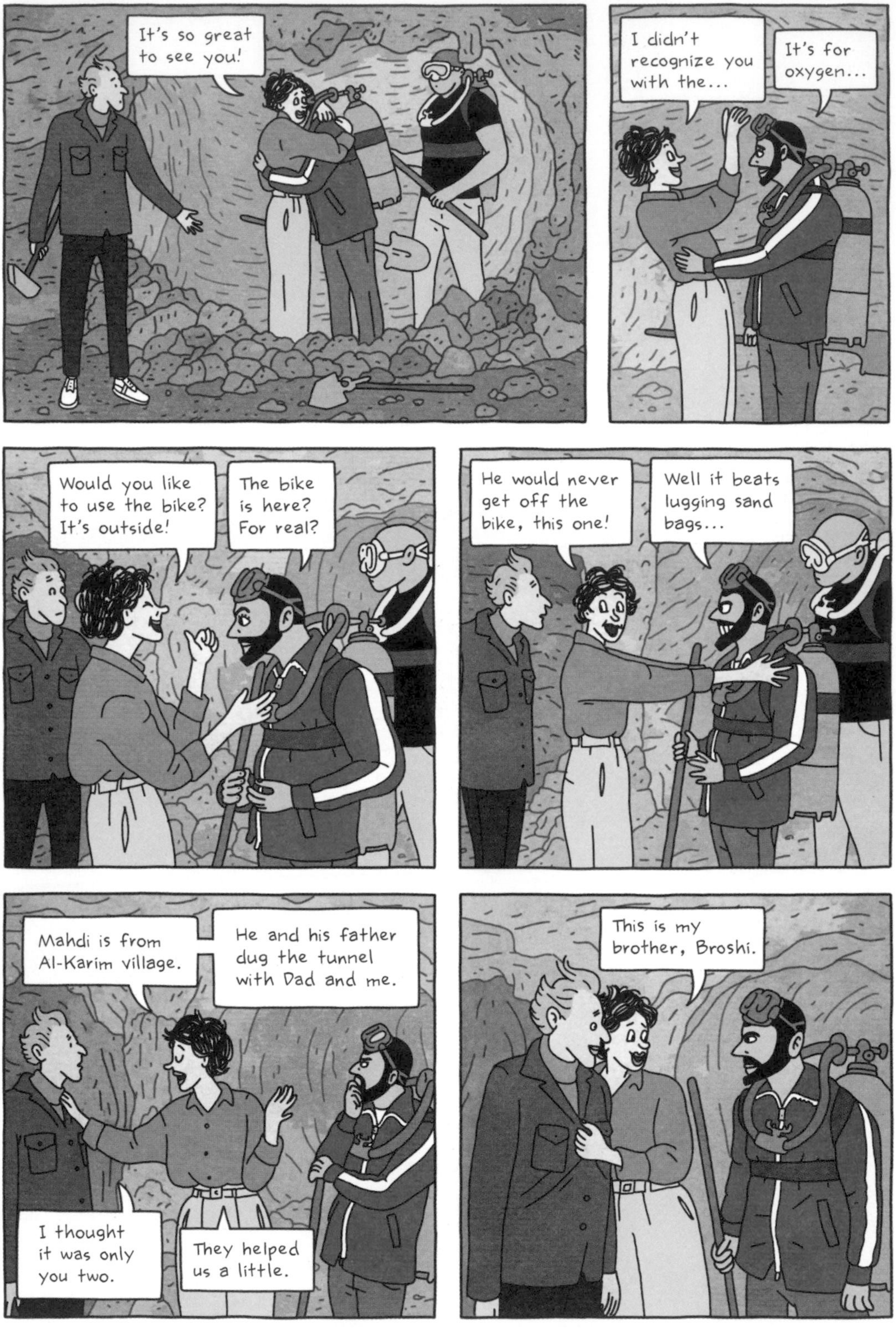
It's so great to see you!
I didn't recognize you with the...
It's for oxygen...
Would you like to use the bike? It's outside!
The bike is here? For real?
He would never get off the bike, this one!
Well it beats lugging sand bags...
Mahdi is from Al-Karim village.
He and his father dug the tunnel with Dad and me.
I thought it was only you two.
They helped us a little.
This is my brother, Broshi.

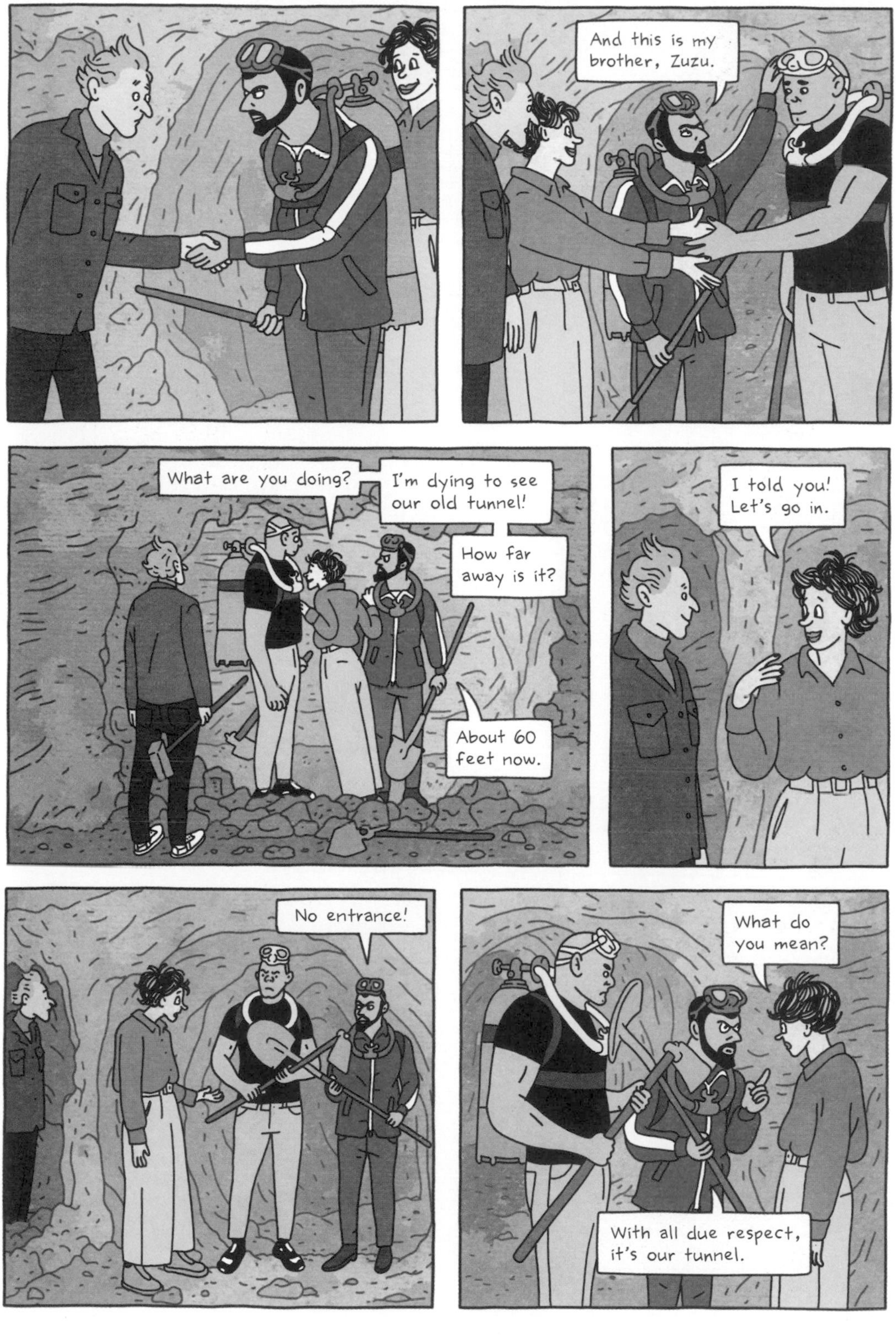
And this is my brother, Zuzu.
What are you doing?
I'm dying to see our old tunnel!
How far away is it?
About 60 feet now.
I told you! Let's go in.
No entrance!
What do you mean?
With all due respect, it's our tunnel.

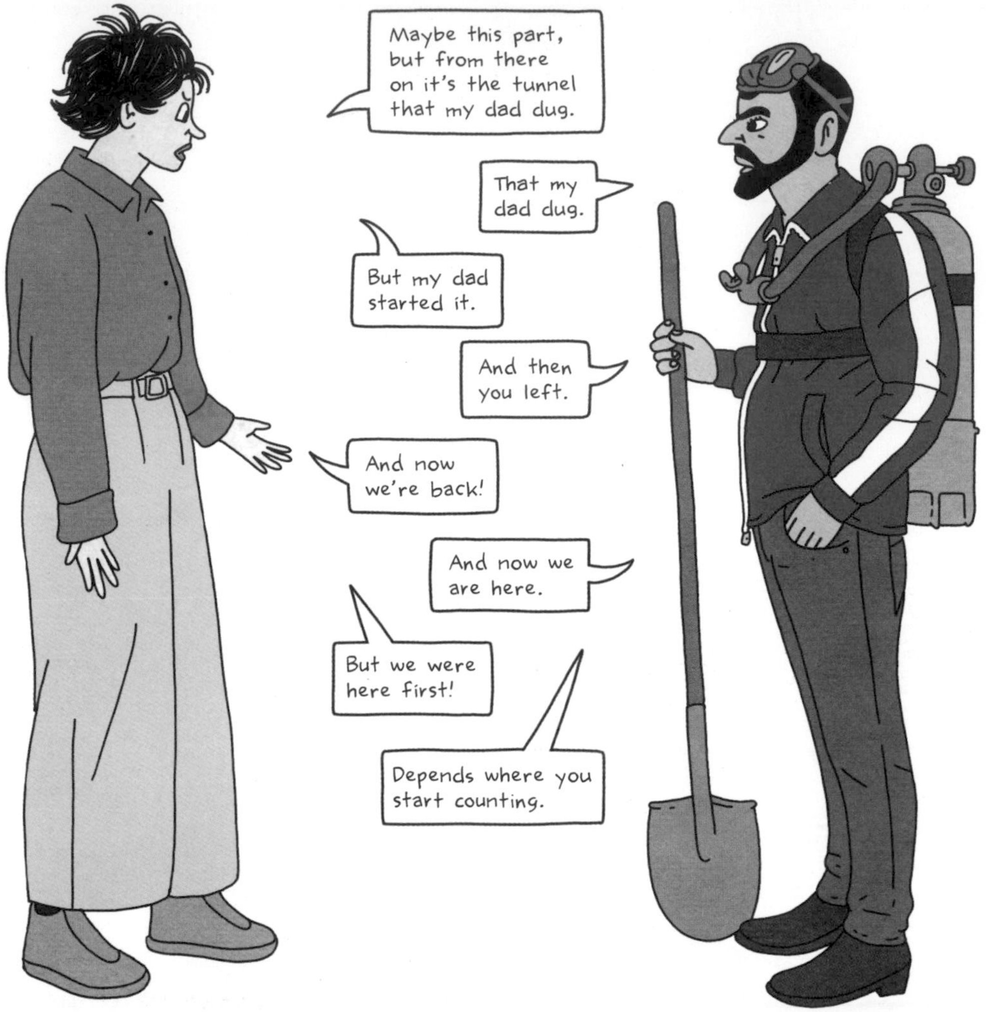
Maybe this part, but from there on it's the tunnel that my dad dug.
That my dad dug.
But my dad started it.
And then you left.
And now we're back!
And now we are here.
But we were here first!
Depends where you start counting.

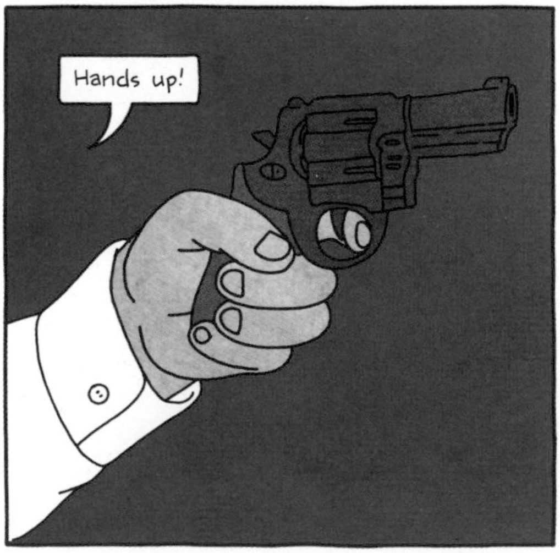
Hands up!

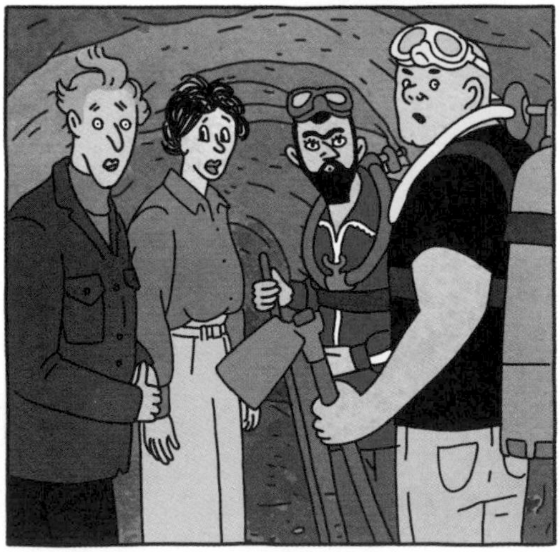

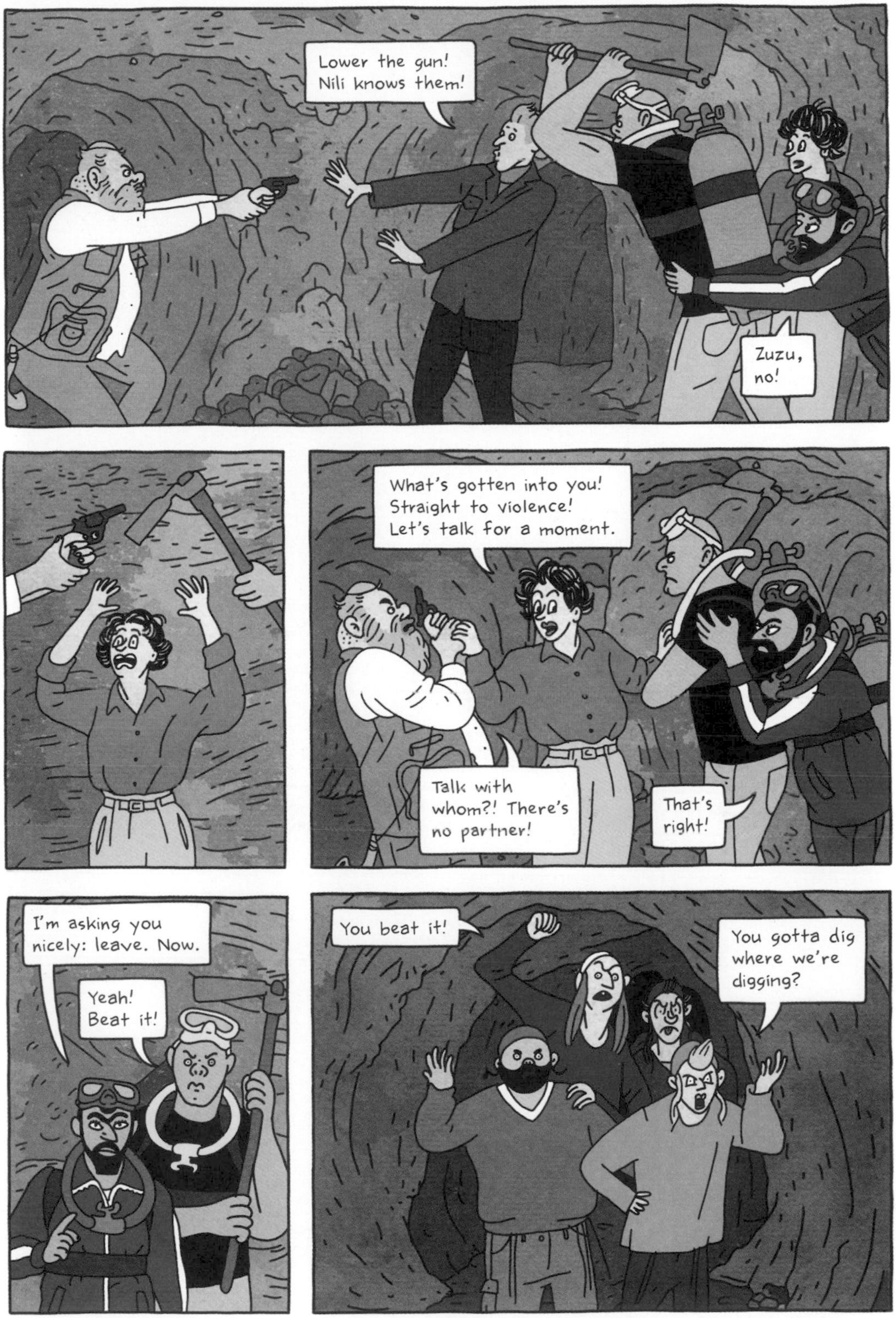
Lower the gun! Nili knows them!
Zuzu, no!
What's gotten into you! Straight to violence! Let's talk for a moment.
Talk with whom?! There's no partner!
That's right!
I'm asking you nicely: leave. Now.
Yeah! Beat it!
You beat it!
You gotta dig where we're digging?

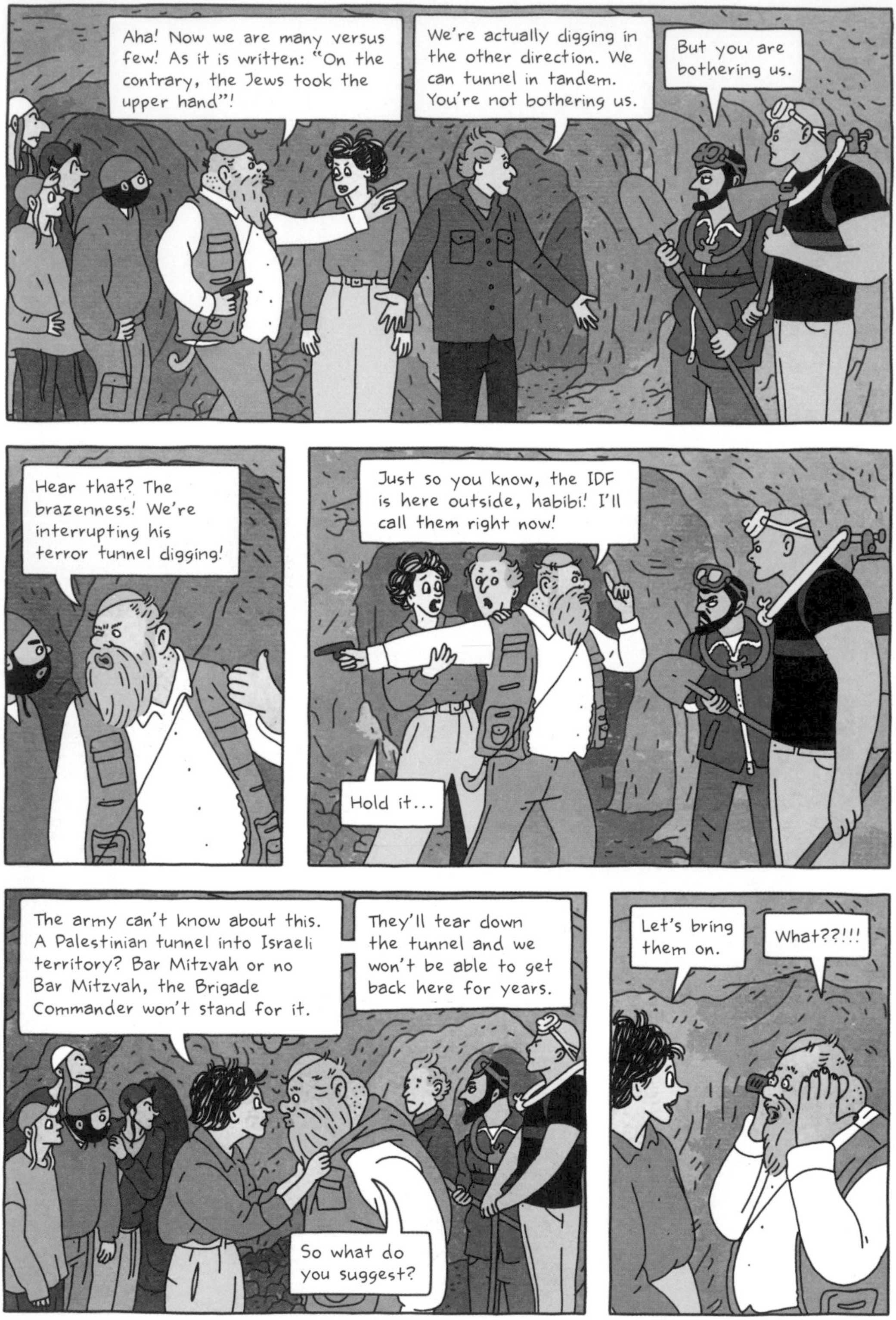

Aha! Now we are many versus few! As it is written: "On the contrary, the Jews took the upper hand"!
We're actually digging in the other direction. We can tunnel in tandem. You're not bothering us.
But you are bothering us.
Hear that? The brazenness! We're interrupting his terror tunnel digging!
Just so you know, the IDF is here outside, habibi! I'll call them right now!
Hold it...
The army can't know about this. A Palestinian tunnel into Israeli territory? Bar Mitzvah or no Bar Mitzvah, the Brigade Commander won't stand for it.
They'll tear down the tunnel and we won't be able to get back here for years.
So what do you suggest?
Let's bring them on.
What??!!!

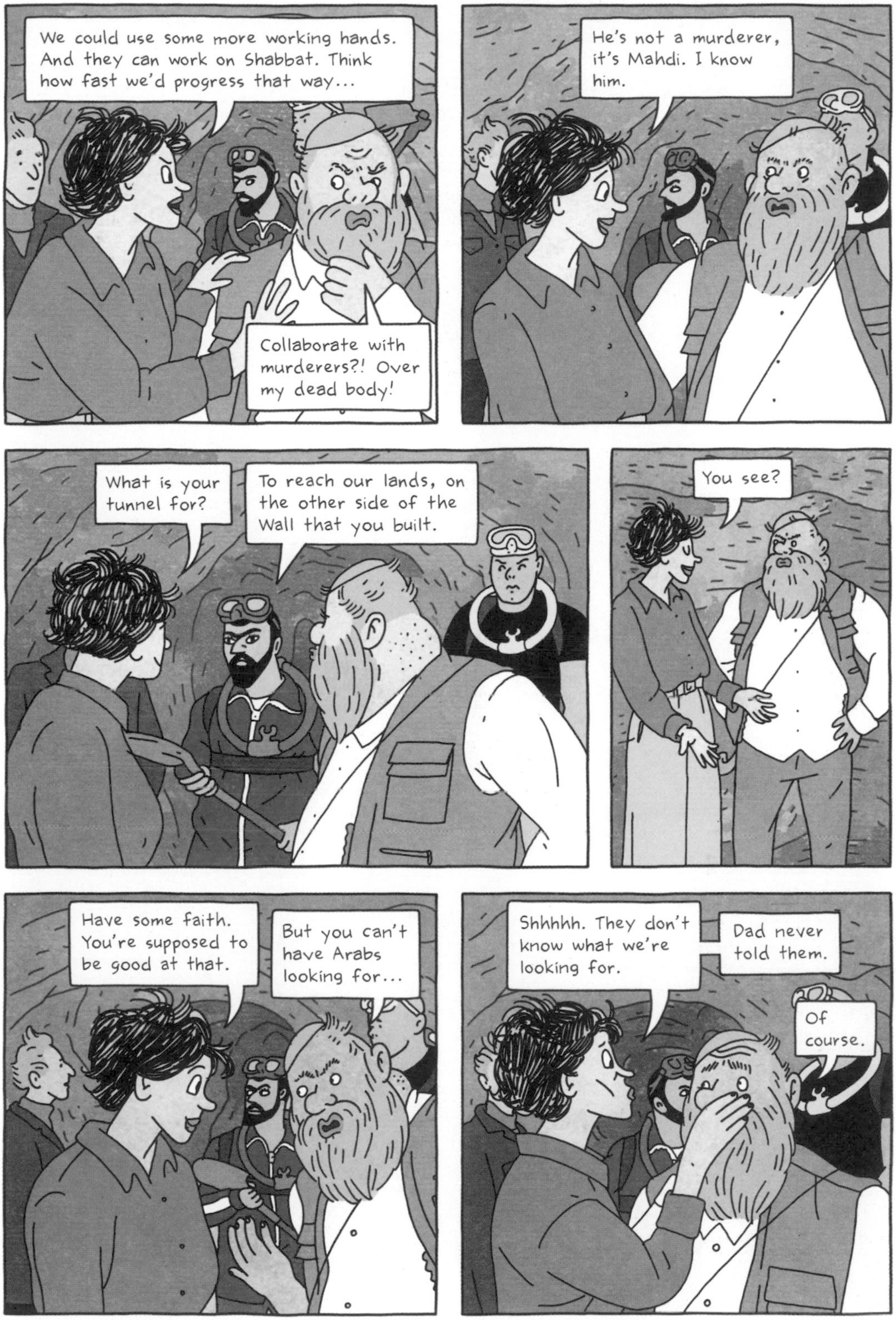
We could use some more working hands. And they can work on Shabbat. Think how fast we'd progress that way...
Collaborate with murderers?! Over my dead body!
He's not a murderer, it's Mahdi. I know him.
What is your tunnel for?
To reach our lands, on the other side of the Wall that you built.
You see?
Have some faith. You're supposed to be good at that.
But you can't have Arabs looking for...
Shhhhh. They don't know what we're looking for.
Dad never told them.
Of course.

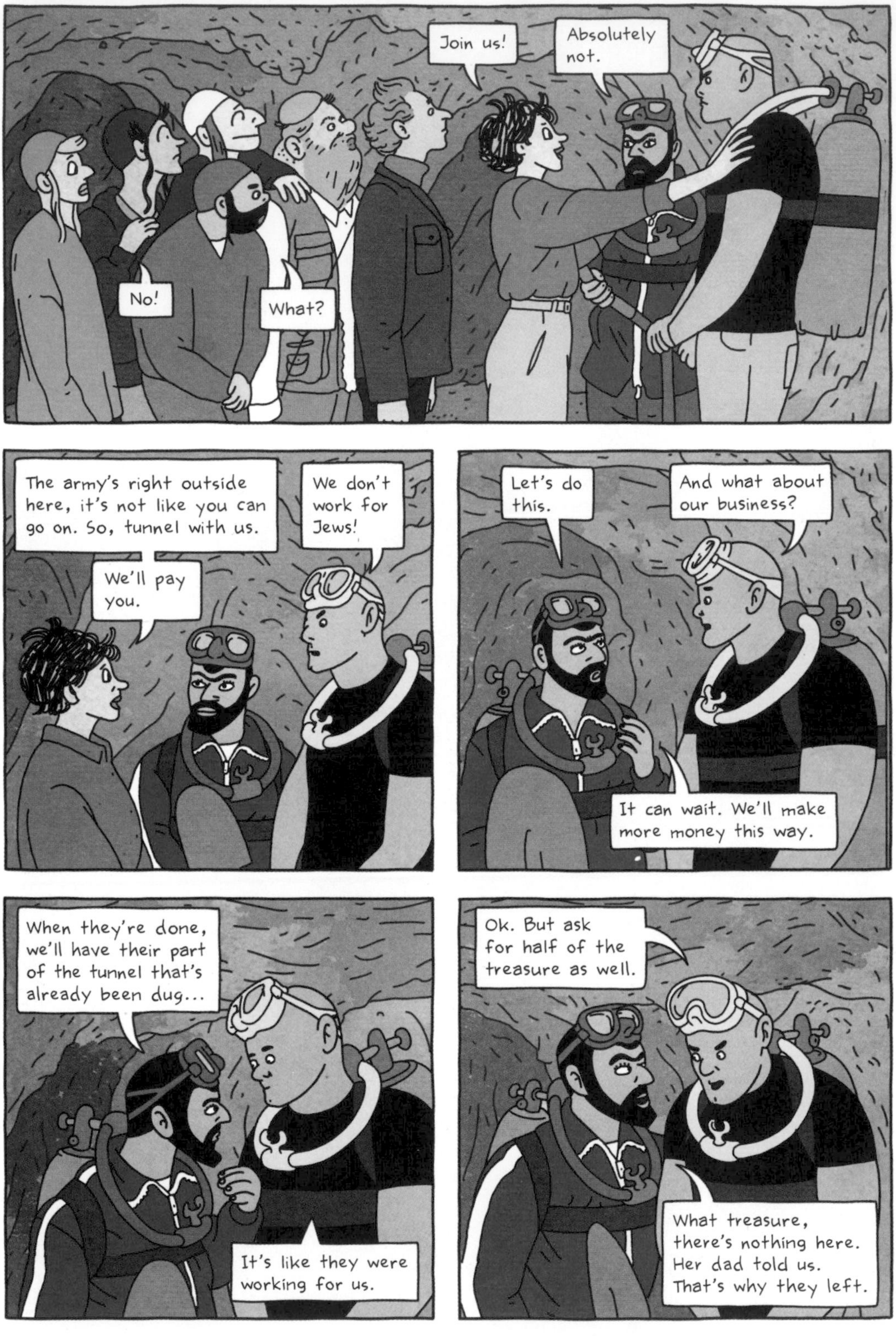
Join us!
Absolutely not.
No!
What?
The army's right outside here, it's not like you can go on. So, tunnel with us.
We'll pay you.
We don't work for Jews!
Let's do this.
And what about our business?
It can wait. We'll make more money this way.
When they're done, we'll have their part of the tunnel that's already been dug...
It's like they were working for us.
Ok. But ask for half of the treasure as well.
What treasure, there's nothing here. Her dad told us. That's why they left.

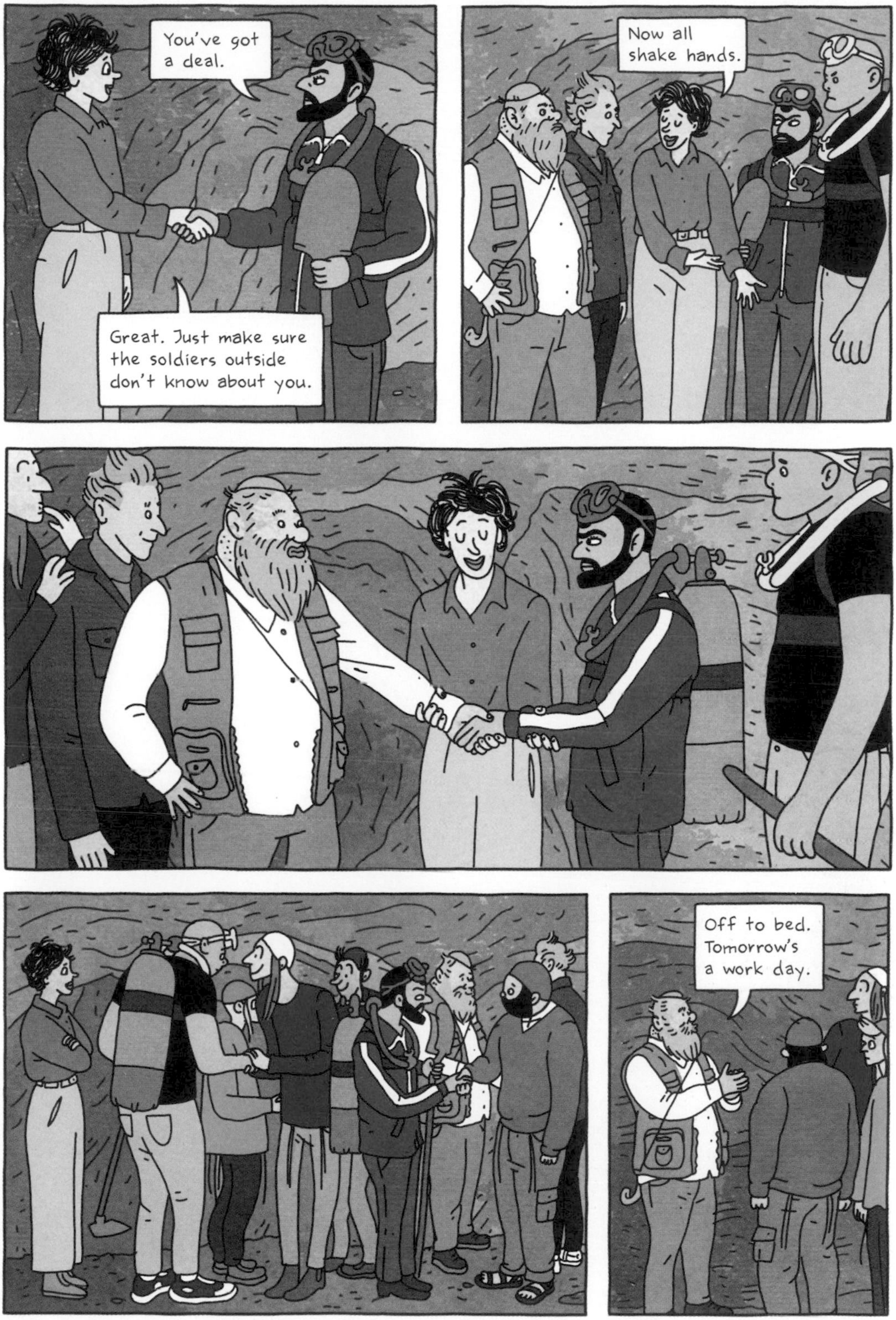
You've got a deal.
Great. Just make sure the soldiers outside don't know about you.
Now all shake hands.
Off to bed. Tomorrow's a work day.

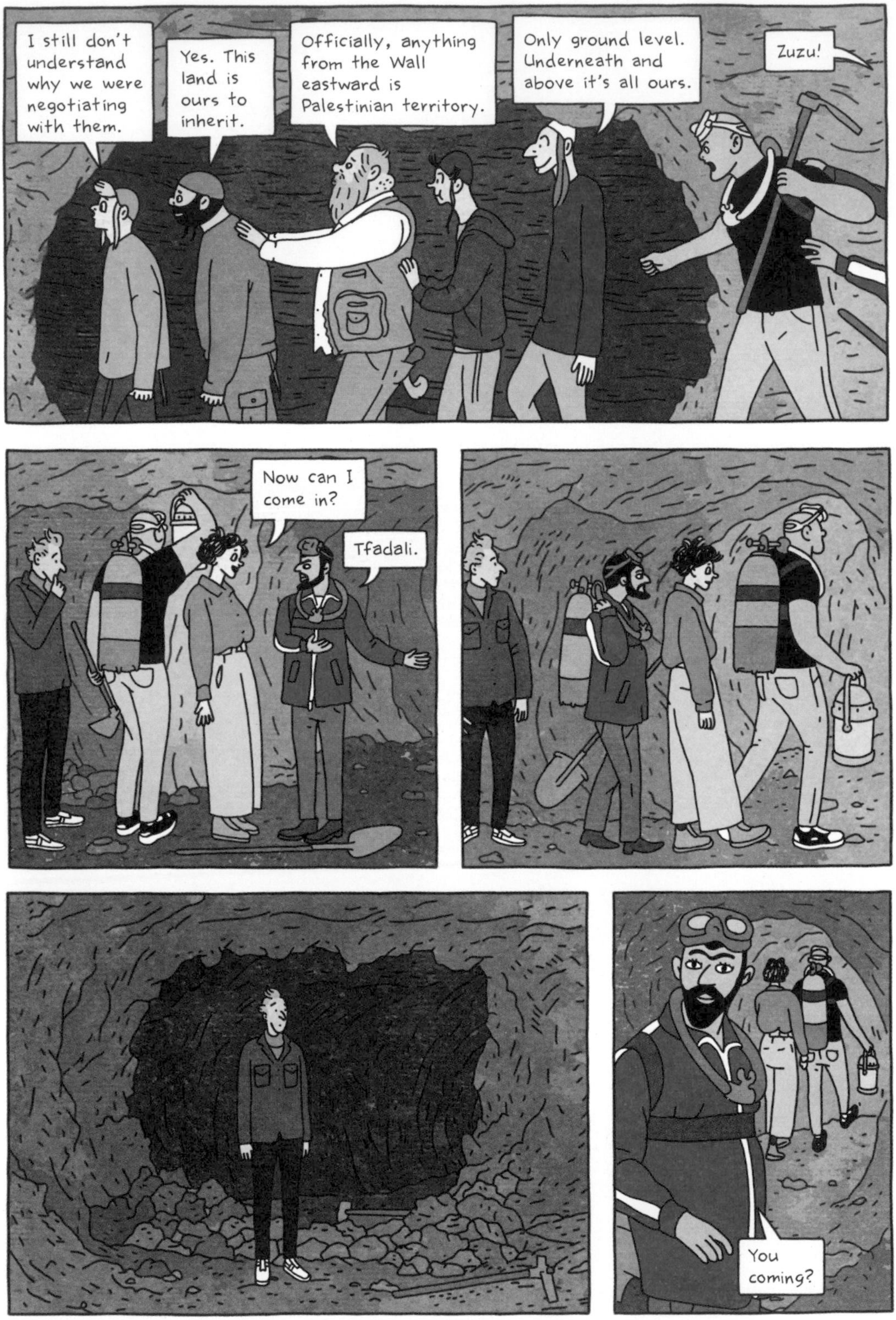
I still don't understand why we were negotiating with them.
Yes. This land is ours to inherit.
Officially, anything from the Wall eastward is Palestinian territory.
Only ground level. Underneath and above it's all ours.
Zuzu!
Now can I come in?
Tfadali.
You coming?

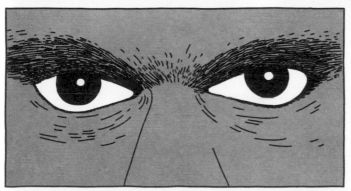

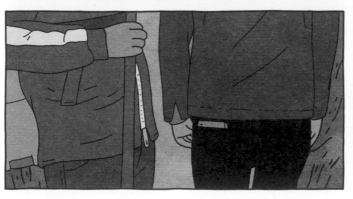

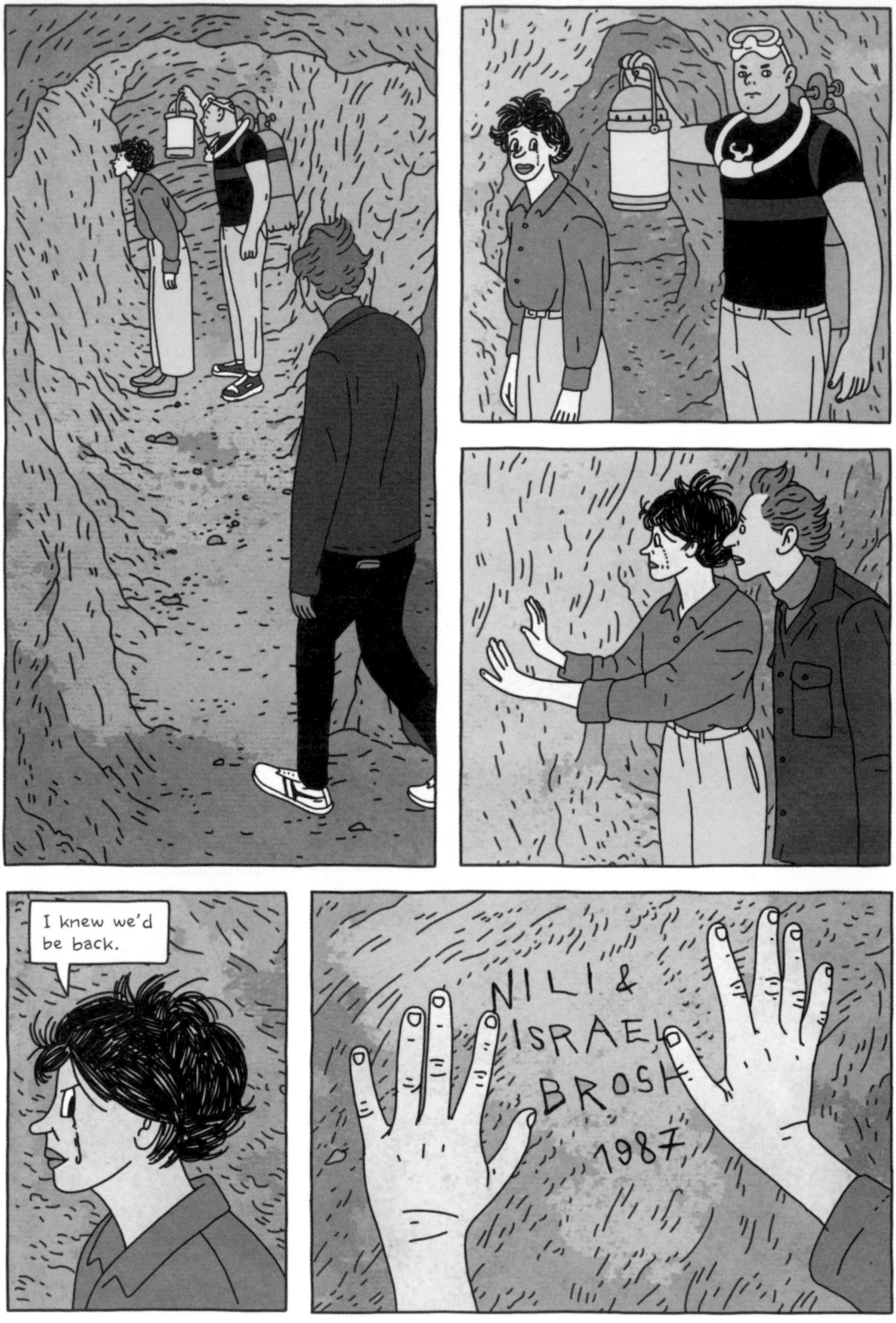
I knew we'd be back.
NILI &
ISRAEL
BROSH
1987

Part 3: The Old Tunnel

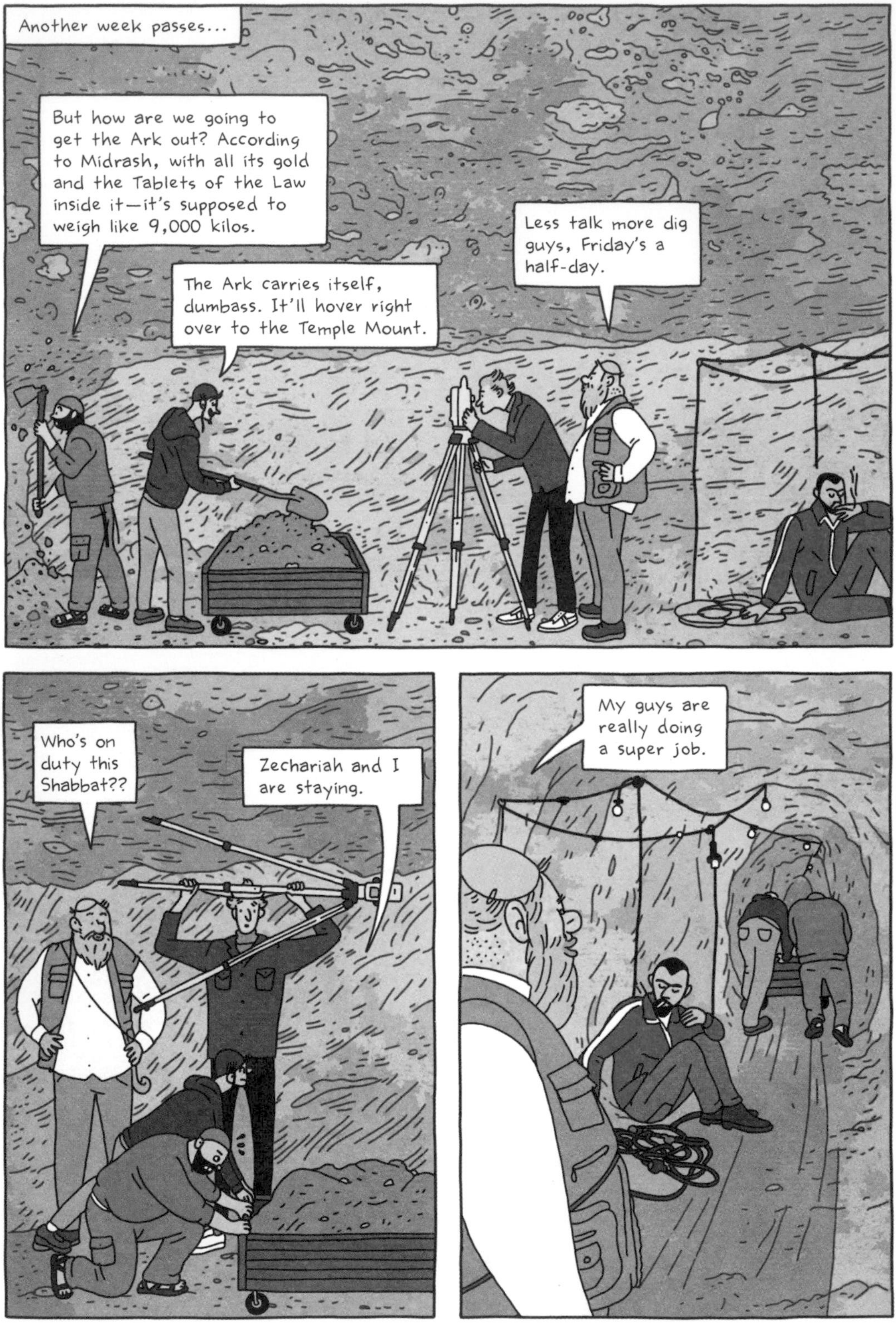

Another week passes...
But how are we going to get the Ark out? According to Midrash, with all its gold and the Tablets of the Law inside it—it's supposed to weigh like 9,000 kilos.
The Ark carries itself, dumbass. It'll hover right over to the Temple Mount.
Less talk more dig guys, Friday's a half-day.
Who's on duty this Shabbat??
Zechariah and I are staying.
My guys are really doing a super job.

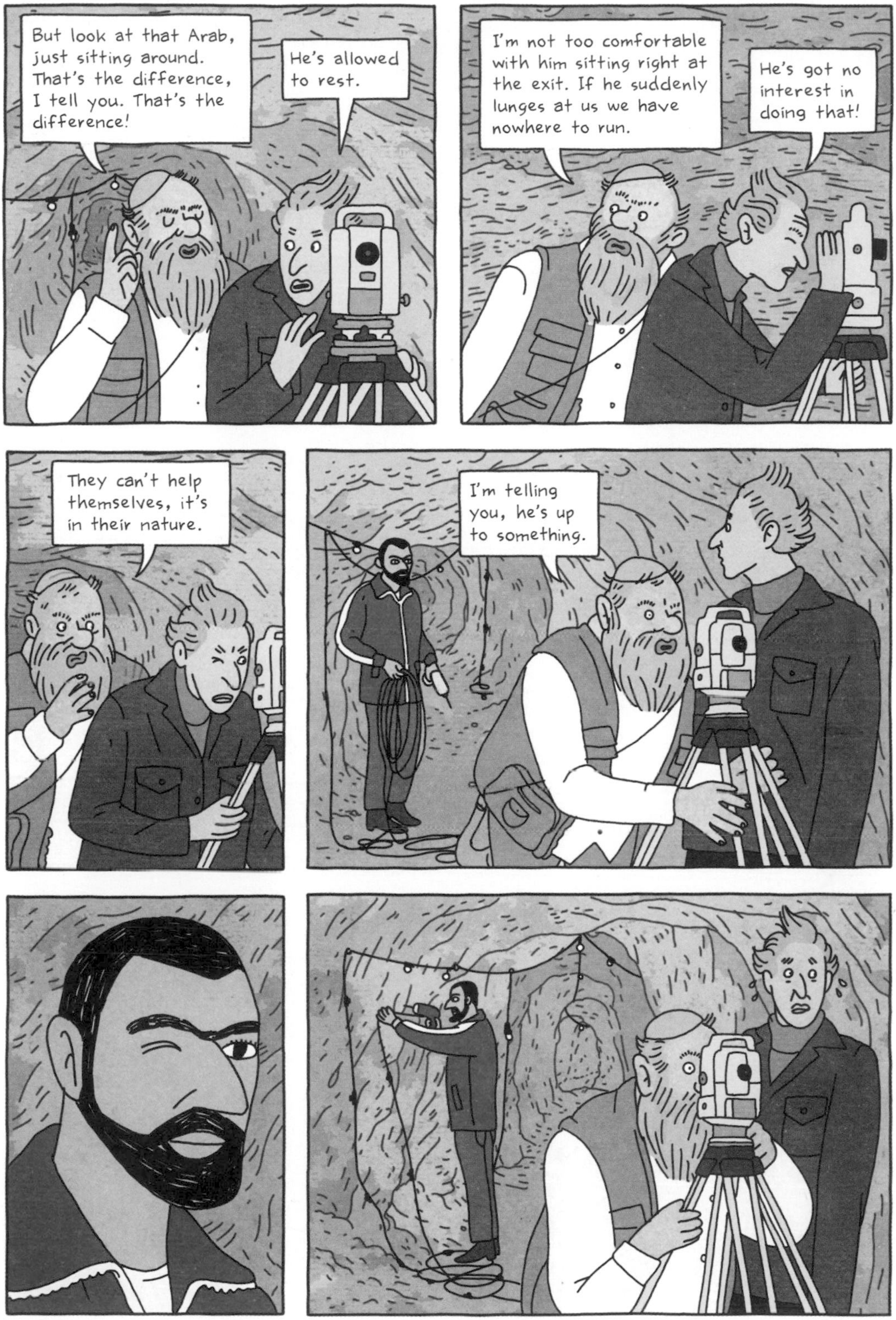
But look at that Arab, just sitting around. That's the difference, I tell you. That's the difference!
He's allowed to rest.
I'm not too comfortable with him sitting right at the exit. If he suddenly lunges at us we have nowhere to run.
He's got no interest in doing that!
They can't help themselves, it's in their nature.
I'm telling you, he's up to something.

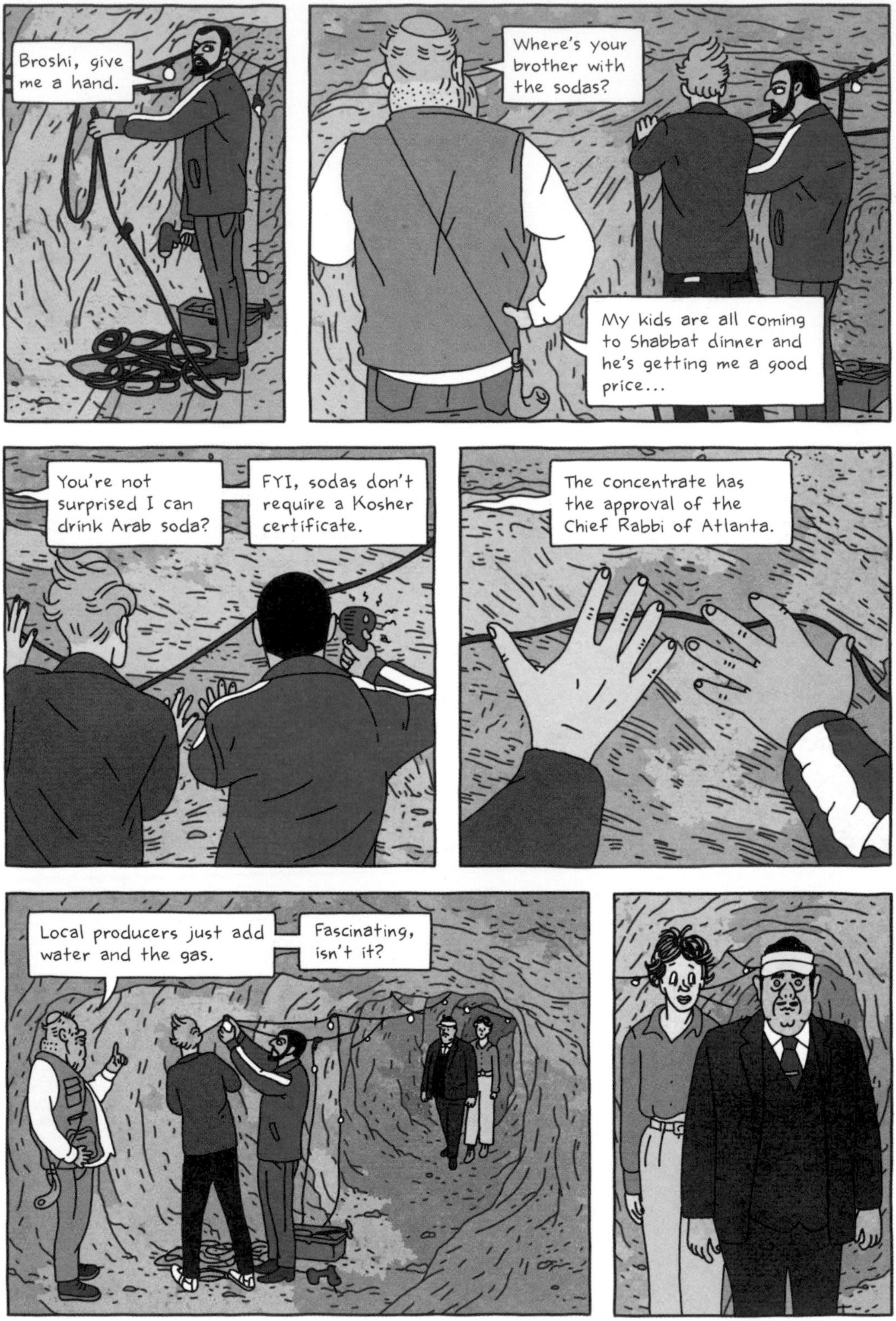
Broshi, give me a hand.
Where's your brother with the sodas?
My kids are all coming to Shabbat dinner and he's getting me a good price...
You're not surprised I can drink Arab soda?
FYI, sodas don't require a Kosher certificate.
The concentrate has the approval of the Chief Rabbi of Atlanta.
Local producers just add water and the gas.
Fascinating, isn't it?

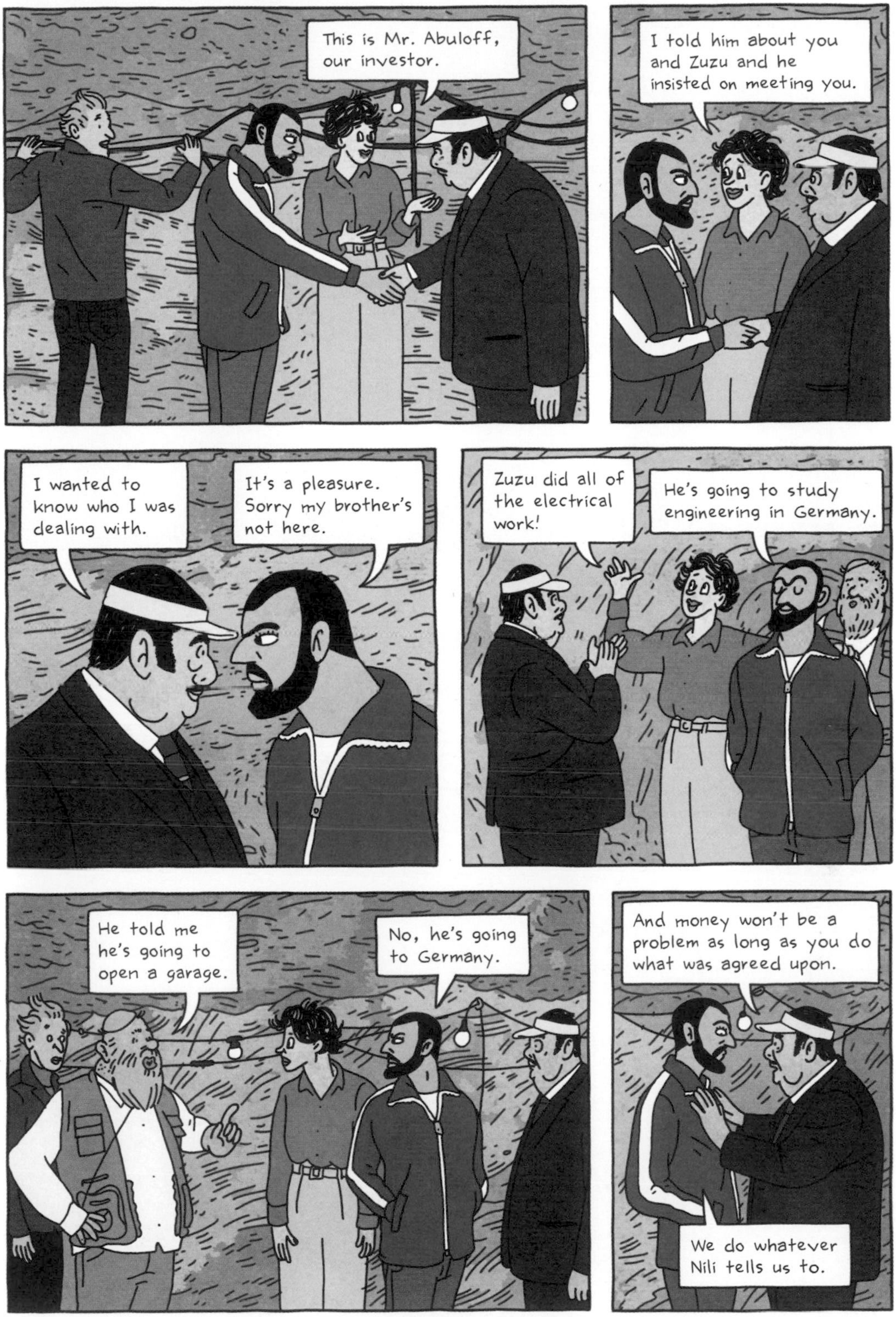
This is Mr. Abuloff, our investor.
I told him about you and Zuzu and he insisted on meeting you.
I wanted to know who I was dealing with.
It's a pleasure. Sorry my brother's not here.
Zuzu did all of the electrical work!
He's going to study engineering in Germany.
He told me he's going to open a garage.
No, he's going to Germany.
And money won't be a problem as long as you do what was agreed upon.
We do whatever Nili tells us to.

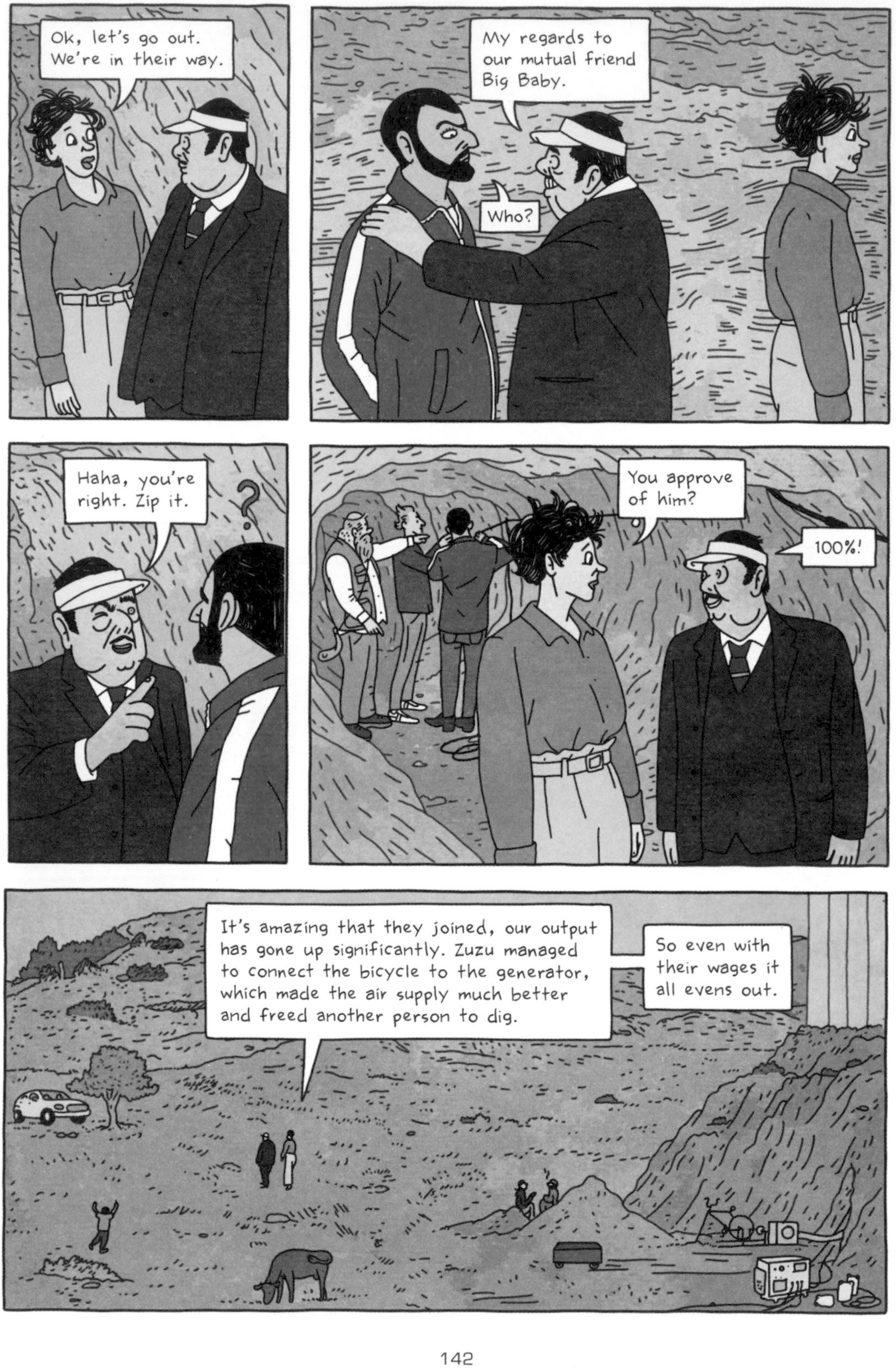

Ok, let's go out. We're in their way.
My regards to our mutual friend Big Baby.
Who?
Haha, you're right. Zip it.
?
You approve of him?
100%!
It's amazing that they joined, our output has gone up significantly. Zuzu managed to connect the bicycle to the generator, which made the air supply much better and freed another person to dig.
So even with their wages it all evens out.

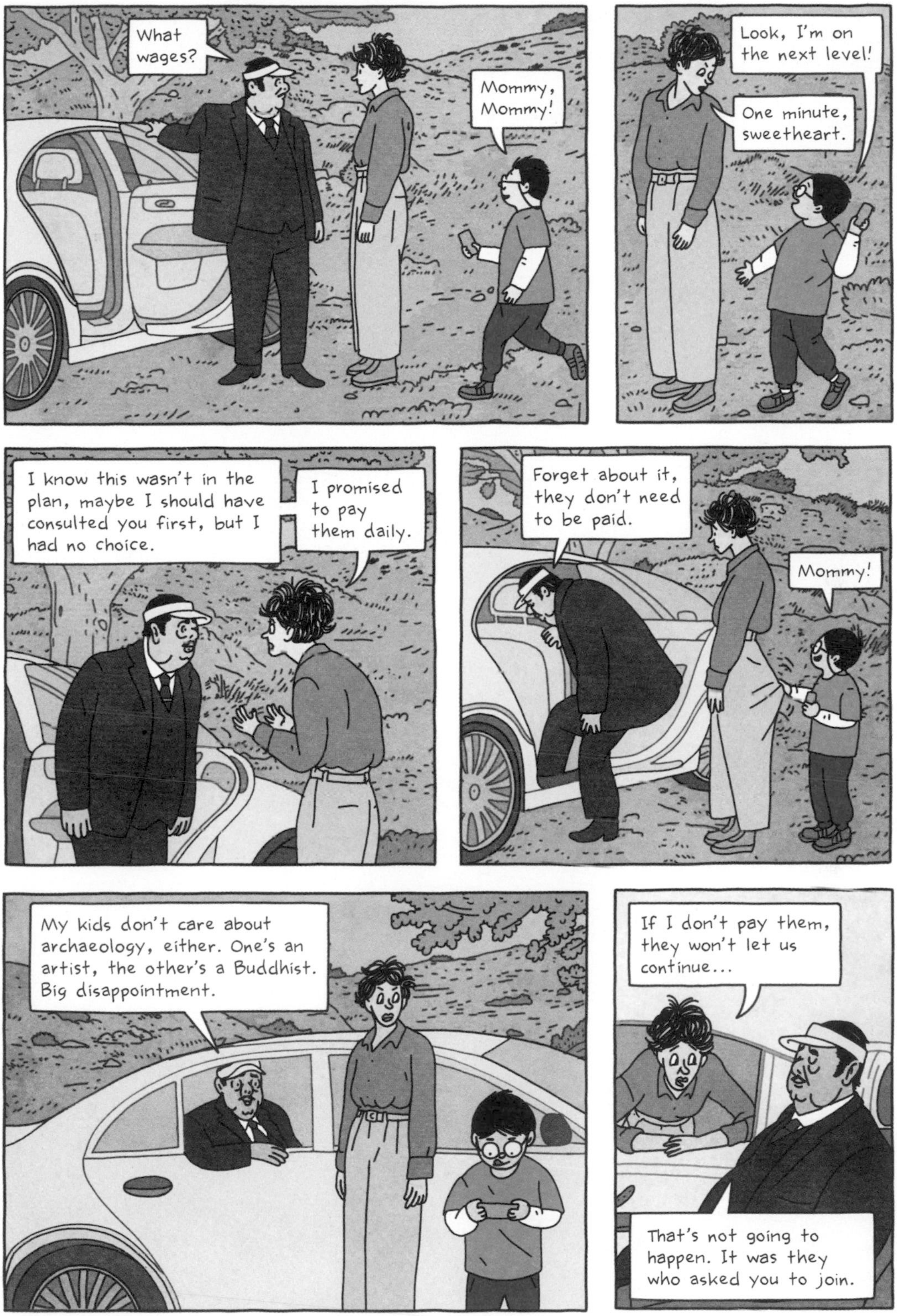
What wages?
Mommy, Mommy!
Look, I'm on the next level!
One minute, sweetheart.
I know this wasn't in the plan, maybe I should have consulted you first, but I had no choice.
I promised to pay them daily.
Forget about it, they don't need to be paid.
Mommy!
My kids don't care about archaeology, either. One's an artist, the other's a Buddhist. Big disappointment.
If I don't pay them, they won't let us continue...
That's not going to happen. It was they who asked you to join.

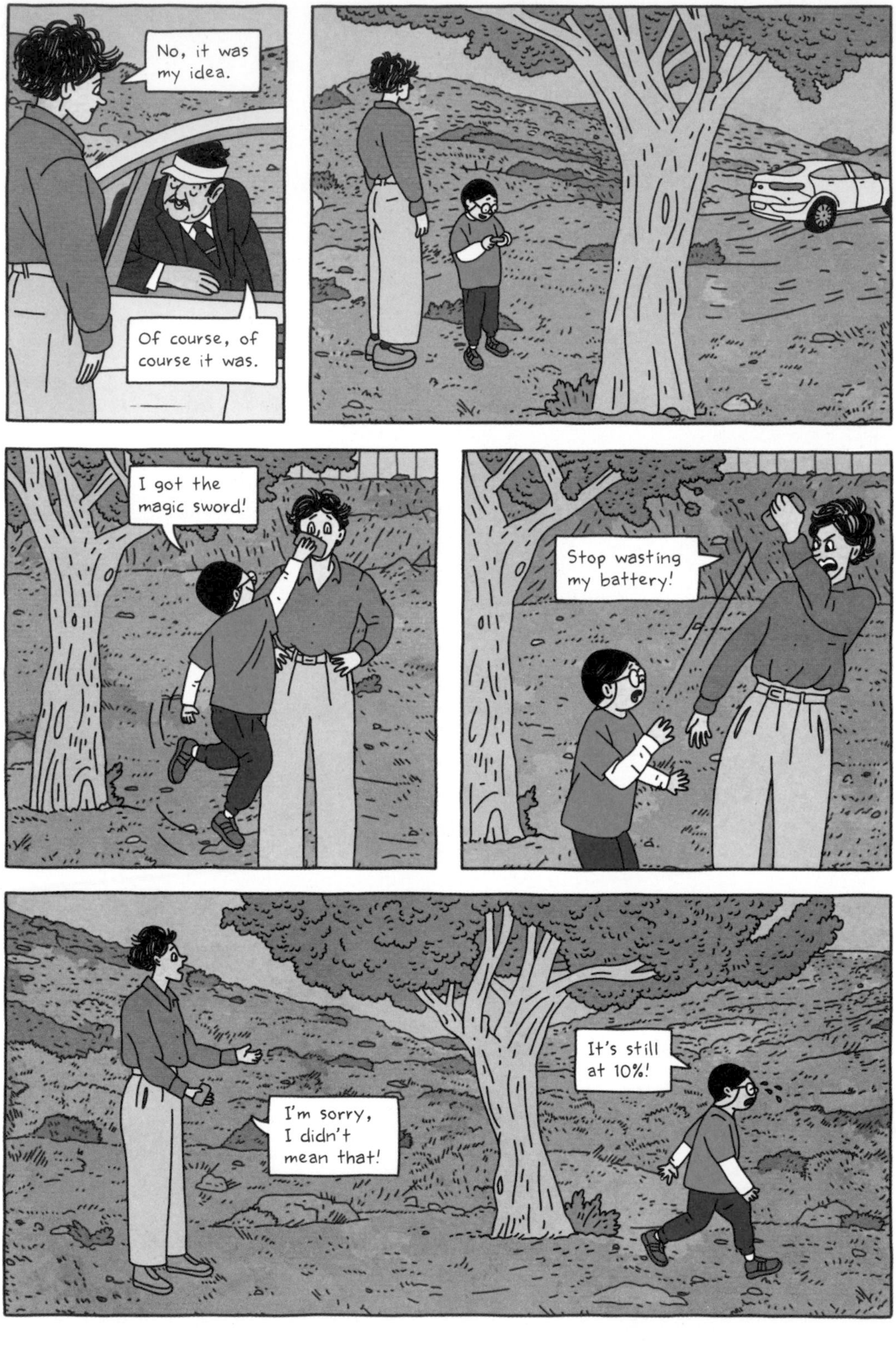
No, it was my idea.
Of course, of course it was.
I got the magic sword!
Stop wasting my battery!
I'm sorry, I didn't mean that!
It's still at 10%!

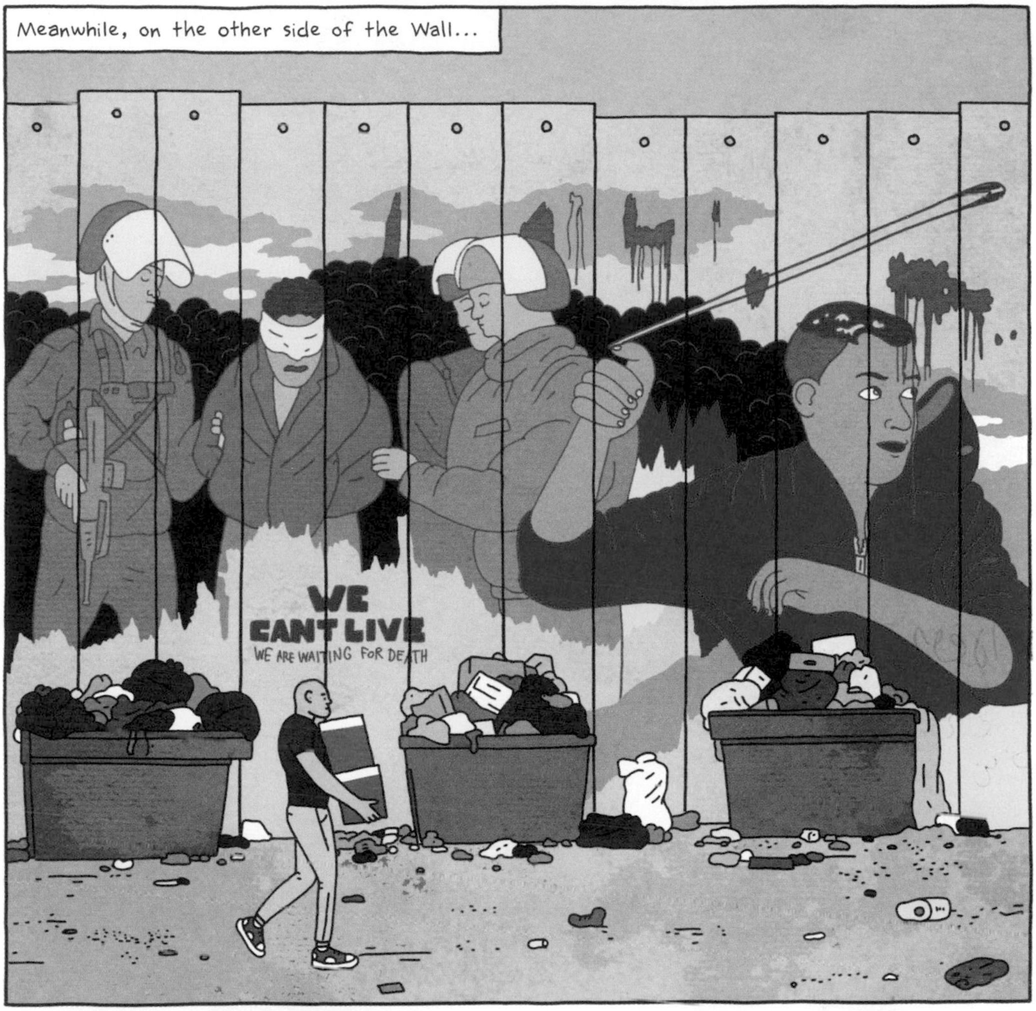
Meanwhile, on the other side of the Wall...
WE CANT LIVE
WE ARE WAITING FOR DEATH

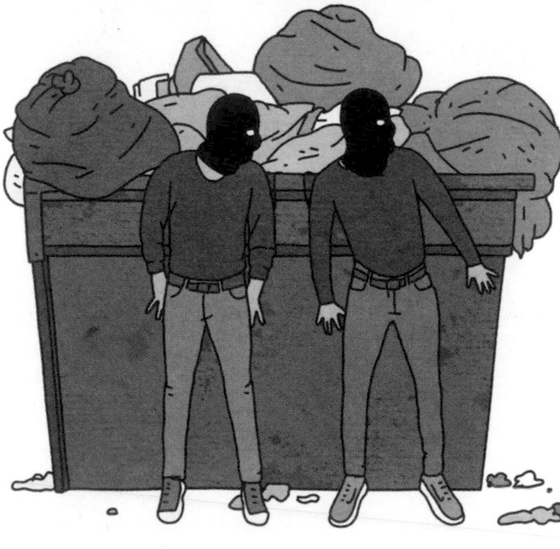

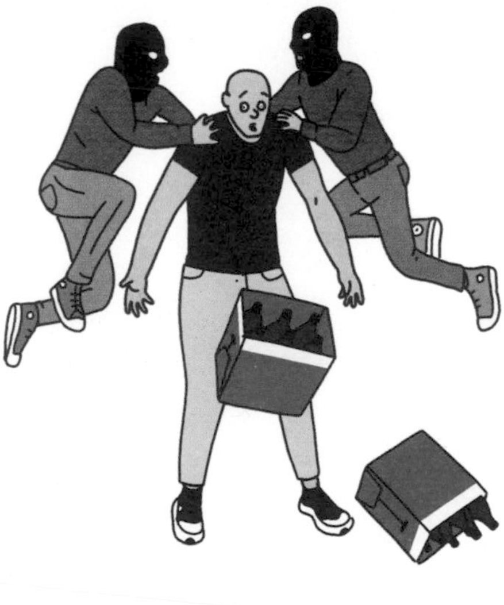

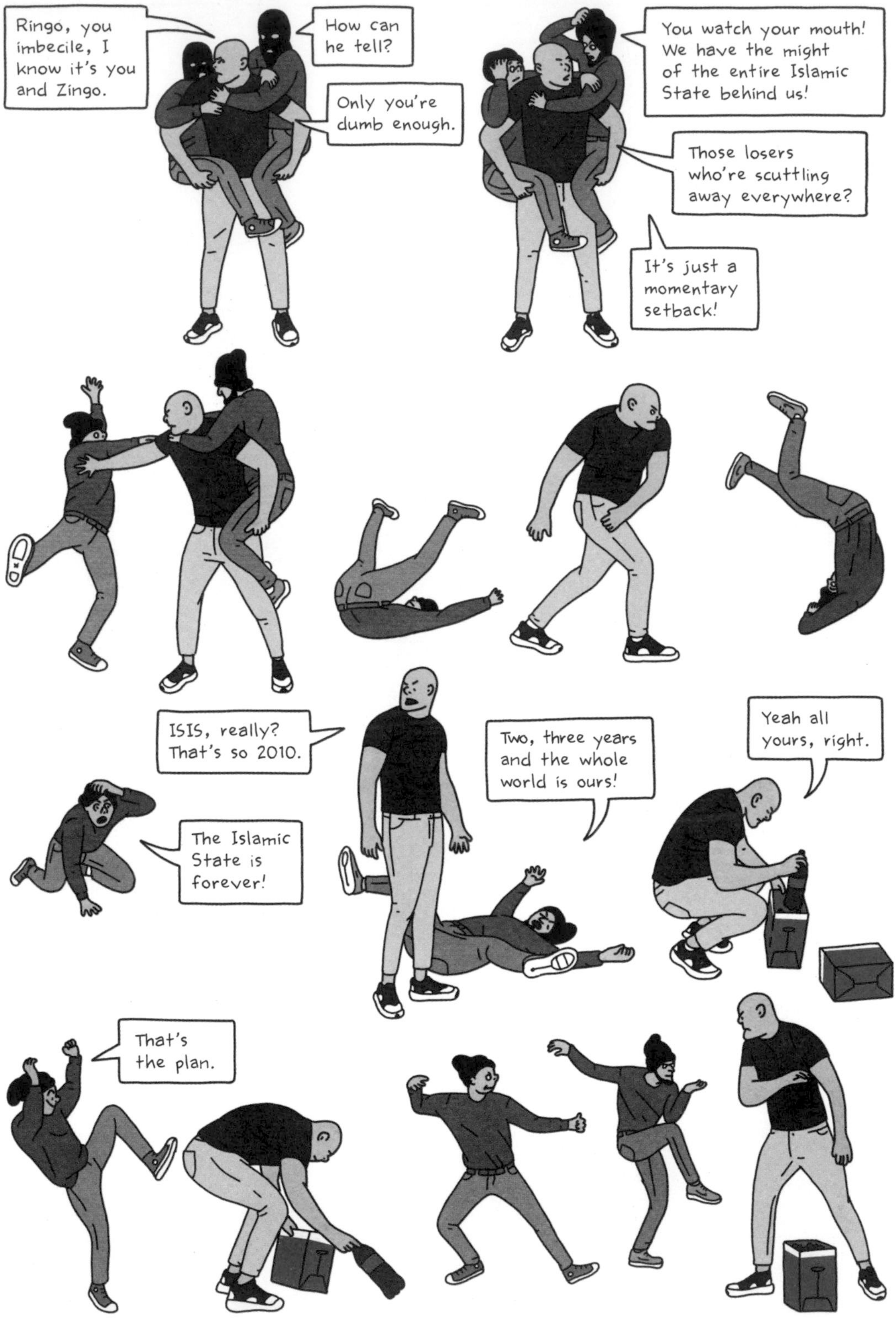
Ringo, you imbecile, I know it's you and Zingo.
How can he tell?
Only you're dumb enough.
You watch your mouth! We have the might of the entire Islamic State behind us!
Those losers who're scuttling away everywhere?
It's just a momentary setback!
ISIS, really? That's so 2010.
The Islamic State is forever!
Two, three years and the whole world is ours!
Yeah all yours, right.
That's the plan.

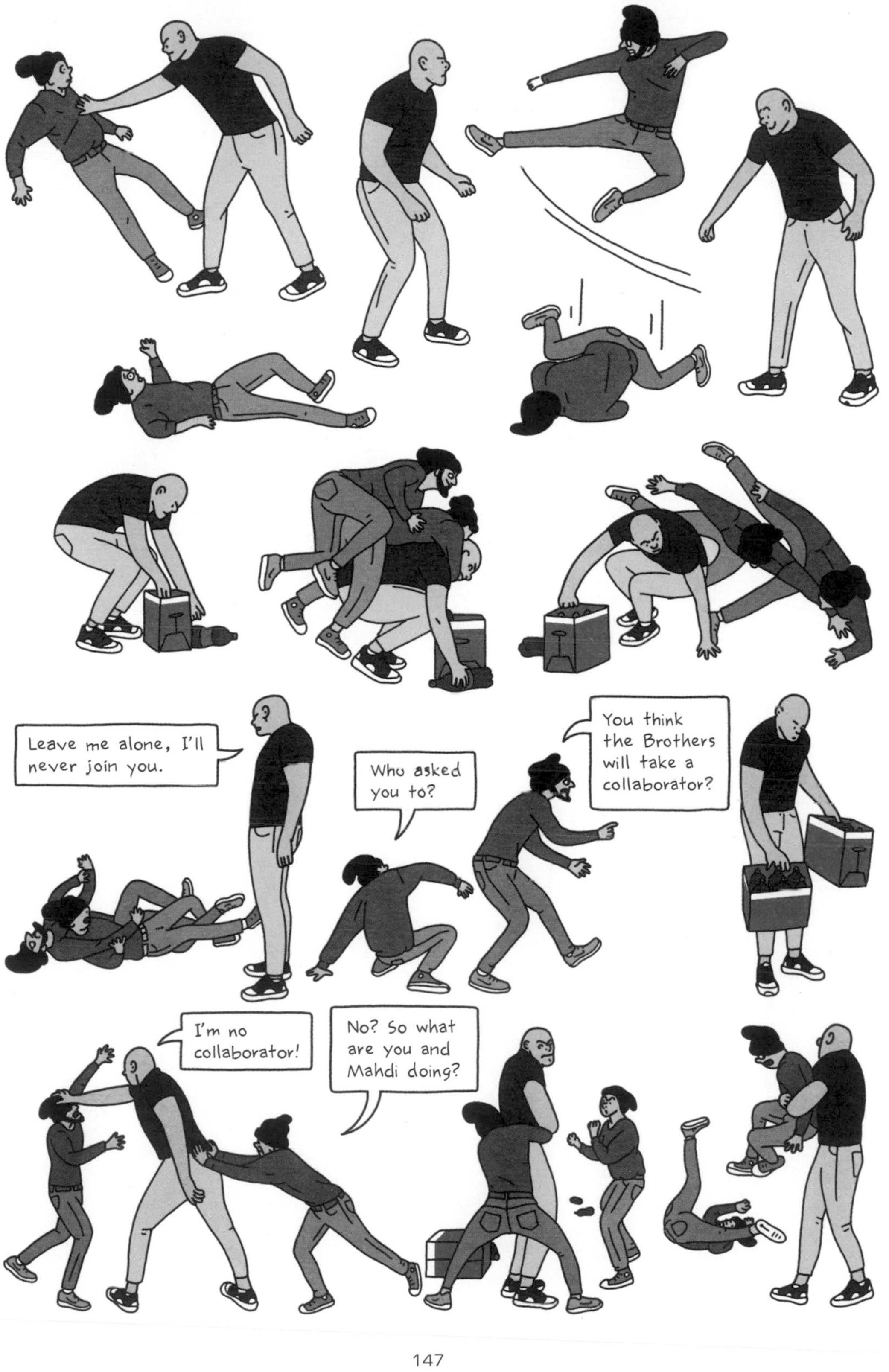
Leave me alone, I'll never join you.
Who asked you to?
You think the Brothers will take a collaborator?
I'm no collaborator!
No? So what are you and Mahdi doing?

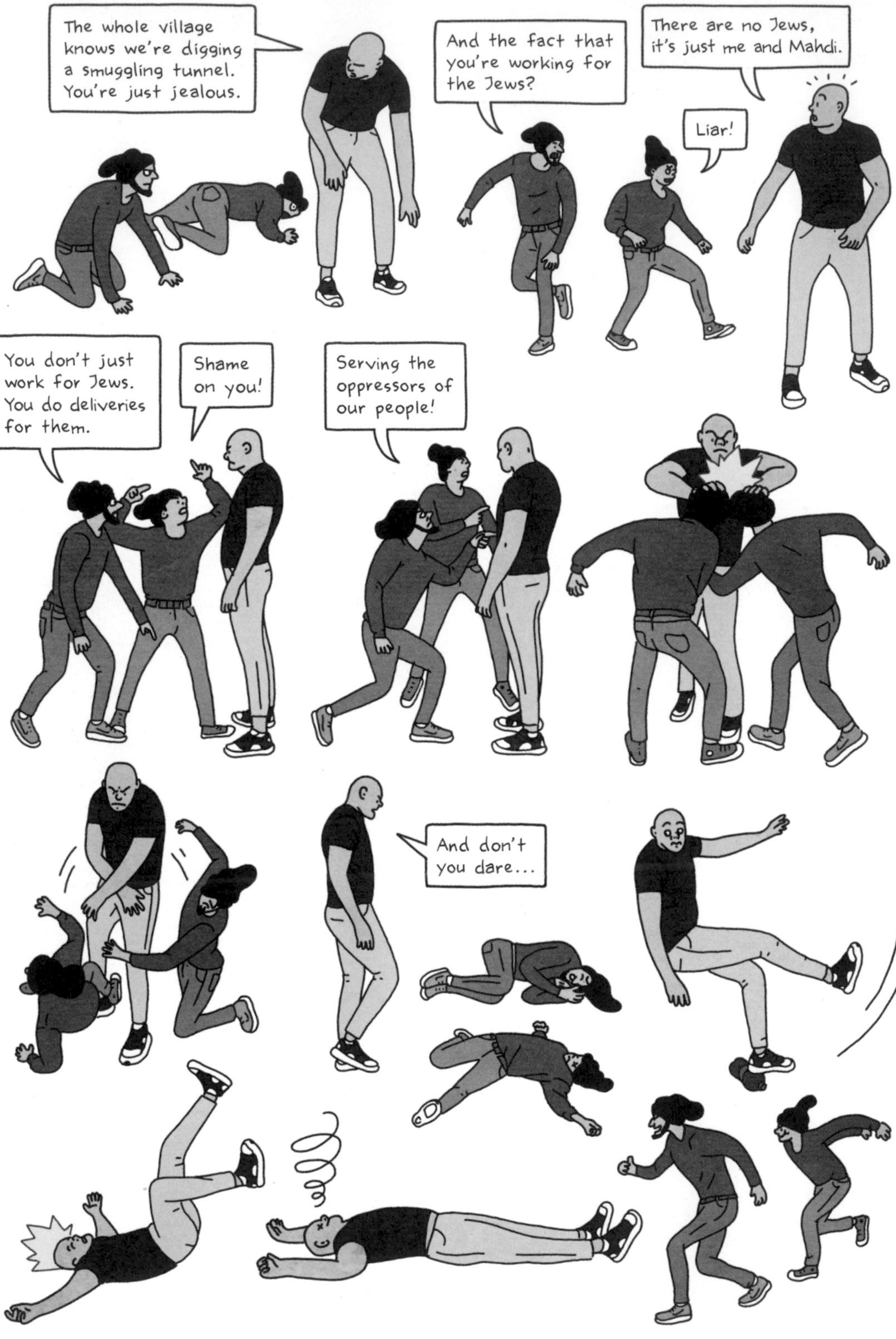
The whole village knows we're digging a smuggling tunnel. You're just jealous.
And the fact that you're working for the Jews?
There are no Jews, it's just me and Mahdi.
Liar!
You don't just work for Jews. You do deliveries for them.
Shame on you!
Serving the oppressors of our people!
And don't you dare...

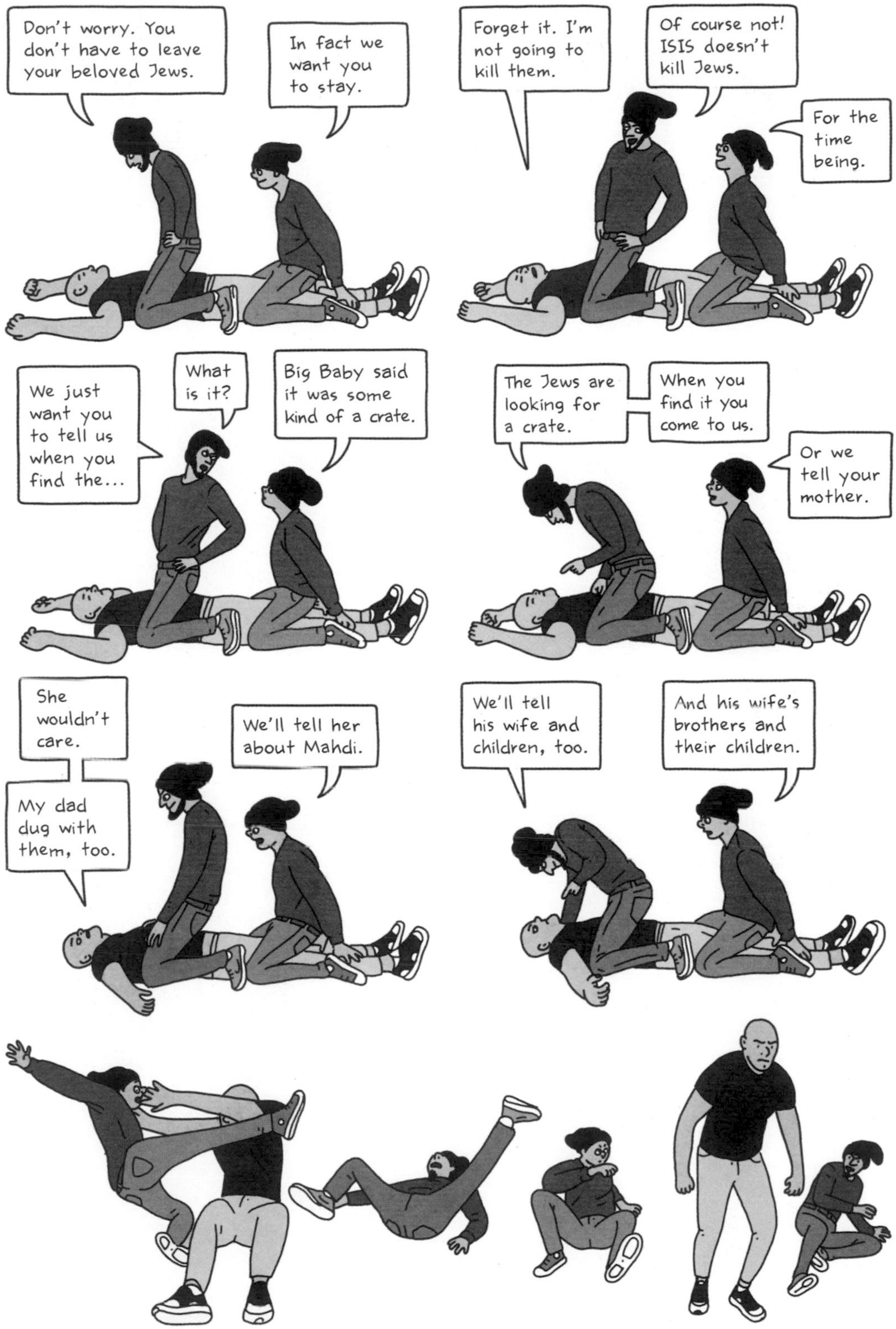

Don't worry. You don't have to leave your beloved Jews.
In fact we want you to stay.
Forget it. I'm not going to kill them.
Of course not! ISIS doesn't kill Jews.
For the time being.
We just want you to tell us when you find the...
What is it?
Big Baby said it was some kind of a crate.
The Jews are looking for a crate.
When you find it you come to us.
Or we tell your mother.
She wouldn't care.
My dad dug with them, too.
We'll tell her about Mahdi.
We'll tell his wife and children, too.
And his wife's brothers and their children.

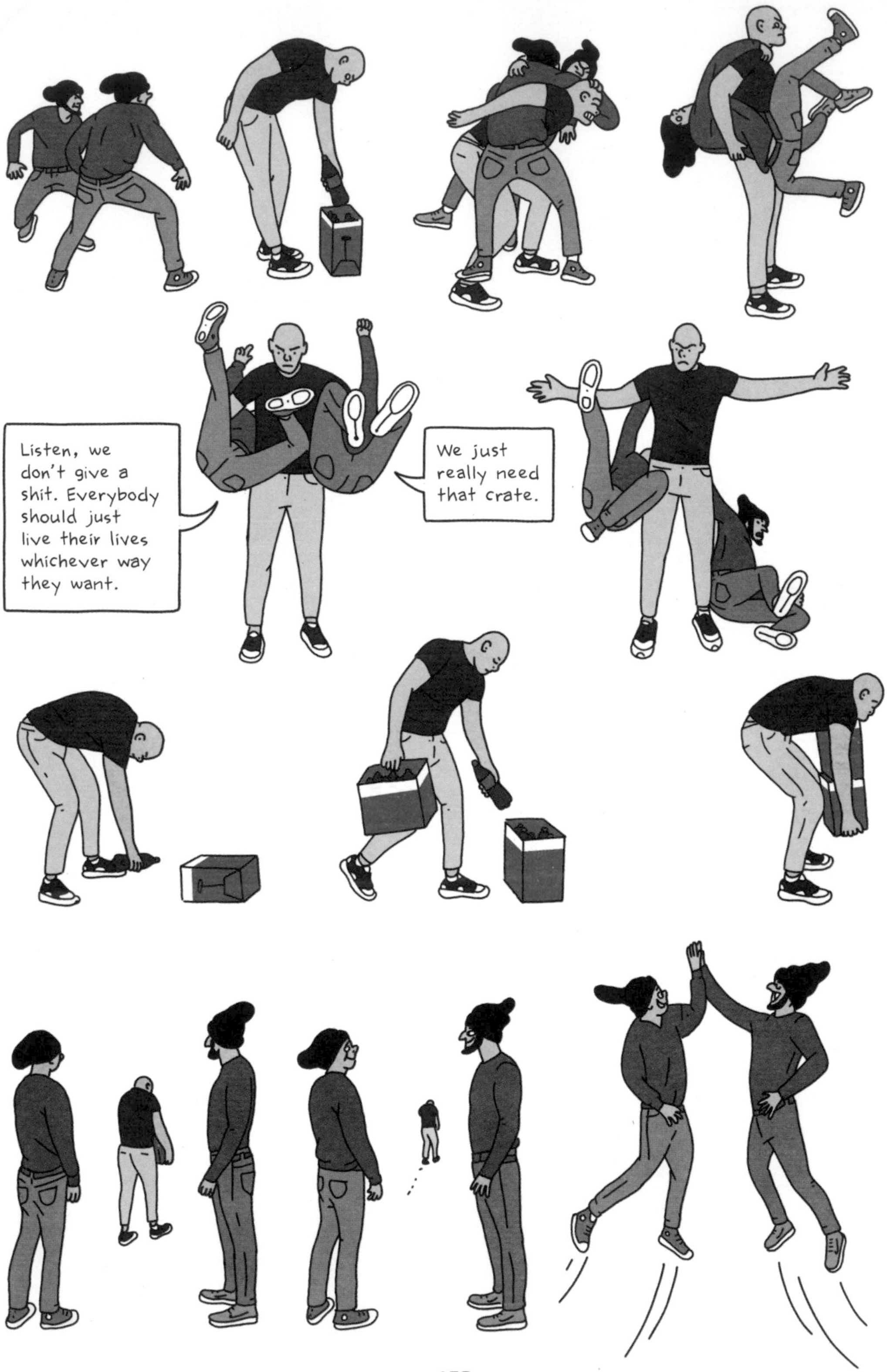
Listen, we don't give a shit. Everybody should just live their lives whichever way they want.
We just really need that crate.

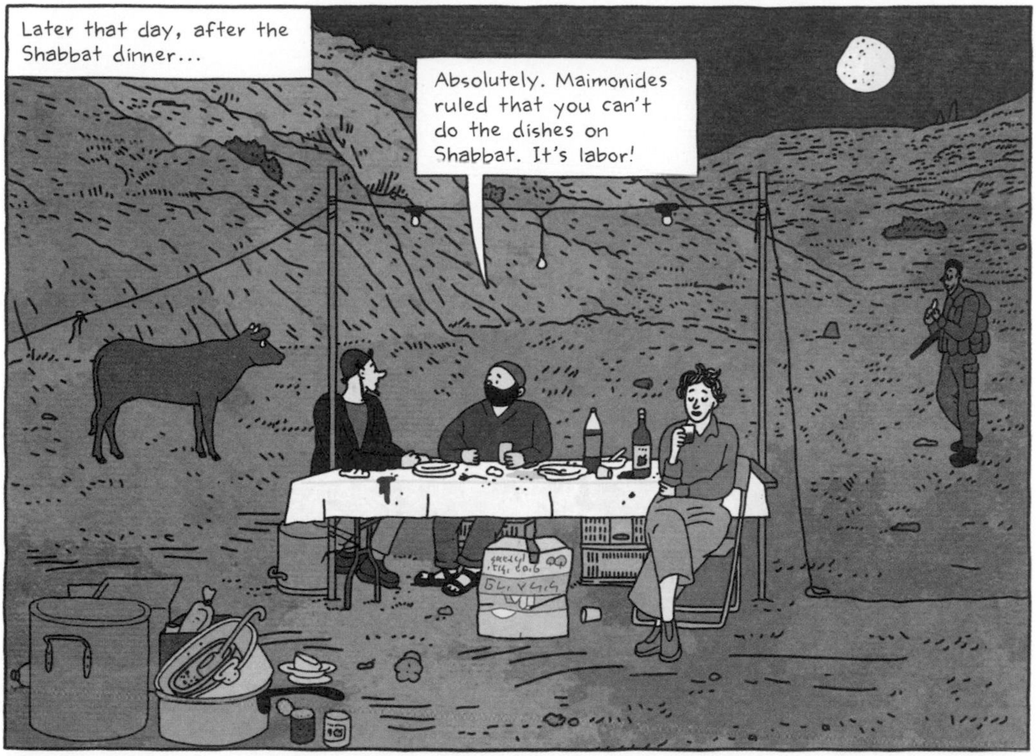
Later that day, after the Shabbat dinner...
Absolutely. Maimonides ruled that you can't do the dishes on Shabbat. It's labor!

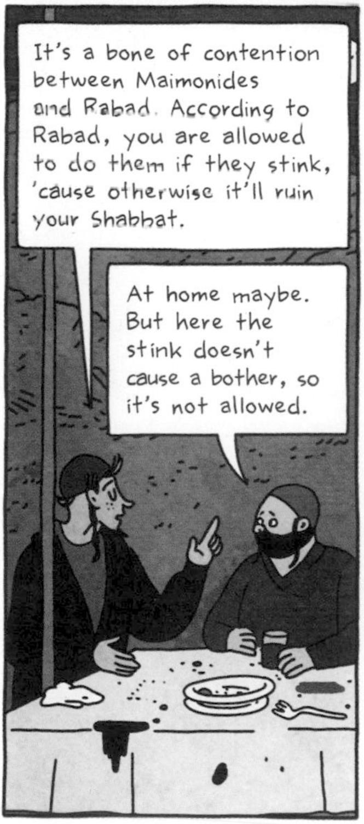
It's a bone of contention between Maimonides and Rabad. According to Rabad, you are allowed to do them if they stink, 'cause otherwise it'll ruin your Shabbat.
At home maybe. But here the stink doesn't cause a bother, so it's not allowed.

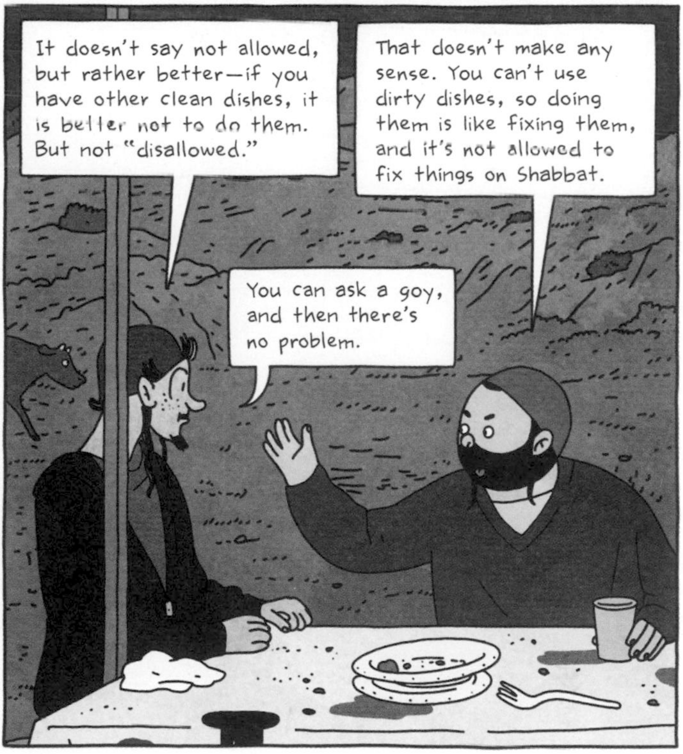
It doesn't say not allowed, but rather better—if you have other clean dishes, it is better not to do them. But not "disallowed."
That doesn't make any sense. You can't use dirty dishes, so doing them is like fixing them, and it's not allowed to fix things on Shabbat.
You can ask a goy, and then there's no problem.

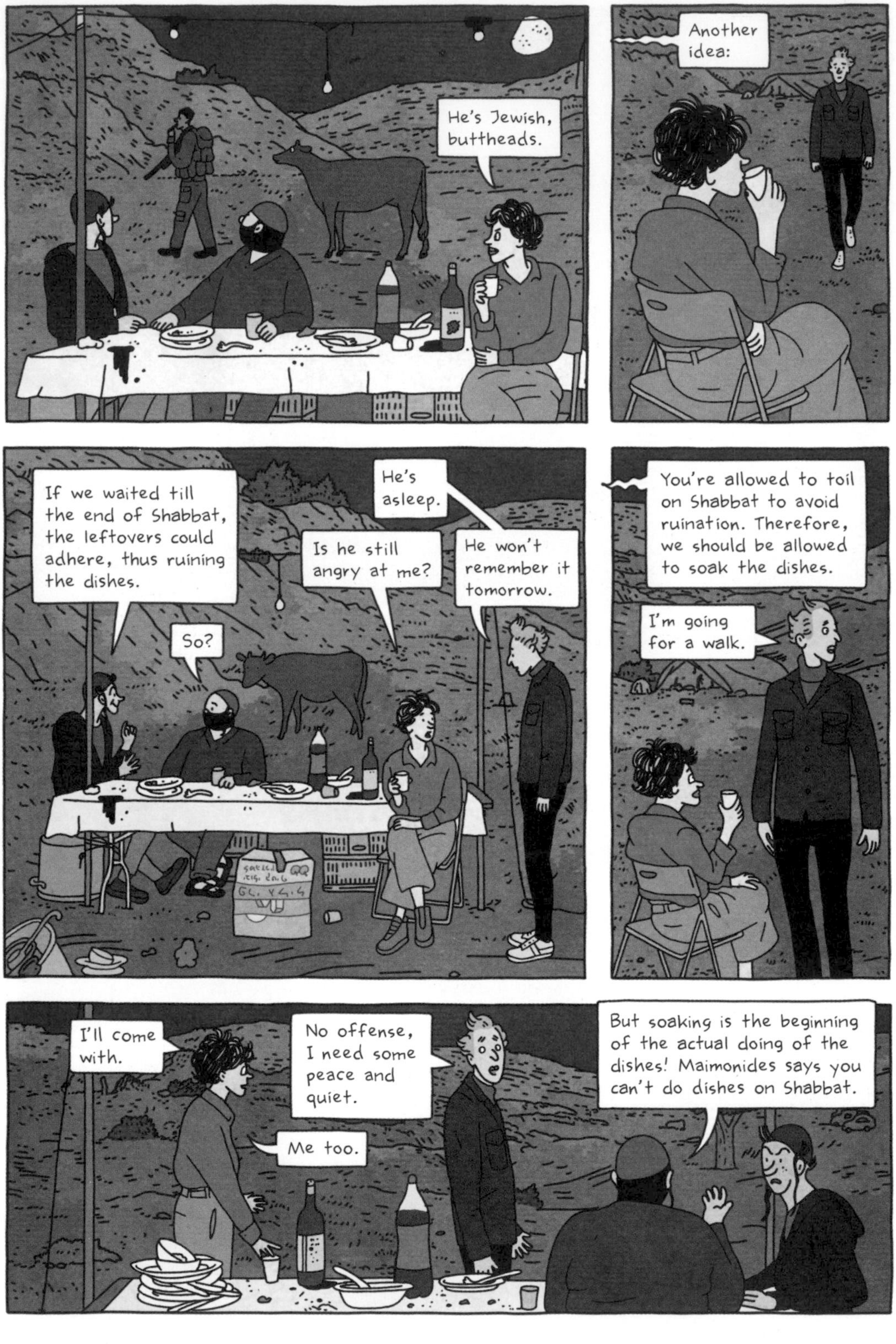
He's Jewish, buttheads.
Another idea:
If we waited till the end of Shabbat, the leftovers could adhere, thus ruining the dishes.
So?
Is he still angry at me?
He's asleep.
He won't remember it tomorrow.
You're allowed to toil on Shabbat to avoid ruination. Therefore, we should be allowed to soak the dishes.
I'm going for a walk.
I'll come with.
No offense, I need some peace and quiet.
Me too.
But soaking is the beginning of the actual doing of the dishes! Maimonides says you can't do dishes on Shabbat.

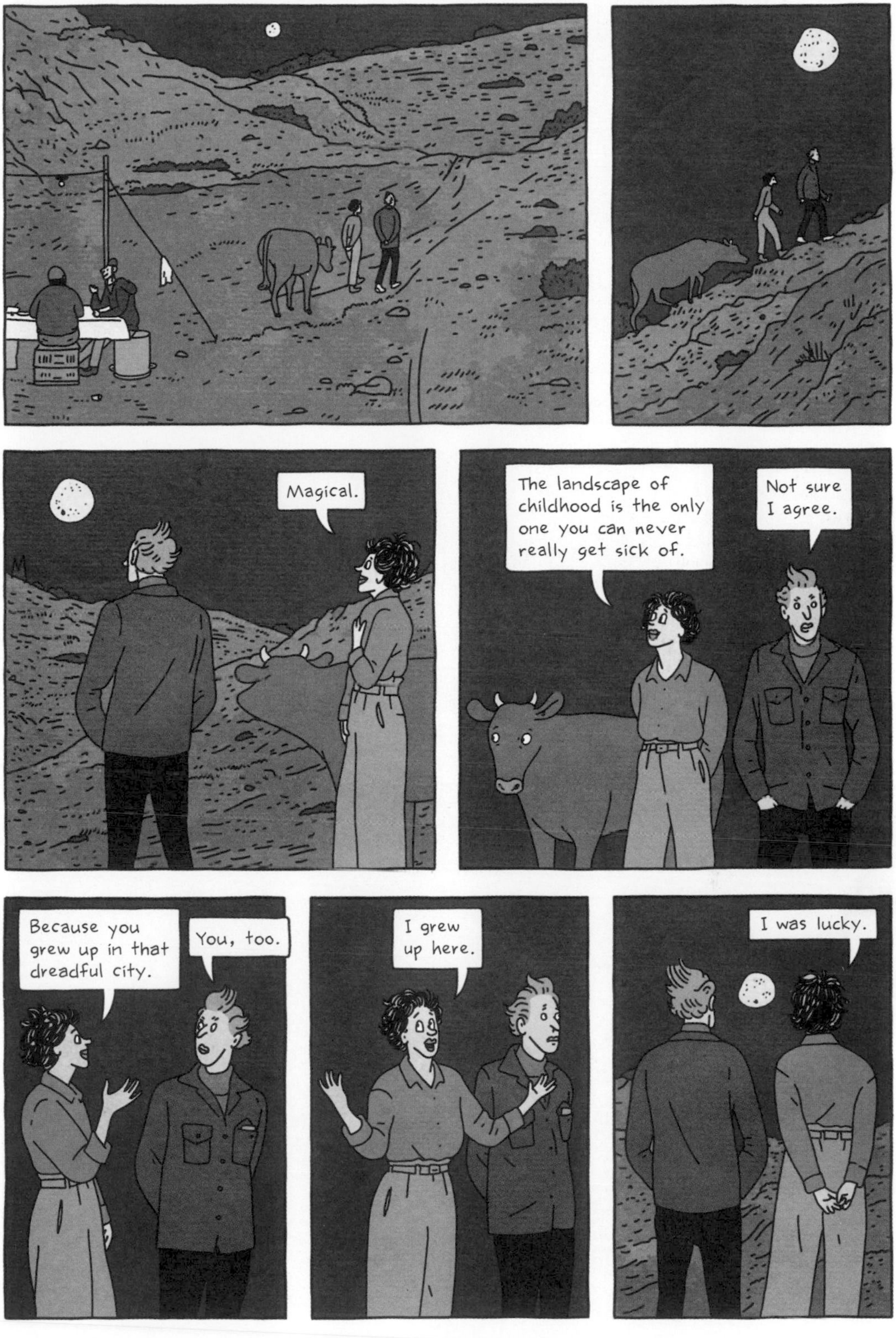

Magical.
The landscape of childhood is the only one you can never really get sick of.
Not sure I agree.
Because you grew up in that dreadful city.
You, too.
I grew up here.
I was lucky.

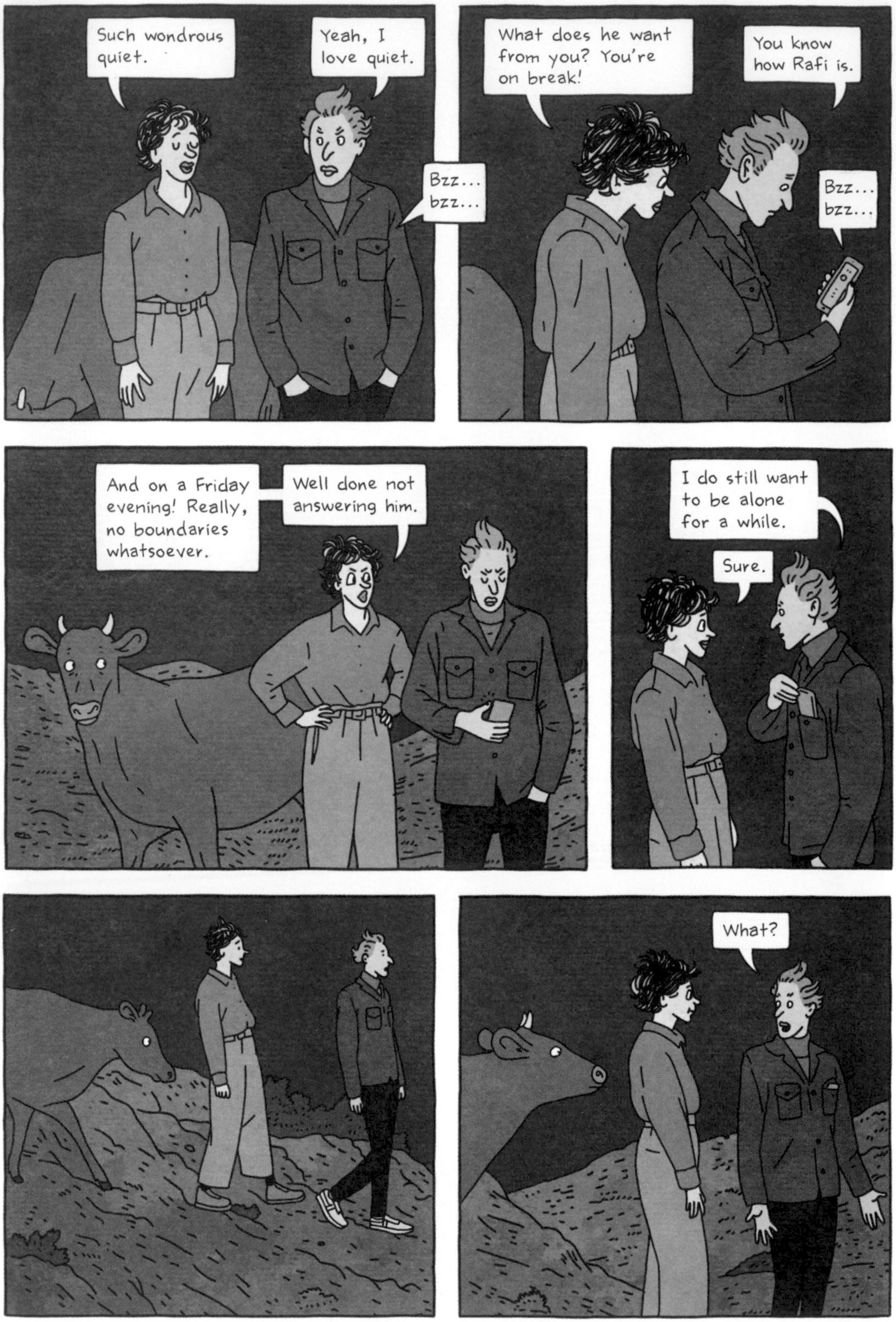
Such wondrous quiet.
Yeah, I love quiet.
Bzz... bzz...
What does he want from you? You're on break!
You know how Rafi is.
Bzz... bzz...
And on a Friday evening! Really, no boundaries whatsoever.
Well done not answering him.
I do still want to be alone for a while.
Sure.
What?

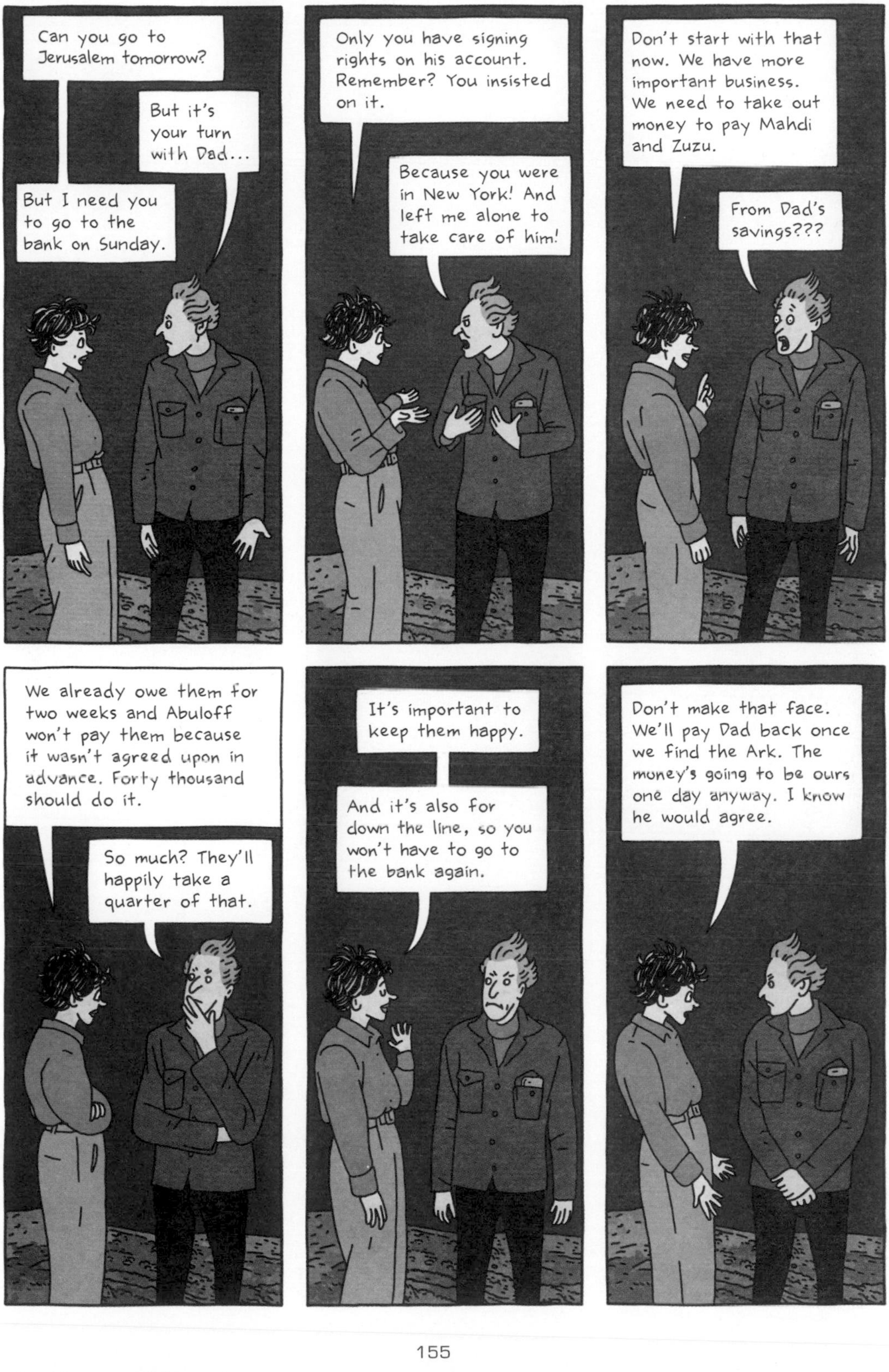
Can you go to Jerusalem tomorrow?
But it's your turn with Dad...
But I need you to go to the bank on Sunday.
Only you have signing rights on his account. Remember? You insisted on it.
Because you were in New York! And left me alone to take care of him!
Don't start with that now. We have more important business. We need to take out money to pay Mahdi and Zuzu.
From Dad's savings???
We already owe them for two weeks and Abuloff won't pay them because it wasn't agreed upon in advance. Forty thousand should do it.
So much? They'll happily take a quarter of that.
It's important to keep them happy.
And it's also for down the line, so you won't have to go to the bank again.
Don't make that face. We'll pay Dad back once we find the Ark. The money's going to be ours one day anyway. I know he would agree.

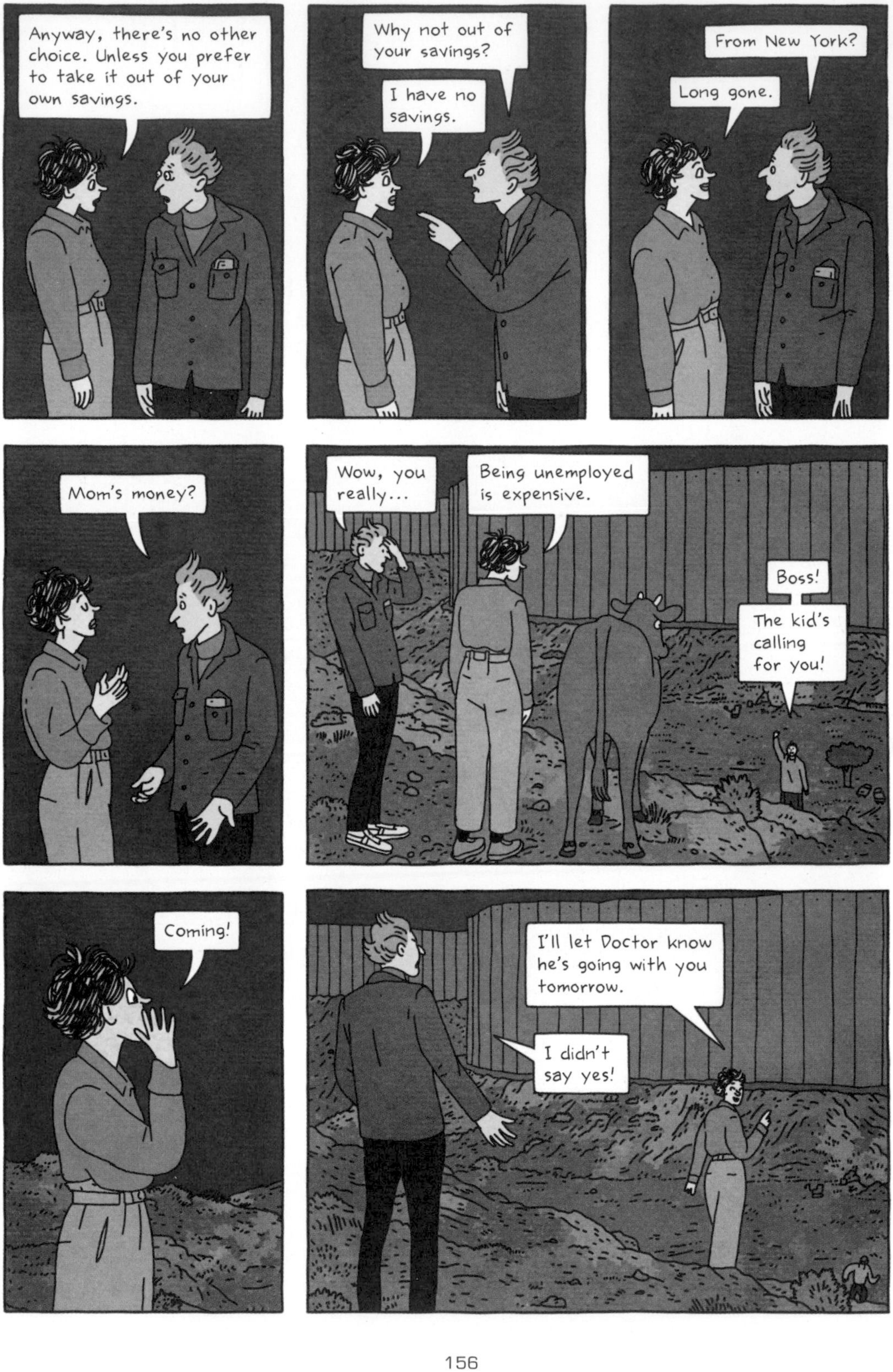
Anyway, there's no other choice. Unless you prefer to take it out of your own savings.
Why not out of your savings?
I have no savings.
From New York?
Long gone.
Mom's money?
Wow, you really...
Being unemployed is expensive.
Boss!
The kid's calling for you!
Coming!
I'll let Doctor know he's going with you tomorrow.
I didn't say yes!

C'mon. A little privacy, please.

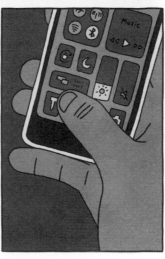

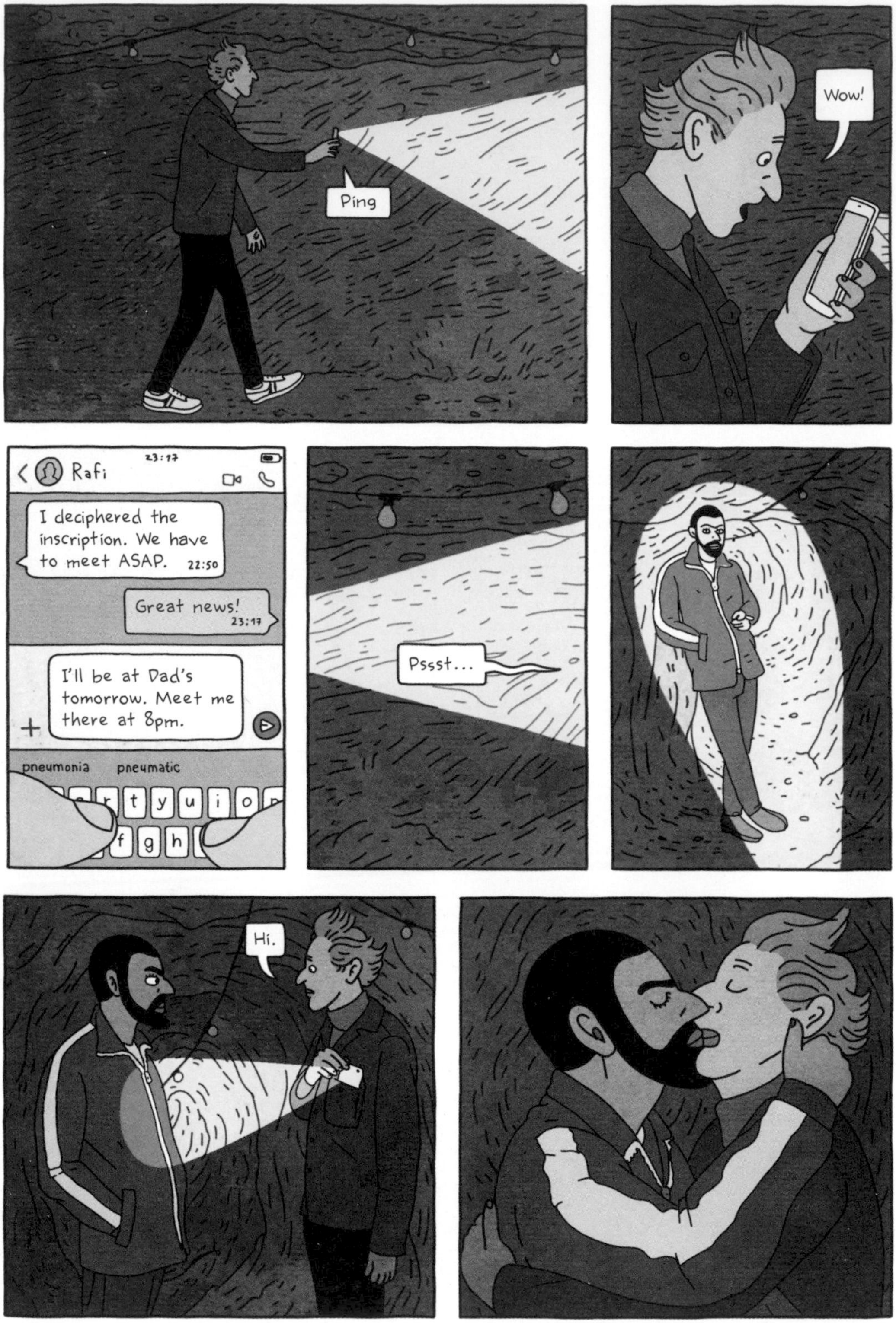
Ping
Wow!
Rafi
23:17
I deciphered the inscription. We have to meet ASAP. 22:50
Great news! 23:17
I'll be at Dad's tomorrow. Meet me there at 8pm.
pneumonia
pneumatic
Pssst...
Hi.

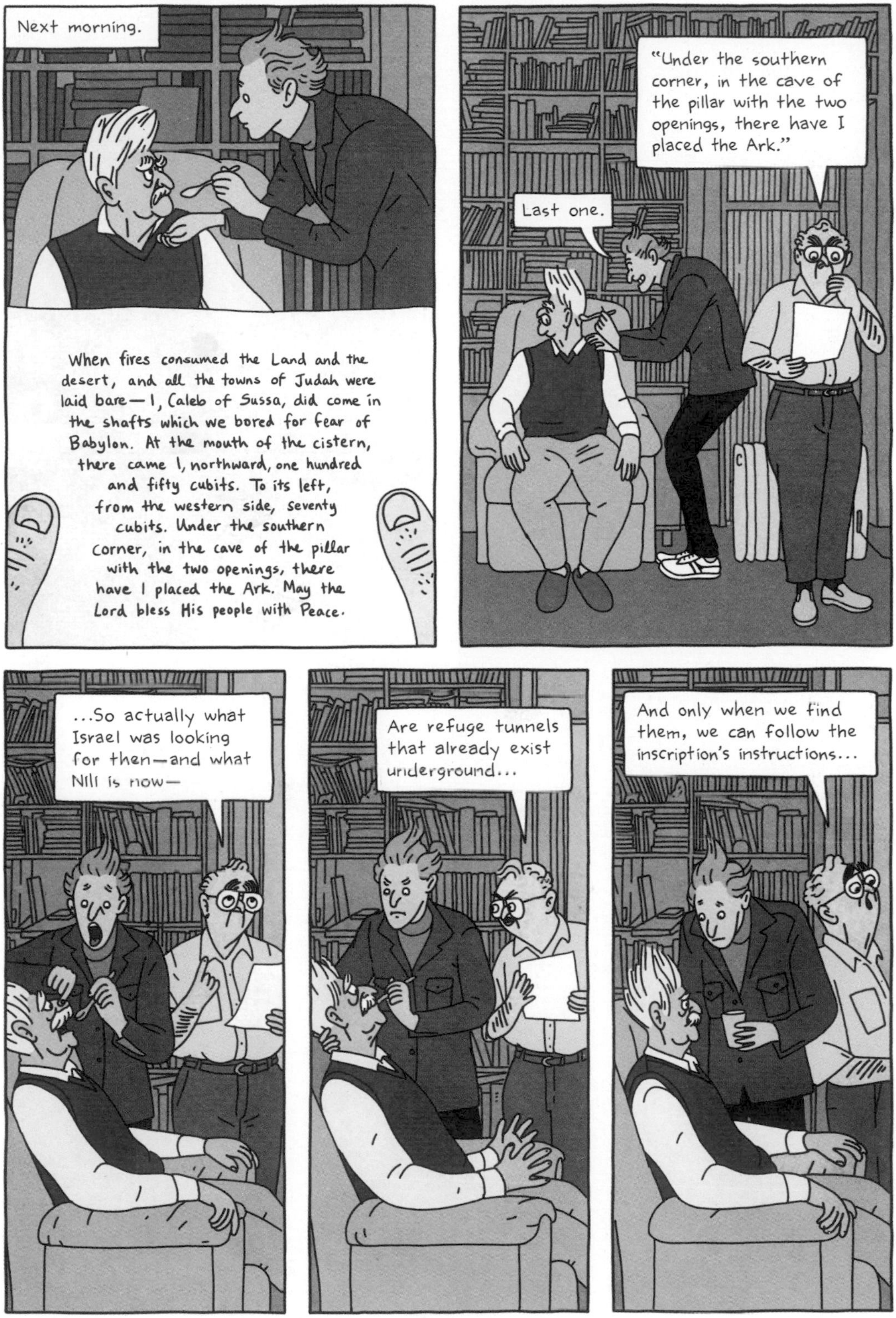
Next morning.
When fires consumed the Land and the desert, and all the towns of Judah were laid bare—I, Caleb of Sussa, did come in the shafts which we bored for fear of Babylon. At the mouth of the cistern, there came I, northward, one hundred and fifty cubits. To its left, from the western side, seventy cubits. Under the southern corner, in the cave of the pillar with the two openings, there have I placed the Ark. May the Lord bless His people with Peace.
"Under the southern corner, in the cave of the pillar with the two openings, there have I placed the Ark."
Last one.
...So actually what Israel was looking for then—and what Nili is now—
Are refuge tunnels that already exist underground...
And only when we find them, we can follow the inscription's instructions...

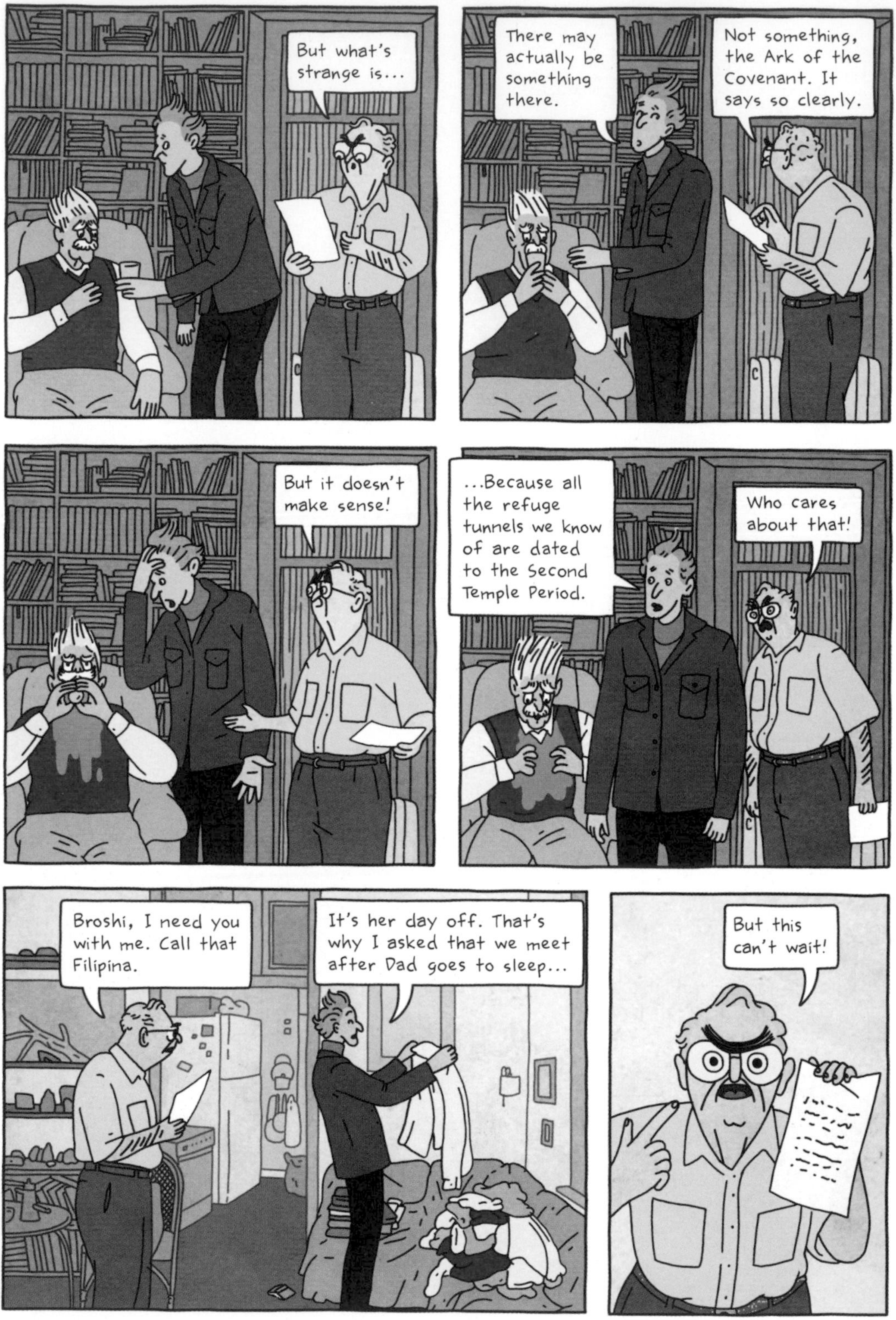
But what's strange is...
There may actually be something there.
Not something, the Ark of the Covenant. It says so clearly.
But it doesn't make sense!
...Because all the refuge tunnels we know of are dated to the Second Temple Period.
Who cares about that!
Broshi, I need you with me. Call that Filipina.
It's her day off. That's why I asked that we meet after Dad goes to sleep...
But this can't wait!

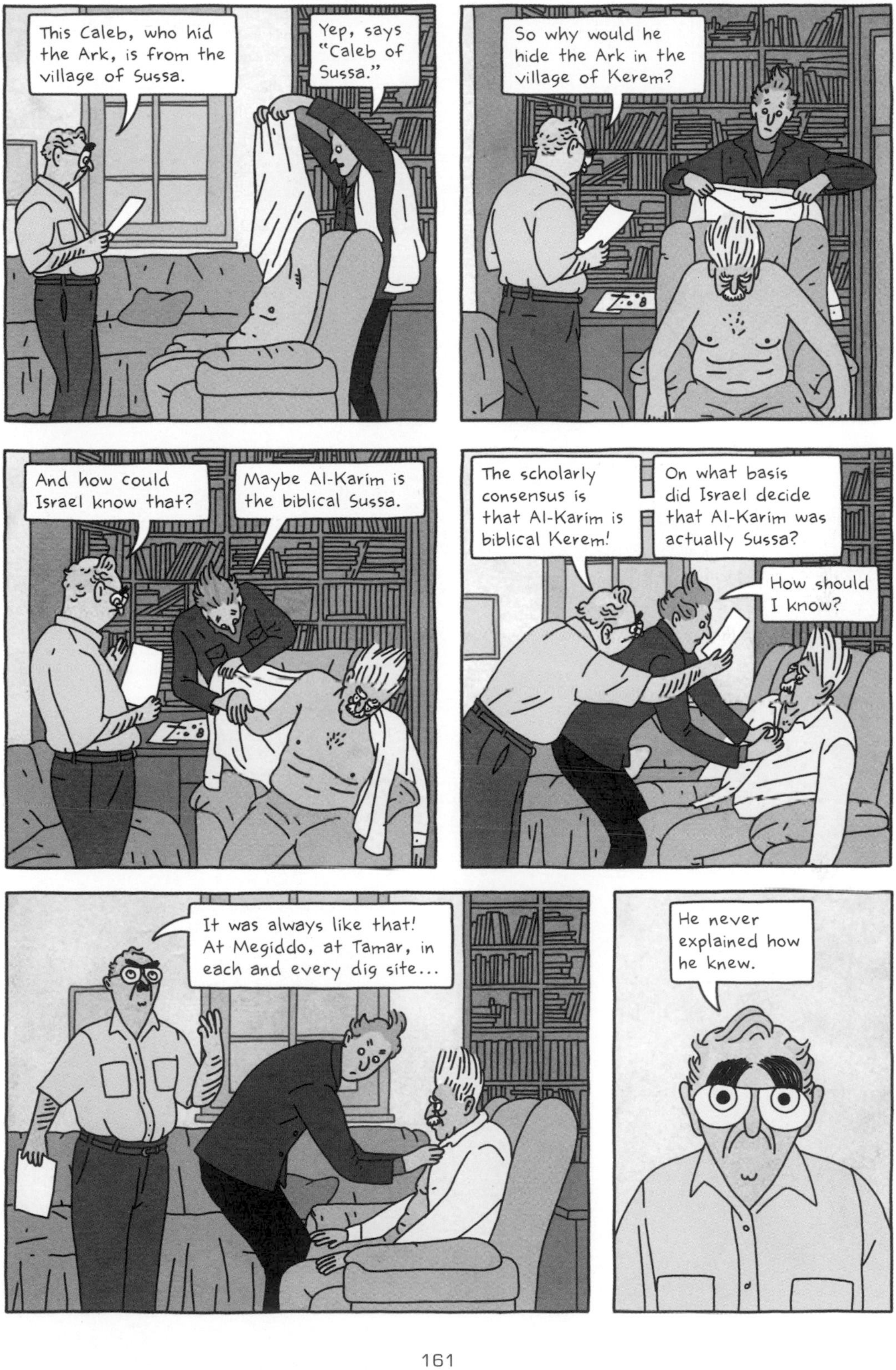

This Caleb, who hid the Ark, is from the village of Sussa.
Yep, says "Caleb of Sussa."
So why would he hide the Ark in the village of Kerem?
And how could Israel know that?
Maybe Al-Karim is the biblical Sussa.
The scholarly consensus is that Al-Karim is biblical Kerem!
On what basis did Israel decide that Al-Karim was actually Sussa?
How should I know?
It was always like that! At Megiddo, at Tamar, in each and every dig site...
He never explained how he knew.

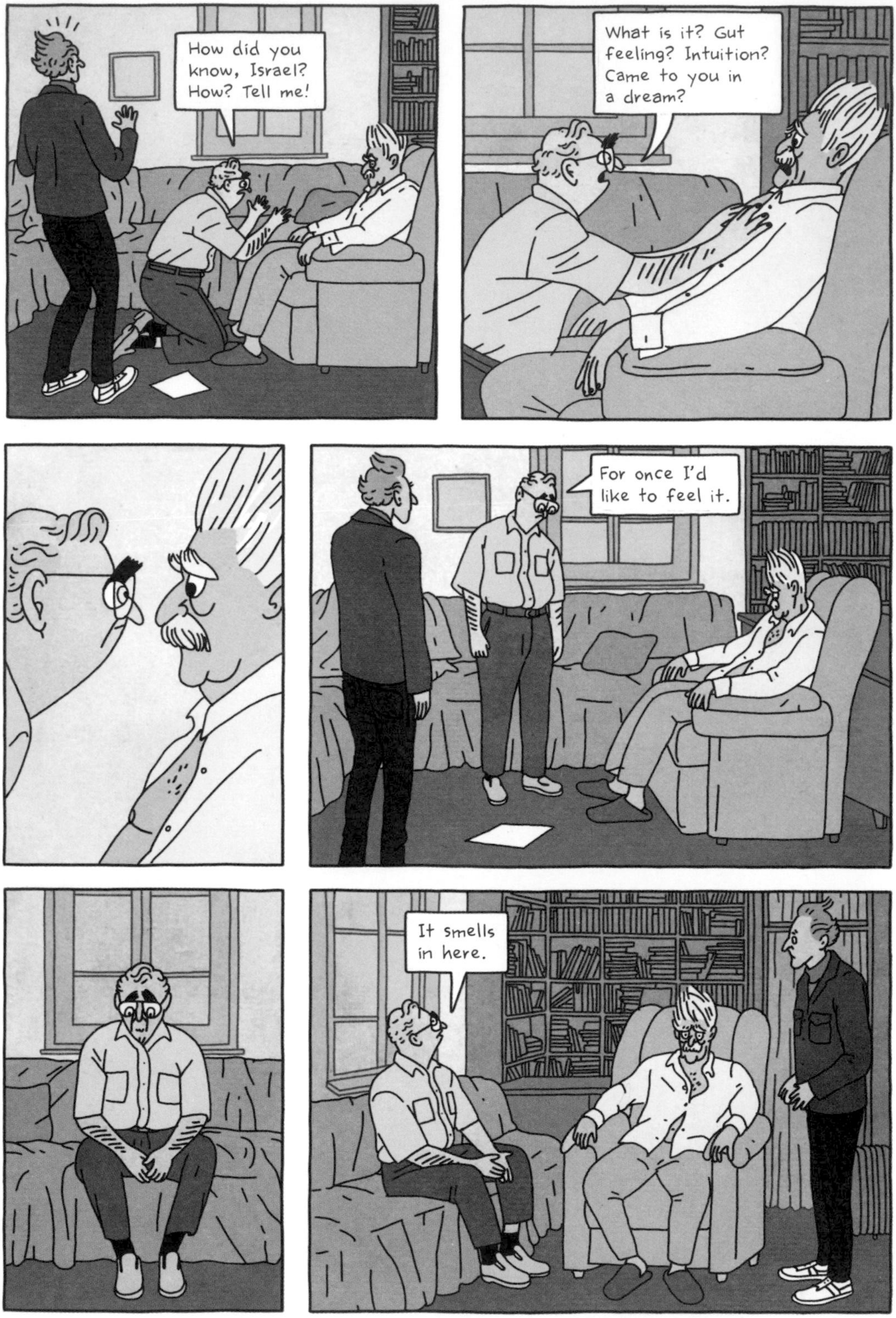
How did you know, Israel? How? Tell me!
What is it? Gut feeling? Intuition? Came to you in a dream?
For once I'd like to feel it.
It smells in here.

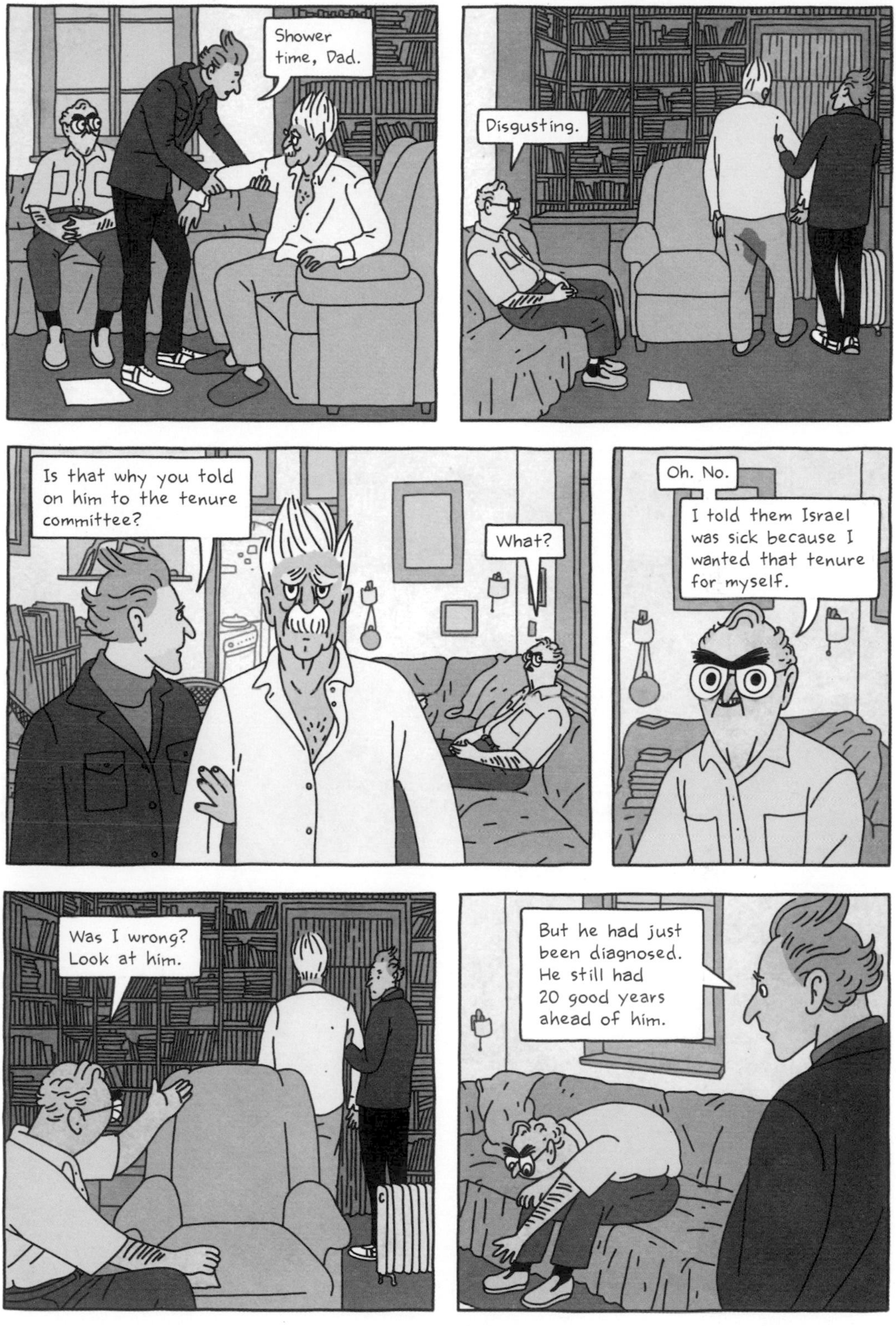
Shower time, Dad.
Disgusting.
Is that why you told on him to the tenure committee?
What?
Oh. No.
I told them Israel was sick because I wanted that tenure for myself.
Was I wrong? Look at him.
But he had just been diagnosed. He still had 20 good years ahead of him.

That's why I suggested that we keep working like before. Me getting tenure would have only helped us both.

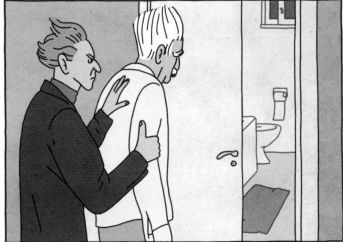

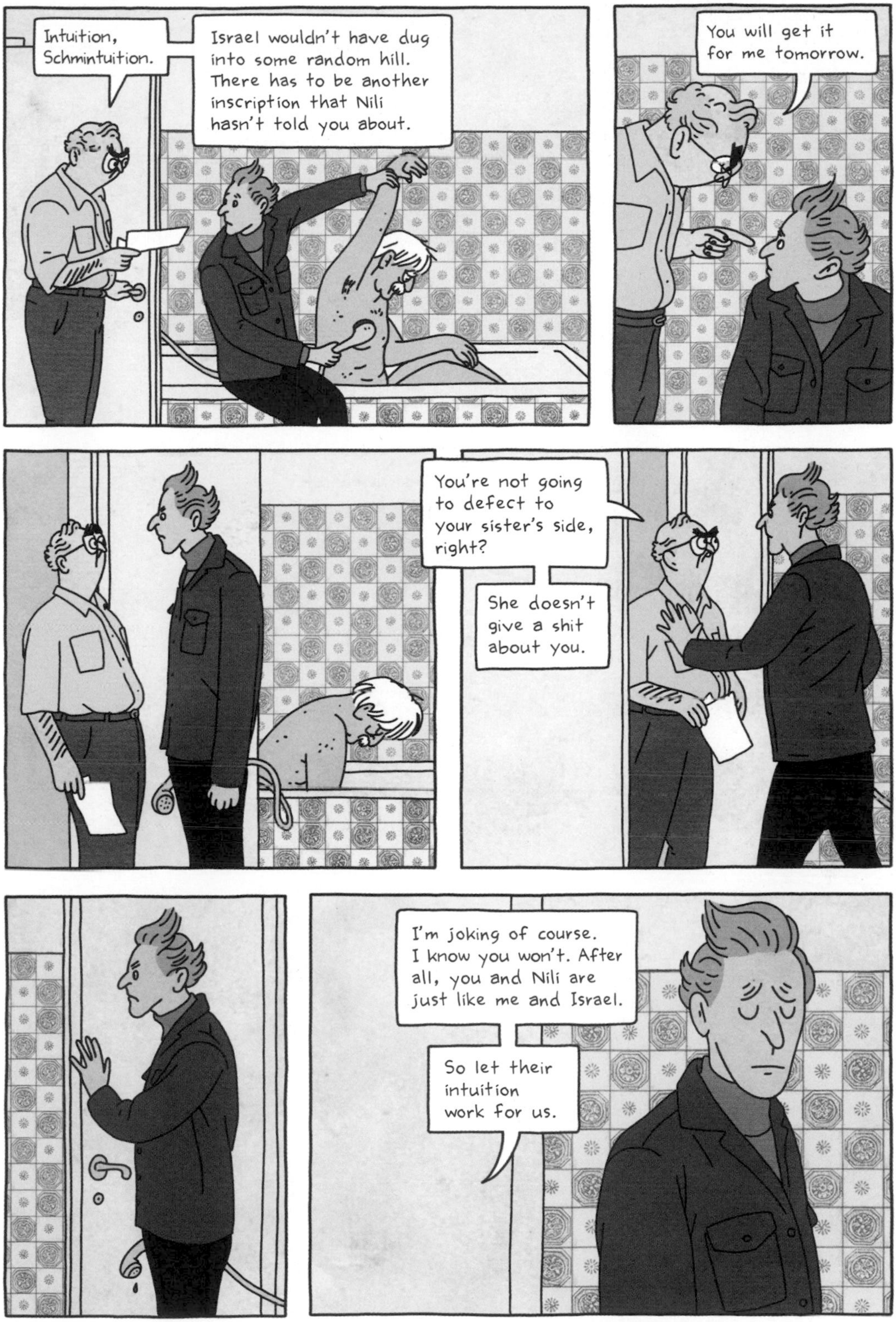
Intuition, Schmintuition.
Israel wouldn't have dug into some random hill. There has to be another inscription that Nili hasn't told you about.
You will get it for me tomorrow.
You're not going to defect to your sister's side, right?
She doesn't give a shit about you.
I'm joking of course. I know you won't. After all, you and Nili are just like me and Israel.
So let their intuition work for us.

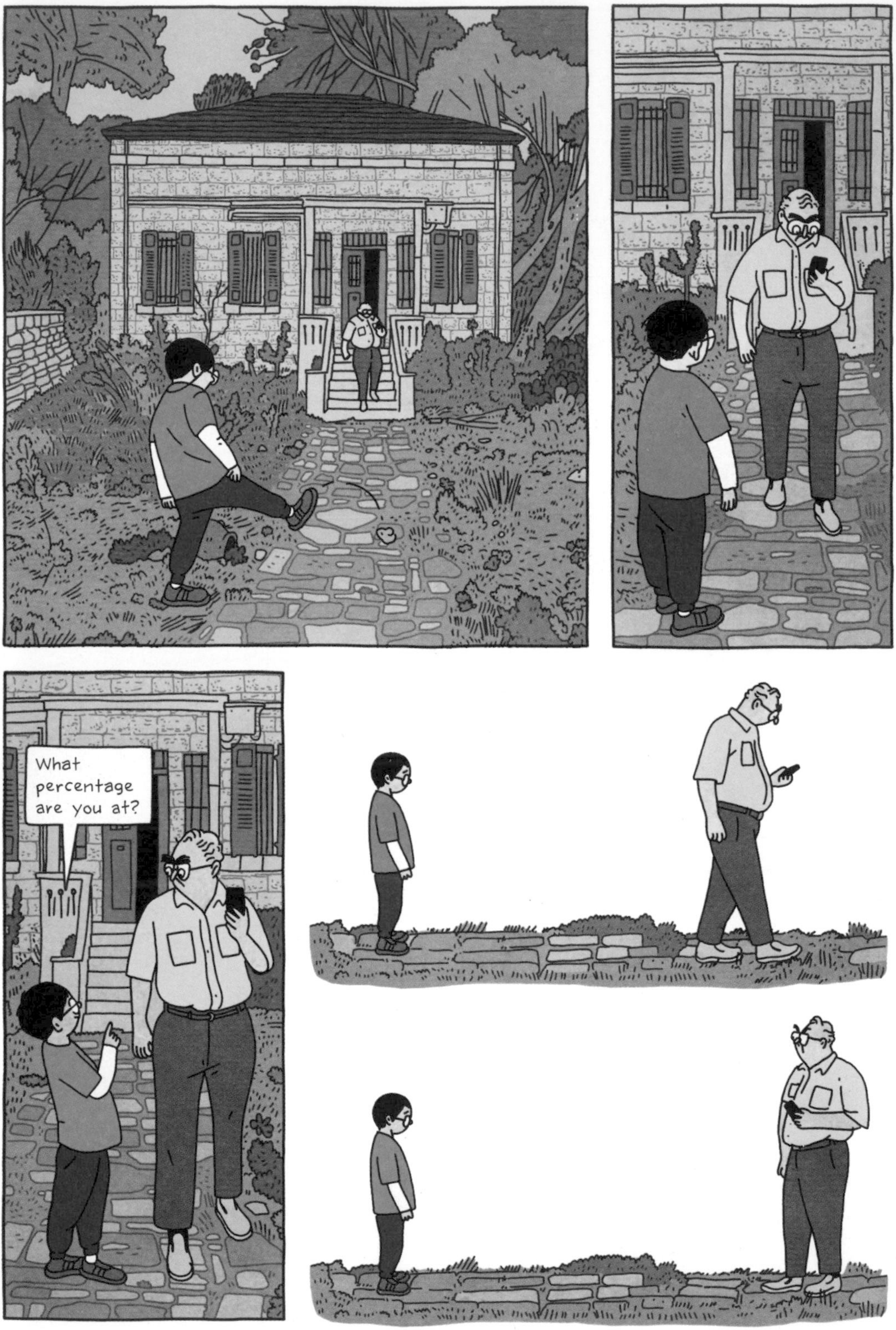
What percentage are you at?

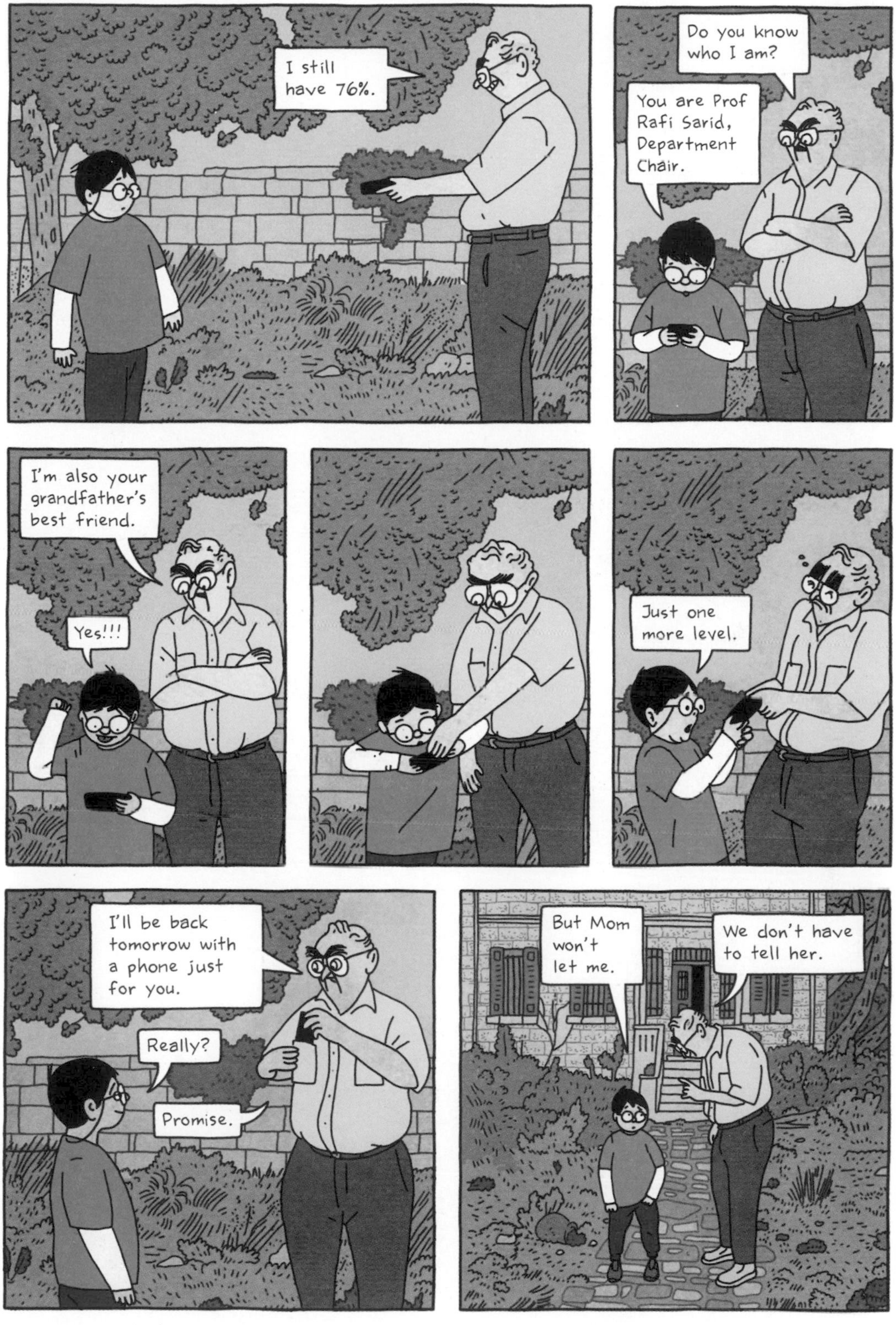
I still have 76%.
Do you know who I am?
You are Prof Rafi Sarid, Department Chair.
I'm also your grandfather's best friend.
Yes!!!
Just one more level.
I'll be back tomorrow with a phone just for you.
Really?
Promise.
But Mom won't let me.
We don't have to tell her.

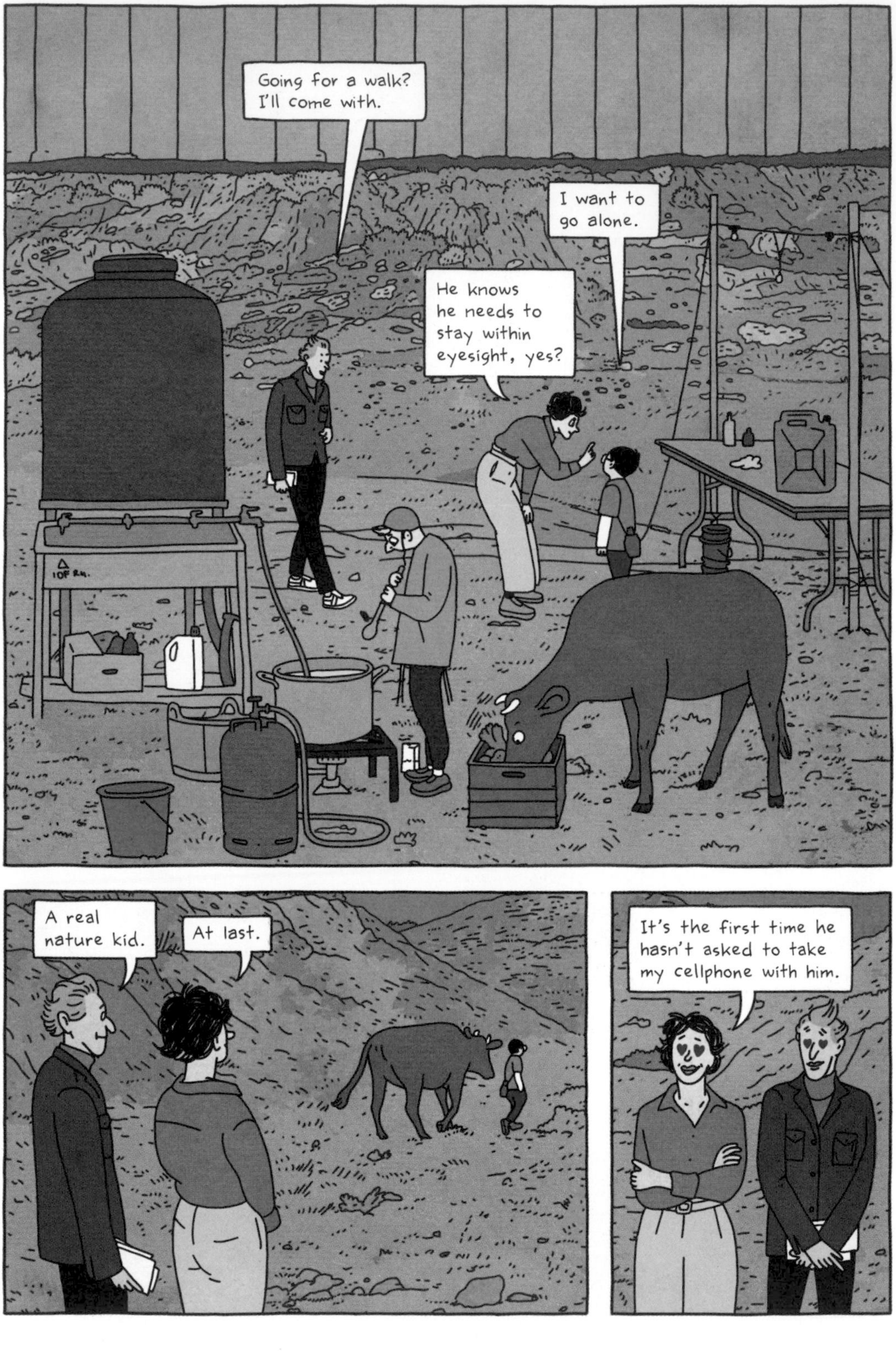
Going for a walk? I'll come with.
I want to go alone.
He knows he needs to stay within eyesight, yes?
A real nature kid.
At last.
It's the first time he hasn't asked to take my cellphone with him.

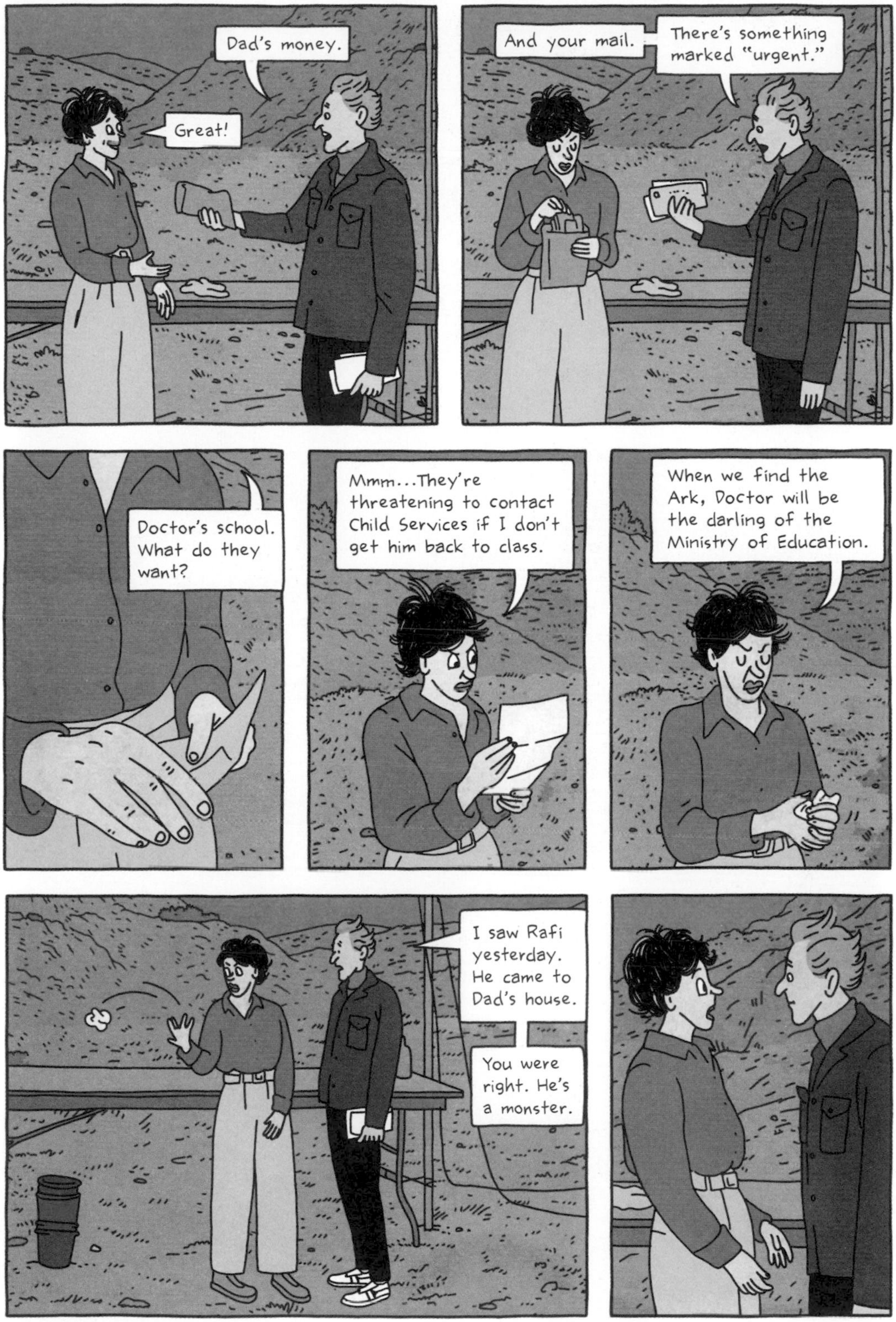
Dad's money.
Great!
And your mail.
There's something marked "urgent."
Doctor's school. What do they want?
Mmm...They're threatening to contact Child Services if I don't get him back to class.
When we find the Ark, Doctor will be the darling of the Ministry of Education.
I saw Rafi yesterday. He came to Dad's house.
You were right. He's a monster.

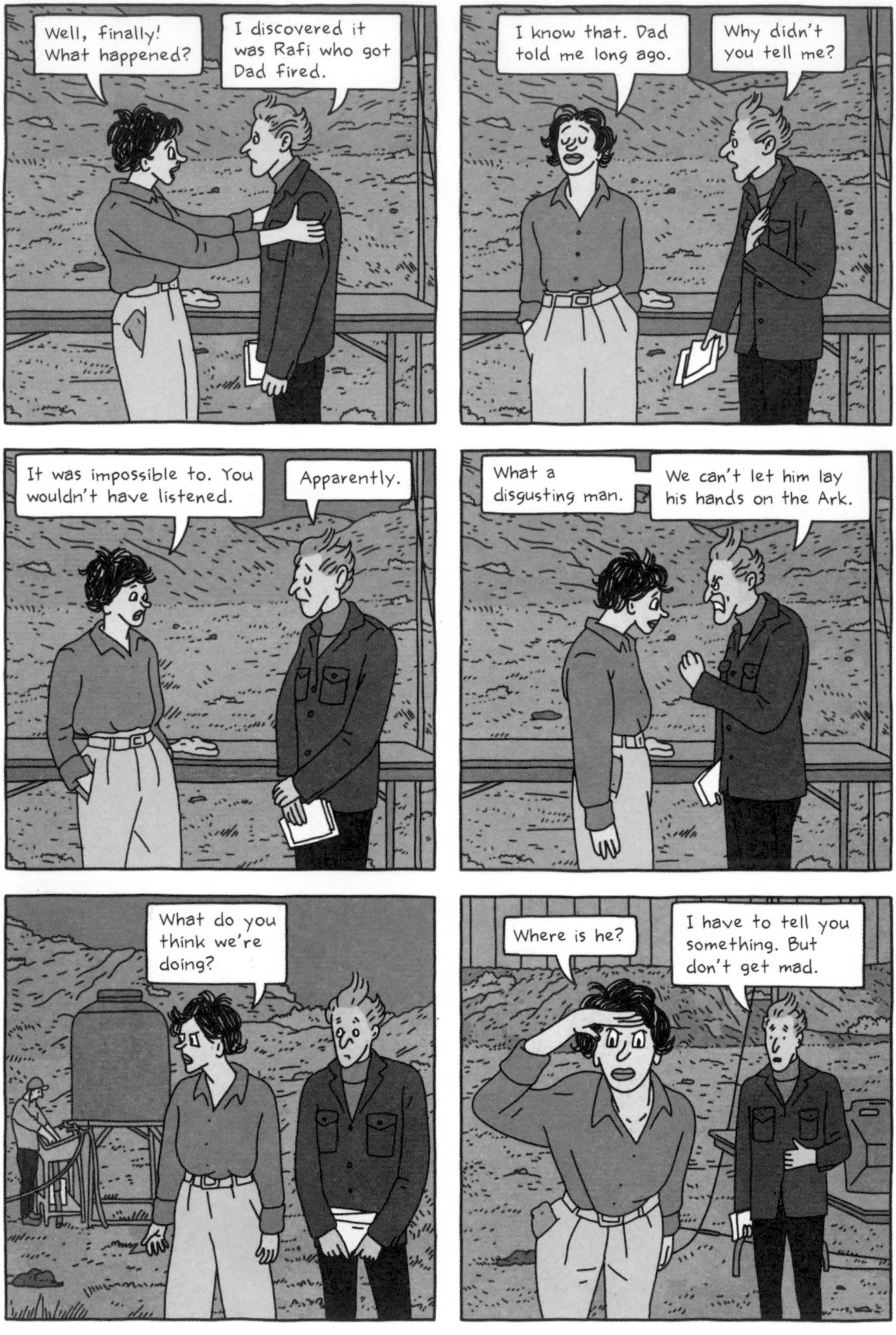
Well, finally! What happened?
I discovered it was Rafi who got Dad fired.
I know that. Dad told me long ago.
Why didn't you tell me?
It was impossible to. You wouldn't have listened.
Apparently.
What a disgusting man.
We can't let him lay his hands on the Ark.
What do you think we're doing?
Where is he?
I have to tell you something. But don't get mad.

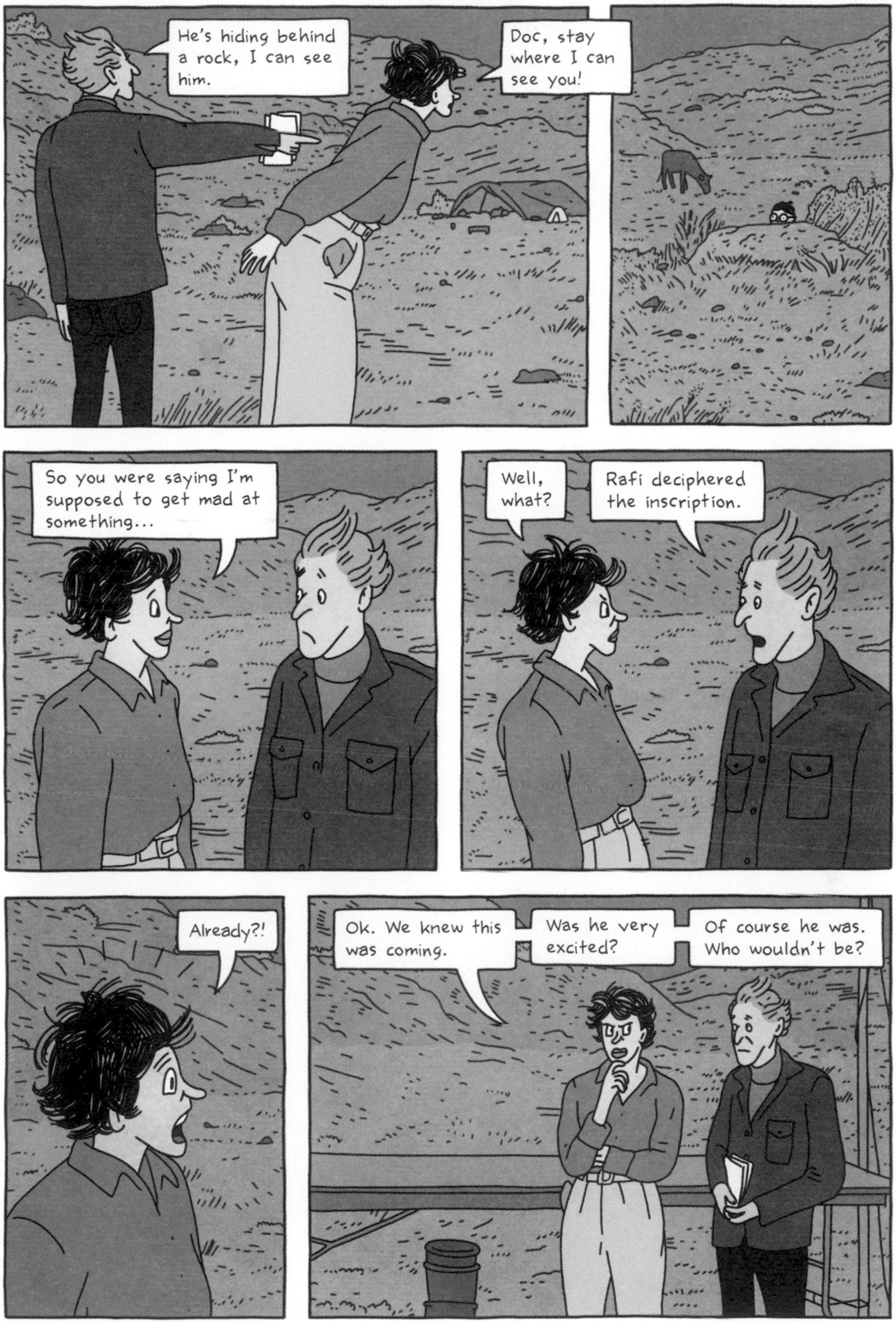
He's hiding behind a rock, I can see him.
Doc, stay where I can see you!
So you were saying I'm supposed to get mad at something...
Well, what?
Rafi deciphered the inscription.
Already?!
Ok. We knew this was coming.
Was he very excited?
Of course he was. Who wouldn't be?

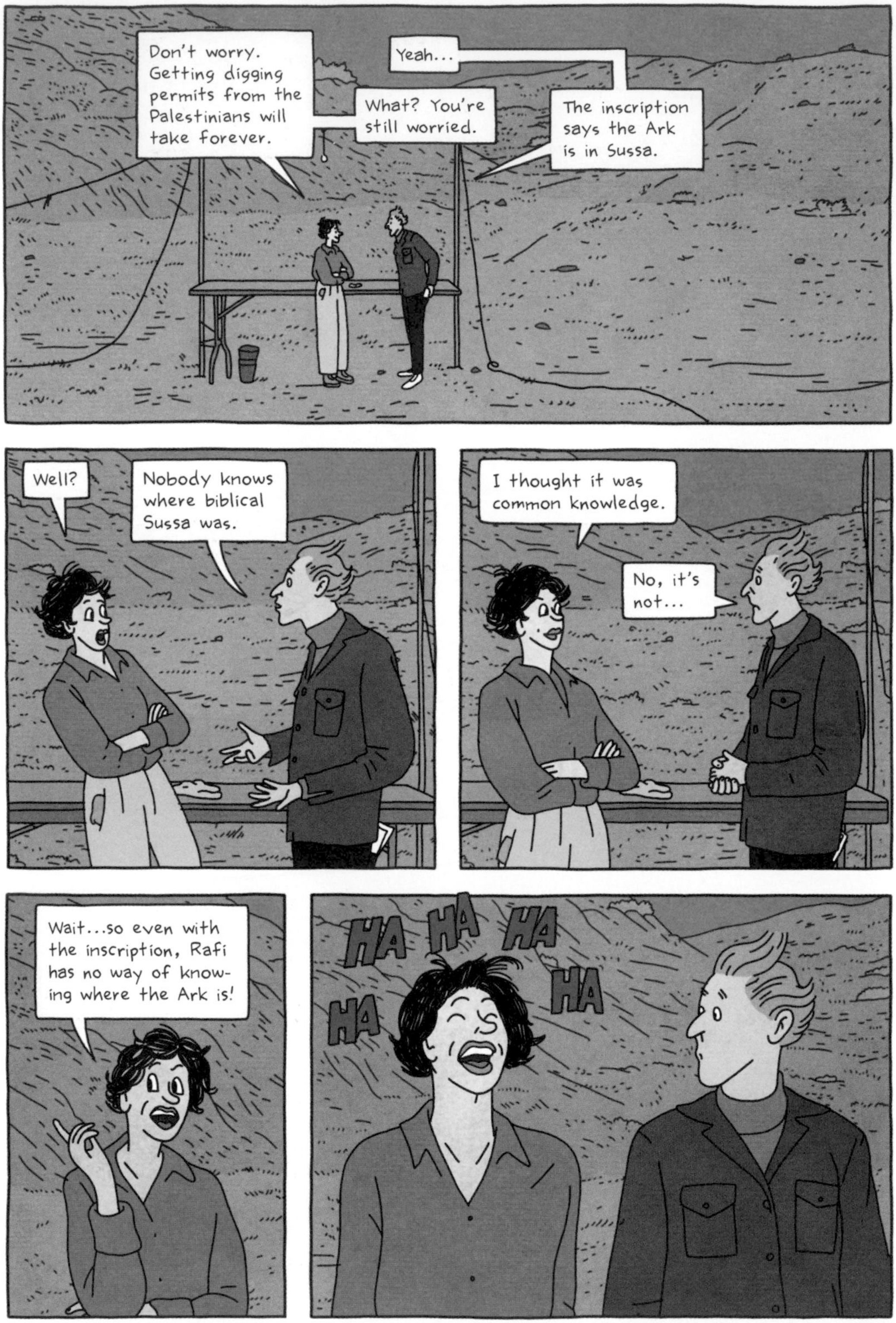
Don't worry. Getting digging permits from the Palestinians will take forever.
What? You're still worried.
Yeah...
The inscription says the Ark is in Sussa.
Well?
Nobody knows where biblical Sussa was.
I thought it was common knowledge.
No, it's not...
Wait...so even with the inscription, Rafi has no way of knowing where the Ark is!
HA HA HA HA HA

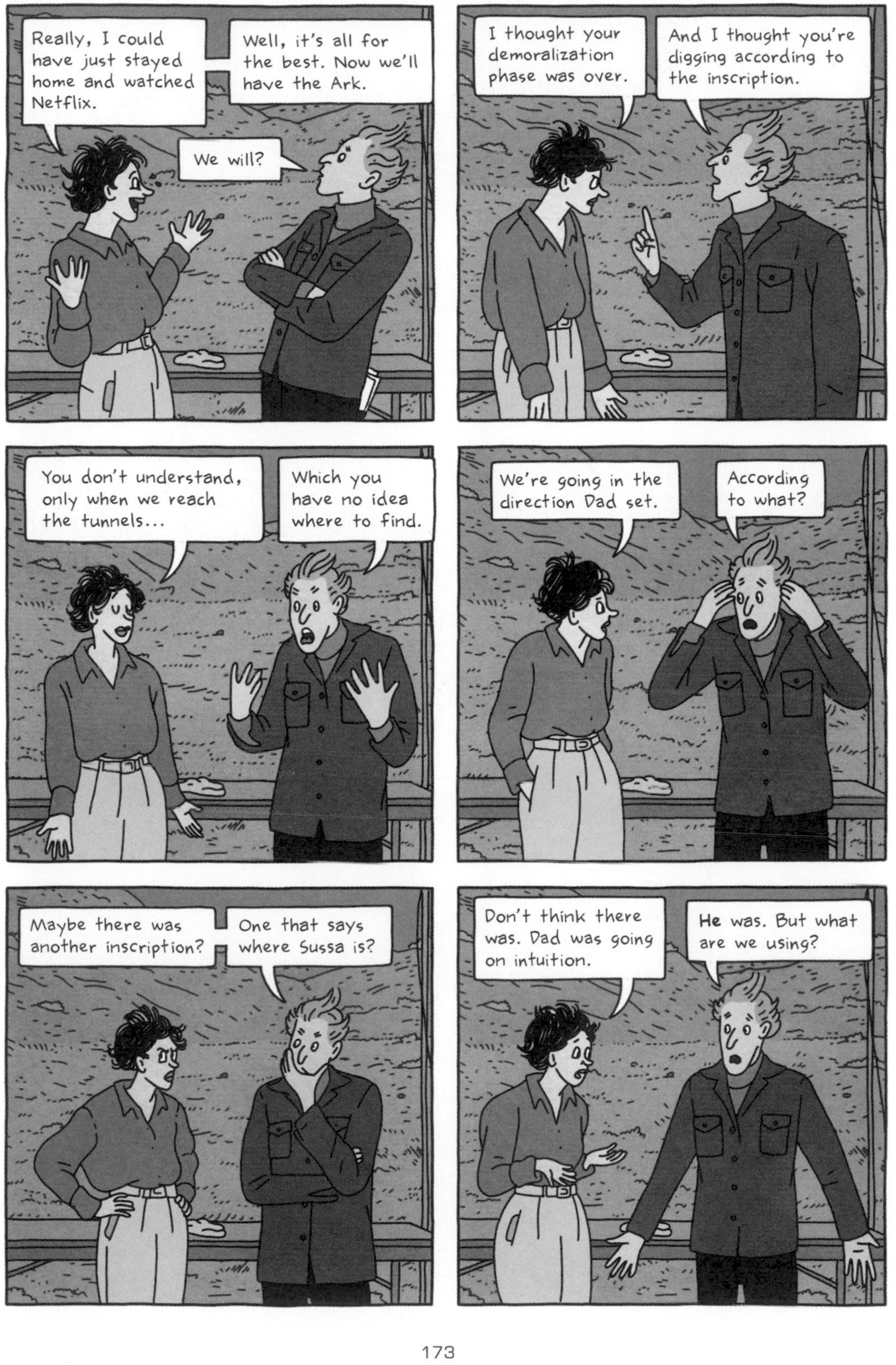

Really, I could have just stayed home and watched Netflix.
Well, it's all for the best. Now we'll have the Ark.
We will?
I thought your demoralization phase was over.
And I thought you're digging according to the inscription.
You don't understand, only when we reach the tunnels...
Which you have no idea where to find.
We're going in the direction Dad set.
According to what?
Maybe there was another inscription?
One that says where Sussa is?
Don't think there was. Dad was going on intuition.
He was. But what are we using?

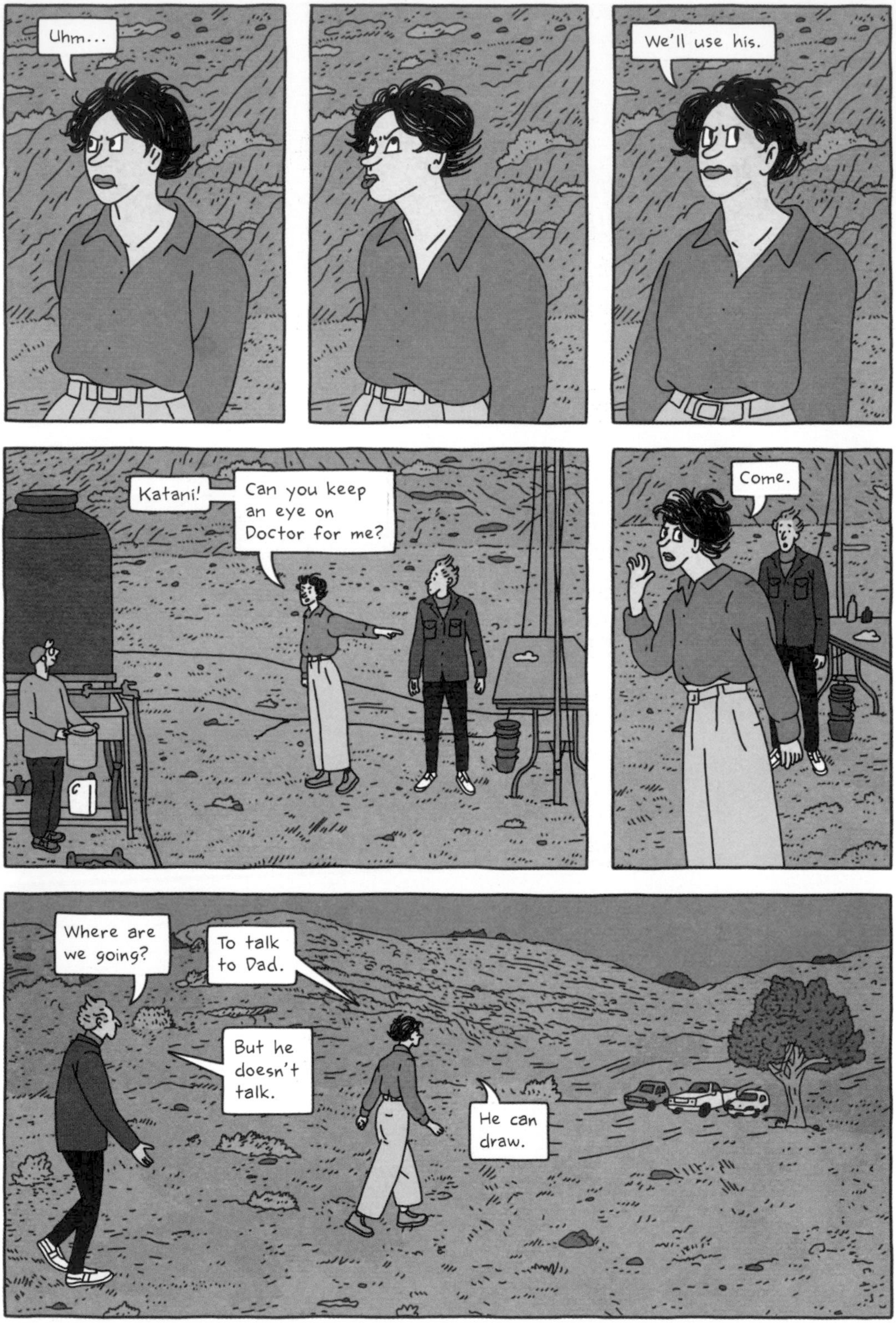
Uhm...
We'll use his.
Katani!
Can you keep an eye on Doctor for me?
Come.
Where are we going?
To talk to Dad.
But he doesn't talk.
He can draw.

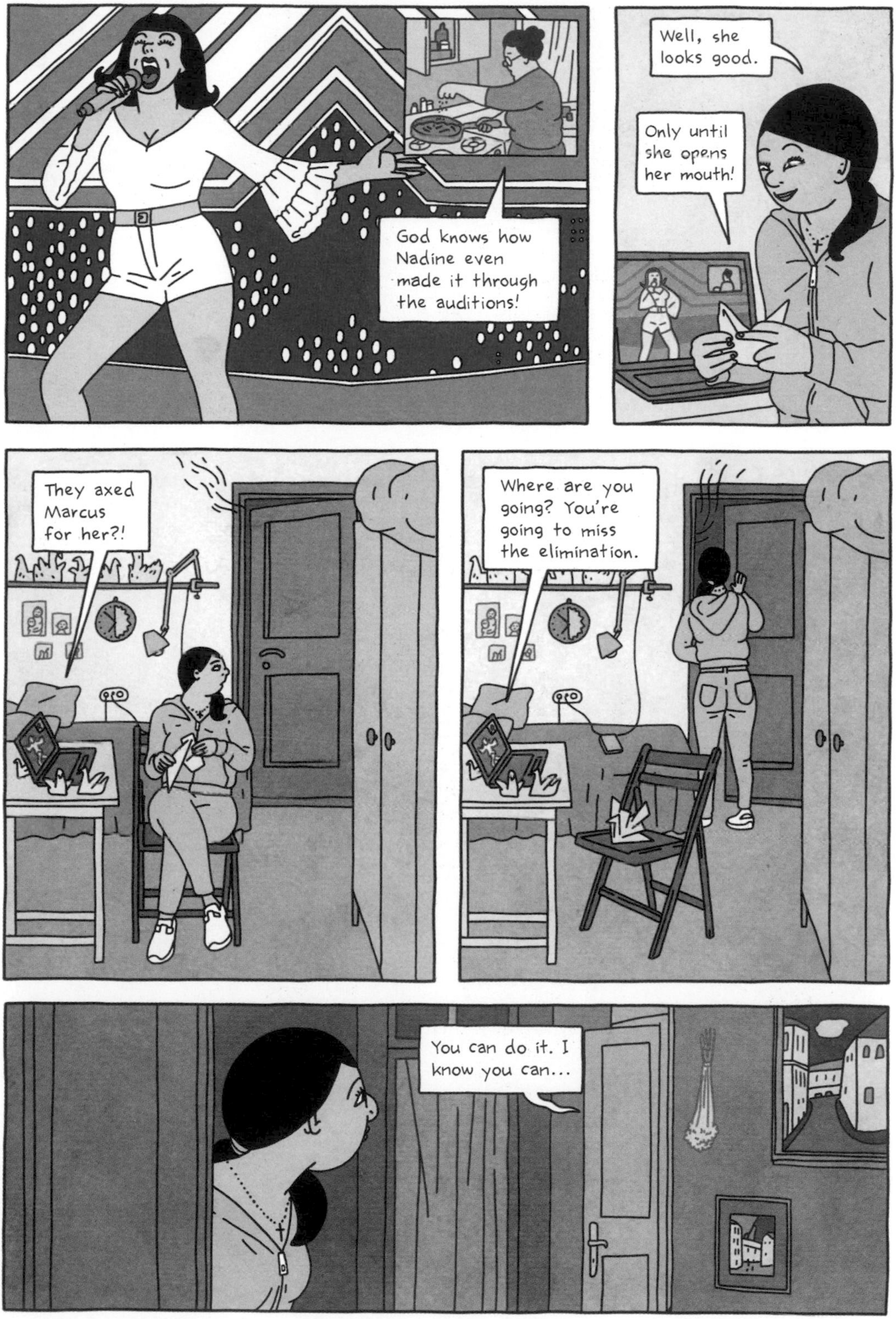
God knows how Nadine even made it through the auditions!
Well, she looks good.
Only until she opens her mouth!
They axed Marcus for her?!
Where are you going? You're going to miss the elimination.
You can do it. I know you can...

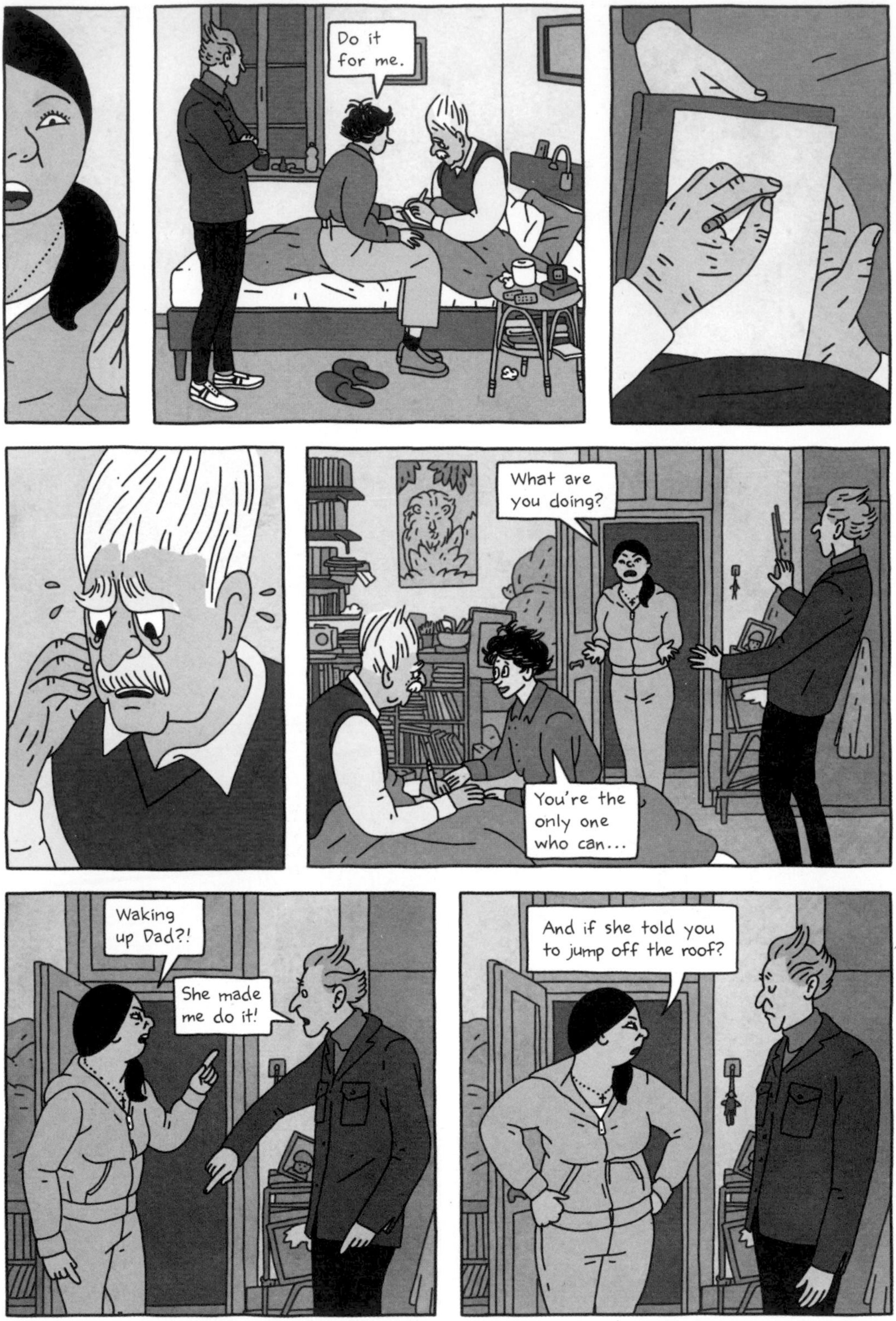
Do it for me.
What are you doing?
You're the only one who can...
Waking up Dad?!
She made me do it!
And if she told you to jump off the roof?

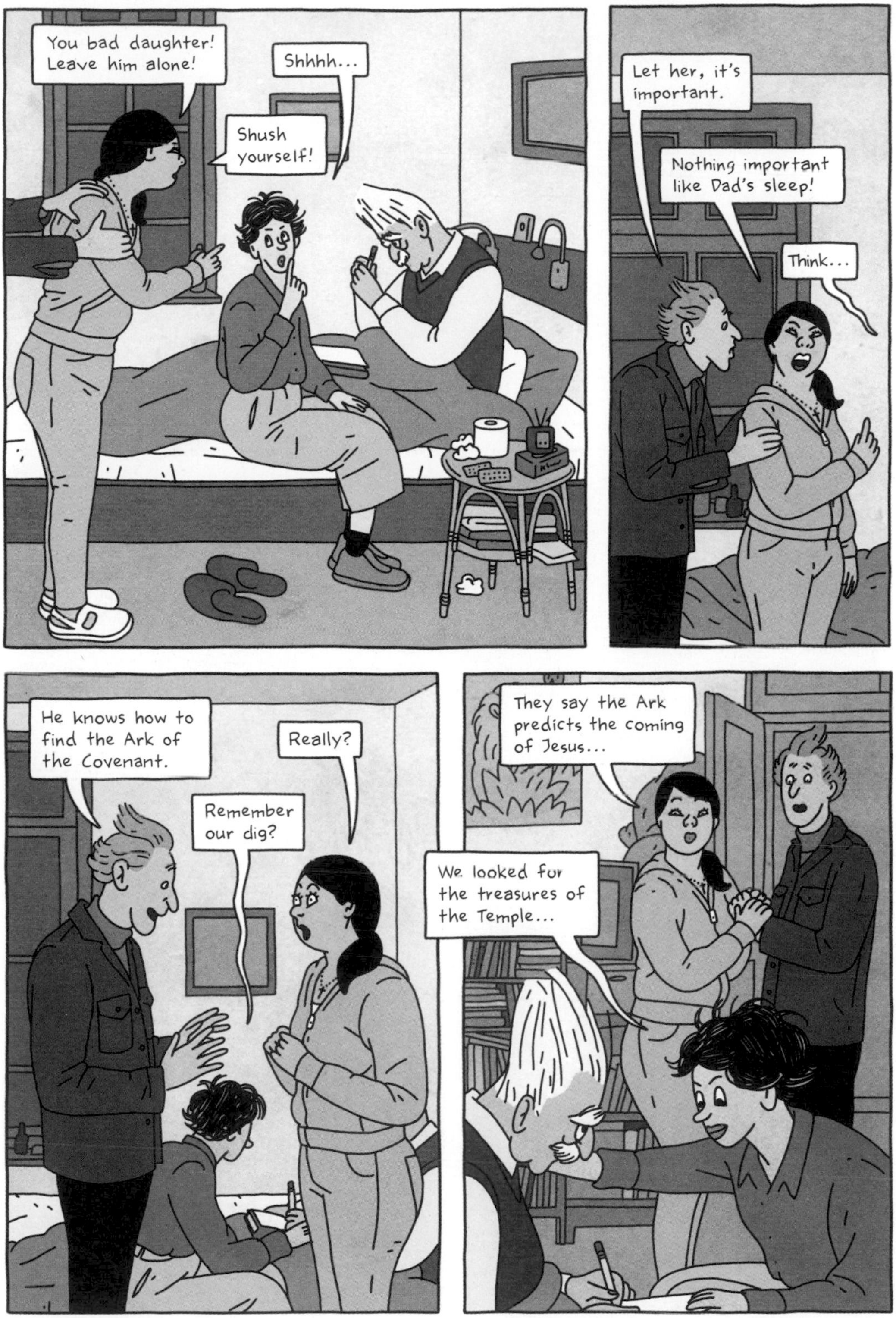
You bad daughter! Leave him alone!
Shhhh...
Shush yourself!
Let her, it's important.
Nothing important like Dad's sleep!
Think...
He knows how to find the Ark of the Covenant.
Really?
Remember our dig?
They say the Ark predicts the coming of Jesus...
We looked for the treasures of the Temple...

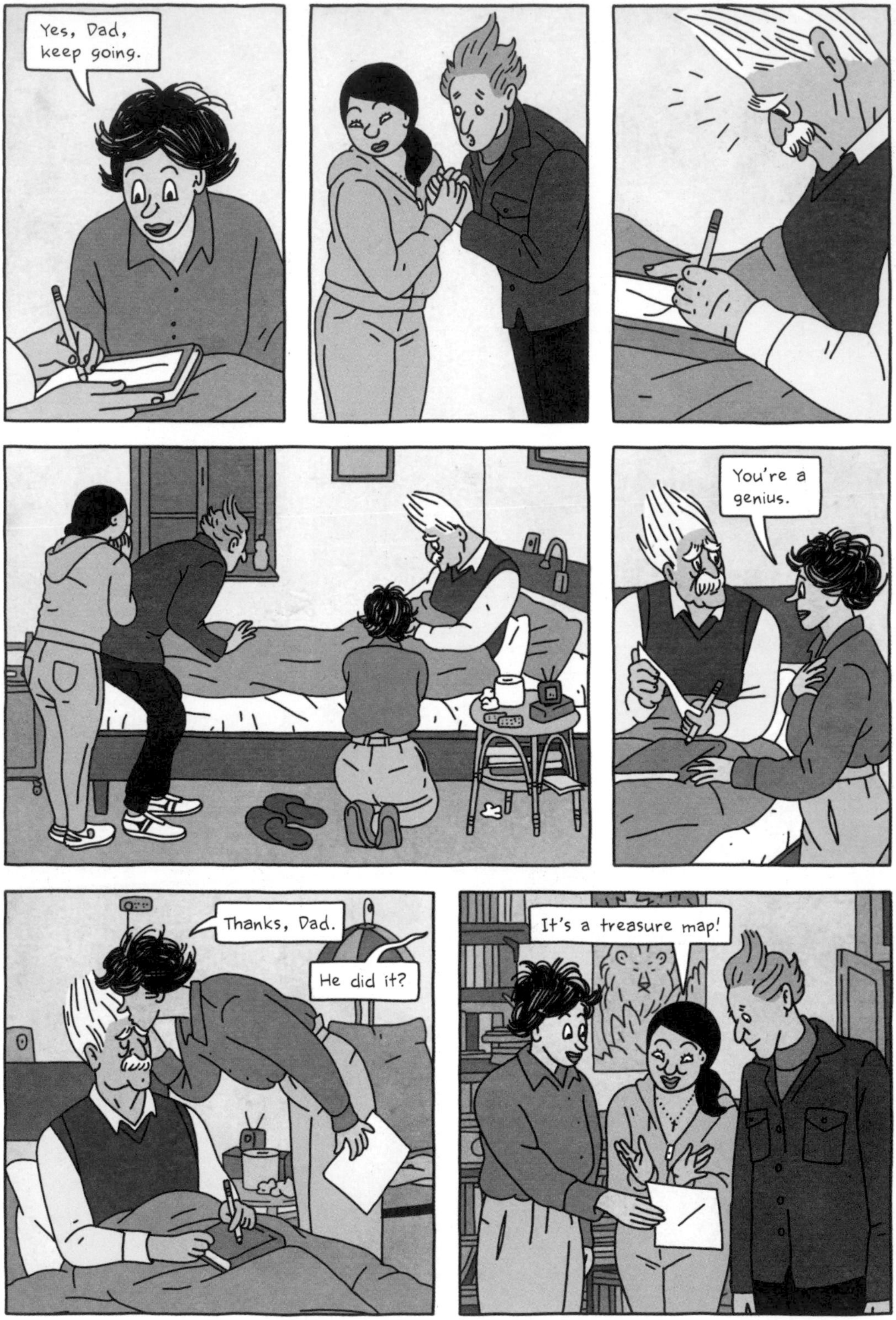
Yes, Dad, keep going.
You're a genius.
Thanks, Dad.
He did it?
It's a treasure map!

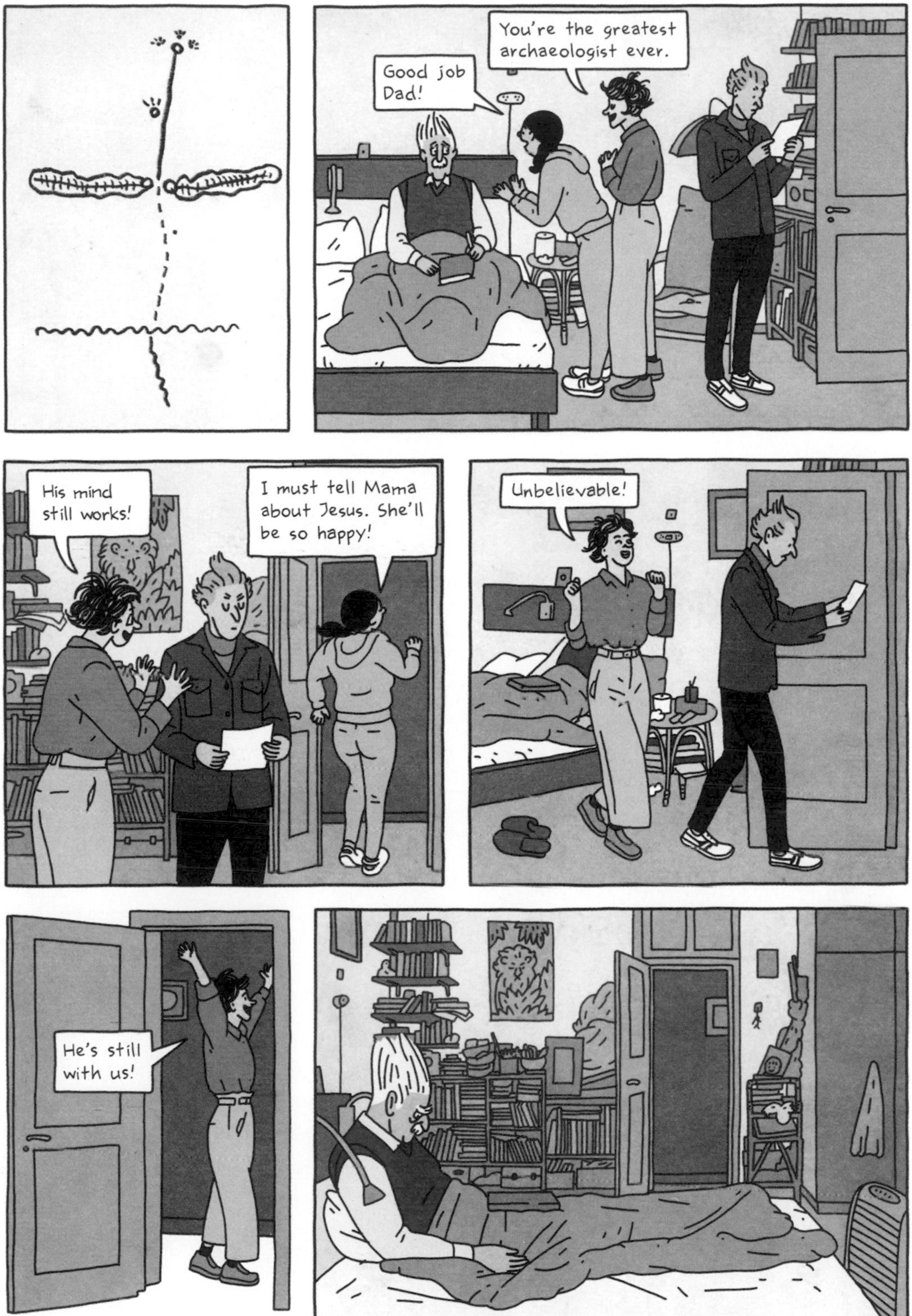
Good job Dad!
You're the greatest archaeologist ever.
His mind still works!
I must tell Mama about Jesus. She'll be so happy!
Unbelievable!
He's still with us!

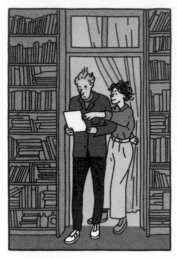

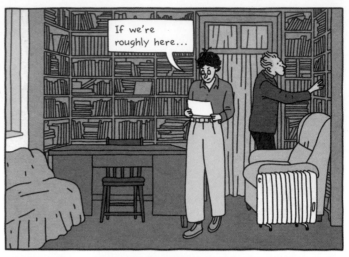

If we're roughly here...
We might actually be...
...Closer than I thought...
What's that?
A book from when Dad was a child.
King Solomon's Mines
by H.R. Haggard

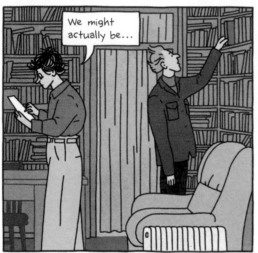

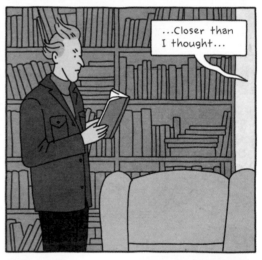

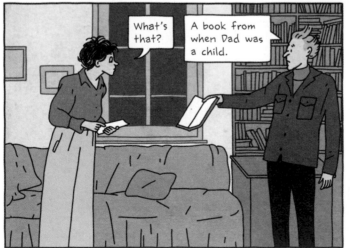

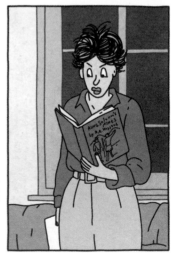

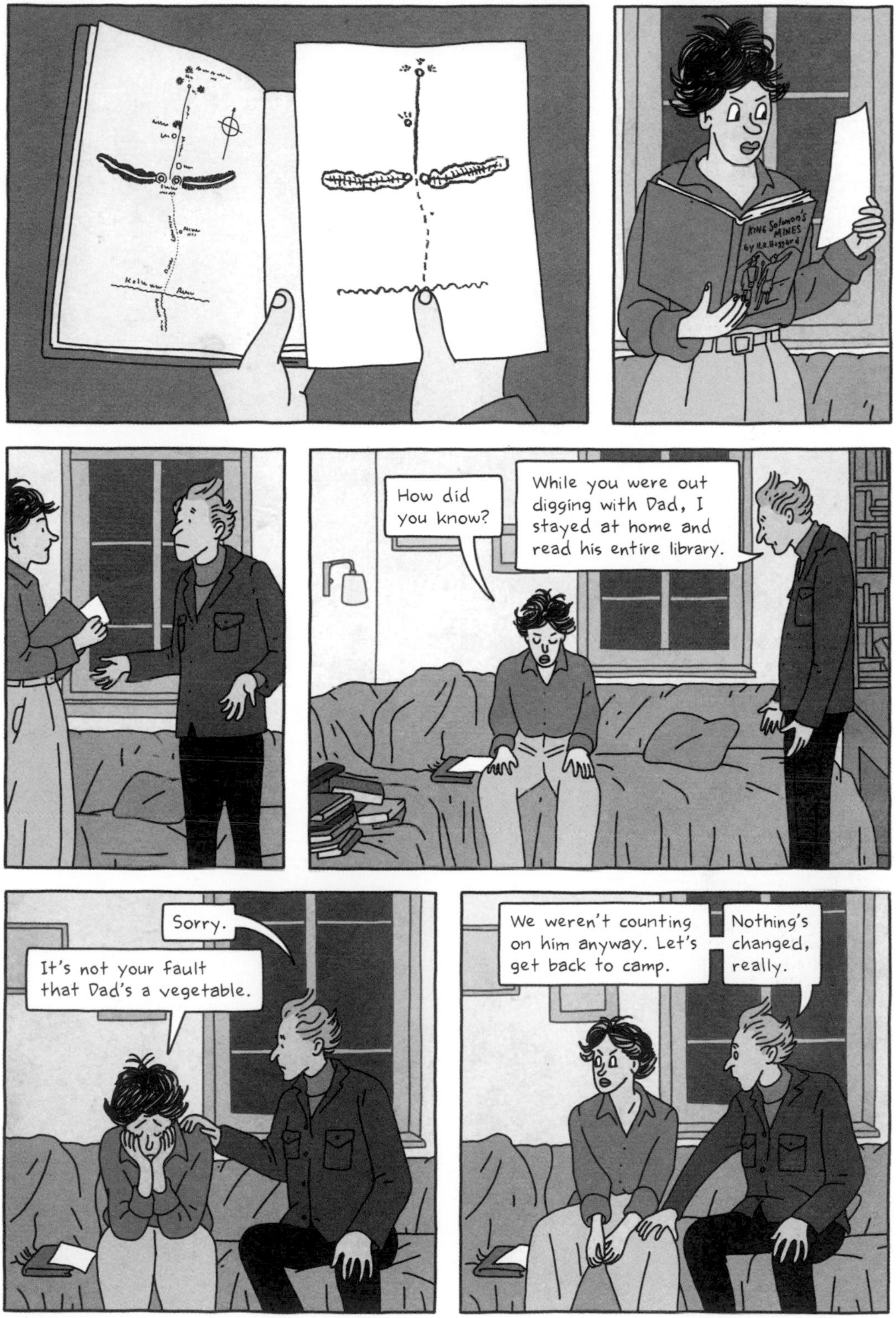
KING Solomon's MINES
by H.R. Haggard
How did you know?
While you were out digging with Dad, I stayed at home and read his entire library.
Sorry.
It's not your fault that Dad's a vegetable.
We weren't counting on him anyway. Let's get back to camp.
Nothing's changed, really.

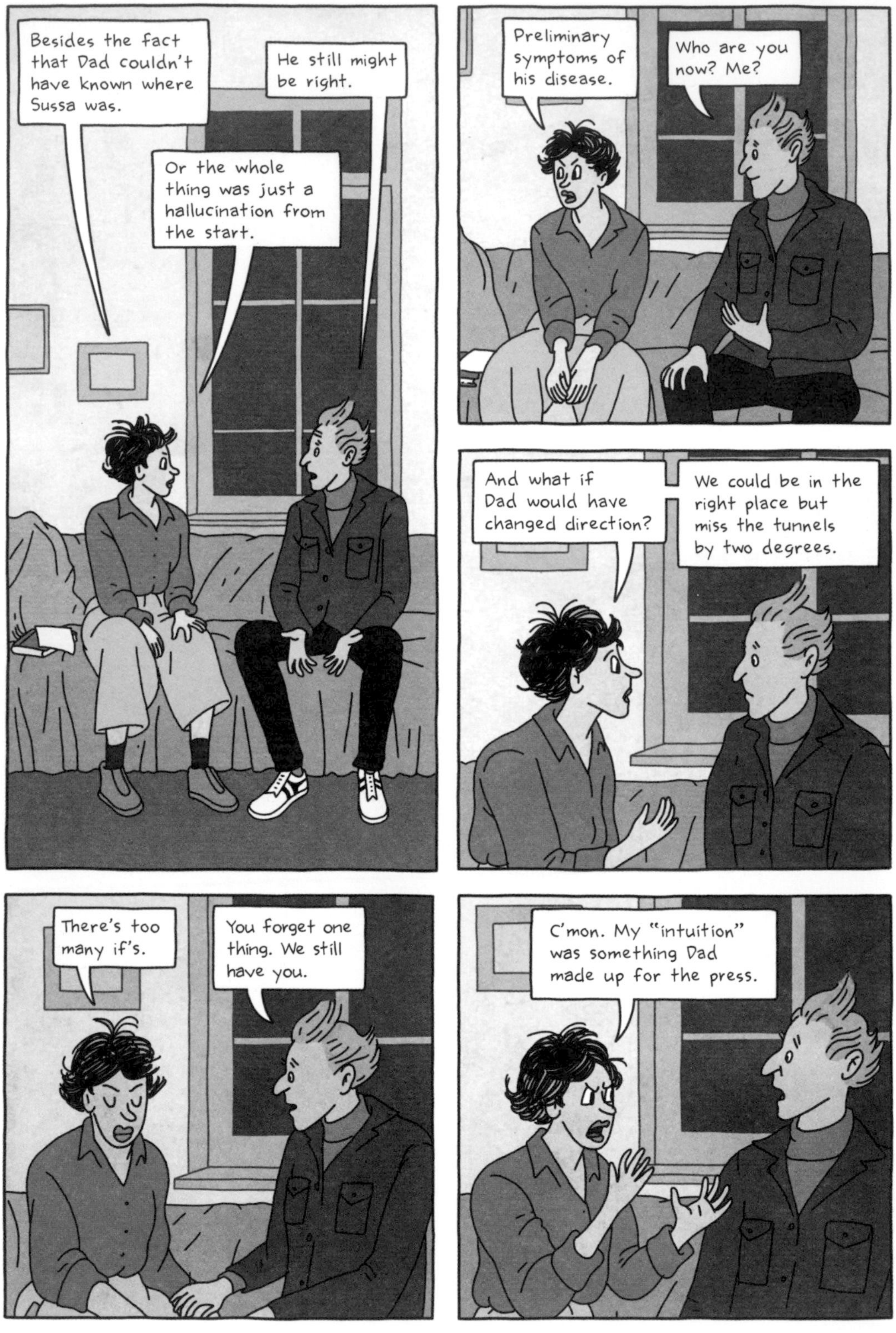
Besides the fact that Dad couldn't have known where Sussa was.
He still might be right.
Or the whole thing was just a hallucination from the start.
Preliminary symptoms of his disease.
Who are you now? Me?
And what if Dad would have changed direction?
We could be in the right place but miss the tunnels by two degrees.
There's too many if's.
You forget one thing. We still have you.
C'mon. My "intuition" was something Dad made up for the press.

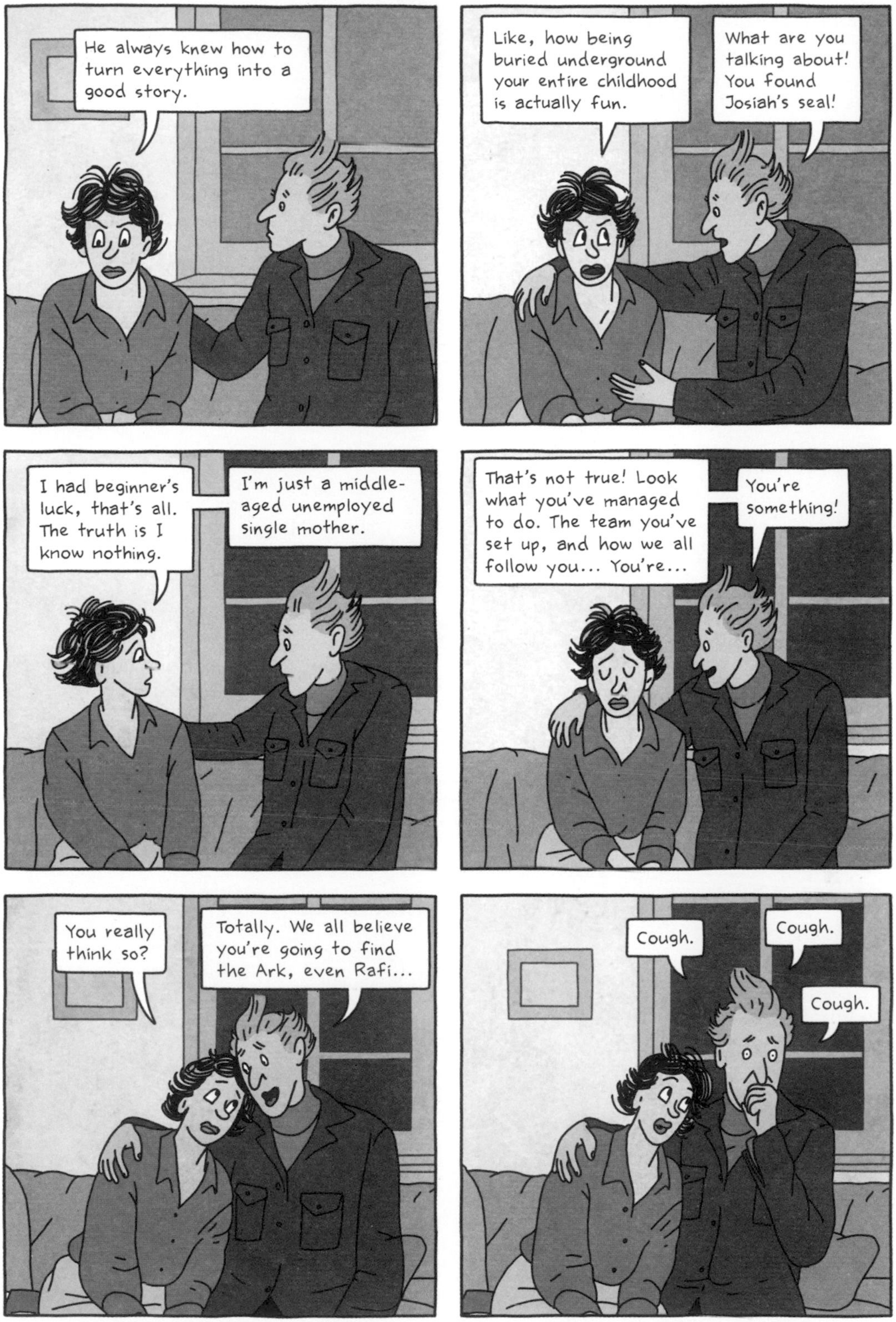
He always knew how to turn everything into a good story.
Like, how being buried underground your entire childhood is actually fun.
What are you talking about! You found Josiah's seal!
I had beginner's luck, that's all. The truth is I know nothing.
I'm just a middle-aged unemployed single mother.
That's not true! Look what you've managed to do. The team you've set up, and how we all follow you... You're...
You're something!
You really think so?
Totally. We all believe you're going to find the Ark, even Rafi...
Cough.
Cough.
Cough.

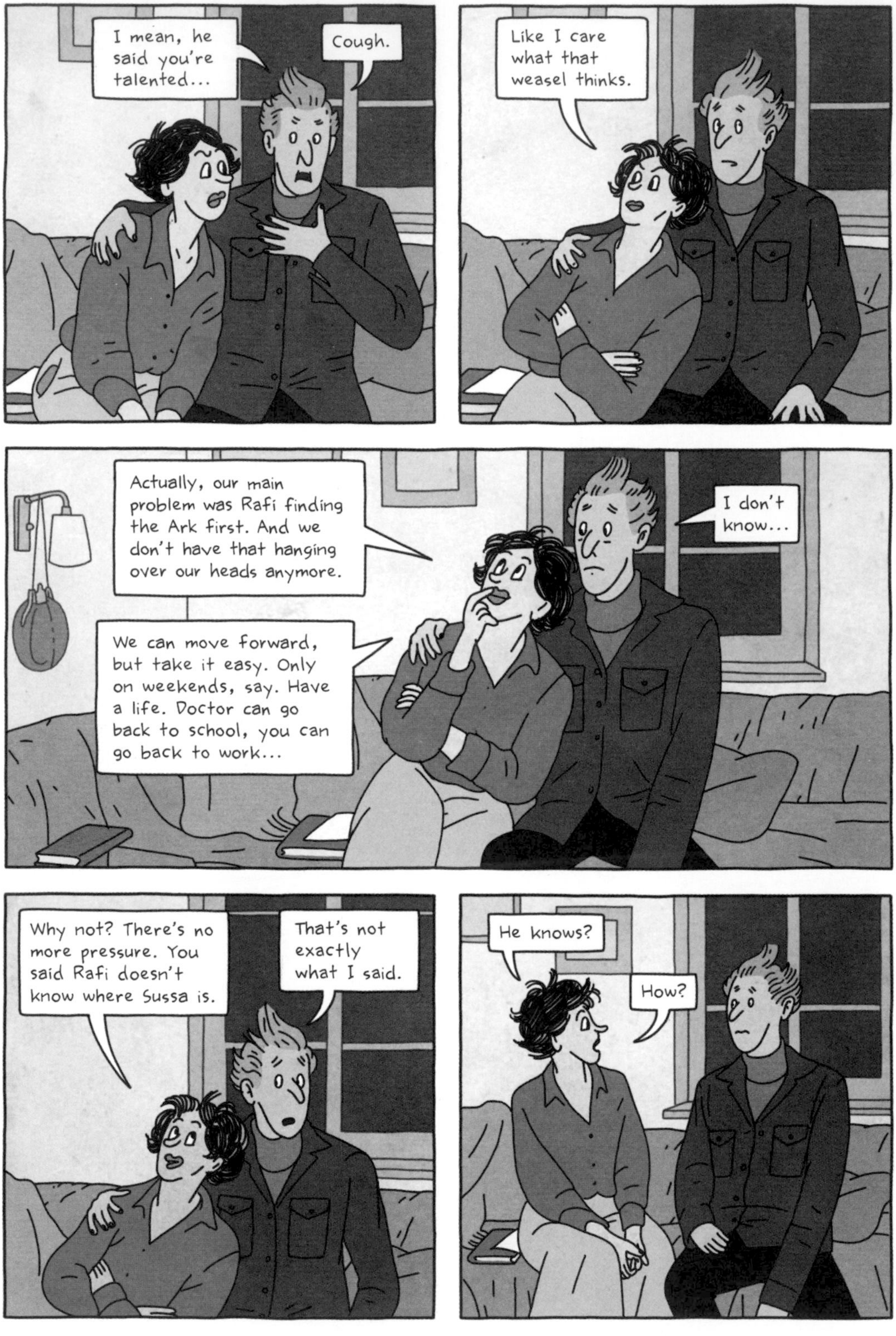
I mean, he said you're talented...
Cough.
Like I care what that weasel thinks.
Actually, our main problem was Rafi finding the Ark first. And we don't have that hanging over our heads anymore.
I don't know...
We can move forward, but take it easy. Only on weekends, say. Have a life. Doctor can go back to school, you can go back to work...
Why not? There's no more pressure. You said Rafi doesn't know where Sussa is.
That's not exactly what I said.
He knows?
How?

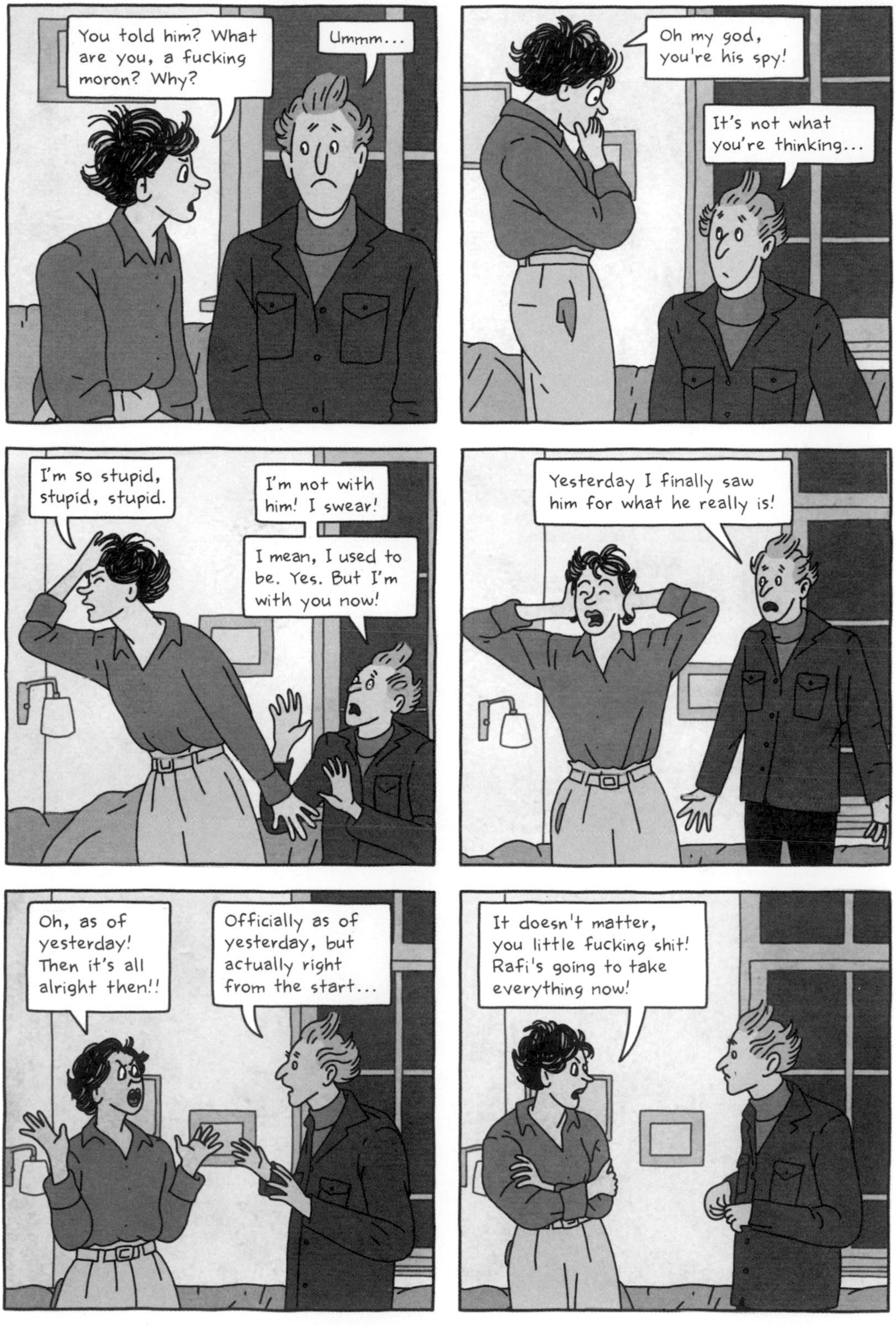
You told him? What are you, a fucking moron? Why?
Ummm...
Oh my god, you're his spy!
It's not what you're thinking...
I'm so stupid, stupid, stupid.
I'm not with him! I swear!
I mean, I used to be. Yes. But I'm with you now!
Yesterday I finally saw him for what he really is!
Oh, as of yesterday! Then it's all alright then!!
Officially as of yesterday, but actually right from the start...
It doesn't matter, you little fucking shit! Rafi's going to take everything now!

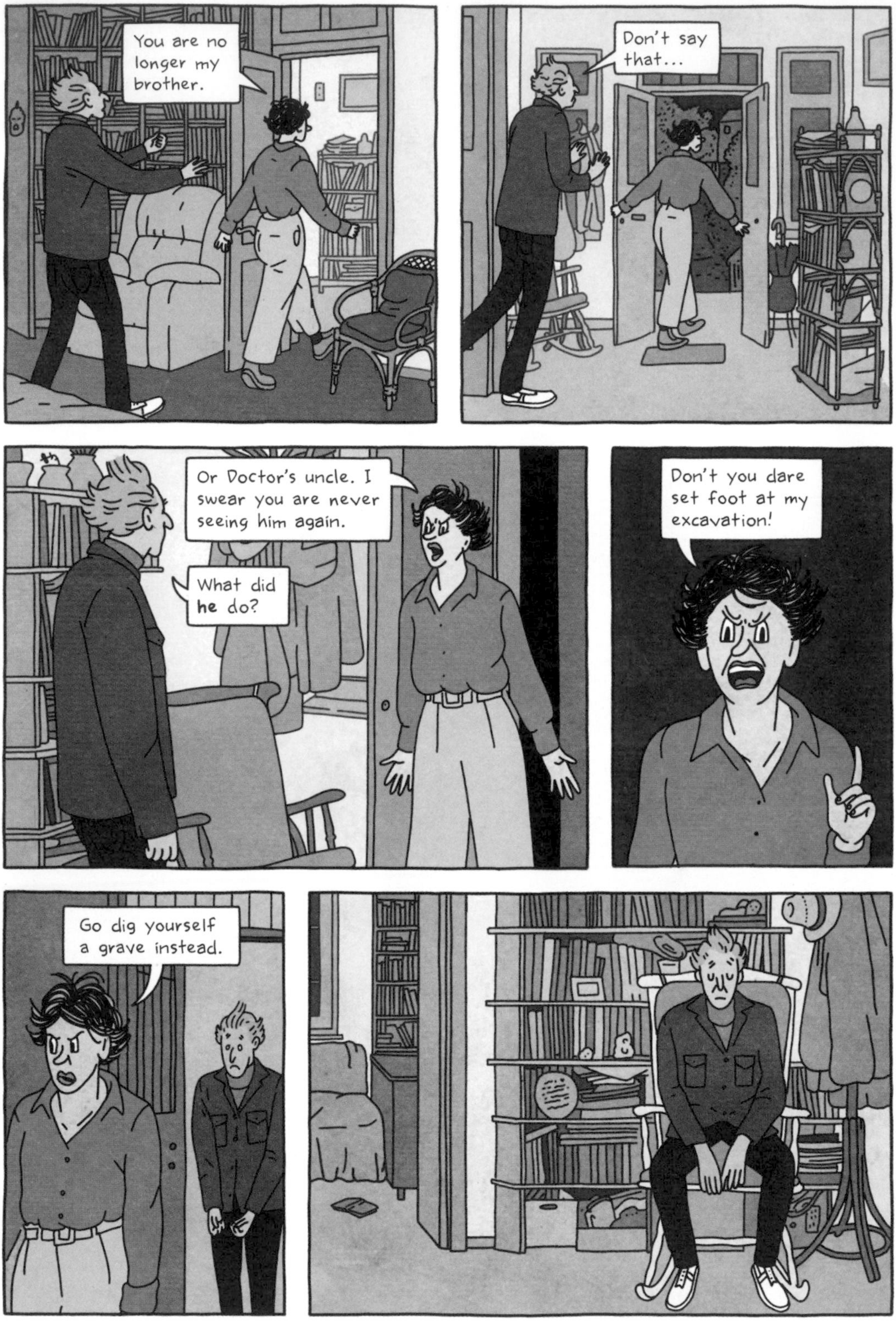
You are no longer my brother.
Don't say that...
Or Doctor's uncle. I swear you are never seeing him again.
What did **he** do?
Don't you dare set foot at my excavation!
Go dig yourself a grave instead.

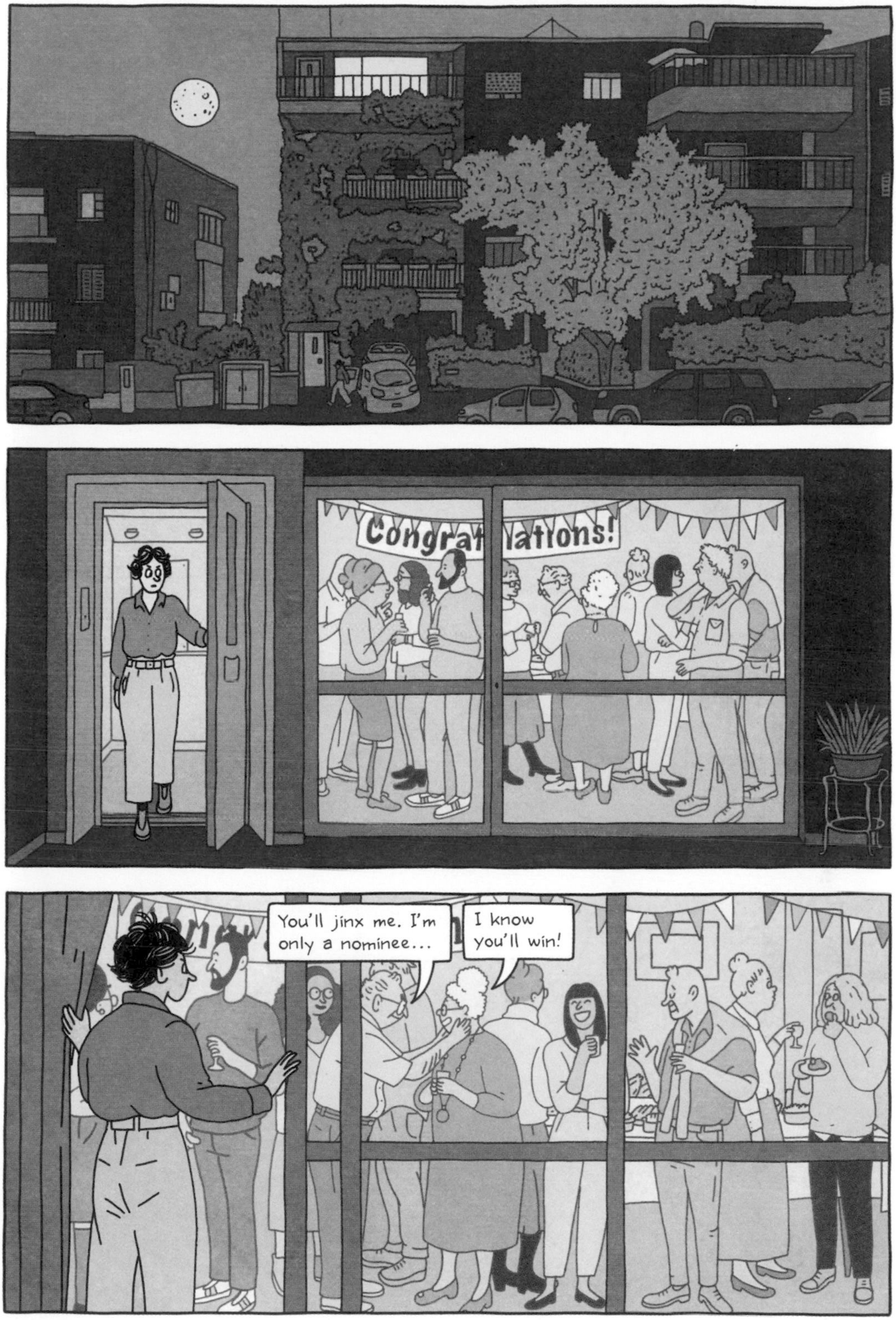
Congrat lations!
You'll jinx me. I'm only a nominee...
I know you'll win!

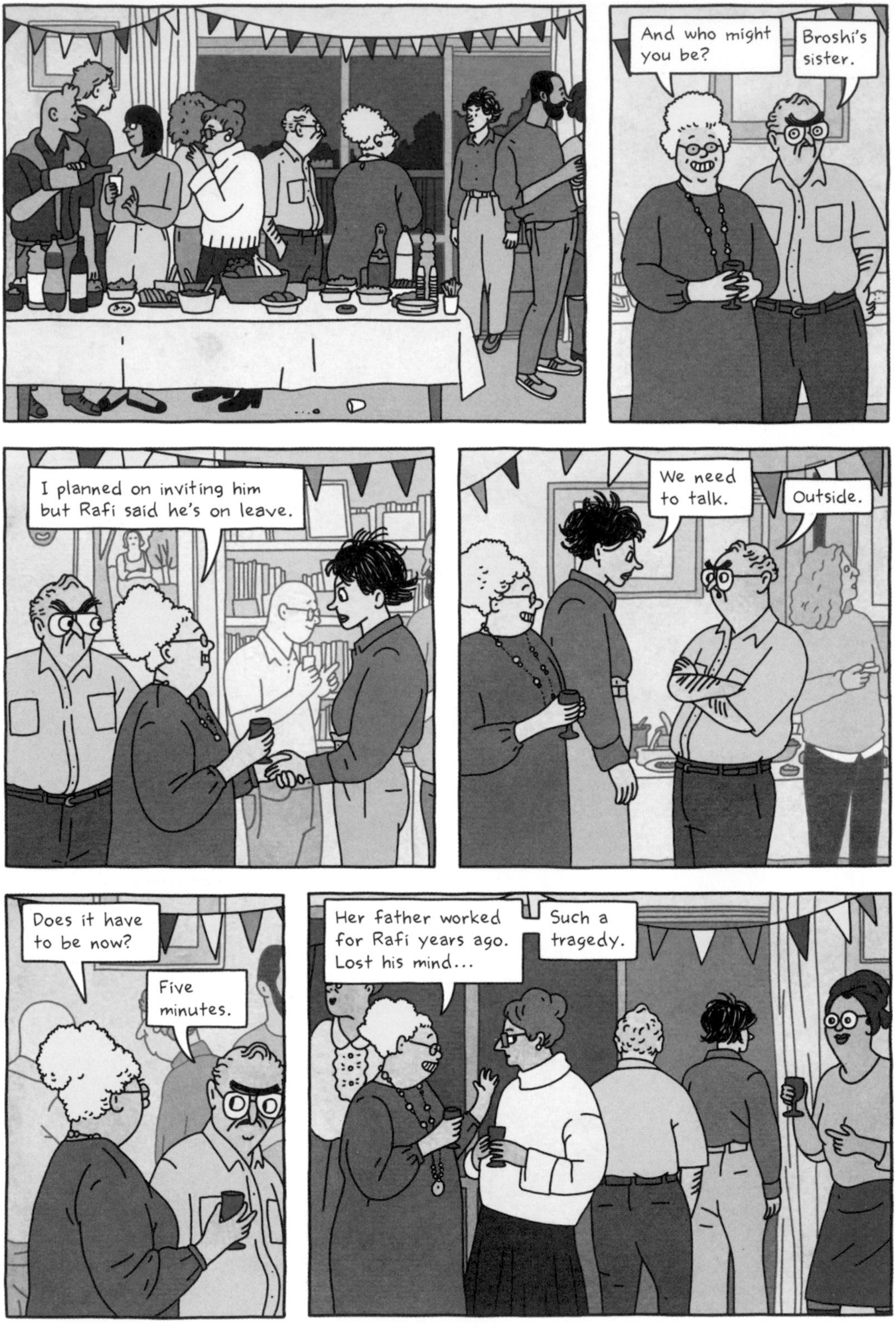
And who might you be?
Broshi's sister.
I planned on inviting him but Rafi said he's on leave.
We need to talk.
Outside.
Does it have to be now?
Five minutes.
Her father worked for Rafi years ago. Lost his mind...
Such a tragedy.

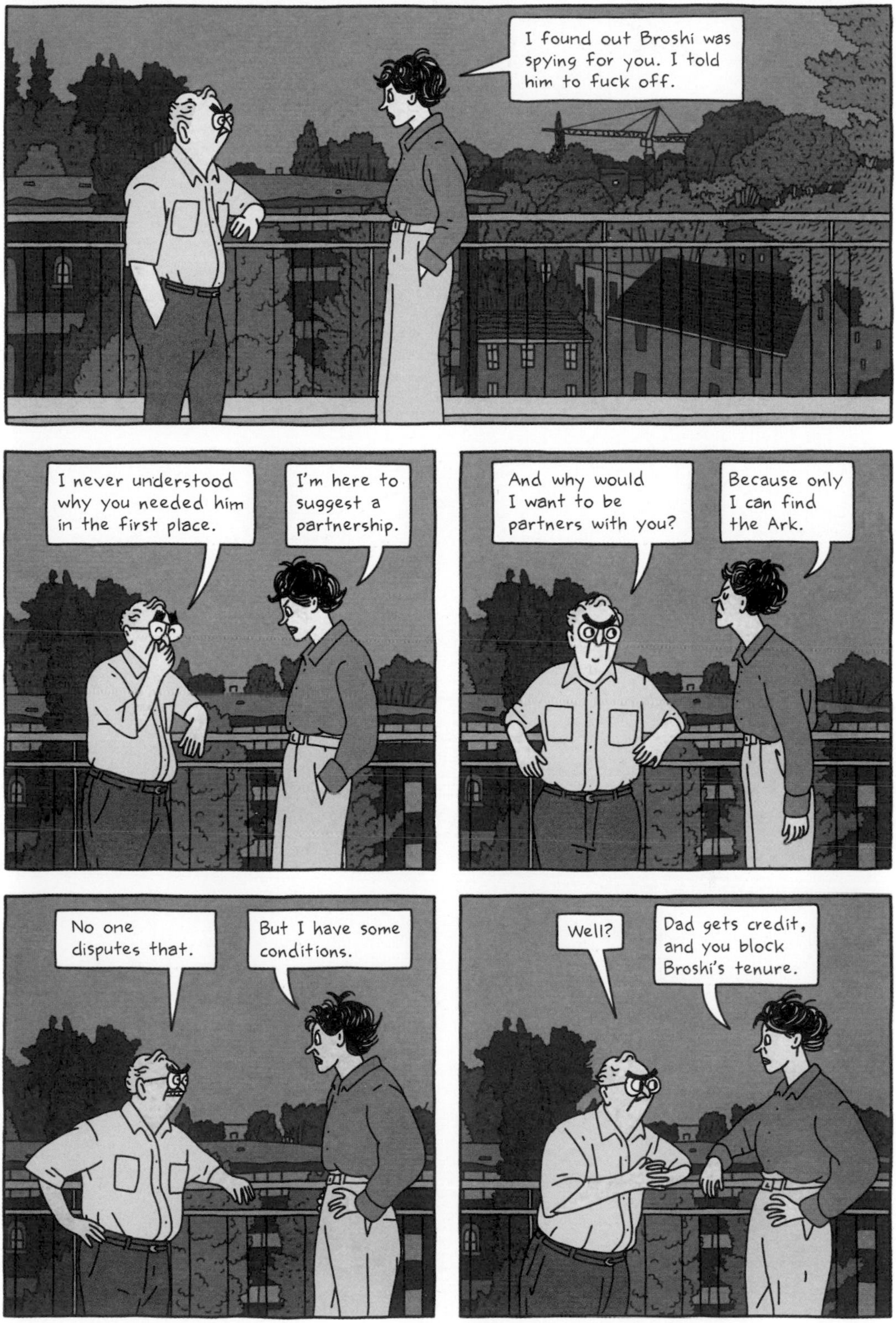
I found out Broshi was spying for you. I told him to fuck off.
I never understood why you needed him in the first place.
I'm here to suggest a partnership.
And why would I want to be partners with you?
Because only I can find the Ark.
No one disputes that.
But I have some conditions.
Well?
Dad gets credit, and you block Broshi's tenure.

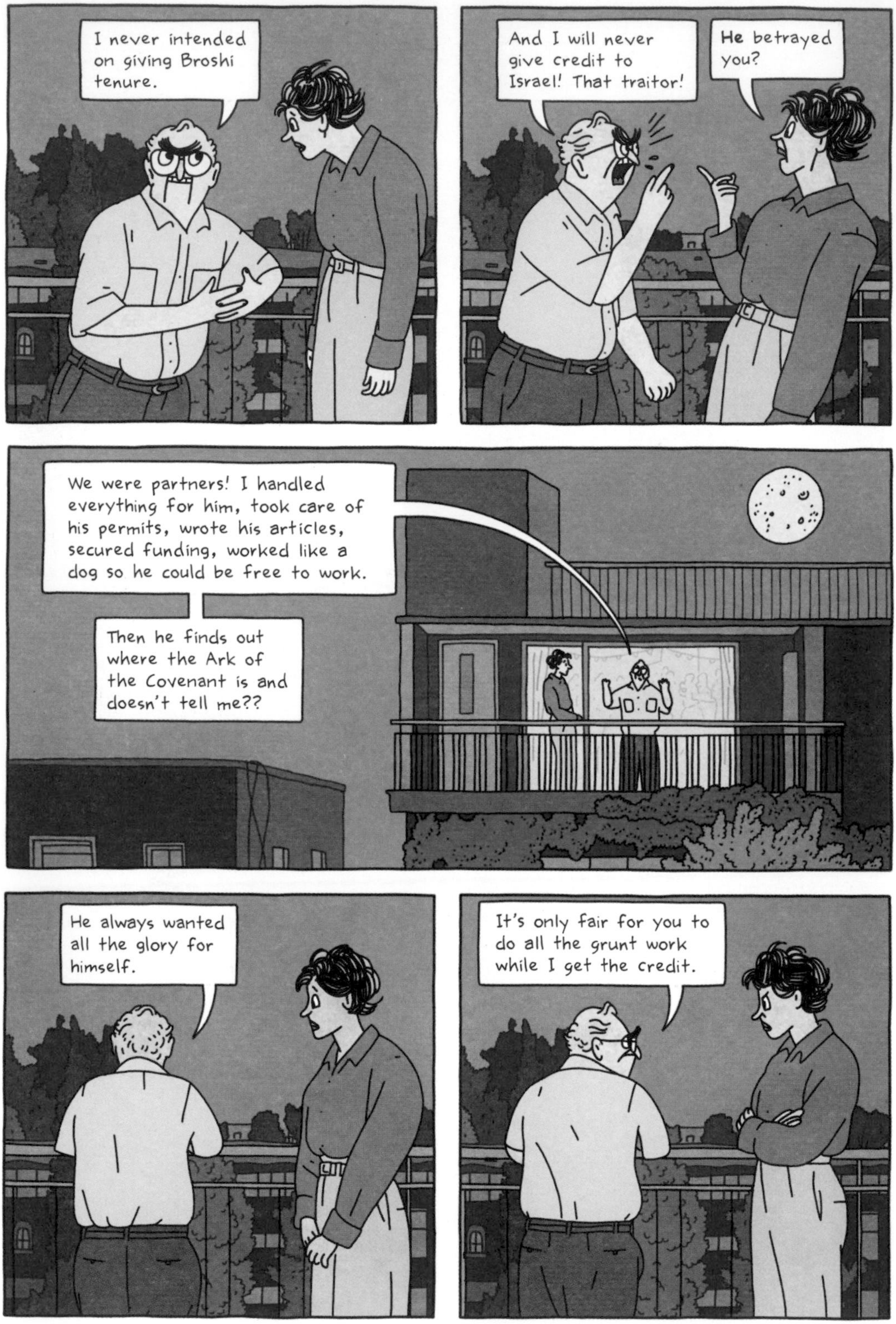
I never intended on giving Broshi tenure.
And I will never give credit to Israel! That traitor!
He betrayed you?
We were partners! I handled everything for him, took care of his permits, wrote his articles, secured funding, worked like a dog so he could be free to work.
Then he finds out where the Ark of the Covenant is and doesn't tell me??
He always wanted all the glory for himself.
It's only fair for you to do all the grunt work while I get the credit.

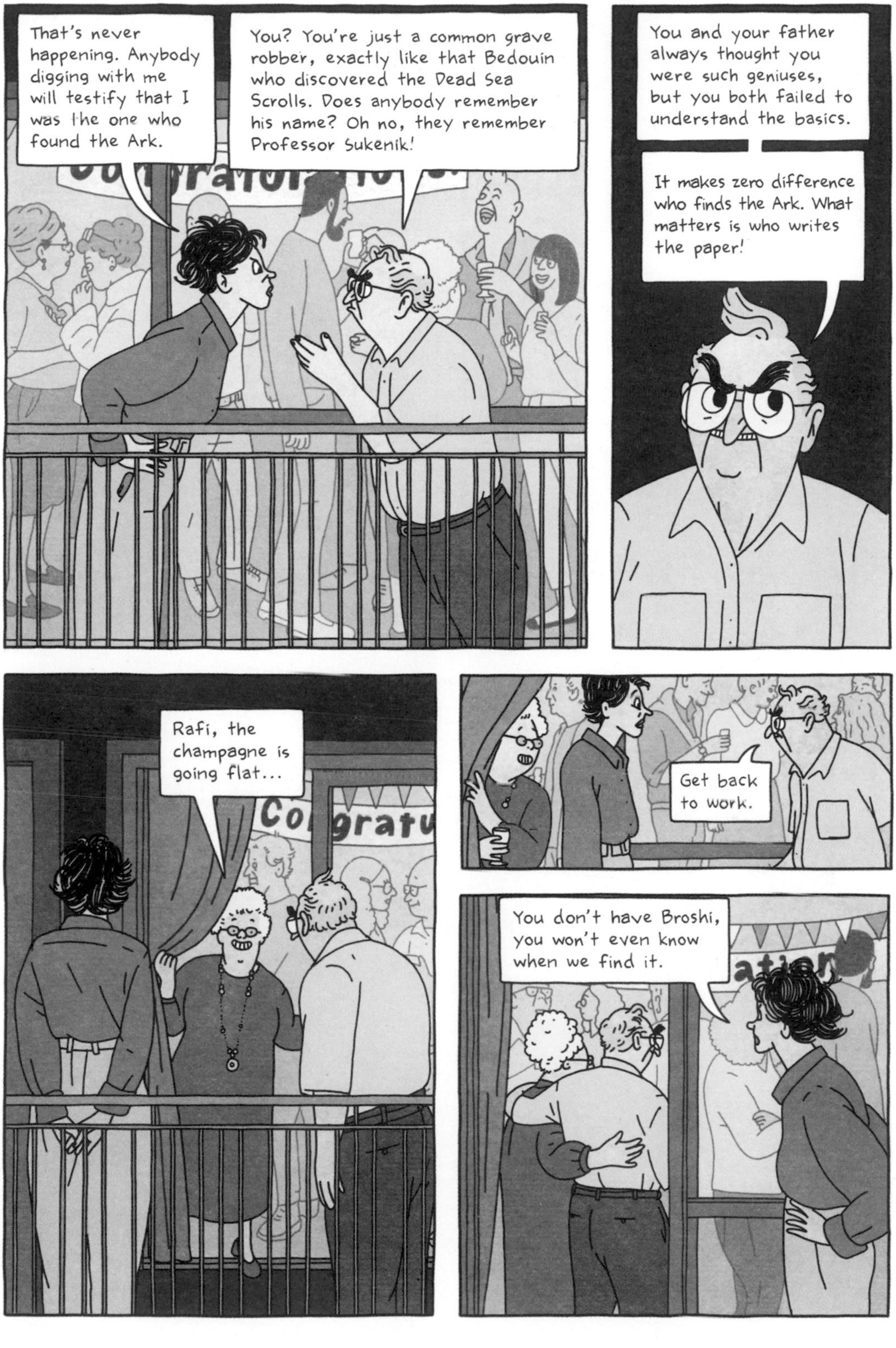
That's never happening. Anybody digging with me will testify that I was the one who found the Ark.
You? You're just a common grave robber, exactly like that Bedouin who discovered the Dead Sea Scrolls. Does anybody remember his name? Oh no, they remember Professor Sukenik!
You and your father always thought you were such geniuses, but you both failed to understand the basics.
It makes zero difference who finds the Ark. What matters is who writes the paper!
Rafi, the champagne is going flat...
Get back to work.
You don't have Broshi, you won't even know when we find it.

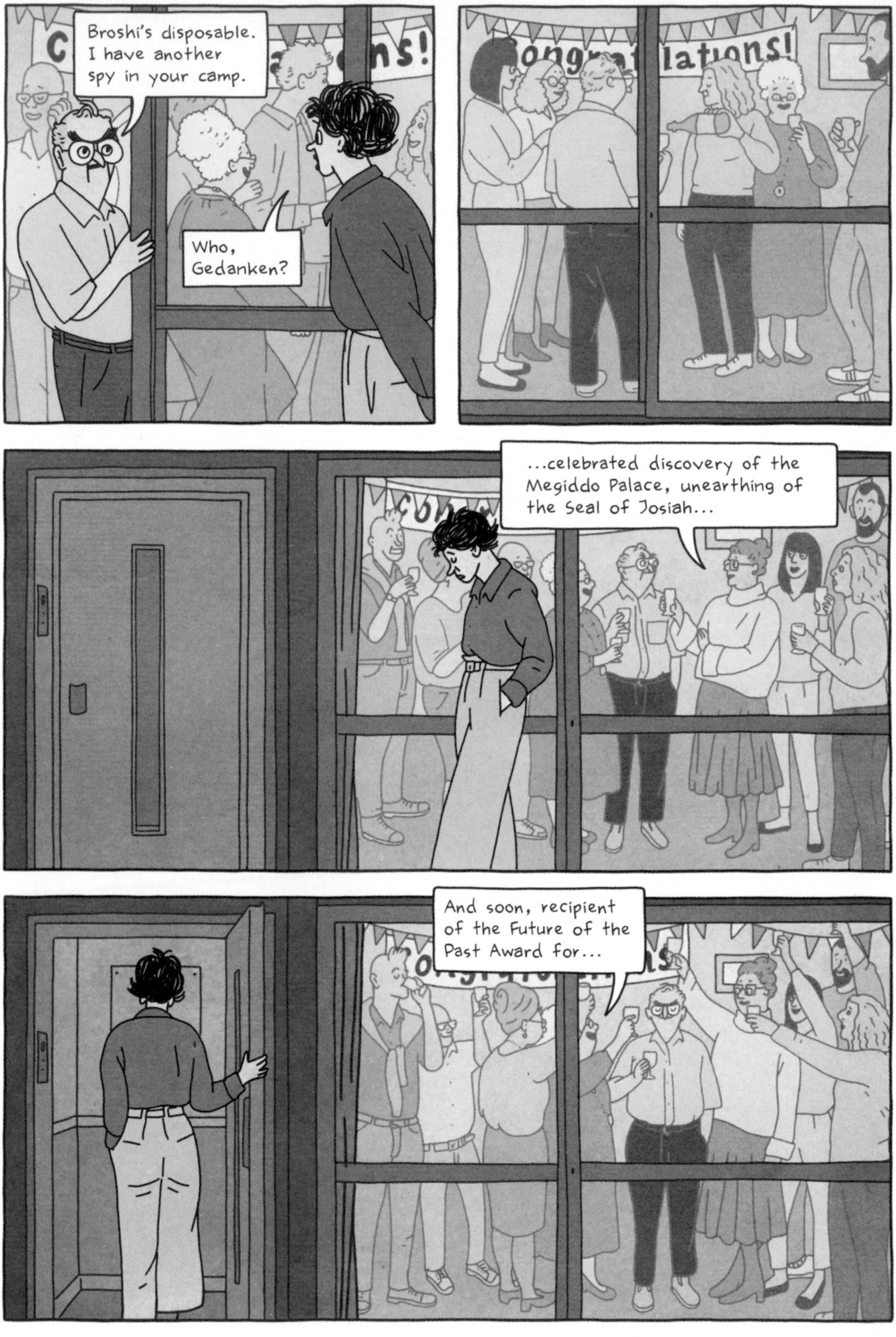

Broshi's disposable. I have another spy in your camp.
Who, Gedanken?
Congratulations!
...celebrated discovery of the Megiddo Palace, unearthing of the Seal of Josiah...
And soon, recipient of the Future of the Past Award for...

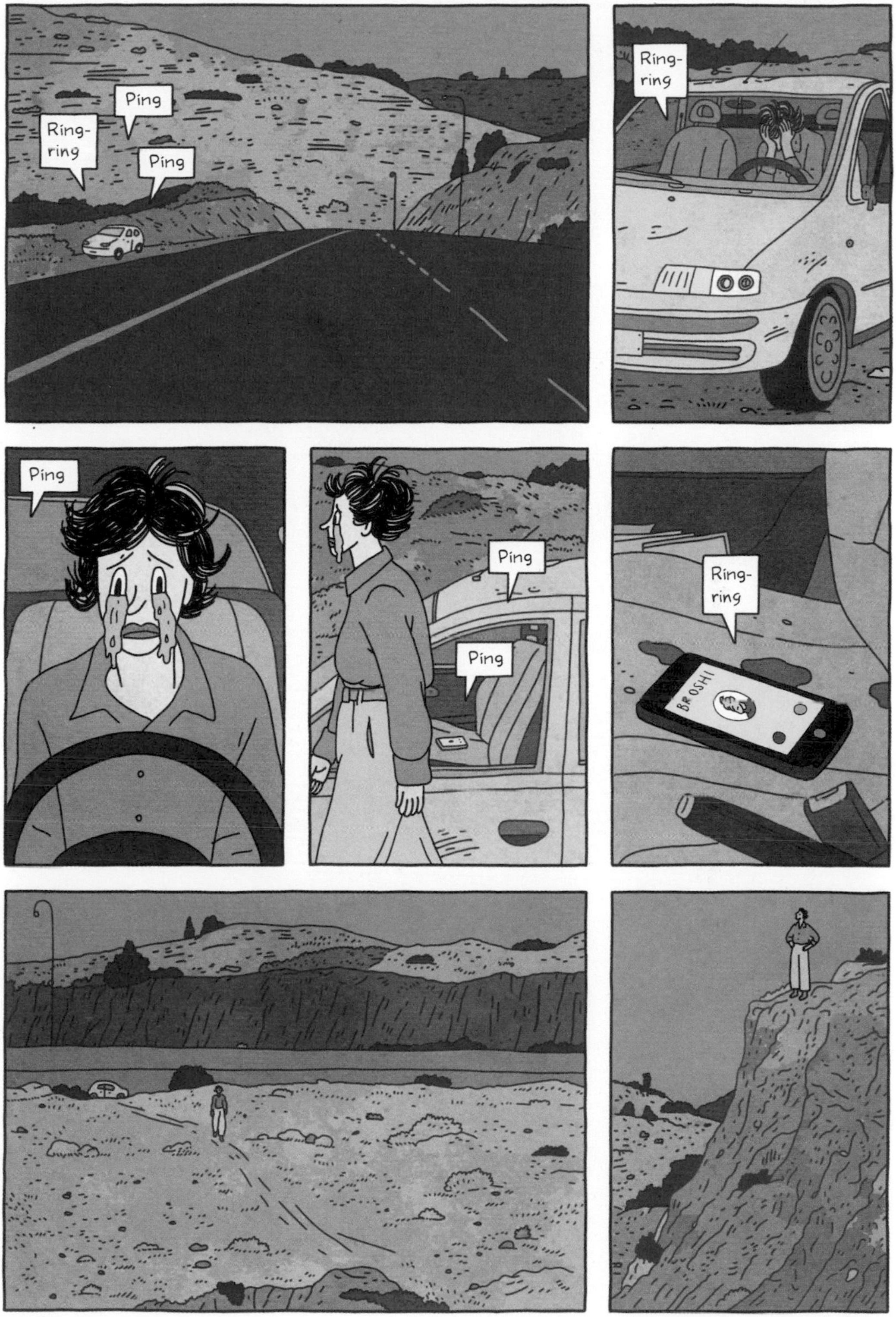
Ring-
ring
Ping
Ping
Ring-
ring
Ping
Ping
Ping
Ring-
ring
BROSHI

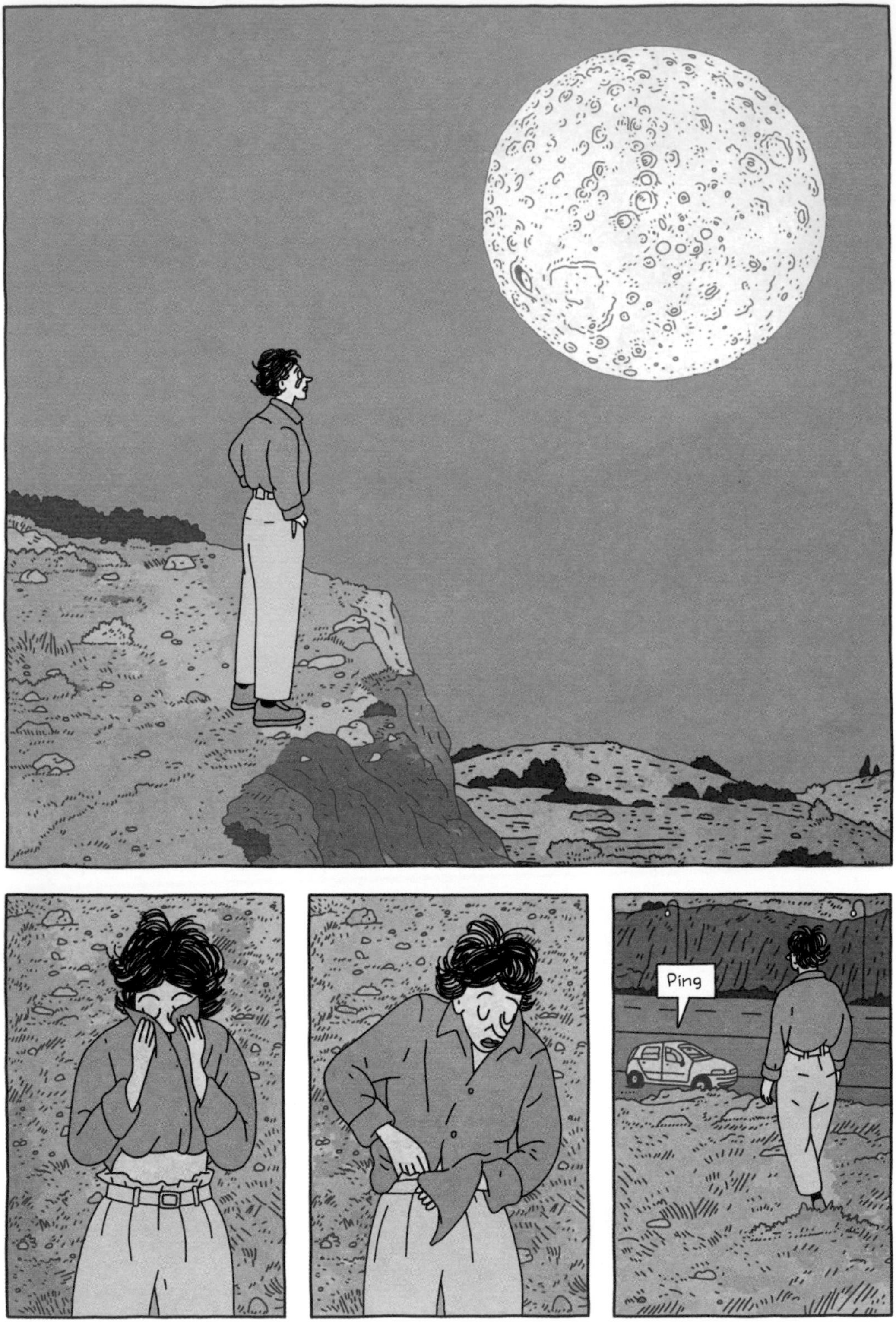
Ping

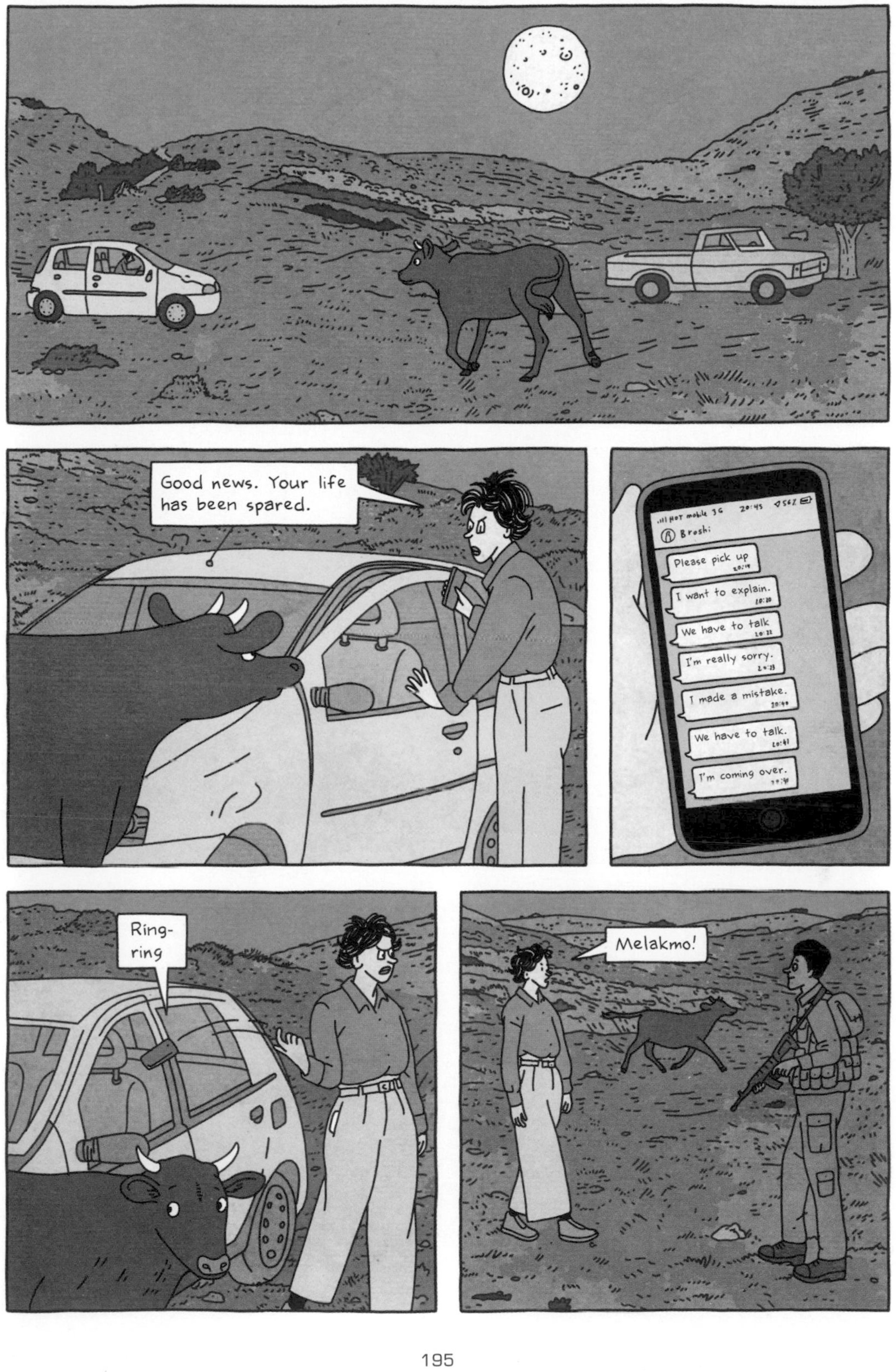
Good news. Your life has been spared.
HOT mobile 3G 20:45 56%
Broshi
Please pick up 20:19
I want to explain. 20:20
We have to talk 20:22
I'm really sorry. 20:23
I made a mistake. 20:40
We have to talk. 20:41
I'm coming over.
Ring-ring
Melakmo!

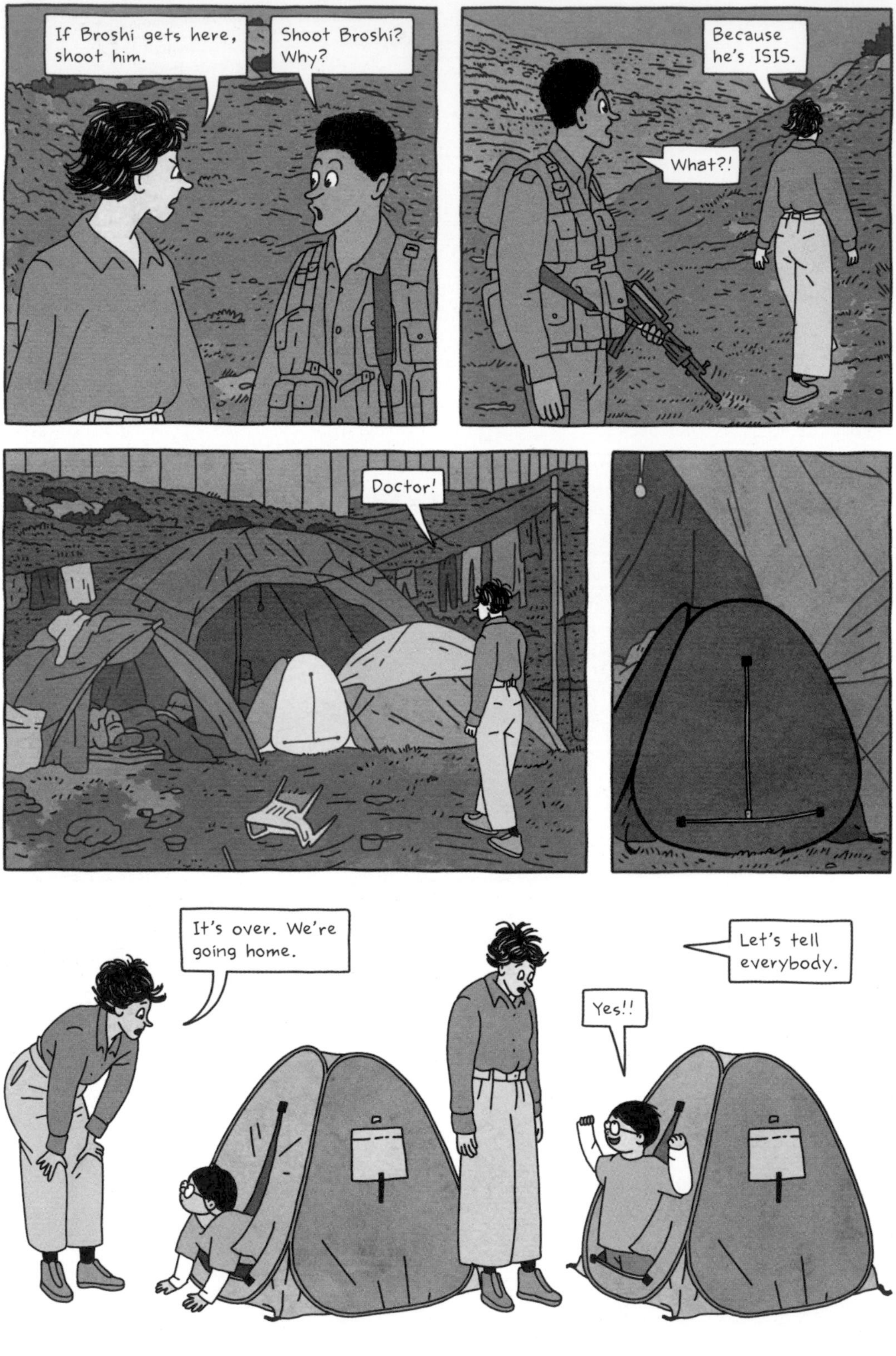
If Broshi gets here, shoot him.
Shoot Broshi? Why?
Because he's ISIS.
What?!
Doctor!
It's over. We're going home.
Let's tell everybody.
Yes!!

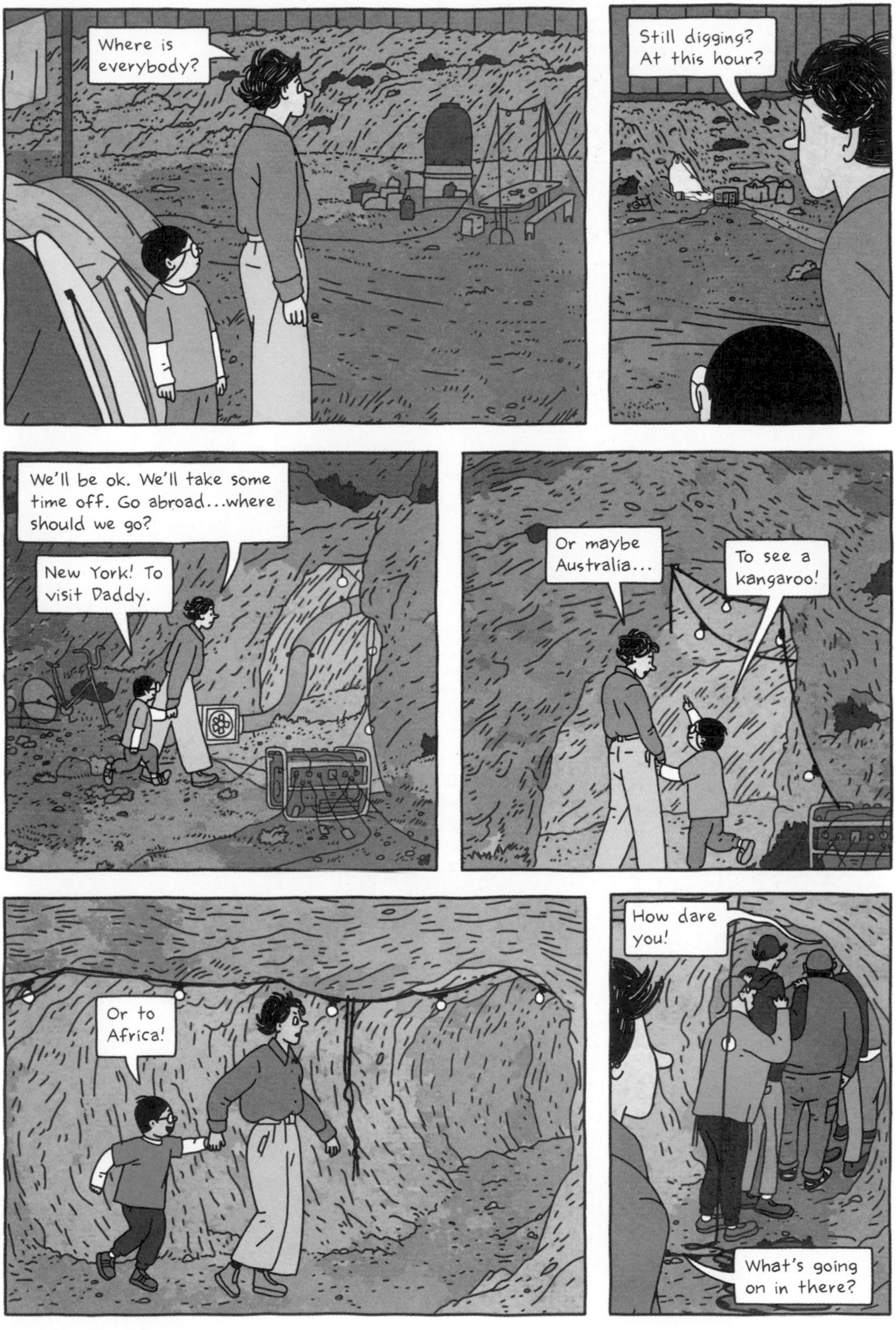
Where is everybody?
Still digging? At this hour?
We'll be ok. We'll take some time off. Go abroad...where should we go?
New York! To visit Daddy.
Or maybe Australia...
To see a kangaroo!
Or to Africa!
How dare you!
What's going on in there?

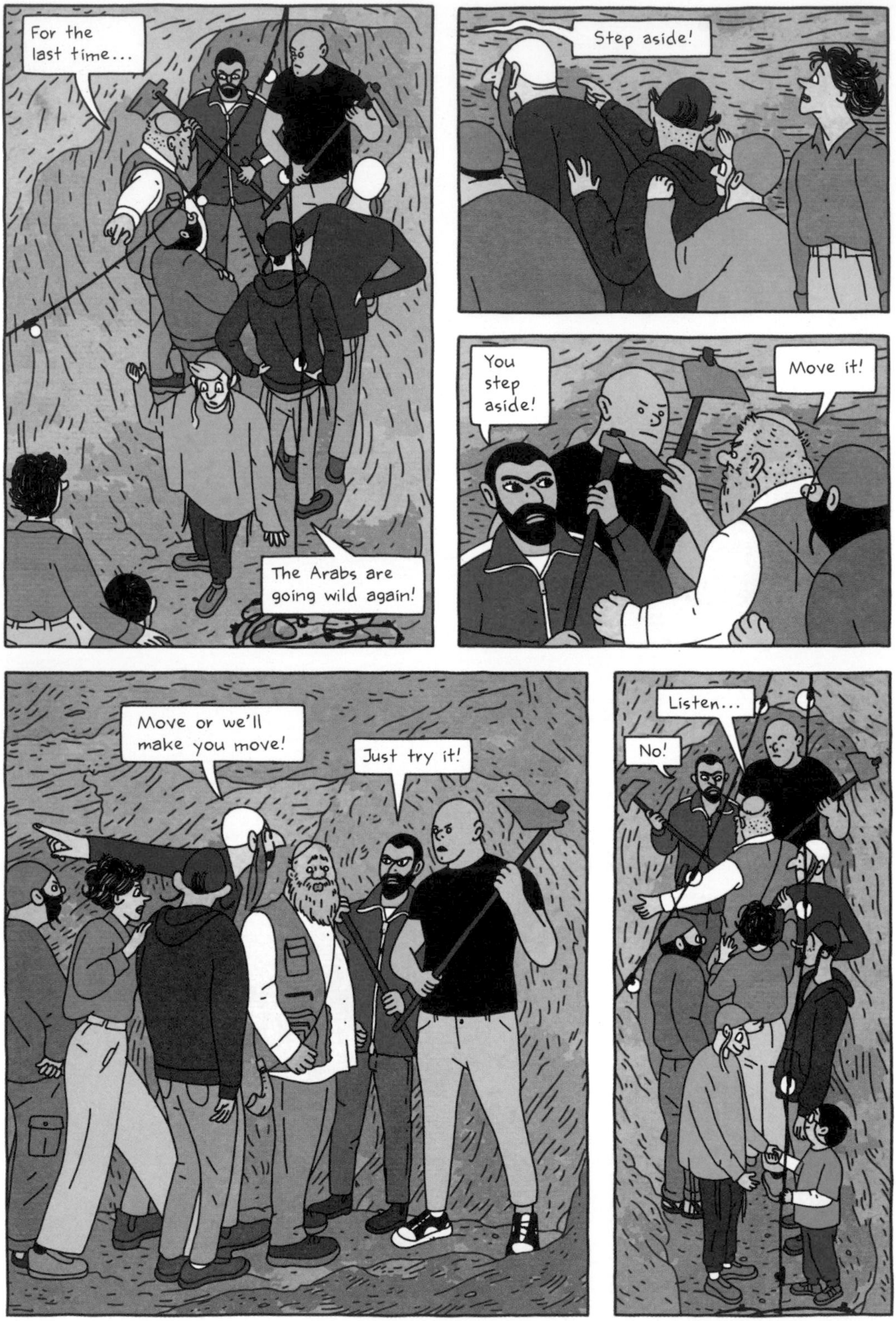
For the last time...
The Arabs are going wild again!
Step aside!
You step aside!
Move it!
Move or we'll make you move!
Just try it!
Listen...
No!

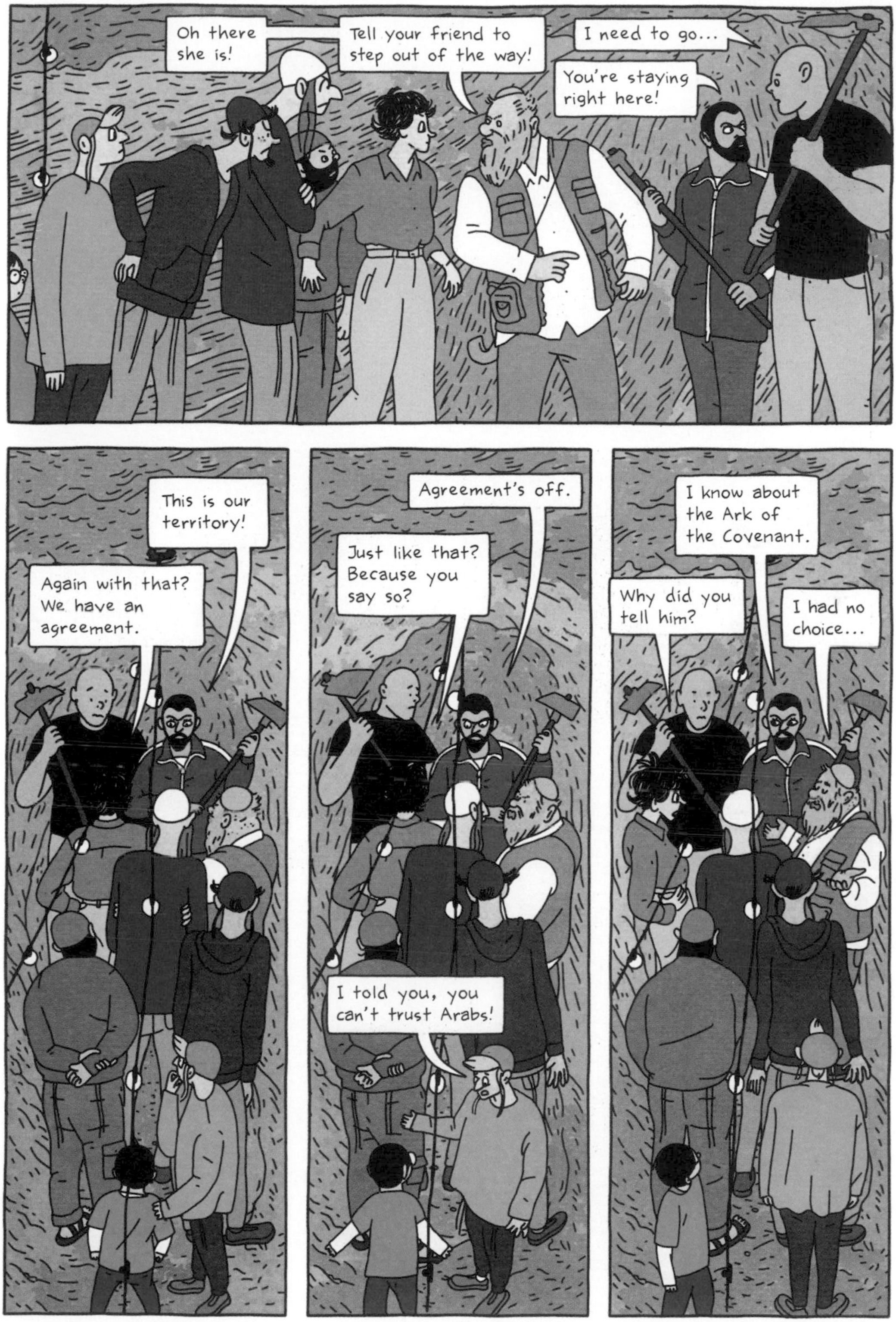
Oh there she is!
Tell your friend to step out of the way!
I need to go...
You're staying right here!
This is our territory!
Again with that? We have an agreement.
Agreement's off.
Just like that? Because you say so?
I told you, you can't trust Arabs!
I know about the Ark of the Covenant.
Why did you tell him?
I had no choice...

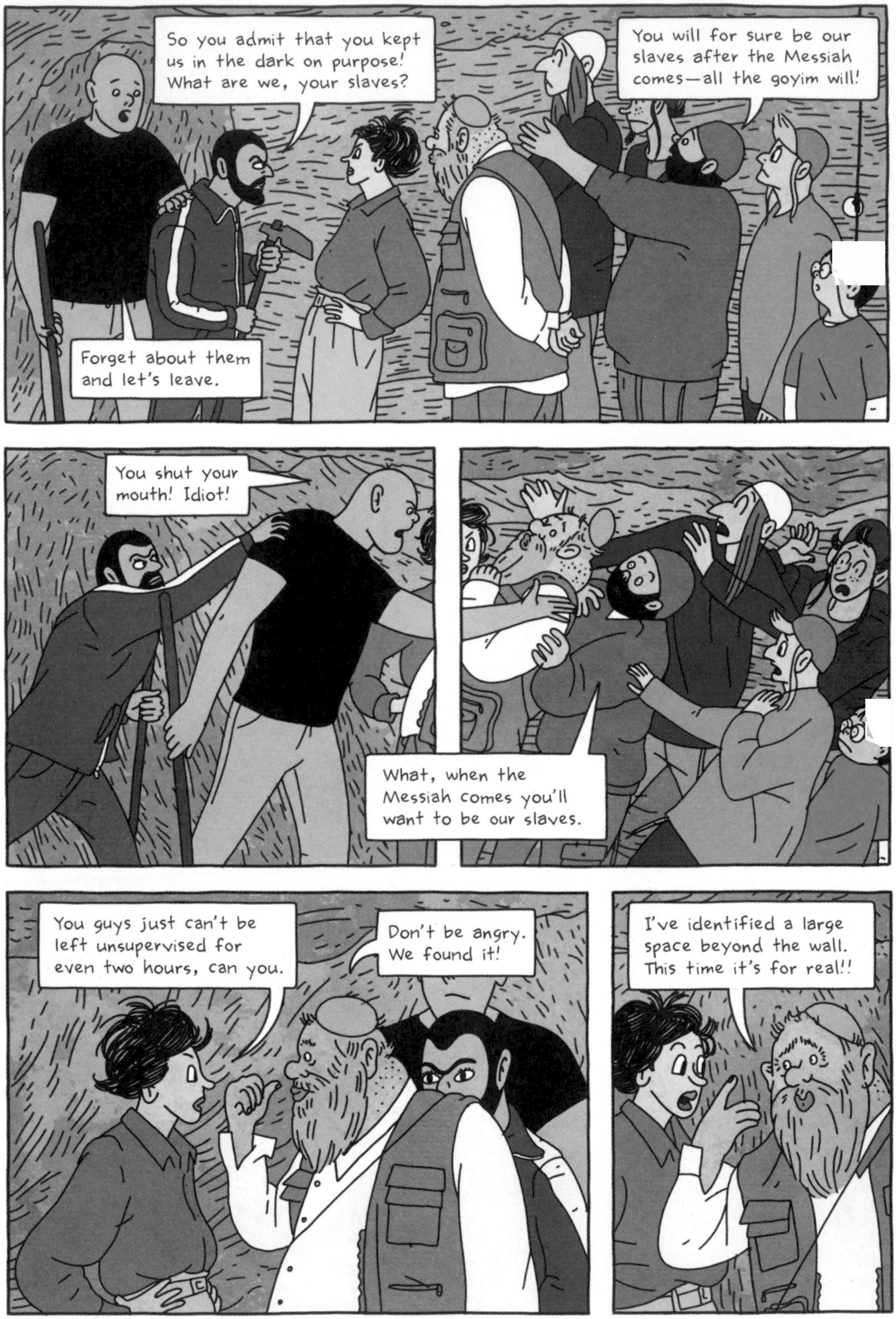
So you admit that you kept us in the dark on purpose! What are we, your slaves?
You will for sure be our slaves after the Messiah comes—all the goyim will!
Forget about them and let's leave.
You shut your mouth! Idiot!
What, when the Messiah comes you'll want to be our slaves.
You guys just can't be left unsupervised for even two hours, can you.
Don't be angry. We found it!
I've identified a large space beyond the wall. This time it's for real!!

And goyim aren't allowed to approach the holy vessel.
They have to leave.
It's for your own good. The demon guarding the Ark would smite you.
Out.
Not you.
Are you crazy?
No way!
We leave and they stay?
And you call yourself Jewish?
Mahdi...
Don't move!
Only someone of priestly descent can touch the Ark and Doctor is the only Cohen among us. Leave, or I'm taking him out of here.
You don't even believe in any of this!
Please. Trust me. Do what I tell you to.

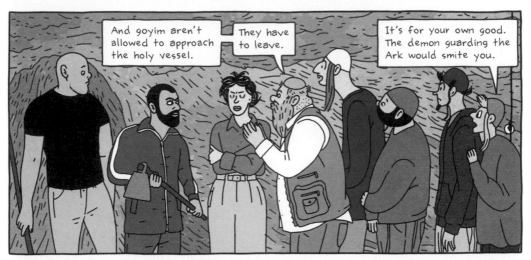

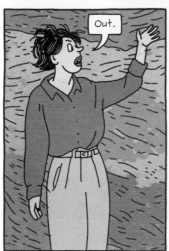

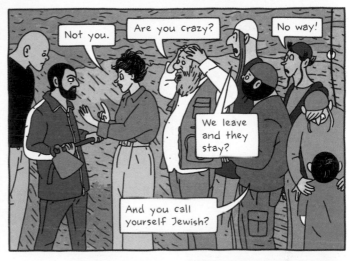

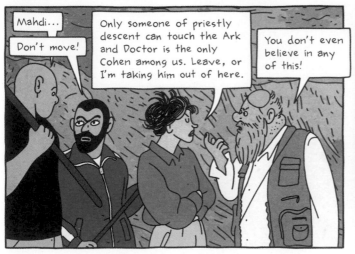

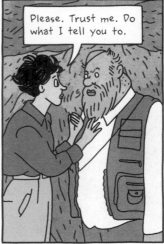

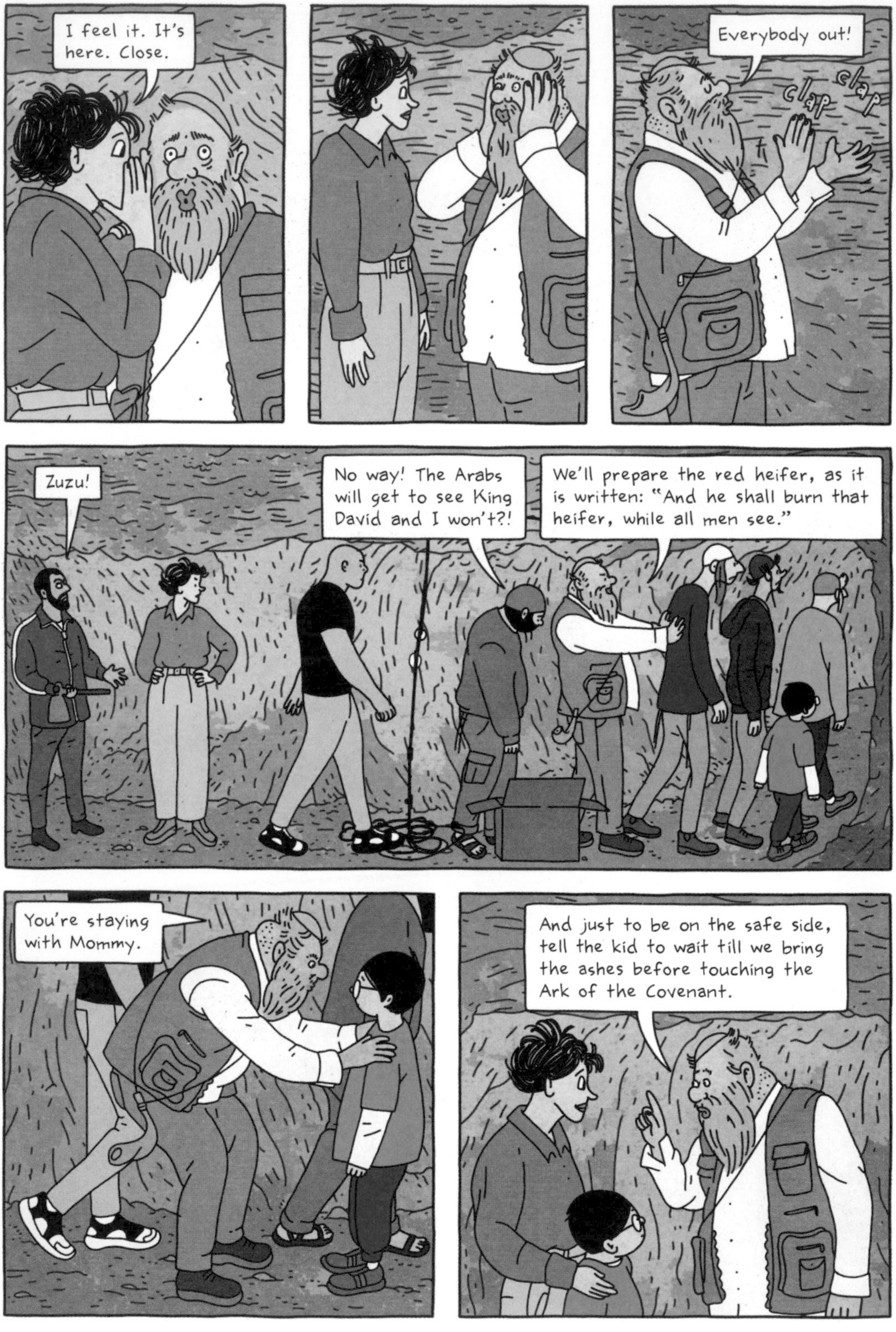
I feel it. It's here. Close.
Everybody out!
clap clap
Zuzu!
No way! The Arabs will get to see King David and I won't?!
We'll prepare the red heifer, as it is written: "And he shall burn that heifer, while all men see."
You're staying with Mommy.
And just to be on the safe side, tell the kid to wait till we bring the ashes before touching the Ark of the Covenant.

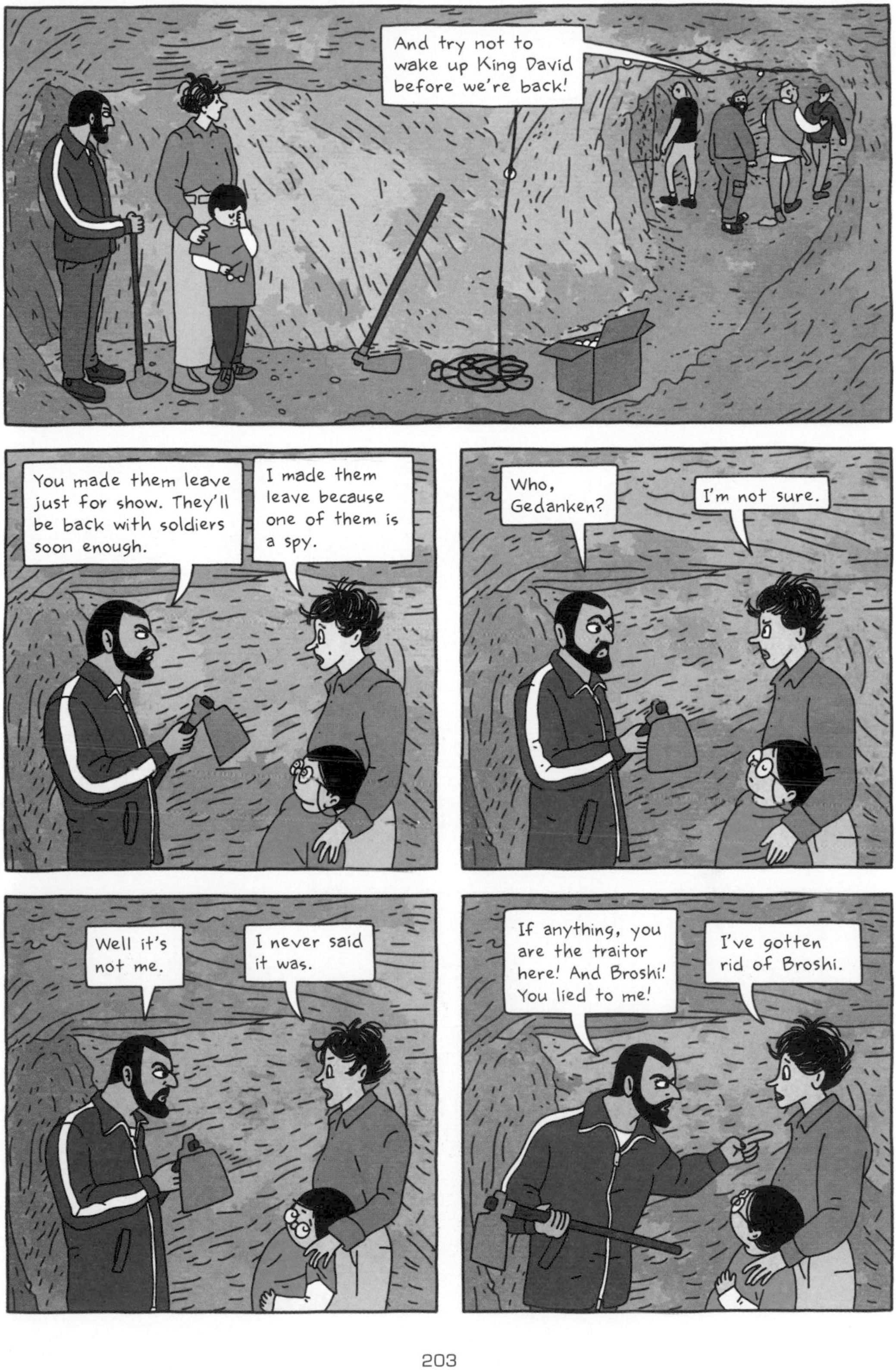
And try not to wake up King David before we're back!
You made them leave just for show. They'll be back with soldiers soon enough.
I made them leave because one of them is a spy.
Who, Gedanken?
I'm not sure.
Well it's not me.
I never said it was.
If anything, you are the traitor here! And Broshi! You lied to me!
I've gotten rid of Broshi.

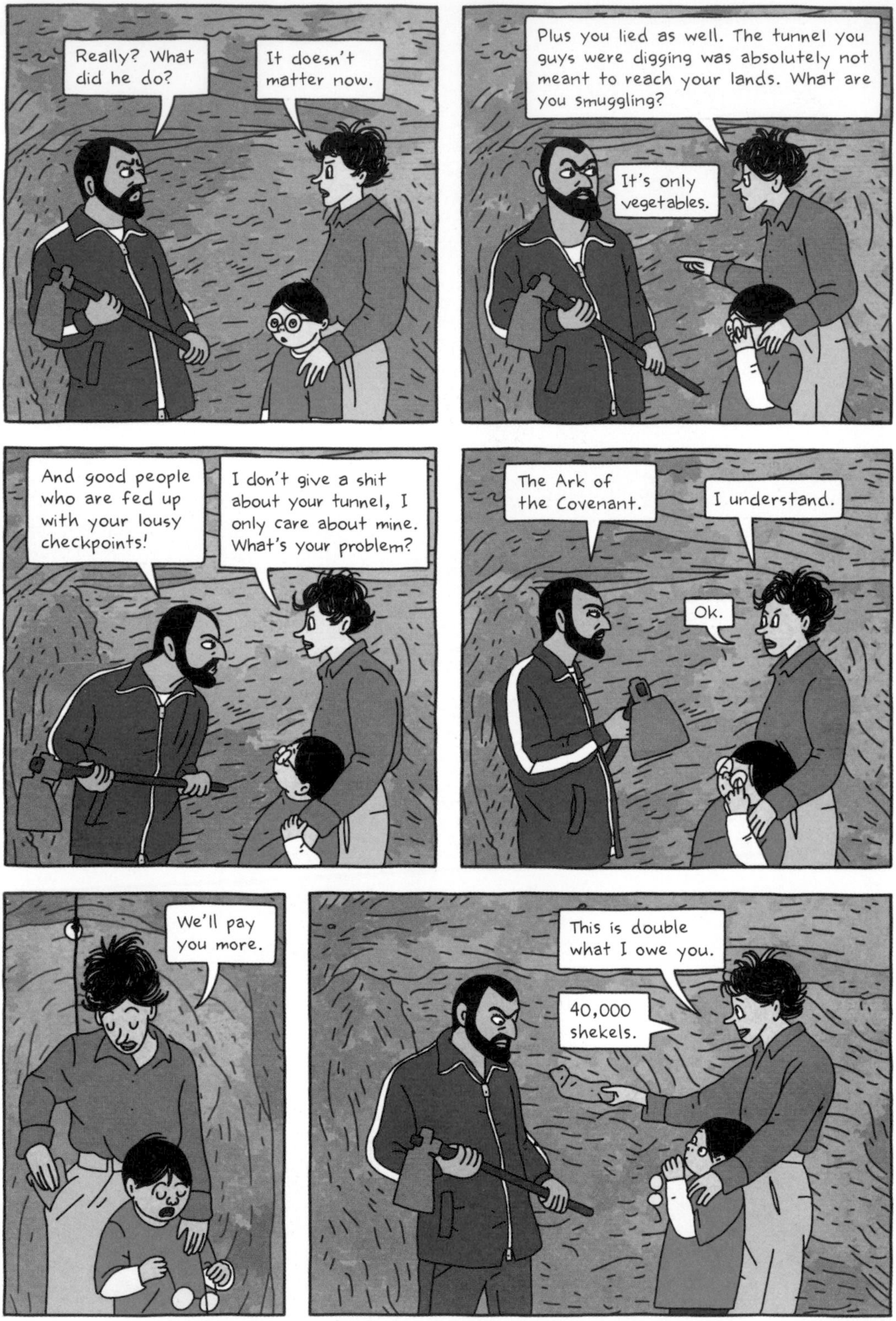
Really? What did he do?
It doesn't matter now.
Plus you lied as well. The tunnel you guys were digging was absolutely not meant to reach your lands. What are you smuggling?
It's only vegetables.
And good people who are fed up with your lousy checkpoints!
I don't give a shit about your tunnel, I only care about mine. What's your problem?
The Ark of the Covenant.
I understand.
Ok.
We'll pay you more.
This is double what I owe you.
40,000 shekels.

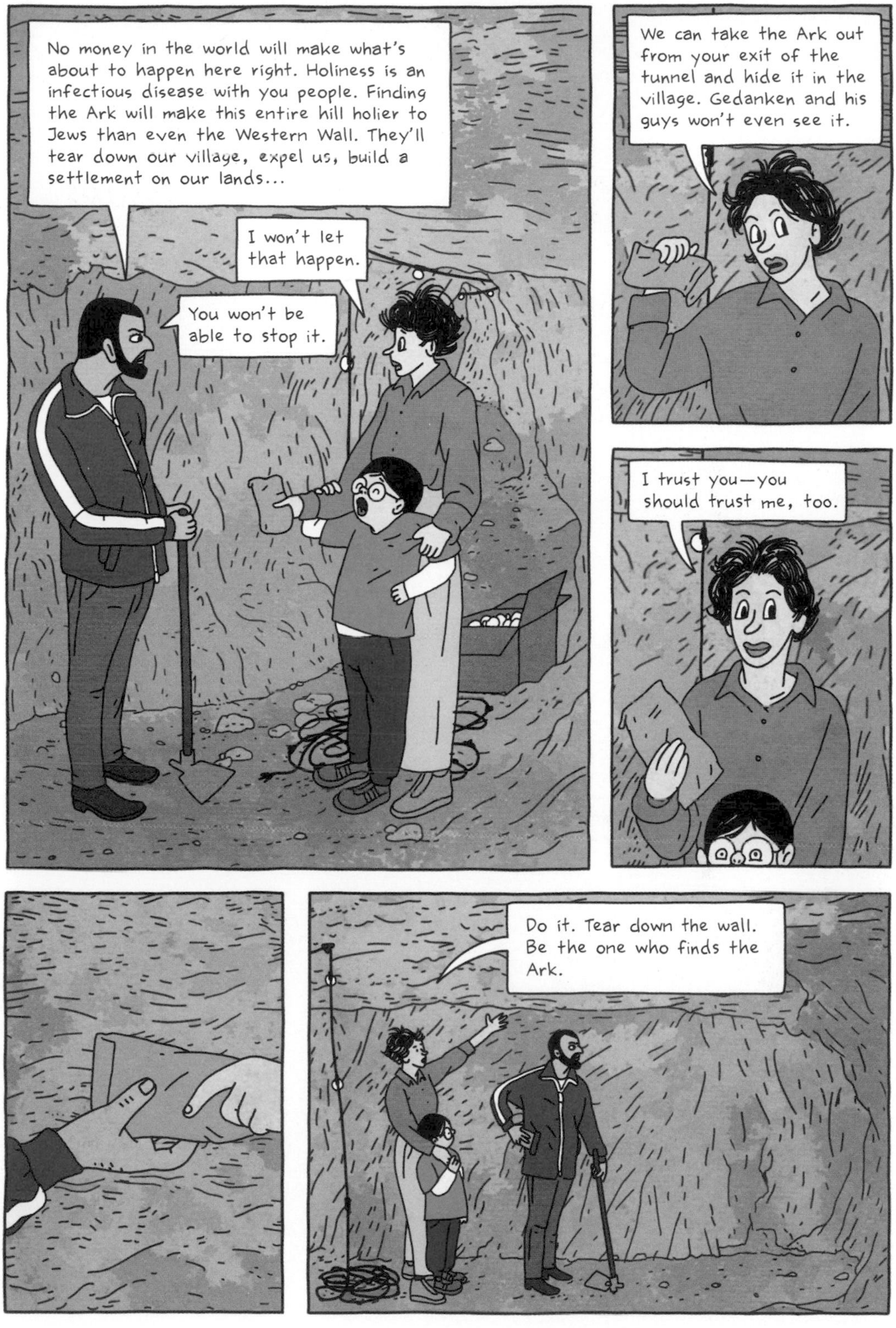
No money in the world will make what's about to happen here right. Holiness is an infectious disease with you people. Finding the Ark will make this entire hill holier to Jews than even the Western Wall. They'll tear down our village, expel us, build a settlement on our lands...
You won't be able to stop it.
I won't let that happen.
We can take the Ark out from your exit of the tunnel and hide it in the village. Gedanken and his guys won't even see it.
I trust you—you should trust me, too.
Do it. Tear down the wall. Be the one who finds the Ark.

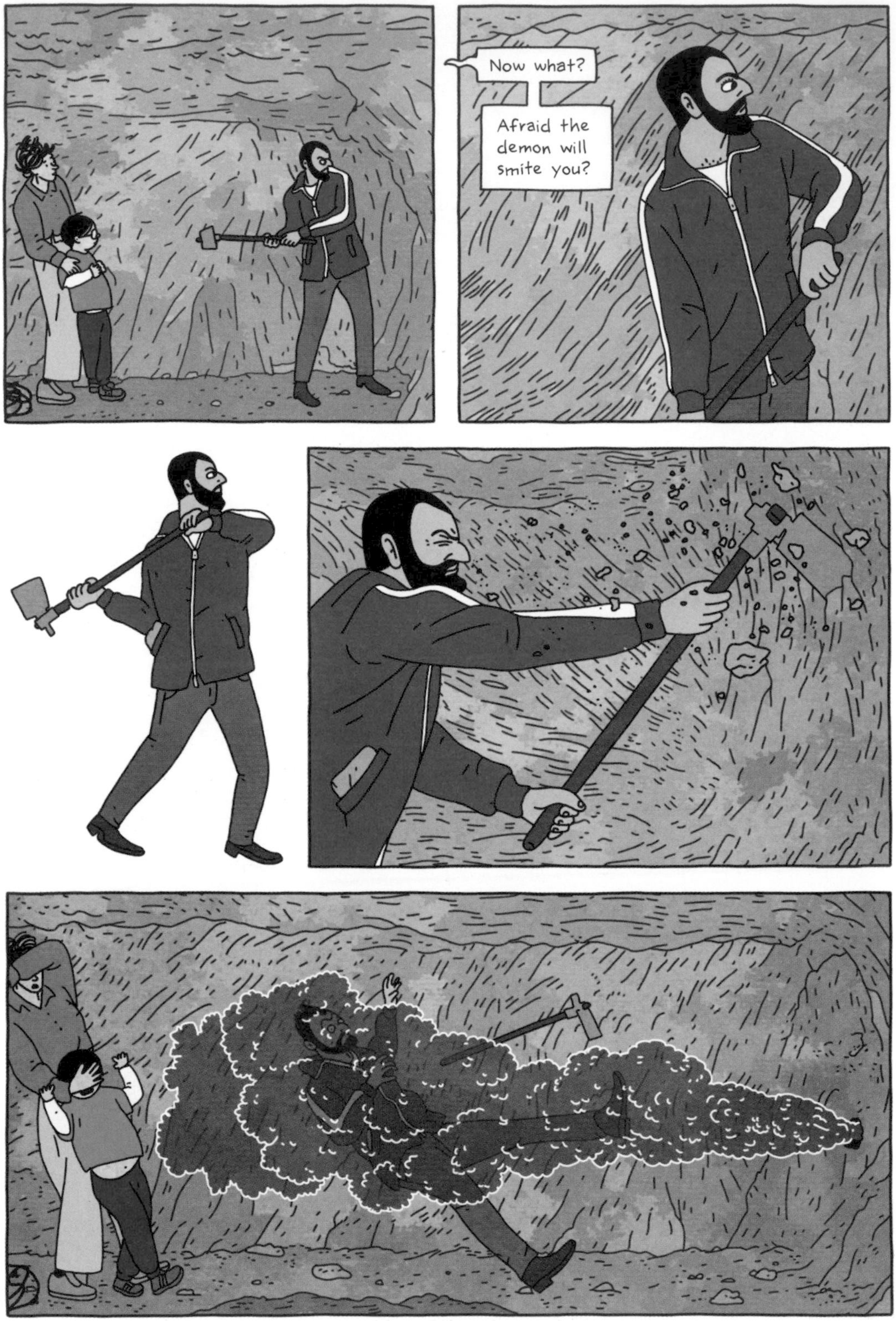
Now what?
Afraid the demon will smite you?

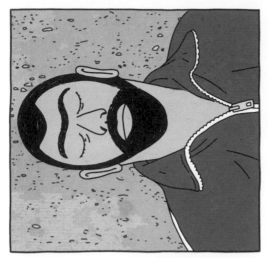

You're alive. You just fainted.

What was that?

Underground gas bubble—a common enough phenomenon in enclosed spaces.

It's a good sign!

There's something in there. Bring the lights.

So dark!

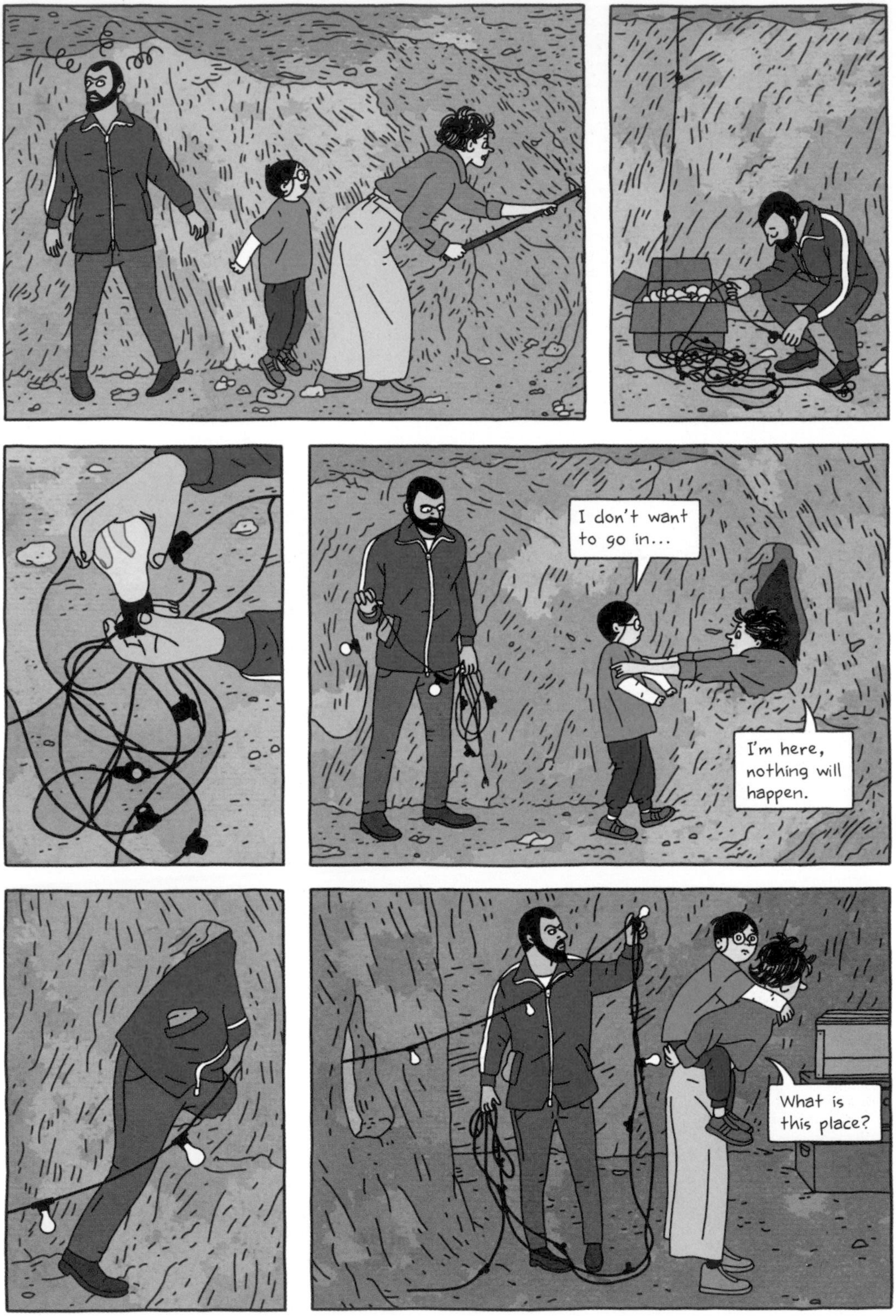
I don't want to go in...
I'm here, nothing will happen.
What is this place?

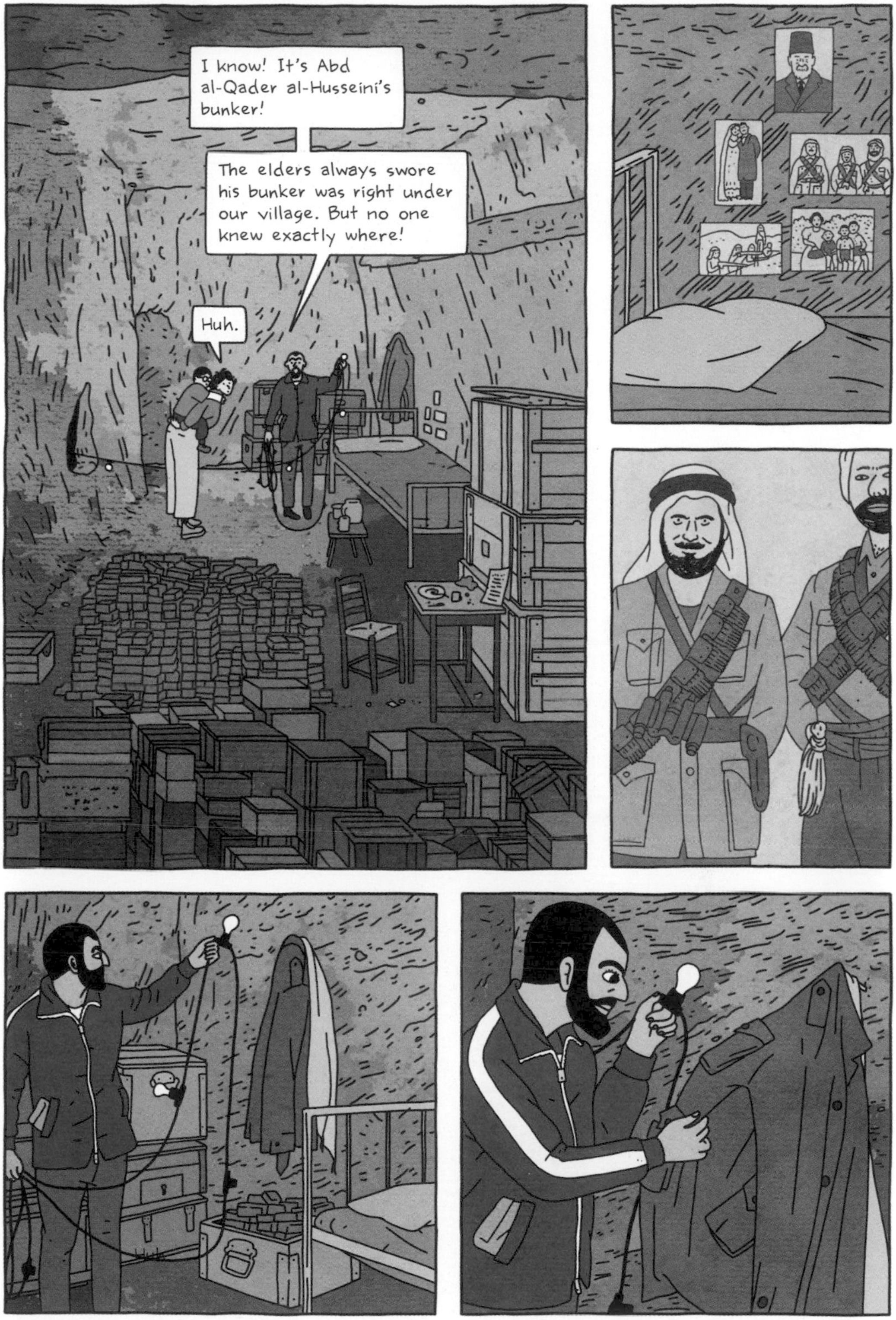
I know! It's Abd al-Qader al-Husseini's bunker!
The elders always swore his bunker was right under our village. But no one knew exactly where!
Huh.

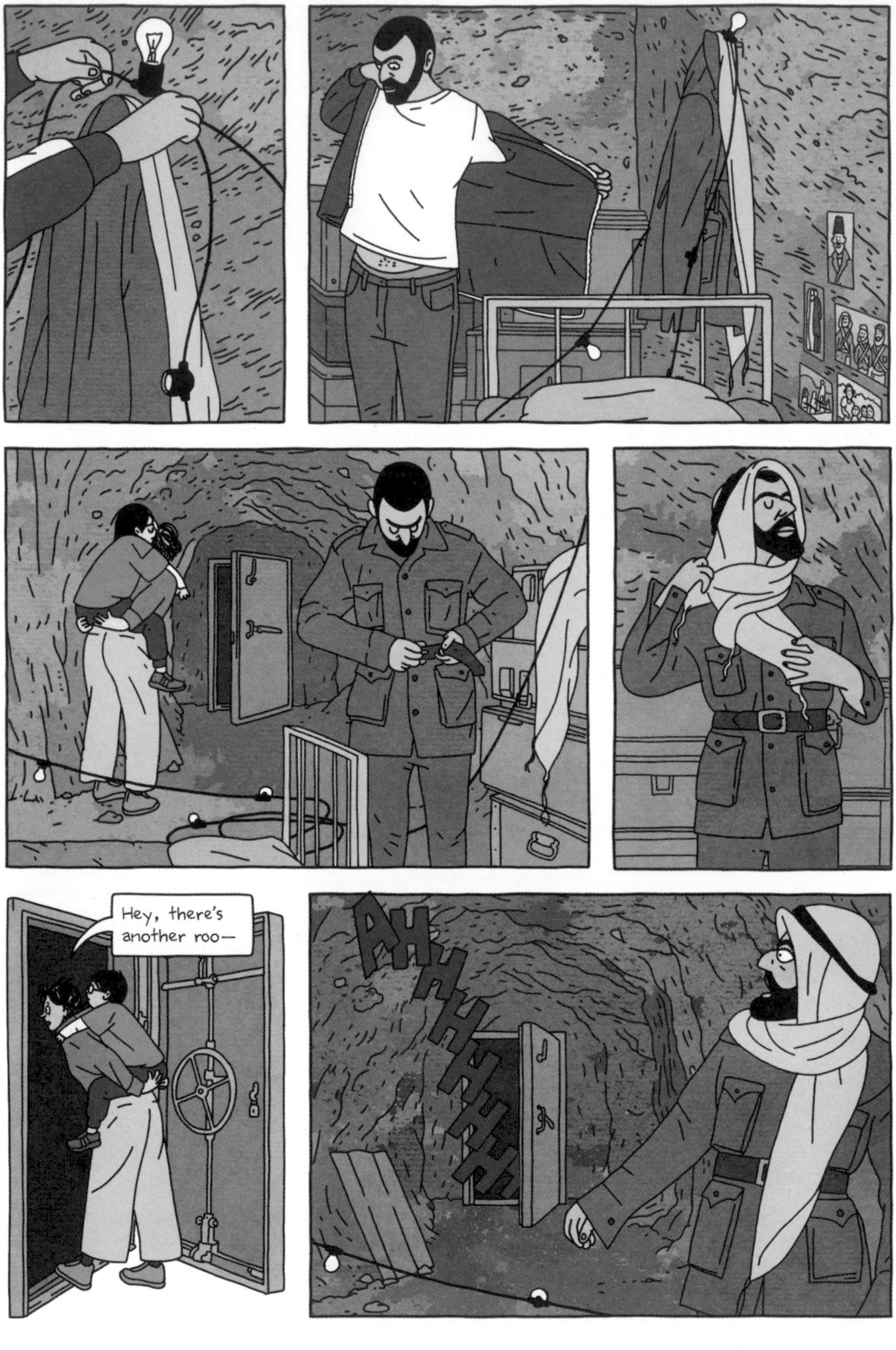

Hey, there's another roo—
AHHHHHHH

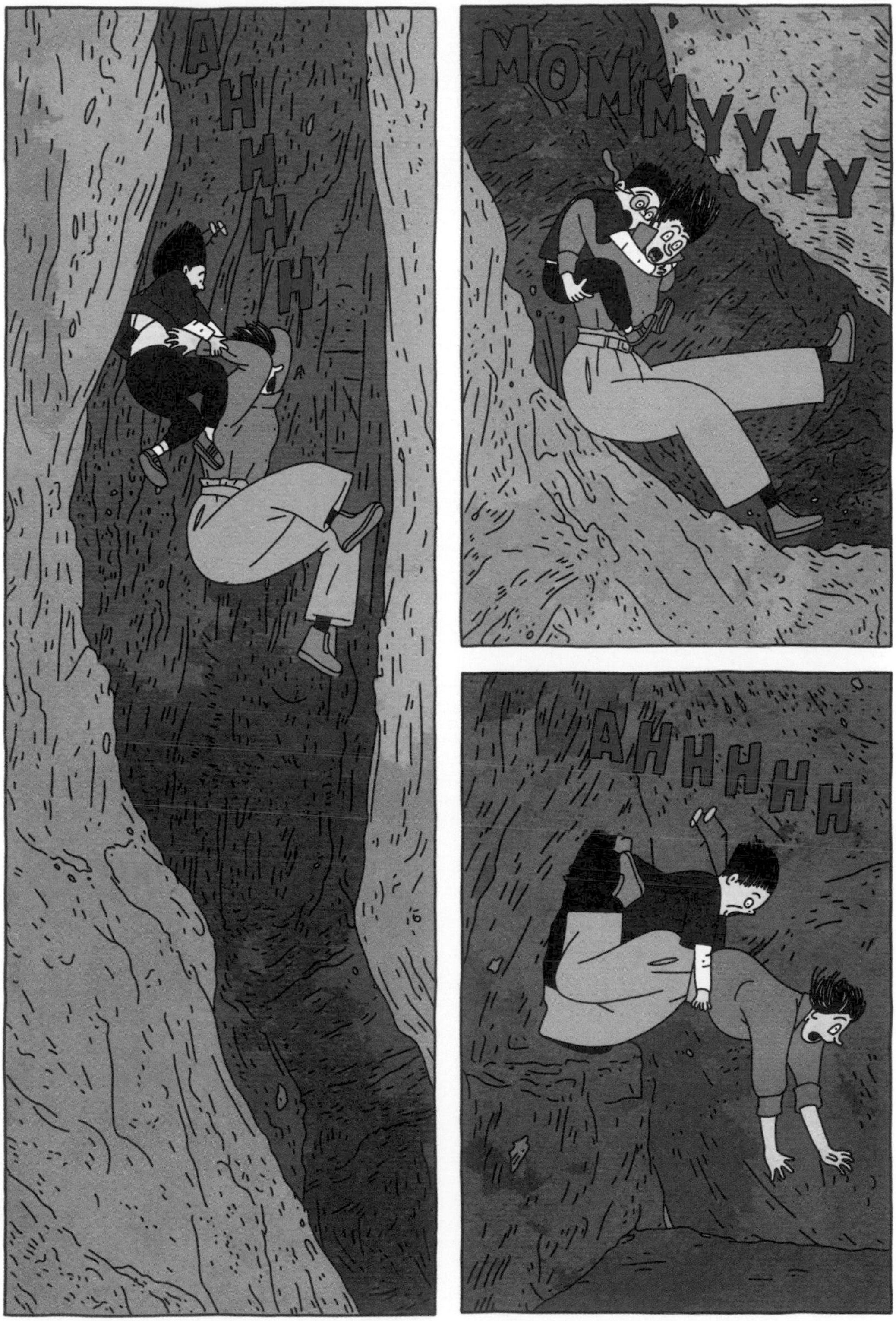
AHHHHH
MOMMYYYYY
AHHHHHH

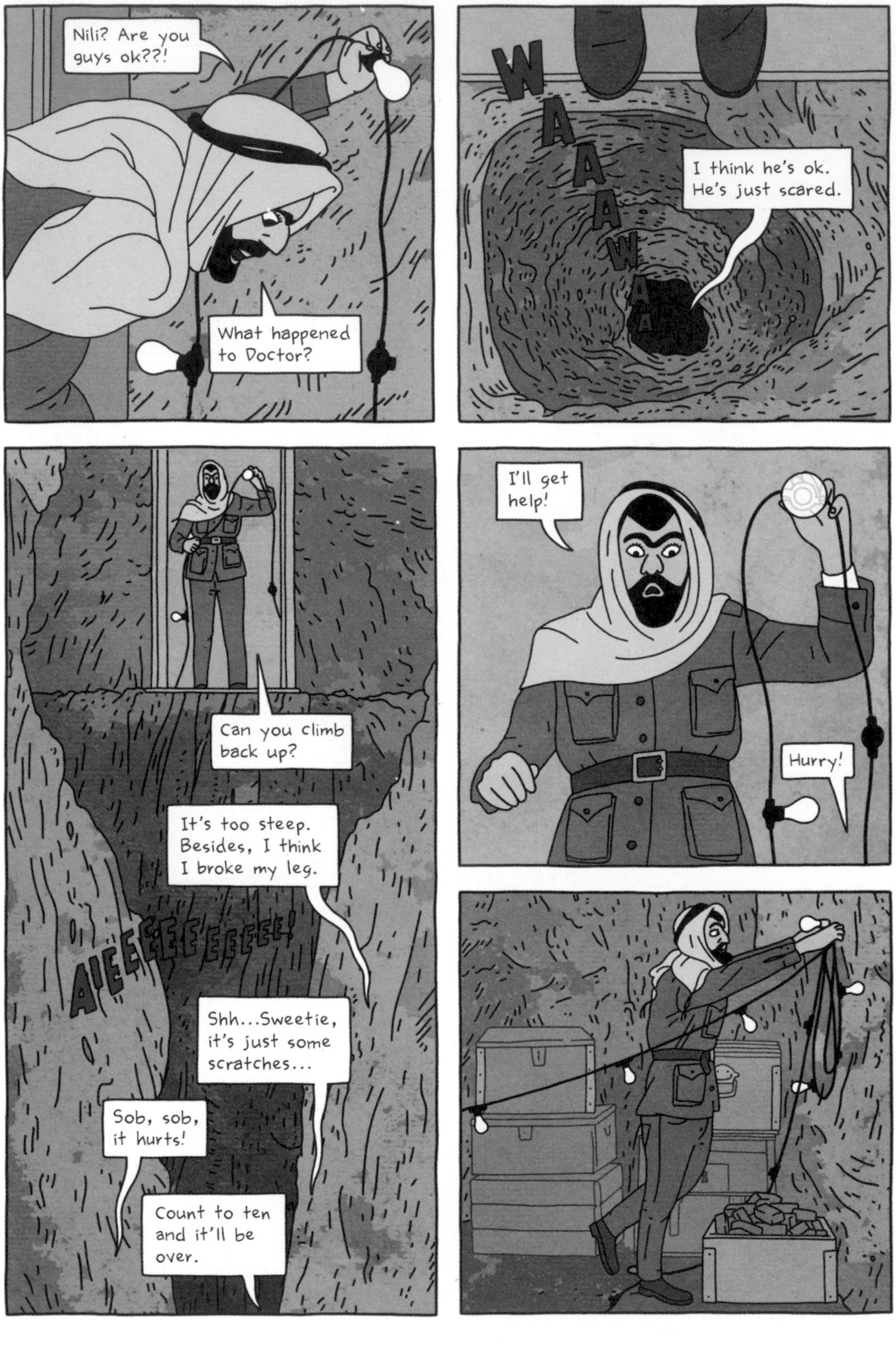
Nili? Are you guys ok??!
What happened to Doctor?
WAAAAWAA
I think he's ok. He's just scared.
Can you climb back up?
It's too steep. Besides, I think I broke my leg.
AIEEEEEEEEEEE!
Shh...Sweetie, it's just some scratches...
Sob, sob, it hurts!
Count to ten and it'll be over.
I'll get help!
Hurry!

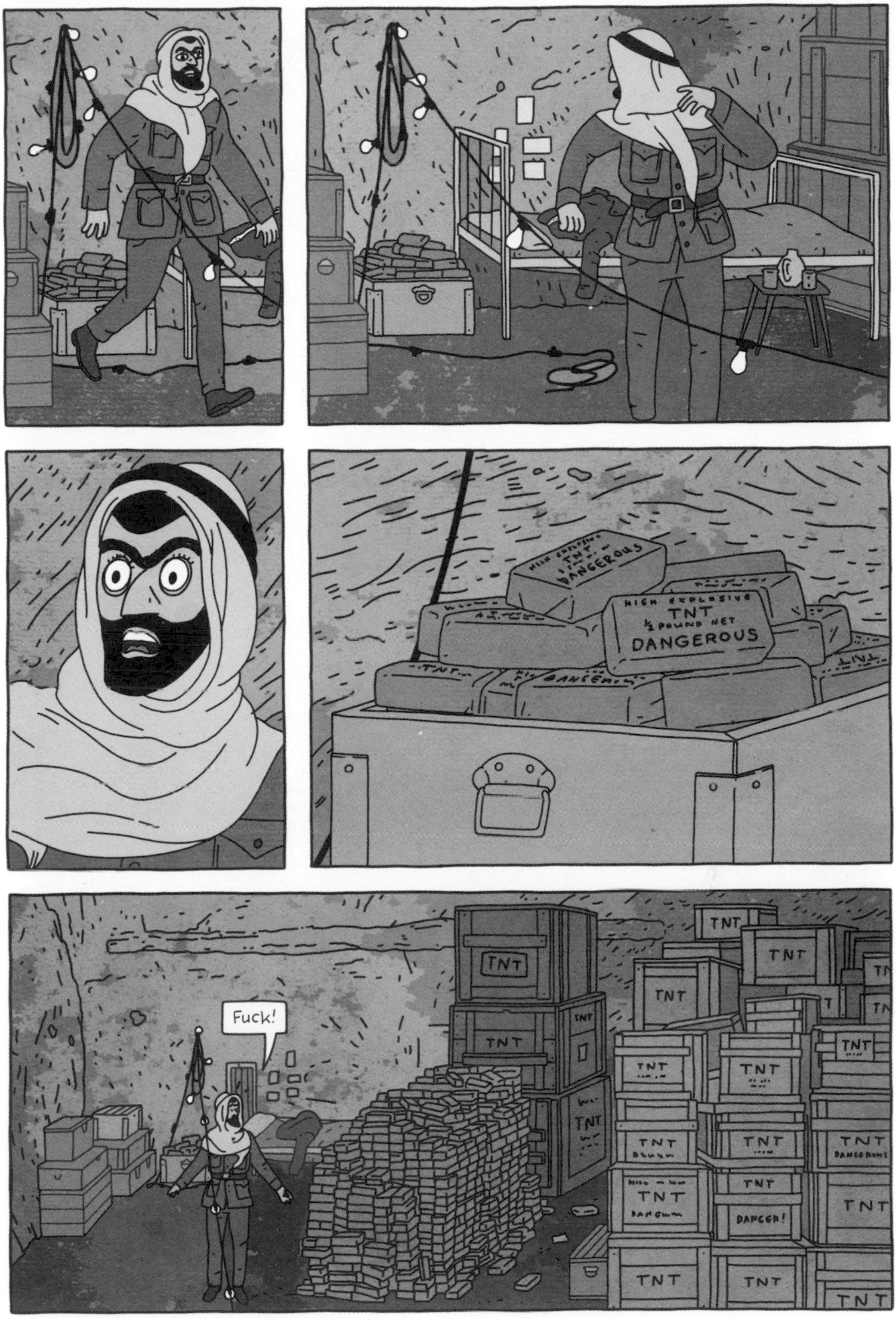
DANGEROUS
HIGH EXPLOSIVE
TNT
½ POUND NET
DANGEROUS
Fuck!
TNT
TNT
TNT
TNT
TNT
TNT
TNT
TNT
TNT
DANGER!
TNT
TNT
TNT

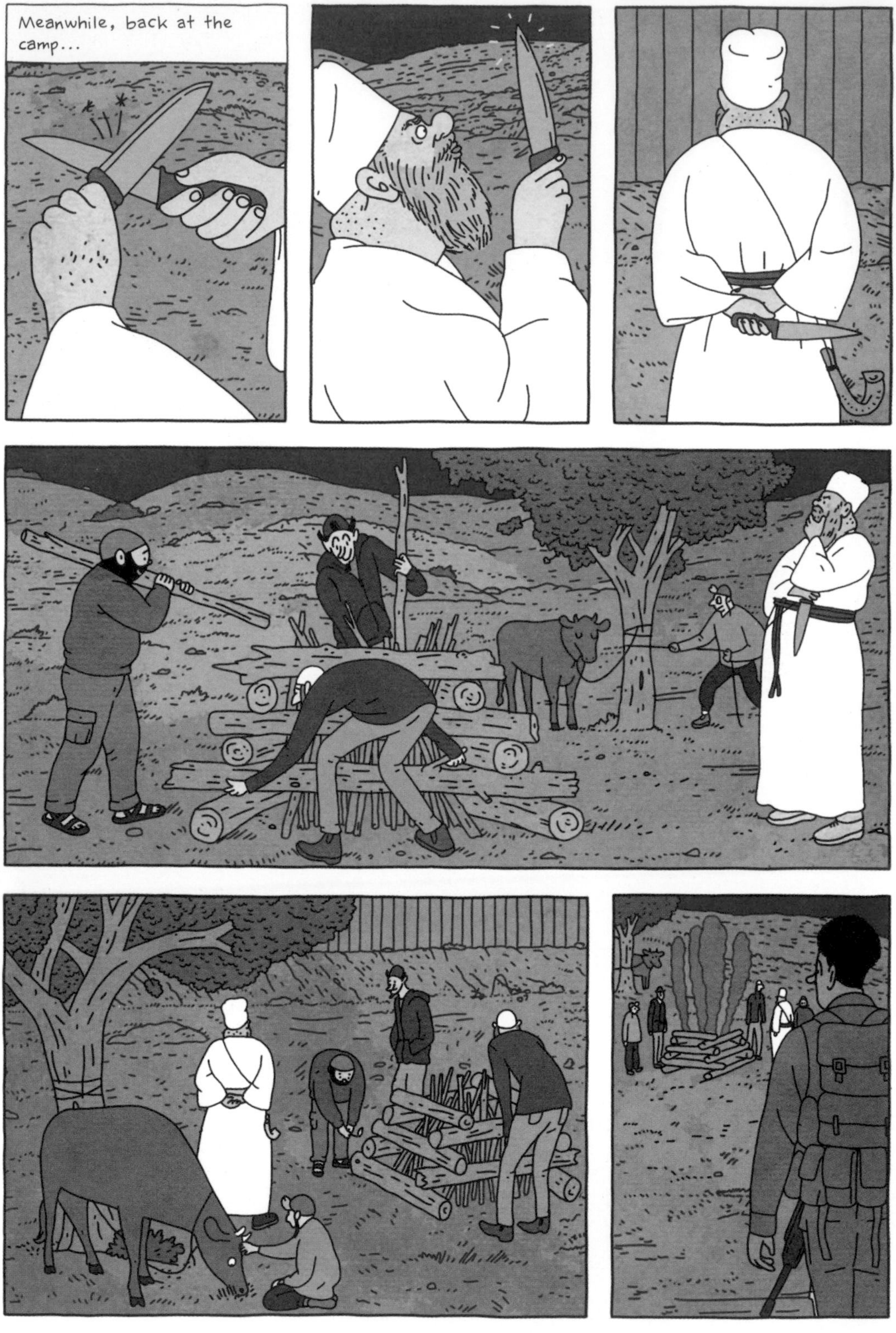
Meanwhile, back at the camp...

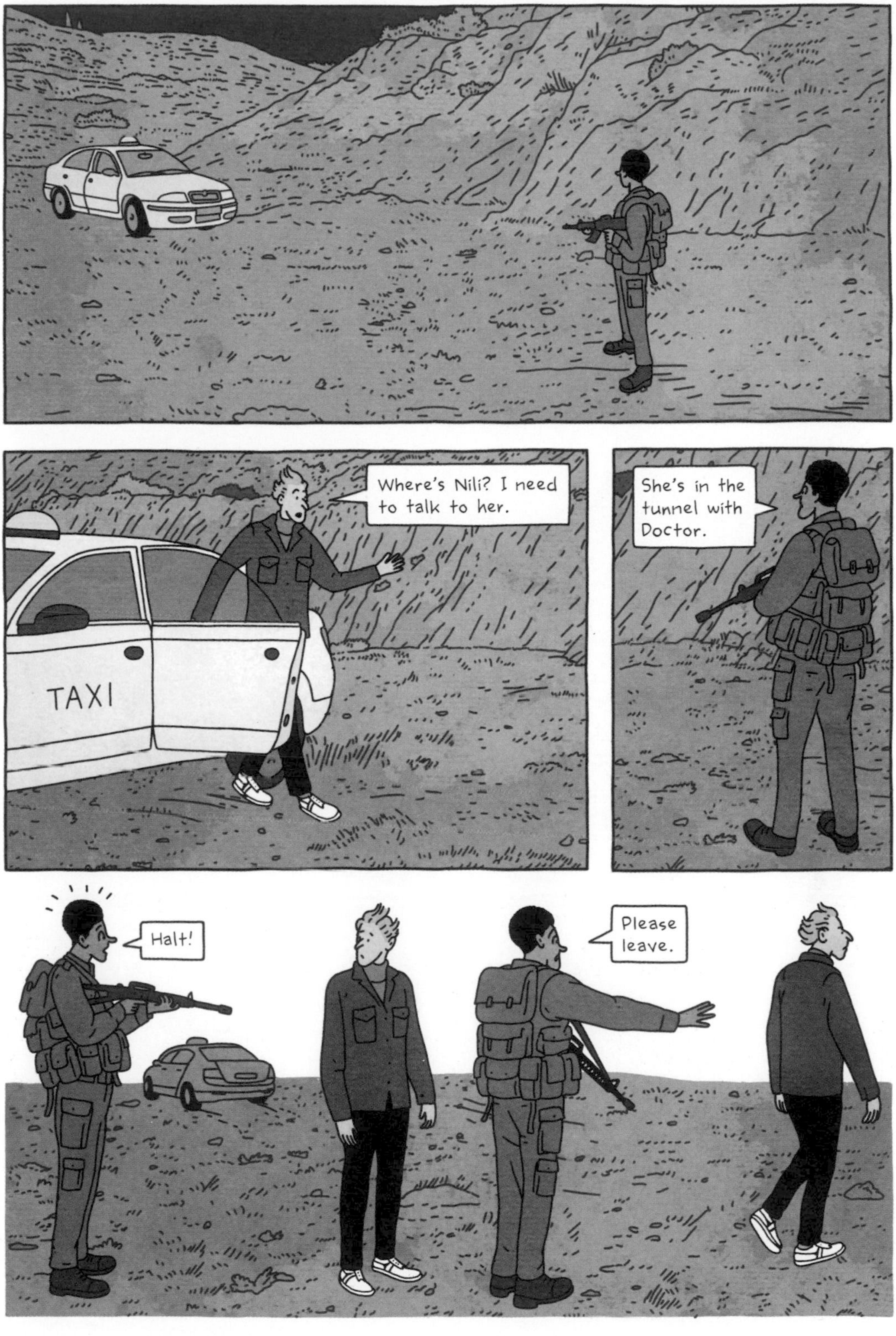
Where's Nili? I need to talk to her.
She's in the tunnel with Doctor.
Halt!
Please leave.

Nili doesn't want you here.
She already told you about me?
So it's true?
Broshi! Quick! The tunnel is full of explosives!!
Don't shoot! He's a friend!
I'm with him! I'm with him!
You really are ISIS!

BANG!

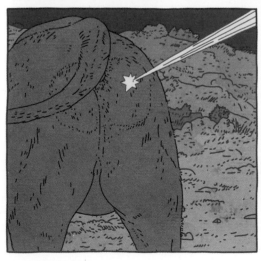

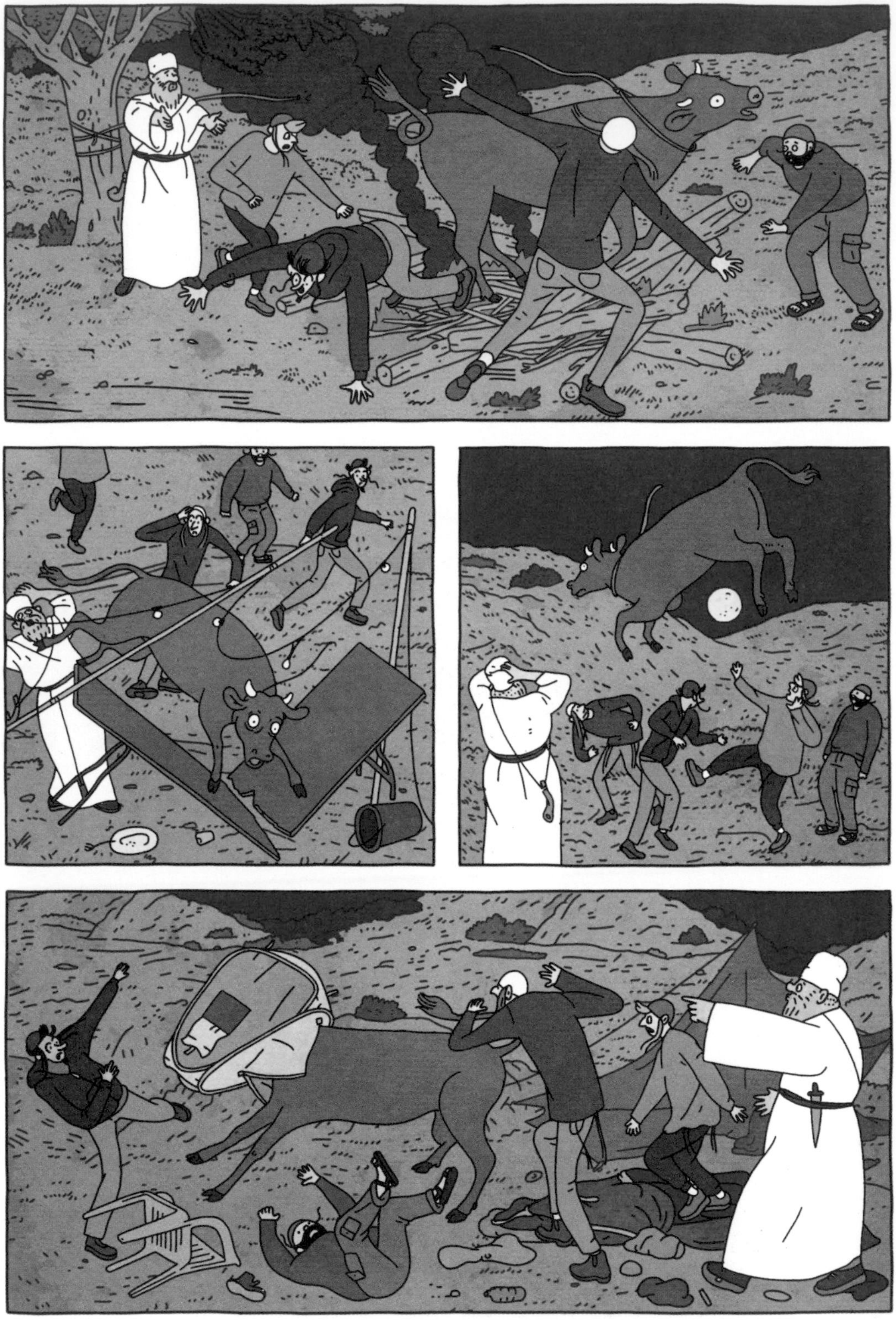

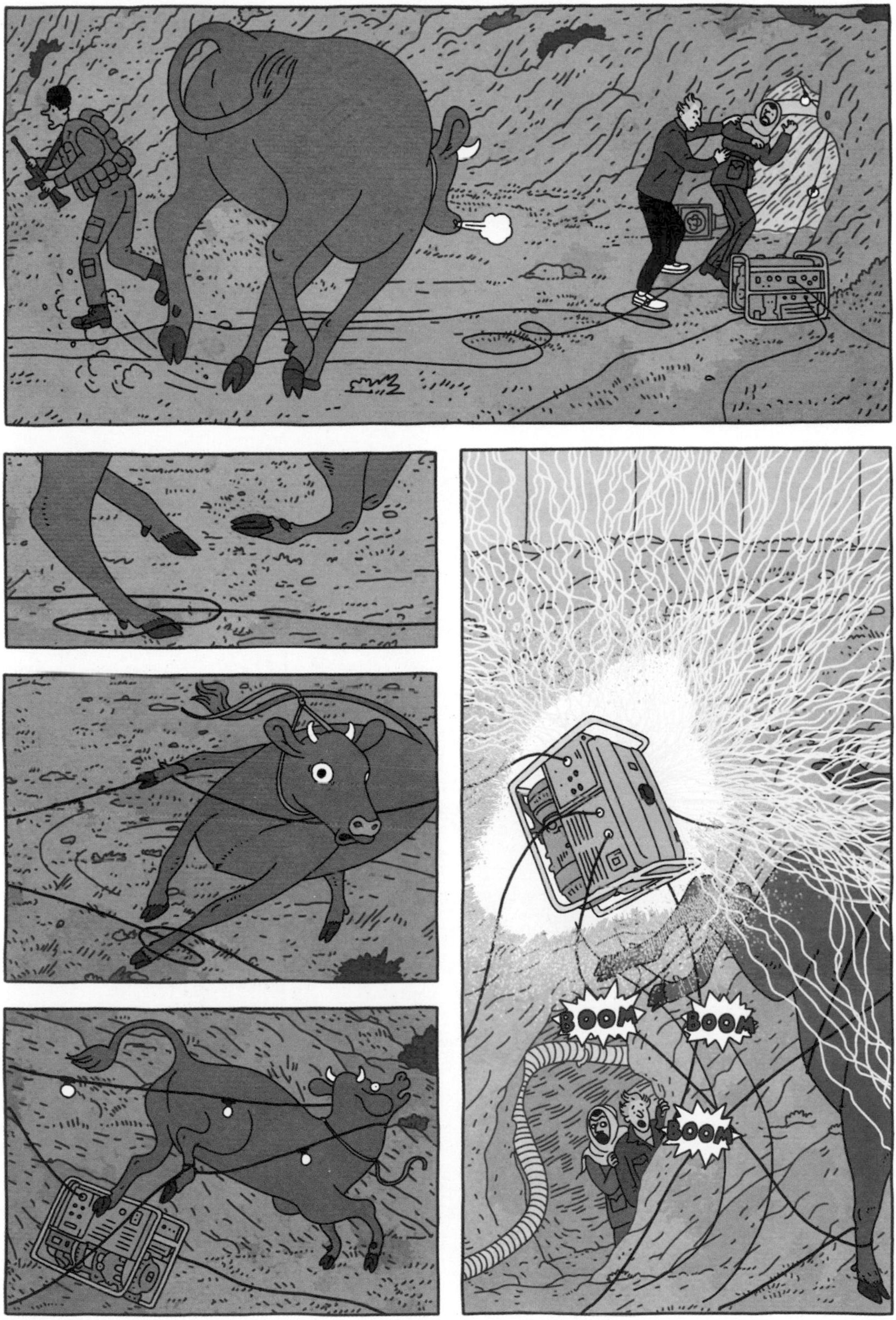
BOOM
BOOM
BOOM

BOOM
BOOM
BOOM
BOOM
Run! Explosives!!
BOOM
BOOM
BOOM
BOOM
Nili! Doctor!

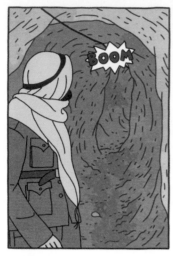

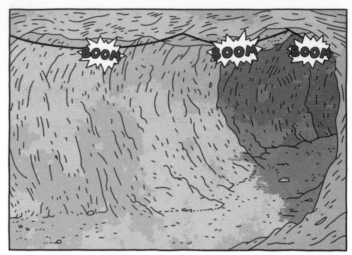

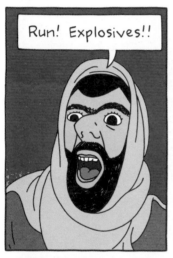

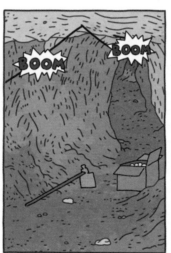

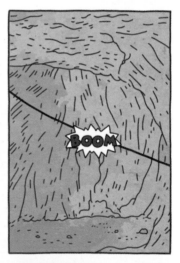

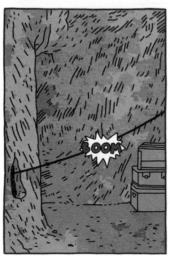

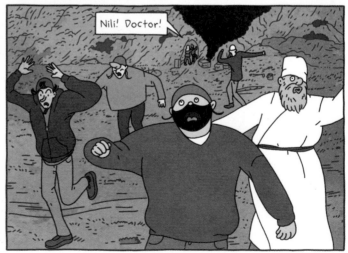

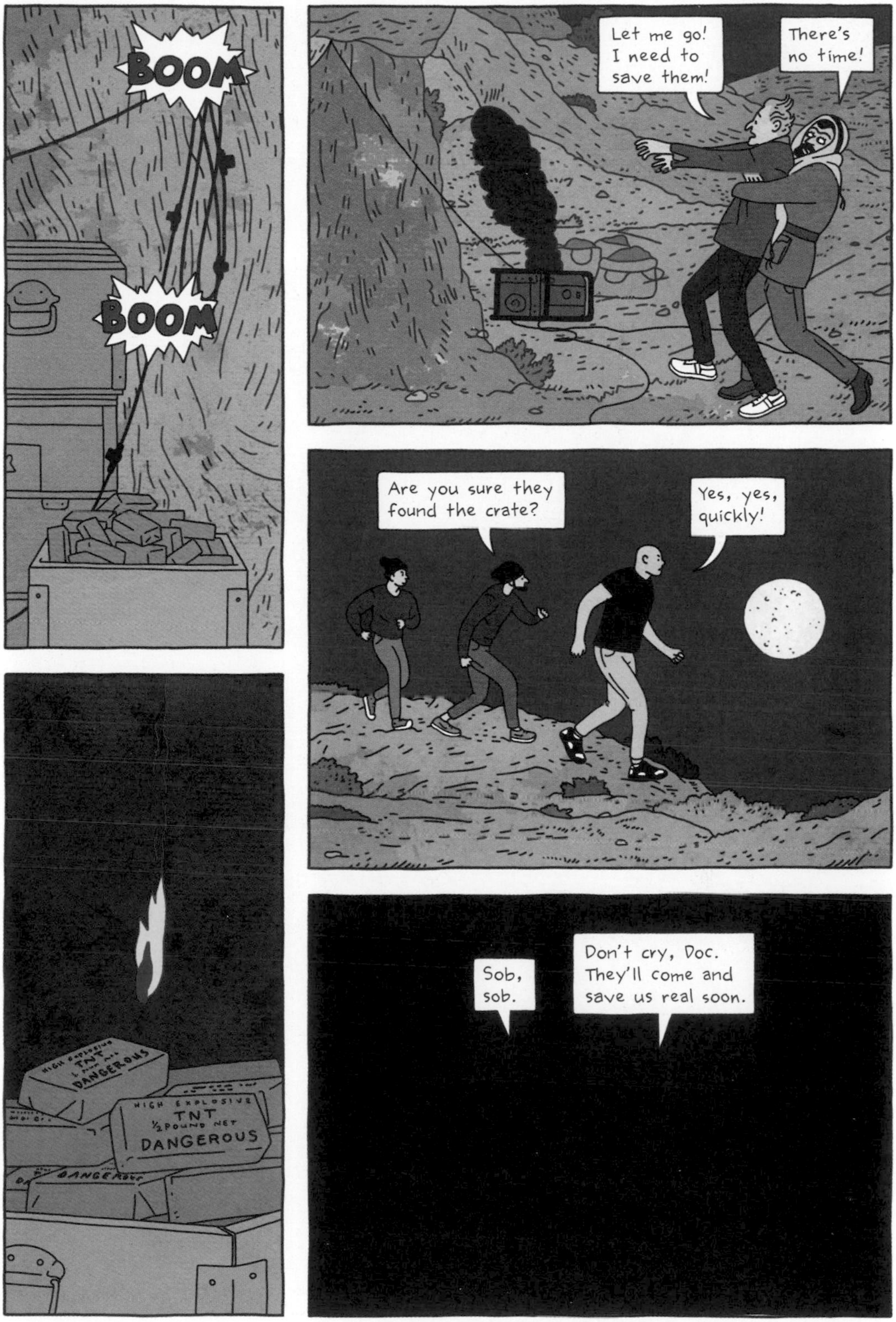
BOOM
BOOM
Let me go! I need to save them!
There's no time!
Are you sure they found the crate?
Yes, yes, quickly!
HIGH EXPLOSIVE TNT 1/2 POUND NET DANGEROUS
DANGEROUS
Sob, sob.
Don't cry, Doc. They'll come and save us real soon.

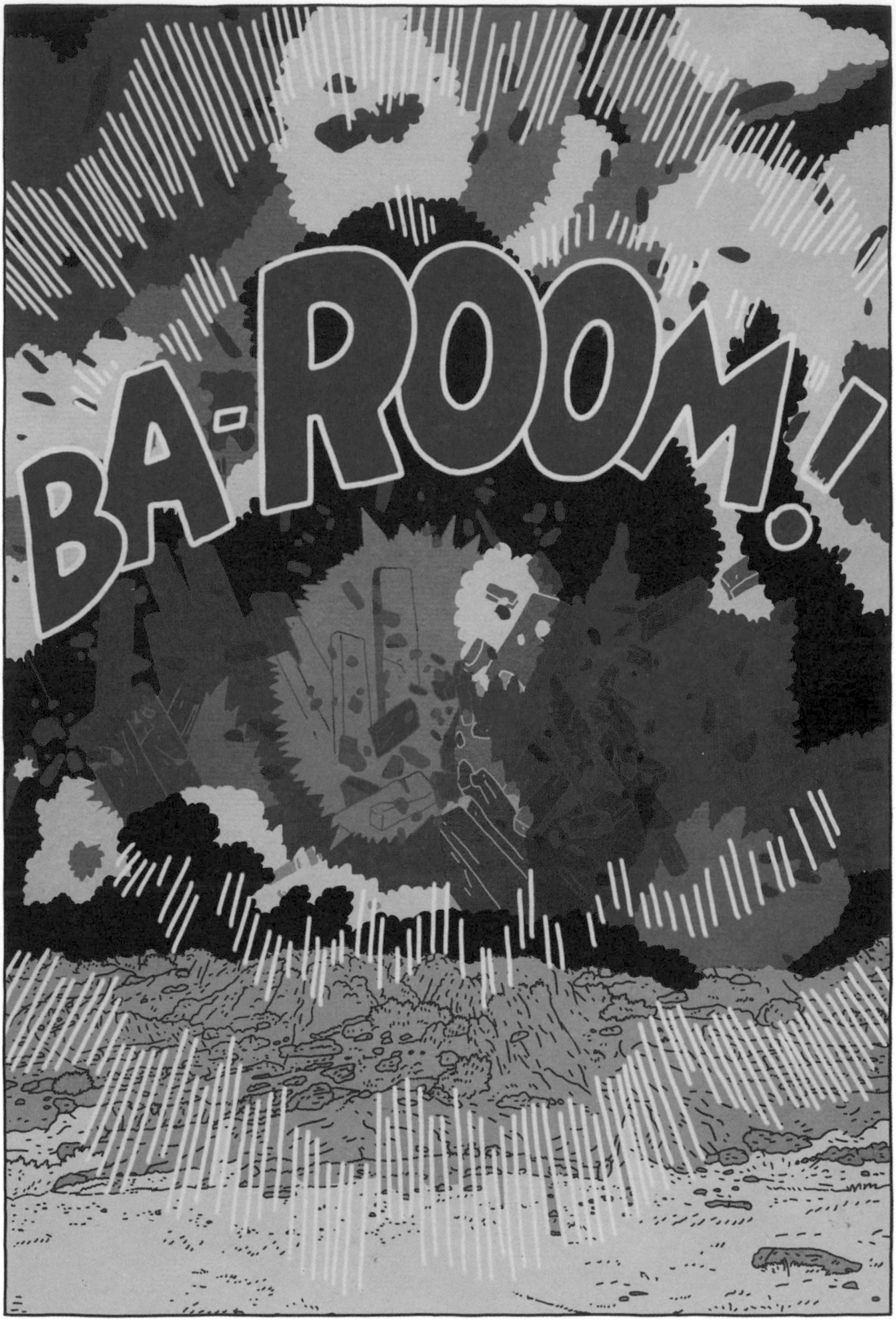
BA-ROOM!!

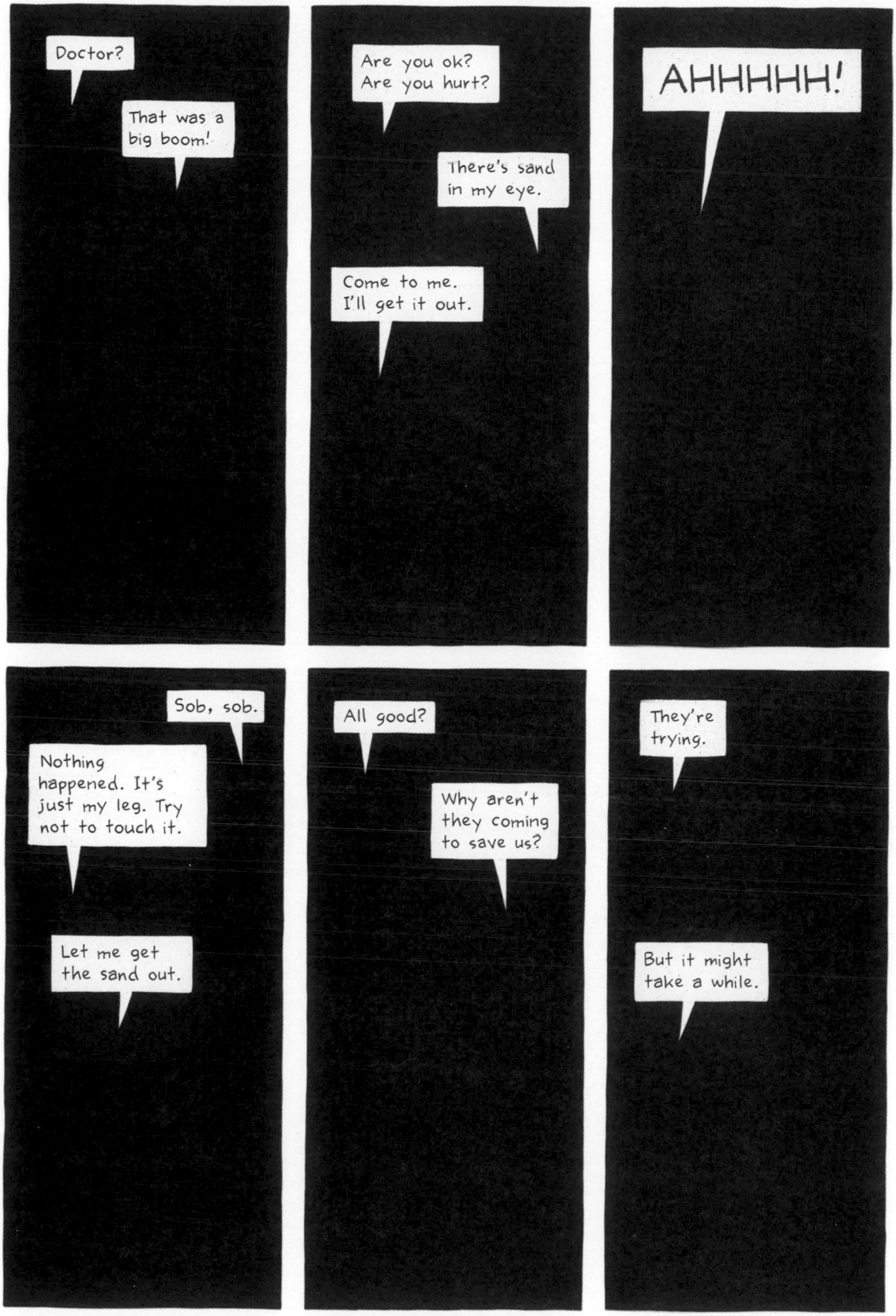
Doctor?
That was a big boom!
Are you ok? Are you hurt?
There's sand in my eye.
Come to me. I'll get it out.
AHHHHH!
Sob, sob.
Nothing happened. It's just my leg. Try not to touch it.
Let me get the sand out.
All good?
Why aren't they coming to save us?
They're trying.
But it might take a while.

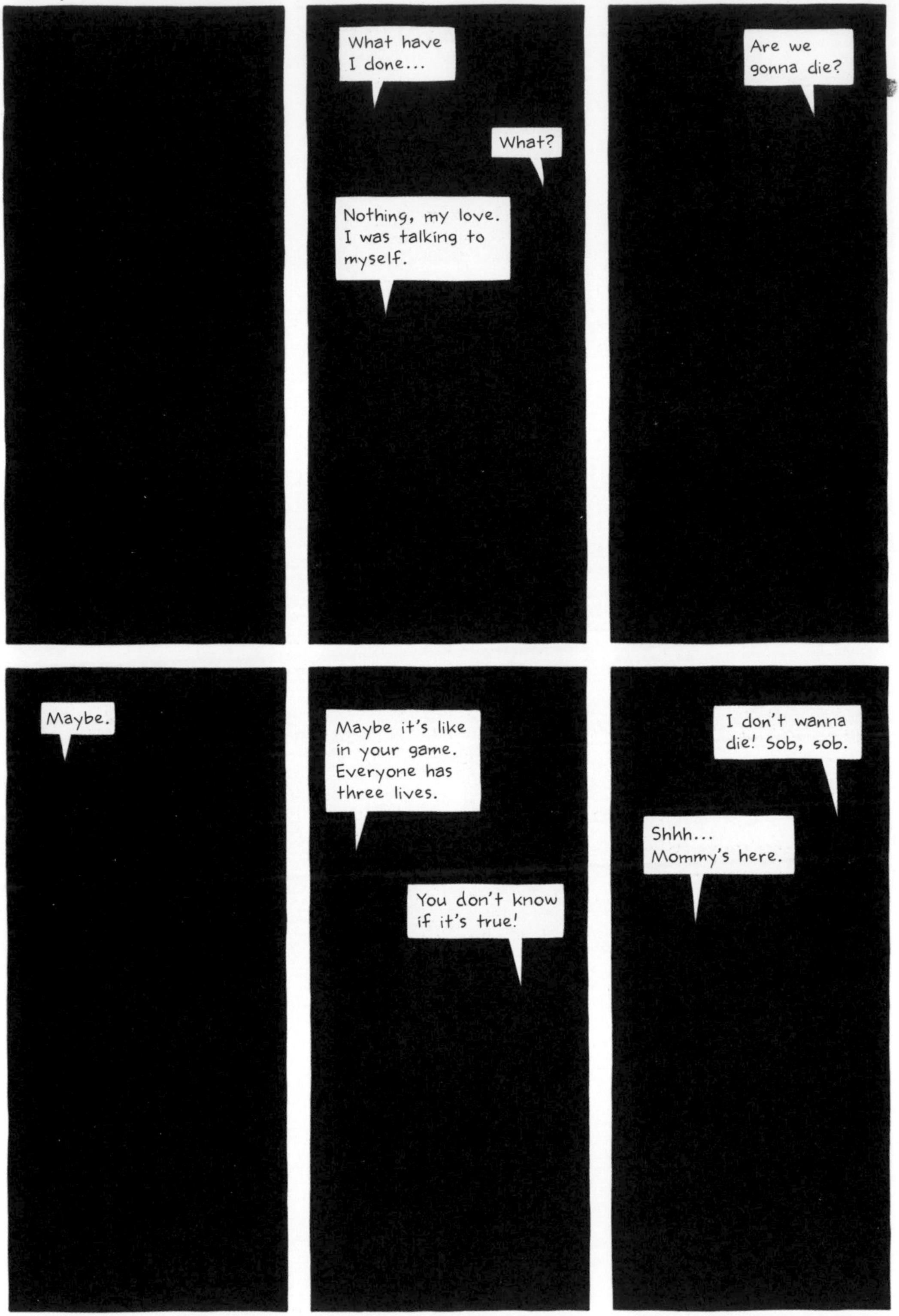
What have I done...
What?
Nothing, my love. I was talking to myself.
Are we gonna die?
Maybe.
Maybe it's like in your game. Everyone has three lives.
You don't know if it's true!
I don't wanna die! Sob, sob.
Shhh... Mommy's here.

Part 4: The Pit

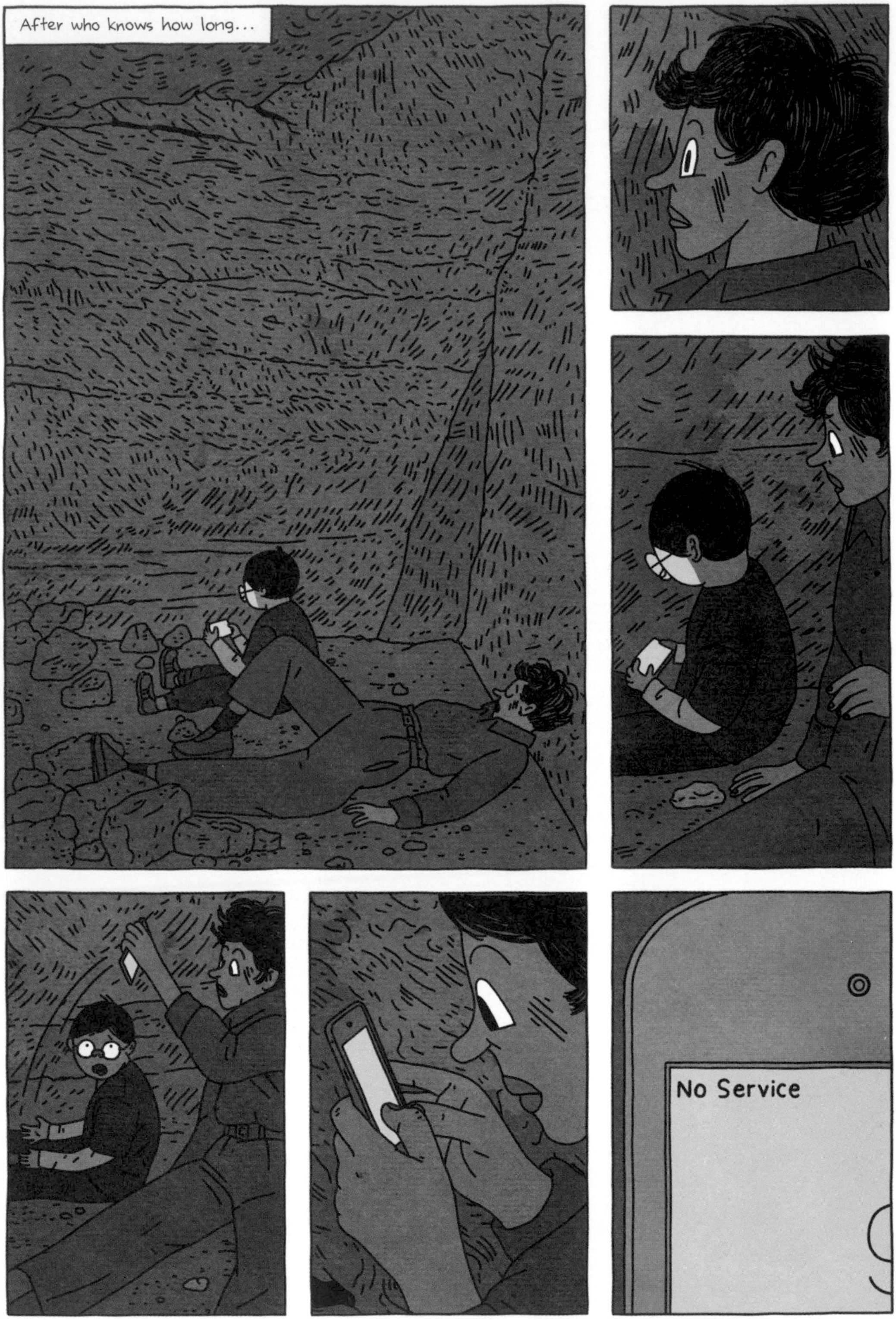
After who knows how long...
No Service

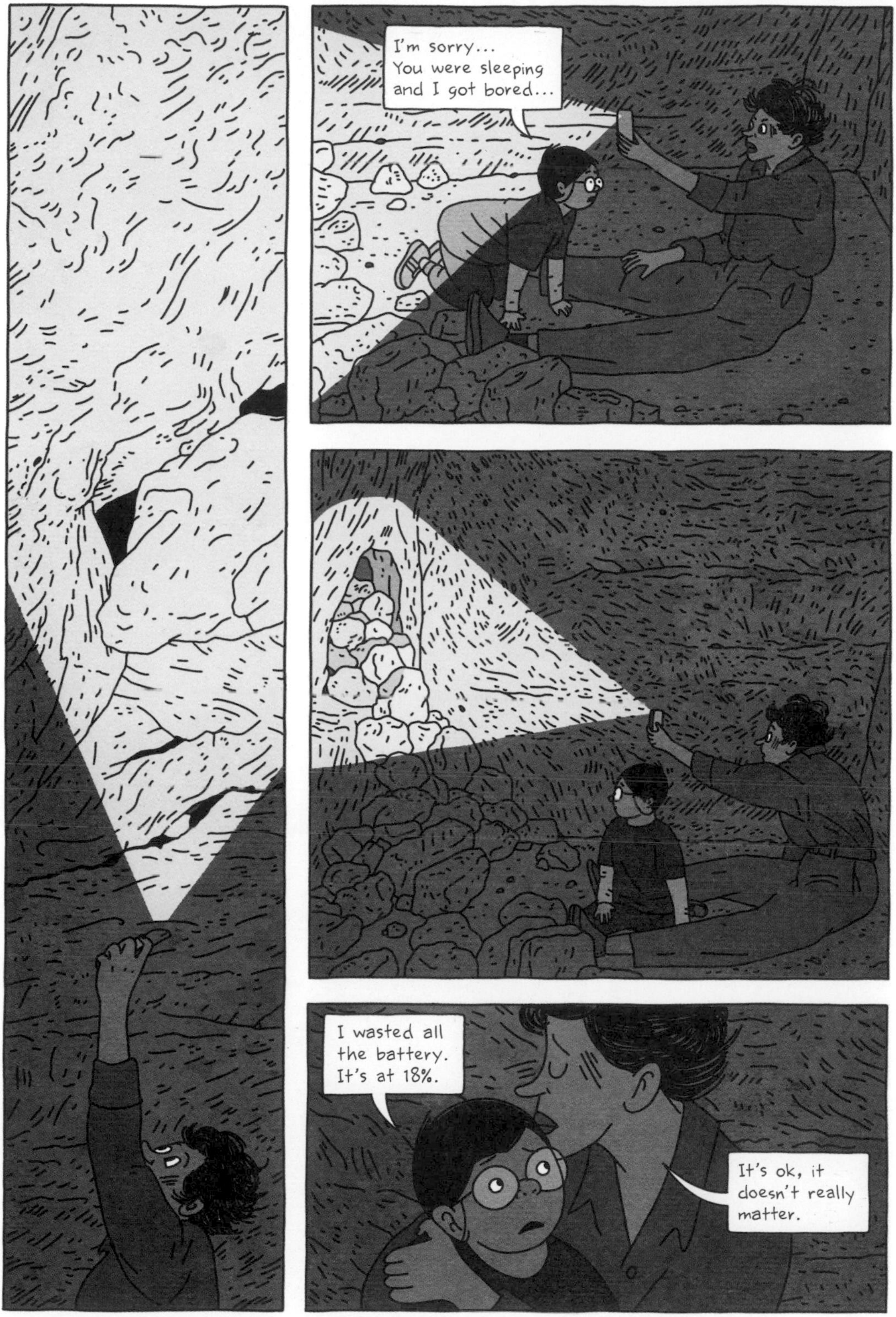
I'm sorry...
You were sleeping
and I got bored...
I wasted all
the battery.
It's at 18%.
It's ok, it
doesn't really
matter.

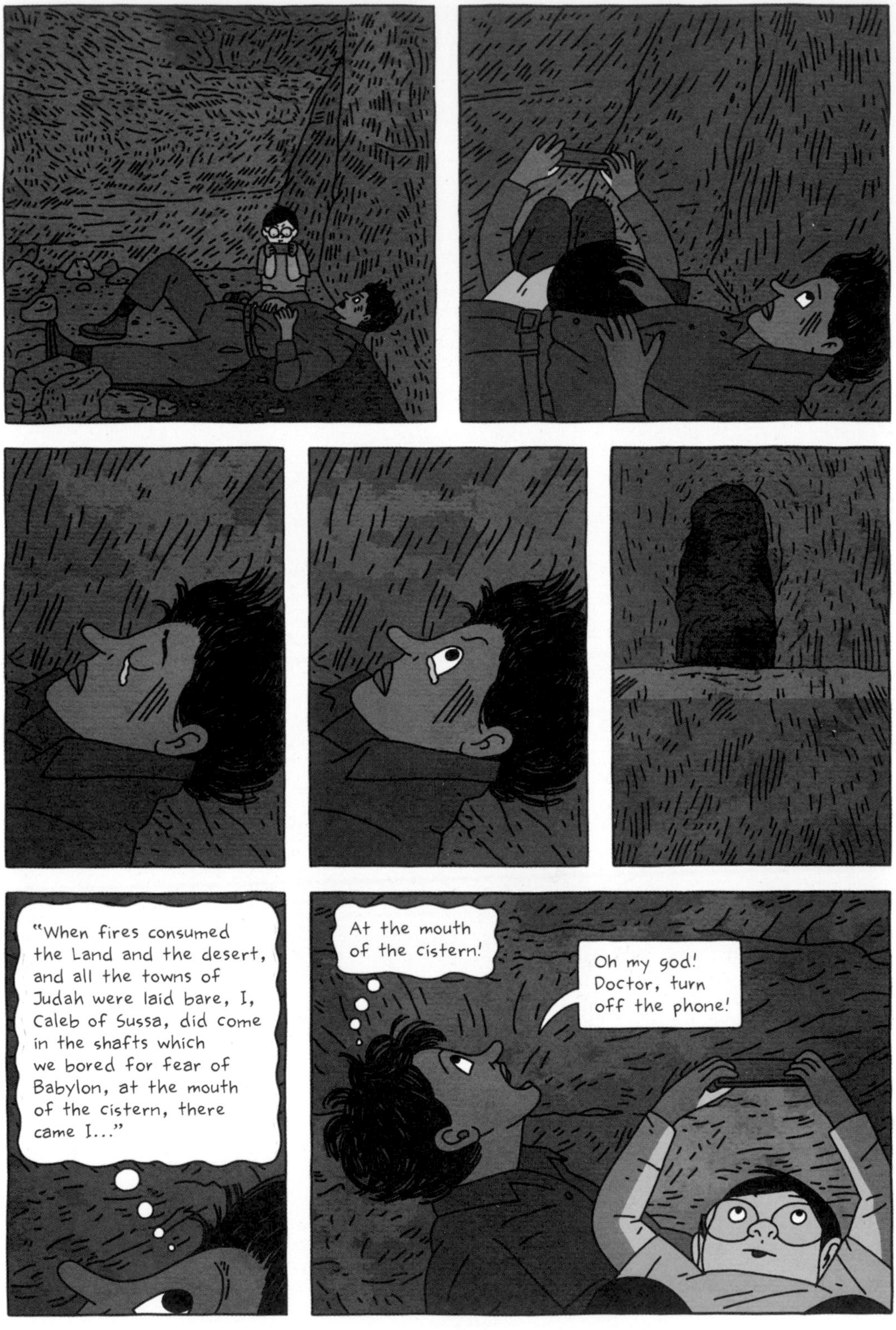
"When fires consumed the Land and the desert, and all the towns of Judah were laid bare, I, Caleb of Sussa, did come in the shafts which we bored for fear of Babylon, at the mouth of the cistern, there came I..."
At the mouth of the cistern!
Oh my god! Doctor, turn off the phone!

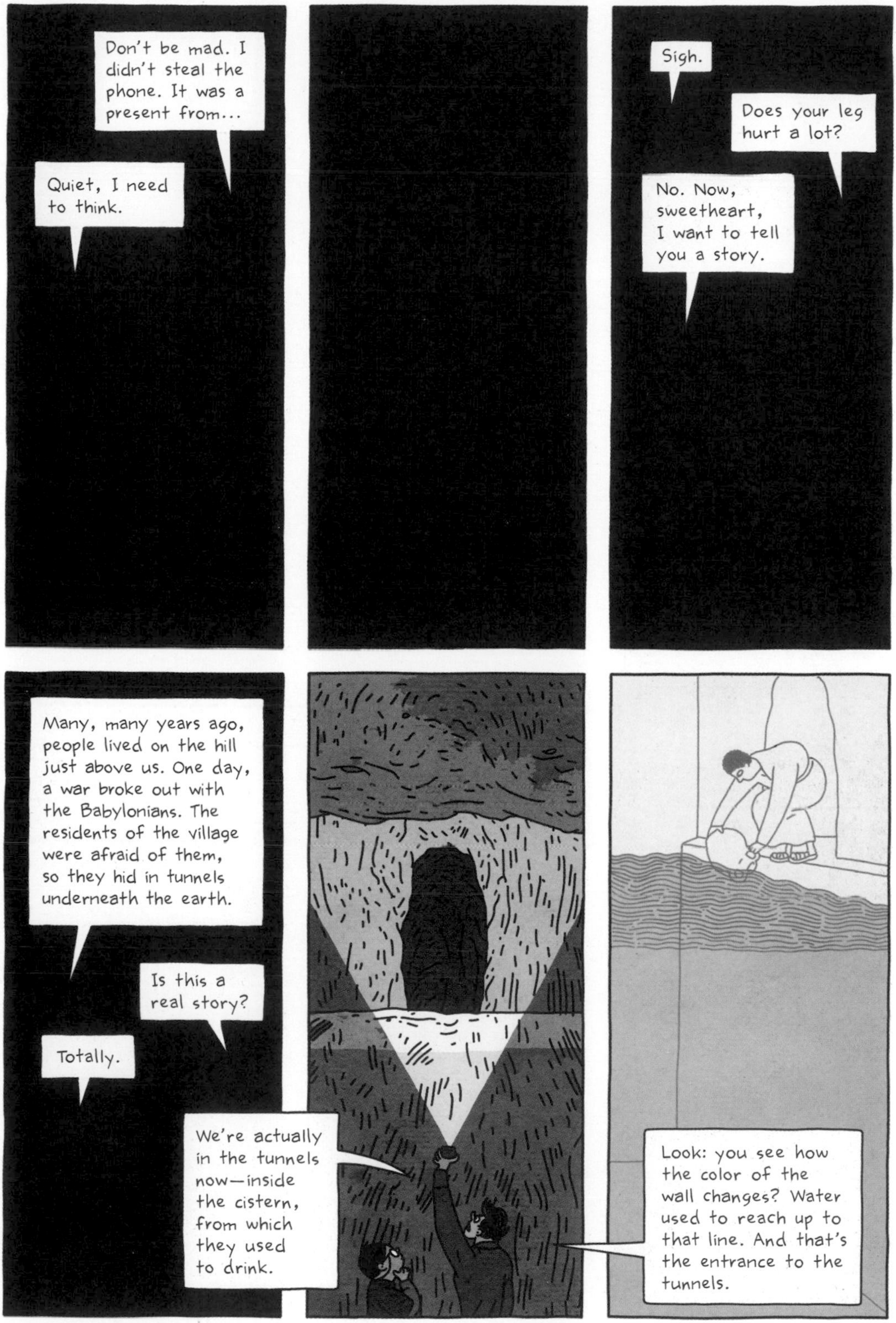

Don't be mad. I didn't steal the phone. It was a present from...
Quiet, I need to think.
Sigh.
Does your leg hurt a lot?
No. Now, sweetheart, I want to tell you a story.
Many, many years ago, people lived on the hill just above us. One day, a war broke out with the Babylonians. The residents of the village were afraid of them, so they hid in tunnels underneath the earth.
Is this a real story?
Totally.
We're actually in the tunnels now—inside the cistern, from which they used to drink.
Look: you see how the color of the wall changes? Water used to reach up to that line. And that's the entrance to the tunnels.

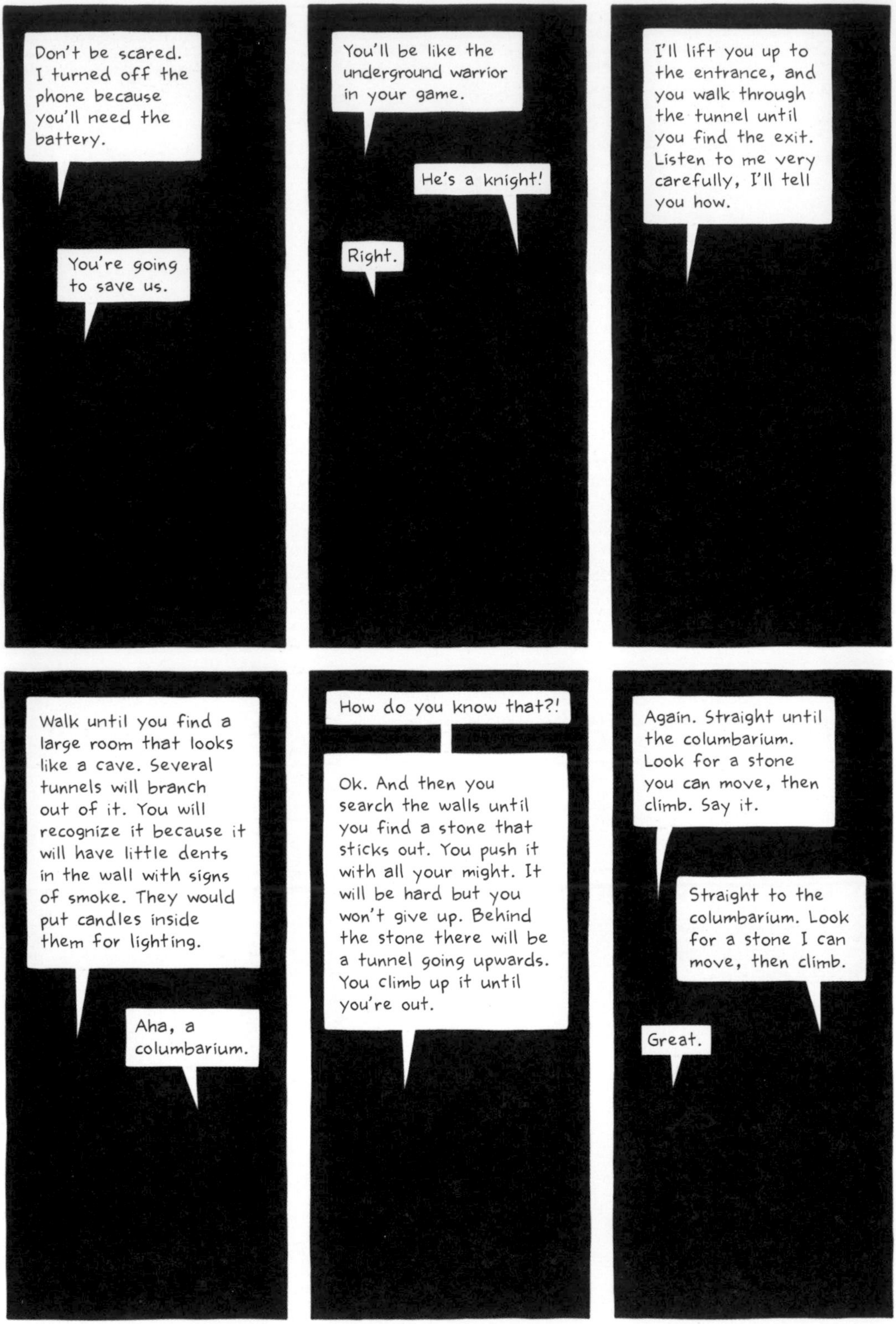
Don't be scared. I turned off the phone because you'll need the battery.
You're going to save us.
You'll be like the underground warrior in your game.
He's a knight!
Right.
I'll lift you up to the entrance, and you walk through the tunnel until you find the exit. Listen to me very carefully, I'll tell you how.
Walk until you find a large room that looks like a cave. Several tunnels will branch out of it. You will recognize it because it will have little dents in the wall with signs of smoke. They would put candles inside them for lighting.
Aha, a columbarium.
How do you know that?!
Ok. And then you search the walls until you find a stone that sticks out. You push it with all your might. It will be hard but you won't give up. Behind the stone there will be a tunnel going upwards. You climb up it until you're out.
Again. Straight until the columbarium. Look for a stone you can move, then climb. Say it.
Straight to the columbarium. Look for a stone I can move, then climb.
Great.

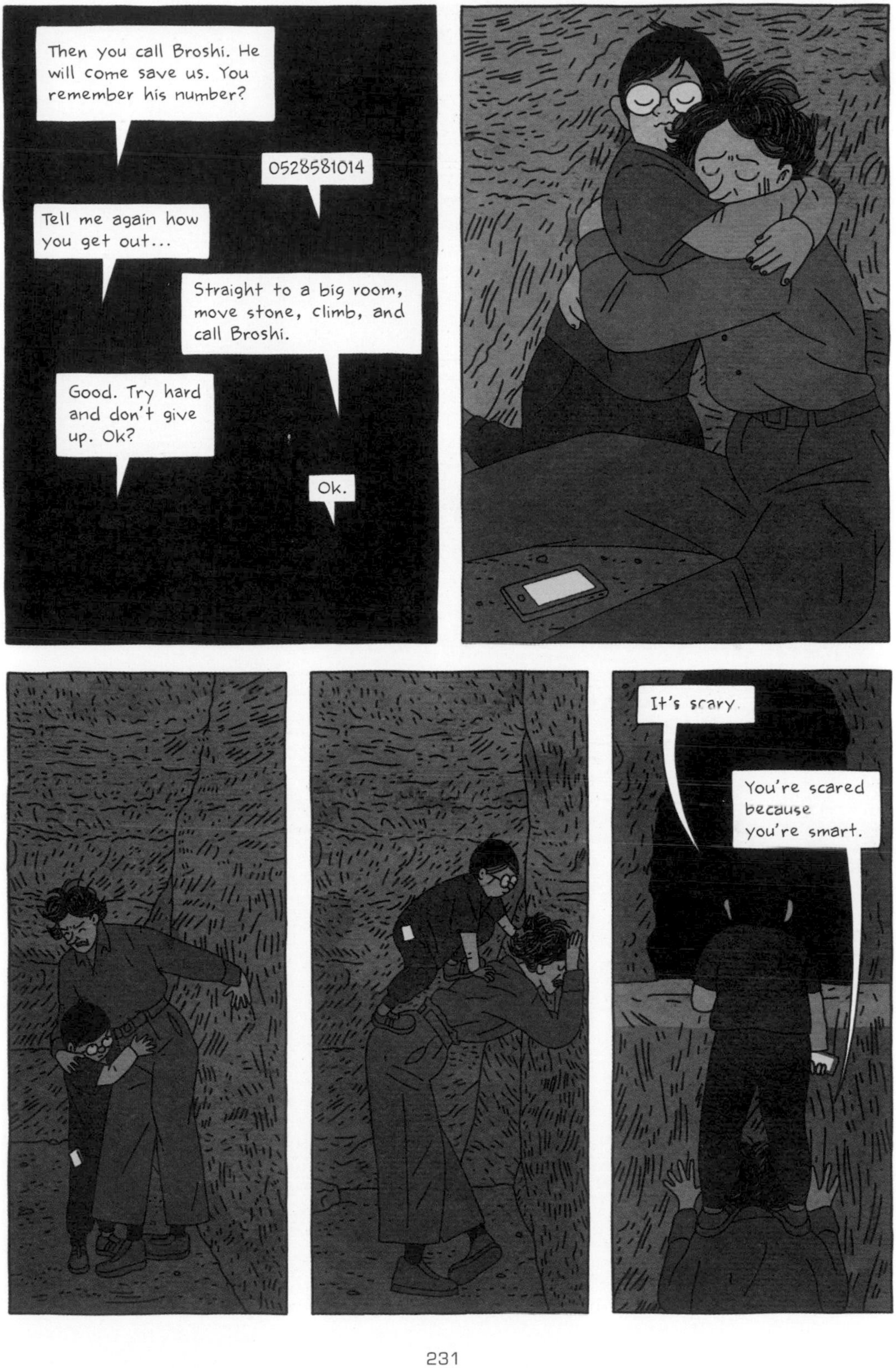
Then you call Broshi. He will come save us. You remember his number?
0528581014
Tell me again how you get out...
Straight to a big room, move stone, climb, and call Broshi.
Good. Try hard and don't give up. Ok?
Ok.
It's scary.
You're scared because you're smart.

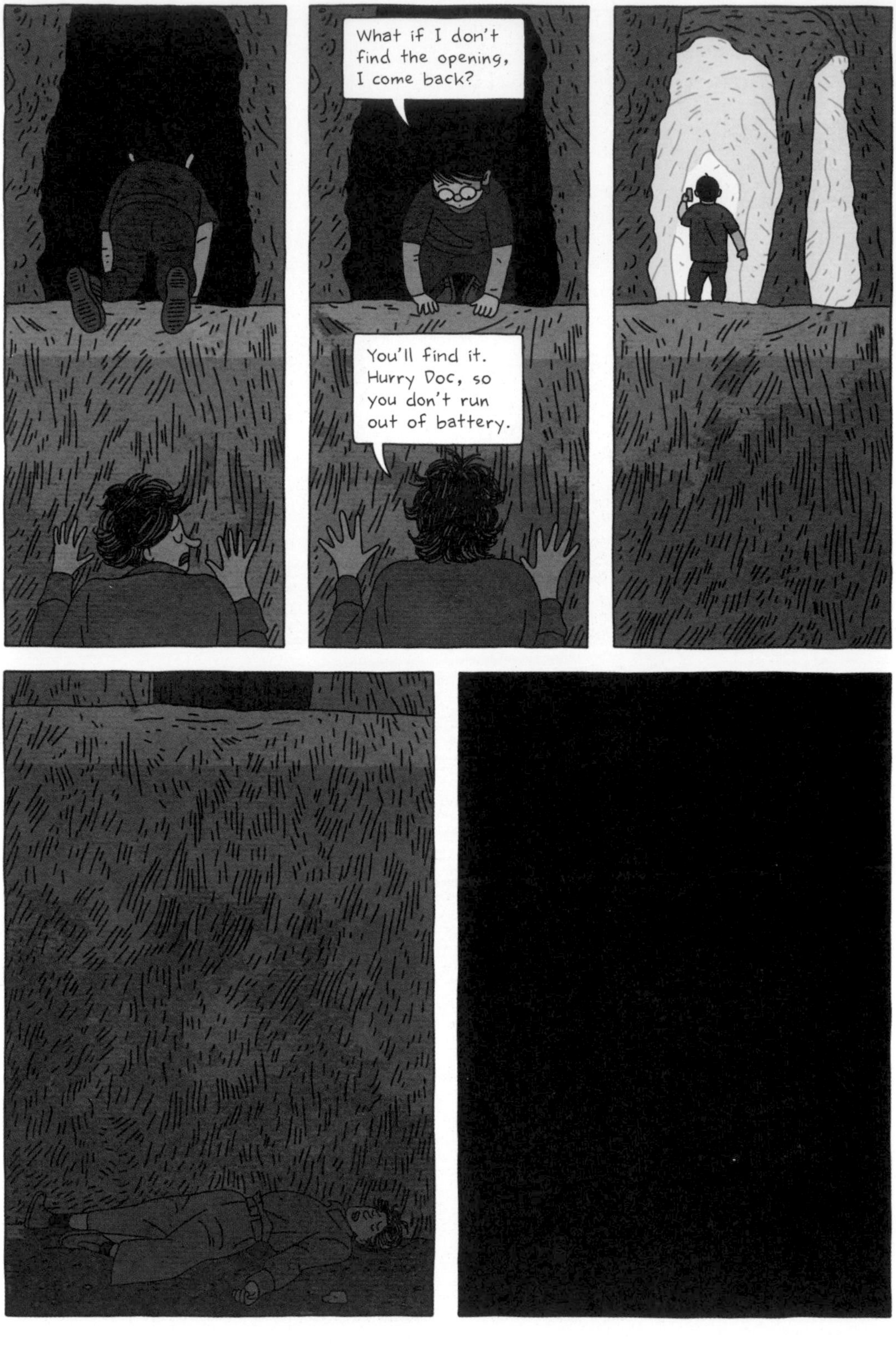
What if I don't find the opening, I come back?
You'll find it. Hurry Doc, so you don't run out of battery.

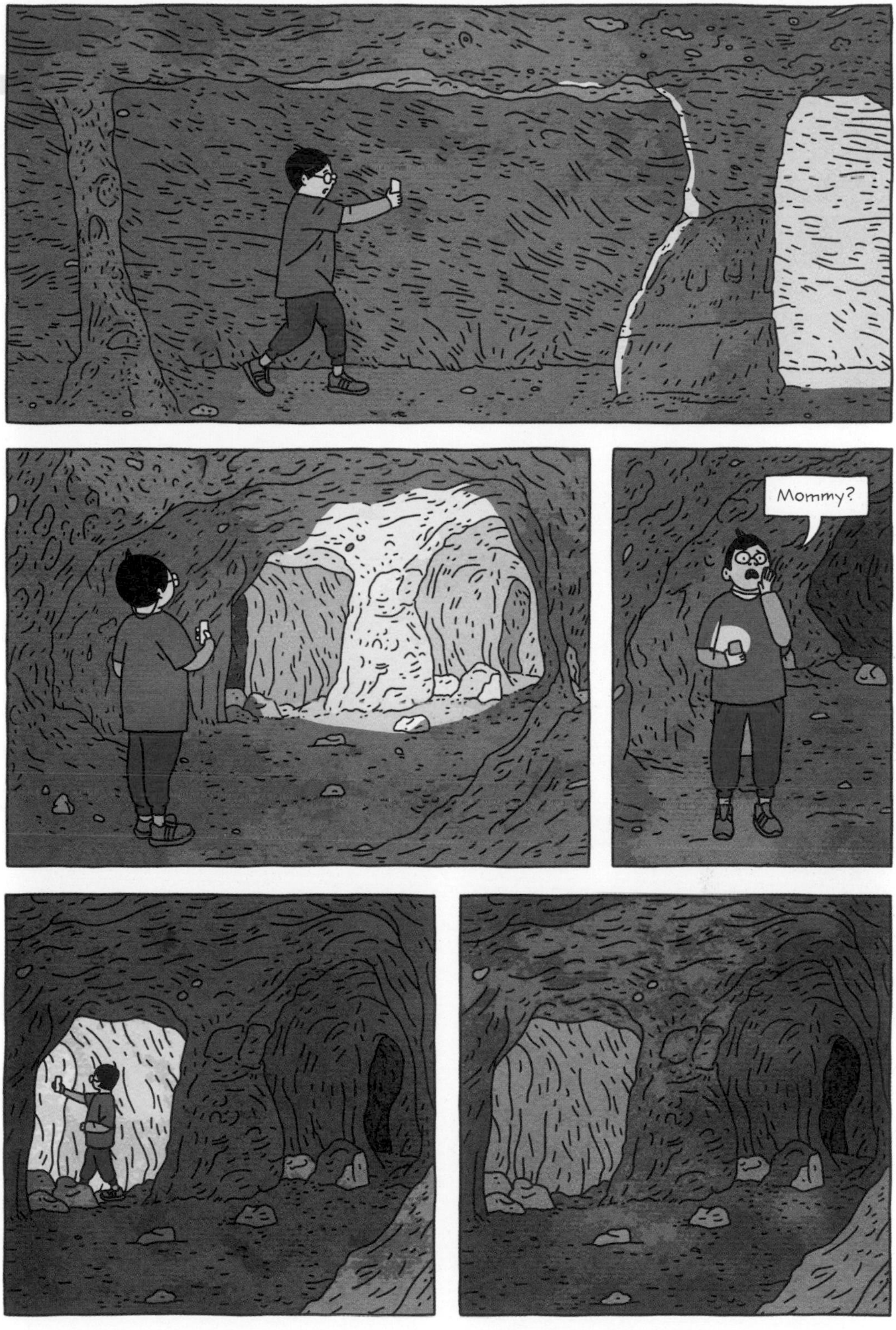
Mommy?

Columbarium.

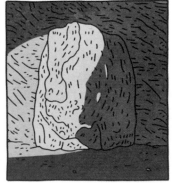

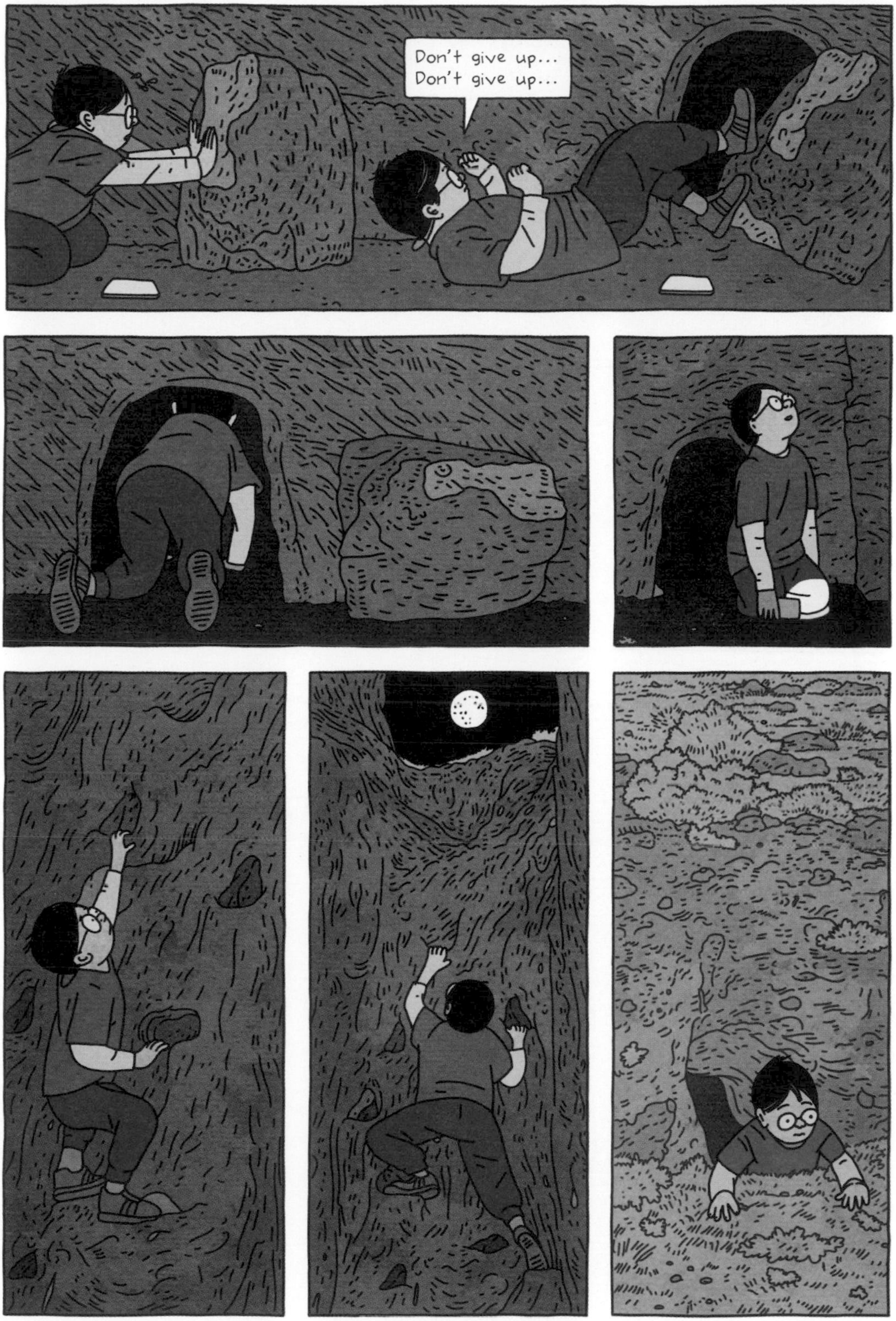
Don't give up...
Don't give up...

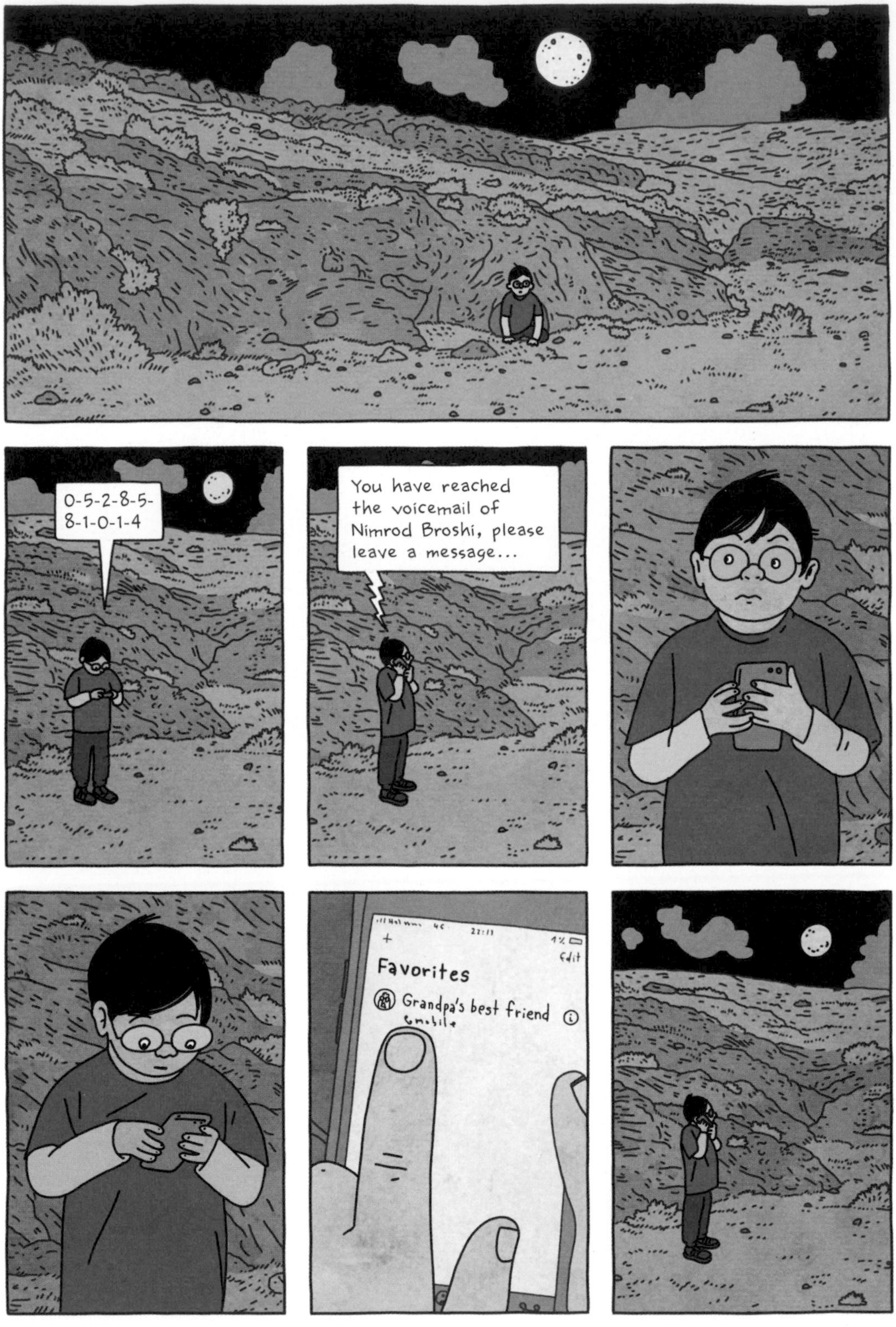
0-5-2-8-5-8-1-0-1-4
You have reached the voicemail of Nimrod Broshi, please leave a message...
Favorites
Grandpa's best friend
Edit

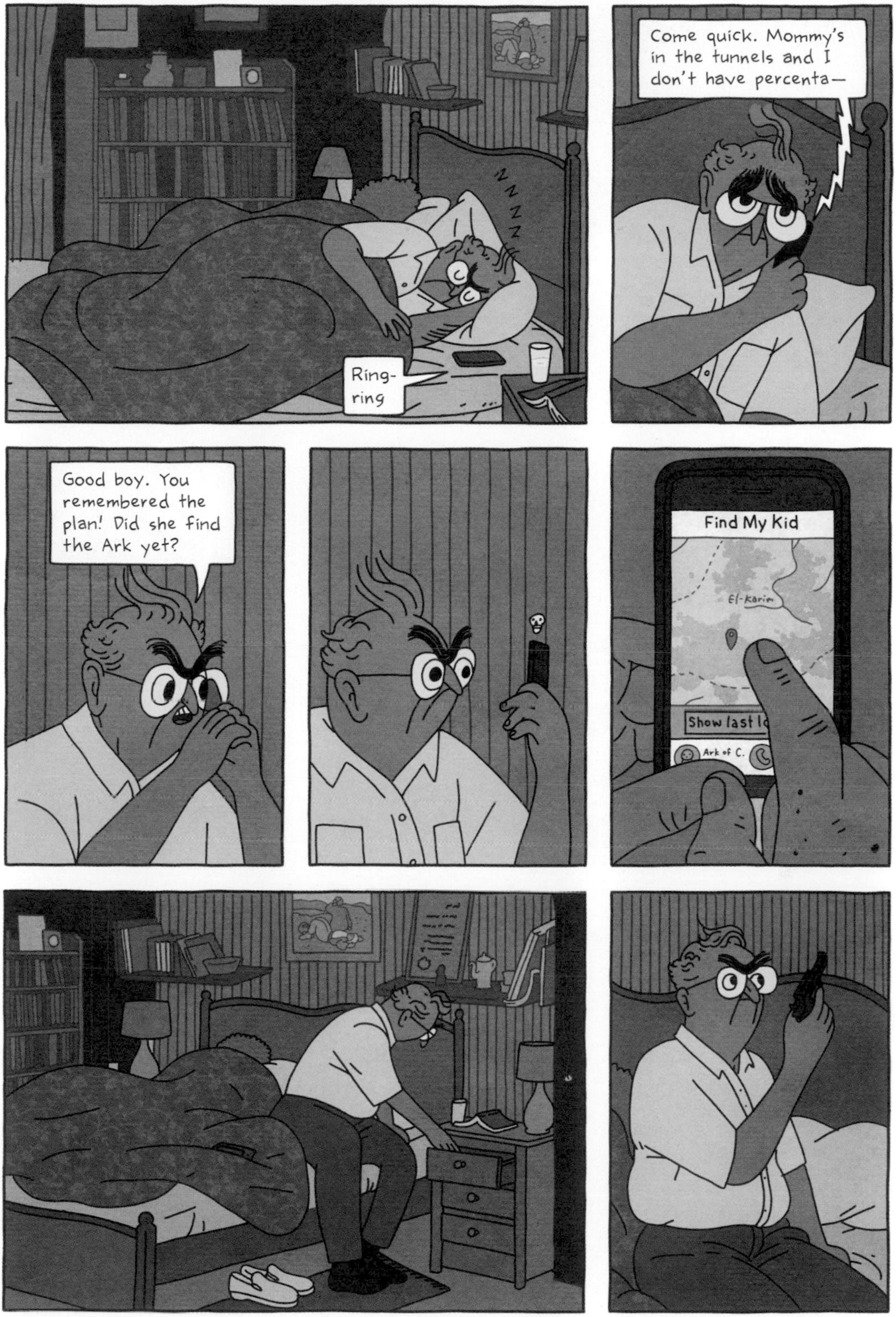

Ring-
ring
Come quick. Mommy's in the tunnels and I don't have percenta—
Good boy. You remembered the plan! Did she find the Ark yet?
Find My Kid
El-Karim
Show last lo
Ark of C.

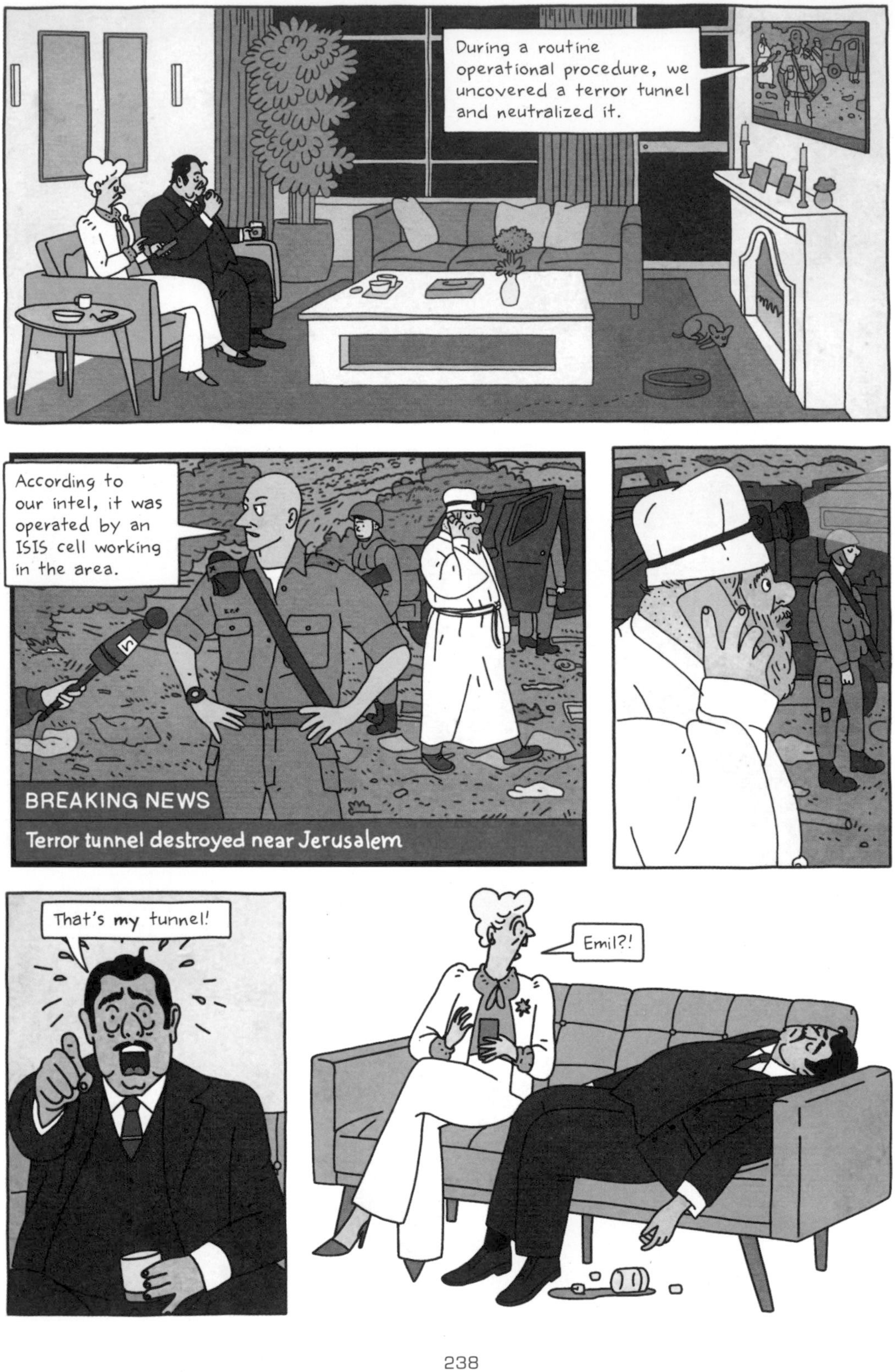
During a routine operational procedure, we uncovered a terror tunnel and neutralized it.
According to our intel, it was operated by an ISIS cell working in the area.
BREAKING NEWS
Terror tunnel destroyed near Jerusalem
That's **my** tunnel!
Emil?!

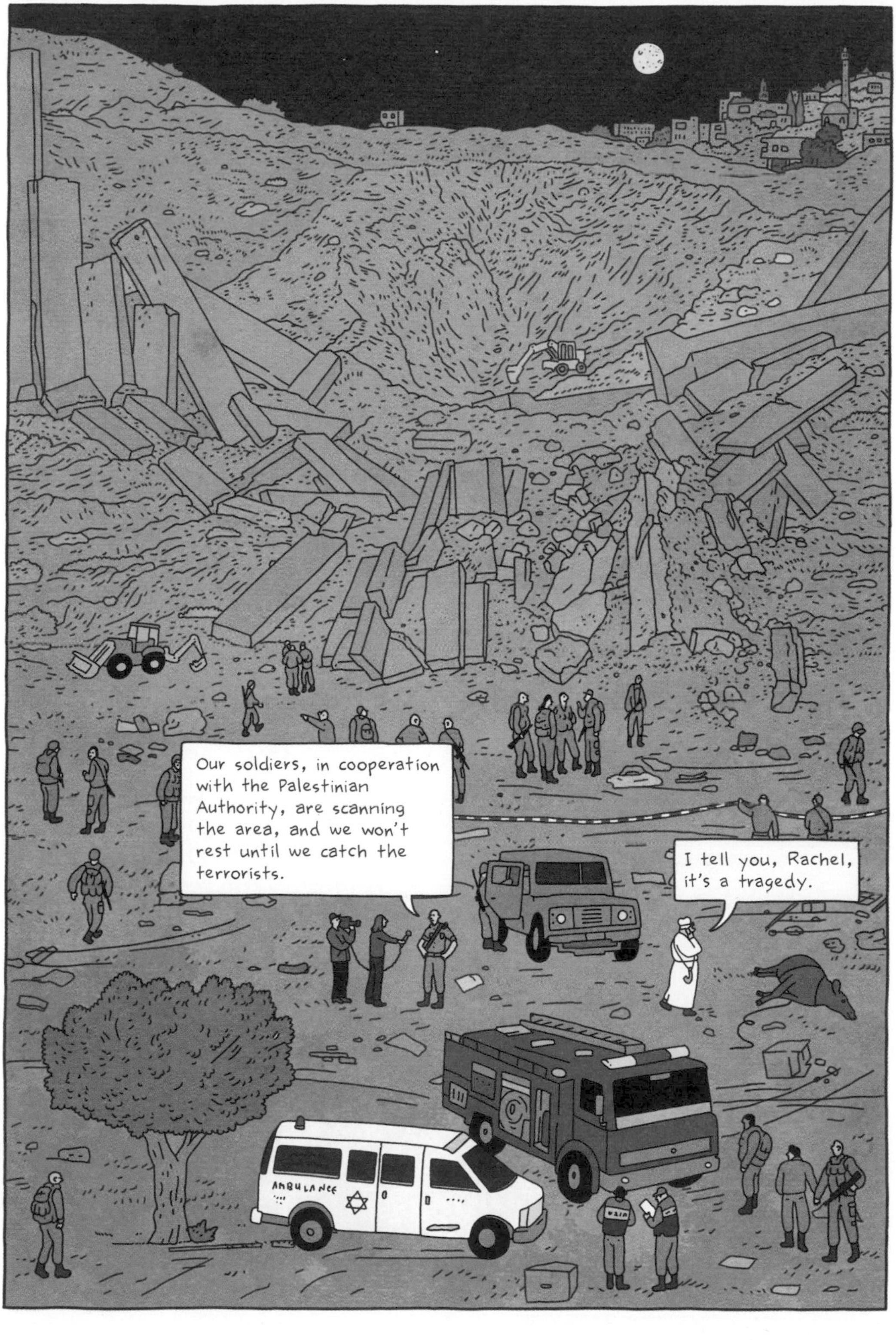
Our soldiers, in cooperation with the Palestinian Authority, are scanning the area, and we won't rest until we catch the terrorists.
I tell you, Rachel, it's a tragedy.
AMBULANCE

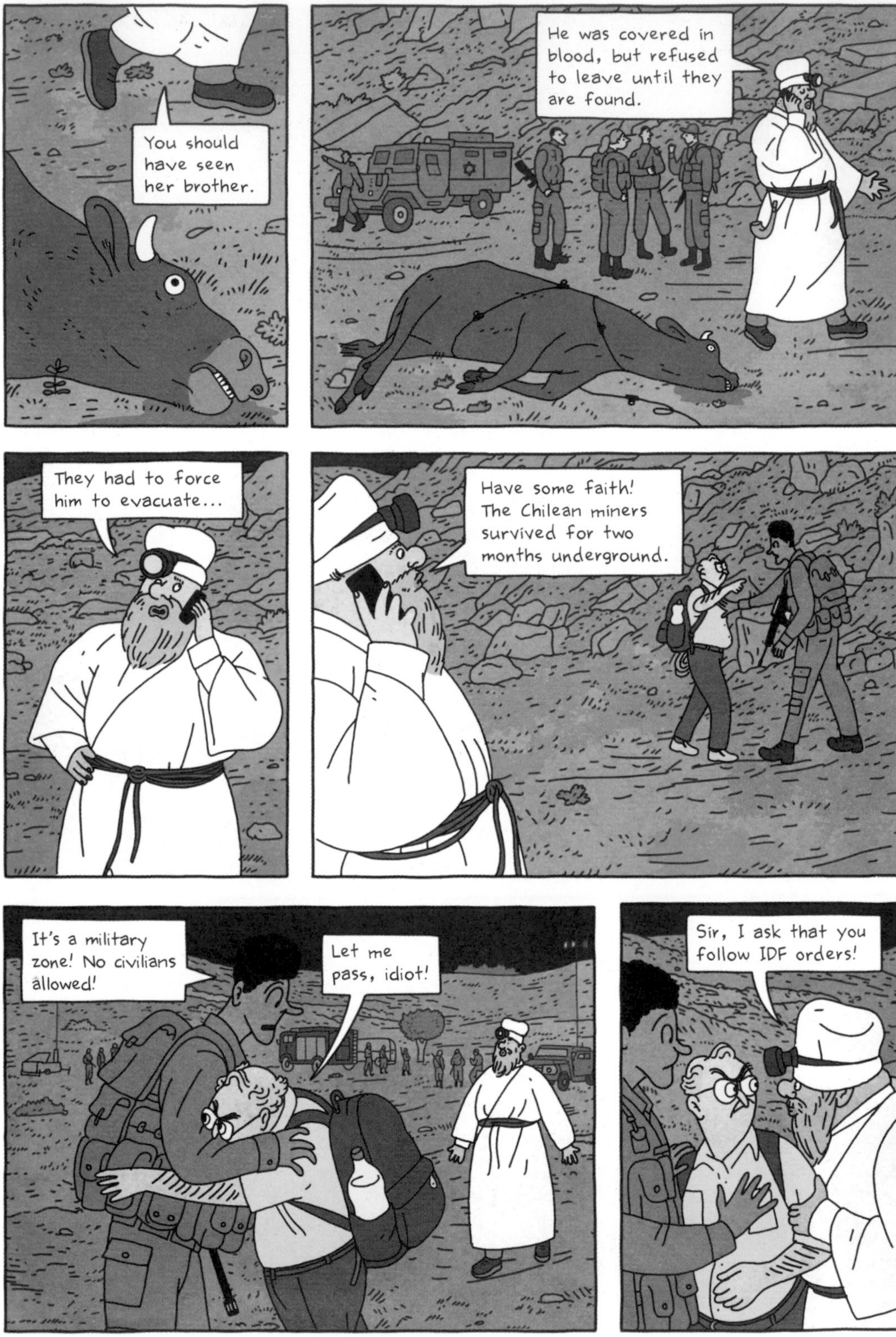
You should have seen her brother.
He was covered in blood, but refused to leave until they are found.
They had to force him to evacuate...
Have some faith! The Chilean miners survived for two months underground.
It's a military zone! No civilians allowed!
Let me pass, idiot!
Sir, I ask that you follow IDF orders!

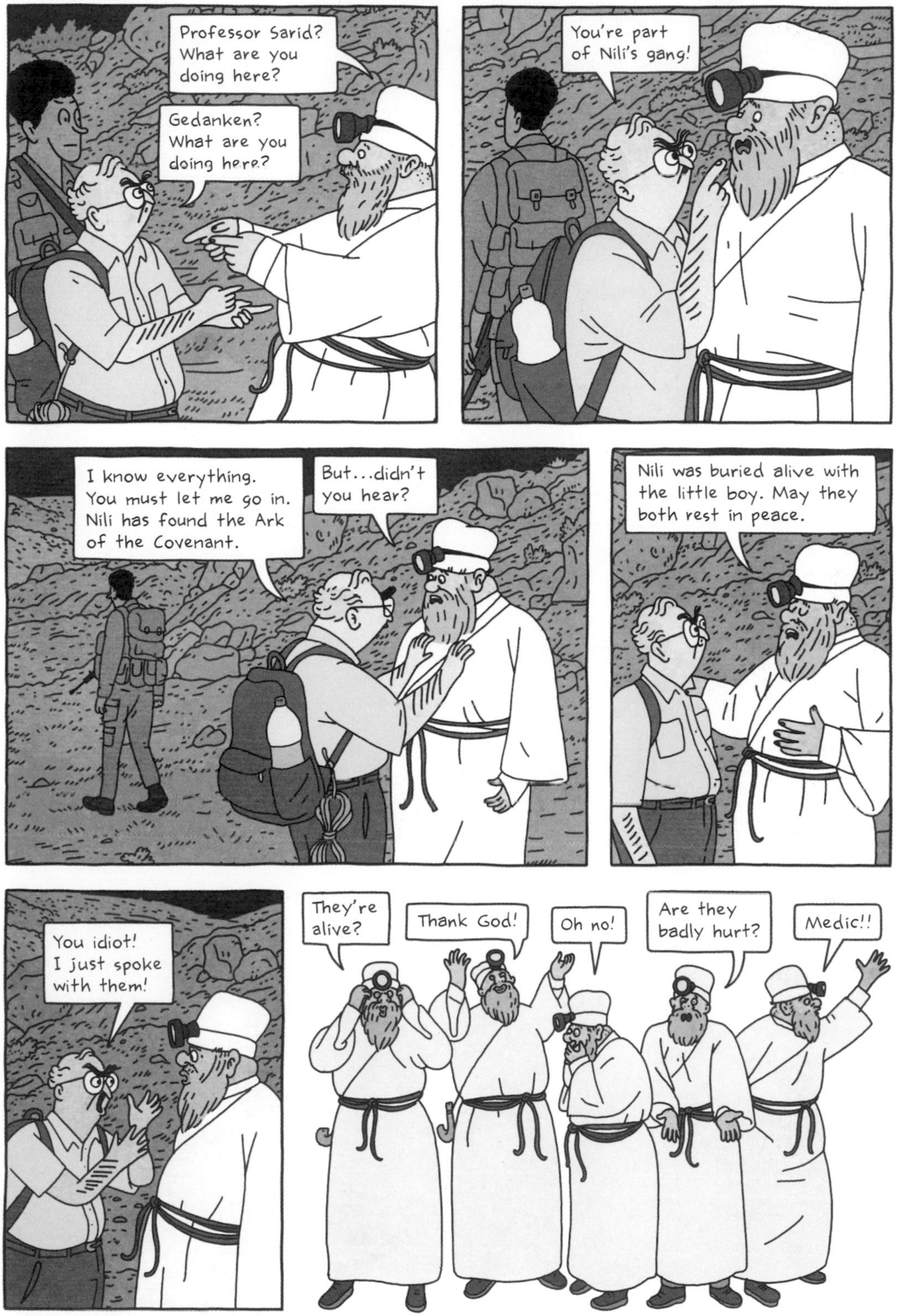
Professor Sarid? What are you doing here?
Gedanken? What are you doing here?
You're part of Nili's gang!
I know everything. You must let me go in. Nili has found the Ark of the Covenant.
But...didn't you hear?
Nili was buried alive with the little boy. May they both rest in peace.
You idiot! I just spoke with them!
They're alive?
Thank God!
Oh no!
Are they badly hurt?
Medic!!

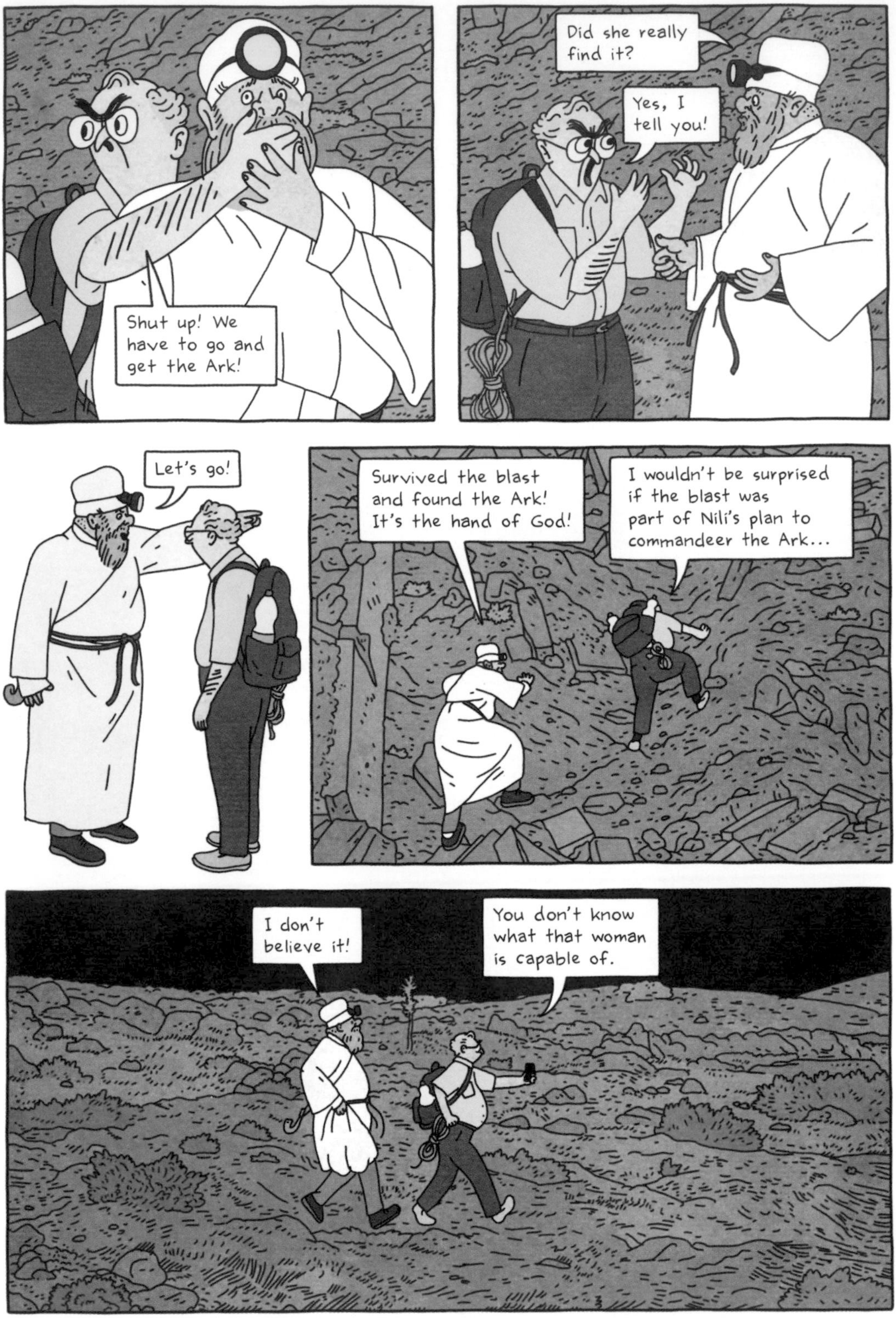

Shut up! We have to go and get the Ark!
Did she really find it?
Yes, I tell you!
Let's go!
Survived the blast and found the Ark! It's the hand of God!
I wouldn't be surprised if the blast was part of Nili's plan to commandeer the Ark...
I don't believe it!
You don't know what that woman is capable of.

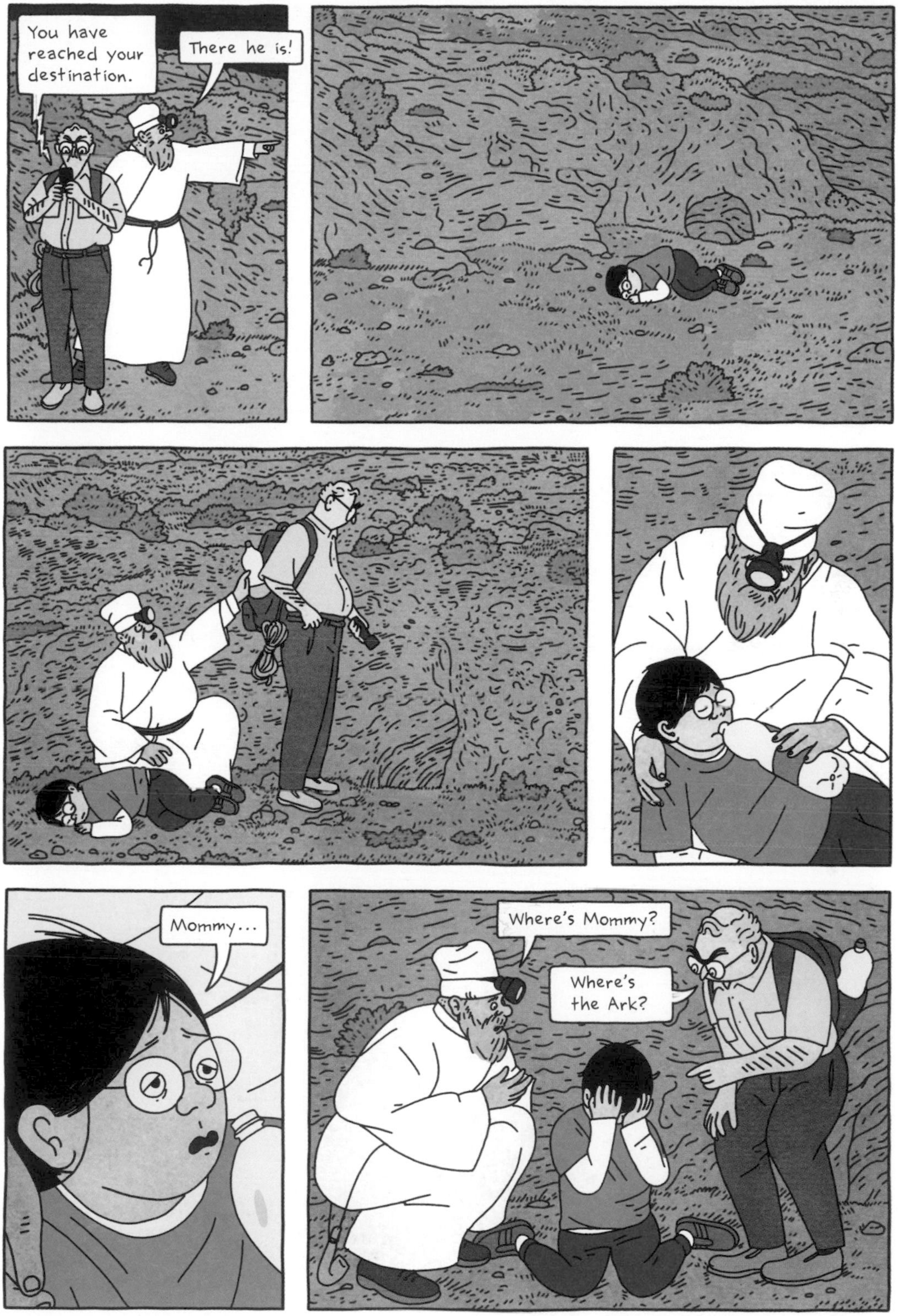
You have reached your destination.
There he is!
Mommy...
Where's Mommy?
Where's the Ark?

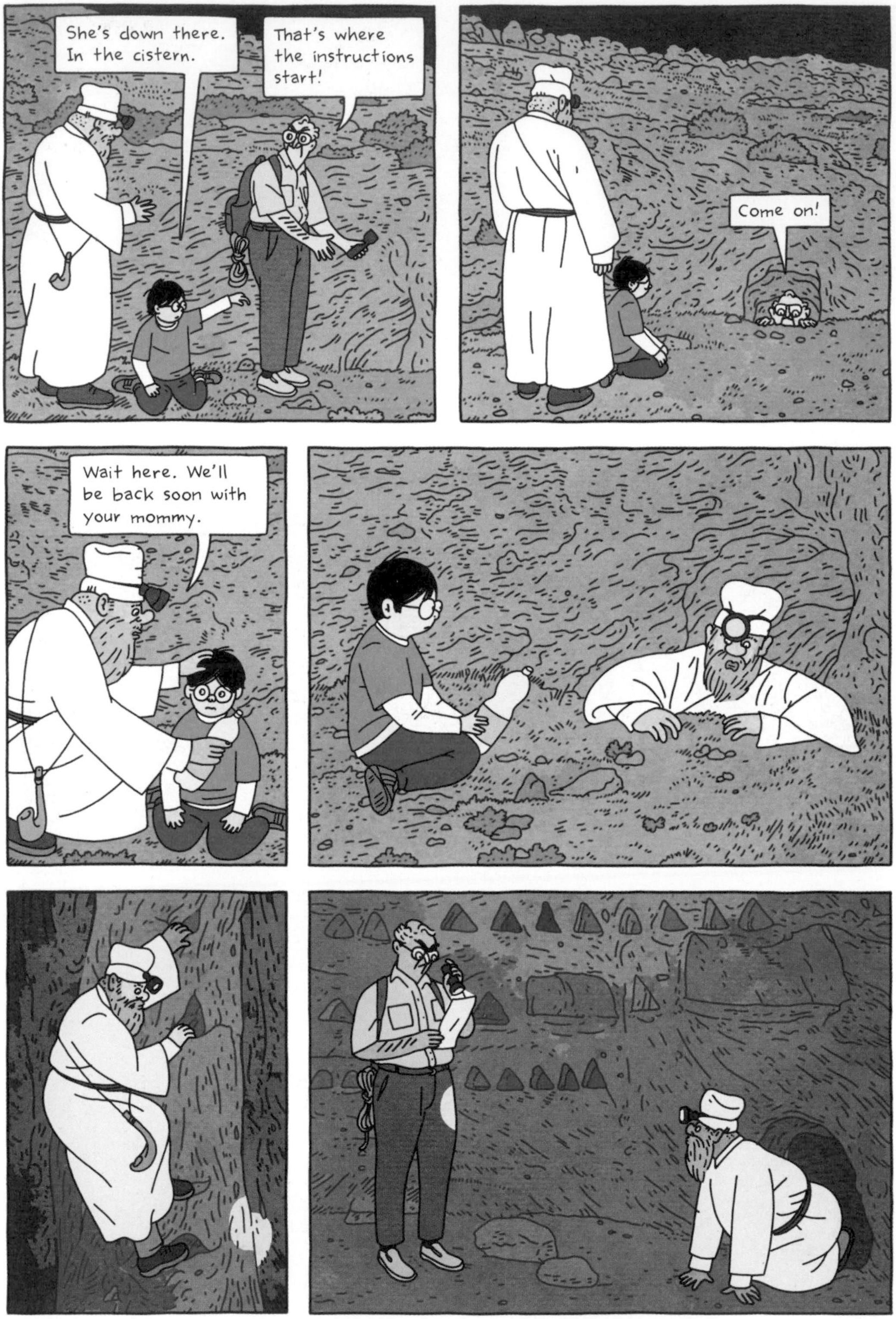
She's down there. In the cistern.
That's where the instructions start!
Come on!
Wait here. We'll be back soon with your mommy.

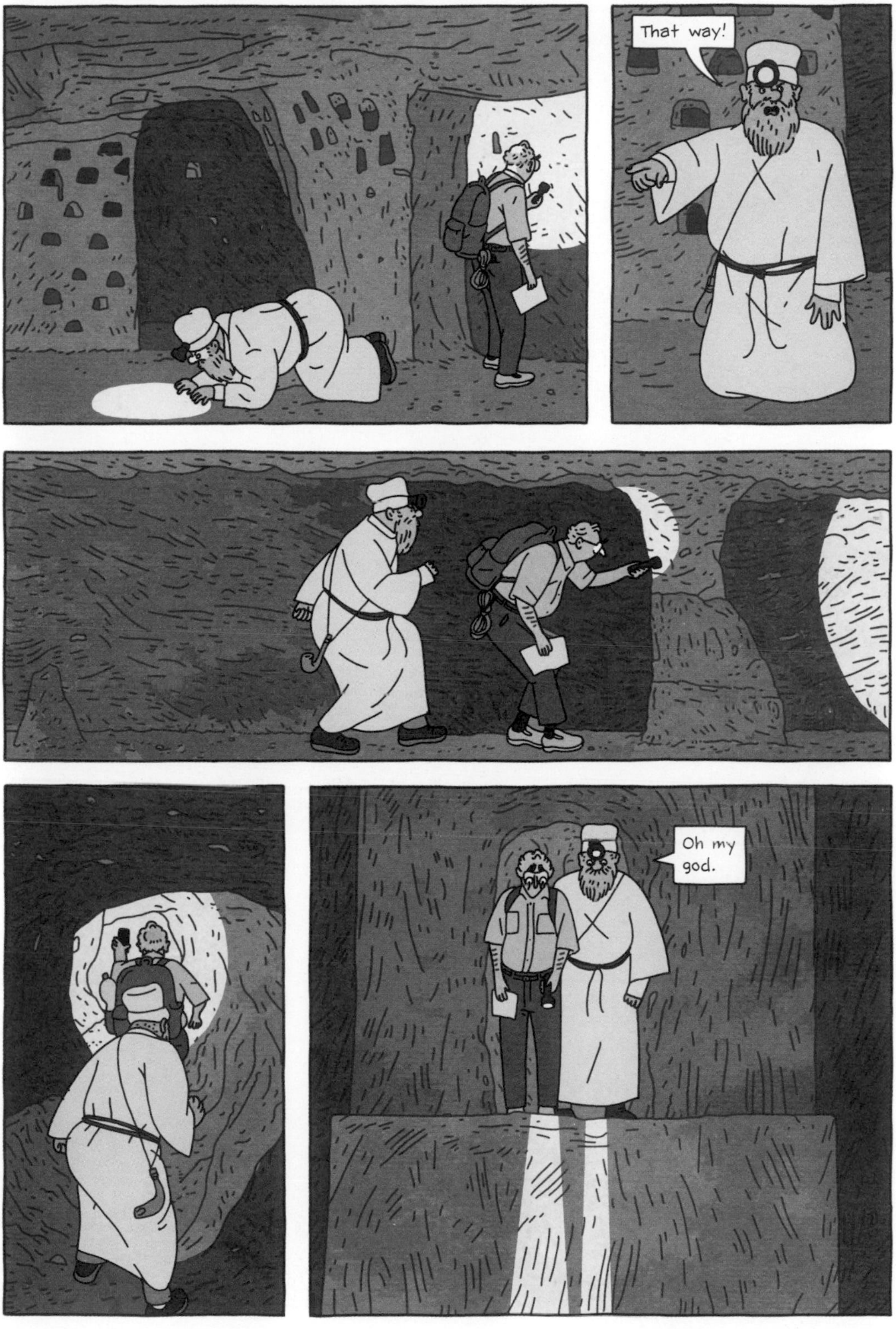
That way!
Oh my god.

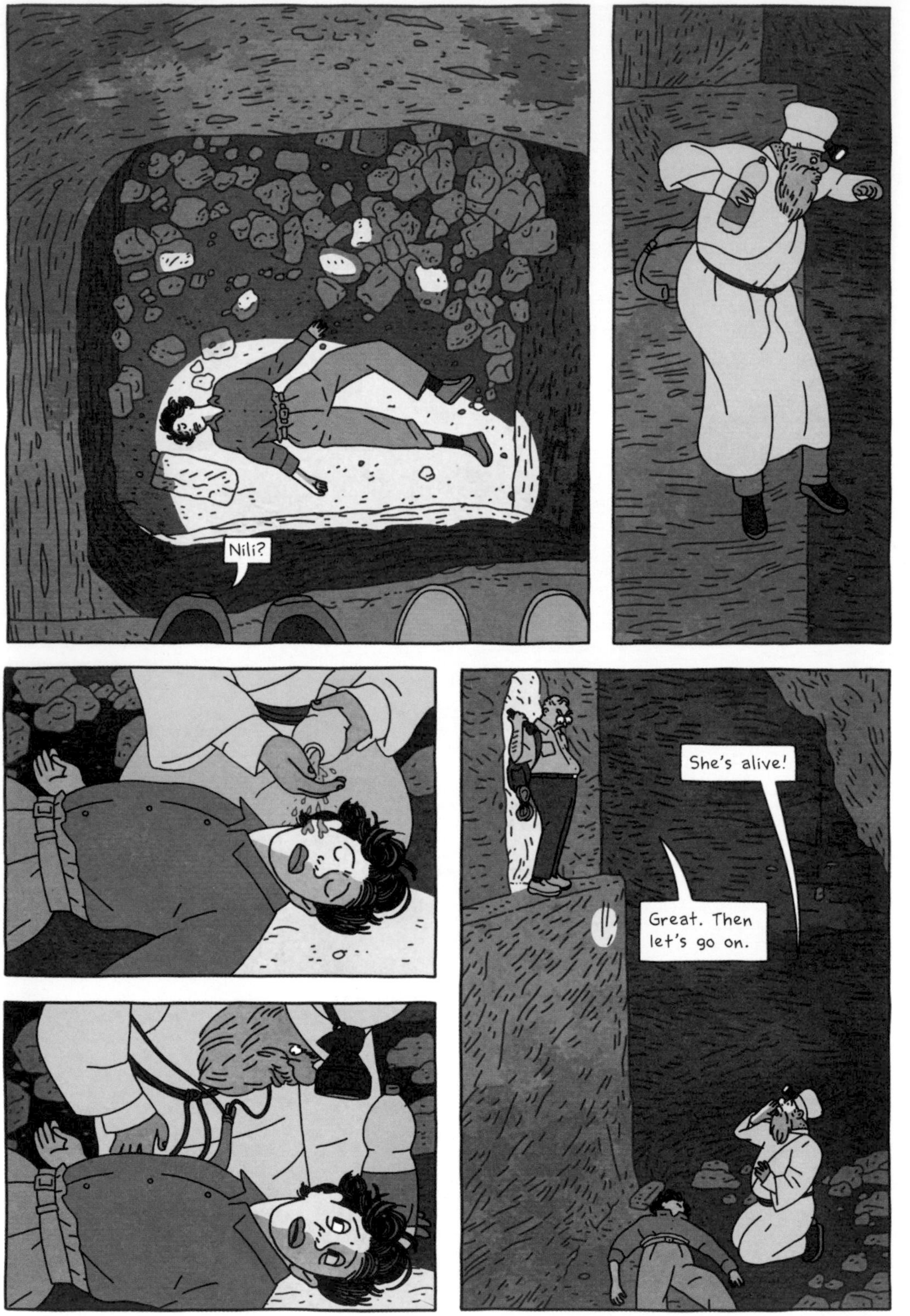

Nili?
She's alive!
Great. Then let's go on.

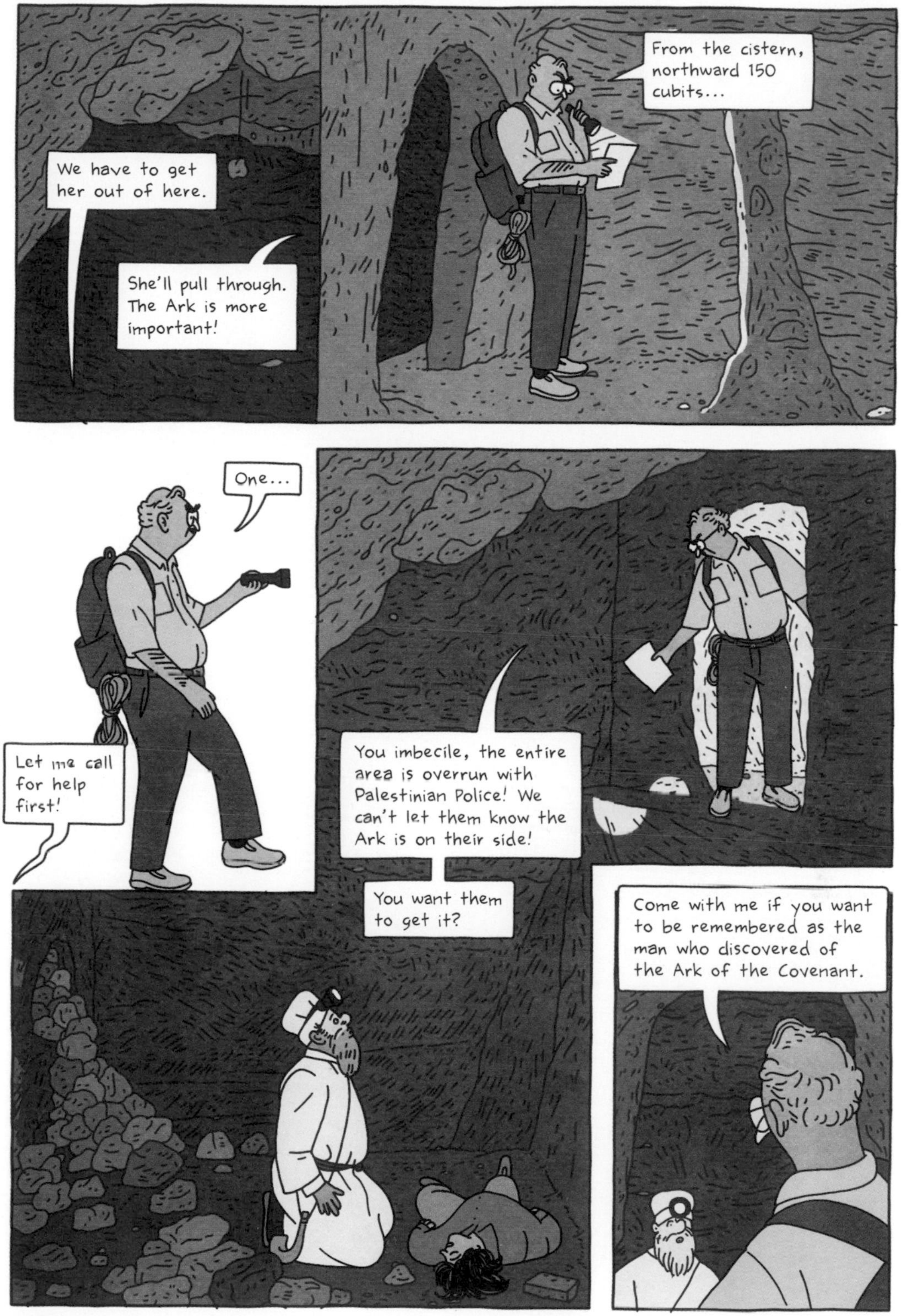

We have to get her out of here.
She'll pull through. The Ark is more important!
From the cistern, northward 150 cubits...
One...
Let me call for help first!
You imbecile, the entire area is overrun with Palestinian Police! We can't let them know the Ark is on their side!
You want them to get it?
Come with me if you want to be remembered as the man who discovered of the Ark of the Covenant.

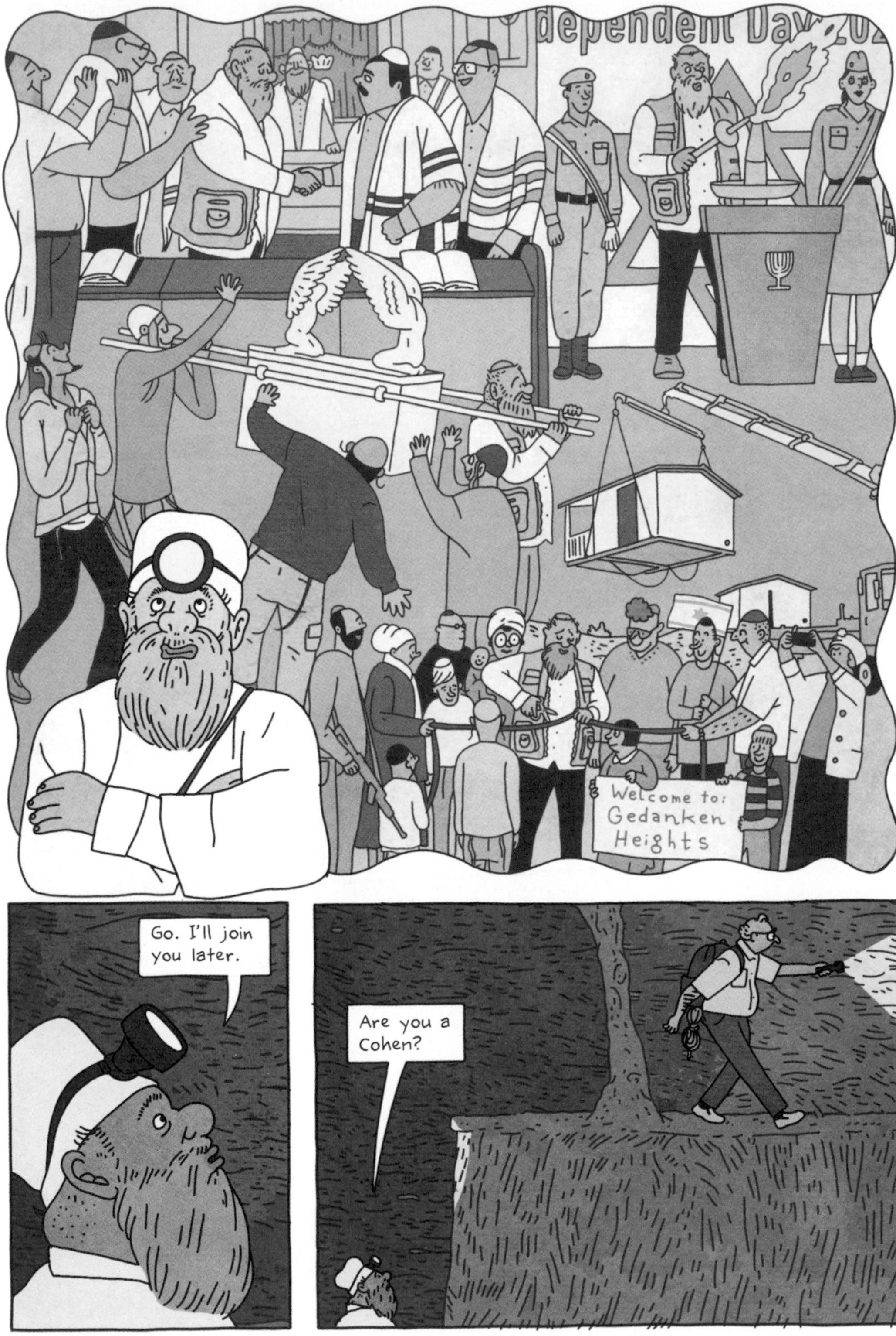
dependent Day 202
Welcome to:
Gedanken
Heights
Go. I'll join you later.
Are you a Cohen?

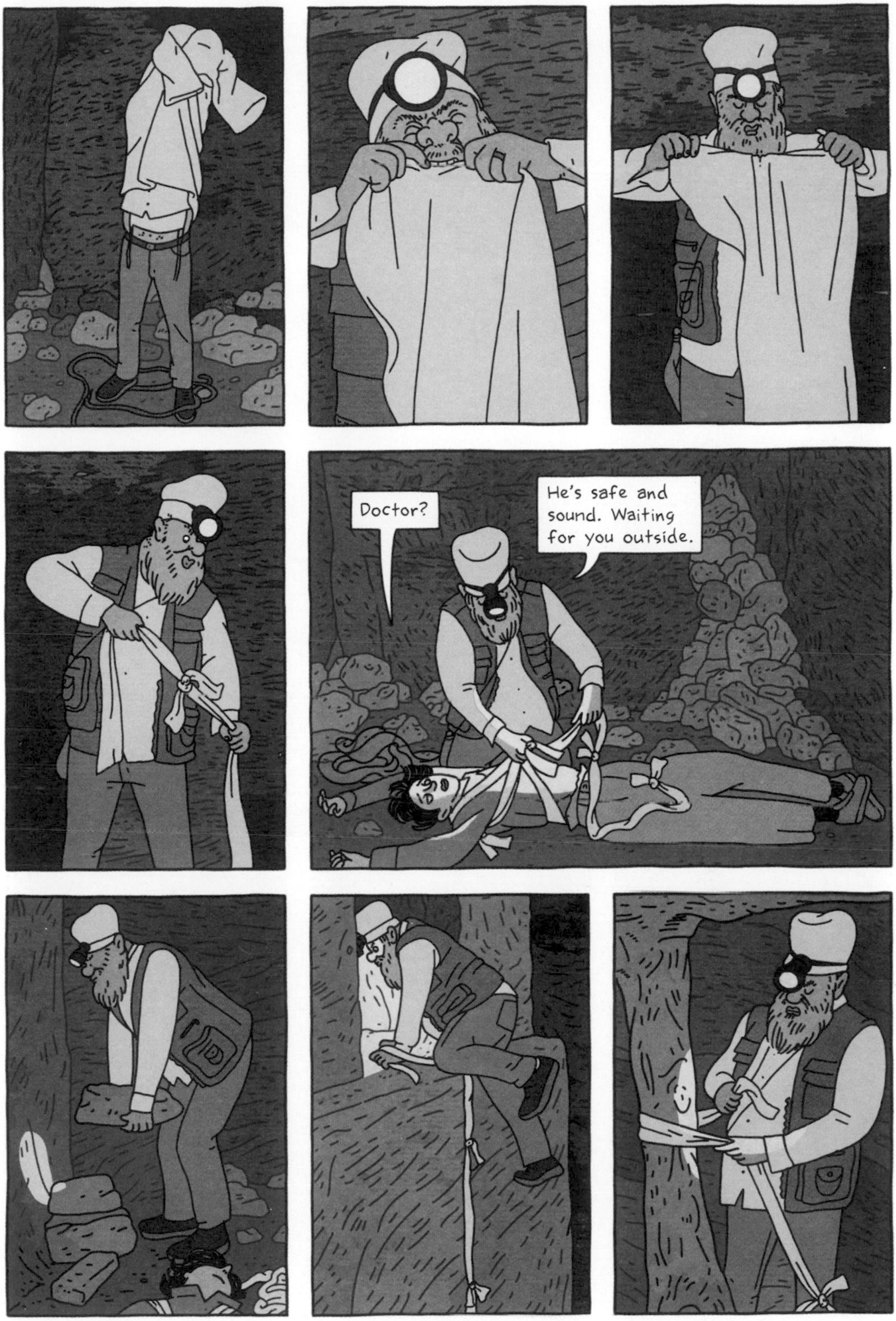
Doctor?
He's safe and sound. Waiting for you outside.

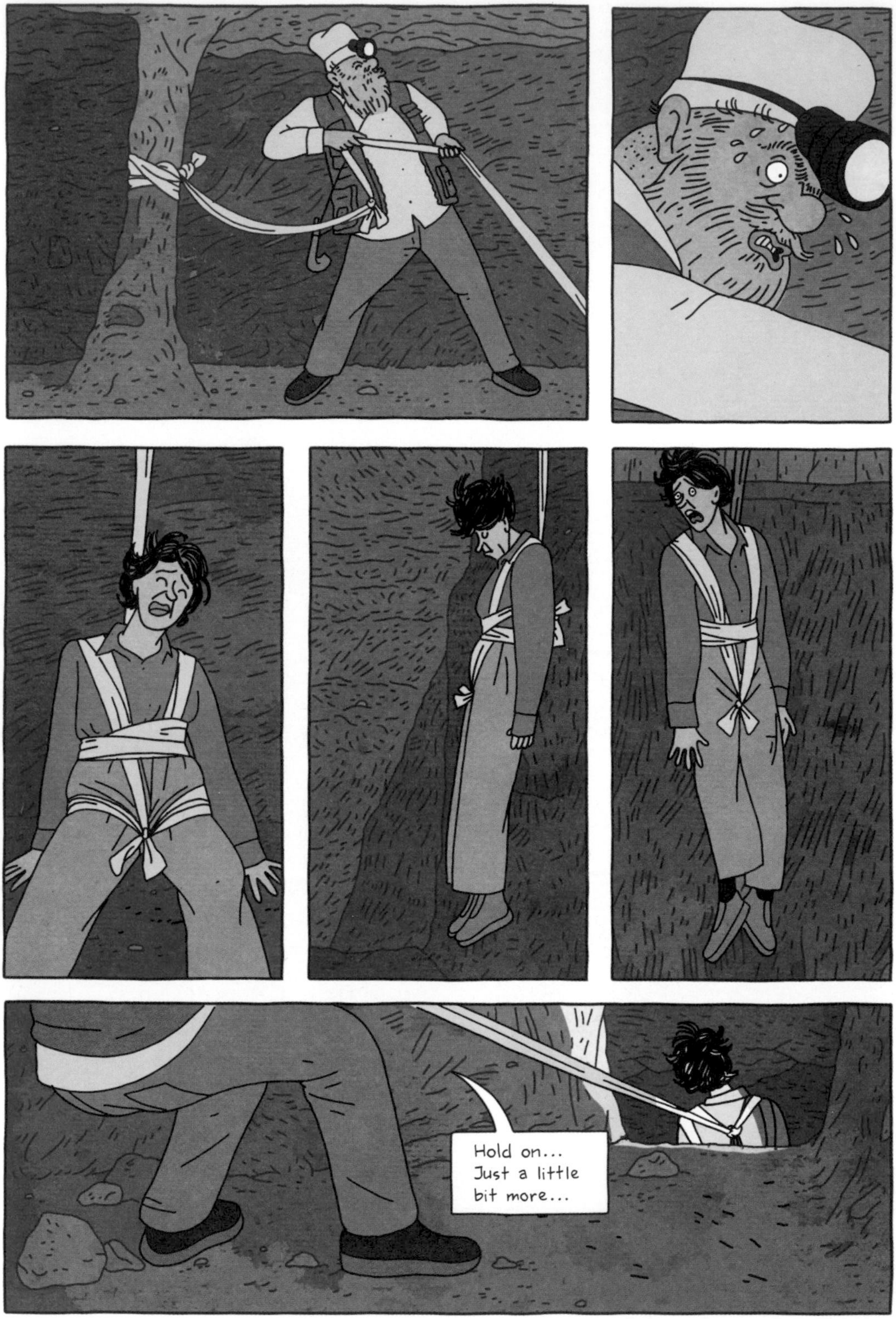
Hold on...
Just a little
bit more...

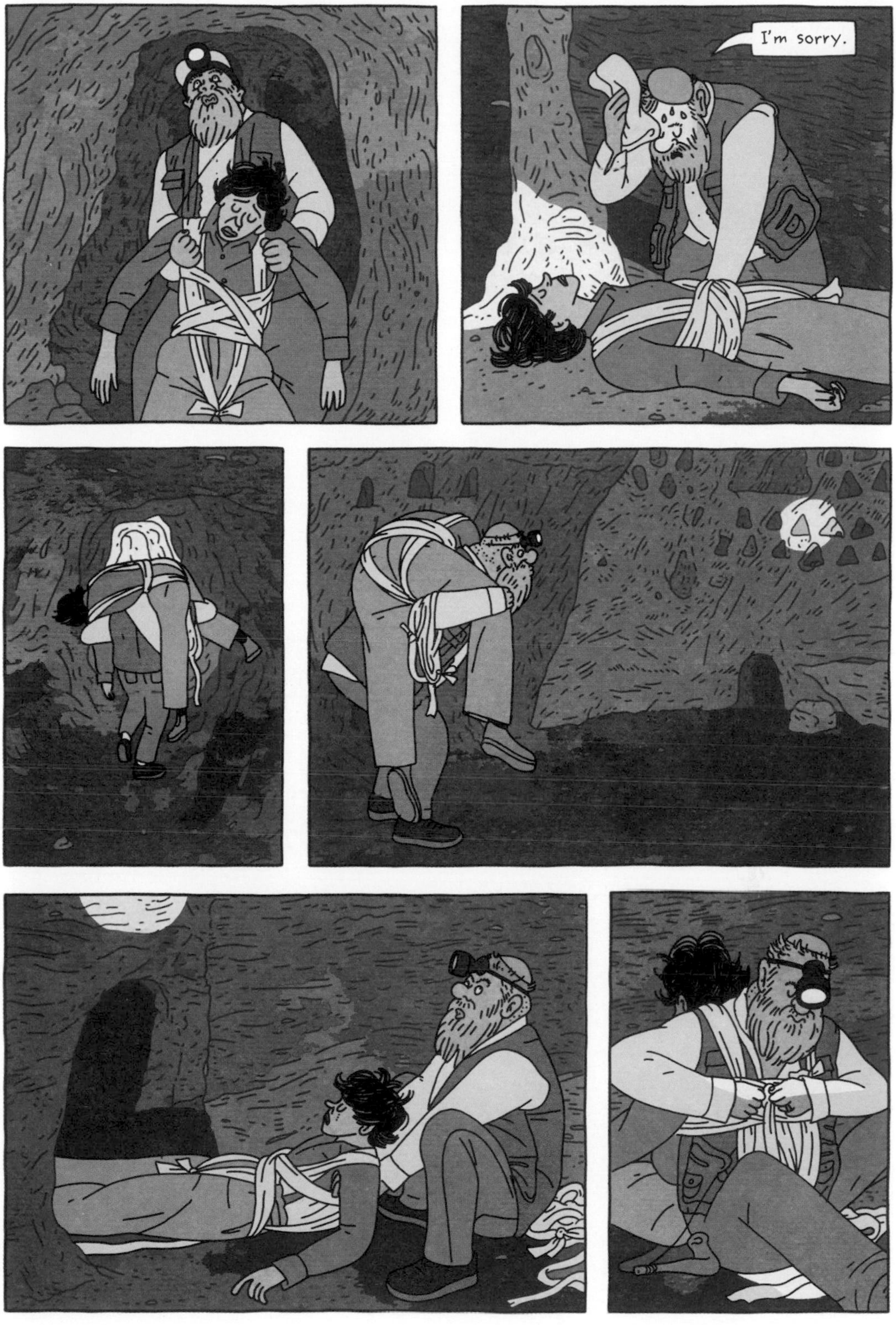
I'm sorry.

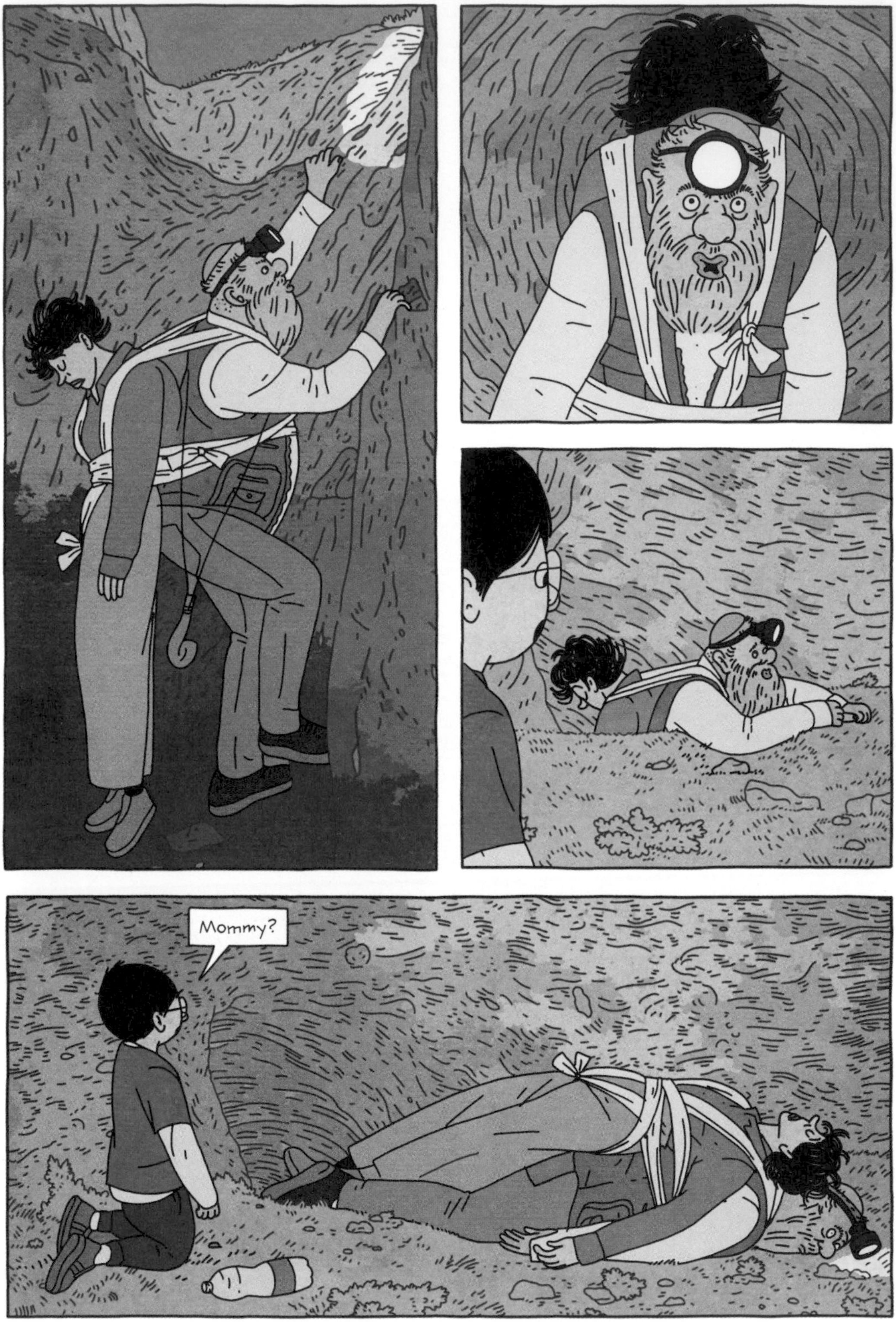
Mommy?

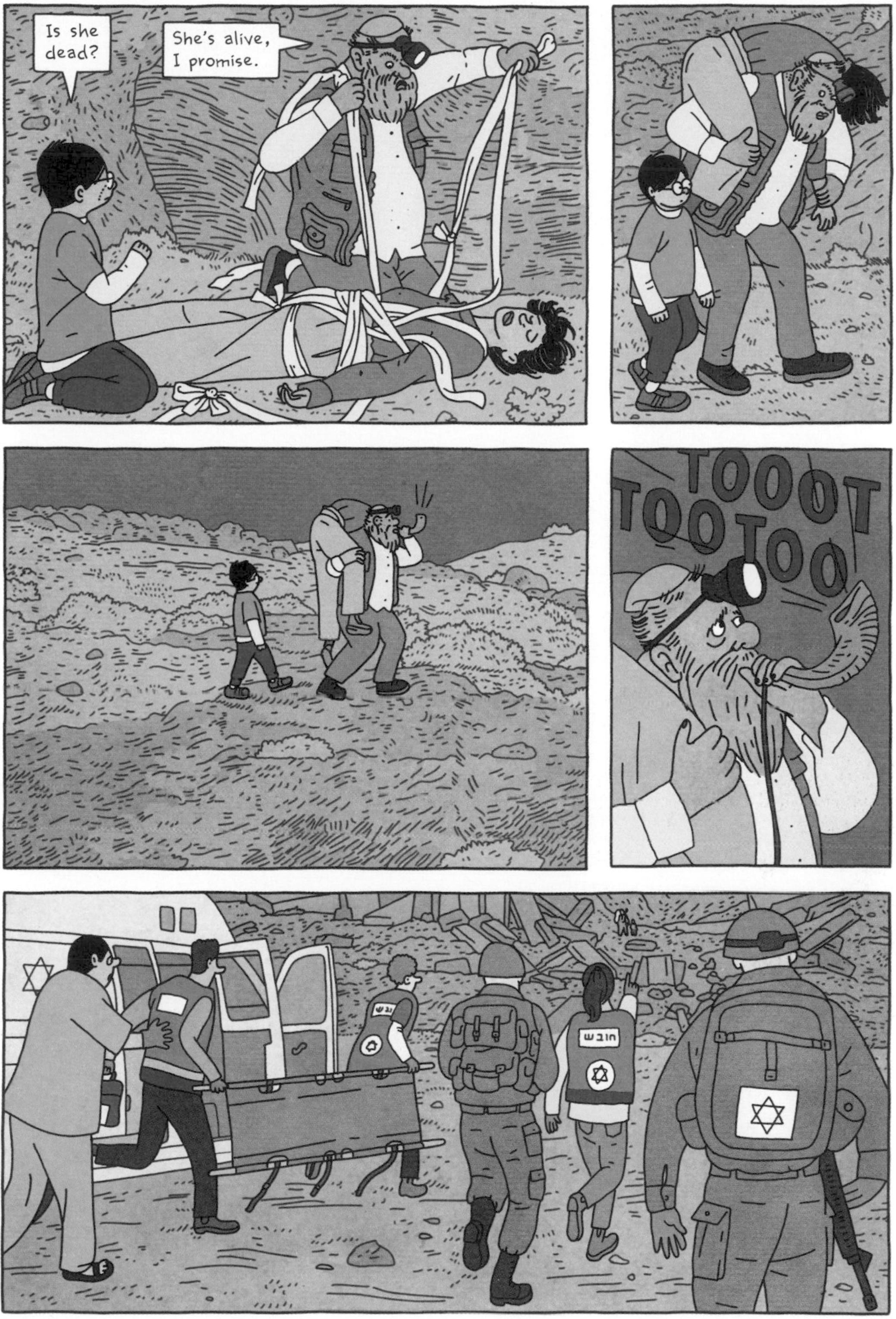
Is she dead?
She's alive, I promise.
TOOOT
TOOTOOO

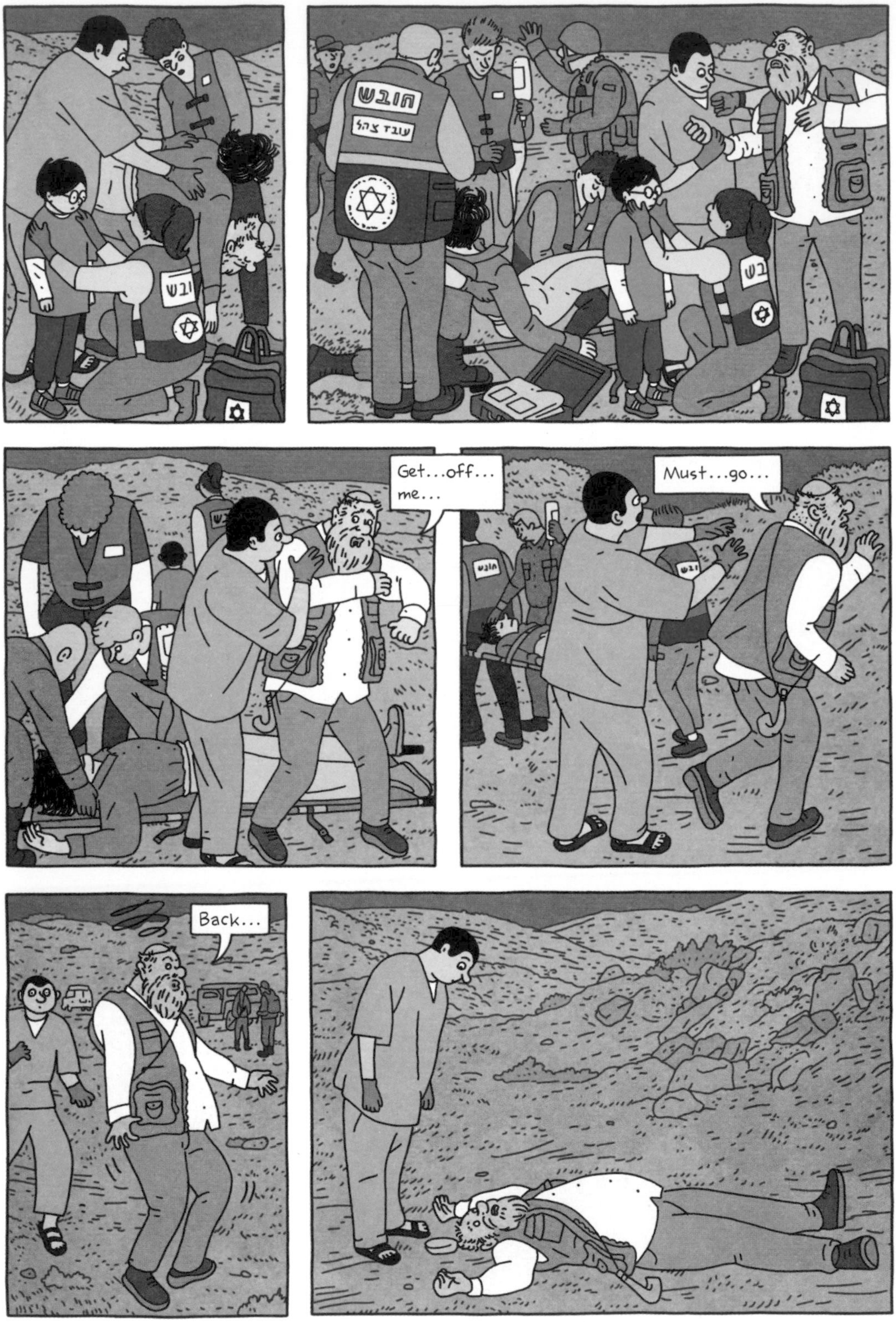
חובש
עובד צה״ל
Get...off... me...
Must...go...
Back...

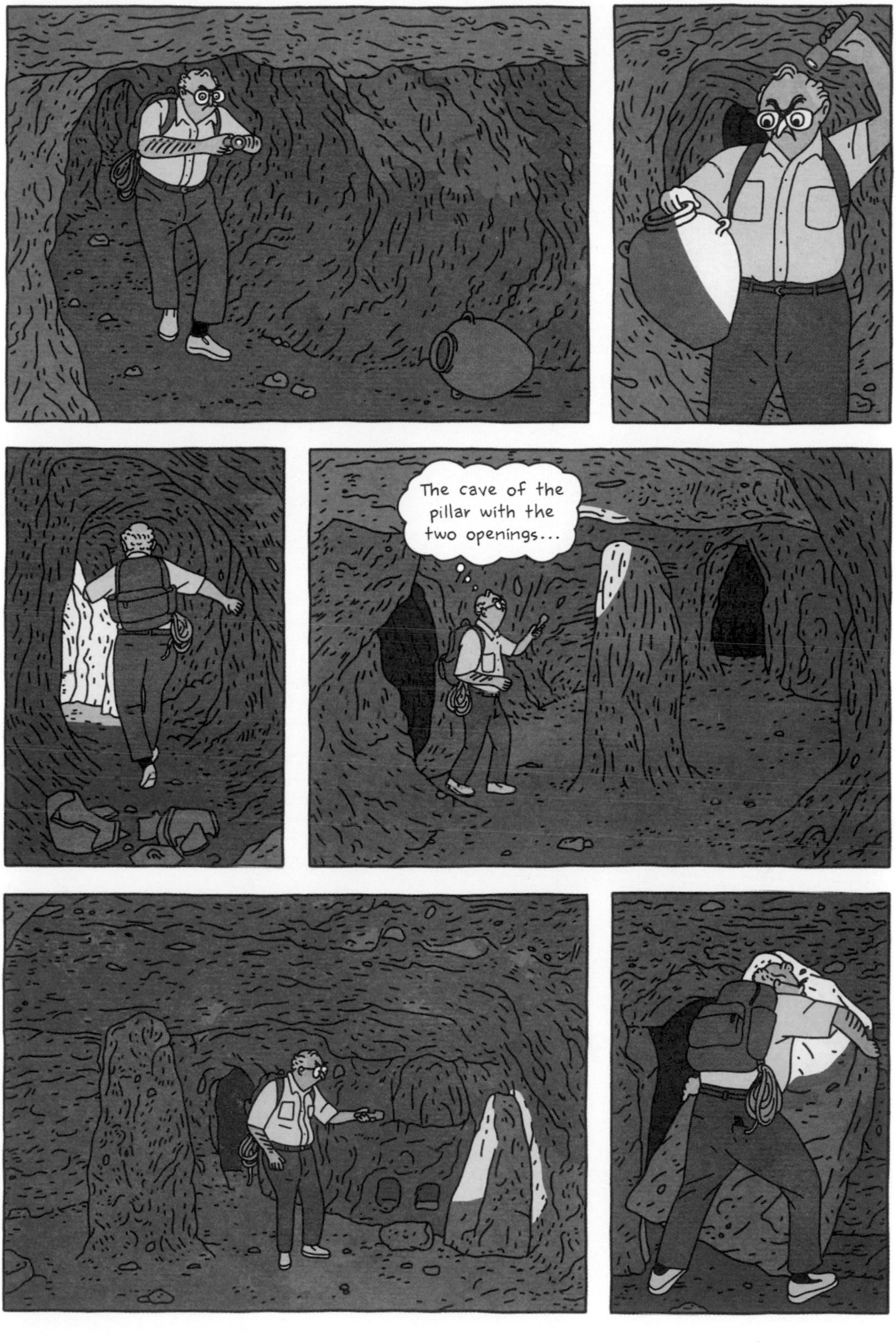
The cave of the pillar with the two openings...

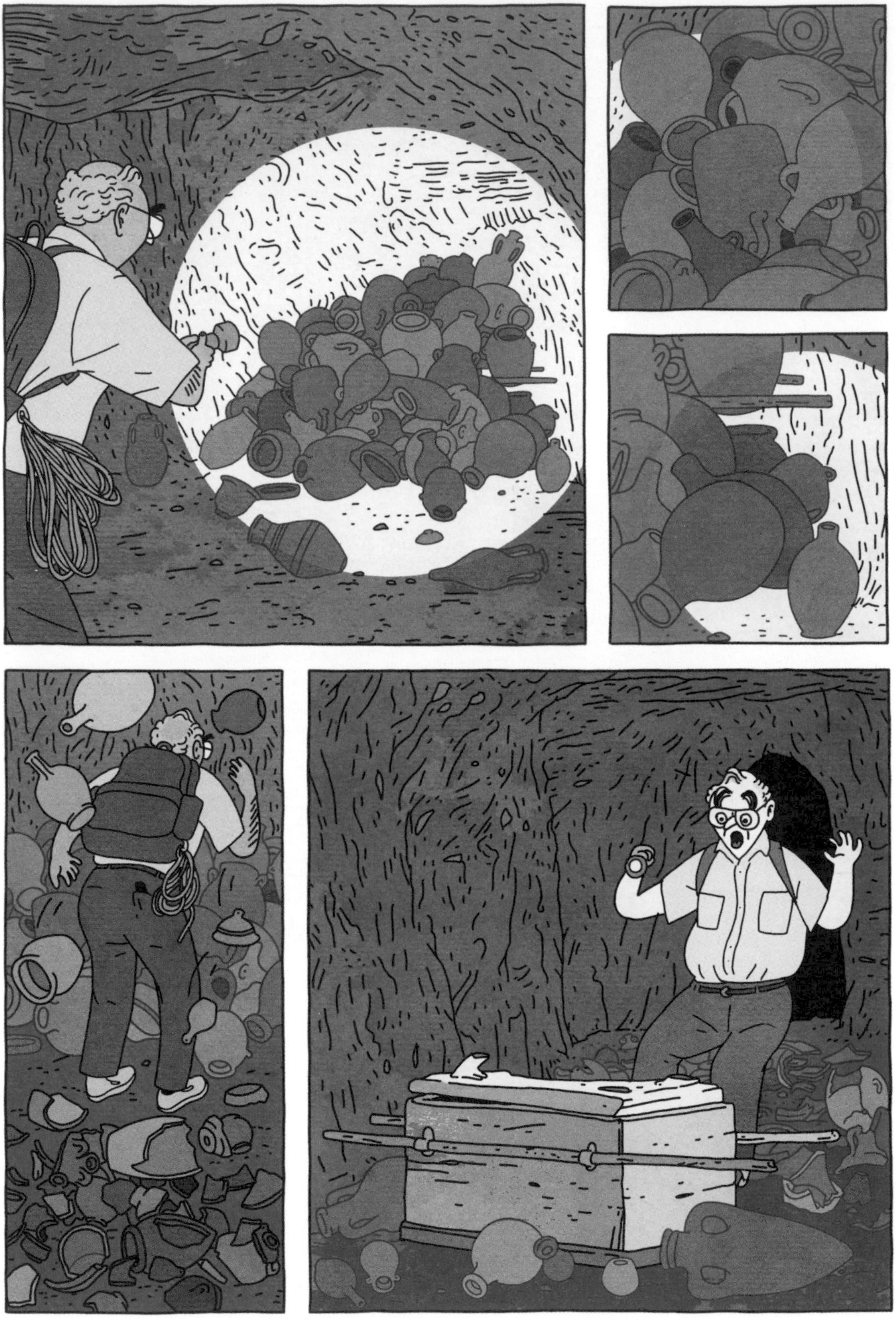

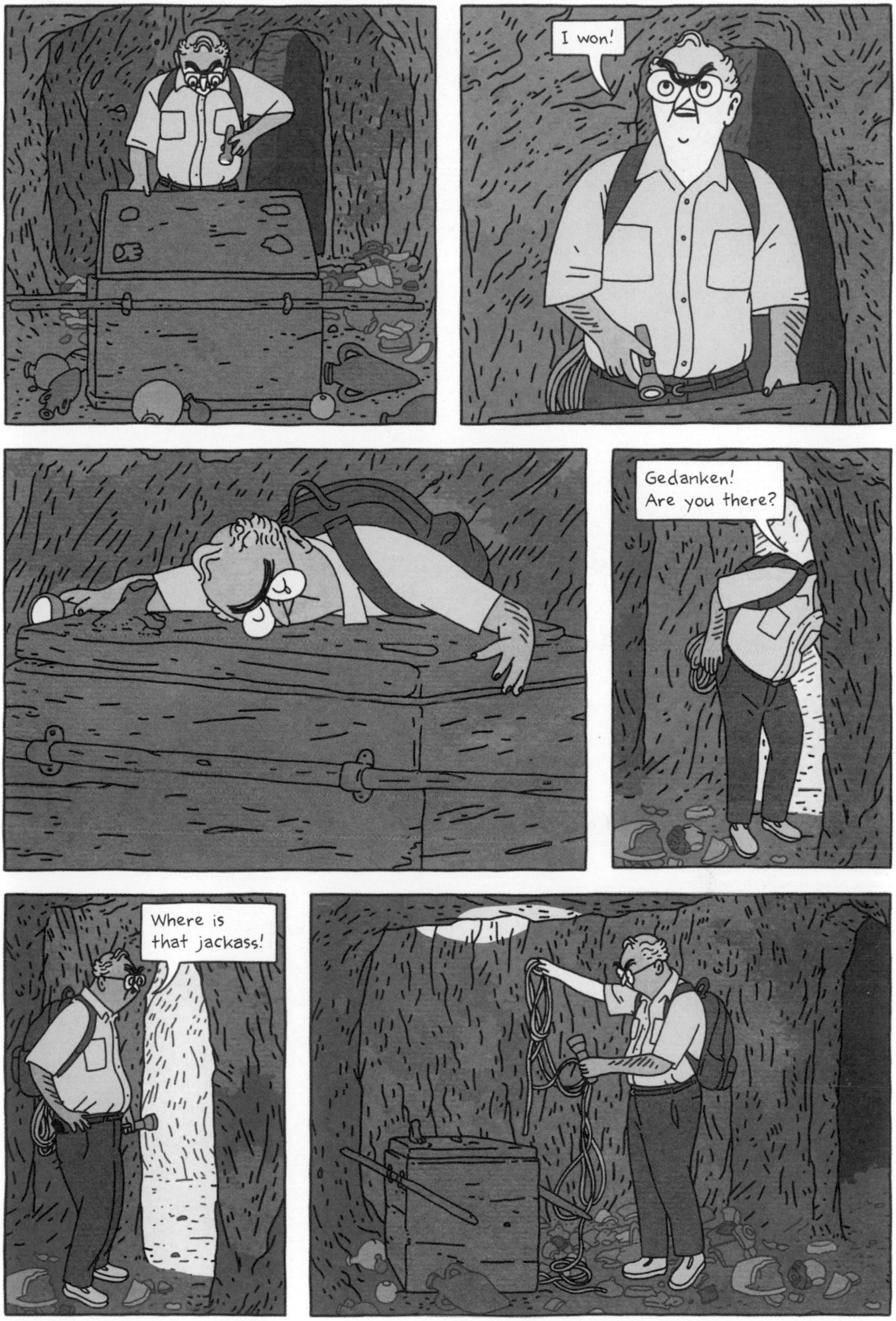
I won!
Gedanken! Are you there?
Where is that jackass!

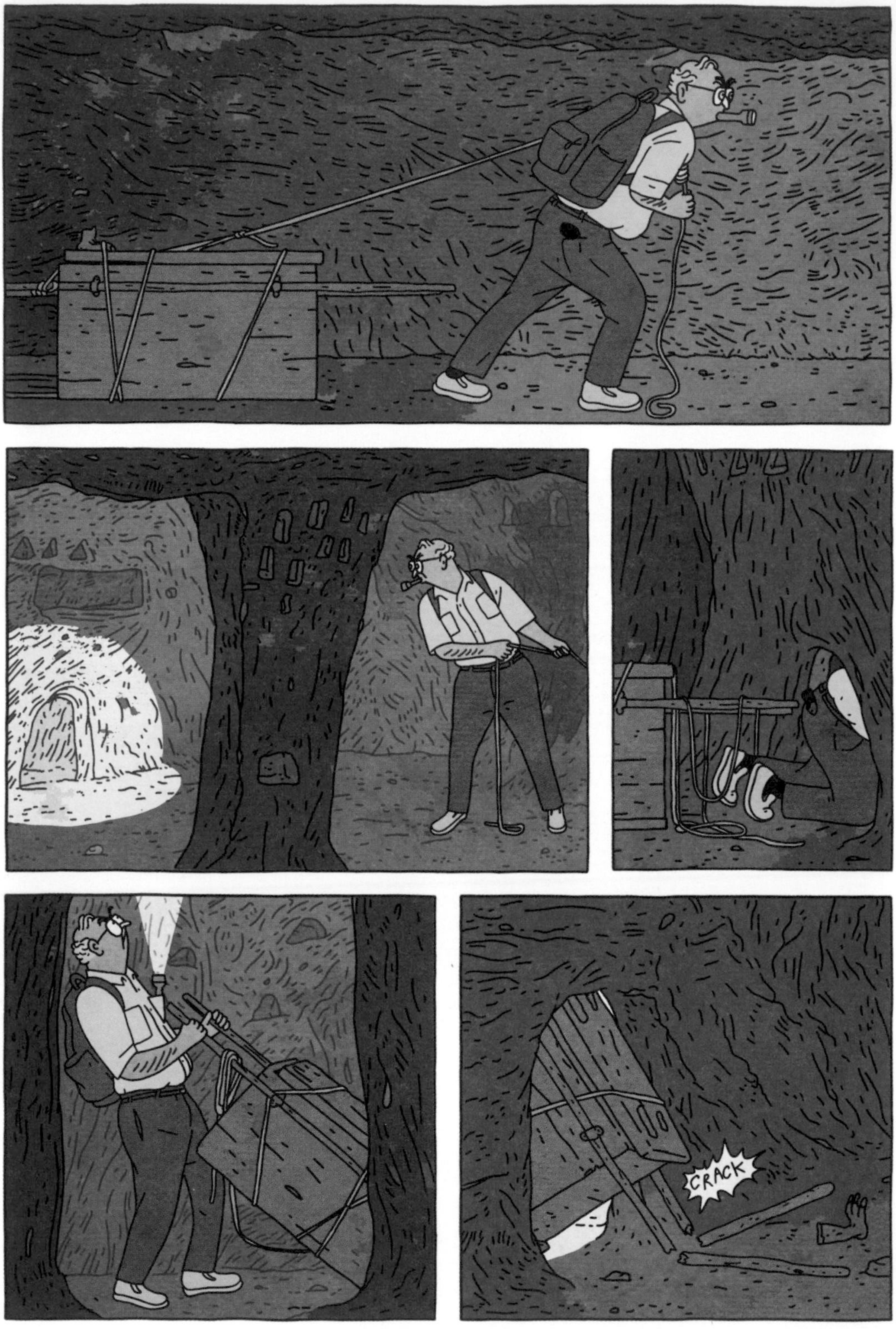
CRACK

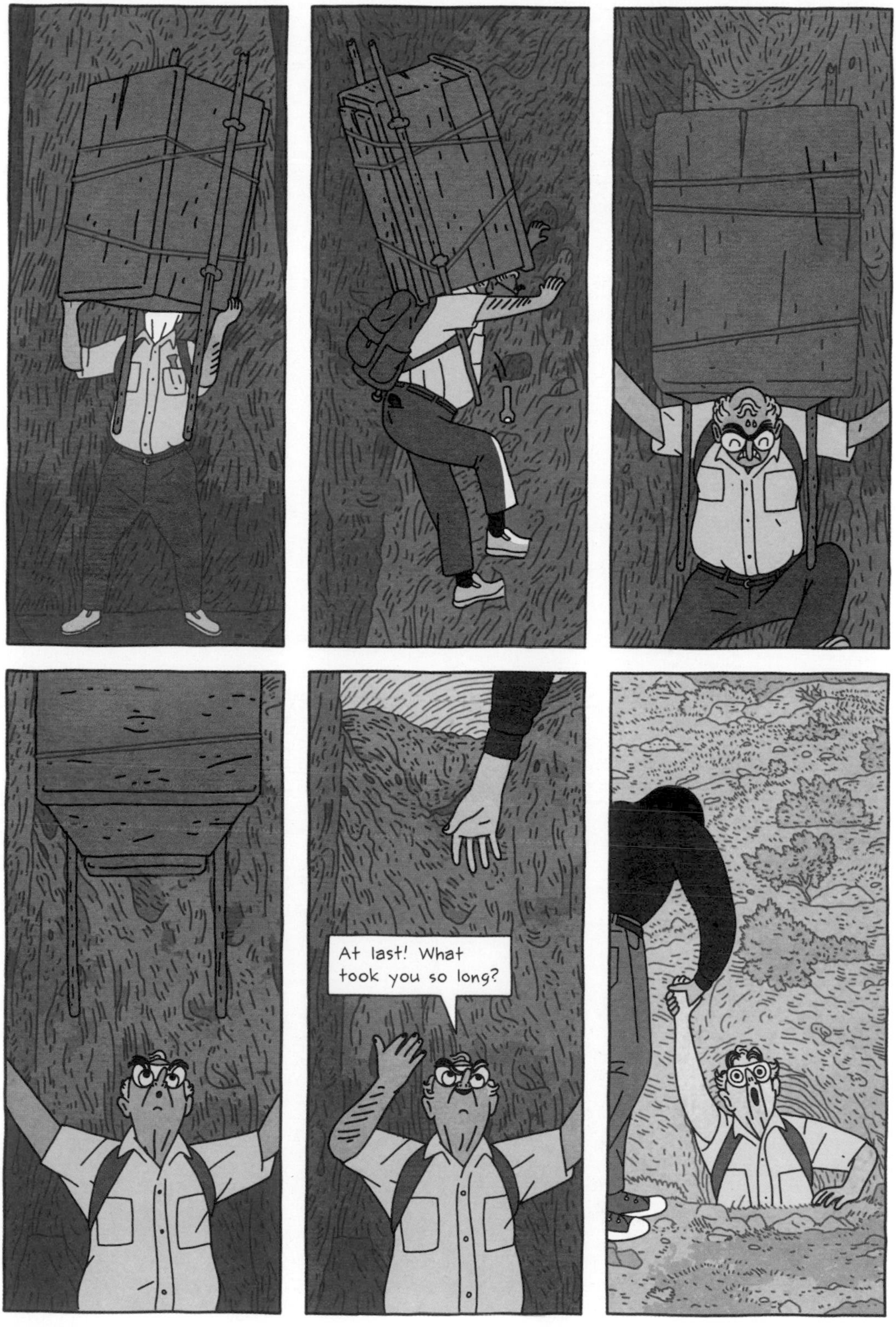
At last! What took you so long?

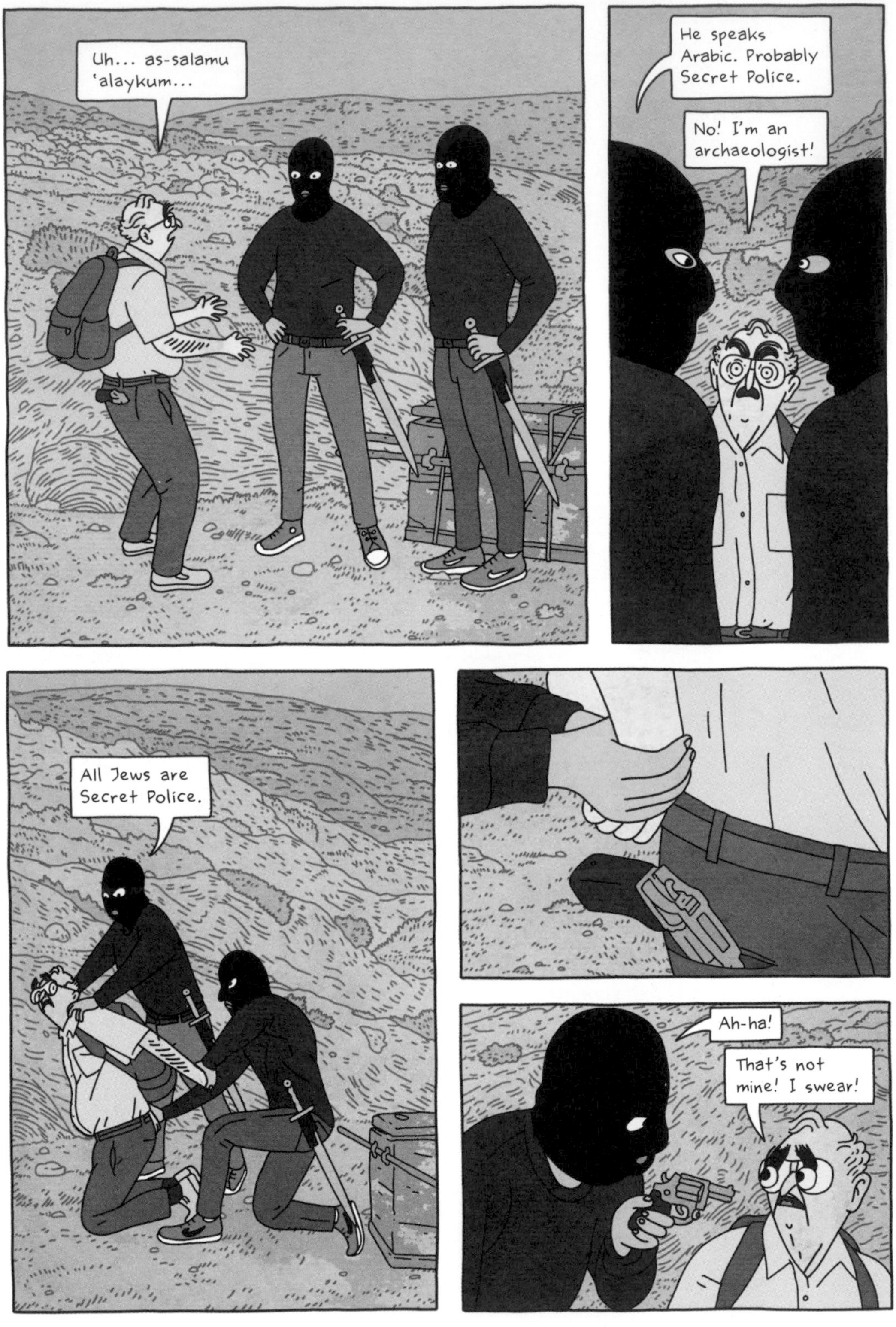
Uh... as-salamu 'alaykum...
He speaks Arabic. Probably Secret Police.
No! I'm an archaeologist!
All Jews are Secret Police.
Ah-ha!
That's not mine! I swear!

Shall we shoot a video?
No time. They're gonna pick us up any minute.
Please, have mercy on me...
Can't. Whole world's after us.
I'll give you... uh... Half a million dollars.
You got half a million dollars on you?
I will soon, if you just let me go... with...this...
And that's worth half a million dollars! Fancy story, man.
Wait!
Isn't this the crate the Jew was looking for?
Wallah?
Which Jew?

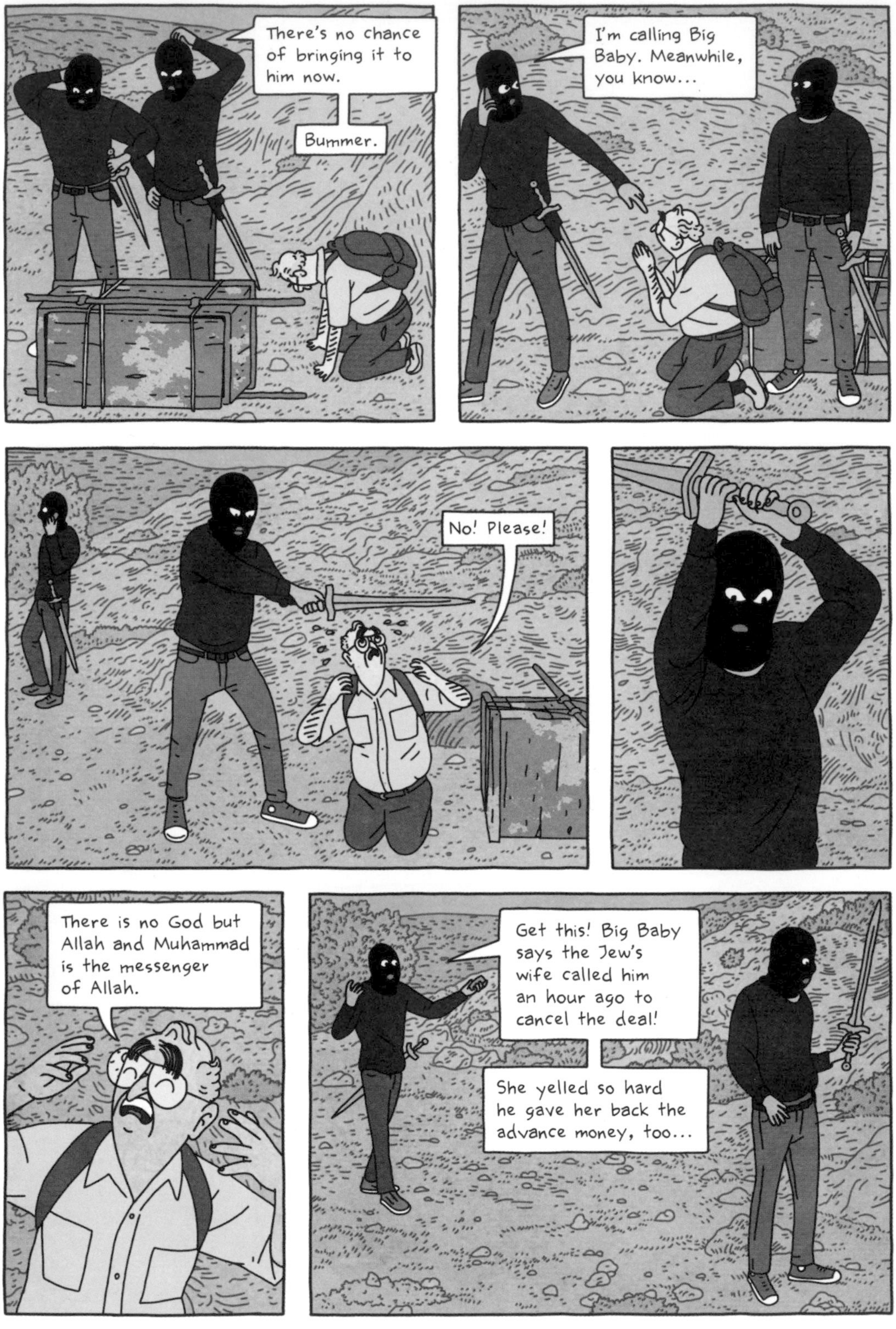
There's no chance of bringing it to him now.
Bummer.
I'm calling Big Baby. Meanwhile, you know...
No! Please!
There is no God but Allah and Muhammad is the messenger of Allah.
Get this! Big Baby says the Jew's wife called him an hour ago to cancel the deal!
She yelled so hard he gave her back the advance money, too...

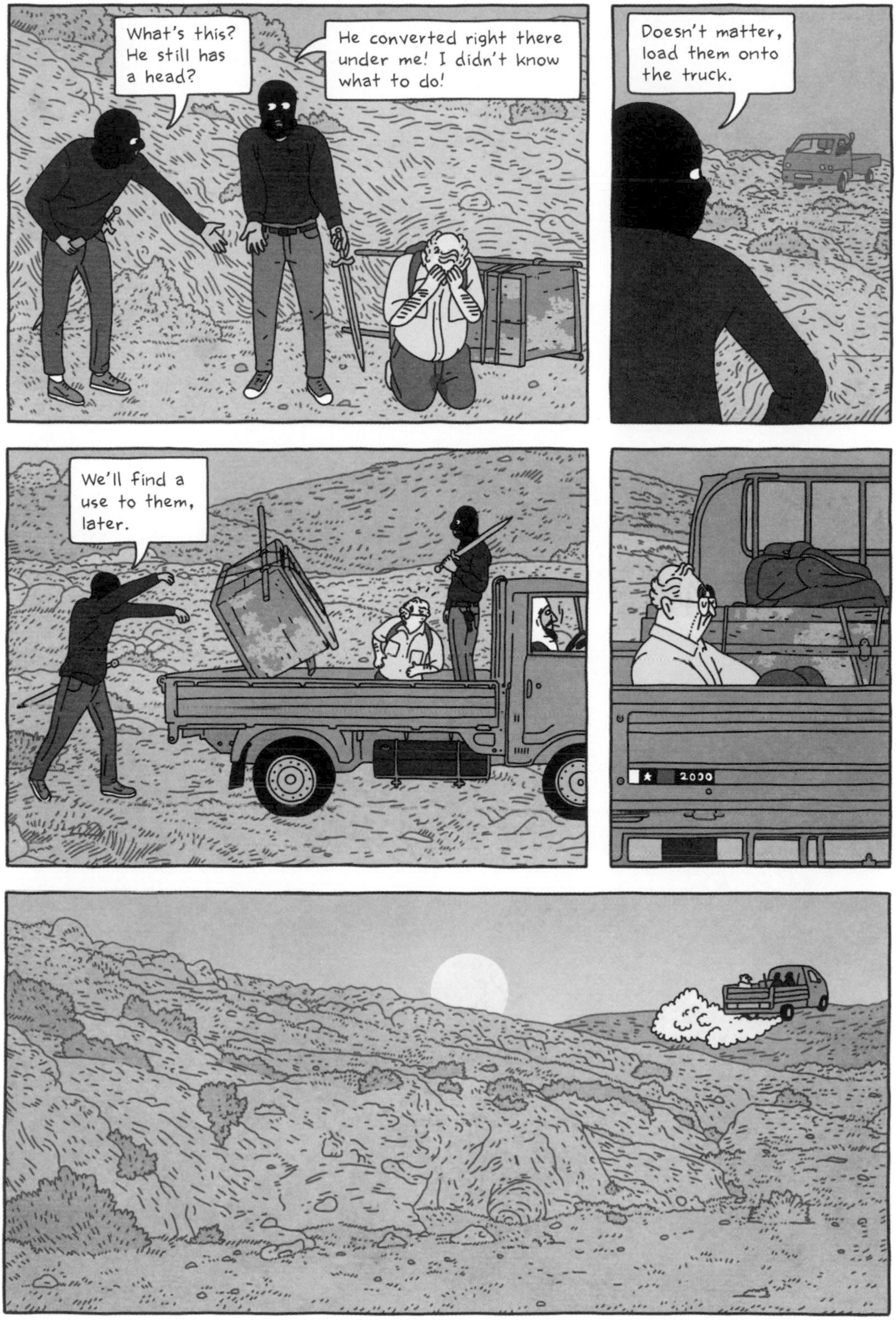
What's this? He still has a head?
He converted right there under me! I didn't know what to do!
Doesn't matter, load them onto the truck.
We'll find a use to them, later.
2000

Three Months Later...

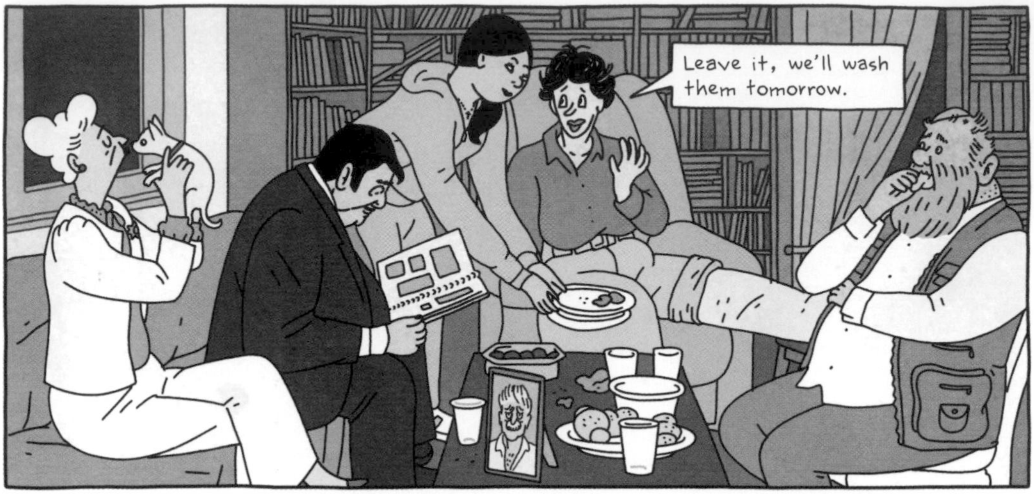
Leave it, we'll wash them tomorrow.

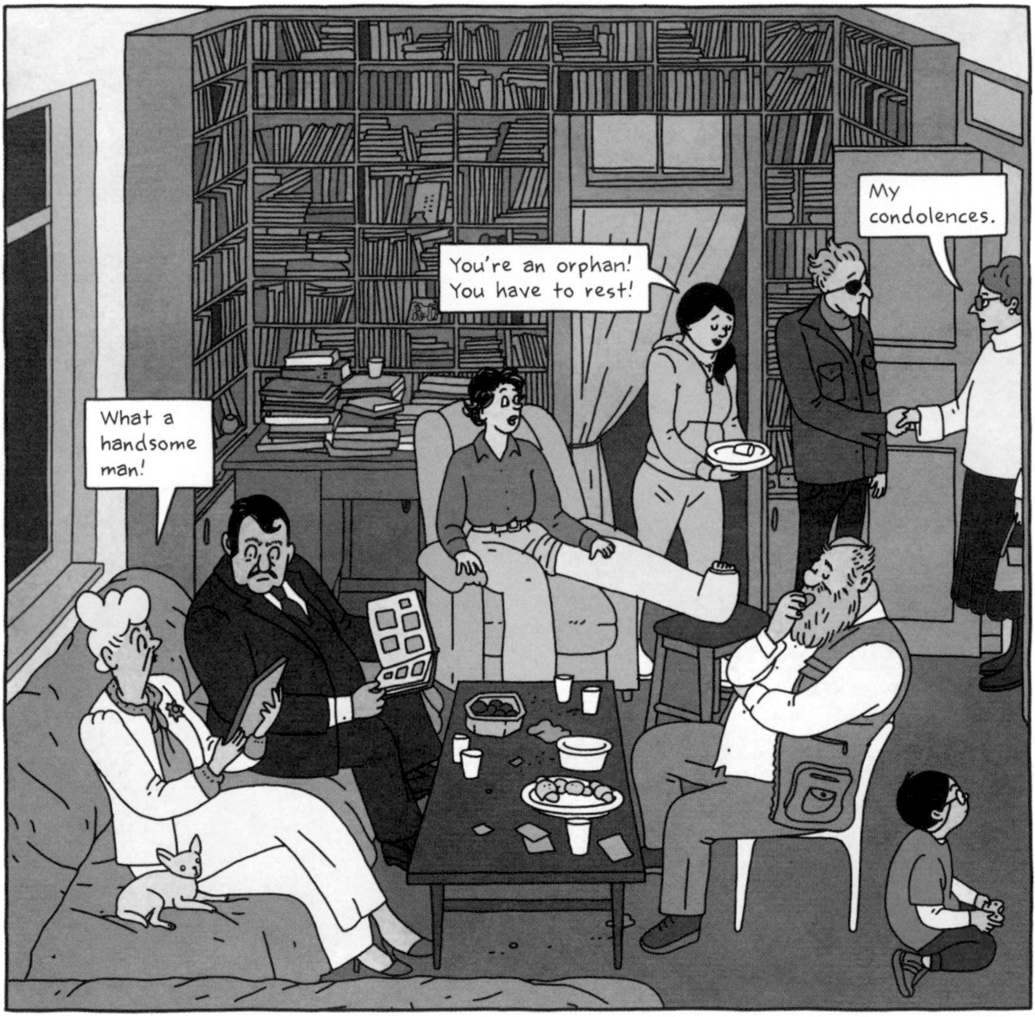
My condolences.
You're an orphan! You have to rest!
What a handsome man!

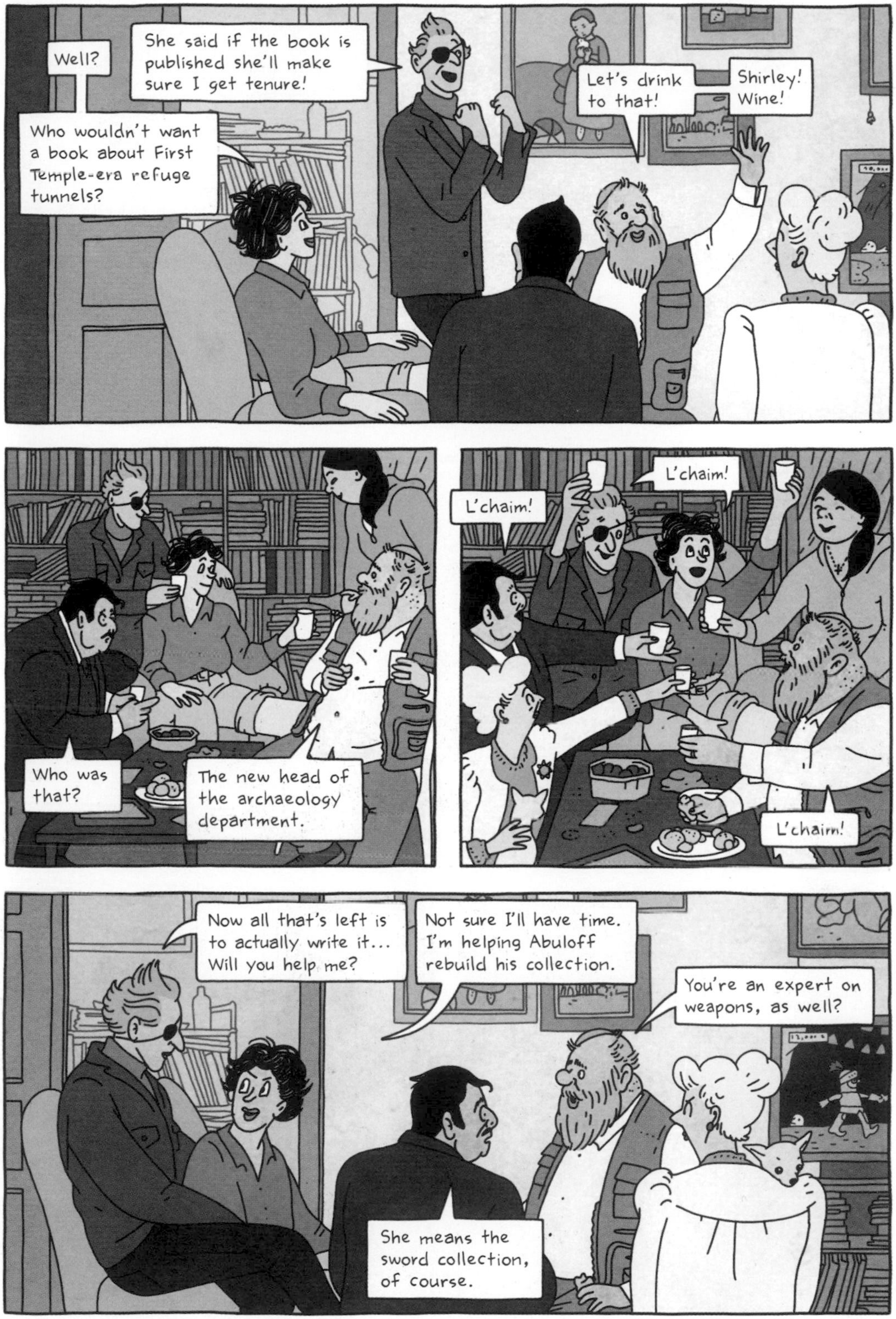
Well?
She said if the book is published she'll make sure I get tenure!
Who wouldn't want a book about First Temple-era refuge tunnels?
Let's drink to that!
Shirley! Wine!
Who was that?
The new head of the archaeology department.
L'chaim!
L'chaim!
L'chaim!
Now all that's left is to actually write it... Will you help me?
Not sure I'll have time. I'm helping Abuloff rebuild his collection.
You're an expert on weapons, as well?
She means the sword collection, of course.

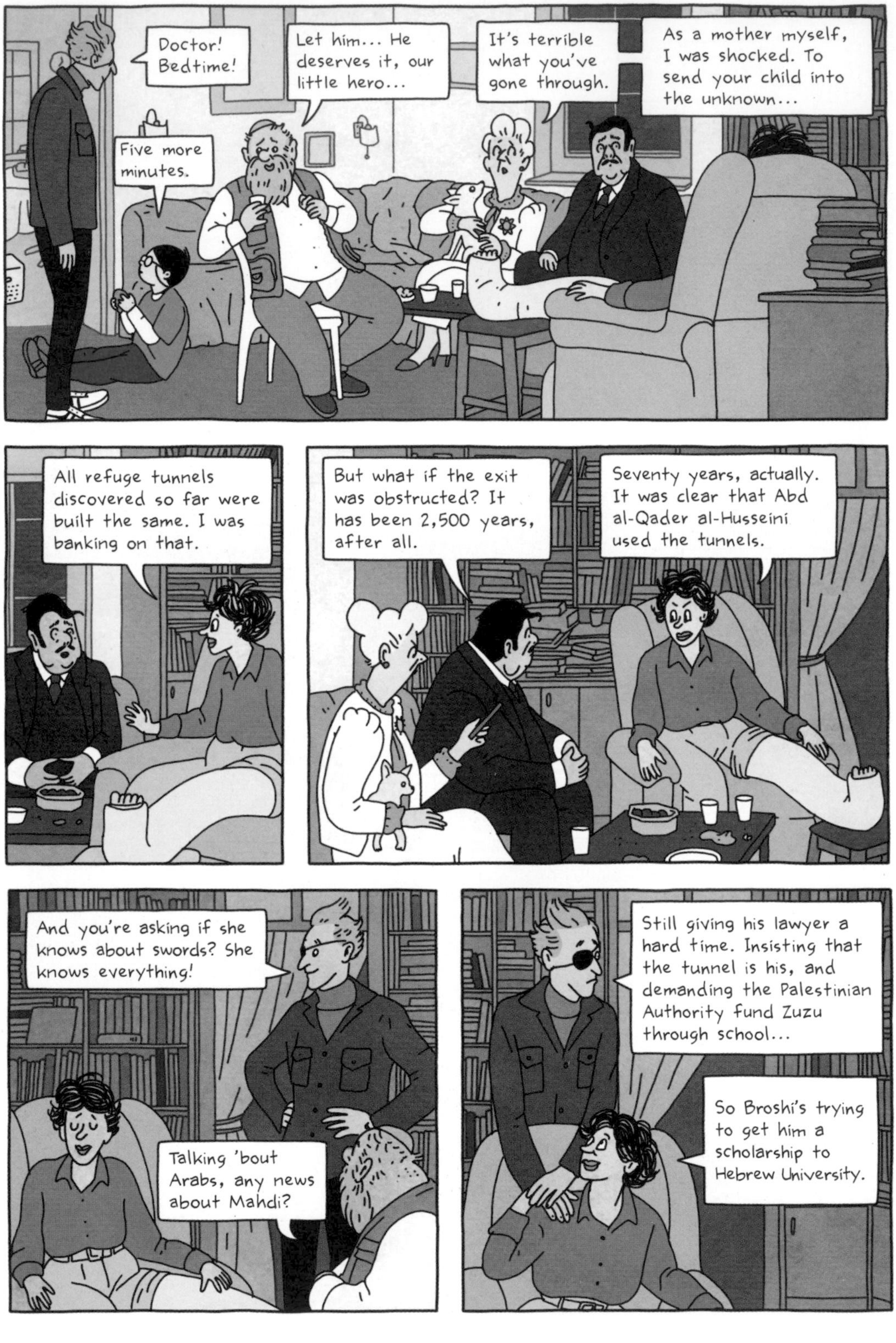
Doctor! Bedtime!
Five more minutes.
Let him... He deserves it, our little hero...
It's terrible what you've gone through.
As a mother myself, I was shocked. To send your child into the unknown...
All refuge tunnels discovered so far were built the same. I was banking on that.
But what if the exit was obstructed? It has been 2,500 years, after all.
Seventy years, actually. It was clear that Abd al-Qader al-Husseini used the tunnels.
And you're asking if she knows about swords? She knows everything!
Talking 'bout Arabs, any news about Mahdi?
Still giving his lawyer a hard time. Insisting that the tunnel is his, and demanding the Palestinian Authority fund Zuzu through school...
So Broshi's trying to get him a scholarship to Hebrew University.

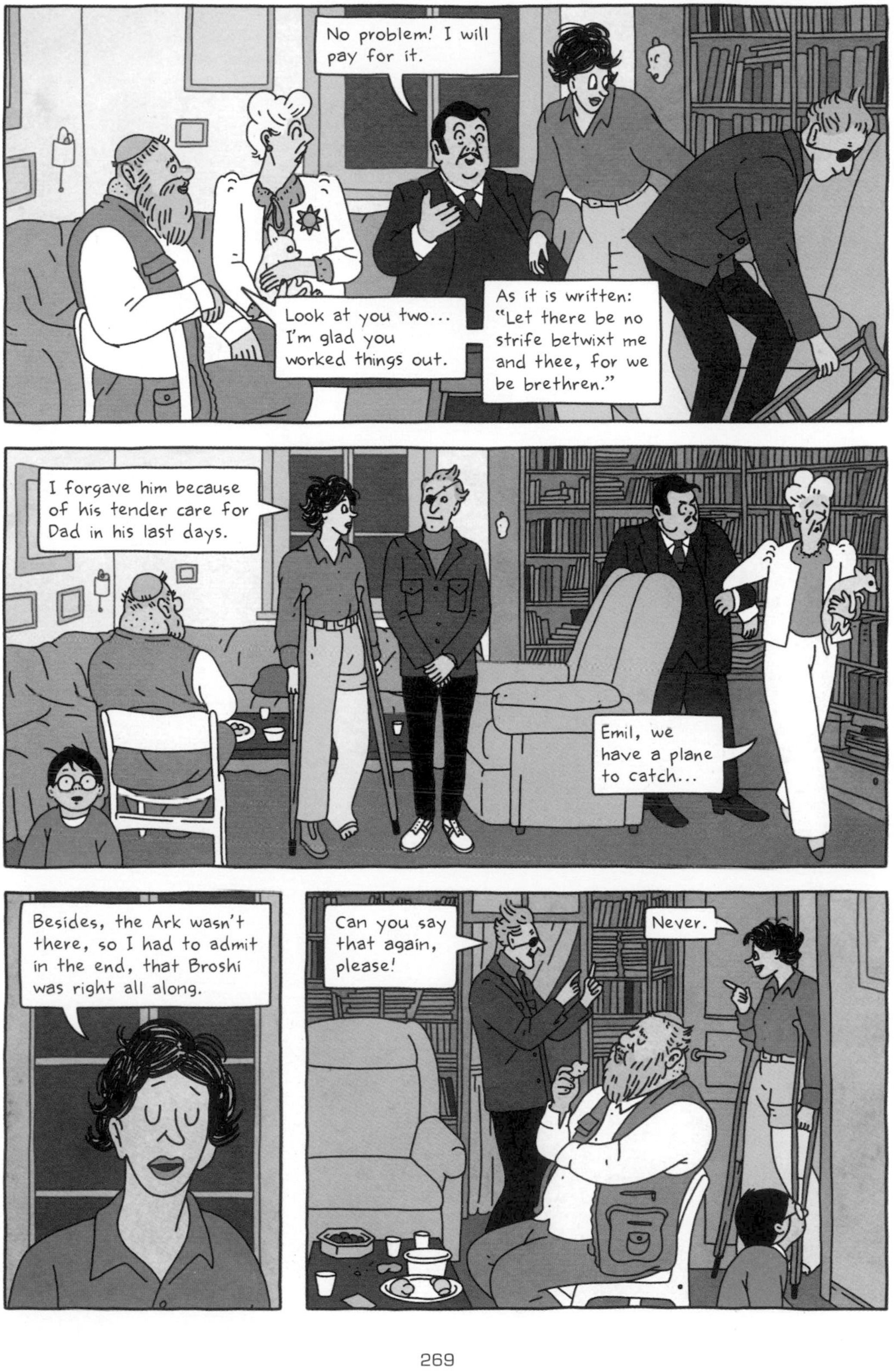
No problem! I will pay for it.
Look at you two... I'm glad you worked things out.
As it is written: "Let there be no strife betwixt me and thee, for we be brethren."
I forgave him because of his tender care for Dad in his last days.
Emil, we have a plane to catch...
Besides, the Ark wasn't there, so I had to admit in the end, that Broshi was right all along.
Can you say that again, please!
Never.

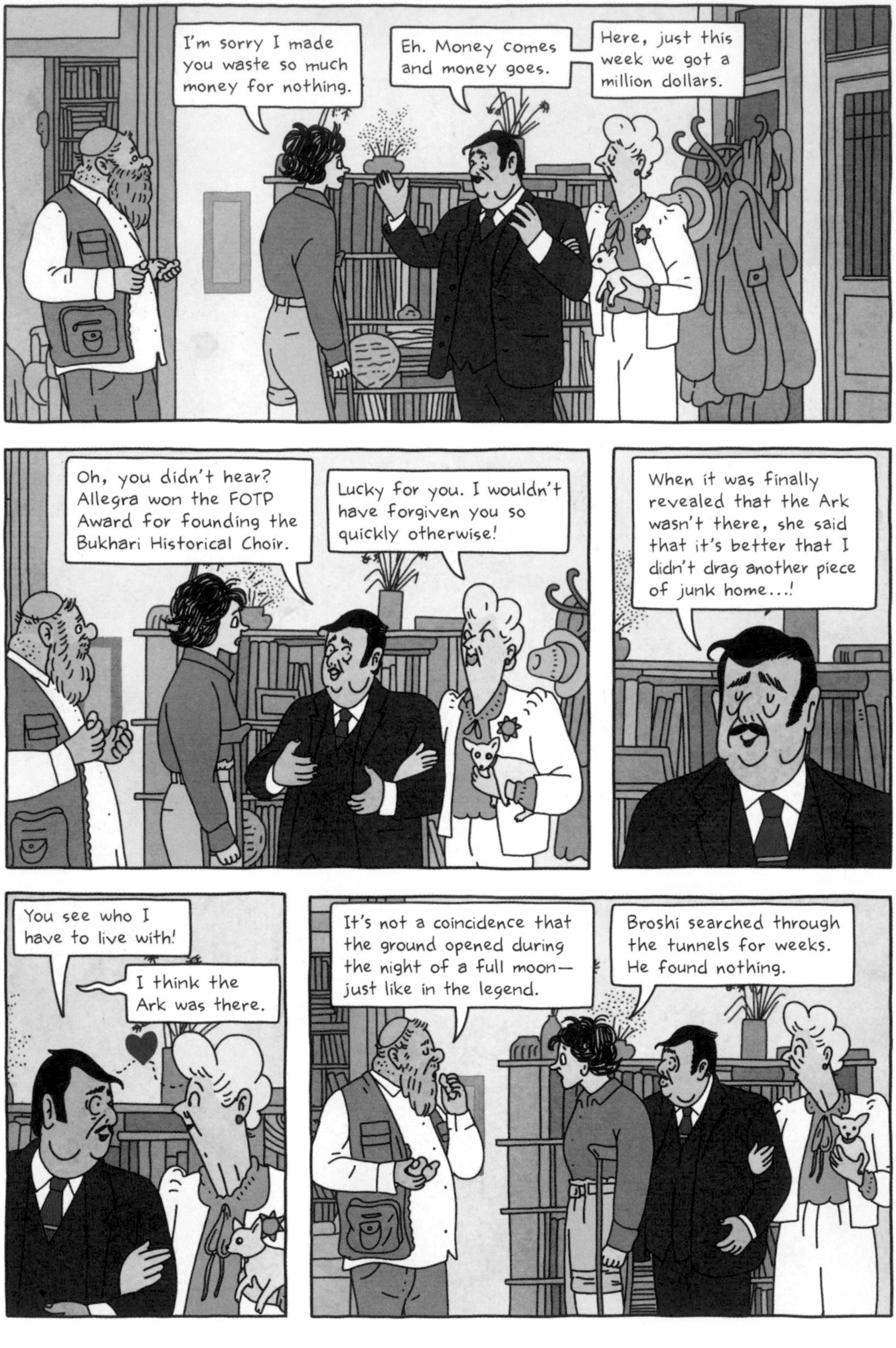
I'm sorry I made you waste so much money for nothing.
Eh. Money comes and money goes.
Here, just this week we got a million dollars.
Oh, you didn't hear? Allegra won the FOTP Award for founding the Bukhari Historical Choir.
Lucky for you. I wouldn't have forgiven you so quickly otherwise!
When it was finally revealed that the Ark wasn't there, she said that it's better that I didn't drag another piece of junk home...!
You see who I have to live with!
I think the Ark was there.
It's not a coincidence that the ground opened during the night of a full moon—just like in the legend.
Broshi searched through the tunnels for weeks. He found nothing.

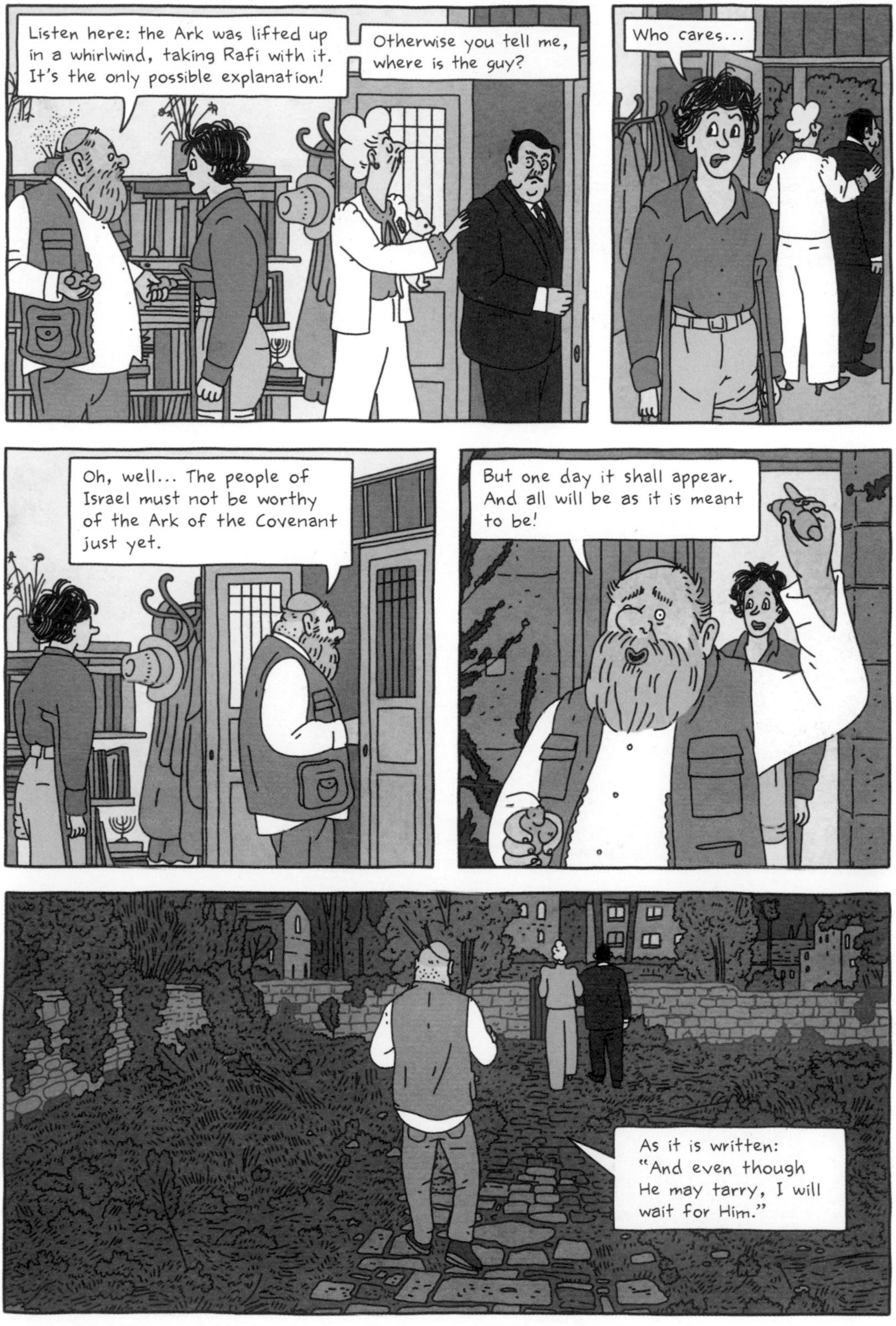
Listen here: the Ark was lifted up in a whirlwind, taking Rafi with it. It's the only possible explanation!
Otherwise you tell me, where is the guy?
Who cares...
Oh, well... The people of Israel must not be worthy of the Ark of the Covenant just yet.
But one day it shall appear. And all will be as it is meant to be!
As it is written: "And even though He may tarry, I will wait for Him."

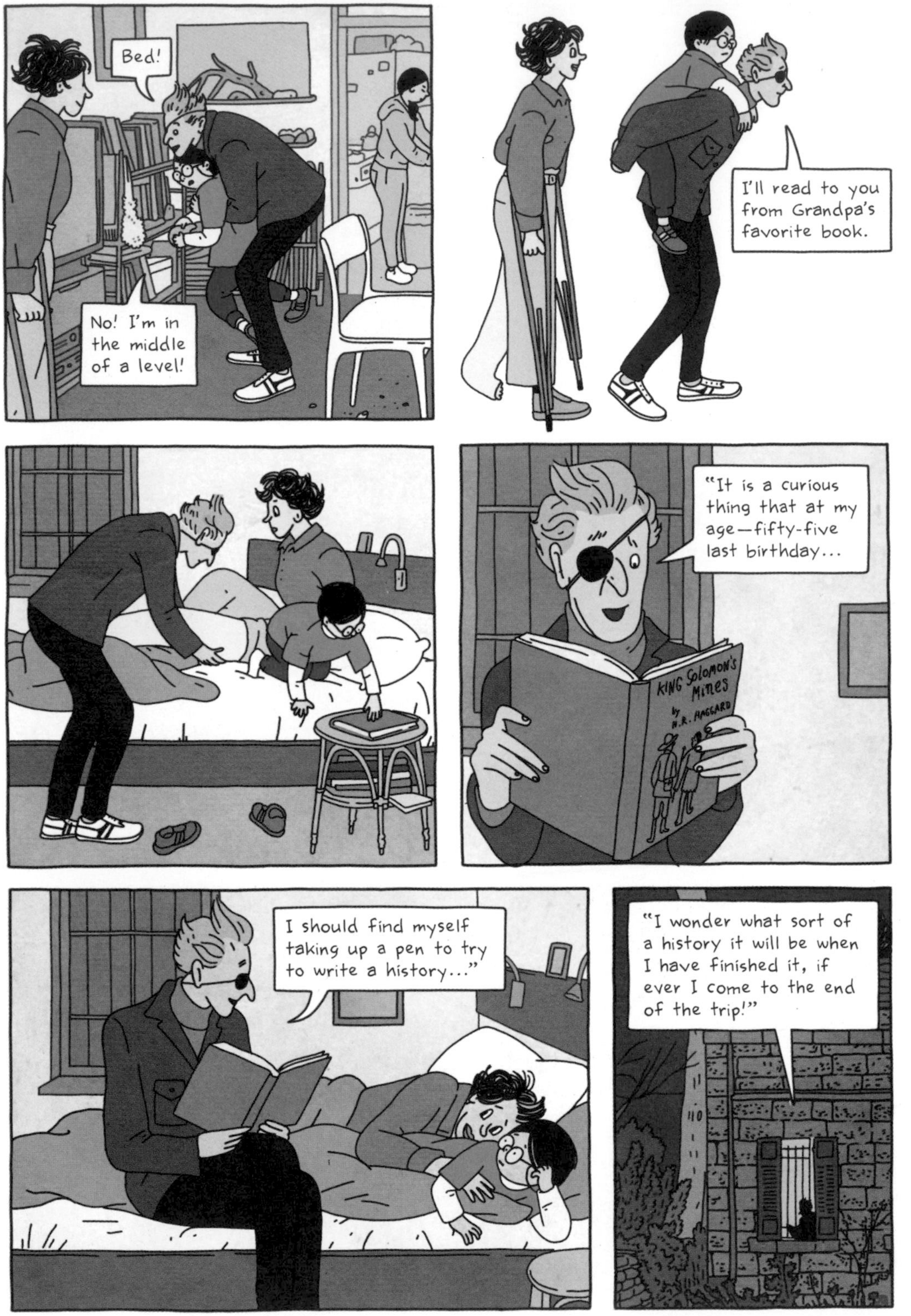
Bed!
No! I'm in the middle of a level!
I'll read to you from Grandpa's favorite book.
"It is a curious thing that at my age—fifty-five last birthday...
KING SOLOMON'S MINES by H.R. HAGGARD
I should find myself taking up a pen to try to write a history..."
"I wonder what sort of a history it will be when I have finished it, if ever I come to the end of the trip!"

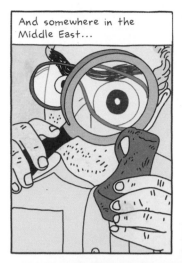

And somewhere in the Middle East...

Garbage.

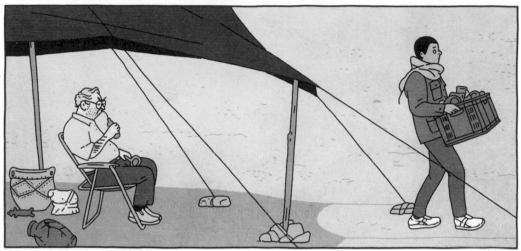

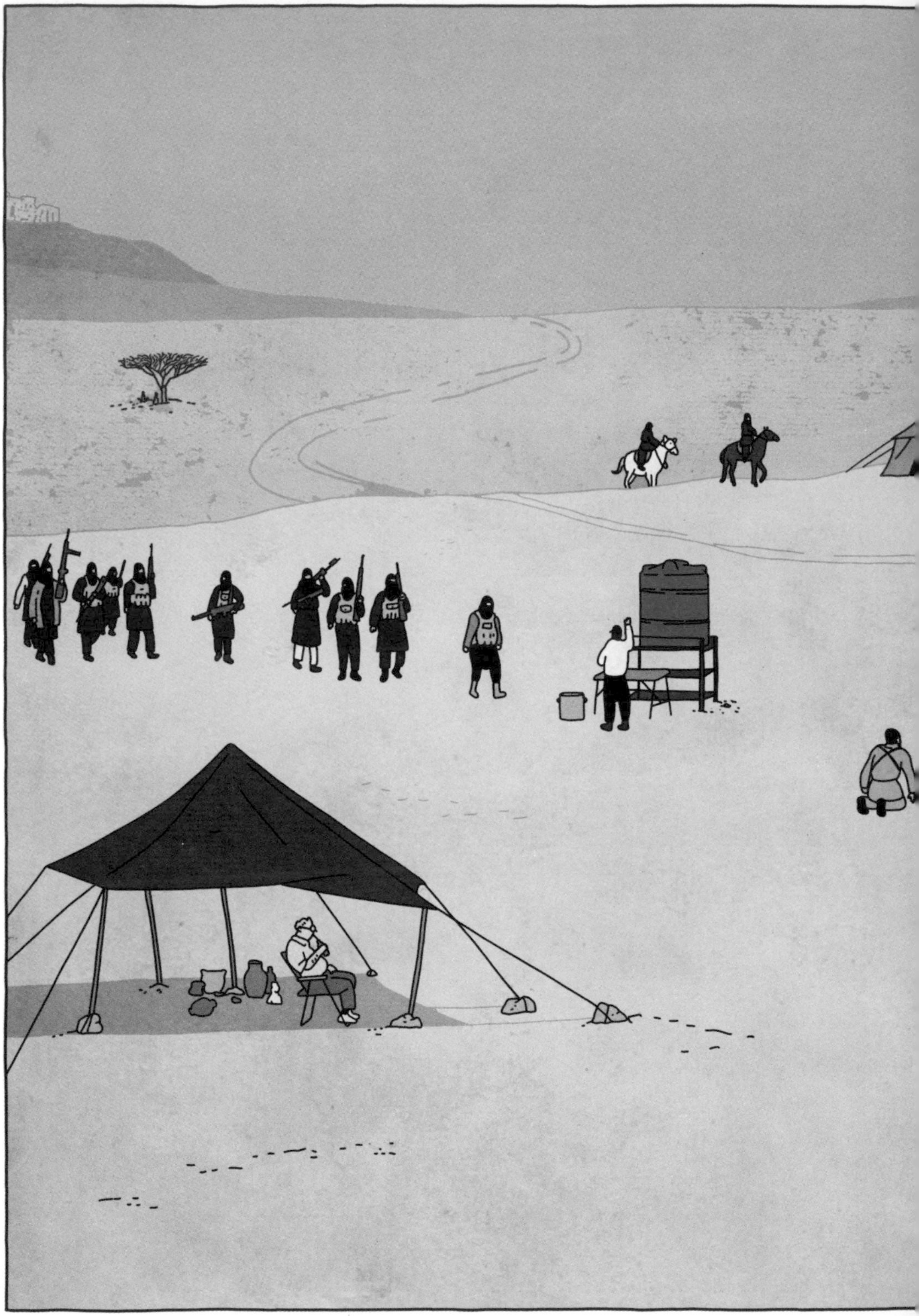

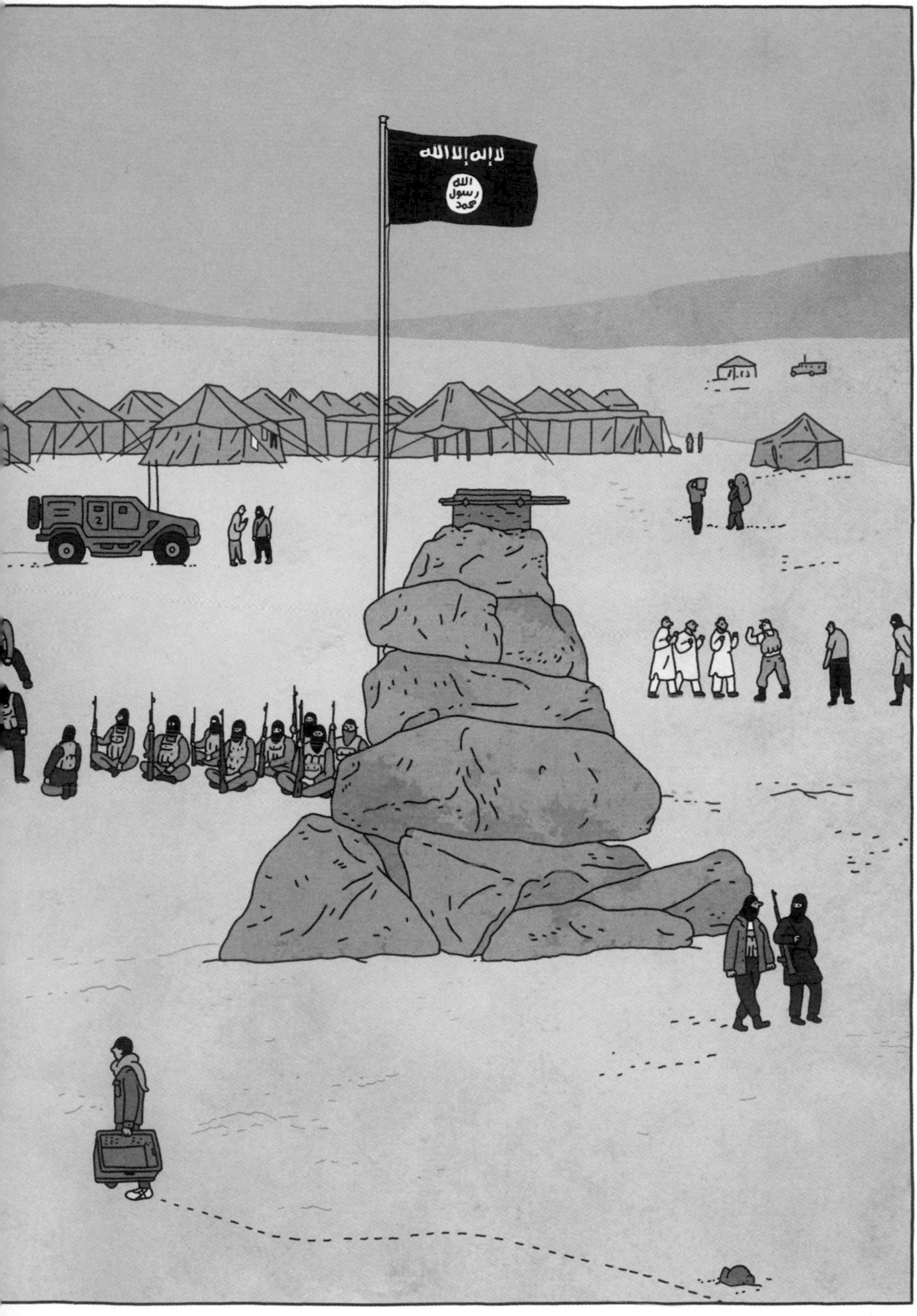
لا إله إلا الله
الله
رسول
محمد

End

AFTERWORD

INCLUDES SPOILERS

At the time of these words' writing, we are—hopefully—nearing the end of a global pandemic. It will be years before we can tell for sure if it completely transformed our world, or if it will only be remembered as a bizarre episode with which we will be left regaling our yawning grandchildren.

What is already evident, though, is that the pandemic hastened a process that began much earlier: a loss of agreement regarding reality. The fact is that not even one single authoritative figure that all are willing to believe is to be found anywhere. That even numbers, whose rigidity we complained about in school when told that one and one always equals two, cannot be totally counted upon. They, too, we have discovered, can be powerful tools in the hands of interested parties who throw one graph or another our way.

In this confusing state of affairs, when each fact is immediately contrasted with a counter-fact and everyone is branded a liar, when the word truth can be used only in apology and within quotation marks, it seems that the only object that can claim total honesty is fiction itself. The fictional story (as long as it is not disguised propaganda) a priori never claims to narrate the truth. Humbly, it confesses to being mere fantasy, told from the viewpoint of one limited, and patently not all-knowing, person. Among billion of voices that noisily hurtle unequivocal opinions at each other on social media, always trying to persuade and convince, the fictional story's only desire is to be listened to and enjoyed. How refreshing! All hail storytellers. But this comes with a hefty responsibility—declaring something "non truth" does not mean complete unaccountability.

Tunnels is the most complex story I have ever written. I knew going in that the only viewpoint I could tell it from would be my own: a Jewish-Israeli woman of the present. Still, in my attempt to tunnel, as it were, to the roots of even this limited truth, I had to put several stories that are an inseparable part of my identity—stories told to me as facts—to the test, and juxtapose them with the stories and facts of others, even my so-called enemies.

Facts. Another word that can be used only ironically. Even those that randomly survived and were discovered by chance, lay buried under layers of earth and time, distorted by interpretation, manipulations, prejudice, and nostalgia.

Still, I tried. I read history books, listened to lectures on archaeology, went on tours, and spoke with many people who generously opened their world to me, enriching my story with their knowledge, insight, and some wonderful sentences—which I shamelessly stole. I can't thank them enough. Unfortunately, they are too many to enumerate here. They include archaeologists and mystics, settlers and Palestinians, tunnel diggers and explosives experts, collectors and antiquity dealers. One of the latter, for example, a Palestinian man in his thirties, turned out to be seven times more knowledgeable in Israelite history than I have ever been. His merchandise mainly interests Jews, so he has become professionally conversant in biblical events and ancient Israelite royal history (so as to be able to price the items he owns according to importance). He translated for me a coin from his collection, bearing an ancient Hebrew letter inscription of the words "the temple of Jerusalem." The same temple which, according to an oft-heard Palestinian opinion, never existed. Against the background of the ongoing conflict around the Al-Aqsa Mosque, which according to Jewish tradition is built on the ruins of that same temple, I was curious about the clash between this young antiquity trader's national allegiance and his professional one. I asked him how he settles the two. "There was a temple in Jerusalem," he answered immediately, "but now Al-Aqsa is there." I liked his surprisingly sincere and simple answer very much: if only more of us found the present adequate, instead of squabbling over the past. His answer also speaks to the profound, almost unbridgeable, misunderstanding between the eternal wanderer and the indigenous resident. Between a group yearning to set down roots and a group that feels no need to prove theirs.

The fascinating people that I met—as different as can be from each other and from me—share the same land and one main desire: to be left alone in peace. The rollicking events, more than troubling them ideologically, only serve to block them from devoting themselves to their personal obsessions. As with them, so with me and with *Tunnels*' characters: a bevy of weird and (to me) familiar characters who band around Nili in common cause—finding the Arc of the Covenant. On the surface they agree to collaborate with each other, but mistrust, prejudice, and miscommunication drive them to strike alliance after contradictory alliance behind each other's backs, only to break them at the drop of a hat as soon as they feel threatened. Sadly, it is exactly their inability to trust each other that costs them all the ultimate treasure, a pretty fair summation of life here, which reminds me of a childhood joke:

> A traveler passes a cave when he suddenly hears a voice come out of it: "Don't make waves.... Don't make waves..." His curiosity piqued, the man enters the cave. There, in a deep pit, several people are submerged in shit up to their chins. Every once in a while one of them whispers: "Don't make waves..."

The waves that Nili makes almost cost her own life and that of her young son. Perhaps a more sober and realistic ending to the story would have had the Palestinians and the Israelis murdering each other in argument over ownership of the tunnel, with Nili and Doctor buried alive (or in the better case, fleeing to New York), and the Arc of the Covenant forgotten for another eternity.

Whether out of self-delusion or from a mystical fear of prophecies' power to self-fulfill, *Tunnels* ends differently. The bad guys are exiled to the desert, the others give up their grandiose plans for much more practical dreams, and no one is really hurt (except for Aviva the cow, the most innocent of all and without a doubt the one least invested in the Arc). On the other hand, the Arc is kept by the most dangerous extremists. If we choose to believe in the Arc's supernatural powers, and in the fact that ownership over it promises unlimited divine support in any military campaign, then the ending is perhaps not the most optimistic.

Israel—Palestine—is the most excavated place in the world. The first archaeologists who arrived here, devout Christians, were adamant to prove that the stories of the Bible were real. The Zionist archaeologists that followed them had the exact same goal, but different motivations. And Palestinian archaeologists have had their own. As opposed to the extreme effort expended, and everybody's sky-high expectations, the actual findings have been disappointingly neutral. Broken tools, barren stone walls, bone mounds. Here and there, a coin or a miniscule clay bulla are unearthed and their discovery makes front page news. Israel Finkelstein, one of Israel's most celebrated living archaeologists, has ruefully summed up the state of the research: "a formless, tasteless mound of trash compared to the illustrious cultures neighboring us, such as Egypt, Greece, and Babylon." Once, I visited an enthusiastic antiquities collector and he pointed to the walls of his home, which were easily more well-stocked and impressive than the Israel Museum's entire archaeological wing. "Look!" he gesticulated mournfully, "it all looks like a second-grade clay art project!"

It has been the historical misfortune of this not specially beautiful or resource-rich thin strip of land to be a bridge between three continents. Empires rose and fell, and each in turn desired it as a strategic stronghold. The poor residents of the land stood no actual chance of building anything serious, because every few years a giant army invaded them on its way to tackle an enemy empire, burning and looting everything in sight. Many left the land for more convenient places to live. Those who chose to stay always had a harder life. Perhaps that's why they chose to invent fantastic reasons for their devotion to it—and perhaps that is how they developed their storytelling abilities. Stories—especially those transmitted orally—can't be burned and looted. When the worst happens, they are easily moved from home to home, from continent to continent, from generation to generation. And the more the story is tossed, thrown around, and shaken, the more it grows, gradually becoming as elaborate and as immutable as the pyramids themselves.

For many centuries, the Jewish people based its identity not on territory, not even on religious worship, but on shared stories. This strategy—of basing communal identity on abstract rather than material grounds—has been revealed as an effective survival strategy, if not personal then at least cultural. It was a daring proposition, innovative even by the terms of the present. It was, to say the least, not always accepted amicably by others.

The attempt to return, to make the abstract story concrete, failed to take into account another people with its own story, which has proven no less tenacious. The War of Absolute Rightness began, and the gates of hell were thrown open.

It's a pity. Several stories can happily coexist simultaneously in our brains—as long as they don't try to be reality. Let's say I have become convinced that historically and archaeologically, the story of the Exodus from Egypt has no real bearing in reality—it would not, by that power, have lost any of its meaningfulness to me. Real or not, I certainly prefer the Exodus story over genetics, which as a basis for identity I find insulting and, when applied on a group level, tends to lead to frightful things.

I concede that it is not simple to accept any story just because it's a good one. Relinquishing the desire to ascertain "what actually happened" is problematic, especially when removed from antiquity to the recent past. In the best case, it sounds like despair with the project of justice-making. Used politically, this renunciation is a dangerous tool: it can lead to the suppression of any questioning of the status quo and to a reconsolidation of the aggressor's position.

Here is the story of just such a case:
There used to be two small kingdoms that lived side by side, both ruled by a fearsome empire. The two kingdoms shared a language and similar customs, sometimes cooperating against shared enemies and sometimes fighting between themselves. One time, one of the kingdoms rebelled against the

empire. The outcome was foreseeably terrible: the kingdom was destroyed and its residents exiled. Many of them sought refuge in the neighboring kingdom.

The refugees numbered about a half of the neighboring kingdom's population. So many, in fact, that the central government feared for its stability. The solution the government found was to convince the members of both peoples that in fact they were originally members of one people.

This wasn't so simple. Each of the peoples had their own histories and mythological memories, passed down through the generations for centuries, and both did not necessarily fit with the other, as recently, each considered the other to be an actual enemy. Each people had their own creation myth and god, and the same battles were narrated as crushing defeats or glorious victories, depending on whose point of view—the leader of one people, considered a paragon of virtue, was perceived by the other people as a mad scoundrel, etc.

It was impossible to expect the newly-arrived residents to give up their own stories and forget them. At best that would have created a deep resentment. All other avenues exhausted, it was decided to commit both peoples' stories down to writing, enmeshed into each other with all their possible contradictions. Where two versions existed, both were included. All the stories were unified into one book, about one people, with one god and one history, and one especially illustrious king—who just so happened to be the ancient forerunner of the current local monarch.

The plan was wildly successful. Residents of the kingdom—both the original and those newly-arrived—loved the book, and believed in it. It became a hysterical, and historical, best-seller. Hundreds of millions read it to this day—more readers than the Ikea catalogue. Many are willing to die or (even better) murder each other to defend its ideas. So much has it become a symbol of truth that people to this day swear in court while laying their hand on it.

The book is, of course, the Bible; the ancient kingdoms are Israel and Judah; and the two unified peoples have since been called either Israel or the Jewish people. Though that is not exactly the story I was told in school, it is one theory among several possible and considered pretty mainstream today, and it has a degree of archaeological and textual evidence to support it.

At any rate, I like to think that is what happened in Jerusalem about 2,700 years ago. What seems to me to be the book's greatest success was exactly the suturing of two stories into one—exactly because of their contradictions. It is because King David is represented in the Bible as both poet and celebrated military leader and as a ruthless and treacherous terrorist that he is such an unforgettable character—so much so that it is not simply the Jewish people but many others that see him as related to the Messiah (whether the one crucified or the one to come). Even the Queen of England professes to be related to him.

Combining the two peoples' narratives resulted in complex and convincing plots, and in believable and identifiable heroes. They did terrible and wonderful things, erred and triumphed and suffered—just like us. The audience disregarded the blatant holes in the plot and the story took so well that even non-believers quote it; and even those who wish they were rid of it can't be, because it is so assimilated into their own life-story. In desperation, they try and interpret it differently or weave their own story into it, but it's very hard to trounce a best-seller.

The years passed, and we now find ourselves in the same place: two rival peoples, fighting each other to the death for the same land, trying to overcome each other, each one screaming its own truth and claim to justice. Are we really that limited that we cannot imagine the conflict coming to an end one day? Can we not, at least in our minds, jump over the tectonic events, still hidden from our eyes, that would lead, three thousand years hence, to a time when the Israeli and Palestinian narratives have been assimilated into one story? So convincing that anybody who objects to it would be branded as a traitor? And if we can already imagine such a situation, why can't we try and avoid the usually unsavory tribulations of history and strive for it already now?

It is almost embarrassing to admit, but only about two weeks ago, the full meaning of the 'covenant' in 'Arc of the Covenant' suddenly dawned on me. A covenant is not simply a solemn agreement between parties to cooperate: in Hebrew, the term for it (berit) signifies the kind of pact—signed metaphorically or materially in blood—that it is better to die than to break. If that is so, then the characters of Tunnels can actually be said to be collaborating in the name of cooperation, and Nili is even more heroic than I'd thought. In her attempt to dig under the separation barrier, in her efforts to bring together all the crazies around her, without them giving up on their dreams or even their prejudices. She does all this to get to the greatest treasure: the ultimate agreement, the one that will bring the Messiah and everybody can live happily ever after. It is not the Arc she is after but the covenant—and that is what slips between her fingers because of her own fear and impatience, and those of the men around her. And maybe Israel Broshi's map isn't just the ravings of a demented old man. Maybe in pointing to an illustration copied from a fictional adventure book, he was trying to signify to his children that the search suffices. The backbreaking, arduous search after what may even not be there. Don't call it a nightmare, Israel was trying to say, call it an adventure, despite—and because of—its many perils.

It is now May 2021. Jews and Palestinians are again killing each other in ways that are becoming ever more cruel and murderous. The killing is never symmetrical, and that's important to say and write. But if I may, just momentarily, move beyond calculus and symmetry—the dreams I have never sat well with mathematics, anyway—couldn't I suggest that we write one story from all the old stories, a story that will be bigger than all combined? A terrible and wonderful and turbulent story full of holes and contradictions? One that people can live inside. Let's sign a covenant worth dying for among us. In these dark times, I would happily settle for just the search.

In the meantime, please, no more waves.

—RUTU MODAN

GLOSSARY

BIRTHRIGHT

A controversial program, established with the purpose of strengthening the bond between Jewish young adults around the world and the state of Israel. The project, partially funded by the government of Israel, pays for participants to visit Israel and sends them on a ten-day tour all over the country. The Hebrew name for the project is the less-loaded title *taglit* which means "discovery" or "finding."

IR DAVID (THE CITY OF DAVID)

An archaeological excavation on the site of ancient Jerusalem, where the city existed from its inception until medieval times. Today, the site is located in the Palestinian village Silwan. Ir David is considered a national heritage site by Israelis, but is a source of ideological and political conflicts—among other things, Palestinian residents allegedly have been displaced from their homes.

INTIFADA

"Intifada" means "an uprising" in Arabic.

The first Palestinian Intifada broke out in 1987; it was a struggle to end the Israeli occupation of the West Bank. When the Oslo Accords were signed in the 90s, the Intifada subsided.

The second Intifada started in 2000 after a long period of relative peace. The question "who is to blame" for the new uprising is under debate. Unlike the first Intifada that took place within the West Bank borders, and where the rebels used mostly "cold" weapons such as rocks and Molotov cocktails, the Second Intifada took place all over the country and was characterized by frequent suicide bombings. The violence on both sides of the conflict collapsed the Oslo Accords and led to the building of the Barrier (or the Separation Wall, as it is called by the Israelis) between the West Bank and Israel's internationally recognized territory.

OSLO ACCORDS

The Oslo Accords were signed between the state of Israel, led by Prime Minister Yitzhak Rabin, and the Palestine Liberation Organization (PLO), led by Yasser Arafat, in order to end the Israeli-Palestinian conflict. The first accord was signed in 1993, wherein Israel recognized the PLO as the representative of the Palestinians and agreed to withdraw from territories in the West Bank and Gaza, while the PLO recognized the legitimate existence of the Jewish state and pledged to stop the violent resistance. The second accord was signed in 1995. In this accord, the West Bank's civilian and military control would be divided between the PLO and Israel and into three parts:

Area A: Areas under civilian and military control of the Palestinian Authority.
Area B: Areas under civilian control of the Palestinian Authority and military control of the State of Israel.
Area C: Areas under the civilian and military control of the State of Israel.

The implementation of the agreement was delayed over and over again. Each party argued that the other had failed to comply with the terms of the agreement. Opponents in both nations tried to undermine the agreement in political and violent ways, including the assassination of Prime Minister Yitzhak Rabin by an Israeli Jew. Following the wave of suicide bombings in the Second Intifada, the Israel Defense Forces reoccupied the West Bank and since then, military control of the area has been in the hands of Israel.

PIT OF JEREMIAH

Jeremiah was a prophet who lived at the end of the First Temple period, in the seventh century BC. Jeremiah opposed the Jewish kings in Jerusalem who sought independence from the Babylonian Empire. He claimed that this would wreak havoc on the kingdom of Judah and so he called for cooperation with the Babylonians. These prophecies, in addition to his irritable and argumentative nature, made him hated by the king and the people alike. To silence him, Jeremiah was imprisoned in a mud pit underground. He was liberated by Babylonian soldiers after their army conquered and burned Jerusalem and exiled its inhabitants, just as Jeremiah had prophesied. In the City of David, there is a pit called Jeremiah's Pit even though it only dates back to from the Byzantine period, about 1,000 years after the time of the Prophet.

PRESUMPTION OF PRIESTLY DESCENT (COHEN)

In biblical times, priests (*Cohen* in Hebrew) were responsible for the temples' operations and ceremonies. Having no land of their own, they would make their living from donations. The head of priests is known as the high priest (*Ha-Cohen Ha'Gadol* in Hebrew). According to the Hebrew faith, only the high priest could be in the presence of the Ark of the Covenant without danger, and only after satisfying rigorous prerequisites, such as performing a ritual purification using a red cow's ashes. After the destruction of the Second Temple and the exile of the Jews to Babylon, the priests lost most of their functions. In time, just the symbolic laws and ceremonies, like their prohibition on entering a cemetery, remained to distinguish their high priest status. Today, anyone whose last name is Cohen (or other names derived from the same root, such as Kahana, Kohn, etc.) is given the "Presumption of Priestly Descent," even though there is no evidence showing genetic links between today's Cohens and past priests.

SETTLERS

Israeli Jews who created settlements in the West Bank, outside the internationally agreed borders of the State of Israel. Some moved there with the support of the Israeli government, while some, the extremists and religious zealots (also known as the idealists), created settlements illegally with the aim of "establishing facts on the ground," i.e. make their territorial claims harder to reverse. They often confront the Israeli army which tries to evacuate them from the area.

CREDITS

TRANSLATOR .... Ishai Mishory

STORY EDITOR .... Noah Stollman

COVER DESIGNER .... Michal Sahar

COLORING ASSISTANTS .... Omer Porat & Michal Bergman

ACTORS

DOCTOR .... Adam Smooha-Modan

NILI .... Batia Kolton

BROSHI .... Ami Smolarchik

GEDANKEN .... Uri Hochman

RAFI SARID .... Dov Navon

MAHDI .... Yami Wisler

ZUZU .... Ibrahim Alam

EMIL ABULOFF .... Victor Ida

ALLEGRA ABULOFF .... Meital Raz

COLONEL KAFRI .... Assi Cohen

MOSHE & DAYAN .... Uri Magen-Garbuz

CORAL .... Michal Bergman

SHIMSHON .... Omer Porat

KATANI .... Itamar Koren

KABIRI .... Yair Israel

ZECHARIAH .... Amir Kiper

BIG BABY .... Arik Kneler

RINGO .... Eldad Babay

ZINGO .... Daniel Edvardson

RAFI'S WIFE .... Merav Salomon

TALL SOLDIER .... Hilel Berman

MELAKMO .... Salomon Chekol

LUGASSI .... Ofer Bergman

ISRAEL BROSHI .... Yirmi Pinkus

SHIRLEY .... Zohar Elazar

NEW HEAD OF DEPARTMENT .... Dana Modan

PARTY GUESTS .... Roni Levit, Uri Nisim, Amitay Gilad,
Guy Saggee, Noa Alfia, Shir Hay,
Ayal Zakin, Irit Hemo, Michal Sahar

PRODUCTION MANAGERS .... Gail Philosof & Karin Etedgi

RUTU MODAN is an illustrator, comics artist, and Associate Professor at the Bezalel Academy of Art & Design, Jerusalem. After publishing several comics strips in the Israeli media, Modan co-founded the Actus Comics group. In 2008 her book *Exit Wounds* won the Eisner Award. Her 2013 graphic novel *The Property* won the Eisner award for Best Graphic Novel, the Special Jury Prize in the International Comics Festival in Angoulême, France, and the first prize for best book of the year in Lucca Comics & Games Festival, Italy. Modan's comics and children's books have been translated into fifteen languages. In 2013, she and Yirmi Pinkus established an independent publishing house specialising in comics for young children.

ISHAI MISHORY is a longtime New York City— and newly Bay Area—based translator and sometimes illustrator. He is currently conducting research for a PhD dissertation on 16th century Italian printing.